List of Acronyms

ACSE	Association Control Service Element
ANSI	American National Standards Institute
ASN.1	Abstract Syntax Notation One
FTP	File Transfer Protocol
IAB	Internet Activities Board
ICMP	Internet Central Message Protocol
IEEE	Institute of Electrical and Electronics Engineers
IETF	Internet Engineering Task Force
IP	Internet Protocol
ISO	International Organization for Standardization
LAN	Local Area Network
MIB	Management Information Base
NMA	Network Management app
NME	Network Management entity
OSI	Open Systems Interconnection
PDU	Protocol Data Unit
RFC	Request for Comment
RPC	Remote Procedure Call
RMON	Remote Network Monitoring
SMI	Structure of Management Information
SMP	Simple Management Protocol
SNMP	Simple Network Management Protocol
TCP	Transmission Control Protocol
TFTP	Trivial File Transfer Protocol
UDP	User Datagram Protocol
USM	User-Based Security Model
VACM	View-Based Access Control Model
WAN	Wide Area Network

SNMP, SNMPv2, SNMPv3, and RMON 1 and 2

SNMP, SNMPv2, SNMPv3, and RMON 1 and 2

Third Edition

William Stallings

ADDISON-WESLEY

An imprint of Addison Wesley Longman, Inc.

Reading, Massachusetts • Harlow, England • Menlo Park, California
Berkeley, California • Don Mills, Ontario • Sydney
Bonn • Amsterdam • Tokyo • Mexico City

Many of the designations used by manufacturers and sellers to distinguish their products are claimed as trademarks. Where those designations appear in this book and Addison-Wesley was aware of a trademark claim, the designations have been printed in initial caps or all caps.

The author and publisher have taken care in the preparation of this book, but make no expressed or implied warranty of any kind and assume no responsibility for errors or omissions. No liability is assumed for incidental or consequential damages in connection with or arising out of the use of the information or programs contained herein.

The publisher offers discounts on this book when ordered in quantity for special sales. For more information, please contact:

Corporate, Government, and Special Sales Group
Addison Wesley Longman, Inc.
One Jacob Way
Reading, Massachusetts 01867

Library of Congress Cataloging-in-Publication Data
Stallings, William.
    SNMP, SNMPv2, SNMPv3, and RMON 1 and 2 / William Stallings. — 3rd ed.
        p.   cm.
    Rev. ed. of: SNMP, SNMPv2, and RMON. 2nd ed. © 1996.
    Includes bibliographical references and index.
    ISBN 0-201-48534-6   (alk. paper)
    1. Computer networks—Management.   2. Computer network protocols—
Standards.   3. Simple Network Management Protocol (Computer network
protocol)   I. Stallings, William. SNMP, SNMPv2, and RMON.
II. Title.
TK5105.5.S732   1999
004.6'2--dc21   98-43316
                                                                           CIP

ISBN 0-201-48534-6
Text printed on recycled and acid-free paper.

1 2 3 4 5 6 7 8 9 10 – MA – 02 01 00 99 98
First printing, December 1998

As Always for A.T.S.
Exotic
Elegant
Ebullient
And those are only the Es!

Contents

APPENDICES

Preface

The relentless growth in the information processing needs of organizations has been accompanied by rapid development in computer and data networking technology to support those needs, and an explosion in the variety of equipment and networks offered by vendors. Gone are the days when an organization would rely on a single vendor and a relatively straightforward architecture to support its needs. The world is no longer divided into the pure mainframe-based, IBM-compatible centralized environment and the PC-based, single-LAN-type, distributed environment. Today's typical organization has a large and growing but amorphous architecture, with a variety of local area networks (LANs) and wide area networks (WANs), supported by bridges and routers, and a variety of distributed computing services and devices, including PCs, workstations, and servers. And, of course, despite over two decades of premature eulogies, the mainframe lives on in countless distributed and a few centralized configurations.

To manage these systems and networks, which continue to grow in scale and diversity, a rich set of automated network management tools and applications is needed. Fundamental to the operation of such tools and applications in a multivendor environment are standardized techniques for representing and exchanging information relating to network management.

In response to these needs, managers and users have turned overwhelmingly to one standard: SNMP and the related RMON specification. SNMP (Simple Network Management Protocol) was initially specified in the late 1980s and quickly became the standard means for multivendor network management. However, SNMP was too limited to meet all critical network management needs. Three enhancements have solidified the role of SNMP as the indispensable network management tool.

First the RMON (Remote Network Monitoring) specification, which is built on SNMP, was released in 1991. RMON was revised in 1995, and an enhancement to RMON, known as RMON2, was issued in 1997. RMON defines algorithms and databases for managing remote LANs. Second, an enhanced version of SNMP, known as SNMPv2, was released in 1993 and revised in 1995. SNMPv2 provides more functionality and greater efficiency than in the original version of SNMP. Finally, SNMPv3 was issued in 1998. SNMPv3 defines an overall framework for present and future versions of SNMP and adds security features to SNMP. This book covers the latest versions of SNMPv1, SNMPv2, and RMON 1 and 2, as well as the new SNMPv3. All these versions are in active use.

Objective

To manage today's systems effectively and to plan intelligently for the future use of network management systems, the systems manager needs an understanding of the technology of network management and a thorough grasp of the details of the existing and evolving standards. This book's objective is to fill that need.

This book provides a comprehensive introduction to SNMP-based network and internetwork management. Part I of the book is a survey of network management technology and techniques, to enable the reader to place the various vendor offerings into the context of his or her requirements. Part II presents the original SNMP family of standards, which is still the most widely deployed version. Part III looks at the revised version of RMON1, plus RMON2, which extends RMON functionality. Part IV examines SNMPv2, which provides expanded functionality to SNMP. Part V of the book examines SNMPv3, which provides security features for use with SNMPv1 or SNMPv2. Throughout, practical issues related to the use of these standards, and products based on these standards, are examined.

Intended Audience

This book is intended for a broad range of readers interested in network management, including:

- *Students and professionals in data processing and data communications:* This book is intended as a basic tutorial and reference source for this exciting area.

- *Network management designers and implementers:* This book discusses critical design issues and explores approaches to meeting communication requirements.

- *Network management system customers and system managers:* This book is meant to help the reader understand what features and structures are needed in a network management facility, and it provides information about current and evolving standards to enable the reader to assess a specific vendor's offering.

Acknowledgments

Thanks to Uri Blumenthal of IBM for providing insight and answering questions concerning SNMPv3.

I would also like to thank the following reviewers, who generously provided feedback on part or all of the second edition: K. K. Ramakrishnan of AT&T, Russell Dietz of Technically Elite Concepts, Ravi Prakash of FTP Software, Ole Jacobsen of Cisco, Cliff Baker of the Research Libraries Group, Sandra Durham of Cisco, and Ian Taylor of Cygnus. In addition, the two main authors of RMON2, Andy Bierman of Bierman Consulting and Robin Iddon of AXON Networks, provided detailed reviews of the RMON material.

In addition, I am grateful to the people who reviewed the original proposal for this book, and an early draft: Lyman Chapin of BBN, Radia Perlman of Novell, Glen Glater and Christopher Heigham of Midnight Networks, and Peter Schmidt of Midnight Networks.

CHAPTER 1 *Introduction*

Networks and distributed processing systems are of growing importance and, indeed, have become critical in the business world. Within a given organization, the trend is toward larger, more complex networks supporting more applications and more users. As these networks grow in scale, two facts become painfully evident:

- The network and its associated resources and distributed applications become indispensable to the organization.
- More things can go wrong, disabling the network or a portion of the network or degrading performance to an unacceptable level.

A large network cannot be put together and managed by human effort alone. The complexity of such a system dictates the use of automated network management tools. The urgency of the need for such tools is increased, and the difficulty of supplying such tools is also increased, if the network includes equipment from multiple vendors.

As networked installations become larger, more complex, and more heterogeneous, the cost of network management rises. To control costs, standardized tools are needed that can be used across a broad spectrum of product types, including end systems, bridges, routers, and telecommunications equipment, and that can be used in a mixed-vendor environment. In response to this need, the simple network management protocol (SNMP) has been developed to provide a tool for multivendor, interoperable network management.

SNMP actually refers to a set of standards for network management, including a protocol, a data base structure specification, and a set of data objects. SNMP was adopted as the standard for TCP/IP-based internets in 1989 and has enjoyed widespread popularity. In 1991, a supplement to SNMP, known as remote network monitoring (RMON), was issued; RMON extended the capabilities of SNMP to include management of local area networks (LANs) as well as the devices attached to those networks. In 1993, an upgrade to SNMP, known as SNMP version 2 (SNMPv2), was proposed, and a revision of SNMPv2 was issued in 1995. SNMPv2 adds functional enhancements to SNMP and codifies the use of SNMP on OSI-based networks. Also in 1995, RMON was extended with an addition known as RMON2. Finally, in 1998, SNMPv3 was issued; this set of documents defines a security capability for SNMP and an architecture for future enhancements. SNMPv3 is intended for use with the functionality provided by SNMPv2, but can also be used with the initial version of SNMP, now known as SNMPv1.

The bulk of this book is devoted to a study of SNMP, RMON 1 and 2, SNMPv2, and SNMPv3, and to some of the practical issues associated with each. The remainder of this chapter, and the next two, provide an overview of network management in general.

1.1   *Network Management Requirements*

Table 1.1 lists the key functional areas of network management as defined by the International Organization for Standardization (ISO). Although this functional classification was developed for the OSI environment, it has gained broad acceptance by vendors of both standardized and proprietary network management systems. These categories provide a useful way of organizing our discussion of requirements.

1.1.1   Fault Management

1.1.1.1   Overview

To maintain proper operation of a complex network, care must be taken that systems as a whole, and each essential component individually, are in proper working order. When a fault occurs, it is important, as rapidly as possible, to:

- Determine exactly where the fault is.
- Isolate the rest of the network from the failure so that it can continue to function without interference.
- Reconfigure or modify the network in such a way as to minimize the impact of operation without the failed component or components.
- Repair or replace the failed components to restore the network to its initial state.

Central to the definition of fault management is the fundamental concept of a fault. Faults are to be distinguished from errors. A *fault* is an abnormal condition that requires management attention (or action) to repair, whereas an error is a single event. A fault is usually indicated by failure to operate correctly or by excessive errors. For example, if a communications line is physically cut, no signals can get through. Or a crimp in the cable may cause wild distortions so that there is a persistently high bit error rate. Certain errors (for example, a single bit error on a communication line) may occur occasionally and are not normally considered to be faults. It is usually possible to compensate for errors using the error control mechanisms of the various protocols.

TABLE 1.1   OSI Management Functional Areas

Fault management
  The facilities that enable the detection, isolation, and correction of abnormal operation of the OSI environment

Accounting management
  The facilities that enable charges to be established for the use of managed objects and costs to be identified for the use of those managed objects

Configuration and name management
  The facilities that exercise control over, identify, collect data from, and provide data to managed objects for the purpose of assisting in providing for the continuous operation of interconnection services

Performance management
  The facilities needed to evaluate the behavior of managed objects and the effectiveness of communication activities

Security management
  The facilities that address those aspects of OSI security essential to operate OSI network management correctly and to protect managed objects

1.1.1.2   User Requirements

End users expect fast and reliable problem resolution. Most end users will tolerate occasional outages. When these infrequent outages do occur, however, the end user generally expects to receive immediate notification and expects that the problem will be corrected almost immediately. To provide this level of fault resolution requires very rapid and reliable fault detection and diagnostic management functions. The impact and duration of faults can also be minimized by the use of redundant components and alternate communication routes to give the network a degree of "fault tolerance." The fault management capability itself should be redundant to increase network reliability.

Users expect to be kept informed of the network status, including both scheduled and unscheduled disruptive maintenance. Users expect reassurance of correct network operation through mechanisms that use confidence tests or analyze dumps, logs, alerts, or statistics. After correcting a fault and restoring a system to its full operational state, the fault management service must ensure that the problem is truly resolved and that no new problems are introduced. This requirement is called problem tracking and control. As with other areas of network management, fault management should have minimal effect on network performance.

1.1.2   Accounting Management

1.1.2.1   Overview

In many corporate networks, individual divisions or cost centers, or even individual project accounts, are charged for the use of network services. These are internal accounting procedures rather than actual cash transfers, but they are important to the participating end users nevertheless. Furthermore, even if no such internal charging is employed, the network manager needs to be able to track the use of network resources by end user or end user class for a number of reasons, including the following.

- An end user or group of end users may be abusing their access privileges and burdening the network at the expense of other end users.
- End users may be making inefficient use of the network, and the network manager can assist in changing procedures to improve performance.
- The network manager is in a better position to plan for network growth if end user activity is known in sufficient detail.

1.1.2.2   User Requirements

The network manager needs to be able to specify the kinds of accounting information to be recorded at various nodes, the desired interval between sending the recorded information to higher-level management nodes, and the algorithms to be used in calculating the charging. Accounting reports should be generated under network manager control.

To limit access to accounting information, the accounting facility must provide the capability to verify end users' authorization to access and manipulate that information.

1.1.3   Configuration and Name Management

1.1.3.1   Overview

Modern data communication networks are composed of individual components and logical subsystems (for example, the device driver in an operating system) that can be configured to perform many different applications. The same device, for example, can be configured to act either as a router or as an end system node or both. Once it is decided how a device is to be used, the configuration manager can choose the appropriate software and set of attributes and values (for example, a transport layer retransmission timer) for that device.

Configuration management is concerned with initializing a network and gracefully shutting down part or all of the network. It is also concerned with maintaining, adding, and updating the relationships among components and the status of components themselves during network operation.

1.1.3.2   User Requirements

Start-up and shut-down operations on a network are the specific responsibilities of configuration management. It is often desirable for these operations on certain components to be performed unattended (for example, starting or shutting down a network interface unit). The network manager needs the capability to identify initially the components that comprise the network and to define the desired connectivity of these components. Those who regularly configure a network with the same or a similar set of resource attributes need ways to define and modify default attributes and to load these predefined sets of attributes into the specified network components. The network manager needs the capability to change the connectivity of network components when end users' needs change. Reconfiguration of a network is often desired in response to performance evaluation or in support of network upgrade, fault recovery, or security checks.

End users often need to, or want to, be informed of the status of network resources and components. Therefore, when changes in configuration occur, end users should be notified of these changes. Configuration reports can be generated either on some routine periodic basis or in response to a request for such a report. Before reconfiguration, end users often want to inquire about the upcoming status of resources and their attributes. Network managers usually want only authorized end users (operators) to manage and control network operation (for example, software distribution and updating).

1.1.4   Performance Management

1.1.4.1   Overview

Modern data communications networks are composed of many and varied components, which must intercommunicate and share data and resources. In some cases, it is critical to the effectiveness of an application that the communication over the network be within certain performance limits.

Performance management of a computer network comprises two broad functional categories—monitoring and controlling. Monitoring is the function that tracks activities on the network. The controlling function enables performance management to make adjustments to improve network performance. Some of the performance issues of concern to the network manager are:

- What is the level of capacity utilization?
- Is there excessive traffic?
- Has throughput been reduced to unacceptable levels?
- Are there bottlenecks?
- Is response time increasing?

To deal with these concerns, the network manager must focus on some initial set of resources to be monitored in order to assess performance levels. This includes associating appropriate metrics and values with relevant network resources as indicators of different levels of performance. For example, what count of retransmissions on a transport connection is considered to be a performance problem requiring attention? Performance management, therefore, must monitor many resources to provide information in determining network operating level. By collecting this information, analyzing it, and then using the resultant analysis as feedback to the prescribed set of values, the network manager can become more and more adept at recognizing situations indicative of present or impending performance degradation.

1.1.4.2   User Requirements

Before using a network for a particular application, an end user may want to know such things as the average and worst case response times and the reliability of network services. Thus performance must be known in sufficient detail to assess specific end user queries. End users expect network services to be managed in such a way as to consistently afford their applications good response time.

Network managers need performance statistics to help them plan, manage, and maintain large networks. Performance statistics can be used to recognize potential bottlenecks before they cause problems to the end users. Appropriate corrective action can then be taken. This action can take the form of changing routing tables to balance or redistribute traffic load during times of peak use or when a bottleneck is identified by a rapidly growing load in one area. Over the long term, capacity planning based on such performance information can indicate the proper decisions to make, for example, with regard to expansion of lines in that area.

1.1.5   Security Management

1.1.5.1   Overview

Security management is concerned with managing information protection and access control facilities. These include generating, distributing, and storing encryption keys. Passwords, and other authorization or access control information, must be maintained and distributed. Security management is also concerned with monitoring and controlling access to computer networks and access to all or part of the network management information obtained from the network nodes. Logs are an important security tool, and therefore, security management is very much involved with the collection, storage, and examination of audit records and security logs, as well as with the enabling and disabling of these logging facilities.

1.1.5.2   User Requirements

Security management provides facilities for protection of network resources and end user information. Network security facilities should be available for authorized users only. End users want to know that the proper security policies are in force and effective and that the management of security facilities is itself secure.

1.2   *Network Management Systems*

A network management system is a collection of tools for network monitoring and control that is integrated in the following senses.

- It is a single operator interface with a powerful but user-friendly set of commands for performing most or all network management tasks.

- A minimal amount of separate equipment is necessary. That is, most of the hardware and software required for network management is incorporated into the existing user equipment.

A network management system consists of incremental hardware and software additions implemented among existing network components. The software used in accomplishing the network management tasks resides in the host computers and communications processors (for example, front-end processors, terminal cluster controllers, bridges, routers). A network management system is designed to view the entire network as a unified architecture, with addresses and labels assigned to each point and the specific attributes of each element and link known to the system. The active elements of the network provide regular feedback of status information to the network control center.

1.2.1   Network Management Configuration

Figure 1.1 suggests the architecture of a network management system. Each network node contains a collection of software devoted to the network management task, referred to in the diagram as a network management entity (NME). Each NME performs the following tasks:

- Collect statistics on communications and network-related activities.

- Store statistics locally.

- Respond to commands from the network control center, including commands to:
    1. Transmit collected statistics to network control center.
    2. Change a parameter (for example, a timer used in a transport protocol).
    3. Provide status information (for example, parameter values, active links).
    4. Generate artificial traffic to perform a test.

- Send messages to the network control center when local conditions undergo significant change.

At least one host in the network is designated as the network control host, or **manager**. In addition to the NME software, the network control host includes a collection of software called the network management application (NMA). The NMA includes an operator interface to allow an authorized user to manage the network. The NMA responds to user commands by displaying information and/or by issuing commands to NMEs throughout the network. This communication is carried out using an application-level network management protocol that employs the communications architecture in the same fashion as any other distributed application.

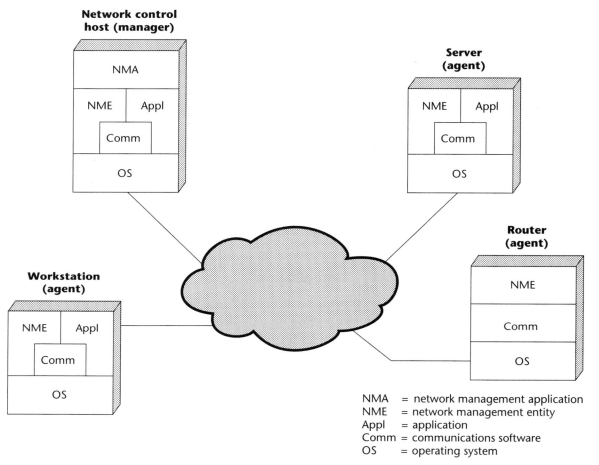

FIGURE 1.1 Elements of a network management system

Other nodes in the network that are part of the network management system include an NME that responds to requests from a manager system. The NME in such managed systems is generally referred to as an agent module, or simply an *agent*. Agents are implemented in end systems that support end user applications as well as nodes that provide a communications service, such as front-end processors, cluster controllers, bridges, and routers.

Several observations are in order.

1. Since the network management software relies on the host operating system and on the communications architecture, most offerings to date are designed for use on a

single vendor's equipment. Recent years have seen the emergence of standardized network management systems designed to manage a multiple-vendor network.

2. As depicted in Figure 1.1, the network control host communicates with and controls the NMEs in other systems.

3. For maintaining high availability of the network management function, two or more network control hosts are used. In normal operation, one of the centers is idle or simply collecting statistics, while the other is used for control. If the primary network control host fails, the backup system can be used.

1.2.2   Network Management Software Architecture

The actual architecture of the network management software in a manager or agent varies greatly, depending on the functionality of the platform and the details of the network management capability. Figure 1.2 presents a generic view of such an architecture. The software can be divided into three broad categories:

- User presentation software
- Network management software
- Communications and database support software

1.2.2.1   User Presentation Software

Interaction between a user of network management and the network management software takes place across a user interface. Such an interface is needed in any manager system, to allow a user to monitor and control the network. It may also be useful to have such an interface in some agent systems for purposes of testing and debugging, and also to allow some parameters to be viewed or set locally.

The key to an effective network management system is a *unified* user interface. The interface should be the same at any node, regardless of vendor. This allows a user to manage a heterogeneous configuration with a minimum of training.

One danger in any network management system is information overload. If a configuration is instrumented properly, a tremendous amount of information is available to the network management user. Presentation tools are needed to organize, summarize, and simplify this information as much as possible. Ideally, there will be an emphasis on graphical presentations over textual or tabular outputs.

1.2.2.2   Network Management Software

The software that specifically provides the network management application may be very simple, as in the case of SNMP, or very complex, as in the case of OSI systems management. The central box in Figure 1.2 shows a rather complex structure that reflects the

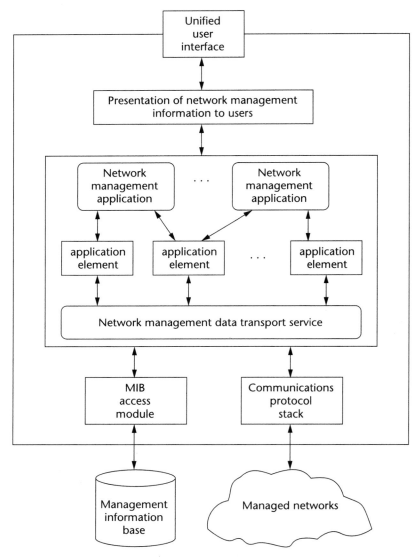

FIGURE 1.2   Architectural model of a network management system

architecture of OSI systems management and that is also suggestive of a typical proprietary network management system.

The network management software in the figure is organized into three layers. The
top layer consists of a collection of network management applications that provide the
services of interest to users. For example, these applications could correspond to the OSI

management functional areas: fault management, accounting management, configuration management, performance management, and security. Each application covers a broad area of network management. Each application should exhibit a consistent behavior over various types of configurations, although there may be detailed differences depending on the nature of the network facility (for example, LAN, WAN, T1 multiplexer network).

The small number of network management applications is supported by a larger number of application elements. These are modules that implement more primitive and more general-purpose network management functions, such as generating alarms or summarizing data. The application elements implement basic tools that are of use to one or more of the network management applications. Organizing the software in terms of applications and application elements follows traditional modular design principles and enables a more efficient implementation to be developed based on software reuse.

The lowest level of management-specific software is a network management data transport service. This module consists of a network management protocol used to exchange management information among managers and agents and a service interface to the application elements. Typically, the service interface provides very primitive functions, such as get information, set parameters, and generate notifications.

1.2.2.3   Network Management Support Software

To perform its intended functions, network management software needs access to a local management information base (MIB) and to remote agents and managers.

The local MIB at an agent contains information of use to network management, including information that reflects the configuration and behavior of this node, and parameters that can be used to control the operation of this node. The local MIB at a manager contains such node-specific information as well as summary information about agents under the manager's control. The MIB access module includes basic file management software that enables access to the MIB. In addition, the access module may need to convert from the local MIB format to a form that is standardized across the network management system.

Communication with other nodes (agents and managers) is supported by a communications protocol stack, such as OSI or the TCP/IP stack. The communications architecture thus supports the network management protocol, which is at an application level.

1.2.3   Distributed Network Management

The configuration depicted in Figure 1.1 suggested a centralized network management strategy, with a single network control center and perhaps a standby center. This is the strategy that has traditionally been favored by both mainframe vendors and information system executives. A centralized network management system implies central control. This makes sense in a mainframe-dominated configuration, where the key resources reside in a computer center and service is provided to remote users. The strategy also makes sense to managers responsible for the total information system assets of an organization. A centralized network management system enables the manager to maintain control over the entire configuration, balancing resources against needs and optimizing the overall utilization of resources.

But, just as the centralized computing model has given way to a distributed computing architecture, with applications shifted from data centers to remote departments, network management is also becoming distributed. The same factors come into play: the proliferation of low-cost, high-power PCs and workstations, the proliferation of departmental LANs, and the need for local control and optimization of distributed applications.

A distributed management system replaces the single network control center with interoperable workstations located on LANs distributed throughout the enterprise. This strategy gives departmental-level managers, who must watch over downsized applications and PC LANs, the tools they need to maintain responsive networks, systems, and applications for their local end users. To prevent anarchy a hierarchical architecture is typically used, with the following elements.

- Distributed management stations are given limited access for network monitoring and control, usually defined by the departmental resources they serve.
- One central workstation, with a backup, has global access rights and the ability to manage all network resources. It can also interact with less-enabled management stations to monitor and control their operation.

While maintaining the capacity for central control, the distributed approach offers a number of benefits.

1. Network management traffic overhead is minimized. Much of the traffic is confined to the local environment.
2. Distributed management offers greater scalability. Adding additional management capability is simply a matter of deploying another inexpensive workstation at the desired location.
3. The use of multiple, networked stations eliminates the single point of failure that exists with centralized schemes.

Figure 1.3 illustrates the basic structure used for most distributed network management systems now on the market. Closest to the users are the management clients. These give the user access to management services and information and provide an easy-to-use graphical user interface. Depending on access privileges, a client workstation may access one or more management servers. The management servers are the heart of the system. Each server supports a set of management applications and a management information base (MIB). They also store common management data models and route management

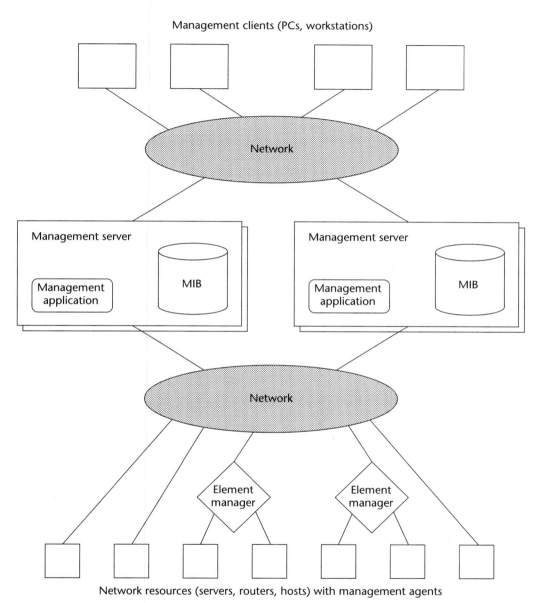

Management clients (PCs, workstations)

Network resources (servers, routers, hosts) with management agents

FIGURE 1.3   Typical distributed management system architecture information to applications and clients. Those devices to be managed that share the same network management protocol as the management servers contain agent software and are managed directly by one or more management servers. For other devices, management servers can only reach the resources through a vendor-specific element manager, or proxy. The concept of proxy is explored in the next subsection.

The flexibility and scalability of the distributed management model is evident from Figure 1.3. As additional resources are added to the configuration, each is equipped with agent software or linked to a proxy. In a centralized system, this growth might eventually overwhelm a central station. But in a distributed system, additional management servers and client workstations can be added to cope with the additional resources. Furthermore, the growth of the overall configuration will occur in a structured way (for example, adding an additional LAN with a number of attached PCs); the growth of the management system mirrors this underlying resource growth, with servers and clients added where the new resources are located.

1.2.4   Proxies

The configuration of Figure 1.1 suggests that each component of the configuration that is of management interest includes a network management entity, with common network management software across all managers and agents. In an actual configuration, this may not be practical or even possible. For example, the configuration may include older systems that do not support the network management standards that are being used, small systems that would be unduly burdened by a full-blown NME implementation, or components such as modems and multiplexers that do not support additional software.

To handle such cases, it is common to have one of the agents in the configuration serve as a proxy for one or more other nodes. We will have more to say about proxies in Part II, but for now we provide a brief introduction to the concept.

When an agent performs in a proxy role, it acts on behalf of one or more other nodes. A network manager that wishes to obtain information from or control the node communicates with the proxy agent. The proxy agent then translates the manager request into a form appropriate for the target system and uses whatever network management protocol is appropriate to communicate with the target system. Responses from the target system back to the proxy are similarly translated and passed on to the manager.

Figure 1.4 illustrates a structured architecture that enables a management application to manage a proprietary resource through standard operations and event reports which are translated by the proxy system into proprietary operations and event reports. In this case, a remote procedure call (RPC) mechanism is used. The RPC mechanism is frequently found with distributed system software and provides a flexible and easy-to-use facility for supporting the proxy function.

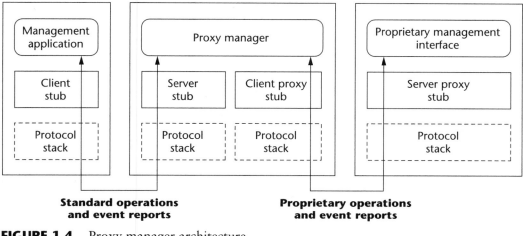

FIGURE 1.4 Proxy manager architecture

1.3 Outline of the Book

This chapter serves as an introduction to the entire book. A brief synopsis of the remaining chapters follows.

1.3.1 Chapter 2 Network Monitoring

Fundamental to network management is the ability to gather information about the status and behavior of the networked configuration, which is the function of network monitoring. Indeed, many network management systems provide only a network monitoring capability. This chapter examines the basic architectural and design issues of network monitoring and then looks at three specific areas: performance monitoring, fault monitoring, and accounting monitoring.

1.3.2 Chapter 3 Network Control

A complete network management system will include the capability of controlling a configuration as well as monitoring it. Chapter 3 examines the basic mechanisms of network control and then looks at two specific aspects of network control: configuration control and security control.

1.3.3 Chapter 4 SNMP Network Management Concepts

A network management framework for TCP/IP-based internets has been developed and standardized for use in conjunction with the TCP/IP protocol suite. The framework includes the simple network management protocol (SNMP), a structure of management information, and a management information base. This chapter provides an overview of the concepts that underlie SNMP and the related standards.

1.3.4   Chapter 5   SNMP Management Information

Management information accessible via SNMP is maintained in a management information base (MIB) at each manager and agent node. This chapter summarizes the structure of SNMP management information, which consists of a simple, hierarchical structure of objects. Each object represents some attribute of a managed resource. The chapter looks at the formal methods for defining and representing management information and examines some of the practical issues in the use of such information in a multivendor, interoperable environment.

1.3.5   Chapter 6   Standard MIBs

Chapter 6 examines MIB-II, which is a structured set of standard objects that includes many of the objects commonly required in an SNMP-based network management system. It also describes the important Ethernet Interface MIB, which along with MIB-II, is an Internet Standard.

1.3.6   Chapter 7   Simple Network Management Protocol

This chapter examines the basic principles of operation of SNMP. Then, the protocol specification itself is examined in detail. The chapter also discusses the type of transport-level service that may be used to support SNMP, and then looks at the MIB objects used to monitor and manage the operation of the protocol itself.

1.3.7   Chapter 8   Remote Network Monitoring: Statistics Collection

A network management system is concerned not only with the status and behavior of individual nodes on a network, but with the traffic on the network itself. Remote monitoring is a term used to refer to the monitoring of a network by one of the nodes on the network, for the purposes of network management. In the context of SNMP, a remote monitoring (RMON) MIB has been defined. The RMON MIB specifies the information that is to be collected and stored by a remote monitor. The specification also defines the functionality of the monitor and the functionality of the manager-monitor interaction. Chapter 8 introduces the fundamental concepts of RMON and then examines those elements of the RMON MIB that are principally concerned with statistics collection.

1.3.8   Chapter 9   Remote Network Monitoring: Alarms and Filters

Chapter 9 completes the discussion of the original RMON with a look at those elements that have to do with generating alarms on the basis of specified events and with filtering and capturing packet traffic. The chapter also looks at some of the practical issues involved in the use of RMON in a multivendor, interoperable environment.

1.3.9   Chapter 10   RMON2

This chapter examines the recent extension of the RMON MIB to encompass a broader range of managed objects. This extension of RMON, known as RMON2, focuses on traffic and addressing at protocol layers above the medium access control (MAC) layer, with emphasis on IP traffic and application-level traffic.

1.3.10   Chapter 11   SNMPv2: Management Information

As the name suggests, SNMP provides a simple facility for network management, one that is easy to implement and should consume minimal processing resources. Many users of SNMP have felt the need for a more powerful and comprehensive facility, without going to the full-blown capability represented by OSI systems management. In response to this need, version 2 of SNMP (SNMPv2) was developed. SNMPv2 includes functional enhancements to SNMP as well as features that improve the efficiency of SNMP operation. This chapter examines the management information aspects of SNMPv2.

1.3.11   Chapter 12   SNMPv2: Protocol

This chapter provides a description of the SNMPv2 protocol. This is followed by a discussion of transport mappings defined for SNMPv2. Finally, the chapter examines strategies for coexistence between SNMPv2 and SNMPv1 entities on the same network.

1.3.12   Chapter 13   SNMPv2: MIBs and Conformance

We begin this chapter with a description of the SNMPv2 MIB, which instruments both SNMPv2 and SNMPv1. Next, conformance statements are examined; these are used to specify conformance requirements for standardized MIBs and to enable vendors to document the scope of their implementation. Finally, the chapter discusses the MIB extensions to the interfaces group, which are defined using SNMPv2 SMI, and depend on some of the protocol features of SNMPv2.

1.3.13   Chapter 14   Cryptographic Algorithms Used in SNMPv3

SNMPv3 was developed to provide a security capability for SNMP. For the reader with little or no background in security, Chapter 14 provides an overview. The chapter begins with a discussion of network security threats and requirements. Then, conventional encryption using DES is examined. The remainder of the chapter describes the message authentication code HMAC and two related secure hash functions, MD5 and SHA-1.

1.3.14 Chapter 15   SNMPv3: Architecture and Applications

This chapter introduces SNMPv3 and provides some of the basic details. SNMPv3 defines an overall architecture that incorporates the functional elements of SNMPv1 and SNMPv2, as well as the security features defined in SNMPv3; this architecture also provides a framework for future revision and enhancement of SNMP. Chapter 15 also examines the basic services provided by SNMP in terms of primitive applications, and looks at MIBs defined to support SNMP applications.

1.3.15 Chapter 16   SNMPv3: Message Processing and User-Based Security Model

Chapter 16 discusses the message processing functions defined in the SNMPv3 documents. The chapter begins with a general discussion of message processing that is intended to work not only with SNMPv3 security features but with future enhancements to security. The chapter then examines in some detail the user-based security model (USM) for SNMPv3. USM defines the functions and procedures for providing authentication and privacy services for SNMPv3 messages.

1.3.16 Chapter 17   SNMPv3: View-Based Access Control Model

SNMPv3 also defines a view-based access control model (VACM) to regulate manager access to management information maintained on agent systems. Chapter 17 defines the functionality of VACM and describes the MIB used to support access control processing.

1.3.17 Appendix A   The TCP/IP Protocol Suite

This appendix summarizes the TCP/IP protocol suite, including the protocol architecture and each layer of the architecture.

1.3.18 Appendix B   Abstract Syntax Notation One

ASN.1 is the language used to define the syntax of objects in the management information base for both the SNMP family and OSI systems management. In addition, the syntax of application-level protocol data units for both the SNMP family and OSI systems management is defined using ASN.1. The basic elements of ASN.1 and examples of its use are provided in this appendix.

APPENDIX 1A   *INTERNET RESOURCES*

It is the author's hope that this book will serve as both a tutorial for learning about the field of network management and a reference that can be returned to for help on a specific topic. However, with the rapid changes taking place in both the technology and the standards for this field, no book can hope to stand alone for very long. The reader who is truly interested in this field will need to invest a certain amount of time keeping up with new developments. One of the best ways is through the Internet.

1A.1   Web Sites

The World Wide Web is the most convenient way of gathering information via the Internet. Useful Web sites for SNMP and network management:

- `http://ietf.org/html.charters/snmpv3-charter.html`: Home page of the SNMPv3 working group. This site maintains the most recent copies of SNMPv3-related RFCs and Internet draft documents, plus a schedule of past and future work.

- `http://ietf.org/html.charters/rmonmib-charter.html`: Home page of the RMON MIB working group. This site maintains the most recent copies of RMON-related RFCs and Internet draft documents, plus a schedule of past and future work.

- `http://www.ibr.cs.tu-bs.de/projects/snmpv3`: An SNMPv3 Web site maintained by the Technical University of Braunschweig. It provides links to the RFCs and Internet drafts, copies of clarifications and proposed changes posted by the working group, and links to vendors with SNMPv3 implementations.

- `http://www.simple-times.org`: *The Simple Times* is an on-line free quarterly publication of SNMP technology, comment, and events. The Web site is maintained jointly by the Technical University of Braunschweig and the University of Twente. Each issue features technical articles, columns, a list of Internet documents, and brief announcements of events and products.

- `http://www.snmp.cs.utwente.nl`: This is known as The Simple Web site, maintained by the University of Twente. It is a good source of information on SNMP, including pointers to many public-domain implementations and lists of books and articles.

- `http://netman.cit.buffalo.edu/index.html`: A good overall site for information on network management topics. This site has links to many of the vendors who offer SNMP, RMON, and other network management products.

- `http://www.nmf.org`: This is the home page for the Network Management Forum (NMF). The NMF is a nonprofit organization whose members are vendors, customers, and others concerned with standardizing network management protocol and services. Although the original focus of NMF was OSI network management, it has since expanded its charter to include the promotion of SNMP-based products and solutions.

1A.2   USENET News Groups

Another handy way to track developments and get questions answered is USENET. USENET is a collection of electronic bulletin boards that work in much the same way as the Internet mailing lists. If you subscribe to a particular news group, you receive all messages posted to that group, and you may post a message that is available to all subscribers. The differences between USENET and Internet mailing lists have to do with the mechanics of the systems. USENET is actually a distributed network of sites that collect and broadcast news group entries. To access a news group, for read or write, one must have access to a USENET node. Such nodes are accessible over the Internet, and in a variety of other ways.

Relevant news groups:

- `comp.protocols.snmp`: Discussion of topics related to SNMP.
- `comp.dcom.net-management`: A general discussion of network management topics.

1A.3   Errata

As soon as any typos or other errors are discovered, an errata list for this book will be available at my Web site at `http://www.shore.net/~ws`. The file will be updated as needed. Please send any errors that you spot to me at ws@shore.net.

Errata sheets for all of my other books are at the same Web site, as well as discount ordering information for the books.

PART ONE

Network Management Fundamentals

CHAPTER 2 *Network Monitoring*

The network-monitoring portion of network management is concerned with observing and analyzing the status and behavior of the end systems, intermediate systems, and subnetworks that make up the configuration to be managed.

Chiu and Sudama (1992) suggest that network monitoring consists of three major design areas:

- *Access to monitored information:* how to define monitoring information, and how to get that information from a resource to a manager
- *Design of monitoring mechanisms:* how best to obtain information from resources
- *Application of monitored information:* how the monitored information is used in various management functional areas

The first section in this chapter deals with the first two items in the preceding list, by examining some of the general design considerations for a network-monitoring system. The remainder of the chapter deals with network-monitoring applications. Network monitoring encompasses all five of the functional areas listed in Table 1.1. In this chapter we focus on the three functional areas that generally are most important for network monitoring: performance monitoring, fault monitoring, and accounting monitoring.

2.1 *Network Monitoring Architecture*

Before considering the design of a network-monitoring system, it is best to consider the type of information that is of interest to a network monitor. Then we can look at the alternatives for configuring the network-monitoring function.

2.1.1   Network-Monitoring Information

The information that should be available for network monitoring can be classified as follows:

- *Static:* This is information that characterizes the current configuration and the elements in the current configuration, such as the number and identification of ports on a router. This information will change only infrequently.
- *Dynamic:* This information is related to events in the network, such as a change of state of a protocol machine or the transmission of a packet on a network.
- *Statistical:* This is information that may be derived from dynamic information, such as the average number of packets transmitted per unit time by an end system.

An example of such an information structure, for use in monitoring a real-time system, is suggested in Mazumdar and Lazar (1991). In this scheme, the static database has two major components: a configuration database with basic information about the computer and networking elements, and a sensor database, with information about sensors used to obtain real-time readings. The dynamic database is primarily concerned with collecting information about the state of various network elements and events detected by the sensors. The statistical database includes useful aggregate measures. Figure 2.1 suggests the relationships among these components.

The nature of the monitored information has implications for where it is collected and stored for purposes of monitoring. Static information is typically generated by the element involved. Thus, a router maintains its own configuration information. This information can be made available directly to a monitor if the element has the appropriate agent software. Alternatively, the information can be made available to a proxy that in turn will make it available to a monitor.

Dynamic information, too, is generally collected and stored by the network element responsible for the underlying events. However, if a system is attached to a LAN, then much of its activity can be observed by another system on the LAN. The term "remote monitor" refers to a device on a LAN that observes all of the traffic on the LAN and gathers information about that traffic. For example, the total number of packets issued by an element on a LAN could be recorded by the element itself or by a remote monitor that is listening on the same LAN. Some dynamic information, however, can be generated only by the element itself, such as the current number of network-level connections.

Statistical information can be generated by any system that has access to the underlying dynamic information. The statistical information could be generated back at the network monitor itself. This would require that all of the "raw" data be transmitted to the monitor, where it would be analyzed and summarized. If the monitor does not need access to all of the raw data, then monitor processing time and network capacity could be saved if the system that holds the dynamic data does the summarization and sends the results to the monitor.

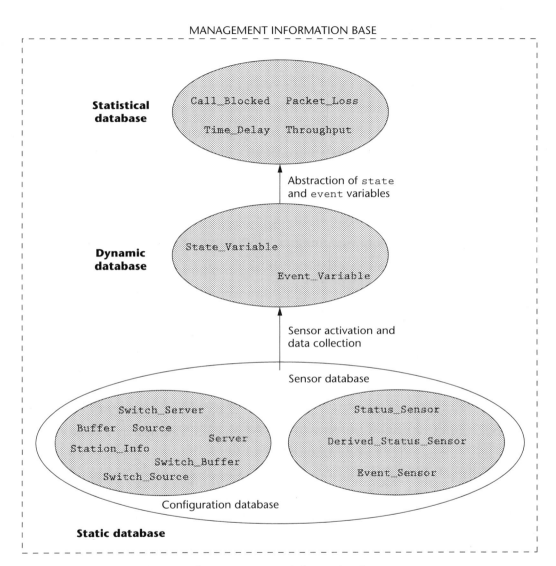

FIGURE 2.1   Organization of a management information base

2.1.2   Network-Monitoring Configurations

Figure 2.2, based on a depiction in Chiu and Sudama (1992), illustrates the architecture for network monitoring in functional terms. Part (a) of the figure shows the four major components of a network-monitoring system:

- *Monitoring application:* This component includes the functions of network monitoring that are visible to the user, such as performance monitoring, fault monitoring, and accounting monitoring.

- *Manager function:* This is the module at the network monitor that performs the basic monitoring function of retrieving information from other elements of the configuration.

- *Agent function:* This module gathers and records management information for one or more network elements and communicates the information to the monitor.

- *Managed objects:* This is the management information that represents resources and their activities.

It is useful to highlight an additional functional module concerned with statistical information (Figure 2.2, part (b)):

- *Monitoring agent:* This module generates summaries and statistical analyses of management information. If remote from the manager, this module acts as an agent and communicates the summarization information to the manager.

These functional modules may be configured in a number of ways. The station that hosts the monitoring application is itself a network element and subject to monitoring. Thus, the network monitor generally includes agent software and a set of managed objects (Figure 2.3 (a)). In fact, it is vital to monitor the status and behavior of the network monitor to assure that it continues to perform its function and to assess the load on itself and on the network. One key requirement is that the network management protocol be instrumented to monitor the amount of network management traffic into and out of the network monitor.

Figure 2.3 (b) illustrates the most common configuration for monitoring other network elements. This configuration requires that the manager and agent systems share the same network management protocol and MIB (management information base) syntax and semantics.

A network-monitoring system may also include one or more agents that monitor traffic on a network. These are often referred to as external monitors or remote monitors; the configuration is depicted in Figure 2.3 (c).

Finally, as was discussed in Section 1.2.4, for network elements that do not share a common network management protocol with the network monitor, a proxy agent is needed (Figure 2.3 (d)).

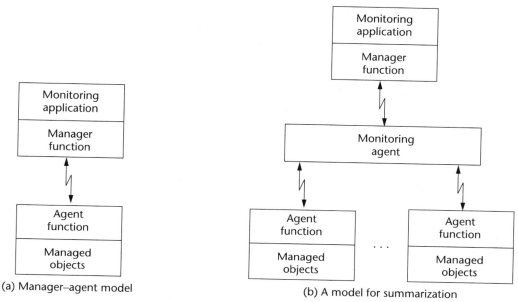

(a) Manager–agent model   (b) A model for summarization

FIGURE 2.2   Functional architecture for network monitoring

2.1.3   Polling and Event Reporting

Information that is useful for network monitoring is collected and stored by agents and made available to one or more manager systems. Two techniques are used to make the agent information available to the manager: polling and event reporting.

Polling is a request–response interaction between a manager and agent. The manager can query any agent (for which it has authorization) and request the values of various information elements; the agent responds with information from its MIB. The request may be specific, listing one or more named variables. A request may also be in the nature of a search, asking the agent to report information matching certain criteria, or to supply the manager with information about the structure of the MIB at the agent. A manager system may use polling to learn about the configuration it is managing, to obtain periodically an update of conditions, or to investigate an area in detail after being alerted to a problem. Polling is also used to generate a report on behalf of a user and to respond to specific user queries.

With *event reporting*, the initiative is with the agent and the manager is in the role of a listener, waiting for incoming information. An agent may generate a report periodically to give the manager its current status. The reporting period may be preconfigured or set

(a) Managed resources in
    manager system

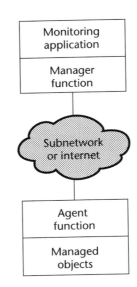

(b) Resources in agent system

(c) External monitor

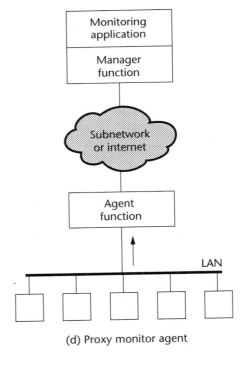

(d) Proxy monitor agent

FIGURE 2.3   Network-monitoring configurations

by the manager. An agent may also generate a report when a significant event (for example, a change of state) or an unusual event (for example, a fault) occurs. Event reporting is useful for detecting problems as soon as they occur. It is also more efficient than polling for monitoring objects whose states or values change relatively infrequently.

Both polling and event reporting are useful, and a network-monitoring system will typically employ both methods. The relative emphasis placed on the two methods varies greatly in different systems. Telecommunications management systems have traditionally placed a very high reliance on event reporting. In contrast, the SNMP approach puts very little reliance on event reporting. OSI systems management tends to fall somewhere between these extremes. However, both SNMP and OSI systems management, as well as most proprietary schemes, allow the user considerable latitude in determining the relative emphasis on the two approaches. The choice of emphasis depends on a number of factors, including the following:

- The amount of network traffic generated by each method
- Robustness in critical situations
- The time delay in notifying the network manager
- The amount of processing in managed devices
- The tradeoffs of reliable versus unreliable transfer
- The network-monitoring applications being supported
- The contingencies required in case a notifying device fails before sending a report

2.2   *Performance Monitoring*

2.2.1   Performance Indicators

An absolute prerequisite for the management of a communications network is the ability to measure the performance of the network, or *performance monitoring*. We cannot hope to manage and control a system or activity unless we can monitor its performance. One of the difficulties facing the network manager is in the selection and use of the appropriate indicators that measure the network's performance. Among the problems that may appear are the following.

- There are too many indicators in use.
- The meanings of most indicators are not yet clearly understood.
- Some indicators are introduced and supported by some manufacturers only.
- Most indicators are not suitable for comparison with each other.
- Frequently, the indicators are accurately measured but incorrectly interpreted.

- In many cases, the calculation of indicators takes too much time, and the final results can hardly be used for controlling the environment.

In this section, we give some general ideas of the types of indicators that are useful for network management. These fall into two categories: service-oriented measures and efficiency-oriented measures; Table 2.1, based on Terplan (1992), gives a breakdown of major indicators in each category. The principal means of judging that a network is meeting its requirements is that specified service levels are maintained to the satisfaction of the users. Thus, service-oriented indicators are of the highest priority. The manager is also concerned with meeting these requirements at minimum cost, hence the need for efficiency-oriented measures.

2.2.1.1 Availability

Availability can be expressed as the percentage of time that a network system, component, or application is available for a user. Depending on the application, high availability can be significant. For example, in an airline reservation network, a one-minute outage may cause $10,000 in losses; in a banking network, a one-hour outage may introduce losses in the millions of dollars.

Availability is based on the reliability of the individual components of a network. Reliability is the probability that a component will perform its specified function for a specified time under specified conditions. Component failure is usually expressed by the *mean time between failures* (MTBF). The availability, *A*, can be expressed as

$$A = \frac{\text{MTBF}}{\text{MTBF} + \text{MTTR}},$$

where MTTR is the *mean time to repair* following a failure.

TABLE 2.1   Network Performance Indicators

	Service-oriented
Availability	The percentage of time that a network system, a component, or an application is available for a user
Response time	How long it takes for a response to appear at a user's terminal after a user action calls for it
Accuracy	The percentage of time that no errors occur in the transmission and delivery of information
	Efficiency-oriented
Throughput	The rate at which application-oriented events (e.g., transaction messages, file transfers) occur
Utilization	The percentage of the theoretical capacity of a resource (e.g., multiplexer, transmission line, switch) that is being used

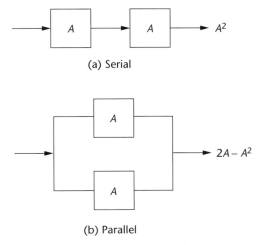

(a) Serial

(b) Parallel

FIGURE 2.4   Availability of serial and parallel connections

The availability of a system depends on the availability of its individual components plus the system organization. For example, some components may be redundant, such that the failure of one component does not affect system operation. Or the configuration may be such that the loss of a component results in reduced capability, but the system still functions.

Figure 2.4 shows two simple configurations. In part (a), two components are connected in series, and both must function properly for the function in question to be available. For example, these might be two modems at opposite ends of a communications link. When two components are connected in series in this fashion, then the availability of the combination is A^2, if the availability of each component is A. Thus, if the availability of each modem is 0.98, then the availability of the link with the two modems is $0.98 \times 0.98 = 0.96$.[1] The second part of the figure shows two devices in parallel. For example, these might be two links connecting a terminal to a host; if one link fails, the other is automatically used for backup. In this case, the dual link is unavailable only if both individual links are unavailable. If the availability of each link is 0.98, then the probability that one of them is unavailable is $1 - 0.98 = 0.02$. The probability that they are both unavailable is $0.02 \times 0.02 = 0.0004$. Thus the availability of the combined unit is $1 - 0.0004 = 0.9996$.

The availability analysis becomes quite complex as the configurations become more complicated and as we take into account not only the availability of the components but

---

[1]This assumes that the availability of the communications link itself is 1.0. If the link has an availability of, say, 0.99, then the overall availability is $0.99 \times 0.98 \times 0.98 = 0.95$.

also the expected load on the system. As an example, consider a dual-link system, such as is shown in Figure 2.4(b). The two links are used to connect a multiplexer to a host system. Nonpeak periods account for 40 percent of requests for service, and during those periods, either link can handle the traffic load. During peak periods, both links are required to handle the full load, but one link can handle 80 percent of the peak load. Functional availability for the system can be expressed as

$$A_f = \text{(capability when one link is up)} \times \Pr[1 \text{ link up}] + \text{(capability when two links are up)} \times \Pr[2 \text{ links up}],$$

where Pr[ ] means "the probability of."

The probability that both links are up is A^2, where A is the availability of either link. The probability that exactly one link is up is $A(1 - A) + (1 - A)A = 2A - 2A^2$. Using a value for A of 0.9, then $\Pr[2 \text{ links up}] = 0.9 \times 0.9 = 0.81$, and $\Pr[1 \text{ link up}] = 0.18$. Recalling that one link is sufficient for nonpeak loads, we have

$$A_f(\text{nonpeak}) = (1.0)(0.18) + (1.0)(0.81) = 0.99$$

and, for peak periods,

$$A_f(\text{peak}) = (0.8)(0.18) + (1.0)(0.81) = 0.954.$$

Overall functional availability, then, is

$$A_f = 0.6 \times A_f(\text{peak}) + 0.4 \times A_f(\text{nonpeak}) = 0.9684.$$

Thus, on average, about 97 percent of requests for service can be handled by the system.

2.2.1.2 Response Time

Response time is the time it takes a system to react to a given input. In an interactive transaction, it may be defined as the time between the last keystroke by the user and the beginning of the resulting display by the computer. For different types of applications, a slightly different definition is needed. In general, it is the time it takes for the system to respond to a request to perform a particular task.

Ideally, one would like the response time for any application to be short. However, it is almost invariably the case that shorter response time imposes greater cost. This cost comes from two sources:

- *Computer processing power:* The faster the computer, the shorter the response time. Of course, increased processing power means increased cost.

- *Competing requirements:* Providing rapid response time to some processes may penalize other processes.

Thus the value of a given level of response time must be assessed versus the cost of achieving that response time.

Table 2.2, based on Martin (1988), lists six general ranges of response times. Design difficulties are faced when a response time of less than one second is required. That a rapid response time is the key to productivity in interactive applications has been confirmed in a number of studies (Guynes 1988; Shneiderman 1984; Thadhani 1981). These studies show that when a computer and a user interact at a pace that ensures that neither has to wait on the other, productivity increases significantly, the cost of the work done on the computer therefore drops, and quality tends to improve. It used to be widely accepted that a relatively slow response—up to two seconds—was acceptable for most interactive

TABLE 2.2   Response-Time Ranges

Greater than 15 seconds

This rules out conversational interaction. For certain types of applications, certain types of users may be content to sit at a terminal for more than 15 seconds waiting for the answer to a single simple inquiry. However, for a busy person, captivity for more than 15 seconds seems intolerable. If such delays will occur, the system should be designed so that the user can turn to other activities and request the response at some later time.

Greater than 4 seconds

These are generally too long for a conversation requiring the operator to retain information in short-term memory (the operator's memory, not the computer's!). Such delays would be very inhibiting in problem-solving activity and frustrating in data entry activity. However, after a major closure, delays of from 4 to 15 seconds can be tolerated.

2 to 4 seconds

A delay longer than 2 seconds can be inhibiting to terminal operations demanding a high level of concentration. A wait of 2 to 4 seconds at a terminal can seem surprisingly long when the user is absorbed and emotionally committed to complete what he or she is doing. Again, a delay in this range may be acceptable after a minor closure has occurred.

Less than 2 seconds

When the terminal user has to remember information throughout several responses, the response time must be short. The more detailed the information remembered, the greater the need for responses of less than 2 seconds. For elaborate terminal activities, 2 seconds represents an important response-time limit.

Subsecond response time

Certain types of thought-intensive work, especially with graphics applications, require very short response times to maintain the user's interest and attention for long periods of time.

Decisecond response time

A response to pressing a key and seeing the character displayed on the screen or clicking a screen object with a mouse needs to be almost instantaneous—less than 0.1 second after the action. Interaction with a mouse requires extremely fast interaction if the designer is to avoid the use of alien syntax (one with commands, mnemonic punctuation, etc.).

applications because the user was thinking about the next task. However, it now appears that productivity increases as rapid response times are achieved.

The results reported on response time are based on an analysis of on-line transactions. A transaction consists of a user command from a terminal and the system's reply. It is the fundamental unit of work for on-line system users. It can be divided into two time sequences:

- *User response time:* the time span between the moment a user receives a complete reply to one command and enters the next command; often referred to as *think time*
- *System response time:* the time span between the moment the user enters a command and the moment a complete response is displayed on the terminal

As an example of the effect of reduced system response time, Figure 2.5 shows the results of a study carried out on engineers using a computer-aided design graphics program for the design of integrated circuit chips and boards (Smith 1983). Each transaction consists of a command by the engineer that alters in some way the graphic image being displayed on the screen. The results show that the rate of transactions increases as system

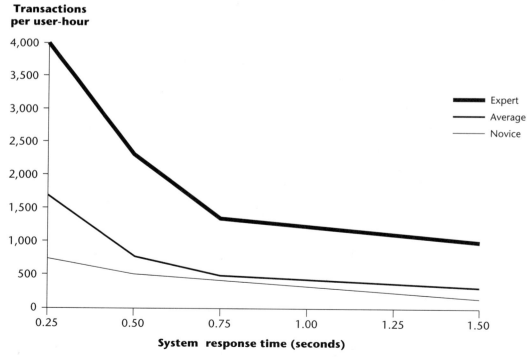

FIGURE 2.5   Response-time results for high-function graphics

response time falls and rises dramatically once system response time falls below one second. What happens is that as the system response time falls, so does the user response time. This has to do with the effects of short-term memory and human attention span.

To measure response time, a number of elements need to be examined. In particular, while it may be possible directly to measure the total response time in a given network environment, this figure alone is of little use in correcting problems or planning for the growth of the network. For these purposes, a detailed breakdown of response time is needed to identify bottlenecks and potential bottlenecks.

Figure 2.6 illustrates a typical networking situation and indicates the seven elements of response time common to most interactive applications. Each of these elements is one step in the overall path an inquiry takes through a communications configuration, and each element contributes a portion of the overall response time:

- *Inbound terminal delay:* the delay in getting an inquiry from the terminal to the communications line. By and large, there is no noticeable delay at the terminal itself, so the delay is directly dependent on the transmission rate from terminal to controller. For example, if the data rate on the line is 2400 bps = 300 characters per second, then the delay is 1/300 = 3.33 milliseconds per character. If the average message length is 100 characters, the delay will be 0.33 seconds.

- *Inbound queuing time:* the time required for processing by the controller or PAD device. The controller is dealing with input from a number of terminals as well as input from the network to be delivered to the terminals. Thus, an arriving message

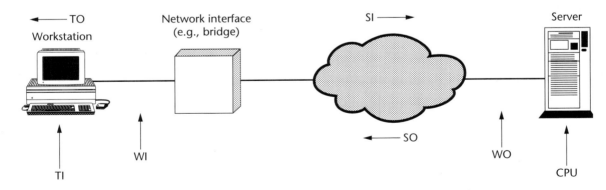

$$RT = TI + WI + SI + CPU + WO + SO + TO$$

RT = response time
TI = inbound terminal delay
WI = inbound queuing time
SI = inbound service time

CPU = CPU processor delay
WO = outbound queuing time
SO = outbound service time
TO = outbound terminal delay

FIGURE 2.6 Elements of response time

will be placed in a buffer to be served in turn. The busier the controller is, the longer the delay for processing will be.

- *Inbound service time:* the time to transmit the communications link, network, or other communications facility from the controller to the host's front-end processor. This element is itself made up of a number of elements based on the structure of the communications facility. If the facility is a public packet-switched network, it must be treated as a single element. However, if it is a private network (wide area or local area), leased line, or other user-configured facility, then a breakdown of this element will be needed for network control and planning.

- *Processor delay:* the time the front-end processor, the host processor, the disk drives, and so on at the computer center spend preparing a reply to an inquiry. This element is usually outside the control of the network manager.

- *Outbound queuing time:* the time a reply spends at a port in the front-end processor waiting to be dispatched to the network or communications line. As with the controller, the front-end processor will have a queue of replies to be serviced, and the delay is greater as the number of replies waiting increases.

- *Outbound service time:* the time to transmit the communications facility from the host's front-end processor to the controller.

- *Outbound terminal delay:* the delay at the terminal itself. Again, this is primarily due to line speed.

Response time is relatively easy to measure and is one of the most important classes of information needed for network management.

2.2.1.3   Accuracy

Accurate transmission of data between user and host or between two hosts is, of course, essential for any network. Because of the built-in error-correction mechanisms in protocols such as the data link and transport protocols, accuracy is generally not a user concern. Nevertheless, it is useful to monitor the rate of errors that must be corrected. This may give an indication of an intermittently faulty line or the existence of a source of noise or interference that should be corrected.

2.2.1.4   Throughput

Throughput is an application-oriented measure. Examples include

- the number of transactions of a given type for a certain period of time
- the number of customer sessions for a given application during a certain period of time
- the number of calls for a circuit-switched environment

It is useful to track these measures over time to get a feel for projected demand and likely performance trouble spots.

2.2.1.5 Utilization

Utilization is a more fine-grained measure than throughput. It refers to determining the percentage of time that a resource is in use over a given period of time.

Perhaps the most important use of utilization is to search for potential bottlenecks and areas of congestion. This is important because response time usually increases exponentially as the utilization of a resource increases; this is a well-known result of queuing theory (see Appendix 2A). Because of this exponential behavior, congestion can quickly get out of hand if it is not spotted early and dealt with quickly.

By looking at a profile of which resources are in use at any given time and which are idle, the analyst may be able to find resources that are overcommitted or underutilized and adjust the network accordingly. Consider the following example of a simple but very effective technique of assessing network efficiency. This technique is useful for assessing the capacity of various communications links in a network. The basic idea is to observe differences between planned load and actual load on various links in a network. The planned load is reflected by the capacity, in bits per second, of each individual link. The actual load, of course, is the measured average traffic, again in bits per second, on each such link. An analogy can be made with a cost accounting technique that looks at the ratios of actual expenditures to planned expenditures by division within a company. Significant divergences across divisions can lead to useful information because they challenge expectations and raise questions about the accuracy of the budget-planning process in each division.

Consider, for example, the simple network configuration of Figure 2.7(a). We will express the load on each channel as the percentage of the total load in the network and the flow on each channel as the percentage of the total flow. Table 2.3 contains the numerical results, and Figure 2.7(b) provides a graphical illustration. As we can see, the total capacity of the network provides a comfortable margin over the total load on the network, and of course no link is carrying a load greater than its capacity. However, by looking at relative capacity and relative loads, we can see that some links are carrying less than a proportionate share of the load and some are carrying more than their share. This indicates an inefficient allocation of resources. By adjusting these ratios—either by redirecting traffic or by changing the relative data rates of the various links—a closer balance between the planned load and the actual load can be achieved, reducing the total required capacity and using resources more efficiently.

2.2.2 Performance-Monitoring Function

Performance monitoring encompasses three components: *performance measurement,* which is the actual gathering of statistics about network traffic and timing; *performance analysis,* which consists of software for reducing and presenting the data; and *synthetic traffic generation,* which permits the network to be observed under a controlled load.

Performance measurement is often accomplished by agent modules within the devices on the network (hosts, routers, bridges, etc.). These agents are in a position to

(a) Network layout

(b) Proportionate share of capacity and load

■ Relative capacity   ▨ Relative load

FIGURE 2.7   Simple efficiency analysis

TABLE 2.3   Load and Capacity Analysis for Network Shown in Figure 2.7(a)

	Link 1	Link 2	Link 3	Link 4	Link 5	Total
Load (Kbps)	30	30	50	40	50	200
Capacity (Kbps)	40	40	60	80	180	400
Percentage of total load	15	15	25	20	25	100
Percentage of total capacity	10	10	15	20	45	100
Ratio	1.5	1.5	1.67	1.0	0.55	—

observe the amount of traffic into and out of a node, the number of connections (network level, transport level, application level) and the traffic per connection, and other measures that provide a detailed picture of the behavior of that node. Of course, all of this measurement comes at the price of processing resources within the node.

In a shared network, such as a LAN, much of the needed information can be collected by an external or remote monitor that simply observes the traffic on the network. This arrangement offloads much of the processing requirement from operational nodes to a dedicated system.

Table 2.4 lists the types of measurements reported in a typical LAN facility and gives some idea of the kind of measurements that are of interest. These measurements can be used to answer a number of questions. One area of inquiry concerns possible errors or inefficiencies.

- Is traffic evenly distributed among the network users or are there source–destination pairs with unusually heavy traffic?
- What is the percentage of each type of packet? Are some packet types of unusually high frequency, indicating an error or an inefficient protocol?
- What is the distribution of data packet sizes?
- What are the channel acquisition and communication delay distributions? Are these times excessive?
- Are collisions a factor in getting packets transmitted, indicating possible faulty hardware or protocols?
- What is the channel utilization and throughput?

TABLE 2.4   Performance Measurement Reports

Name	Variables	Description
Host communication matrix	Source × destination	(Number, %) of (packets, data packets, data octets)
Group communication matrix	Source × destination	As above, consolidated into address groups
Packet type histogram	Packet type	(Number, %) of (packets, original packets) by type
Data packet size histogram	Packet size	(Number, %) of data packets by data octet length
Throughput-utilization distribution	Source	(Total octets, data octets) transmitted
Packet interarrival time histogram	Interarrival time	Time between consecutive carrier (network-busy) signals
Channel acquisition delay histogram	Network interface unit (NIU) acquisition delay	(Number, %) of packets delayed at NIU by given amount
Communication delay histogram	Packet delay	Time from original packet ready at source to receipt
Collision count histogram	Number of collisions	Number of packets by number of collisions
Transmission count histogram	Number of transmissions	Number of packets by transmission attempts

A second area has to do with increasing traffic load and varying packet sizes:

- What is the effect of traffic load on utilization, throughput, and time delays? When does traffic load start to degrade system performance?
- Defining a stable network as one whose utilization is a nondecreasing function of traffic load, what is the tradeoff among stability, throughput, and delay?
- What is the maximum capacity of the channel under normal operating conditions? How many active users are necessary to reach this maximum?
- Do larger packets increase or decrease throughput and delay?
- How does constant packet size affect utilization and delay?

These areas are of interest to the network manager. Other questions of concern have to do with response time and throughput by user class and determining how much growth the network can absorb before certain performance thresholds are crossed.

2.2.3   Statistical Versus Exhaustive Measurement

When an agent in a node or an external monitor is monitoring a heavy load of traffic, it may not be practical to collect exhaustive data. For example, in order for an external monitor to construct a matrix that accurately shows the total number of packets in a given time period between each source–destination pair, the monitor would need to capture every packet transmitted on the LAN under observation and read the source and destination address in each packet header. When the LAN is heavily loaded, the monitor simply may not be able to keep up.

The alternative is to treat each parameter as a random variable and sample the traffic stream in order to estimate the value of the random variable. However, care must be taken in employing and interpreting statistical estimation results. Traditional statistical methods were developed for such areas as agriculture and biology, where it can often be assumed that the probabilities of interest are relatively large (typically 10^{-2} or higher) and that there is independence among observations (where the outcome of one observation indicates nothing about the outcome of another). Neither of these assumptions holds true for data communications, where some events of interest, such as errors, may occur at a rate of 10^{-6} or lower, and where clustering or burstiness is commonly observed. The individual responsible for designing sampling functions and for interpreting the results needs to have some familiarity with statistical principles.[2]

---

[2]See Appendix 2B for a brief introduction to statistical principles.

2.3   *Fault Monitoring*

The objective of *fault monitoring* is to identify faults as quickly as possible after they occur and to identify the cause of the fault so that remedial action may be taken.

2.3.1   Problems of Fault Monitoring

In a complex environment, locating and diagnosing faults can be difficult. Dupuy et al. (1989) list the following specific problems associated with fault observation.

- *Unobservable faults:* Certain faults are inherently unobservable locally. For example, the existence of a deadlock between cooperating distributed processes may not be observable locally. Other faults may not be observable because the vendor equipment is not instrumented to record the occurrence of a fault.

- *Partially observable faults:* A node failure may be observable but the observation may be insufficient to pinpoint the problem. For example, a node may not be responding due to the failure of some low-level protocol in an attached device.

- *Uncertainty in observation:* Even when detailed observations of faults are possible, there may be uncertainty and even inconsistencies associated with the observations. For example, lack of response from a remote device may mean that the device is stuck, the network is partitioned, congestion caused the response to be delayed, or the local timer is faulty.

Once faults are observed, it is necessary to isolate the fault to a particular component. Problems arise here also, including the following suggested in Fried and Tjong (1990):

- *Multiple potential causes:* When multiple technologies are involved, the potential points of failure and the types of failures increase. This makes it harder to locate the source of a fault. In Figure 2.8, for example, data transmitted between the client workstation and the server must traverse LAN, router, multiplexer, and transmission subsystems. If connectivity is lost or if error rates are high, the trouble could be due to problems in any one of these subsystems.

- *Too many related observations:* A single failure can affect many active communication paths. The failure of the T1 line in Figure 2.8 will affect all active communication between the token ring stations and stations on the two Ethernet LANs, as well as voice communication between the PBXs. Furthermore, a failure in one layer of the communications architecture can cause degradations or failures in all the dependent higher layers, as illustrated in Figure 2.9. Thus, a failure in the T1 line will be detected in the routers as a link failure and in the workstations as transport

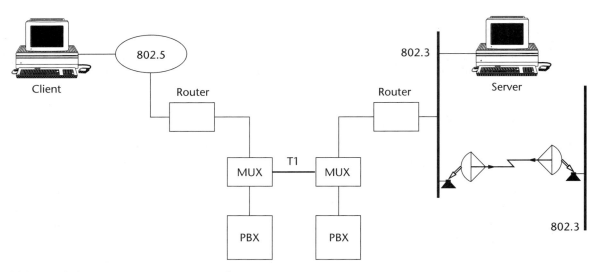

FIGURE 2.8   Heterogeneous network environment

and application failures. Because a single failure may generate many secondary failures, the proliferation of fault-monitoring data that can be generated in this way can obscure the single underlying problem.

- *Interference between diagnosis and local recovery procedures:* Local recovery procedures may destroy important evidence concerning the nature of the fault, disabling diagnosis.

- *Absence of automated testing tools:* Testing to isolate faults is difficult and costly to administer.

2.3.2   Fault-Monitoring Functions

The first requirement of a fault-monitoring system is that it be able to detect and report faults. At a minimum, a fault-monitoring agent will maintain a log of significant events and errors. These logs, or summaries, are available to authorized manager systems. Thus, a system that operates primarily by polling would rely on these logs. Typically, the fault-monitoring agent has the capability to report errors independently to one or more managers. To avoid overloading the network, the criteria for issuing a fault report must be reasonably tight.

In addition to reporting known, existing faults, a good fault-monitoring system will be able to anticipate faults. Generally, this involves setting up thresholds and issuing a report when a monitored variable crosses a threshold. For example, if the fraction of

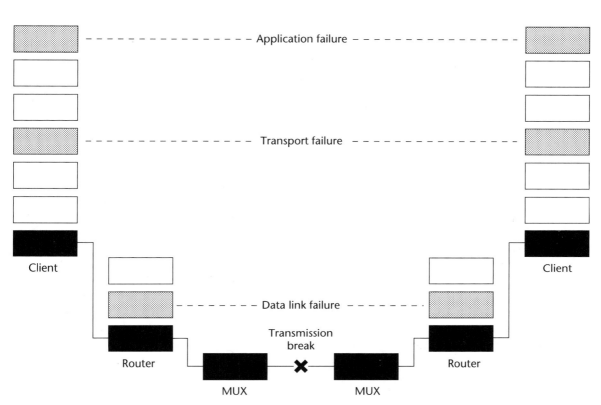

FIGURE 2.9　Propagation of failures to higher layers

transmitted packets that suffers an error exceeds a certain value, this may indicate that a problem is developing along the communications path. If the threshold is set low enough, the network manager may be alerted in time to take action that avoids a major failure in the system.

The fault-monitoring system should also assist in isolating and diagnosing the fault. Examples of tests that a fault-monitoring system should have at its command include a

- Connectivity test
- Data integrity test
- Protocol integrity test
- Data saturation test
- Connection saturation test
- Response-time test

- Loopback test
- Function test
- Diagnostic test

Perhaps more than in other areas of network monitoring, an effective user interface is required for fault monitoring. In complex situations, faults will be isolated, diagnosed, and ultimately corrected only by the cooperative effort of a human user and the monitor software.

2.4   *Accounting Monitoring*

Accounting monitoring is primarily a matter of keeping track of users' usage of network resources. The requirements for this function vary widely. In some environments, accounting may be of a quite general nature. For example, an internal accounting system may be used only to assess the overall usage of resources and to determine what proportion of the cost of each shared resource should be allotted to each department. In other cases, particularly for systems that offer a public service, but also for many systems with only internal users, it is required that usage be broken down by account, by project, or even by individual user for the purposes of billing. In this latter case, the information gathered by the monitor system must be more detailed and more accurate than that required for a general system.

Examples of resources that may be subject to accounting include the following:

- *Communications facilities:* LANs, WANs, leased lines, dial-up lines, and PBX systems
- *Computer hardware:* workstations and servers
- *Software and systems:* applications and utility software in servers, a data center, and end-user sites
- *Services:* includes all commercial communications and information services available to network users

For any given type of resource, accounting data are collected, based on the requirements of the organization. For example, the following communications-related accounting data might be gathered and maintained on each user:

- *User identification:* provided by the originator of a transaction or a service request
- *Receiver:* identifies the network component to which a connection is made or attempted
- *Number of packets:* count of data transmitted
- *Security level:* identifies the transmission and processing priorities

- *Time stamps:* associated with each principal transmission and processing event (for example, transaction start and stop times)
- *Network status codes:* indicates the nature of any detected errors or malfunctions
- *Resources used:* indicates which resources are invoked by this transaction or service event

2.5   Summary

Network monitoring is the most fundamental aspect of automated network management. Although many network management systems—because of a lack of security mechanisms—do not include network control features, all network management systems include a network-monitoring component.

The purpose of network monitoring is to gather information about the status and behavior of network elements. Information to be gathered includes static information, related to the configuration; dynamic information, related to events in the network; and statistical information, summarized from dynamic information. Typically, each managed device in the network includes an agent module responsible for collecting local management information and transmitting it to one or more management stations. Each management station includes network management application software plus software for communicating with agents. Information may be collected actively, by means of polling by the management station, or passively, by means of event reporting by the agents.

In the area of performance management, the most important categories of management information are

- Availability
- Response time
- Accuracy
- Throughput
- Utilization

The objective of fault monitoring is to identify faults as quickly as possible and to identify the cause of the fault so that corrective action may be taken. The fault-monitoring function is complicated by the fact that, by definition, it is needed at a time when some portion of the network is not functioning properly. Thus, it may be difficult to learn of and identify certain faults.

In the area of accounting management, network monitoring is concerned with gathering usage information to the level of detail required for proper accounting.

QUEUING THEORY CONCEPTS

Queuing theory is an invaluable tool in performance management. This appendix gives a brief overview of the basic queuing theory concepts.

2A.1 Why Queuing Analysis?

There are many situations in the field of data communications and computer networking when it is important to be able to project the effect of some change in a design: Either the load on a system is expected to increase or a design change is contemplated. For example, an organization supports a number of terminals, personal computers, and workstations on a 4-Mbps token ring LAN. An additional department in the building is to be cut over onto the network. Can the existing LAN handle the increased workload, or would it be better to provide a second LAN with a bridge between the two? There are other situations in which no facility exists but, on the basis of expected demand, a system design needs to be created. For example, a department intends to equip each of its personnel with a personal computer and to configure these into a LAN with a file server. Based on experience elsewhere in the company, the load generated by each PC can be estimated.

The focus of queuing analysis is system performance. In an interactive or real-time application, often the parameter of concern is response time. In other cases, throughput is the principal issue. In any event, performance projections are to be made on the basis of either existing load information or estimated load for a new environment. A number of approaches are possible.

1. Do an after-the-fact analysis based on actual values.
2. Make a simple projection by scaling up from existing experience to the expected future environment.
3. Develop an analytic model based on queuing theory.
4. Program and run a simulation model.

Option 1 is no option at all: We will wait and see what happens. This often leads to unhappy users and to unwise purchases.

Option 2 sounds more promising. The analyst may take the position that it is impossible to project future demand with any degree of certainty. Therefore, it is pointless to attempt some exact modeling procedure. Rather, a rough-and-ready projection will provide ballpark estimates. The problem with this approach is that the behavior of most communications systems is not what one would intuitively expect. If the environment includes a shared facility (for example, a network, a transmission line, or a time-sharing system), then the performance of that system typically responds in an exponential way to increases in demand.

FIGURE 2.10   Projected versus actual response time

Figure 2.10 is a typical example. The upper line shows what usually happens to user response time on a shared facility as the load on that facility increases. The load is expressed as a fraction of capacity. Thus, if we are dealing with a router that is capable of processing 1,000 packets per second, then a load of 0.5 represents an input of 500 packets per second, and the response time is the amount of time it takes to retransmit any incoming packet. The lower line is a simple projection[3] based on a knowledge of the behavior of the system up to a load of 0.5. Note that while things appear rosy when the simple projection is made, performance on the system will in fact collapse beyond a load of about 0.8 to 0.9.

Thus, a more exact prediction tool is needed. Option 3 is to make use of an analytic model, which is one that can be expressed as a set of equations that can be solved to yield the desired parameters (response time, throughput, etc.). For networking and communications problems, and indeed for many practical real-world problems, analytic models based on queuing theory provide a reasonably good fit to reality. The disadvantage of queuing theory is that a number of simplifying assumptions must be made to derive equations for the parameters of interest.

---

[3]In fact, the lower line is based on fitting a third-order polynomial to the data available up to a load of 0.5.

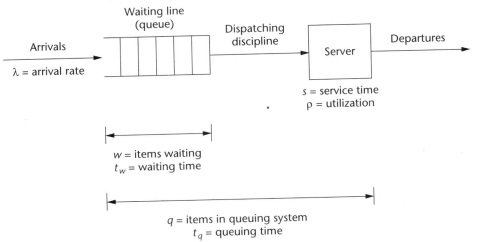

FIGURE 2.11   Queuing system structure and parameters for single-server queue

The final approach is a simulation model. Here, given a sufficiently powerful and flexible simulation programming language, the analyst can model reality in great detail and avoid making the many assumptions required of queuing theory. However, in most cases, a simulation model is not needed or at least is not advisable as a first step in the analysis. First, both existing measurements and projections of future load carry with them a certain margin of error. Thus, no matter how good the simulation model is, the value of the results is limited by the quality of the input. Second, despite the many assumptions required of queuing theory, the results that are produced usually come quite close to those that would be produced by a more careful simulation analysis. Furthermore, a queuing analysis can literally be accomplished in a matter of minutes for a well-defined problem, whereas simulation exercises can take days, weeks, or longer to program and run.

2A.2   Single-Server Queuing Model

The most basic queuing system is depicted in Figure 2.11. The central element of the system is a server, which provides some service to items. Items from some population of items arrive at the system to be served. If the server is idle, an item is served immediately. Otherwise, an arriving item joins a waiting line.[4] When the server has completed serving an item, the item departs. If items are waiting in the queue, one is immediately dispatched to the server.

The figure also illustrates the basic parameters associated with a queuing model. Items arrive at the facility at some average arrival rate (items arriving per second), λ. At

---

[4]The waiting line is referred to as a queue in some treatments in the literature; it is also common to refer to the entire system as a queue. The latter is preferred here.

any given time, a certain number of items will be waiting in the queue (zero or more); the average number waiting is w, and the mean time that an item must wait is t_w. Note that t_w is averaged over all incoming items, including those that do not wait at all. The server handles incoming items with an average service time s; this is the time interval between the dispatching of an item to the server and the departure of that item from the server. Utilization is the fraction of time that the server is busy, measured over some interval of time. Finally, two parameters apply to the system as a whole: The average number of items in the system, including the item being served (if any) and the items in the queue (if any), is q; and the average time that an item spends in the system, waiting and being served, is t_q.

Table 2.5 provides some equations for single-server queues. Making use of a scaling factor, A, the equations for some of the key output variables are straightforward. Note that the key factor in the scaling parameter is the ratio of the standard deviation of service time to the mean. No other information about the service time is needed. Two special cases are of some interest. When the standard deviation is equal to the mean, the service time distribution is exponential. This is the simplest case, and the easiest one for calculating results. Part (b) of the table shows the simplified versions of equations. The other interesting case is a standard deviation of service time equal to zero, that is, a constant service time. The corresponding equations are shown in part (c) of the table.

Figures 2.12 and 2.13 plot values of average queue size and queuing time versus utilization of three values of σ_s/s. Note that the poorest performance is exhibited by the exponential service time, and the best by a constant service time. Usually, one can consider the exponential service time to be a worst case. An analysis based on this assumption will give conservative results.

What value of σ_s/s is one likely to encounter? We can consider four regions:

- *Zero:* This is the rare case of constant service time. If all transmitted messages are of the same length, they would fit this category.

- *Ratio less than 1:* Since this ratio is better than the exponential case, using exponential results will give queue sizes and times that are slightly larger than they should be, and therefore one will be on the safe side. An example of this category might be a data entry application from a particular form.

- *Ratio close to 1:* This is the most common occurrence and corresponds to exponential service time. That is, service times are essentially random. Consider message lengths to a computer terminal: A full screen might be 1,920 characters, with message sizes falling anywhere in the full range. Airline reservations, file look-ups on inquiries, shared LANs, and packet-switching networks are examples of systems that often fit this category.

- *Ratio greater than 1:* If you observe this, you need to use the general model and not rely on the exponential model. The most common occurrence of this in a communications system is a bimodal distribution, with a wide spread between the peaks. An example is a system that experiences many short messages, many long messages, and few in between.

TABLE 2.5 Formulas for Single-Server Queues

Parameters

λ = mean number of arrivals per second

s = mean service time for each arrival

σ_s = standard deviation of service time

ρ = utilization; fraction of time facility is busy

q = mean number of items in system (waiting and being served)

t_q = mean time an item spends in system

σ_q = standard deviation of number of items in system

σ_{tq} = standard deviation of time an item spends in system

Assumptions

1. Poisson arrival rate is assumed.
2. Dispatching discipline does not give preference to items based on service times.
3. Formulas for standard deviation assume first-in, first-out dispatching.
4. No items leave the queue (lost calls delayed).

(a) General service times

$$A = \frac{1}{2}\left[1 + \left(\frac{\sigma_s}{s}\right)^2\right] \quad \text{(useful parameter)}$$

$$q = \rho + \frac{\rho^2 A}{1-\rho}; \quad t_q = s + \frac{\rho s A}{1-\rho}; \quad \rho = \lambda s$$

(b) Exponential service times

$$q = \frac{\rho}{1-\rho}$$

$$t_q = \frac{s}{1-\rho}$$

$$\sigma_q = \frac{\sqrt{\rho}}{1-\rho}$$

$$\sigma_{tq} = \frac{s}{1-\rho}$$

(c) Constant service times

$$q = \frac{\rho^2}{2(1-\rho)} + \rho$$

$$t_q = \frac{s(2-\rho)}{2(1-\rho)}$$

$$\sigma_q = \frac{1}{1-\rho}\sqrt{\rho - \frac{3\rho^2}{2} + \frac{5\rho^3}{6} - \frac{\rho^4}{12}}$$

$$\sigma_{tq} = \frac{s}{1-\rho}\sqrt{\frac{\rho}{2} - \frac{\rho^2}{12}}$$

Incidentally, the same consideration applies to the arrival rate. For a Poisson arrival rate, the interarrival times are exponential, and the ratio of standard deviation to mean is 1. If the observed ratio is much less than 1, then arrivals tend to be evenly spaced (not much variability), and the Poisson assumption will overestimate queue sizes and delays. On the other hand, if the ratio is greater than 1, then arrivals tend to cluster and congestion becomes more acute.

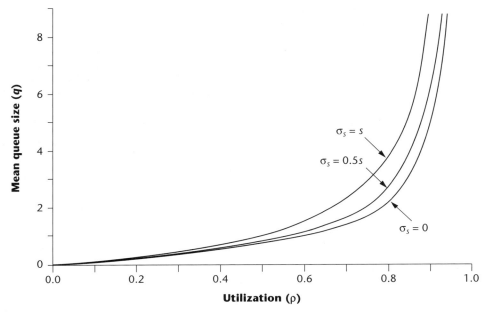

FIGURE 2.12 Mean queue sizes for single-server queue

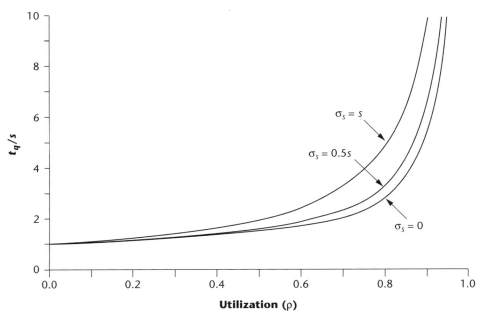

FIGURE 2.13 Mean queueing time for single-server queue

APPENDIX 2B   *STATISTICAL ANALYSIS CONCEPTS*

For many parameters of interest to a performance-monitoring system, it is impossible or impractical to measure the parameter by counting all relevant events. In these cases, we need to estimate the values of the parameters; usually we are interested in the mean and the standard deviation.

Measurements are taken in the form of samples. A particular parameter—for example, the rate of packets generated by a terminal or the size of packets—is estimated by observing some of the packets generated during a period of time.

To estimate a quantity, such as the length of a packet, the following equations can be used:

sample mean:
$$\overline{X} = \frac{1}{n}\sum_{i=1}^{n} X_i,$$

sample variance:
$$S^2 = \frac{\sum_{i=1}^{n}(X_i - \overline{X})^2}{n-1}$$

$$= \frac{\left(n\sum_{i=1}^{n} X_i^2\right) - \left(\sum_{i=1}^{n} X_i\right)^2}{n(n-1)},$$

sample standard deviation: $S = \sqrt{S^2},$

where

n = sample size,
X_i = ith sample.

It is important to note that the sample mean and sample standard deviation are themselves random variables. For example, if you take a sample from some population and calculate the sample mean, and do this a number of times, the calculated values will differ. Thus, we can talk of the mean and the standard deviation of the sample mean, or even of the entire probability distribution of the sample mean.

It follows that the probabilistic nature of our estimated values is a source of error, known as *sampling error*. In general, the greater the size of the sample taken, the smaller the standard deviation of the sample mean, and therefore the closer that our estimate is likely to be to the actual mean. By making certain reasonable assumptions about the nature of the random variable being tested and the randomness of the sampling procedure, one can in fact determine the probability that a sample mean or sample standard deviation is within a certain distance from the actual mean or standard deviation. This concept is often reported with the results of a sample. For example, it is common for the result of an opinion poll to include a comment such as, "The result is within 5% of the true value with a confidence (probability) of 99%." The interval around the actual value is known as the *confidence interval,* and the probability that the sample mean is within that interval is known as the *confidence level.*

In designing a sampling scheme, we can specify any two of the following three quantities, and the remaining quantity can be determined:

- Confidence level
- Sample size
- Length of confidence interval

It is customary first to specify the confidence level. Then either the sample size or the length of the confidence interval is specified and the remaining parameter is calculated. The sample size is specified, and the length of the confidence interval is derived from it, when the budget (amount of resources devoted to sampling) is the more important criterion. Conversely, when the precision of the estimate is the more important criterion, the length of the confidence interval is specified, and the sample size is derived from the interval.

There is, however, another source of error, which is less widely appreciated among nonstatisticians, namely *bias.* For example, if an opinion poll is conducted, and only members of a certain socioeconomic group are interviewed, the results are not necessarily representative of the entire population. In a communications context, sampling done during one time of day may not reflect the activity at another time of day. If we want to design a system that will handle the peak load that is likely to be experienced, then we should observe the traffic during the time of day that is most likely to produce the greatest load.

CHAPTER 3 · *Network Control*

The network control portion of network management is concerned with modifying parameters in and causing actions to be taken by the end systems, intermediate systems, and subnetworks that make up the configuration to be managed.

All of the five major functional areas of network management (performance, fault, accounting, configuration, and security) involve both monitoring and control. Traditionally, however, the emphasis in the first three of these areas has been on monitoring, while the last two areas are more concerned with control. Hence, Chapter 2 focuses on performance, fault, and accounting monitoring. This chapter examines the network control aspects of configuration management and security management.

3.1 Configuration Control

Configuration management is concerned with the initialization, maintenance, and shutdown of individual components and logical subsystems within the total configuration of computer and communications resources of an installation. Configuration management can dictate the initialization process by identifying and specifying the characteristics of the network components and resources that will constitute the "network." Managed resources include both identifiable physical resources (for example, a server or a router) and lower-level logical objects (for example, a transport-layer retransmission timer). Configuration management can specify initial or default values for attributes so that managed resources commence operation in the desired states, possess the proper parameter values, and form the desired relationships with other network components.

While the network is in operation, configuration management is responsible for monitoring the configuration and making changes in response to user commands or in response to other network management functions. For example, if the performance-monitoring function detects that response time is degrading due to an imbalance in load, configuration management may adjust the configuration to achieve load leveling. Similarly, if fault management detects and isolates a fault, configuration management may alter the configuration to bypass the fault.

Configuration management includes the following functions:

- Define configuration information.
- Set and modify attribute values.
- Define and modify relationships.
- Initialize and terminate network operations.
- Distribute software.
- Examine values and relationships.
- Report on configuration status.

The final two items in the preceding list are configuration-monitoring functions. Through a query–response interaction, a manager station may examine configuration information maintained by an agent station. Via an event report, an agent may report a change in status to a manager. The remainder of the items on the list are configuration control functions; these are the subject of this chapter and will be described in the following subsections.

3.1.1   Define Configuration Information

Configuration information describes the nature and status of resources that are of interest to network management. The configuration information includes a specification of the resources under management and the attributes of those resources. Network resources include physical resources (end systems, routers, bridges, communications facilities and services, communications media, and modems) and logical resources (timers, counters, and virtual circuits). Attributes include, for example, name, address, identification number, states, operational characteristics, software version number, and release level.

Configuration information (indeed, all management information) may be structured in a number of ways:

- As a simple structured list of data fields, with each field containing a single value. This is the approach taken by SNMP.
- As an object-oriented database. Each element of interest to management is represented by one or more objects. Each object contains attributes whose values reflect the characteristics of the represented element. An object may also contain behaviors, such as notifications to be issued if certain events relating to this element occur. The use of containment and inheritance relationships allows relationships among objects to be defined. This is the approach taken by OSI network management.
- As a relational database. Individual fields in the database contain values that reflect characteristics of network elements. The structure of the database reflects the relationships among network elements.

Although this information is to be accessible to a manager station, it is generally stored near the resource in question, either in an agent node, if the resource is part of that node, or in a proxy node, if the node containing the resource does not support agent software.

The network control function should enable the user to specify the range and type of values to which the specified resource attributes at a particular agent can be set. The range can be a list of all possible states or the allowed upper and lower limits for parameters and attributes. The type of value allowable for an attribute may also be specified.

The network control function should also be able to define new object types, or data element types, depending on the database type. Ideally, it should be possible to define these new objects on-line and to have such objects created at the appropriate agents and proxies. In virtually all systems today, this function is performed off-line, as part of configuring a network element, rather than being possible dynamically.

3.1.2   Set and Modify Attribute Values

The configuration control function should enable a manager station to remotely set and modify attribute values in agents and proxies. There are two limitations on this capability.

1. A manager must be authorized to make the modification of a particular attribute at a particular agent or proxy at a particular time. This is a security concern, addressed in Section 3.2.

2. Some attributes reflect the "reality" at a resource and cannot, by their nature, be modified remotely. For example, one item of information could be the number of physical ports on a router. Although each port may be enabled or disabled at any particular time, the actual number of ports can be changed only by a physical action at the router, not by a remote parameter-setting action.

The modification of an attribute will obviously modify the configuration information at the agent or proxy. In general, modifications fall into three categories:

- *Database update only:* When a manager issues a modify command to an agent, one or more values in the agent's configuration database are changed (if the operation succeeds). In some cases, there is no other immediate response on behalf of the agent. For example, a manager may change contact information (name and address of person responsible for this resource). The agent responds by updating the appropriate data values and returning an acknowledgment to the manager.

- *Database update plus resource modification:* In addition to updating values in the configuration database at an agent, a modify command can affect an underlying resource. For example, if the state attribute of a physical port is set to "disabled," then the agent not only updates the state attribute but also disables the port, so that it is no longer in use.

- *Database update plus action:* In some network management systems, there are no direct "action commands" available to managers. Rather, there are parameters in the database that, when set, cause the agent to initiate a certain action. For example, a router might maintain a reinitialize parameter in its database. If an authorized manager sets this parameter to TRUE, the router would go through a reinitialization procedure, which would set the parameter to FALSE and reinitialize the router.

The user should be able to load predefined default attribute values such as default states, values, and operational characteristics of resources on a systemwide, individual node, or individual layer basis.

3.1.3   Define and Modify Relationships

A relationship describes an association, connection, or condition that exists between network resources or network components. Examples of relationships are a topology, a hierarchy, a physical or logical connection, or a management domain. A management domain is a set of resources that share a set of common management attributes or a set of common resources that share the same management authority.

Configuration management should allow on-line modification of resources without taking all or part of the network down. The user should be able to add, delete, and modify the relationships among network resources.

One example of the use of relationships is to manage the link-layer connection between LAN nodes, at the level of the service access point (SAP) of logical link control (LLC). An LLC connection can be set up in one of two ways. First, the LLC protocol in one node can issue a connection request to another node, either in response to higher-layer software or a terminal user command; these could be referred to as "switched" connections. Second, a network manager station could set up a fixed, or permanent, LLC connection between two nodes. This connection setup would designate the SAP in each node that served as an endpoint for the connection. The manager software, under operator command, should also be able to break a connection, permanent or switched. Another useful feature is to be able to designate a backup or alternate address to be used in case the primary destination fails to respond to a connection request.

3.1.4   Initialize and Terminate Network Operations

Configuration management should include mechanisms to enable users to initialize and close down network or subnetwork operation. Initialization includes verification that all settable resource attributes and relationships have been properly set, notifying users of any resource, attribute, or relationship still needing to be set, and validating users' initialization commands. For termination, mechanisms are needed to allow users to request retrieval of specified statistics, blocks, or status information before the termination procedures have completed.

3.1.5 Distribute Software

Configuration management should provide the capability to distribute software throughout the configuration to end systems (hosts, servers, and workstations) and intermediate systems (bridges, routers, and application-level gateways). This requires facilities to permit software loading requests, to transmit the specified versions of software, and to update the configuration tracking systems.

In addition to executable software, the software distribution function should also encompass tables and other data that drive the behavior of a node. Foremost in this category is the routing table, used by bridges and routers. There may be accounting, performance, or security concerns that require management intervention into routing decisions that cannot be solved by mathematical algorithms alone.

The user needs mechanisms to examine, update, and manage different versions of software and routing information. For example, users should be able to specify the loading of different versions of software or routing tables based on particular conditions, such as error rates.

3.2 *Security Control*

The requirements of information security within an organization have undergone two major changes in the last several decades. Prior to the widespread use of data-processing equipment, the security of an organization's valuable information was provided primarily by physical and administrative means. An example of the former is the use of rugged filing cabinets with a combination lock for storing sensitive documents. An example of the latter is personnel screening procedures used during the hiring process.

With the introduction of the computer, the need for automated tools for protecting files and other information stored on the computer became evident. This is especially the case for a shared system, such as a time-sharing system, and the need is even more acute for systems that can be accessed over a public telephone or data network. The generic name for the collection of tools designed to protect data and thwart hackers is *computer security*.

The second major change that affects security is the introduction of distributed systems and the use of networks and communications facilities for carrying data between terminal user and computer and between computer and computer. *Network security* measures are needed to protect data during their transmission.

The security management portion of network management deals with the provision of both computer and network security for the resources under management, including of course the network management system itself. Before examining some of the details of security management, it will be useful to characterize the security threat.

3.2.1   Security Threats

In order to be able to understand the types of threats that exist to security, we need to have a definition of security requirements. Computer and network security address three requirements:

- *Secrecy:* requires that the information in a computer system be accessible only for reading by authorized parties (This type of access includes printing, displaying, and other forms of disclosure, including simply revealing the existence of an object.)
- *Integrity:* requires that computer system assets can be modified only by authorized parties; modification includes writing, changing, changing status, deleting, and creating
- *Availability:* requires that computer system assets are available to authorized parties

3.2.1.1   Types of Threats

The types of threats to the security of a computer system or network are best characterized by viewing the function of the computer system to be providing information. In general, there is a flow of information from a source, such as a file or a region of main memory, to a destination, such as another file or a user. This normal flow is depicted in Figure 3.1(a). The remainder of the figure shows four general categories of threats:

- *Interruption:* An asset of the system is destroyed or becomes unavailable or unusable. This is a threat to **availability**. Examples include the destruction of a piece of hardware, such as a hard disk, the cutting of a communication line, or the disabling of the file management system.
- *Interception:* An unauthorized party gains access to an asset. This is a threat to *secrecy.* The unauthorized party could be a person, a program, or a computer. Examples include wiretapping to capture data in a network, and the illicit copying of files or programs.
- *Modification:* An unauthorized party not only gains access but tampers with an asset. This is a threat to *integrity.* Examples include changing values in a data file, altering a program so that it performs differently, and modifying the content of messages being transmitted in a network.
- *Fabrication:* An unauthorized party inserts counterfeit objects into the system. This is also a threat to integrity. Examples include the insertion of spurious messages in a network or the addition of records to a file.

The assets of a computer system can be categorized as hardware, software, data, and communication lines and networks. Figure 3.2 and Table 3.1 indicate the nature of the threats each category of asset faces. Let us consider each of these in turn.

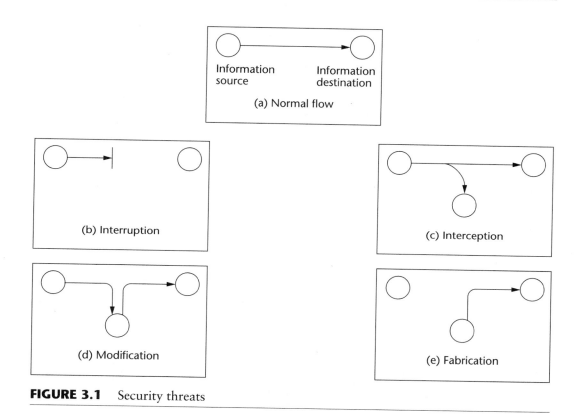

FIGURE 3.1   Security threats

3.2.1.2   Threats to Hardware

The main threat to computer system hardware is in the area of availability. Hardware is the most vulnerable to attack and the least amenable to automated controls. Threats include accidental and deliberate damage to equipment as well as theft. The proliferation of personal computers and workstations and the increasing use of local area networks increase the potential for losses in this area. Physical and administrative security measures are needed to deal with these threats.

3.2.1.3   Threats to Software

The operating system, utilities, and application programs are what make computer systems hardware useful to businesses and individuals. Several distinct threats need to be considered.

A key threat to software is availability. Software, especially application software, is surprisingly easy to delete. Software can also be altered or damaged to render it useless. Careful software configuration management, which includes making backups of the most recent version of software, can maintain high availability.

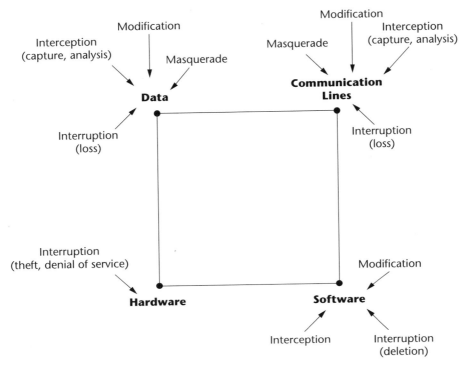

FIGURE 3.2   Security threats and computer system assets

A more difficult problem to deal with is software modification that results in a program that still functions but that behaves differently than before. Computer viruses and related attacks fall into this category.

A final problem is software secrecy. Although certain countermeasures are available, by and large the problem of unauthorized copying of software has not been solved.

3.2.1.4   Threats to Data

Hardware and software security are typically concerns of computing center professionals, or individual concerns of personal computer users. A much more widespread problem is data security, which involves files and other forms of data controlled by individuals, groups, and business organizations.

Security concerns with respect to data are broad, encompassing availability, secrecy, and integrity. In the case of availability, the concern is with the destruction of data files, which can occur either accidentally or maliciously.

The obvious concern with secrecy, of course, is the unauthorized reading of data files or databases, and this area has been the subject of perhaps more research and effort than

TABLE 3.1   Security Threats and Assets

	Availability	Secrecy	Integrity
Hardware	Equipment is stolen or disabled, thus denying service.	—	—
Software	Programs are deleted, denying access by users.	An unauthorized copy of software is made.	A working program is modified, to cause it either to fail during execution or to do some unintended task.
Data	Files are deleted, denying access to users.	An unauthorized read of data is performed. An analysis of statistical data reveals underlying data.	Existing files are modified, or new files are fabricated.
Communication lines	Messages are destroyed or deleted. Communication lines or networks are rendered unavailable.	Messages are read. The traffic pattern of messages is observed.	Messages are modified, delayed, reordered, or duplicated. False messages are fabricated.

any other area of computer security. A less obvious secrecy threat involves the analysis of data and manifests itself in the use of so-called statistical databases, which provide summary or aggregate information. Presumably, the existence of aggregate information does not threaten the privacy of the individuals involved. However, as the use of statistical databases grows, the potential for disclosure of personal information increases. In essence, characteristics of constituent individuals may be identified through careful analysis. To take a simple example, if one table records the aggregate of the incomes of respondents A, B, C, and D and another records the aggregate of the incomes of A, B, C, D, and E, the difference between the two aggregates would be the income of E. This problem is exacerbated by the increasing desire to combine data sets. In many cases, matching several sets of data for consistency at levels of aggregation appropriate to the problem requires a retreat to elemental units in the process of constructing the necessary aggregates. Thus, the elemental units, which are the subject of privacy concerns, are available at various stages in the processing of data sets.

Finally, data integrity is a major concern in most installations. Modifications to data files can have consequences ranging from minor to disastrous.

3.2.1.5   Threats to Communication Lines and Networks

Communication systems are used to transmit data. Thus, the concerns of availability, security, and integrity that are relevant to data security apply as well to network security. In this context, threats are conveniently categorized as passive or active (Figure 3.3).

FIGURE 3.3   Active and passive network security threats

Passive threats are in the nature of eavesdropping on or monitoring the transmissions of an organization. The goal of the attacker is to obtain information that is being transmitted. Two types of threats are involved here: release of message contents and traffic analysis.

The threat of *release of message contents* is clearly understood by most observers. A telephone conversation, an electronic mail message, or a transferred file may contain sensitive or confidential information. We would like to prevent the attacker from learning the contents of these transmissions.

The second passive threat, *traffic analysis*, is more subtle and often less applicable. Suppose that we had a way of masking the contents of messages or other information traffic so that an attacker, even if he or she captured the message, would be unable to extract the information from the message. The common technique for doing this is *encryption*, discussed at length subsequently. If we had such protection in place, it might still be possible for an attacker to observe the pattern of these messages. The attacker can determine the location and identity of communicating hosts and can also observe the frequency and length of messages being exchanged. This information might be useful in guessing the nature of the communication that is taking place.

Passive threats are very difficult to detect since they do not involve any alteration of the data. However, it is feasible to prevent these attacks from being successful. Thus, the emphasis in dealing with passive threats is on prevention and not detection.

The second major category of threat is *active threats*. These involve some modification of the data stream or the creation of a false stream. We can subdivide these threats into three categories: message-stream modification, denial of message service, and masquerade.

Message-stream modification simply means that some portion of a legitimate message is altered, or that messages are delayed, replayed, or reordered, in order to produce an unauthorized effect. For example, a message meaning "allow John Smith to read confidential file accounts" is modified to mean "allow Fred Brown to read confidential file accounts."

The *denial of service* prevents or inhibits the normal use or management of communications facilities. This attack may have a specific target; for example, an entity may suppress all messages directed to a particular destination (for example, the security audit service). Another form of service denial is the disruption of an entire network, either by disabling the network or by overloading it with messages so as to degrade performance.

A *masquerade* takes place when one entity pretends to be a different entity. A masquerade attack usually includes one of the other two forms of active attack. Such an attack can take place, for example, by capturing and replaying an authentication sequence.

Active threats present the opposite characteristics of passive threats. Whereas passive attacks are difficult to detect, measures are available to prevent their success. On the other hand, it is quite difficult to prevent active attacks absolutely, since this would require the physical protection of all communications facilities and paths at all times. Instead, the goal with respect to active attacks is to detect these attacks and to recover from any disruptions or delays caused by the attacks. Because the detection has a deterrent effect, this may also contribute to prevention.

3.2.1.6 Threats to the Network Management System

Since network management is a set of applications and databases on various hardware platforms distributed throughout the configuration, all of the threats discussed earlier in this chapter can be considered threats to the network management system. In addition, three security concerns specific to network management may be cited:

- *User masquerade:* A user who is not authorized to perform network management functions may attempt to access network management applications and information.
- *Network manager masquerade:* A computer system may masquerade as a network manager station (a management server in Figure 1.5).
- *Interference with manager–agent interchange:* One threat is the observation of manager–agent protocol traffic to extract sensitive management information. More damaging would be the modification of such traffic to disrupt the operation of the agent or the resources that it is managing.

3.2.2 Security Management Functions

The security facility of a system or network of systems consists of a set of security services and mechanisms. It is beyond the scope of this book to describe these services and mechanisms;[1] instead our focus is on the management of the security facility.

---

[1] See Stallings (1999) for a discussion.

The functions of security management can be grouped into three categories.

- Maintain security information.
- Control resource-access service.
- Control the encryption process.

3.2.2.1 Maintain Security Information

As with other areas of network management, security management is based on the use of management information exchanges between managers and agents. The same sorts of operations are employed for security management as for other areas of network management; the difference is only in the nature of the management information used. Examples of objects appropriate for security management include keys, authentication information, access right information, and operating parameters of security services and mechanisms.

Security management keeps account of activity, or attempted activity, with these security objects in order to detect and recover from attempted or successful security attacks. This includes the following functions related to the maintenance of security information:

- Event logging
- Monitoring security audit trails
- Monitoring usage and the users of security-related resources
- Reporting security violations
- Receiving notification of security violations
- Maintaining and examining security logs
- Maintaining backup copies for all or part of the security-related files
- Maintaining general network user profiles, and usage profiles for specific resources, to enable references for conformance to designated security profiles

3.2.2.2 Control Resource-Access Service

One of the central services of any security facility is access control. Access control involves authentication and authorization services and the actual decision to grant or refuse access to specific resources. The access-control service is designed to protect a broad range of network resources. Among those resources of particular concern for the network management function are

- Security codes
- Source routing and route recording information
- Directories
- Routing tables

- Alarm threshold levels
- Accounting tables

Security management manages the access-control service by maintaining general network user profiles and usage profiles for specific resources and by setting priorities for access. The security management function enables the user to create and delete security-related objects, change their attributes or state, and affect the relationships between security objects.

3.2.2.3   Control the Encryption Process

Security management must be able to encrypt any exchanges between managers and agents, as needed. In addition, security management should facilitate the use of encryption by other network entities. This function is also responsible for designating encryption algorithms and providing for key distribution.

3.3   *Summary*

Network control is concerned with altering parameters of various components of the configuration and causing predefined actions to be performed by these components.

In the area of configuration control, a variety of functions relating to the configuration of network and computing elements is included. These include the initialization, maintenance, and shut-down of individual components and logical subsystems.

In the area of security control, the responsibility of the network management system is to coordinate and control the security mechanisms built into the configuration of networks and systems under its management control. These security mechanisms are intended to protect user and system resources, including the network management system itself.

SNMPv1

CHAPTER 4   *SNMP Network Management Concepts*

The term Simple Network Management Protocol (SNMP) is actually used to refer to a collection of specifications for network management that include the protocol itself, the definition of data structures, and associated concepts. In this chapter, we provide a brief overview of the key concepts of SNMP. The details are developed in the remaining chapters of this part of the book.

4.1   *Background*

The development of SNMP follows a historical pattern similar to the development of the entire TCP/IP protocol suite, of which it is a part. It is perhaps useful to consider this pattern.

4.1.1   The Origins of TCP/IP

The starting point for TCP/IP[1] dates back to 1969, when the U.S. Department of Defense (DoD) funded, through the Advanced Research Projects Agency, the development of one of the first packet-switching networks, ARPANET. The purpose of ARPANET was to study technologies related to the sharing of computer resources and to spin off these technologies into data networks useful for day-to-day DoD requirements. As ARPANET evolved, it rapidly grew in size to accommodate first dozens and then hundreds of hosts and thousands of terminals. It soon became clear that a major issue was interoperability. With terminals and hosts from many vendors, specialized software needed to be developed to support everything from file transfer to terminal–host interaction. The problem became even greater as ARPANET evolved in the Internet, a collection of wide area and local area networks with ARPANET as the core.

---

[1]See Appendix A for a brief technical discussion of TCP/IP. A more detailed discussion can be found in Stallings (1997).

To solve the interoperability problem, ARPANET researchers developed a standardized set of protocols, which by the late 1970s had evolved into the present TCP/IP protocol suite. These protocols were standardized as official Internet Architecture Board (IAB) standards issued as requests for comments (RFCs). Ultimately, the core protocols of the suite were issued as military standards.

TCP/IP met the requirements of the DoD and became standard in DoD procurements. An interesting and generally unexpected development was the growth of the use of TCP/IP in nonmilitary applications. This growth began to take off in the mid-1980s, just when efforts were being made to develop an international consensus around OSI. Despite OSI, TCP/IP grew rapidly and is today the dominant standardized communications architecture. Although many (perhaps most) observers continue to predict that OSI will ultimately be the foundation for the bulk of interoperable computer communications, the life expectancy of TCP/IP grows with every passing year.

It is natural to ask why these military protocols have found favor in a commercial marketplace that should, on the face of it, prefer international standards. The commercial motivation is much the same as that of the DoD: The TCP/IP protocol suite is a mature, working set of protocols that provides interoperability and a high level of functionality. The international standards have been slow to develop, indeed are still evolving, and have only recently become commercially available. Furthermore, although the OSI protocol suite provides a much richer functionality than TCP/IP, this very richness implies a complexity that has made the implementation of conformant, interoperable software more difficult than with TCP/IP.

4.1.2   The Origins of TCP/IP Network Management

As TCP/IP was being developed, little thought was given to network management. Initially, virtually all of the hosts and subnetworks attached to ARPANET were based in an environment that included systems programmers and protocol designers working on some aspect of the ARPANET research. Therefore, management problems could be left to protocol experts who could tweak the network with the use of some basic tools.

Through the late 1970s, there were no management protocols as such. The one tool that was effectively used for management was the Internet Control Message Protocol (ICMP). ICMP provides a means for transferring control messages from routers and other hosts to a host, to provide feedback about problems in the environment. ICMP is available on all devices that support IP. From a network management point of view, the most useful feature of ICMP is the echo/echo-reply message pair. These messages provide a mechanism for testing that communication is possible between entities. The recipient of an echo message is obligated to return the contents of that message in an echo-reply message. Another useful pair of messages are time stamp and time stamp reply, which provide a mechanism for sampling the delay characteristics of the network.

These ICMP messages can be used, along with various IP header options such as source routing and record route, to develop simple but powerful management tools. The most notable example of this is the widely used PING (Packet Internet Groper) program. Using ICMP, plus some additional options such as the interval between requests and the number of times to send a request, PING can perform a variety of functions. Examples include determining if a physical network device can be addressed, verifying that a network can be addressed, and verifying the operation of a server on a host. The PING capability can be used to observe variations in round-trip times and in datagram loss rates, which can help to isolate areas of congestion and points of failure.

With some supplemental tools, the PING capability was a satisfactory solution to the network management requirement for many years. It was only in the late 1980s, when the growth of the Internet became exponential, that attention was focused on the development of a more powerful network management capability.

The number of hosts attached to the Internet has grown explosively. This growth in sheer size has been accompanied by a growth in complexity. There has been an equally rapid and exponential growth in the number of subnetworks that are part of the Internet and of the number of distinct administrative domains. This latter parameter reflects the number of different entities that have "management" responsibility for part of the Internet.

With the number of hosts on the network in the hundreds of thousands, and the number of individual networks in the thousands, it is no longer possible to rely on a small cadre of network experts to solve management problems. What was required was a standardized protocol with far more functionality than PING and yet one that could be easily learned and used by a wide variety of people with network management responsibilities.

The starting point in providing specific network management tools was the Simple Gateway Monitoring Protocol (SGMP) issued in November 1987. SGMP provided a straightforward means for monitoring gateways. As the need for a more general-purpose network management tool grew, three promising approaches emerged:

- *High-Level Entity Management System (HEMS):* This was a generalization of perhaps the first network management protocol used in the Internet, the Host Monitoring Protocol (HMP).

- *Simple Network Management Protocol (SNMP):* This was an enhanced version of the Simple Gateway Management Protocol (SGMP).

- *CMIP over TCP/IP (CMOT):* This was an attempt to incorporate, to the maximum extent possible, the protocol (common management information protocol), services, and database structure being standardized by ISO for network management.

In early 1988, the Internet Architecture Board (IAB) reviewed these proposals and approved further development of SNMP as a short-term solution and CMOT as the long-range solution (Cerf 1988). It was felt that within a reasonable period of time, TCP/IP installations would transition to OSI-based protocols. Thus, there was a reluctance to invest substantial effort in application-level protocols and services on TCP/IP that might soon have to be abandoned. In order to meet immediate needs, SNMP would be quickly developed to provide some basic management tools and support the development of an experience base for doing network management. HEMS was more capable than SNMP, but the extra effort on a dead end seemed unwarranted. Meanwhile, if CMIP could be implemented to run on top of TCP, then it might be possible to deploy CMOT even before the transition to OSI. Then, when the time came to move to OSI, the network management aspect of the move would require minimal effort.

To further solidify this strategy, the IAB dictated that both SNMP and CMOT use the same database of managed objects. That is, both protocols were to use the same set of monitoring and control variables, in the same formats, within any host, router, bridge, or other managed device. Thus, only a single structure of management information (SMI: the basic format conventions for objects) and a single management information base (MIB: the actual structure, or schema, of the database) would be defined for both protocols. This identity of databases would greatly facilitate the transition: Only the protocol and supporting software would need to be changed; the actual database would be the same in format and content at the time of transition.

It soon became apparent that this binding of the two protocols at the object level was impractical. In OSI network management, managed objects are seen as sophisticated entities with attributes, associated procedures, and notification capabilities, and other complex characteristics associated with object-oriented technology. To keep SNMP simple, it is not designed to work with such sophisticated concepts. In fact, the objects in SNMP are not really objects at all from the viewpoint of object-oriented technology; rather, objects in SNMP are simply variables with a few basic characteristics, such as data type and read-only or read-write attributes. Accordingly, the IAB relaxed its condition of a common SMI/MIB and allowed SNMP and CMOT development to proceed independently and in parallel (Cerf 1989).

4.1.3 The Evolution of SNMP

With the SNMP developers freed from the constraint of OSI compatibility, progress was rapid and it mirrors the history of TCP/IP. SNMP soon became widely available on vendor equipment and flourished within the Internet. In addition, SNMP quickly became the standardized management protocol of choice for the general user. Just as TCP/IP has outlasted all predictions of its useful lifetime, so SNMP appears to be around for the long haul, and widespread deployment of OSI network management continues to be delayed. Meanwhile, the CMOT effort languishes.

The "basic" SNMP is now in widespread use. Virtually all major vendors of host computers, workstations, bridges, routers, and hubs offer basic SNMP. Work is even progressing on the use of SNMP over OSI and other non-TCP/IP protocol suites. In addition, enhancements to SNMP have been pursued in a number of directions.

Perhaps the most important of these initiatives, so far, is the development of a remote monitoring capability for SNMP. The Remote Monitoring (RMON) specification defines additions to the basic SNMP MIB as well as the functions that exploit the RMON MIB.

RMON gives the network manager the ability to monitor subnetworks as a whole, rather than just individual devices on the subnetwork. Both vendors and users view RMON as an essential extension to SNMP, and RMON, though relatively new, is already widely deployed. Because of its importance, a separate part of this book (Part III) is devoted to RMON.

In addition to RMON, other extensions to the basic SNMP MIB have been developed. Some of these are vendor-independent and have to do with standardized network interfaces, such as token ring and FDDI. Others are vendor-specific, private extensions to the MIB. In general, these extensions do not add any new technology or concepts to SNMP. Therefore, other than some discussion of the practical issues related to these extensions, they are not covered in this book.

There is a limit to how far SNMP can be extended by simply defining new and more elaborate MIBs. RMON perhaps represents as far as one would want to go in trying to enhance the functionality of SNMP by adding to the semantics of the MIB. However, as SNMP is applied to larger and more sophisticated networks, its deficiencies become more apparent. Some of these deficiencies are addressed in SNMPv2, which is discussed in Part IV, and SNMPv3, which is discussed in Part V.

4.1.4   SNMP-Related Standards

The set of specifications that define SNMP and its related functions and databases is comprehensive and still growing. Table 4.1 lists the nonobsolete specifications issued in the RFC series as of the time of this writing. The three foundation specifications are:

- Structure and Identification of Management Information for TCP/IP-based networks (RFC 1155): describes how managed objects contained in the MIB are defined
- Management Information Base for Network Management of TCP/IP-based Internets: MIB-II (RFC 1213): describes the managed objects contained in the MIB
- Simple Network Management Protocol (RFC 1157): defines the protocol used to manage these objects

The remaining RFCs listed in Table 4.1 define various extensions to the SMI or MIB.

4.2   Basic Concepts

4.2.1   Network Management Architecture

The model of network management that is used for TCP/IP network management includes the following key elements:

- Management station
- Management agent

TABLE 4.1   SNMP-Related RFCs (excluding RMON, SNMPv2, and SNMPv3)

RFC	Date	Title
		FULL STANDARDS
1155	May 1990	Structure and Identification of Management Information for TCP/IP-based Internets
1157	May 1990	A Simple Network Management Protocol (SNMP)
1212	March 1991	Concise MIB Definitions
1213	March 1991	Management Information Base for Network Management of TCP/IP-based Internets: MIB-II
1643	July 1994	Definition of Managed Objects for the Ethernet-like Interface Types
		DRAFT STANDARDS
1493	July 1993	Definitions of Managed Objects for Bridges
1559	December 1993	DECnet Phase IV MIB
1657	July 1994	Definitions of Managed Objects for the Border Gateway Protocol (Version 4)
1658	July 1994	Definitions of Managed Objects for Character Stream Devices
1659	July 1994	Definitions of Managed Objects for RS-232-like Hardware Devices
1660	July 1994	Definitions of Managed Objects for Parallel-Printer-like Hardware Devices
1694	August 1994	SMDS Interface Protocol (SIP) MIB
1724	November 1994	RIP Version 2 MIB Extension
1748	December 1994	IEEE 802.5 Token Ring Interface Type MIB
1850	November 1995	OSPF Version 2 MIB
2115	September 1997	Frame Relay DTE Interface Type MIB
		PROPOSED STANDARDS
1285	January 1992	FDDI Interface Type (SMT 6.2) MIB
1381	November 1992	X.25 LAPB MIB
1382	November 1992	SNMP MIB Extension for the X.25 Packet Layer
1406	January 1993	DS1 Interface Type MIB
1407	January 1993	DS3 Interface Type MIB
1414	February 1993	Identification MIB
1461	May 1993	SNMP MIB Extension for Multiprotocol Interconnect over X.25
1471	June 1993	Definitions of Managed Objects for the Link Control Protocol of PPP
1472	June 1993	Definitions of Managed Objects for the Security Protocols of PPP
1473	June 1993	Definitions of Managed Objects for the IP Network Control Protocol of PPP
1474	June 1993	Definitions of Managed Objects for Bridge Network Control Protocol of PPP
1512	September 1993	FDDI MIB
1514	September 1993	Host Resources MIB
1525	September 1993	Definitions of Managed Objects for Source Routing Bridges
1567	January 1994	X.500 Directory Monitoring MIB
1573	January 1994	Extensions to the Generic-Interface MIB
1595	March 1994	Definitions of Managed Objects for the SONET/SDH Interface Type

TABLE 4.1   *continued*

RFC	Date	Title
1604	March 1994	Definitions of Managed Objects for Frame Relay Service
1611	March 1994	DNS Server MIB Extensions
1612	March 1994	DNS Resolver MIB Extensions
1628	March 1994	UPS MIB
1650	August 1994	Ether-like Interface Type (SMIv2)
1666	August 1994	SNA NAU MIB
1695	August 1994	Definitions of Managed Objects for ATM Management Version 8.0
1696	August 1994	Modem MIB
1697	August 1994	Relational Database Management System MIB
1742	January 1995	Appletalk MIB
1747	January 1995	SDLC MIB
1749	December 1994	IEEE 802.5 MIB
1759	March 1995	Printer MIB
2006	October 1996	Mobile IP MIB
2020	October 1996	IEEE 802.12 Interfaces MIB
2024	October 1996	Data Link Switching MIB
2037	October 1996	Entity MIB
2051	October 1996	APPC MIB
2096	January 1997	IP Forwarding Table MIB
2108	February 1997	IEEE 802.3 Repeater MIB
2127	March 1997	ISDN MIB
2128	March 1997	Dial Control MIB
2155	June 1997	APPN MIB
2206	September 1997	Resource Reservation Protocol MIB
2213	September 1997	Integrated Services MIB
2214	September 1997	Integrated Services Guaranteed Service Extensions MIB
2232	November 1997	DLUR MIB
2233	November 1997	Interfaces Group MIB
2238	November 1997	High Performance Routing MIB
2239	November 1997	IEEE 802.3 Medium Attachment Unit (MAU) MIB
2248	January 1998	Network Services Monitoring MIB
2249	January 1998	Mail Monitoring MIB
2266	January 1998	IEEE 802.12 Repeater MIB
2287	February 1998	System-Level Managed Objects for Applications
2320	April 1998	Classical IP and ARP over ATM MIB
	INFORMATIONAL	
1215	March 1991	A Convention for Defining Traps for Use with the SNMP

- Management information base
- Network management protocol

The *management station* is typically a stand-alone device, but it may be a capability implemented on a shared system. In either case, the management station serves as the interface for the human network manager into the network management system. At a minimum, the management station will have

- A set of management applications for data analysis, fault recovery, and so on
- An interface by which the network manager may monitor and control the network
- The capability of translating the network manager's requirements into the actual monitoring and control of remote elements in the network
- A database of information extracted from the MIBs of all the managed entities in the network

Only the last two elements are the subject of SNMP standardization.

The other active element in the network management system is the *management agent*. Key platforms, such as hosts, bridges, routers, and hubs, may be equipped with SNMP agents so that they may be managed from a management station. The management agent responds to requests for information and actions from the management station and may asynchronously provide the management station with important but unsolicited information.

Resources in the network may be managed by representing these resources as objects. Each object is, essentially, a data variable that represents one aspect of the managed agent. The collection of objects is referred to as a *management information base* (MIB). The MIB functions as a collection of access points at the agent for the management station. These objects are standardized across systems of a particular class (for example, a common set of objects is used for the management of various bridges). A management station performs the monitoring function by retrieving the value of MIB objects. A management station can cause an action to take place at an agent or can change the configuration settings at an agent by modifying the value of specific variables.

The management station and agents are linked by a *network management protocol*. The protocol used for the management of TCP/IP networks is the Simple Network Management Protocol (SNMP), which includes the following key capabilities:

- `get`: enables the management station to retrieve the value of objects at the agent
- `set`: enables the management station to set the value of objects at the agent
- `trap`: enables an agent to notify the management station of significant events

The standards do not specify the number of management stations or the ratio of management stations to agents. In general, it is prudent to have at least two systems capable of performing the management station function, to provide redundancy in case of failure. The other issue is the practical one of how many agents a single management station can handle. As long as SNMP remains relatively "simple," that number can be quite high, certainly in the hundreds.

4.2.2   Network Management Protocol Architecture

SNMP was designed to be an application-level protocol that is part of the TCP/IP protocol suite. It is intended to operate over the User Datagram Protocol (UDP).[2] Figure 4.1 suggests the typical configuration of protocols for SNMP. For a stand-alone management station, a manager process controls access to a central MIB at the management station and provides an interface to the network manager. The manager process achieves network management by using SNMP, which is implemented on top of UDP, IP, and the relevant network-dependent protocols (for example, Ethernet, FDDI, and X.25).

Each agent must also implement SNMP, UDP, and IP. In addition, an agent process interprets the SNMP messages and controls the agent's MIB. For an agent device that supports other applications, such as FTP, both TCP and UDP are required. The shaded portions in the figure depict the operational environment—that which is to be managed. The unshaded portions provide support to the network management function.

Figure 4.2 provides a somewhat closer look at the protocol context of SNMP. From a management station, three types of SNMP messages are issued on behalf of a management application: `GetRequest`, `GetNextRequest`, and `SetRequest`. The first two are two variations of the `get` function. All three messages are acknowledged by the agent in the form of a `GetResponse` message, which is passed up to the management application. In addition, an agent may issue a trap message in response to an event that affects the MIB and the underlying managed resources.

Because SNMP relies on UDP, which is a connectionless protocol, SNMP is itself connectionless. No ongoing connections are maintained between a management station and its agents. Instead, each exchange is a separate transaction between a management station and an agent.

4.2.3   Trap-Directed Polling

If a management station is responsible for a large number of agents, and if each agent maintains a large number of objects, then it becomes impractical for the management station regularly to poll all agents for all of their readable object data. Instead, SNMP and the associated MIB are designed to encourage the manager to use a technique referred to as *trap-directed polling*.

---

[2]See Appendix A for a brief description of UDP.

FIGURE 4.1   Configuration of SNMP

The preferred strategy is this. At initialization time, and perhaps at infrequent intervals, such as once a day, a management station can poll all of the agents it knows for some key information, such as interface characteristics and perhaps some baseline performance statistics, such as the average number of packets sent and received over each interface over a given period of time. Once this baseline is established, the management station refrains from polling. Instead, each agent is responsible for notifying the management station of any unusual event; for example, the agent crashes and is rebooted, a link fails, or an overload condition as defined by the packet load crosses some threshold. These events are communicated in SNMP messages known as *traps*.

FIGURE 4.2   The role of SNMP

Once a management station is alerted to an exception condition, it may choose to take some action. At this point, the management station may direct polls to the agent reporting the event and perhaps to some nearby agents in order to diagnose any problem and to gain more specific information about the exception condition.

Trap-directed polling can result in substantial savings of network capacity and agent processing time. In essence, the network is not made to carry management information that the management station does not need, and agents are not made to respond to frequent requests for uninteresting information.

4.2.4   Proxies

The use of SNMP requires that all agents, as well as management stations, must support a common protocol suite, such as UDP and IP. This limits direct management to such devices and excludes other devices, such as some bridges and modems, that do not support any part of the TCP/IP protocol suite. Further, there may be numerous small systems (personal computers, workstations, programmable controllers) that do implement TCP/IP to support their applications, but for which it is not desirable to add the additional burden of SNMP, agent logic, and MIB maintenance.

To accommodate devices that do not implement SNMP, the concept of proxy was developed. In this scheme an SNMP agent acts as a proxy for one or more other devices; that is, the SNMP agent acts on behalf of the proxied devices.

Figure 4.3 indicates the type of protocol architecture that is often involved. The management station sends queries concerning a device to its proxy agent. The proxy agent converts each query into the management protocol that the device is using. When the agent receives a reply to a query, it passes that reply back to the management station. Similarly, if an event notification of some sort from the device is transmitted to the proxy, the proxy sends that on to the management station in the form of a trap message.

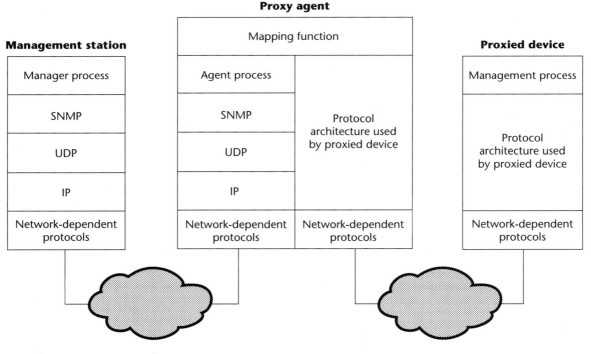

FIGURE 4.3   Proxy configuration

4.3   *Summary*

The Simple Network Management Protocol was designed to be an easily implemented, basic network management tool that could be used to meet short-term network management needs. Because of the slow progress in OSI systems management, SNMP has filled the gap and become the dominant standardized network management scheme in use today.

The SNMP set of standards provides a framework for the definition of management information and a protocol for the exchange of that information. The SNMP model assumes the existence of managers and agents. A manager is a software module in a management system responsible for managing part or all of the configuration on behalf of network management applications and users. An agent is a software module in a managed device responsible for maintaining local management information and delivering that information to a manager via SNMP. A management information exchange can be initiated by the manager (via polling) or by the agent (via a trap).

SNMP accommodates the management of devices that do not implement the SNMP software by means of proxies. A proxy is an SNMP agent that maintains information on behalf of one or more non-SNMP devices.

SNMP Management Information

As with any network management system, the foundation of a TCP/IP-based network management system is a database containing information about the elements to be managed. In both the TCP/IP and the OSI environments, the database is referred to as a management information base (MIB). Each resource to be managed is represented by an object. The MIB is a structured collection of such objects. For SNMP, the MIB is, in essence, a database structure in the form of a tree. Each system (workstation, server, router, bridge, etc.) in a network or internetwork maintains a MIB that reflects the status of the managed resources at that system. A network management entity can monitor the resources at that system by reading the values of objects in the MIB and may control the resources at that system by modifying those values.

In order for the MIB to serve the needs of a network management system, it must meet certain objectives.

1. *The object or objects used to represent a particular resource must be the same at each system.* For example, consider information stored concerning the TCP entity at a system. The total number of connections opened over a period of time consists of active opens and passive opens. The MIB at the system could store any two of the three relevant values (number of active opens, number of passive opens, total number of opens), from which the third could be derived when needed. However, if different systems select different pairs for storage, it is difficult to write a simple protocol to access the required information. As it happens, the MIB definition for TCP/IP specifies that the active and passive open counts be stored.

2. *A common scheme for representation must be used to support interoperability.*

The second point is addressed by defining a structure of management information (SMI), which we examine in this chapter, together with a look at some of the practical issues involved in managing by means of managed objects. The first point is addressed by defining the objects and the structuring of those objects in the MIB; Chapter 6 looks at some important examples.

This chapter makes use of the ASN.1 notation. The reader not familiar with this notation should first consult Appendix B.

5.1 *Structure of Management Information*

The *structure of management information* (SMI), which is specified in RFC 1155, defines the general framework within which a MIB can be defined and constructed.[1] The SMI identifies the data types that can be used in the MIB and specifies how resources within the MIB are represented and named. The philosophy behind SMI is to encourage simplicity and extensibility within the MIB. Thus, the MIB can store only simple data types: scalars and two-dimensional arrays of scalars. We will see that SNMP can retrieve only scalars, including individual entries in a table. The SMI does not support the creation or retrieval of complex data structures. This philosophy is in contrast to that used with OSI management, which provides for complex data structures and retrieval modes to support greater functionality.

SMI avoids complex data types to simplify the task of implementation and to enhance interoperability. MIBs will inevitably contain vendor-created data types, and unless tight restrictions are placed on the definition of such data types, interoperability will suffer.

To provide a standardized way of representing management information, the SMI must do the following.

- Provide a standardized technique for defining the structure of a particular MIB.
- Provide a standardized technique for defining individual objects, including the syntax and the value of each object.
- Provide a standardized technique for encoding object values.

Let us consider each of these aspects in turn.

5.1.1 MIB Structure

All managed objects in the SNMP environment are arranged in a hierarchical or tree structure. The leaf objects of the tree are the actual managed objects, each of which represents some resource, activity, or related information that is to be managed. The tree structure itself defines a grouping of objects into logically related sets.

Associated with each type of object in a MIB is an identifier of the ASN.1 type OBJECT IDENTIFIER. The identifier serves to name the object. In addition, because the

---

[1]As part of the standardization effort for SNMPv2, a more elaborate SMI has been defined (SMIv2). In time, all of the existing MIB specifications are to be rewritten using SMIv2. However, for preexisting MIBs, the changes are minor. For the purposes of Part II, we will confine ourselves to a discussion of SMIv1.

value associated with the type OBJECT IDENTIFIER is hierarchical, the naming convention also serves to identify the structure of object types.

To summarize from Appendix B, the object identifier is a unique identifier for a particular object type. Its value consists of a sequence of integers. The set of defined objects has a tree structure, with the root of the tree being the object referring to the ASN.1 standard. Beginning with the root of the object identifier tree, each object identifier component value identifies an arc in the tree. Starting from the root, there are three nodes at the first level: iso, ccitt, and joint-iso-ccitt. Under the iso node, one subtree is for the use of other organizations, one of which is the U.S. Department of Defense (dod). RFC 1155 makes the assumption that one subtree under dod will be allocated for administration by the Internet Activities Board as follows:

```
internet OBJECT IDENTIFIER ::= { iso (1) org(3) dod(6) 1 }
```

This is illustrated in Figure 5.1. Thus, the internet node has the object identifier value of 1.3.6.1. This value serves as the prefix for the nodes at the next lower level of the tree.

As shown, the SMI document defines four nodes under the internet node:

- directory: reserved for future use with the OSI directory (X.500)
- mgmt: used for objects defined in IAB-approved documents
- experimental: used to identify objects used in Internet experiments
- private: used to identify objects defined unilaterally

The mgmt subtree contains the definitions of management information bases that have been approved by the IAB. At present, two versions of the MIB have been developed, mib-1 and mib-2. The second MIB is an extension of the first. Both are provided with the same object identifier in the subtree since only one of the MIBs would be present in any configuration.

Additional objects can be defined for a MIB in one of three ways:

1. The mib-2 subtree can be expanded or replaced by a completely new revision (presumably mib-3). To expand mib-2, a new subtree is defined. For example, the remote network monitoring MIB, described in Part III, is defined as the sixteenth subtree under mib-2 (mib-2 (16)).

2. An experimental MIB can be constructed for a particular application. Such objects may subsequently be moved to the mgmt subtree. Examples of these include the various transmission media MIBs that have been defined, such as the one for IEEE 802.5 token ring LAN (RFC 1231).

3. Private extensions can be added to the private subtree. One that is documented as an RFC is the MUX MIB (RFC 1227).

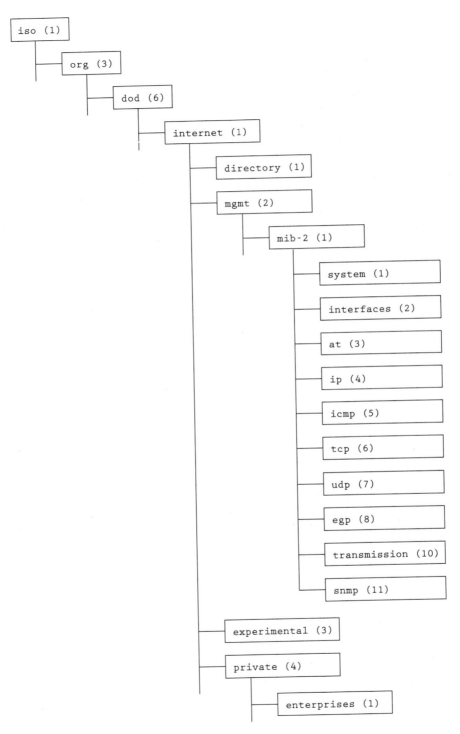

FIGURE 5.1 MIB-II object groups

The `private` subtree currently has only one child node defined, the `enterprises` node. This portion of the subtree is used to allow vendors to enhance the management of their devices and to share this information with other users and vendors who might need to interoperate with their systems. A branch within the `enterprise` subtree is allocated to each vendor that registers for an `enterprise` object identifier.

The division of the `internet` node into four subtrees provides a strong foundation for the evolution of MIBs. As vendors and other implementors experiment with new objects, they are in effect gaining a good deal of practical know-how before these objects are accepted as part of the standardized (`mgmt`) specification. Thus, the MIB is useful immediately for managing objects that fit within the standardized portion of the MIB and is flexible enough to adapt to changes in technology and product offerings. This evolutionary character mirrors that of the protocols within the TCP/IP suite: All of these protocols underwent extensive experimental use and debugging before being finalized as standard protocols.

5.1.2 Object Syntax

Every object within an SNMP MIB is defined in a formal way; the definition specifies the data type of the object, its allowable forms and value ranges, and its relationship to other objects within the MIB. The ASN.1 notation is used to define each individual object and also to define the entire MIB structure. In keeping with the objective of simplicity, only a restricted subset of the elements and features of ASN.1 are used.

5.1.2.1 Universal Types

The UNIVERSAL class of ASN.1 consists of application-independent data types that are of general use. Within the UNIVERSAL class, only the following data types are permitted to be used to define MIB objects:

- `integer` (UNIVERSAL 2)
- `octetstring` (UNIVERSAL 4)
- `null` (UNIVERSAL 5)
- `object identifier` (UNIVERSAL 6)
- `sequence`, `sequence-of` (UNIVERSAL 16)

The first four are primitive types that are the basic building blocks of other types of objects. Note that the `enumerated` type is not included. Therefore, when an enumerated list of integers is to be defined, it must be done with the integer type. Two conventions are associated with the use of enumerations.

- The value 0 may not be used. This allows for common encoding errors to be caught.

- Only the enumerated integer values may be used. There is typically one enumerated value labeled *other,* or something similar, to handle cases that don't fit the other enumerated labels.

The object identifier is a unique identifier of an object, consisting of a sequence of integers, known as subidentifiers. The sequence, read from left to right, defines the location of the object in the MIB tree structure. For example, looking ahead to Figure 6.10, the object identifier for the object tcpConnTable is derived as follows:

iso	org	dod	internet	mgmt	mib-2	tcp	tcpConnTable
1	3	6	1	2	1	6	13

This identifier would normally be written as 1.3.6.1.2.1.6.13.

The last item in the preceding list consists of the constructor types sequence and sequence-of. These types are used to construct tables, as explained later in this chapter.

5.1.2.2   Application-Wide Types

The APPLICATION class of ASN.1 consists of data types that are relevant to a particular application. Each application, including SNMP, is responsible for defining its own APPLICATION data types. RFC 1155 lists a number of application-wide data types; other types may be defined in future RFCs. The following types are defined:

- networkaddress: This type is defined using the CHOICE construct, to allow the selection of an address format from one of a number of protocol families. Currently, the only defined address is IpAddress.
- ipaddress: This is a 32-bit address using the format specified in IP.
- counter: This is a non-negative integer that may be incremented but not decremented. A maximum value of $2^{32} - 1$ (4,294,967,295) is specified; when the counter reaches its maximum, it wraps around and starts increasing again from zero (Figure 5.2(a)).
- gauge: This is a non-negative integer that may increase or decrease, with a maximum value of $2^{32} - 1$. If the maximum value is reached, the gauge remains latched at that value until reset (Figure 5.2(b)).
- timeticks: This non-negative integer counts the time in hundredths of a second since some epoch. When an object type is defined in the MIB that uses this type, the definition of the object type identifies the reference epoch.
- opaque: This type supports the capability to pass arbitrary data. The data is encoded as OCTET STRING for transmission. The data itself may be in any format defined by ASN.1 or another syntax.

The counter, also known as the rollover counter, is one of the most common types used in defining objects. Typical applications are to count the number of packets or octets

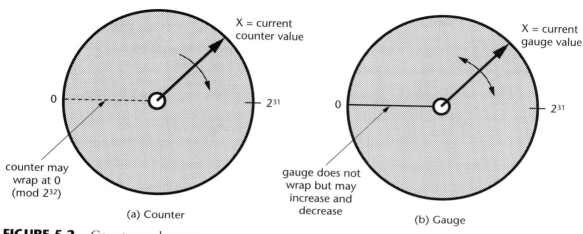

FIGURE 5.2   Counter and gauge

sent or received. An alternative type of counter that the SMI designers considered is the latch counter, which sticks at its maximum value and must be reset. The latch counter was rejected because of the following potential problem. Suppose that more than one management system is allowed access to a particular counter; that is, more than one management system can monitor a device. When a latch counter reaches its maximum and needs to be reset, there are two alternatives:

1. Designate one management system as responsible for latch reset. The problem with this approach is that if that system fails, the counter remains stuck at its latched value.
2. Allow any management system the authority to reset the counter when it deems it appropriate. The problem here has to do with the time lag involved in communication across a distributed system. Several systems may reset the same counter, with the result that some information is lost (counts that take place between the arrival of the two resets at the managed object).

With rollover counters, these difficulties are avoided. However, after a rollover counter has wrapped around several times, it is difficult for a management system to know whether a counter value of x means that the quantity observed is x or $(N \times 2^{32}) + x$. The only way around this is for the management station periodically to poll the object to keep track of wraparounds. Because 32-bit counters are used, this should not have to be done very often.

Typically, a gauge is used to measure the current value of some entity, such as the current number of packets stored in a queue. A gauge can also be used to store the difference in the value of some entity from the start to the end of a time interval. This enables a gauge to be used to monitor the rate of change of the value of an entity.

The gauge type is referred to as a latched value. There is, unfortunately, some ambiguity concerning the meaning of the word "latch." It is certainly the case that, once a gauge reaches its maximum value, it will not roll over to zero. Rather, if the gauge represents a value that increases beyond the maximum, the gauge remains stuck at its maximum value. If the represented value subsequently falls below the gauge maximum, one of two policies could be adopted:

1. Allow the gauge to decrease so that the gauge always has the same value as the modeled value so long as the modeled value remains in the range of the gauge.

2. Leave the gauge stuck at its maximum value until it is reset by management action.

There is no consensus on the correct interpretation. Thus, the preceding discussion on latched counters does not necessarily apply to latched gauges. If the second interpretation in the preceding list is used, then there is a potential problem of multiple managers being allowed to reset the gauge, as discussed for latched counters. One positive feature of using the second interpretation in the preceding list is that if the latched value is not immediately reset, it tells management stations that some parameter has been exceeded (for example, maximum queue size).

The timeticks type is a relative timer: Time is measured relative to some event (such as startup or reinitialization) within the managed system. While such values are unambiguous within the managed system, they cannot be directly compared to timer values in other systems. Some designers would have preferred an absolute time value using the standard ASN.1 representation. Unfortunately, most systems running the TCP/IP protocol suite do not support a time synchronization protocol. Thus, an absolute time type is impractical for SNMP.

One important type that is left out of the SNMP SMI is the threshold type. A threshold is used in the following way: If the threshold value is crossed (in either a positive or negative direction, depending on the definition of the threshold), an event is triggered and an event notification is sent to the management station(s). The SMI designers feared that this capability could lead to *event floods,* in which a managed system's threshold is repeatedly crossed and the system floods the network with numerous event notifications. Such event floods have been experienced on ARPANET and other networks. A particularly deadly kind of event flood is one in which the event is triggered by congestion. The creation of an event flood due to congestion exacerbates the condition being reported! However, we will see that the Remote Monitoring (RMON) MIB defines a form of threshold (Chapter 9).

5.1.2.3   Defining Objects

A management information base consists of a set of objects. Each object has a type and a value. The **object type** defines a particular kind of managed object. The definition of an object type is therefore a syntactic description. An **object instance** is a particular instance of an object type that has been bound to a specific value.

How are we to define objects for inclusion in the MIB? The notation that will be used is ASN.1. As explained in Appendix B, ASN.1 includes a number of predefined universal types and a grammar for defining new types that are derived from existing types. One alternative for defining managed objects would be to define a new type called `Object`. Then, every object in the MIB would be of this type. This approach is technically possible, but would result in unwieldy definitions. We need to allow for a variety of value types, including counters, gauges, and so forth. In addition, the MIB supports the definition of two-dimensional tables, or arrays, of values. Thus a general-purpose object type would have to somehow include parameters that encompass all of these possibilities and alternatives.

Because managed objects may contain a variety of information to represent a variety of entities being managed, it makes more sense to define an open-ended set of new types, one for each general category of managed object. This could be done directly in ASN.1. However, this alternative also has a drawback. If the only restriction on the definition of a new managed object type is that the definition be written in ASN.1, we can expect to see considerable variation in the format of object definitions. This variety will make it more difficult for the user or implementor of a MIB to incorporate a variety of object types. More seriously, the use of relatively unstructured object type definitions complicates the task of using SNMP for interoperable access to managed objects.

A more attractive alternative, and the one used with SNMP, is to use a macro to define a set of related types used to define managed objects. As explained in Appendix B, a macro definition gives the syntax of a set of related types, while a macro instance defines a specific type. Thus we have the following levels of definition:

- *Macro definition:* defines the legal macro instances; specifies the syntax of a set of related types
- *Macro instance:* an instance generated from a specific macro definition by supplying arguments for the parameters in the macro definition; specifies a particular type
- *Macro instance value:* represents a specific entity with a specific value

The macro used for the SNMP MIBs was initially defined in RFC 1155 (Structure of Management Information) and later expanded in RFC 1212 (Concise MIB Definitions). The RFC 1155 version is used for defining objects in MIB-I. The RFC 1212 version, which includes more information, is used for defining objects in MIB-II and other recent additions to the MIB.

Figure 5.3 is the definition of the `OBJECT-TYPE` macro from RFC 1212.[2] The key components are as follows:

- `SYNTAX`: the abstract syntax for the object type. This must resolve to an instance of the `ObjectSyntax` type defined in RFC 1155 (see Figure 5.4). Essentially, the syntax

---

[2]Several elements of the definition are not used in MIB-II (`ReferPart` and `DefValPart`). They may, however, be used in other MIB definitions.

```
IMPORTS    ObjectName, Object Syntax FROM RFC-1155-SMI

OBJECT-TYPE MACRO ::=
BEGIN
     TYPE NOTATION ::=     "SYNTAX"    type (TYPE ObjectSyntax)
                           "ACCESS"    Access
                           "STATUS"    Status
                           DescrPart
                           ReferPart
                           IndexPart
                           DefValPart
     VALUE NOTATION ::= value (VALUE ObjectName)

     Access ::= "read-only"|"read-write"|"write-only"|"not-accessible"

     Status ::= "mandatory|"optional"|"obsolete"|"deprecated"

     DescrPart ::= "DESCRIPTION" value (description DisplayString)|empty

     ReferPart ::= "REFERENCE" value (reference DisplayString)|empty

     IndexPart ::= "INDEX" "{" IndexTypes "}"

     IndexTypes ::= IndexType|IndexTypes "," IndexType

     IndexType ::= value (indexobject ObjectName)   --if indexobject, use the SYNTAX
                                                     --value of the correspondent
                                                     --OBJECT-TYPE invocation
                        |type (indextype)            --otherwise use named SMI type;
                                                     --must conform to IndexSyntax below

     DefValPart ::= "DEFVAL" "{" value (defvalue ObjectSyntax) "}" |empty

     DisplayString ::= OCTET STRING SIZE (0..255)

END

IndexSyntax ::= CHOICE { number INTEGER (0..MAX),
                         string OCTET STRING,
                         object OBJECT IDENTIFIER,
                         address NetworkAddress,
                         IpAddress IpAddress }
```

FIGURE 5.3   Macro for managed objects (RFC 1212)

```
RFC1155-SMI DEFINITIONS ::= BEGIN

EXPORTS -- EVERYTHING
            internet, directory, mgmt, experimental, private, enterprises, OBJECT-TYPE,
            ObjectName, ObjectSyntax, SimpleSyntax, ApplicationSyntax, Network Address,
            IpAddress, Counter, Gauge, TimeTicks, Opaque;

-- the path to the root

internet            OBJECT IDENTIFIER ::= { iso org(3) dod(6) 1 }
directory           OBJECT IDENTIFIER ::= { internet 1 }
mgmt                OBJECT IDENTIFIER ::= { internet 2 }
experimental        OBJECT IDENTIFIER ::= { internet 3 }
private             OBJECT IDENTIFIER ::= { internet 4 }
enterprises         OBJECT IDENTIFIER ::= { private 1 }

-- definition of object types

OBJECT-TYPE MACRO ::=
BEGIN
     TYPE NOTATION ::= "Syntax"    type (TYPE ObjectSyntax)
                       "ACCESS"    Access
                       "STATUS"    Status
     VALUE NOTATION ::= value (VALUE ObjectName)
     Access  ::= "read-only"|"read-write"|"write-only"|"not-accessible"
     Status  ::= "mandatory"|"optional"|"obsolete"
END

-- names of objects in the MIB

ObjectName ::= OBJECT IDENTIFIER

--syntax of objects in the MIB

ObjectSyntax ::= CHOICE {simple SimpleSyntax,

       --note that simple SEQUENCES are not directly mentioned here to keep things
       --simple (i.e., prevent misuse). However, application-wide types which are
       --IMPLICITly encoded simple SEQUENCEs may appear in the following CHOICE

                       application-wide ApplicationSyntax}

SimpleSyntax ::= CHOICE {number INTEGER,
                        string OCTET STRING,
                        object OBJECT IDENTIFIER
                        empty NULL}
```

continued

FIGURE 5.4   Structure of management information (RFC 1155)

```
ApplicationSyntax ::= CHOICE {address     NetworkAddress,
                              counter     Counter,
                              gauge       Gauge,
                              ticks       TimeTicks,
                              arbitrary   Opaque
             --other application-wide types, as they are defined, will be added here}

--application-wide types

NetworkAddress ::= Choice {internet IpAddress}

IpAddress ::= [APPLICATION 0]                        --in network-byte order
              IMPLICIT OCTET STRING (SIZE (4))

Counter ::= [APPLICATION 1] IMPLICIT INTEGER (0..4294967295)

Gauge ::= [APPLICATION 2] IMPLICIT INTEGER (0..4294967295)

TimeTicks ::= [APPLICATION 3] IMPLICIT INTEGER (0..4294967295)

Opaque ::= [APPLICATION 4] OCTET STRING       --arbitrary ASN.1 value, "double-wrapped"

END
```

FIGURE 5.4   Structure of management information (RFC 1155)   *Continued*

must be constructed using the universal and application-wide types allowed in the SMI.

- ACCESS: defines the way in which an instance of the object may be accessed, via SNMP or another protocol. The access clause specifies the minimum level of support required for that object type. Implementation-specific additions or restrictions to the access are permissible. The options are *read-only, read-write, write-only*, and *not-accessible*. In the latter case, the object's value may not be read and may not be set.

- STATUS: Indicates the implementation support required for this object. Support may be *mandatory* or *optional*. Alternatively, an object can be specified as *deprecated*. A deprecated object is one that must be supported, but that will most likely be removed from the next version of the MIB. Finally, the status may be *obsolete*, which means that managed systems need no longer implement this object.

- DescrPart: a textual description of the semantics of the object type. This clause is optional.

- ReferPart: a textual cross-reference to an object defined in some other MIB module. This clause is optional.

- `IndexPart`: used in defining tables. This clause may be present only if the object type corresponds to a conceptual row. The use of this clause is described later in this chapter.
- `DefValPart`: defines an acceptable default value that may be used when an object instance is created, at the discretion of the agent. This clause is optional.
- `VALUE NOTATION`: This indicates the name used to access this object via SNMP.

Figure 5.5 shows an example of an object type definition.

Because the complete definition of the MIB using the `OBJECT-TYPE` macro is contained in the MIB documents, and because of the length of such definitions, we will generally refrain from their use. Instead we will use a more compact representation, based on tree structures and a tabular presentation of object characteristics, as will be seen ahead.

5.1.2.4   Defining Tables

The SMI supports only one form of structuring of data: a simple two-dimensional table with scalar-valued entries. The definition of tables involves the use of the `sequence` and `sequence-of` ASN.1 types and the `IndexPart` of the `OBJECT-TYPE` macro.

The best way to explain the table-definition convention is by example. Consider the object type `tcpConnTable`, which, as was mentioned earlier, has the object identifier 1.3.6.1.2.1.6.13. This object, the TCP Connection Table, contains information about TCP connections maintained by the corresponding managed entity. For each such connection, the following information is stored in the table:

- *State:* the state of the TCP connection [The value of this entry may be one of the 11 TCP states as defined in the standard (see Appendix 5A to this chapter); the value is set by the TCP entity and is changed by the TCP entity to reflect the state of the connection. In addition, the entry may take on the value `deleteTCB`; this is a value set

```
tcpMaxConn OBJECT-TYPE
    SYNTAX INTEGER
    ACCESS read-only
    STATUS mandatory
    DESCRIPTION
        "The limit on the total number of TCP connections the entity can
        support. In entities where the maximum number of connections is
        dynamic, this object should contain the value -1."
    ::= { tcp 4 }
```

FIGURE 5.5   Example of an object definition

by a management station. When this value is set, it causes the TCP entity to delete the transmission control block for this connection, thereby destroying the connection; this is equivalent to a transition to the CLOSED state.]

- *Local address:* the IP address of this end of the connection
- *Local port:* the TCP port of this end of the connection
- *Remote address:* the IP address of the other end of the connection
- *Remote port:* the TCP port of the other end of the connection

Before proceeding, it is instructive to note that the TCP connection table is a part of the MIB and, as such, is maintained by a managed station to provide visibility to the management station of some underlying entity represented by the managed object. In this case, each entry in tcpConnTable represents the state information stored in the managed station for one connection. As indicated in Appendix 5A, this state information consists of 22 separate items of information for each connection. Only five of these items are actually visible to network management by means of the tcpConnTable. This illustrates the emphasis of SNMP on keeping network management simple: Only a limited, useful subset of information on a managed entity is contained in the corresponding managed object.

Figure 5.6, taken from RFC 1213, shows the MIB-II specification of tcpConn-Table. The technique for defining the table structure, which is invariably followed in all table definitions, is to use the sequence and sequence-of constructs as follows.

- The overall table consists of a SEQUENCE OF TcpConnEntry. As discussed in Appendix B, the ASN.1 construct SEQUENCE OF consists of one or more elements, all of the same type. In this case (and in all other SNMP SMI cases), each element is a row of the table. Thus, a table consists of zero or more rows.
- Each row consists of a SEQUENCE that includes five scalar elements. Again, as discussed in Appendix B, the ASN.1 construct SEQUENCE consists of a fixed number of elements, possibly of more than one type. While ASN.1 allows any of these elements to be options, the SMI restricts the use of this construct to mandatory elements only. In this case, each row of the table contains elements of type INTEGER, IpAddress, INTEGER (..65535), IpAddress, INTEGER (..65535).

Finally, the INDEX component of the entry definition determines which object value(s) will be used to distinguish one row in the table. In TCP, a single socket (IP address, TCP port) may support many connections, but at any one time, there may only be a single connection between any given pair of sockets. Thus, the last four elements in the row are necessary and sufficient to unambiguously distinguish a single row from the table.

Figure 5.7 is an example. In this case, the table contains three rows. The entire table represents a single instance of the object type tcpConnTable. Each row is an instance of the object type tcpConnEntry, for a total of three instances. There are also three in-

```
tcpConn Table OBJECT-TYPE
        SYNTAX     SEQUENCE OF TcpConnEntry
        ACCESS     not-accessible
        STATUS     mandatory
        DESCRIPTION
              "A table containing TCP connection-specific information."
        ::= { tcp 13 }

tcpConnEntry OBJECT-TYPE
        SYNTAX     TcpConnEntry
        ACCESS     not-accessible
        STATUS     mandatory
        DESCRIPTION
              "Information about a particular TCP connection. An object of this type is
              transient, in that it ceases to exist when (or soon after) the connection
              makes the transition to the CLOSED state."
        INDEX      { tcpConnLocalAddress,
                     tcpConnLocalPort,
                     tcpConnRemAddress,
                     tcpConnRemPort }
        ::= { tcpConnTable 1 }

TcpConnEntry ::= SEQUENCE { tcpConnState INTEGER,
                           tcpConnLocalAddress IpAddress,
                           tcpConnLocalPort INTEGER (0..65535),
                           tcpConnRemAddress IpAddress
                           tcpConnRemPort INTEGER (0..65535)}

tcpConnState OBJECT-TYPE
        SYNTAX     INTEGER {closed (1),
                            listen (2),
                            synSent (3),
                            synReceived (4),
                            established (5),
                            finWait1 (6),
                            finWait2 (7),
                            closeWait (8),
                            lastAck (9),
                            closing (10),
                            timeWait (11),
                            delete TCB (12) }

        ACCESS     read-write
        STATUS     mandatory
        DESCRIPTION
              "The state of this TCP connection.
```

FIGURE 5.6   MIB-II specification of TCP connection table (RFC 1213)

continued

The only value which may be set by a management station is deleteTCB(12)."
Accordingly, it is appropriate for an agent to return a 'badValue'
response if a management station attempts to set this object to any other
value.

If a management station sets this object to the value deleteTCB(12), then
this has the effect of deleting the TCB (as defined in RFC 793) of the
corresponding connection on the managed node, resulting in immediate termination of the connection.

As an implementation-specific option, a RST segment may be sent from the
managed node to the other TCP endpoint (note however that RST segments are
not sent reliably)."
```
        ::= { tcpConnEntry 1 }

tcpConnLocalAddress OBJECT-TYPE
        SYNTAX      IpAddress
        ACCESS      read-only
        STATUS      mandatory
        DESCRIPTION
            "The local IP address for this TCP connection. In the case of a connec-
            tion in the listen state which is willing to accept connections for any
            IP interface associated with the node, the value 0.0.0.0 is used."
        ::= { tcpConnEntry 2 }

tcpConnLocalPort OBJECT-TYPE
        SYNTAX      INTEGER (0..65535)
        ACCESS      read-only
        STATUS      mandatory
        DESCRIPTION
            "The local port number for this TCP connection."
        ::= { tcpConnEntry 3 }

tcpConnRemAddress OBJECT-TYPE
        SYNTAX      IpAddress
        ACCESS      read-only
        STATUS      mandatory
        DESCRIPTION
            "The remote IP address for this TCP connection."
        ::= { tcpConnEntry 4 }

tcpConnRemPort OBJECT-TYPE
        SYNTAX      INTEGER (0..65535)
        ACCESS      read-only
        STATUS      mandatory
        DESCRIPTION
            "The remote port number for this TCP connection."
        ::= { tcpConnEntry 5 }
```

FIGURE 5.6   MIB-II specification of TCP connection table (RFC 1213)   *Continued*

FIGURE 5.7 Instance of a TCP connection table

stances of each of the scalar elements of the table. Thus there are three instances of the object type `tcpConnState`, and so on. In RFC 1212, these scalar objects are referred to as *columnar objects,* emphasizing the fact that each such object corresponds to a number of instances in one column of the table.

The SMI does not permit nesting. That is, it is not allowed to define an element of a table to be another table. This restriction reduces the utility and flexibility of the SMI.

5.1.3 Encoding

Objects in the MIB are encoded using the basic encoding rules (BER) associated with ASN.1 (see Appendix B). While not the most compact or efficient form of encoding, BER is a widely used, standardized encoding scheme.

5.2 Practical Issues

5.2.1 Measurement

As was discussed in Part I of this book, one of the two key functions of a network management system is monitoring, which involves measuring certain quantities and reporting the results to a management system. In SNMP, the MIB supports monitoring through the use of scalar values, such as counters and gauges. The risk with SNMP and, indeed, with any network management scheme, is that the manager will believe reported values that are in fact erroneous.

At first glance, this risk might seem small. For example, consider a device such as a bridge or a router, whose primary function is as an intermediate system that captures and forwards packets going from host to host within an internet. The manager concerned with the sizing of the design (how many bridges or routers, how much throughput each can sustain) will naturally want to monitor the amount of traffic through each bridge or router. What could be more straightforward? Surely any network management package worth its name would be able accurately to count and report the total number of packets moving through the device? That is exactly the question asked by a group of AT&T researchers, in a series of experiments sponsored by the publication *Network World.* The results of these experiments are somewhat discouraging and, at the very least, serve as a sobering reminder to network managers that one cannot simply believe vendor claims and protocol specifications. It is necessary to verify that the network management products do what they are advertised to do.

The first experiment that was run was to test various SNMP-managed bridge products (Mier 1991a). The primary objectives were to determine the accuracy of the data collected and reported by the agent entity and the interoperability of the agent with

SNMP management stations. In this section, we focus on the first objective; we return to the second in Chapter 6.

The test environment was designed to simulate a large user organization's network management center and was structured to show how the various products could be integrated into an existing SNMP-managed multivendor network. The configuration consisted of two Ethernet LANs with the following key components:

- *Bridge:* The two LANs were connected by a single bridge. Seven different bridge products were tested, each with its own SNMP agent software.
- *Network management station:* Each experiment was run twice, using two different network management stations from different vendors. This assured that any anomalous results were not the artifact of the station manager but of the bridge agent.
- *LAN analyzer:* The LAN analyzer generated test packets addressed to off-LAN destinations (MAC and IP addresses) and captured and analyzed messages issued by SNMP agents.

Table 5.1 reports on the results of an experiment (Mier 91a) to test the accuracy with which bridges count, then report, specific traffic statistics for each interface. The test consisted of a stream of 100 packets generated by the LAN analyzer, consisting of 88 normal unicast packets ranging in size from 64 to 1,500 octets and 12 packets with intentional frame check sequence errors. In addition, the management station issued some packets containing SNMP messages to retrieve the data from the agents; these packets were deducted from the reported counts to produce the results shown in the table.

As the table shows, three objects from the Interfaces group were tested. Unfortunately, the MIB standard is ambiguous regarding which traffic bridges are supposed to count: It hinges on whether the bridge relay function is considered a higher-layer protocol.[3] Even so, the test results show that some bridge agents are able to provide an SNMP management station with accurate, consistent counts of packets received while others are not.

The second experiment that was run was to test various SNMP-managed IP router products (Mier 1991b). With routers, there is no such ambiguity concerning which packets to count and so the results are more definitive; those relating to traffic statistics are shown in Tables 5.2 and 5.3.

Essentially the same test environment was used, including a LAN analyzer, two different SNMP management stations, and two Ethernets. In this case, the LANs were connected by a router rather than a bridge. Nine different router products were tested, each with its own SNMP agent software.

---

[3]In most traditional bridge implementations, the relay function simply picks up frames from one LAN and deposits them on another; the relay function is viewed as occurring within the MAC layer. However, in the IEEE 802 standards for transparent and source-routing bridges, there is a *MAC relay entity*, which is in fact at a higher layer than, and uses the services of, a *MAC entity*. See Stallings (1996a) for a discussion.

TABLE 5.1 SNMP Bridge Agents Count Differently (Mier 1991a)

Vendor	IfIn-Octets[1]	Comments	Evaluation	IfIn-Ucast Pkts[2]	Comments	Evaluation	ifIn-Errors[3]	Comments	Evaluation	Overall
A	67,000 to 86,000	Reasonable, but different, values reported from each of 5 tests.	Fair	100[4]	Agent counts SNMP packets and errored packets in total.	Excellent	12	Agent reported value accurately.	Excellent	Very good
B	66,400 ± 500	Agent reported value accurately and consistently.	Excellent	88[4]	Agent counts only SNMP packets.	Excellent	12	Agent reported value accurately.	Excellent	Excellent
C	64,700 ± 100	Agent reported value accurately and consistently.	Excellent	88[4]	Agent counts SNMP packets.	Excellent	12	Agent reported value accurately.	Excellent	Excellent
D	64,900 ± 100	Agent reported value accurately and consistently.	Excellent	100[4]	Agent counts SNMP packets and errored packets in total.	Excellent	12	Agent reported value accurately.	Excellent	Excellent
E	0	Agent always returns a value of 0 for this object.	Poor	0	Agent counts no packets.	Poor	0	Agent does not count or report errored packets.	Poor	Poor

F	250 to 1,500	Agent apparently counts only SNMP packet traffic.	Poor	0 (4)	Agent apparently counts only SNMP packets.	Fair	0	Agent does not count or report errored packets.	Poor	Poor
G	500 to 1,500	Agent apparently counts only SNMP packet traffic.	Poor	0 (4)	Agent apparently counts only SNMP packets.	Fair	0	Agent does not count or report errored packets.	Poor	Poor

[1]Acceptable response: 64,000 to 68,000 octets. Based on interpretation of MIB standards and reporting requirements by a consensus of experts. A total of 67,640 octets were sent over the LAN in the 100-packet test transmission. However, the acceptable response range takes into account SNMP packets sent to retrieve the values, which added from 500 to 1,500 octets to this count. In addition, some agents discounted 12 "errored" packets (total of 2,988 octets), which were included as part of the 100-packet test stream (see footnote 3 below).

[2]Optimum response: 88 to 100 packets. Per MIB standard, this is the number of packets "delivered to a higher-layer protocol." Bridges could technically report 0 (except for SNMP packets, which must be included in this count), but this provides no useful SNMP management information. Errored packets, which are discarded, may legitimately be excluded.

[3]Optimum response: 12 packets. The 100-packet test transmission sent 12 errored packets with misaligned frame check sequences.

[4]After deducting SNMP packets

105

TABLE 5.2 Router SNMP Agent Counts of Interface-Level Traffic (Mier 1991b)

Vendor	ifInOctets[1]	Comments	Evaluation	IfInUcastPkts[2]	Comments	Evaluation
1	15,500 ± 500	Consistent count, but low; not clear what traffic was omitted	Fair	145	Apparently adds discarded unknown-protocol packets to count	Good
2	19,000 ± 500	Consistent count within acceptable range	Excellent	145	Apparently adds discarded unknown-protocol packets to count	Good
3	20,000 ± 100	Consistent, accurate count	Excellent	120	Consistent, accurate count	Excellent
4	20,000 ± 100	Consistent, accurate count	Excellent	210	Apparently adds broadcast and unknown-protocol packets to count	Fair
5	20,000 ± 100	Consistent, accurate count	Excellent	180	Apparently adds errored and unknown-protocol packets to count	Fair
6	20,000 ± 100	Consistent, accurate count	Excellent	145	Apparently adds discarded unknown-protocol packets to count	Good
7	19,000 ± 500	Consistent count within acceptable range	Excellent	145	Apparently adds discarded unknown-protocol packets to count	Good
8	14,000 ± 200	Consistent count, but low; not clear what traffic was omitted	Fair	120	Consistent, accurate count	Excellent
9	19,000 ± 500	Consistent count within acceptable range	Excellent	210	Apparently adds broadcast and unknown-protocol packets to count	Fair

TABLE 5.2 *Continued*

Vendor	IfInNUcastPkts[3]	Comments	Evaluation	IfInUnknownProtos[4]	Comments	Evaluation	IfInErrors[5]	Comments	Evaluation
1	65	Consistently correct	Excellent	0	Packets not reported	Poor	35	Consistently correct	Excellent
2	65	Consistently correct	Excellent	0	Packets not reported	Poor	35	Consistently correct	Excellent
3	65	Consistently correct	Excellent	25	Consistently correct	Excellent	0	Packets not reported	Poor
4	0	No count of broadcast packets	Poor	0	Packets not reported	Poor	35	Consistently correct	Excellent
5	65	Consistently correct	Excellent	0	Packets not reported	Poor	35	Consistently correct	Excellent
6	55	Reasonable but incorrect count	Fair	25	Consistently correct	Excellent	0	Packets not reported	Poor
7	65	Consistently correct	Excellent	25	Consistently correct	Excellent	35	Consistently correct	Excellent
8	65	Consistently correct	Excellent	25	Consistently correct	Excellent	0	Packets not reported	Poor
9	0	Consistently correct	Excellent	0	Packets not reported	Poor	35	Consistently correct	Excellent

[1]The test packet stream delivered a total of 23,290 octets on the LAN. After deducting 12 octets per packet (8 for the preamble and 4 for the frame check sequence, which are stripped off at the physical layer of the receiving LAN adapter and not passed on as part of incoming packet traffic), a net total of 20,350 octets should have been recorded.

[2]The count should be 120: the total of 4 test packet stream types addressed to the physical address of the router under test, which should have been delivered to higher protocol layers within the router.

[3]The count should be 65: the total of 2 test broadcast packet stream types that should have been delivered to higher protocol layers within the router.

[4]The test packet stream contained 25 packets with an invalid protocol type in the Ethernet header. These could not have been passed to a higher protocol layer within the router and would have been discarded.

[5]Thirty-five packets in the test stream had misaligned frame check sequences.

TABLE 5.3 Router SNMP Agent Counts of IP Traffic (Mier 1991b)

Vendor	ipIn-Delivers[1]	Comments	Evaluation	ipInHdr-Errors[2]	Comments	Evaluation	ipOutNo-Routes[3]	Comments	Evaluation
1	40	Consistently correct	Excellent	0	Datagrams not counted	Poor	5	Consistently correct	Excellent
2	40	Consistently correct	Excellent	0	Datagrams not counted	Poor	5 or 6	Count was often slightly off	Good
3	20	Consistent but incorrect; unclear what agent counts	Fair	45	Consistent, accurate count	Excellent	5 or 35	Possible configuration problem	Inconclusive
4	40	Consistently correct	Excellent	45	Consistent, accurate count	Excellent	3 or 9	Inaccurate and inconsistent	Fair
5	37	Consistent but slightly low	Good	0	Datagrams not counted	Poor	80	Possible configuration problem	Inconclusive
6	40	Consistently correct	Excellent	45	Consistent, accurate count	Excellent	0	Configuration did not enable count	Inconclusive
7	40	Consistently correct	Excellent	0	Datagrams not counted	Poor	5 or 6	Count was often slightly off	Good
8	0	Datagrams not counted	Poor	0	Datagrams not counted	Poor	5	Consistently correct	Excellent
9	40	Consistently correct	Excellent	45	Consistent, accurate count	Excellent	2	Inaccurate	Fair

[1]Forty of the 245 test stream packets were addressed to the router's IP address and should have been delivered to the router's IP layer for processing.

[2]Forty-five packets sent to the router and addressed to a destination on a distant subnetwork had a 0 time-to-live value in the IP header. These should have been discarded.

[3]Five packets of the test stream were sent to an invalid network address.

Again, a test was conducted using objects from the Interfaces group; objects from the IP group were also included. The test stream consisted of 245 packets broken down as follows.

- 120 packets contained IP datagrams with the unicast MAC address of the router, of which:
  - 40 contained the router's IP address;
  - 45 contained a distant IP address with a 0 time-to-live;
  - 5 contained an invalid IP address;
  - 30 contained a valid distant IP address and a nonzero time-to-live.
- 65 packets contained a broadcast MAC address that included the router and that should have been delivered to a higher layer within the router.
- 25 packets had an invalid protocol type in the Ethernet header.
- 35 packets had an incorrect frame check sequence.

Table 5.2 shows the results for some of the counters in the Interfaces group. Not a single vendor reported accurate values for all five counters. Table 5.3 shows the results for counters in the IP group; again, not one vendor got all of the numbers right. In a few cases, it is possible that the fault lies not with the SNMP agent software but with the entities being managed. For example, five of the routers failed to report datagrams that had expired.[4] This could be either because the agent failed to count datagrams that were discarded because they expired or because the IP entity forwarded expired datagrams. In the latter case, the SNMP agent is a useful tool for detecting faults in other software.

The results of all of these tests are clearly cause for concern. These statistics are critical to the network manager. For example, if a router agent fails to report the presence of errored packets, then a serious condition threatening the network could remain unnoticed until a catastrophic failure occurs.

Compared to the OSI network management scheme, SNMP sacrifices functionality for simplicity. One of the strengths of the SNMP standards is their relative clarity and succinctness. Yet, despite this emphasis on simplicity, products from reputable, well-established vendors cannot agree on some of the most basic parameters that a network management system must measure. Several cautionary observations can be made.

1. There is a need for some sort of verification or certification procedure for SNMP/MIB to increase the likelihood that vendor offerings are "correct."
2. In the absence of such certification, the customer/user needs to know that, like any other piece of software, SNMP manager–agent software may contain errors.

---

[4]The time-to-live parameter in the IP header is used to prevent a datagram from remaining in circulation indefinitely. Each router is supposed to decrement this value prior to forwarding a datagram. If an IP module receives a datagram with a time-to-live value of zero, and it is not addressed to this IP module, the datagram is supposed to be discarded.

3. If these are the problems one faces with the relatively simple SNMP, one can imagine the potential for misinformation and miscontrol in OSI network management.[5]

5.2.2   Private MIBs

One of the strengths of the SNMP approach is the way in which the MIB has been designed to accommodate growth and to provide flexibility for adding new objects. As was mentioned, private extensions can be added to the private subtree (Figure 5.1). This allows vendors to create objects to manage specific entities on their products and to make those objects visible to a management station. Because of the use of a standardized SMI and a standardized object identifier scheme, it should be possible to manage private objects from a management station of a different vendor. In other words, interoperability should extend to private extensions to the MIB.

With SNMP, a management station can access only the information for which it knows how to ask. Recall that this approach was taken in the design of SNMP to prevent the network from being clogged with management information that devices were mindlessly broadcasting. Thus, in order for a management station to be able to manage private MIB objects, the management station must be loaded with the private MIB structure. Otherwise, the management station cannot offer the user the benefits of those private extensions. Of course, loading the private MIB into the management station should present no problem if the management station and the agent station are from the same vendor. The potential for difficulty arises when the two are from different vendors.

Most vendors supply both a text version and a formal description of their MIB extensions. Without the formal description, it would be necessary to type many (perhaps hundreds) object definitions into the management station. With a formal description, the management station should be able to read a MIB file from disk and compile it into the management station's library of managed objects. One difficulty that occurs is that vendors currently use three different formats to define private MIBs:

*   The original SNMP SMI specification, RFC 1155
*   The newer Concise MIB Format, RFC 1212
*   The OSI SMI specification

Converting from one MIB to another is currently a manual process that requires a person to be knowledgeable in both formats and to have hours of time available. RFC 1212 provides guidelines in "de-osifying" OSI MIBs to the SNMP MIB format and describes the process as "straightforward though tedious."

---

[5]Fortunately, a mechanism is in place for developing certification/verification procedures for OSI-based standards, based on conformance testing. As of this writing, approved conformance tests for OSI management have not yet been developed, but should be forthcoming as the OSI management standards stabilize.

It is likely that vendors using the SNMP format will all sooner or later convert from RFC 1155 to RFC 1212. Also, an experience base in converting between OSI SMI and SNMP SMI is gradually accumulating. But another problem is in the actual parsing and compiling of a MIB specification. Despite the fact that MIB objects are defined using formal techniques, different management systems seem to apply different criteria in determining whether a vendor's private MIB is syntactically correct.

For a concrete example of these difficulties, we again turn to the Bell Labs studies of bridges and routers, reported in Table 5.4. Again, the results are discouraging to the customer/user who believes the "simple" in "SNMP." In the case of the bridge products, half of the products equipped with private MIBs produced major problems. In all cases of both bridge and router products, the process was less than smooth.

Again, the conclusions to be drawn from all of these tests is that one should be wary of using private SNMP extensions and that greater problems await in OSI systems management. With SNMP, users need to determine how much of the control of SNMP agent products has been embedded in proprietary MIB objects and make sure that the management station they are considering can accommodate such objects.

5.2.3   Limitations of MIB Objects

A network management system is limited by the capabilities of the network management protocol and by the objects used to represent the environment to be managed. In Chapter 7, we examine some of the key limitations of SNMP. These limitations are "fundamental," in the sense that the limitations cannot be removed without changing the SNMP specification and subsequently all of the SNMP implementations in a configuration.

The limitations due to an inadequate set of objects in the MIB are less serious. These can be dealt with by adding more objects. However, it is still true that the implementations in a configuration, including both manager and agent, must be enhanced to deal with the new objects. In any case, the standard MIB-II serves as a common base for all implementations, and it is important to recognize that MIB-II does indeed limit the ability to monitor and control a network.

We give one example here, suggested by Masum Hasan at the University of Toronto's Computer Systems Research Institute. The example makes use of the configuration in Figure 5.8. Suppose that there is substantial traffic to the server from throughout the network, causing a considerable load on router R2 and subnetwork N3, but that the router and network are able to handle this load. Now suppose that a new source of traffic develops between systems on subnetwork N5 and subnetwork N4. This may increase the load on R2 or N3 to unacceptable levels. If we could determine that this increased load is in fact caused by additional N5–N4 traffic, we might be able to design effective countermeasures, such as a new bridge or router linking N4 and N6. However, there is no way to determine this using MIB-II objects. For example, if we could examine TCP traffic on a per-connection basis, then we could examine the traffic on connections terminating at N3

TABLE 5.4 MIB Agent–Manager Compatibility

(a) Bridge Products (Mier 1991a)

Bridge Vendor	Vendor X Management Station		Vendor Y Management Station	
	Able to load vendor-specific MIB on management station?	Was manager able to invoke/access selected private MIB objects?	Able to load vendor-specific MIB on management station?	Was manager able to invoke/access selected private MIB objects?
A	Yes, easily; system adjusted for syntax error in MIB file.	Yes, objects tested worked and provided good data.	Yes, after about one hour[2] but with limited capabilities.	Limited, could retrieve only some object values.
C	Unable to load or to effectively diagnose why not.	Could not be determined.	Yes, after three or more hours.	Yes, objects tested worked and provided good data.
D	Yes, after 30 minutes; a minor syntax error was found and corrected.	Could not test, unable to configure bridge or access bridge's SNMP agent.[1]	Yes, after about one hour of file reformatting and syntax changes.[2]	Could not test, unable to configure bridge or access bridge's SNMP agent.[1]
E	Unable to load or to effectively diagnose why not.	Could not be determined.	Yes, after about one hour of file reformatting and syntax changes.[2]	Agent returned a value of 0 for most objects tested; other values were questionable.
F	Unable to load or to effectively diagnose why not.	Could not be determined.	Unable to load or to effectively diagnose why not.	Could not be determined.
H	Yes, easily.	Yes, objects tested worked and provided good data.	Yes, after about one hour of file reformatting and syntax changes.[2]	Yes, objects tested worked and provided good data.

[1] While vendor's MIB could be loaded in both management systems with relatively minor syntax adjustments, no private MIB objects could be tested because the bridge, containing the SNMP agent, could not be set up and operated with SNMP agent support.

[2] Syntax changes were needed because the systems manager requires that MIBs be in the ISO SMI format; most of the submitted MIBs were in the SNMP MIB format.

TABLE 5.4 *Continued*

(b) Router Products (Mier 1991b)

Bridge Vendor	Vendor X Management Station		Vendor Y Management Station	
	Able to load vendor-specific MIB on management station?	Was manager able to invoke/access selected private MIB objects?	Able to load vendor-specific MIB on management station?	Was manager able to invoke/access selected private MIB objects?
1	Yes, on first attempt; manager adjusted for a logical error in MIB.	Yes, all objects tested, including sets, worked and provided good data.	Yes, after about an hour; a logical error in MIB had to be corrected before MIB would load.	Yes, all objects tested, including sets, worked and provided good data.
2	Yes, on first attempt.	Some. Agent returned no response for others; a read-write object could not be set.	Yes, on first attempt.	Some. Agent returned no response for others; a read-write object could not be set.
3	Yes, after about an hour; three minor syntax corrections were required.	Yes, all objects tested worked and provided good data.	Yes, after about an hour; five minor syntax corrections were required.	Yes, all objects tested worked and provided good data.
4	Yes, on first attempt.	Very few to test; private IP objects and not SNMP-accessible.	Yes, after minor format editing required by manager.	Very few to test; private IP objects and not SNMP-accessible.
5	Yes, after about two hours; many minor syntax corrections were required.	No. No values were returned by the agent for most of the objects tested.	Yes, after about two hours; many minor syntax corrections were required.	No. No values were returned by the agent for most of the objects tested.
6	Yes, in about 10 minutes; two minor syntax corrections were required.	Yes, most; however, numerous objects were inaccessible because of IP configuration.	Yes, on first attempt, after minor format editing required by manager.	Yes, most; however, numerous objects were inaccessible because of IP configuration.
8	After about two hours of editing on manager.	Yes, all objects tested, including sets, worked and provided good data.	Yes, after about 2½ hours; numerous corrections were required.	Yes, all objects tested, including sets, worked and provided good data.
9	Yes, on first attempt.	Very few to test; private IP objects and not SNMP-accessible.	Yes, on first attempt, after minor format editing required by manager.	Very few to test; private IP objects and not SNMP-accessible.

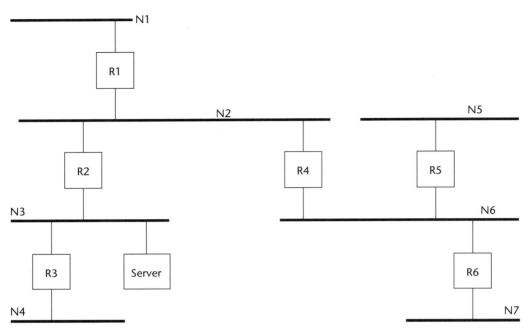

FIGURE 5.8   Example of SNMP management configuration

hosts and terminating at N4 hosts and determine that the source of the new load on R2 and N3 is due to traffic between N5 and N4. But the MIB-II TCP group (Figure 5.6) does not allow this flow to be measured. All that can be measured at a system is the total TCP traffic in and out, not the per-connection TCP traffic.

The tradeoff here is clear: A finer-grained set of MIB objects allows for greater control of the network. The costs are increased storage and processing at the agents and increased SNMP traffic over the network. MIB-II is designed to minimize the burden on systems and networks, which is fine. However, the user must be aware of what is lost by adopting such a strategy.

5.3   Summary

Within the SNMP framework, management information is represented using Abstract Syntax Notation One (ASN.1). A management information base (MIB) consists of a collection of objects organized into groups. Objects hold values that represent managed resources; a group is a unit of conformance.

The structure of management information (SMI) defines the allowable ASN.1 types and the allowable MIB structures. Most objects are scalars; the allowable types are `integer, octet string, null,` and `object identifier`. The `sequence` and `sequence-of` types may be used to construct simple two-dimensional tables of scalar objects. No more elaborate structure is allowed.

APPENDIX 5A   *TCP CONNECTION STATES*

In this chapter, and in Chapter 7, the object `tcpConnTable` is used as an example. It is instructive to look at the underlying protocol information reflected in this managed object. This appendix contains a brief summary. For more detail, see Stallings (1996c) or the actual TCP standard.[6]

Since TCP is designed to run over an unreliable network service (specifically, IP), it must contain elaborate mechanisms to deal with lost, duplicated, misordered, and delayed segments. One of these mechanisms defines the procedure for connection establishment:

1. A TCP entity initiates a connection establishment by sending a SYN to the other side.[7]

2. The other side responds with a SYN, ACK sequence.

3. The initiating TCP entity acknowledges the SYN/ACK with an ACK.

The SYN represents a request for connection, or a willingness to open a connection. With the procedure just outlined, each side explicitly acknowledges the other side's SYN. This procedure is known as a *three-way handshake* and prevents a number of problems that could arise if a two-way handshake (SYN followed by ACK) were used.

It could happen that two TCP entities issue a SYN to each other at about the same time. This is allowed, and a connection results. The sequence listed earlier is modified as follows:

1. A TCP entity initiates a connection establishment by sending a SYN to the other side.

2. The TCP entity receives a SYN from the other side.

3. The TCP entity acknowledges the SYN with a SYN, ACK.

4. The TCP entity receives an ACK from the other side.

A similar three-way handshake is used to close a connection. All of these events can be modeled by a state transition diagram. Figure 5.9, taken from MIL-STD-1778, shows the TCP state transition diagram. The upper part of the label on each state transition shows the input to the TCP entity, which is either a TCP segment from another entity, or a service request from a user of this TCP entity. The lower part shows the TCP segment issued by this TCP entity.

---

[6]RFC 793 (September 1981) is the defining document for TCP as used by the Internet Activities Board. MIL-STD-1778 (October 1983), issued by the Defense Communications Agency, is the military standard document used for government procurements of TCP. The latter document is clearer and more comprehensive and is technically aligned with the RFC definition.

[7]Only one type of protocol data unit is employed in TCP, the TCP segment. When the standard refers to issuing a SYN, it means that the sending entity has sent a TCP segment with the SYN bit in the header set to 1.

SV   = state vector
MSL = maximum segment lifetime

FIGURE 5.9   TCP entity state summary (MIL-STD-1778)

To maintain various connections, a TCP entity retains state information about each connection, in what is referred to as a state vector (MIL-STD-1778) or a transmission control block (RFC 793). The state vector includes the following information:

- state: one of the states of the connection
- source_address: IP address of this system

- `source_port`: port number of the TCP user at this end of the connection
- `destination_address`: IP address of the system at the other end of the connection
- `lcn`: local connection name; shorthand identifier used in service request and response interaction with the TCP user to refer to this connection
- `sec`: security label for this connection
- `sec_ranges`: security structure that specifies the allowed ranges for this connection
- `original_prec`: precedence level specified by the local TCP user in the open request
- `actual_prec`: precedence level negotiated at connection opening and used during connection lifetime
- `ULP_timeout`: longest delay allowed for data delivery before automatic connection termination
- `ULP_timeout_action`: in the event of a timeout, determines whether the connection is terminated or an error is reported to the TCP user
- `open_mode`: the type of open request issued by the local user (unspecified passive open, full specified passive open, active open)
- `send_queue`: storage location of data sent by the local user before transmission to the remote TCP (Each data octet is stored with a time stamp indicating its time of entry.)
- `send_queue_length`: number of entries in the send queue made up of data and time stamp information
- `send_push`: an offset from the front of the send queue indicating the end of push data
- `send_urg`: an offset from the front of the send queue indicating the end of urgent data
- `recv_queue`: storage location of data received from the remote TCP before delivery to the local user
- `recv_queue_length`: number of data octets in receive queue
- `recv_push`: an offset from the front of the receive queue indicating the end of push data
- `recv_urg`: an offset from the front of the receive queue indicating the end of urgent data
- `recv_alloc`: the number of data octets the local TCP user is currently willing to receive

All of this information is needed to correctly manage the TCP connection. Referring to Figure 5.6, we see that only a small fraction of this information is available to a remote manager via SNMP and the MIB. The advantage, indeed the necessity, of limiting the amount of manager-visible information is minimizing the complexity of the manager and agent modules, the amount of storage required for the MIB, and the amount of traffic on the network consumed in communicating management information. The disadvantage, of course, is that the management functionality is limited. For example, if a user complains to a network manager that a connection is somehow malfunctioning, the manager has very little information with which to diagnose the problem. Worse, the MIB provides no mechanism for representing inactive connections. Thus, if a user reports that a connection has failed, the information that the network manager needs concerning the failed connection is not available.

Standard MIBs

As Table 4.1 indicates, a large number of separate MIB documents have been developed. In this chapter, we look at the two MIBs that, at the time of this writing, have achieved full standards status. MIB-II is the most important of the MIB specifications, covering a broad range of managed objects. The Ethernet MIB focuses on the most widely used type of local area network (LAN) and is representative of interface-specific MIBs.

6.1 *MIB-II*

MIB-II (RFC 1213) defines the second version of the management information base; the first version, MIB-I, was issued as RFC 1156. MIB-II is a superset of MIB-I, with some additional objects and groups. The designers of MIB-II used the following criteria, as cited in RFC 1213, for including an object in the newer version.

1. An object needed to be essential for either fault or configuration management.

2. Only weak control objects were permitted (by "weak," it is meant that tampering with them can do only limited damage). This criterion reflects the fact that the current management protocols are not sufficiently secure to do more powerful control operations.

3. Evidence of current use and utility was required.

4. When MIB-I was developed, the number of objects was intentionally limited to about 100 to make it easier for vendors fully to instrument their software. In MIB-II, this limit was eliminated given the wide technological base now implementing MIB-I.

5. To avoid redundant variables, no object that could be derived from others in the MIB could be included.

6. Implementation-specific objects (for example, for BSD UNIX) were excluded.

7. The developers agreed to avoid heavily instrumenting critical sections of code. The general guideline was one counter per critical section per layer.

Since MIB-II contains only those objects its designers deemed essential, none of the objects is optional. The `mib-2` group is subdivided into the following groups (see Figure 5.1):

- `system`: overall information about the system
- `interfaces`: information about each of the interfaces from the system to a subnetwork
- `at` (address translation; deprecated): description of address translation table for internet-to-subnet address mapping
- `ip`: information related to the implementation and execution experience of IP on this system
- `icmp`: information related to the implementation and execution experience of ICMP on this system
- `tcp`: information related to the implementation and execution experience of TCP on this system
- `udp`: information related to the implementation and execution experience of UDP on this system
- `egp`: information related to the implementation and execution experience of EGP on this system
- `dot3` (transmission): information about the transmission schemes and access protocols at each system interface
- `snmp`: information related to the implementation and execution experience of SNMP on this system

(Note that "deprecated" means "replaced.")

The group organization is a convenience in organizing managed objects according to the function of the underlying managed entities. In addition, it provides guidance for the implementor of managed agents to know which objects he or she must implement. For MIB-I and MIB-II, the method is as follows: If the semantics of a group are applicable to an implementation, then it must implement all objects in that group. For example, an implementation must include all of the objects in the `tcp` group if and only if it implements the TCP protocol; thus, a bridge or a router need not implement the `tcp` group. One exception to this rule is the address translation group, as discussed later in this chapter.

We examine each of the MIB-II groups in this section, with the exception of the `snmp` group, whose discussion is deferred until Chapter 7.

6.1.1   Key to Figures and Tables

Figures 6.1, 6.2, 6.4, 6.5, 6.7, 6.8, 6.10, 6.12, and 6.14 illustrate the hierarchical arrangement of the objects in each of the groups. The structure of each group is determined by the tree-structured object identifiers assigned to the members of the group. For example, each table within a group appears as a three-level tree: The name of the table is the top level; the name of each row is the second level; and the name of each scalar table row element (columnar object) is in the third level. Those elements that serve as INDEXes are indicated by an arrow.

Tables 6.1, 6.2, and 6.4 through 6.9 provide information about the objects in each group. The ACCESS characteristic of an object may be read-only (RO), read-write (RW), write-only (WO), or not accessible (NA). Those elements that serve as INDEXes are indicated by a shading of the corresponding row.

6.1.2   system Group

The system group provides general information about the managed system (Figure 6.1, Table 6.1). The objects in this group are largely self-explanatory, but several comments may be helpful.

The sysServices object has a value that is interpreted as a seven-bit code. Each bit of the code corresponds to a layer in the TCP/IP or OSI architecture, with the least significant bit corresponding to layer 1. If a system offers a service at a particular layer, then the corresponding bit is set. The value can be expressed as

$$\text{sysServices} = \sum_{L \varepsilon S} 2^{L-1},$$

where S = set of numbers of layers for which services are provided. For example, a node that is a host offering application services would have a binary value of 1001000, or a decimal value of 72 ($2^{(4-1)}$ + $2^{(7-1)}$). In the context of the TCP/IP protocol suite, the following layer assignment is used:

Layer	Functionality
1	physical (e.g., repeaters)
2	datalink/subnetwork (e.g., bridges)
3	internet (e.g., IP routers)
4	end-to-end (e.g., IP hosts)
7	applications (e.g., mail relays)

The sysUpTime object indicates the amount of time (as counted by the agent) since the network management portion of the system was last reinitialized. This object has many uses. Typically, if a manager is periodically polling an agent for counter values, it will also include a request for the sysUpTime value; in this way the manager can determine how much the counters have changed over a specific time interval. Another example is fault monitoring: A manager can periodically poll each agent for this value, and if

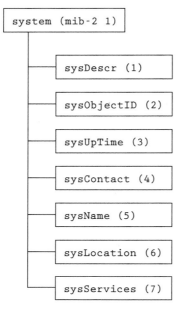

FIGURE 6.1 MIB-II system group

TABLE 6.1 system Group Objects

Object	Syntax	Access	Description
sysDescr	DisplayString (SIZE (0 . . . 255))	RO	A description of the entity, such as hardware, operating system, etc.
sysObjectID	OBJECT IDENTIFIER	RO	The vendor's authoritative identification of the network management subsystem contained in the entity
sysUpTime	TimeTicks	RO	The time since the network management portion of the system was last reinitialized
sysContact	DisplayString (SIZE (0 . . . 255))	RW	The identification and contact information of the contact person for this managed node
sysName	DisplayString (SIZE (0 . . . 255))	RW	An administratively assigned name for this managed node
sysLocation	DisplayString (SIZE (0 . . . 255))	RW	The physical location of this node
sysServices	INTEGER (0 . . . 127)	RO	A value that indicates the set of services this entity primarily offers

the current value for an agent is less than the most recent value, then the agent has been restarted since the last poll.

6.1.3   interfaces Group

The interfaces group contains generic information about the physical interfaces of the entity (Figure 6.2, Table 6.2), including configuration information and statistics on the events occurring at each interface. Each interface is thought of as being attached to a sub-network, although an interface to a point-to-point link is also allowed. Implementation of this group is mandatory for all systems.

The group includes the object ifNumber, which records the total number of network interfaces, regardless of their current state. The remainder of the group consists of the ifTable, which has one row for each interface. The table is indexed by ifIndex, whose value is simply an integer in the range between 1 and the value of ifNumber, with each interface being assigned a unique number.

The object ifType records the type of interface. Table 6.3 indicates the interfaces that have been assigned standard numbers in MIB-II.

The nature of the physical address, ifPhysAddress, will depend on the type of interface. For example, for all IEEE LANs and MANs and FDDI, ifPhysAddress contains the value of the MAC address at that interface.

Two objects in the group relate to the status of the interface. The ifAdminStatus object, which is read-write, enables a manager to specify a desired operational status for the interface. The ifOperStatus object, which is read-only, reflects the actual current operational status of the interface. If both objects have the value down(2), then the interface has been shut off by the manager. If ifAdminStatus has the value up(1) while ifOperStatus has the value down(2), then the interface has failed.

The object ifSpeed is a read-only gauge that estimates the current capacity of the interface in bits per second. This object is useful in the case of an interface whose capacity can vary as a function of demand or other parameters. More commonly, the value of this object is fixed at the nominal data rate of the interface. For example, for an Ethernet interface, the value will be 10^7, reflecting a data rate of 10 Mbps.

All of the information in the interfaces group is generic and thus applicable to any type of interface. The MIB may contain additional information specific to a certain type of interface, such as an IEEE 802.5 token ring. The ifSpecific object contains a pointer to another part of the MIB at this node containing the interface-specific managed objects.

The interfaces group contains basic information that is useful as a starting point for any network management function, such as performance monitoring or fault control. For example, objects in this group can be used to detect congestion, as measured by the total number of octets into or out of the system or the queue length for output. Once congestion has been detected, other group objects can be examined to find out, for example, if protocol activity at the TCP or IP level might be responsible for the congestion.

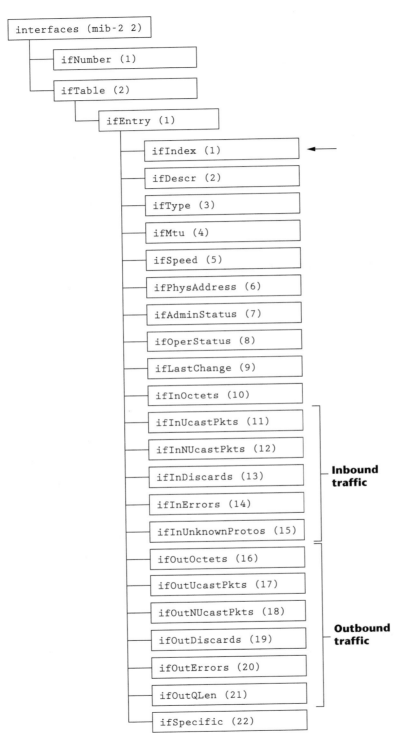

FIGURE 6.2 MIB-II interfaces group

TABLE 6.2 interfaces Group Objects

Object	Syntax	Access	Description
ifNumber	INTEGER	RO	The number of network interfaces
ifTable	SEQUENCE OF ifEntry	NA	A list of interface entries
ifEntry	SEQUENCE	NA	An interface entry containing objects at the subnetwork layer and below for a particular interface
ifIndex	INTEGER	RO	A unique value for each interface
ifDescr	DisplayString (SIZE (0 ... 255))	RO	Information about the interface, including name of manufacturer, product name, and version of the hardware interface
ifType	INTEGER	RO	Type of interface, distinguished according to the physical/link protocol(s)
ifMtu	INTEGER	RO	The size of the largest protocol data unit, in octets, that can be sent/received on the interface
ifSpeed	Gauge	RO	An estimate of the interface's current data rate capacity
ifPhysAddress	PhysAddress	RO	The interface's address at the protocol layer immediately below the network layer
ifAdminStatus	INTEGER	RW	Desired interface state (up(1), down(2), testing(3))
ifOperStatus	INTEGER	RO	Current operational interface state (up(1), down(2), testing(3))
ifLastChange	TimeTicks	RO	Value of sysUpTime at the time the interface entered its current operational state
ifInOctets	Counter	RO	Total number of octets received on the interface, including framing characters
ifInUcastPkts	Counter	RO	Number of subnetwork-unicast packets delivered to a higher-layer protocol
ifInNUcastPkts	Counter	RO	Number of nonunicast packets delivered to a higher-layer protocol
ifInDiscards	Counter	RO	Number of inbound packets discarded, even though no errors had been detected, to prevent their being deliverable to a higher-layer protocol (e.g., buffer overflow)
ifInErrors	Counter	RO	Number of inbound packets that contained errors preventing them from being deliverable to a higher-layer protocol
ifInUnknownProtos	Counter	RO	Number of inbound packets that were discarded because of an unknown or unsupported protocol
ifOutOctets	Counter	RO	Total number of octets transmitted on the interface, including framing characters
ifOutUcastPkts	Counter	RO	Total number of packets that higher-level protocols requested be transmitted to a subnetwork-unicast address, including those that were discarded or otherwise not sent
ifOutNUcastPkts	Counter	RO	Total number of packets that higher-level protocols requested be transmitted to a nonunicast address, including those that were discarded or otherwise not sent
ifOutDiscards	Counter	RO	Number of outbound packets discarded even though no errors had been detected to prevent their being transmitted (e.g., buffer overflow)
ifOutErrors	Counter	RO	Number of outbound packets that could not be transmitted because of errors
ifOutQLen	Gauge	RO	Length of the output packet queue
ifSpecific	OBJECT IDENTIFIER	RO	Reference to MIB definitions specific to the particular media being used to realize the interface

TABLE 6.3 Network Interface Types

Number	Type	Description
1	other	None of the following
2	regular1822	The original ARPANET interface protocol between a host and an Interface Message Processor (IMP)
3	hdh1822	A revised version of 1822, using a synchronous link scheme
4	ddn-x25	Version of X.25 specified for the Defense Data Network
5	rfc877-x25	Version of X.25 defined in RFC 877, intended for carrying IP datagrams
6	ethernetCsmacd	Ethernet Medium Access Control (MAC) protocol
7	iso88023Csmacd	IEEE 802.3 CSMA/CD MAC protocol
8	iso88024TokenBus	IEEE 802.4 Token Bus MAC protocol
9	iso88025TokenRing	IEEE 802.5 Token Ring MAC protocol
10	iso88026Man	IEEE 802.6 DQDB MAC protocol for MANs
11	starLan	A 1-Mbps twisted pair version of Ethernet
12	proteon-10Mbit	A 10-Mbps optical fiber token ring LAN developed by Proteon
13	proteon-80Mbit	An 80-Mbps optical fiber token ring LAN
14	hyperchannel	A 50-Mbps coaxial cable LAN developed by Network Systems
15	fddi	The ANSI Fiber Distributed Data Interface (FDDI) standard LAN
16	lapb	The data link control protocol used with X.25
17	sdlc	The data link control protocol used with IBM's SNA
18	ds1	Interface to a digital transmission line operating with the DS-1 format at 1.544 Mbps
19	e1	A 2.048-Mbps conforming to the ITU-T specification
20	basicISDN	Basic rate ISDN interface, operating at 192 kbps
21	primaryISDN	Primary rate ISDN interface, operating at 1.544 or 2.048 Mbps
22	propPointToPointSerial	Proprietary serial interface
23	ppp	The Internet Point-to-Point Protocol
24	softwareLoopback	Used for transfer between processes in the same system
25	eon	The ISO connectionless network protocol (CLNP) over IP, referred to as experimental OSI-based network, and defined in RFC 1406
26	ethernet-3Mbit	The original 3-Mbps version of Ethernet
27	nsip	XNS over IP
28	slip	The Internet standard Serial Line Interface Protocol
29	ultra	A high-speed fiber interface developed by Ultra Network Technologies

TABLE 6.3   *Continued*

Number	Type	Description
30	ds3	Interface to a digital transmission line operating with the DS-3 format at 44.736 Mbps
31	sip	Transmission of IP datagrams over a SMDS metropolitan-area network
32	frame-relay	Frame relay network interface
33	rs232	RS-232, now EIA-232-D, interface
34	para	Parallel port interface
35	arcnet	ARCnet LAN
36	arcnetPlus	ARCnet Plus LAN
37	atm	Asynchronous transfer-mode network interface
38	miox25	Multiprotocol interconnect on X.25 and ISDN
39	sonet	The synchronous optical network (SONET) and SDH high-speed optical network interfaces
40	x25ple	X.25 packet-level entity
41	iso88021lc	Logical link control, defined in IEEE 802.2
42	localTalk	Old Apple network interface specification
43	smdsDxi	SMDS data exchange interface
44	frameRelayService	Frame relay network-side interface
45	v35	V.35 ITU-T specification
46	hssi	High-speed serial interface
47	hippi	High-performance parallel interface
48	modem	Generic modem
49	aal5	ATM adaption layer 5, providing a simple service interface to ATM
50	sonetPath	SONET path
51	sonetVT	SONET virtual tributary
52	smdsIcip	SMDS intercarrier interface
53	propVirtual	Proprietary virtual/internal
54	propMultiplexor	Proprietary multiplexing

An effective way to visualize the flow of traffic across an interface is by means of a *Case diagram*. Figure 6.3 illustrates the Case diagram for the `interfaces` group. See Appendix 6A for an introduction to this tool.

There have been two extensions to the `interfaces` group. RFC 1229, issued in 1992, defines additional objects and provides more flexibility in handling the wide variety of possible interfaces. Subsequently, RFC 1229 was superseded by RFC 1573, issued in 1994. RFC 1573 clarifies and improves on the scheme proposed in RFC 1229 and uses SMIv2 for definition. Accordingly, we defer a discussion of this topic until Part IV of this book.

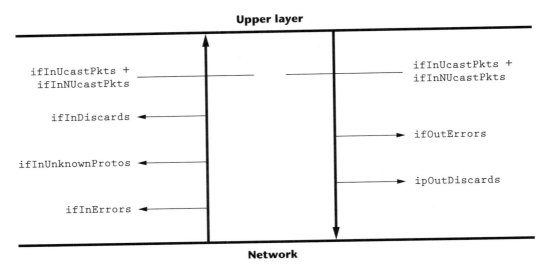

FIGURE 6.3   Case diagram for MIB-II `interfaces` group

6.1.4   Address Translation Group

The address translation group consists of a single table (Figure 6.4, Table 6.4). Each row in the table corresponds to one of the physical interfaces of the system. The row provides a mapping from a network address to a physical address. Typically, the network address is the IP address for this system at this interface. The physical address depends on the nature of the subnetwork. For example, if the interface is to a local area network (LAN), then the physical address is the MAC address for that interface. If the subnetwork is an X.25 packet-switching network, then the physical address may be an X.121 address.

The table is indexed by `atIfIndex`, whose value matches that of `ifIndex` for one of the entries in the `interfaces` group. The table is also indexed by network address. The table contains an entry only for each interface that uses a translation table. Some interfaces use an algorithmic method (for example, DDN-X.25); for these, there is no entry in the table.

This group is deprecated in MIB-II and is included solely for compatibility with MIB-I nodes. In MIB-II, address translation information is provided within each network protocol group. There are two reasons for this change:

- *The need to support multiprotocol nodes:* When a node supports more than one network-level protocol (for example, IP and the ISO connectionless network protocol (CLNP)), then more than one network-level address will be associated with each physical interface.

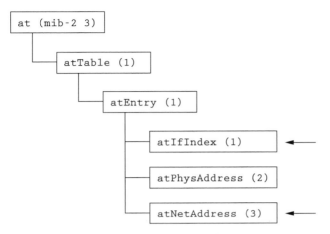

FIGURE 6.4   MIB-II address translation group

TABLE 6.4   Address Translation Group Objects

Object	Syntax	Access	Description
atTable	SEQUENCE OF AtEntry	NA	Contains the NetworkAddress to physical address equivalent
atEntry	SEQUENCE	NA	Contains one NetworkAddress for each physical address
atIfIndex	INTEGER	RW	Interface on which this entry is effective
atPhysAddress	PhysAddress	RW	Media-dependent physical address
atNetAddress	NetworkAddress	RW	The NetworkAddress (e.g., IP address) corresponding to the media-dependent physical address

- *The need for two-way mapping:* The address table in the address translation group is defined to allow mapping to occur only from network address to physical address. Some protocols, such as the ISO end system to intermediate system (ES-IS) routing protocol, also require mapping from physical address to network address.

In MIB-II (and future MIBs), address tables are located within the appropriate network-level protocol groups. Each group may have one or two such tables to support mapping in both directions. The use of two tables allows for ease of implementation but does not prevent the use of a single internal data structure that is visible via SMI as two tables.

This is a rare example in MIB-II where duplicate information is found.

6.1.5   `ip` Group

The `ip` group contains information relevant to the implementation and operation of IP at a node (Figure 6.5, Table 6.5). Since IP is implemented in both end systems (hosts) and intermediate systems (routers), not all of the objects in this group are relevant for any given system. Objects that are not relevant have null values.

6.1.5.1   Original Specification

The `ip` group contains some basic counters of traffic flow into and out of the IP layer. Figure 6.6 depicts these in a Case diagram (see Appendix 6A for an introduction to Case diagrams).

Three tables are included in the `ip` group. The `ipAddrTable` contains information relevant to the IP addresses assigned to this entity, with one row for each IP address. Each address is uniquely assigned to a physical interface, indicated by `ipAdEntIfIndex`, whose value matches that of `ifIndex` for one of the entries in the `interfaces` group. This information is useful in monitoring the configuration of the network in terms of IP addresses. Note, however, that the objects in this table are read-only; thus SNMP cannot be used to change IP addresses. Two of the objects in this table, `ipAdEntNetMask` and `ipAdEnt-BcastAddr`, relate to details of IP addressing, which is explained in Appendix 6B.

The `ipRouteTable` contains information used for Internet routing. The information in the route table is of a relatively general nature and could be extracted from a number of protocol-specific routing tables, such as those for RIP, OSPF, and IS-IS. There is one entry for each route presently known to this entity. The table is indexed by `ip-RouteDest`. For each table route, the local interface for the next hop is identified in `ipRouteIfIndex`, whose value matches that of `ifIndex` for one of the entries in the `interfaces` group. Each entry also indicates, in `ipRouteProto`, the method by which this route was learned. The possible values are as follows:

- `other`: none of the following
- `local`: nonprotocol information, such as manually configured information
- `netmgmt`: route developed by a network management protocol
- `icmp`: Internet Control Message Protocol (RFC 792) (ICMP is a companion to IP, primarily used to provide feedback from routers to end systems about problems. It also includes a `Redirect` message, which provides routing information.)
- `egp`: Exterior Gateway Protocol (RFC 904); a simple router-to-router protocol designed for interchange between routers in different autonomous systems
- `ggp`: Gateway to Gateway Protocol; the routing protocol originally used by routers in the same core domain of the Internet; now obsolete
- `hello`: A simple routing protocol used between routers in the same autonomous system; now obsolete

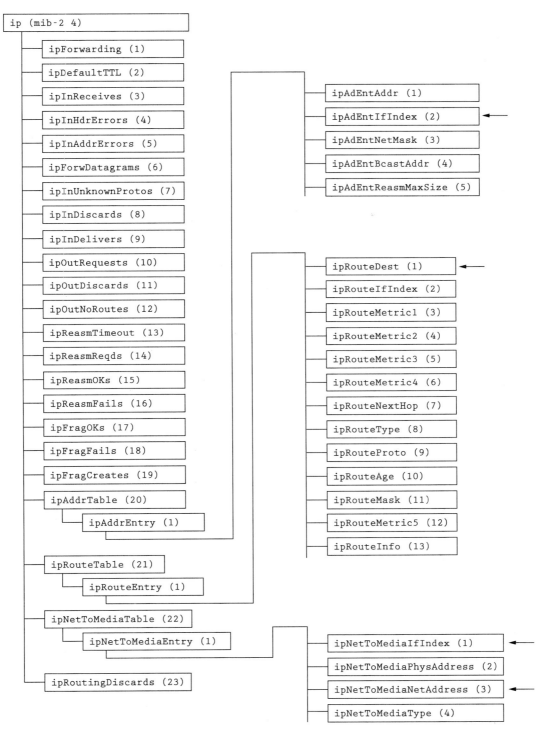

FIGURE 6.5 MIB-II ip group

TABLE 6.5 ip Group Objects

Object	Syntax	Access	Description
ipForwarding	INTEGER	RW	Acting as IP gateway (1); not acting as IP gateway (2)
ipDefaultTTL	INTEGER	RW	Default value inserted into Time-To-Live field of IP header of datagrams originated at this entity
ipInReceives	Counter	RO	Total number of input datagrams received from interfaces, including those received in error
ipInHdrErrors	Counter	RO	Number of input datagrams discarded due to errors in IP header
ipInAddrErrors	Counter	RO	Number of input datagrams discarded because the IP address in the destination field was not valid to be received at this entity
ipForwDatagrams	Counter	RO	Number of input datagrams for which this entity was not their final IP destination, as a result of which an attempt was made to forward
ipInUnknownProtos	Counter	RO	Number of locally addressed datagrams received successfully but discarded because of an unknown or unsupported protocol
ipInDiscards	Counter	RO	Number of input IP datagrams for which no problems were encountered to prevent their continued processing but which were discarded (e.g., for lack of buffer space)
ipInDelivers	Counter	RO	Total number of input datagrams successfully delivered to IP user protocols
ipOutRequests	Counter	RO	Total number of IP datagrams that local IP user protocols supplied to IP in requests for transmission
ipOutDiscards	Counter	RO	Number of output IP datagrams for which no problems were encountered to prevent their continued processing but which were discarded (e.g., for lack of buffer space)
ipOutNoRoutes	Counter	RO	Number of IP datagrams discarded because no route could be found
ipReasmTimeout	INTEGER	RO	Maximum number of seconds that received fragments are held awaiting reassembly at this entity
ipReasmReqds	Counter	RO	Number of IP fragments received that needed to be reassembled at this entity
ipReasmOKs	Counter	RO	Number of IP datagrams successfully reassembled
ipReasmFails	Counter	RO	Number of failures detected by the IP reassembly algorithm
ifFragsOK	Counter	RO	Number of IP datagrams that have been successfully fragmented at this entity
ipFragsFails	Counter	RO	Number of IP datagrams discarded because they needed to be fragmented at this entity but could not be, because the don't-fragment flag was set
ipFragsCreates	Counter	RO	Number of IP datagram fragments generated at this entity
ipAddrTable	SEQUENCE OF IpAddrEntry	NA	Table of addressing information relevant to this entity's IP addresses
ipAddrEntry	SEQUENCE	NA	Addressing information for one of this entity's IP addresses
ipAdEntAddr	IpAddress	RO	IP address to which this entry's addressing information pertains

Name	Type	Access	Description
ipAdEntIfIndex	INTEGER	RO	Index value that uniquely identifies the interface to which this entry is applicable
ipAdEntNetMask	IpAddress	RO	Subnet mask associated with the IP address of this entry
ipAdEntBcastAddr	INTEGER	RO	Value of the least significant bit in the IP broadcast address used for sending datagrams on the logical interface associated with the IP address of this entry
ipAdEntReasmMaxSize	INTEGER	RO	Size of the largest IP datagram which this entity can reassemble from incoming datagrams on this interface
ipRouteTable	SEQUENCE OF IpRouteEntry	NA	This entity's IP routing table
ipRouteEntry	SEQUENCE	NA	A route to a particular destination
ipRouteDest	IpAddress	RW	Destination IP address of this route
ipRouteIfIndex	INTEGER	RW	Index value that uniquely identifies the local interface through which the next hop of this route should be reached
ipRouteMetric1	INTEGER	RW	Primary routing metric for this route
ipRouteMetric2	INTEGER	RW	Alternate routing metric for this route
ipRouteMetric3	INTEGER	RW	Alternate routing metric for this route
ipRouteMetric4	INTEGER	RW	Alternate routing metric for this route
ipRouteNextHop	IpAddress	RW	IP address of next hop of this route
ipRouteType	INTEGER	RW	other (1) ; invalid (2) ; direct (3) ; indirect (4)
ipRouteProto	INTEGER	RO	The routing mechanism by which this route was learned
ipRouteAge	INTEGER	RW	Number of seconds since this route was last updated or verified
ipRouteMask	IpAddress	RW	Mask to be ANDed with destination address before being compared to ipRouteDest
ipRouteMetric5	INTEGER	RW	Alternate routing metric for this route
ipRouteInfo	OBJECT IDENTIFIER	RO	Reference to MIB definitions specific to the routing protocol responsible for this route
ipNetToMediaTable	SEQUENCE OF IpNetToMediaEntry	NA	IP address translation table used for mapping from IP addresses to physical addresses
ipNetToMediaEntry	SEQUENCE	NA	Contains one IpAddress for each physical address
ipNetToMediaIfIndex	INTEGER	RW	Interface for which this entry applies
ipNetToMediaPhysAddress	PhysAddress	RW	Media-dependent physical address
ipNetToMediaNetAddress	IpAddress	RW	IpAddress corresponding to the media-dependent physical address
ipNetToMediaType	INTEGER	RW	Type of mapping: other (1) ; invalid (2) ; dynamic (3) ; static (4)
ipRouting Discards	Counter	RO	Number of routing entries discarded even though valid

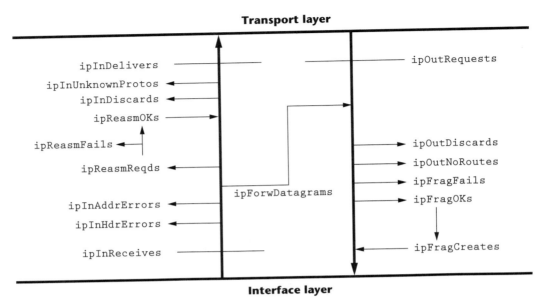

FIGURE 6.6 Case diagram for MIB-II `ip` group

- `rip`: Routing Information Protocol (RFC 1723); a routing protocol used inside a single autonomous system
- `is-is`: Intermediate System to Intermediate System Protocol (ISO 10589); an international standard routing protocol used both within and between autonomous systems; similar in functionality to OSPF
- `es-is`: End System to Intermediate System Protocol (ISO 9542); a simple routing protocol between an end system and a router
- `ciscoIgrp`: a proprietary interior gateway protocol developed by Cisco
- `bbnSpfIgp`: BBN's shortest-path first interior gateway protocol
- `ospf`: Open Shortest Path First (RFC 1583); a routing protocol for use within autonomous systems
- `bgp`: Border Gateway Protocol (RFC 1771); a routing protocol for use between autonomous systems

Another key entry in the `ipRouteTable` is `ipRouteType`. Its possible values are:

- `other`: none of the following
- `invalid`: an invalidated route

- direct: means that the destination address is on a subnetwork directly attached to this router

- indirect: indicates that the destination address is not on a subnetwork directly attached to this router; thus, the route must traverse at least one additional router

The ipRouteTable information is useful for configuration monitoring, and since the objects in the table are read-write, it can be used to control the routing process. In addition, this table can be helpful in fault isolation. For example, if a user is unable to make a connection to a remote host, the fault may lie in inconsistent routing tables among the hosts and routers in the Internet.

The ipNetToMediaTable is an address translation table that provides a correspondence between physical addresses and IP addresses. There is an entry for each interface that does not use an algorithmic mapping technique. The information contained here is the same as that in the address translation group, with the addition of the object ipNet-ToMediaType, which indicates the type of mapping used.

In addition to the three tables, a number of scalar objects in the ip group are useful for performance and fault monitoring.

6.1.5.2   IP Forwarding Table

RFC 1354 was issued as a proposed Internet standard in July 1992. Its purpose was to fix a problem with the ipRouteTable and to make the routing table more flexible, by deprecating ipRouteTable and replacing it with the definitions in RFC 1354.

The specific problem with ipRouteTable is that it is indexed only by ipRoute-Dest, which is the destination IP address for this route. The description clause of ipRouteDest states that

> *Multiple routes to a single destination can appear in the table, but access to such multiple entries is dependent on the table-access mechanism defined by the network management protocol in use.*

No such mechanism has been approved for SNMP (see Section 7.1.3.2 for a discussion). In the absence of such mechanisms, it is possible only to define unambiguously, in ipRouteTable, a single route to a given destination, even if the routing protocol permits the use of alternate routes for load balancing, reliability, or other reasons.

Figure 6.7 illustrates the structure defined in RFC 1354. At the top level, the object ipForward has the object identifier { ip 24 }; thus it becomes the 24th object immediately under ip, directly after ipRoutingDiscards.

Two objects are beneath ipForward: ipForwardNumber is a read-only gauge that records the number of valid entries in ipForwardTable; ipForwardTable defines the routing table that is to replace ipRouteTable.

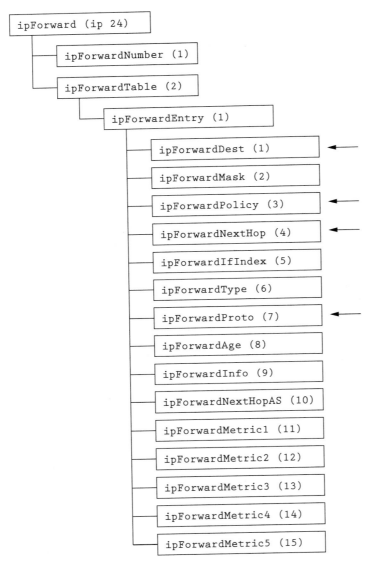

FIGURE 6.7   IP forwarding table MIB

Most of the objects in `ipForwardTable` correspond to objects in `ipRouteTable`, with the same syntax and semantics. The only difference is that the name is prefixed by "`ipForward`" rather than "`ipRoute`." Also, the objects are reorganized for aesthetic reasons. In addition, the following new objects are included in `ipForwardTable`:

- `ipForwardPolicy`: indicates the policy used to select among alternate routes to a destination. In the case of routing of IP datagrams, the policy is based on the IP type-of-service field, which specifies one of eight levels of precedence and a binary value of delay (normal, low), throughput (normal, high), and reliability (normal, high).
- `ipForwardNextHopAS`: the autonomous system number of the next hop. This value is useful to administrators of regional networks.

The `ipRouteTable` is indexed only by `ipRouteDest`. The `ipForwardTable` is indexed by `ipForwardDest`, `ipForwardProto`, `ipForwardPolicy`, and `ipForward-NextHop`. Thus, multiple routes, rather than just a single route, can be managed.

6.1.6   `icmp` Group

The Internet Control Message Protocol (ICMP), defined in RFC 792, is an integral part of the TCP/IP protocol suite. It is a required companion to IP. That is, all systems that implement IP must also provide ICMP. ICMP provides a means for transferring messages from routers and other hosts to a host. In essence, it provides feedback about problems in the communication environment. Examples of its use include: When a datagram cannot reach its destination, when a router does not have the buffering capacity to forward a datagram, and when a router can direct the host to send traffic on a shorter route. In most cases, an ICMP message is sent in response to a datagram, either by a router en route or by the intended destination host.

The `icmp` group contains information relevant to the implementation and operation of ICMP at a node (Figure 6.8, Table 6.6). The group consists solely of counters of the various types of ICMP messages sent and received. Figure 6.9 shows the corresponding Case diagram.

6.1.7   `tcp` Group

The `tcp` group contains information relevant to the implementation and operation of TCP at a node (Figure 6.10, Table 6.7). The only table that is part of this group is the `tcpConnTable`, which was introduced in Section 5.1.2.4.

The first three entries in Table 6.7 deal with retransmission time. When a TCP entity transmits a segment, it expects to receive an acknowledgment. If the segment is lost or

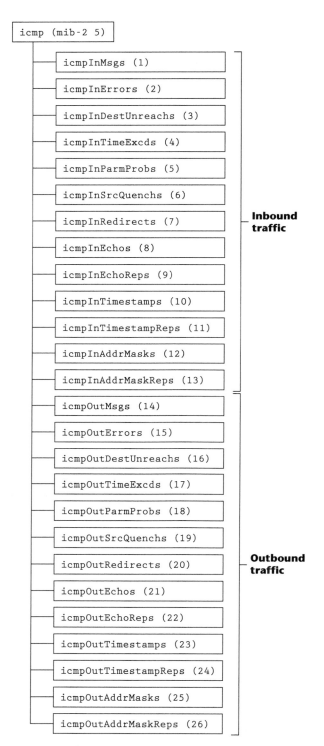

FIGURE 6.8 MIB-II icmp group

TABLE 6.6 `icmp` Group Objects

Object	Syntax	Access	Description
`icmpInMsgs`	Counter	RO	Total number of ICMP messages that the entity received
`icmpInErrors`	Counter	RO	Number of ICMP messages received but determined to have ICMP-specific errors
`icmpInDestUnreachs`	Counter	RO	Number of ICMP Destination Unreachable messages received
`icmpInTimeExcds`	Counter	RO	Number of ICMP Time Exceeded messages received
`icmpInParmProbs`	Counter	RO	Number of ICMP Parameter Problem messages received
`icmpInSrcQuenchs`	Counter	RO	Number of ICMP Source Quench messages received
`icmpInRedirects`	Counter	RO	Number of ICMP Redirect messages received
`icmpInEchos`	Counter	RO	Number of ICMP Echo (request) messages received
`icmpInEchoReps`	Counter	RO	Number of ICMP Echo Reply messages received
`icmpInTimestamps`	Counter	RO	Number of ICMP Timestamp (request) messages received
`icmpInTimestampReps`	Counter	RO	Number of ICMP Timestamp (request) messages received
`icmpInAddrMasks`	Counter	RO	Number of ICMP Address Mask Request messages received
`icmpInAddrMaskReps`	Counter	RO	Number of ICMP Address Mask Reply messages received
`icmpOutMsgs`	Counter	RO	Total number of ICMP messages that the entity attempted to send
`icmpOutErrors`	Counter	RO	Number of ICMP messages that this entity did not send due to problems discovered within ICMP
`icmpOutDestUnreachs`	Counter	RO	Number of ICMP Destination Unreachable messages sent
`icmpOutTimeExcds`	Counter	RO	Number of ICMP Time Exceeded messages sent
`icmpOutParmProbs`	Counter	RO	Number of ICMP Parameter Problem messages sent
`icmpOutSrcQuenchs`	Counter	RO	Number of ICMP Source Quench messages sent
`icmpOutRedirects`	Counter	RO	Number of ICMP Redirect messages sent
`icmpOutEchos`	Counter	RO	Number of ICMP Echo (request) messages sent
`icmpOutEchoReps`	Counter	RO	Number of ICMP Echo Reply messages sent
`icmpOutTimestamps`	Counter	RO	Number of ICMP Timestamp (request) messages sent
`icmpOutTimestampReps`	Counter	RO	Number of ICMP Timestamp (reply) messages sent
`icmpOutAddrMasks`	Counter	RO	Number of ICMP Address Mask Request messages sent
`icmpOutAddrMaskReps`	Counter	RO	Number of ICMP Address Mask Reply messages sent

ICMP logic

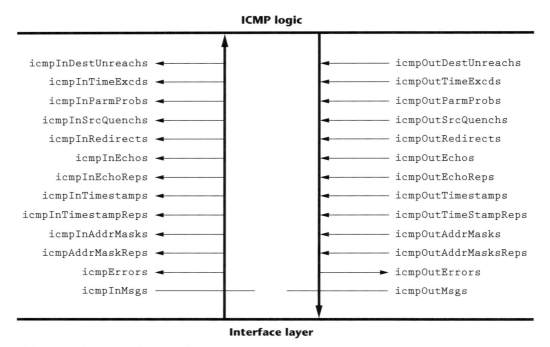

icmpInDestUnreachs ◄	◄ icmpOutDestUnreachs
icmpInTimeExcds ◄	◄ icmpOutTimeExcds
icmpInParmProbs ◄	◄ icmpOutParmProbs
icmpInSrcQuenchs ◄	◄ icmpOutSrcQuenchs
icmpInRedirects ◄	◄ icmpOutRedirects
icmpInEchos ◄	◄ icmpOutEchos
icmpInEchoReps ◄	◄ icmpOutEchoReps
icmpInTimestamps ◄	◄ icmpOutTimestamps
icmpInTimestampReps ◄	◄ icmpOutTimeStampReps
icmpInAddrMasks ◄	◄ icmpOutAddrMasks
icmpAddrMaskReps ◄	◄ icmpOutAddrMasksReps
icmpErrors ◄	► icmpOutErrors
icmpInMsgs	icmpOutMsgs

Interface layer

FIGURE 6.9   Case diagram for MIB-II `icmp` group

damaged, or if the corresponding acknowledgment is lost or damaged, the sending TCP entity receives no acknowledgment and eventually times out and retransmits the segment. The amount of time that a sending TCP entity waits before retransmitting is governed by an algorithm, which is specified in `tcpRtoAlgorithm` as one of the following:

- `other`: It is none of the following.
- `constant`: The retransmission timeout value is constant.
- `rsre`: This algorithm dynamically calculates a timeout value based on traffic conditions. The `rsre` algorithm is based on using a smoothed round-trip time estimate and defining the retransmission timeout as a multiple of this estimate. This algorithm is specified in the military standard version of TCP, MIL-STD-1778.
- `vanj`: This is another dynamic algorithm, developed by Van Jacobson (Jacobson 1988). This algorithm is better suited than the MIL-STD-1778 algorithm in cases in which the round-trip time exhibits a relatively high variance.

Figure 6.11 shows a Case diagram for the `tcp` group.

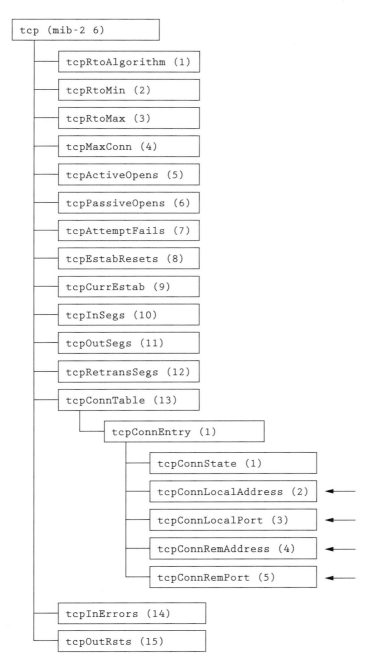

FIGURE 6.10   MIB-II tcp group

TABLE 6.7 tcp Group Objects

Object	Syntax	Access	Description
tcpRtoAlgorithm	INTEGER	RO	Retransmission time (other (1); constant (2); MIL-STD-1778 (3); Jacobson's algorithm (4))
tcpRtoMin	INTEGER	RO	Minimum value for the retransmission timer
tcpRtoMax	INTEGER	RO	Maximum value for the retransmission timer
tcpMaxConn	INTEGER	RO	Limit on total number of TCP connections the entity can support
tcpActiveOpens	Counter	RO	Number of active opens this entity has supported
tcpPassiveOpens	Counter	RO	Number of passive opens this entity has supported
tcpAttemptFails	Counter	RO	Number of failed connection attempts that have occurred at this entity
tcpEstabResets	Counter	RO	Number of resets that have occurred at this entity
tcpCurrEstab	Gauge	RO	Number of TCP connections for which the current state is either ESTABLISHED or CLOSE-WAIT
tcpInSegs	Counter	RO	Total number of segments received, including those received in error
tcpOutSegs	Counter	RO	Total number of segments sent, excluding those containing only retransmitted octets
tcpRetranSegs	Counter	RO	Total number of retransmitted segments
tcpConnTable	SEQUENCE OF TcpConnEntry	NA	Contains TCP connection-specific information
tcpConnEntry	SEQUENCE	NA	Information about a particular current TCP connection
tcpConnState	INTEGER	RW	closed (1); listen (2); synSent (3); synReceived (4); established (5); finWait1 (6); finWait2 (7); closeWait (8); lastAck (9); closing (10); timeWait (11); deleteTCB (12)
tcpConnLocalAddress	IpAddress	RO	Local IP address for this connection
tcpConnLocalPort	INTEGER	RO	Local port number for this connection
tcpConnRemoteAddress	IpAddress	RO	Remote IP address for this connection
tcpConnRemotePort	INTEGER	RO	Remote port number for this connection
tcpInErrors	Counter	RO	Total number of segments received in error
tcpOutRsts	Counter	RO	Number of TCP segments sent containing the RST flag

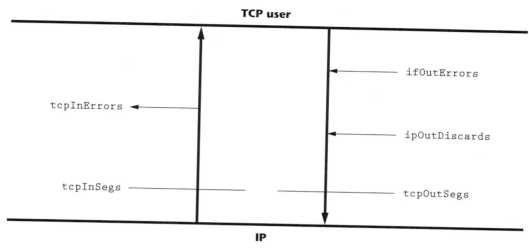

FIGURE 6.11   Case diagram for MIB-II `tcp` group

6.1.8   `udp` **Group**

The `udp` group contains information relevant to the implementation and operation of UDP at a node (Figure 6.12, Table 6.8). In addition to information about datagrams sent and received, the `udp` group includes the `udpTable`. This table contains information about this entity's UDP end-points on which a local application is currently accepting datagrams. For each such UDP user, the table contains the IP address and UDP port for the user.

Figure 6.13 shows a Case diagram for the `udp` group.

6.1.9   `egp` **Group**

The `egp` group contains information relevant to the implementation and operation of the External Gateway Protocol (EGP) at a node (Figure 6.14, Table 6.9). In addition to information about EGP messages sent and received, the `egp` group includes the `egp-NeighTable`. This table contains information about each of the neighbor gateways known to this entity. The table is indexed by `egpNeighAddr`, which is the IP address of a neighbor gateway.

6.1.10 **Transmission Group**

This group is intended to contain objects that provide details about the underlying transmission medium for each interface on a system. In fact, this is not a group at all, but simply a node in the MIB-II hierarchy under which various interface-specific groups are located.

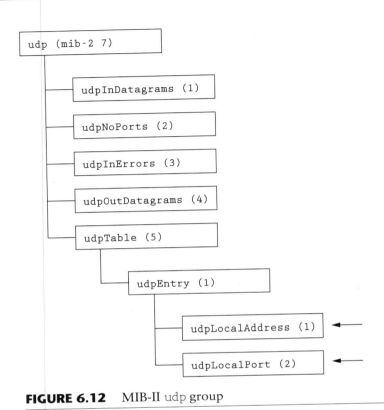

FIGURE 6.12   MIB-II udp group

Whereas the `interfaces` group contains generic information that applies to all interfaces, these interface-specific MIBs contain information that relates to a specific type of subnetwork. An example is the Ethernet MIB, which is discussed in the following section.

6.2   *Ethernet Interface MIB*

The Ethernet Interface MIB, referred to as the EtherLike MIB (RFC 1643), is one of a number of MIBs defined under the transmission node of the MIB-II hierarchy. It is the first of these transmission groups to achieve the status of an Internet standard. The EtherLike MIB defines objects that represent attributes of an interface to an ethernet-like communication medium. Specifically, the following schemes are covered:

- `ethernet-csmacd`: This is the Ethernet standard for operation over a 10-Mbps baseband coaxial cable bus.

TABLE 6.8   udp Group Objects

Object	Syntax	Access	Description
udpInDatagrams	Counter	RO	Total number of UDP datagrams delivered to UDP users
udpNoPorts	Counter	RO	Total number of received UDP datagrams for which there was no application at the destination port
udpInErrors	Counter	RO	Number of received UDP datagrams that could not be delivered for reasons other than the lack of an application at the destination port
udpOutDatagrams	Counter	RO	Total number of UDP datagrams sent from this entity
udpTable	SEQUENCE OF UdpEntry	NA	Contains UDP listener information
udpEntry	SEQUENCE	NA	Information about a particular current UDP listener
udpLocalAddress	IpAddress	RO	Local IP address for this UDP listener
udpLocalPort	INTEGER	RO	Local port number for this UDP listener

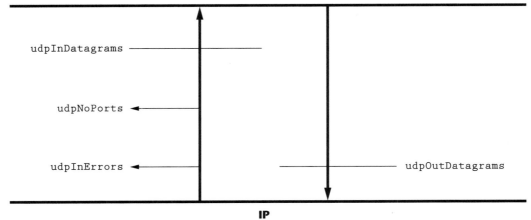

FIGURE 6.13   Case diagram for MIB-II udp group

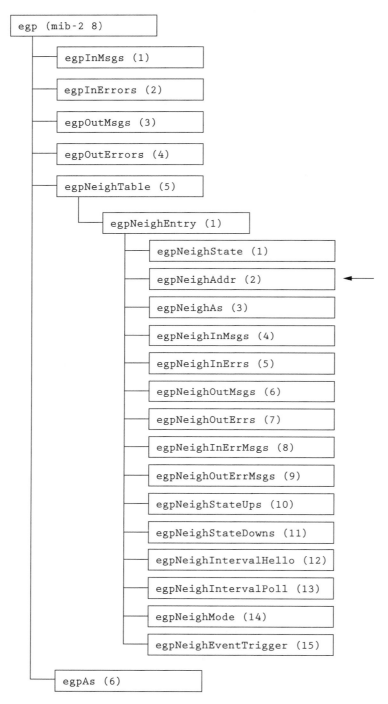

FIGURE 6.14 MIB-II egp group

TABLE 6.9 egp Group Objects

Object	Syntax	Access	Description
egpInMsgs	Counter	RO	Number of EGP messages received without error
egpInErrors	Counter	RO	Number of EGP messages received with an error
egpOutMsgs	Counter	RO	Total number of locally generated EGP messages
egpOutErrors	Counter	RO	Number of locally generated EGP messages not sent due to resource limitations within an EGP entity
egpNeighTable	SEQUENCE OF EgpNeighEntry	NA	The EGP neighbor table
egpNeighEntry	SEQUENCE	NA	Information about this entity's relationship with a particular EGP neighbor
egpNeighState	INTEGER	RO	Idle (1) : acquisition (2) ; down (3) ; up (4) ; cease (5)
egpNeighAddr	IpAddress	RO	IP address of this entry's EGP neighbor
egpNeighAs	INTEGER	RO	Autonomous system of this EGP peer
egpNeighInMsgs	Counter	RO	Number of EGP messages received without error from this EGP peer
egpNeighInErrs	Counter	RO	Number of EGP messages received from this EGP peer with an error
egpNeighOutMsgs	Counter	RO	Number of locally generated EGP messages to this EGP peer
egpNeighOutErrs	Counter	RO	Number of locally generated EGP messages not sent to this EGP peer due to resource limitations within an EGP entity
egpNeighInErrMsgs	Counter	RO	Number of EGP-defined error messages received from this EGP peer
egpNeighOutErrMsgs	Counter	RO	Number of EGP-defined error messages sent to this EGP peer
egpNeighStateUps	Counter	RO	Number of state transitions to the UP state with this EGP peer
egpNeighStateDowns	Counter	RO	Number of state transitions from the UP state to any other state with this EGP peer
egpNeighIntervalHello	INTEGER	RO	Interval between EGP Hello command retransmissions
egpNeighIntervalPoll	INTEGER	RO	Interval between EGP poll command retransmissions
egpNeighMode	INTEGER	RO	Polling mode for this EGP entity (active (1) ; passive (2))
egpNeighEventTrigger	INTEGER	RO	Used to control operator-initiated start and stop events (start (1); stop (2))
egpAs	INTEGER	RO	Autonomous system number of this EGP entity

- `iso88023-csmacd`: This covers a number of standards developed by the IEEE 802.3 committee and subsequently adopted as international standard ISO 8802-3. The 802.3 standards include both 10-Mbps and 100-Mbps data rates operating over twisted pair, baseband coaxial cable, broadband coaxial cable, and optical fiber, and including both bus and star topologies.
- `starLan`: This is an obsolete 1-Mbps, twisted pair star topology LAN, developed by AT&T and formerly part of the IEEE 802.3 standard.

All of these schemes employ a medium access control (MAC) protocol known as Carrier Sense Multiple Access with Collision Detection (CSMA/CD).

Figure 6.15 illustrates the object structure of the EtherLike MIB, and Table 6.10 defines each of the objects. We begin with a brief overview of the CSMA/CD algorithm and then examine the objects in the MIB.

6.2.1   CSMA/CD

CSMA/CD operates over a local area network with a shared transmission medium. The essential characteristic of the medium is that a transmission by any one system attached to the medium is received by all other systems on the medium. This characteristic can be achieved with a simple bus topology, in which all systems attach to the same run of cable. It can also be achieved with a tree topology, in which all systems are connected by point-to-point links to a central repeating element that takes any transmission on an incoming link and repeats it on all outgoing links.

With CSMA/CD, a station wishing to transmit first listens to the medium to determine if another transmission is in progress (carrier sense). If the medium is idle, the station may transmit. It may happen that two or more stations attempt to transmit at about the same time. If this happens, there will be a collision; the data from both transmissions will be garbled and not received successfully. Thus, a procedure is used that specifies what a station should do if the medium is found busy and what it should do if a collision occurs:

1. If the medium is idle, transmit.
2. If the medium is busy, continue to listen until the channel is idle, then transmit immediately.
3. If a collision is detected during transmission, immediately cease transmitting.
4. After a collision, wait a random amount of time, then attempt to transmit again (repeat from step 1).

Figure 6.16 illustrates the technique for a baseband bus. At time t_0, station A begins transmitting a packet addressed to station D. At t_1, both B and C are ready to transmit. B senses a transmission and so defers. C, however, is still unaware of A's transmission and begins its own transmission. When A's transmission reaches C, at t_2, C detects the colli-

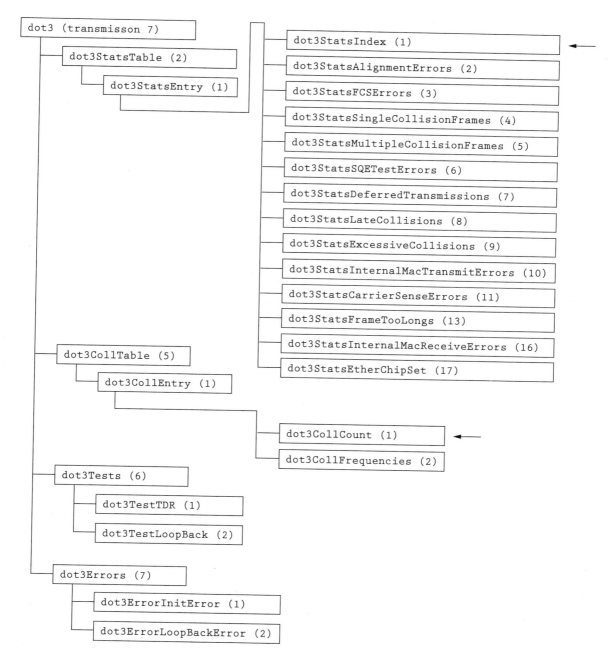

FIGURE 6.15   EtherLike MIB

TABLE 6.10 EtherLike-MIB Group Objects

Object	Syntax	Access	Description
dot3StatsTable	SEQUENCE OF Dot3StatsEntry	NA	IEEE 802.3 statistics table
dot3StatsEntry	SEQUENCE	NA	Statistics for a network interface to an Ethernet-like medium
dot3StatsIndex	INTEGER	RO	Uniquely identifies an interface; same interface as identified by the same value of ifIndex in the interfaces group
dot3StatsAlignmentErrors	Counter	RO	Received frames that are not an integral number of octets
dot3StatsFCSErrors	Counter	RO	Received frames that do not pass the FCS check
dot3StatsSingleCollisionFrames	Counter	RO	Successfully transmitted frames that experience exactly one collision
dot3StatsMultipleCollisionFrames	Counter	RO	Successfully transmitted frames that experience more than one collision
dot3StatsSQETestErrors	Counter	RO	Number of times that the SQE test error message is generated
dot3StatsDeferredTransmissions	Counter	RO	Number of frames for which the first transmission attempt is delayed because medium is busy
dot3StatsLateCollisions	Counter	RO	Number of times a collision is detected later than 512-bit times into the transmission
dot3StatsExcessiveCollisions	Counter	RO	Frames for which transmission fails due to excessive collisions
dot3StatsInternalMacTransmitErrors	Counter	RO	Frames for which transmission fails due to internal MAC transmit error
dot3StatsCarrierSenseErrors	Counter	RO	Number of times that the carrier sense condition was lost or never asserted when attempting to transmit a frame

Name	Type	Access	Description
dot3StatsFrameTooLongs	Counter	RO	Received frames that exceed maximum permitted frame size
dot3StatsInternalMacReceiveErrors	Counter	RO	Frames for which reception fails due to internal MAC transmit error
dot3StatsEtherChipSet	OBJECT IDENTIFIER	RO	Identifies the chipset used to realize this interface
dot3CollTable	SEQUENCE OF Dot3CollEntry	NA	Collection of collision histograms for a set of interfaces
dot3CollEntry	SEQUENCE	NA	One cell (column) in the histogram for a particular interface
dot3CollCount	INTEGER (1..16)	NA	One histogram point for one interface
dot3CollFrequencies	Counter	RO	Number of transmitted frames on a particular interface that experience exactly the number of collisions in the associated dot3CollCount object
dot3Tests	OBJECT IDENTIFIER	RO	A collection of tests that may be invoked from SNMPv2 version of the interfaces group
dot3TestTdr	OBJECT IDENTIFIER	RO	Time domain reflectometry test
dot3TestLoopBack	OBJECT IDENTIFIER	RO	Loopback test
dot3Errors	OBJECT IDENTIFIER	RO	A collection of errors that may occur during a test
dot3ErrorInitError	OBJECT IDENTIFIER	RO	MAC chip for test could not be initialized
dot3ErrorLoopbackError	OBJECT IDENTIFIER	RO	Expected data not received or not received correctly in loop-back test

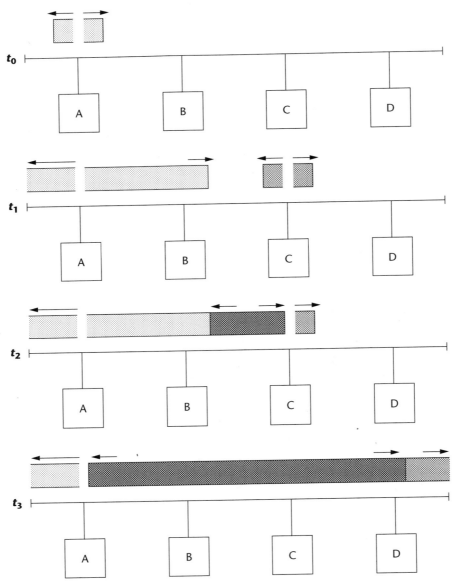

FIGURE 6.16   CSMA/CD operation

sion and ceases transmission. The effect of the collision propagates back to A, where it is detected some time later, t_3, at which time A ceases transmission.

If a collision occurs and the two stations involved were to pause an equal amount of time and then try again, another collision would take place. To avoid this, each station backs off a random amount of time taken from a uniform probability distribution. Furthermore, it should be observed that collisions generate additional LAN traffic. As the medium becomes busier, it is important not to clog the network with retransmissions, which lead to more collisions, which lead to more retransmissions, and so on. Accordingly, when a station experiences repeated collisions, it backs off for longer periods of time to compensate for the extra load on the network.[1]

6.2.2   Ethernet-Like Statistics Table

dot3StatsTable records statistics on the traffic as observed at the interface between the agent and the transmission medium. A table rather than a single set of counters is needed because an agent device (workstation, bridge, etc.) may have more than one physical interface to the medium. Thus, there is one entry in the table for each interface. The table is indexed by dot3StatsIndex; the interface identified by a particular value of this index is the same interface as identified by the same value of ifIndex (see Figure 6.2).

Most of the objects in the table count various outcomes to frame transmission; Figure 6.17 shows their relationship in a Case diagram. Note that two of the objects in the outbound path of the Case diagram are attached to the main path by arrows in both directions. This is to make the counts come out right. The object instance dot3Stats-SingleCollisionFrames is a count of the number of successfully transmitted frames that experience exactly one collision before transmission. This counter is incremented by one for such a frame, even though two attempts are made to transmit the frame. For the same frame, the ifOutUcastPkts or ifOutNUcastPkts counter in the interfaces group for the corresponding interface is also incremented. Similarly, dot3Stats-MultipleCollisionFrames is incremented just once for each successfully transmitted frame, no matter how many times the frame is unsuccessfully transmitted due to a collision, and the ifOutUcastPkts or ifOutNUcastPkts counter for the corresponding interface is also incremented.

6.2.3   Ethernet-Like Collision Statistics Table

The dot3CollTable records a histogram of collision activity as observed at the interface between the agent and the transmission medium. For a single interface, the table consists of up to 16 rows, indexed by dot3CollCount. Figure 6.18 is an example of the resulting histogram. The histogram shows the counted number of transmitted frames

---

[1]For a more detailed description of CSMA/CD, see Stallings (1996a).

FIGURE 6.17   Case diagram for EtherLike MIB

that have experienced a given number of collisions. Thus, since counting began, 426 frames have experienced exactly one collision, 318 frames have experienced exactly two collisions, and so on.

A separate histogram is required for each interface. To accomplish this, the table is indexed not only by dot3CollCount but also by ifIndex from the interfaces group. The use of an object from outside a table as an index into the table is actually a feature of version 2 of the SMI and is described in Part IV of this book.

6.2.4   Test and Error Information

The remainder of the dot3 MIB consists of hierarchical structures of object identifiers used in conducting interface tests and reporting interface errors. These object identifiers are tied into version 2 of the interfaces group, defined in RFC 1573 using SMIv2. The object instances dot3TestTDR and dot3TestLoopBack each have a value of an object identifier that represents a testing action at the agent. When a manager accesses dot3-TestTDR or dot3TestLoopBack, the corresponding test is performed.

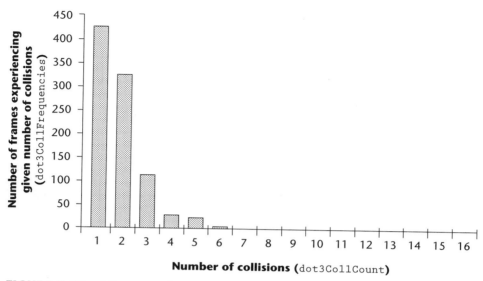

FIGURE 6.18   Histogram from `dot3CollTable`

Similarly, `dot3ErrorInitError` and `dot3LoopbackError` are accessed through the `interfaces` group. The value of each of these objects specifies an object that will contain an error result.

6.3   Summary

The SNMP framework includes the specification of a set of objects that are standardized for use in all implementations. This set is referred to as MIB-II. It contains objects in ten groups, most of which deal with a single protocol entity each. Other MIBs have been designed for specific management areas. In particular, a number of transmission medium interface MIBs have been defined, including the Ethernet-like MIB. These MIBs provide greater detail about an agent interface to a network than is available from the `inter-faces` group.

APPENDIX 6A   *CASE DIAGRAMS*

In 1988, the MIB working group, chartered by the Internet Engineering Task Force, began work on MIB-I for SNMP. It found that it was often difficult to develop clear definitions of the objects needed in the MIB and to make sure that all conditions were represented. Jeffrey Case suggested that the group diagram the flow of packets within individual layers, and he proposed a diagramming technique that was quickly dubbed *Case diagrams* (Case and Partridge 1989). Although these diagrams have been used extensively in the development of MIB-I, MIB-II, and other MIBs, it is only with the SNMPv2 MIB that Case diagrams first appear as part of the official documentation of a standardized MIB.

For many MIB groups, the intent is to record the traffic pattern at a particular protocol layer. A key requirement, obviously, is to make sure that every PDU received at a layer or issued from a layer is accounted for, including valid PDUs and PDUs with various types of errors. However, it is difficult to determine if all cases are accounted for—and that there are no unnecessary duplications—simply by reading a list of object definitions. It is far easier to determine the correctness and completeness of a group of objects if the flow of PDUs can be depicted in a diagram. The purpose of the Case diagram is to illustrate such flows.

The Case diagram also ensures that all implementations record the same information at the same place in the processing sequence. If the information is recorded in a different sequence, or at different places within the processing of a layer, then the semantics of the corresponding counters may actually differ and the results will not be comparable.

Figure 6.19 provides a generic example that illustrates the use of Case diagrams. There is a main path in each direction between the layer below and the layer above. A horizontal line cutting across a main path corresponds to a counter that counts all passing protocol data units (PDUs). An arrow leaving the main path indicates a counter for an error condition or flow that results in a PDU's not continuing on the main path. An arrow into the main path indicates a counter for a point where additional PDUs are injected into the main path. The following relationships hold:

```
InReceives = InErrors + ReasmReqds + ForwPDUs – ReasmOKs
             + InDelivers,
OutSends   = OutRequests + ForwPDUs – FragOKs + FragCreates
```

Relative position on the diagram is significant. For example, on the inbound side, the diagram indicates that all incoming PDUs are counted (InReceives), then those with errors are counted and discarded (InErrors). The line going from the main inbound path to the main outbound path represents PDUs that are forwarded to the outbound path for retransmission. Thus, these PDUs are subtracted from the flow on the inbound path and added to the flow on the outbound path.

The diagram enables a rather concise depiction of the relationships among various counters. For example, the diagram indicates that PDUs requiring reassembly are

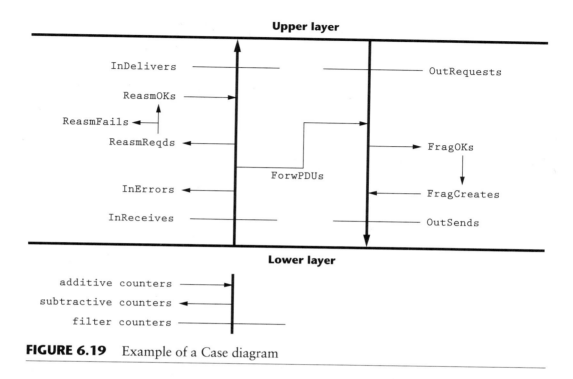

FIGURE 6.19 Example of a Case diagram

removed from the main path. Any resulting reassembled PDUs are returned to the main path, and failed attempts at reassembly are counted. Similarly, on the outbound path, any PDU to be fragmented is removed from the main path, and the resulting fragments are all inserted back into the main path.

APPENDIX 6B *IP ADDRESSING*

To understand the semantics of several of the objects in the `ip` group, it is necessary to understand the conventions for addressing in IP.

6B.1 IP Address Format

IP makes use of 32-bit addresses. In most cases, the address includes a network identifier and a local address. Typically, the network identifier is the unique identifier of a network in the Internet, and the local address is an identifier of a host on a network, with the local address being unique for a particular network. The IP address is coded to allow a variable

FIGURE 6.20   IP address formats

allocation of bits to specify network and host, as depicted in Figure 6.20. This encoding provides flexibility in assigning addresses to hosts and allows a mix of network sizes in an internet. In particular, the three address classes are best suited to the following conditions:

- Class A: few networks, each with many hosts
- Class B: medium number of networks, each with a medium number of hosts
- Class C: many networks, each with a few hosts

In a particular environment, it may be best to use addresses that are all from the same class. For example, a corporate internetwork that consists of a large number of departmental local area networks may need to use Class C addresses exclusively. However, because of the format of the addresses, it is possible to mix all three classes of addresses on the same internet. A mixture of classes is appropriate for an internet that consists of a few large networks, many small networks, and some medium-sized networks.

The extended address format is used for multicasting. In this format, 29 bits are employed in a flat addressing scheme.

6B.2   Subnetting

The typical IP address designates a particular network and a host on that network. This simple scheme has been extended by the concept of "subnets" to allow for more flexible addressing in complex configurations.[2] The objective is to allow complex configurations of local area networks within an organization while insulating the overall internet from the need to be aware of a large number of networks.

With ordinary IP addressing, IP addresses have the following structure:

```
IP-address :: = { <Network-number>, <Local-address> }
```

When an IP datagram is routed, the source host and each intermediate router except the last router in the path can route solely on the basis of network number. The final router in the path must map the local address into the physical address of a host.

With subnetting, IP addresses have the following structure:

```
IP-address :: = { <Network-number>, <Subnet-number>, <Host-number> }
```

The interconnected LANs at a site are given the same network number but different subnet numbers. The distinction between subnets is not visible outside the complex of LANs. Instead, routing outside the complex is based solely on network number. Once an IP datagram reaches a router that is on the "boundary" of the complex, then routing to the final destination depends on the subnet number.

In this structure, the bits allocated to a local address are divided between bits that represent the subnet number and bits that represent the host number. The bit positions containing the subnet number are indicated by a 32-bit subnet mask, which has 1s in the subnet-number bit positions.

6B.3   Broadcast Addresses

IP addressing includes a capability to transmit datagrams with a broadcast address. Using the notation defined in the previous subsection for IP addresses and the notation "−1" to mean a field with all 1 bits, we can define the following formats for broadcasting using Class A, B, and C address formats:

(a) { −1, −1 }: An IP address of all 1s is used for limited broadcast. A datagram with this address is to be delivered to all hosts on the local network or subnetwork but is not transmitted beyond that network.

(b) { <Network-number>, −1 }: This format represents a directed broadcast to a specified network. The datagram is to be delivered to all hosts on the specified network.

---

[2]This is one of a number of examples where the terminology used in TCP/IP-related documents differs from that in OSI-related documents. What are called "networks" in the IP addressing scheme are referred to as "subnetworks" in the OSI documents. The term "subnet" should not be confused with the OSI term "subnetwork."

(c) { <Network-number>, <Subnet-number>, −1 }: This format represents a directed broadcast to a specified subnet on a specified network. The datagram is to be delivered to all hosts on the specified subnet.

(d) { <Network-number>, −1, −1 }: This format represents a directed broadcast to all subnets of a specified network. The datagram is to be delivered to all hosts on the specified subnets.

Simple Network Management Protocol

The Simple Network Management Protocol (SNMP) specification is contained in RFC 1157, dated May 1990. This protocol is obviously at the heart of the SNMP management approach. We begin with an examination of this protocol and then look at the SNMP group of MIB-II. Finally, we address some practical issues.

7.1 Basic Concepts

In this section, we examine some of the basic concepts that relate to the operation of the protocol. We begin with a brief summary of the operations that SNMP supports. Then, the community feature is examined. The remainder of the section deals with the somewhat complicated issue of how to identify objects and instances of objects and with the ordering imposed by the identification convention.

7.1.1 Operations Supported by SNMP

The only operations that are supported in SNMP are the alteration and inspection of variables. Specifically, three general-purpose operations may be performed on scalar objects:

- `Get`: A management station retrieves a scalar object value from a managed station.
- `Set`: A management station updates a scalar object value in a managed station.
- `Trap`: A managed station sends an unsolicited scalar object value to a management station.

It is not possible to change the structure of a MIB by adding or deleting object instances (for example, adding or deleting a row of a table). Nor is it possible to issue commands for an action to be performed. Further, access is provided only to `leaf` objects in the object identifier tree. That is, it is not possible to access an entire table or a row of a table with one atomic action. These restrictions greatly simplify the implementation of SNMP. On the other hand, they limit the capability of the network management system.

7.1.2   Communities and Community Names

Network management can be viewed as a distributed application. Like other distributed applications, network management involves the interaction of a number of application entities supported by an application protocol. In the case of SNMP network management, the application entities are the management station applications and the managed station (agent) applications that use SNMP, which is the supporting protocol.

SNMP network management has several characteristics not typical of all distributed applications. The application involves a one-to-many relationship between a management station and a set of managed stations: The management station is able to get and set objects in the managed stations and is able to receive traps from the managed stations. Thus, from an operational or control point of view, the management station "manages" a number of managed stations. There may be a number of management stations, each of which manages all or a subset of the managed stations in the configuration. These subsets may overlap.

Interestingly, we also need to be able to view SNMP network management as a one-to-many relationship between a managed station and a set of management stations. Each managed station controls its own local MIB and must be able to control the use of that MIB by a number of management stations. There are three aspects to this control:

- *Authentication service:* The managed station may wish to limit access to the MIB to authorized managed stations.

- *Access policy:* The managed station may wish to give different access privileges to different management stations.

- *Proxy service:* A managed station may act as a proxy to other managed stations. This may involve implementing the authentication service and/or access policy for the other managed systems on the proxy system.

All of these aspects relate to security concerns. In an environment in which responsibility for network components is split, such as among a number of administrative entities, managed systems need to protect themselves and their MIBs from unwanted and unauthorized access. SNMP, as defined in RFC 1157, provides only a primitive and limited capability for such security, namely the concept of a community.

An SNMP **community** is a relationship between an SNMP agent and a set of SNMP managers that defines authentication, access control, and proxy characteristics. The community concept is a local one, defined at the managed system. The managed system establishes one community for each desired combination of authentication, access control, and proxy characteristics. Each community is given a unique (within this agent) community name, and the management stations within that community are provided with and must employ the community name in all get and set operations. The agent may establish a number of communities, with overlapping management station membership.

Since communities are defined locally at the agent, the same name may be used by different agents. This identity of names is irrelevant and does not indicate any similarity between the defined communities. Thus, a management station must keep track of the community name or names associated with each of the agents that it wishes to access.

7.1.2.1 Authentication Service

An authentication service is concerned with ensuring that a communication is authentic. In the case of an SNMP message, the function of an authentication service would be to assure the recipient that the message is from the source from which it claims to be. As defined in RFC 1157, SNMP provides for only a trivial scheme for authentication. Every message (get or put request) from a management station to an agent includes a community name. This name functions as a password, and the message is assumed to be authentic if the sender knows the password.

With this limited form of authentication, many network managers will be reluctant to allow anything other than network monitoring; that is, `Get` and `Trap` operations. Network control, via a `Set` operation, is clearly a more sensitive area. The community name could be used to trigger an authentication procedure, with the name functioning simply as an initial password-screening device. The authentication procedure could involve the use of encryption/decryption for more secure authentication functions. This is beyond the scope of RFC 1157.

7.1.2.2 Access Policy

By defining a community, an agent limits access to its MIB to a selected set of management stations. By the use of more than one community, the agent can provide different categories of MIB access to different management stations. There are two aspects to this access control:

- *SNMP MIB view:* a subset of the objects within a MIB. Different MIB views may be defined for each community. The set of objects in a view need not belong to a single subtree of the MIB.

- *SNMP access mode:* an element of the set {READ-ONLY, READ-WRITE}. An access mode is defined for each community.

The combination of a MIB view and an access mode is referred to as an *SNMP community profile*. Thus, a community profile consists of a defined subset of the MIB at the agent, plus an access mode for those objects. The SNMP access mode is applied uniformly to all objects in the MIB view. Thus, if the access mode READ-ONLY is selected, it applies to all objects in the view and limits management stations' access to this view to read-only operations.

Within a community profile, two separate access restrictions must be reconciled. Recall that the definition of each MIB object includes an ACCESS clause (Figure 5.3).

Table 7.1 shows the rules for reconciling an object's ACCESS clause with the SNMP access mode imposed for a particular view. Most of the rules are straightforward. Note, however, that even if an object is declared as write-only, it may be possible with SNMP to read that object; this is an implementation-specific matter.

A community profile is associated with each community defined by an agent; the combination of an SNMP community and an SNMP community profile is referred to as an *SNMP access policy*. Figure 7.1 illustrates the various concepts just introduced.

7.1.2.3   Proxy Service

The community concept is also useful in supporting the proxy service. Recall from Chapter 4 that a proxy is an SNMP agent that acts on behalf of other devices. Typically, the other devices are foreign, in that they do not support TCP/IP and SNMP. In some cases, the proxied system may support SNMP but the proxy is used to minimize the interaction between the proxied device and network management systems.

TABLE 7.1   Relationship Between MIB ACCESS Category and SNMP Access Mode

MIB ACCESS Category	SNMP Access Mode	
	READ-ONLY	READ-WRITE
read-only	Available for get and trap operations	
read-write	Available for get and trap operations	Available for get, set, and trap operations
write-only	Available for get and trap operations, but the value is implementation-specific	Available for get, set, and trap operations, but the value is implementation-specific for get and trap operations
not accessible	Unavailable	

FIGURE 7.1   Administrative concepts

For each device that the proxy system represents, it maintains an SNMP access policy. Thus, the proxy knows which MIB objects can be used to manage the proxied system (the MIB view) and their access mode.

7.1.3 Instance Identification

We have seen that every object in a MIB has a unique object identifier, which is defined by the position of the object in the tree-structured MIB. However, when an access is made to a MIB, via SNMP or some other means, it is a specific instance of an object that is wanted, not an object type.

7.1.3.1 Columnar Objects

For objects that appear in tables, which we refer to as *columnar objects*, the object identifier alone does not suffice to identify the instance: There is one instance of each object for every row in the table. Therefore, some convention is needed by which a specific instance of an object within a table may be identified. In the SMI document (RFC 1155), it states that

> The means whereby object instances are referenced is not defined in the MIB. Reference to object instances is achieved by a protocol-specific mechanism. It is the responsibility of each management protocol adhering to the SMI to define this mechanism.

Thus we must turn to the SNMP document for the referencing convention. SNMP actually defines two techniques for identifying a specific object instance: a serial-access technique and a random-access technique. The serial-access technique is based on a lexicographic ordering of objects in the MIB structure and is examined in Section 7.2. Here, we consider the random-access technique.

It is relatively easy to deduce the type of referencing convention that must be used. A table consists of a set of zero or more rows. Each row contains the same set of scalar object types, or columnar objects. Each columnar object has a unique object identifier that is the same in each row. For example, looking back at Figure 5.7, there are three instances of tcpConnState, but all three instances have the same object identifier: 1.3.6.1.2.1.6.13.1.1. Now, as was described in Chapter 5, the values of the INDEX objects of a table are used to distinguish one row from another. Thus, a combination of the object identifier for a columnar object and one set of values of the INDEX objects specifies a particular scalar object in a particular row of the table. The convention used in SNMP is to concatenate the scalar object identifier with the values of the INDEX objects, listed in the order in which the INDEX objects appear in the table definition.

As a simple example, consider the ifTable in the interfaces group. There is only one INDEX object, ifIndex, whose value is an integer in the range between 1 and the value of ifNumber, with each interface being assigned a unique number. Now suppose that we want to know the interface type of the second interface of a system. The object identifier of `ifType` is 1.3.6.1.2.1.2.2.1.3. The value of `ifIndex` of interest is 2. So the instance identifier for the instance of `ifType` corresponding to the row containing a value of `ifIndex` of 2 is 1.3.6.1.2.1.2.2.1.3.2. We have simply added the value of `ifIndex` as the final subidentifier in the instance identifier.

For a more complicated case, consider the `tcpConnTable` in the `tcp` group. As indicated in Figures 5.6 and 6.10, this table has four INDEX objects. Thus, an instance identifier for any of the five columnar objects in the table consists of the object identifier of that object concatenated with the values for a particular row of the four INDEX objects. Table 7.2 shows the instance identifiers for all of the columnar objects from Figure 5.7. Note that in forming the instance identifier of an object, it makes no difference whether or not that object is an INDEX object. All instance identifiers for `tcpConnTable` are of the form

$$x.i.(\texttt{tcpConnLocalAddress}).(\texttt{tcpConnLocalPort}).$$
$$(\texttt{tcpConnRemAddress}).(\texttt{tcpConnRemPort})$$

where

x = 1.3.6.1.2.1.6.13.1 = object identifier of `tcpConnEntry`,

i = the last subidentifier in the object identifier for a columnar object (that is, its position within the table),

(name) = value of object *name*. For example, (`tcpConnLocalPort`) refers to the value associated with the object `tcpConnLocalPort`.

More generally, we can describe the convention as follows. Given an object whose object identifier is y, in a table with INDEX objects $i1, i2, \ldots, iN$, then the instance identifier for an instance of object y in a particular row is

$$y.(i1).(i2). \ldots .(iN)$$

Table 7.3 shows the form of the instance identifier for all of the tables in MIB-II.

One detail that must be worked out is exactly how the value of an object instance is converted into one or more subidentifiers. Although this issue is not specifically addressed in the SNMP document (RFC 1157), RFC 1212, which defines the OBJECT-TYPE macro used for MIB-II, includes the following rules for each INDEX object instance:

- *Integer-valued:* A single subidentifier takes the integer value (valid only for nonnegative integers).
- *String-valued, fixed-length:* Each octet of the string is encoded as a separate subidentifier, for a total of n subidentifiers for a string of length n octets.
- *String-valued, variable length:* For a string of length n octets, the first subidentifier is n; this is followed by each octet of the string encoded as a separate subidentifier, for a total of $n+1$ subidentifiers.

TABLE 7.2 Instance Identifiers for Objects in Figure 5.7

tcpConnState (1.3.6.1.2.1.6.13.1.1)	tcpConnLocalAddress (1.3.6.1.2.1.6.13.1.2)	tcpConnLocalPort (1.3.6.1.2.1.6.13.1.3)	tcpConnRemAddress (1.3.6.1.2.1.6.13.1.4)	tcpConnRemPort (1.3.6.1.2.1.6.13.1.5)
x.1.10.0.0.99.12.9.1.2.3.15	x.2.10.0.0.99.12.9.1.2.3.15	x.3.10.0.0.99.12.9.1.2.3.15	x.4.10.0.0.99.12.9.1.2.3.15	x.5.10.0.0.99.12.9.1.2.3.15
x.1.0.0.0.0.99.0.0	x.2.0.0.0.0.99.0.0	x.3.0.0.0.0.99.0.0	x.4.0.0.0.0.99.0.0	x.5.0.0.0.0.99.0.0
x.1.10.0.0.99.14.89.1.1.42.84	x.2.10.0.0.99.14.89.1.1.42.84	x.3.10.0.0.99.14.89.1.1.42.84	x.4.10.0.0.99.14.89.1.1.42.84	x.5.10.0.0.99.14.89.1.1.42.84

x = 1.3.6.1.2.1.6.13.1 = object identifier of tcpConnEntry, which is the tcpConnTable row identifier.

TABLE 7.3 Instance Identifiers for MIB-II Table Entries

Group	Table	Row Identifier	Object Identifier
interfaces	ifTable	1.3.6.1.2.1.2.2.1	x.i.(ifIndex)
address translation	atTable	1.3.6.1.2.1.3.1.1	x.i.(atIfIndex).(atNetAddress)
ip	ipAddrTable	1.3.6.1.2.1.4.20.1	x.i.(ipAdEntAddr)
ip	ipRouteTable	1.3.6.1.2.1.4.21.1	x.i.(ipRouteDest)
ip	ipNetToMediaTable	1.3.6.1.2.1.4.22.1	x.i.(ipNetToMediaIfIndex).(ipNetToMediaType)
tcp	tcpConnTable	1.3.6.1.2.1.6.13.1	x.i.(tcpConnLocalAddress).(tcpConnLocalPort).(tcpConnRemAddress).(tcpConnRemPort)
udp	udpTable	1.3.6.1.2.1.7.5.1	x.i.(udpLocalAddress).(udpLocalPort)
egp	egpNeighTable	1.3.6.1.2.1.8.5.1	x.i.(egpNeighAddr)

x = row identifier (sequence of integers); i = columnar object identifier (single integer); (z) = value of object z

- *Object-identifier-valued:* For an object identifier with *n* subidentifiers, the first subidentifier is *n;* this is followed by the value of each subidentifier in order, for a total of *n*+1 subidentifiers.
- `IpAddress`-*valued:* There are four subidentifiers, in the familiar a.b.c.d notation.

7.1.3.2   The Problem of Ambiguous Row References

RFC 1212, which defines the INDEX clause for the OBJECT-TYPE macro, states that the purpose of the INDEX clause is to list the object(s) whose "object value(s) will unambiguously distinguish a conceptual row." Unfortunately, when the INDEX clause is applied to tables that were originally defined in MIB-I, unambiguous reference is not always possible. For example, the INDEX object for `ipRouteTable`, in the `ip` group, is `ipRoute-Dest`. However, it is not always the case that only a single route will be stored for any given destination. In this case, two rows will have the same value for `ipRouteDest`, and the instance identification scheme just described results in two or more object instances with the same instance identifier.

One way around this problem that has been proposed is to add yet another subidentifier to the instance identifier, under the control of the agent. When two or more rows have the same value(s) of INDEX object(s), the agent designates one such row as primary and appends the subidentifier 1, designates another row as secondary and appends the subidentifier 2, and so on.

For example, suppose one were interested in the next hop of an entry in the `ipRouteTable` associated with a destination IP address of 89.1.1.42. Following the rules defined in the preceding subsection, the desired instance identifier is `ipRoute-NextHop.89.1.1.42`. However, if multiple rows have been assigned for the same destination and the manager is interested in the next hop along the primary route, then the instance identifier is `ipRouteNextHop.89.1.1.42.1`.

This proposal has been rejected because of its complexity. For example, either this technique would always have to be used for a particular table—whether or not it contained multiple rows with the same index—or the manager would somehow have to discover which references were ambiguous and required the additional subidentifier.

The strategy that has been adopted is to avoid in the future the definition of tables that cannot be unambiguously referenced and to replace (deprecate) existing tables that suffer from such an ambiguity. An example of this strategy is the `ipForwardTable`, described in Section 5.2.5.2.

7.1.3.3   Conceptual Table and Row Objects

For table and row objects (for example, `tcpConnTable` and `tcpConnEntry`), no instance identifier is defined. This is because these are not `leaf` objects and therefore are not accessible by SNMP. In the MIB definition of these objects, their ACCESS characteristic is listed as "`not-accessible`."

7.1.3.4 Scalar Objects

In the case of scalar objects, there is no ambiguity between an object type and an instance of that object; there is only one object instance for each scalar object type. However, for consistency with the convention for tabular objects—and to distinguish between an object type and an object instance—SNMP dictates that the instance identifier of a nontabular scalar object consists of its object identifier concatenated with 0. For example, Table 7.4 shows the instance identifiers for the nontabular scalar objects in the `tcp` group.

7.1.4 Lexicographical Ordering

An object identifier is a sequence of integers that reflects a hierarchical or tree structure of the objects in the MIB. Given the tree structure of a MIB, the object identifier for a particular object may be derived by tracing a path from the root to the object.

Because object identifiers are sequences of integers, they exhibit a lexicographical ordering. That ordering can be generated by traversing the tree of object identifiers in the MIB, provided that the child nodes of a parent node are always depicted in ascending numerical order (see Appendix 6A). This ordering extends to object instance identifiers, since an object instance identifier is also a sequence of integers.

An ordering of object and object instance identifiers is important because a network management station may not know the exact makeup of the MIB view that an agent presents to it. The management station therefore needs some means of searching for and

TABLE 7.4   Scalar Objects in the `tcp` Group

Object Name	Object Identifier	Instance Identifier
tcpRtoAlgorithm	1.3.6.1.2.1.6.1	1.3.6.1.2.1.6.1.0
tcpRtoMin	1.3.6.1.2.1.6.2	1.3.6.1.2.1.6.2.0
tcpRtoMax	1.3.6.1.2.1.6.3	1.3.6.1.2.1.6.3.0
tcpMaxConn	1.3.6.1.2.1.6.4	1.3.6.1.2.1.6.4.0
tcpActiveOpens	1.3.6.1.2.1.6.5	1.3.6.1.2.1.6.5.0
tcpPassiveOpens	1.3.6.1.2.1.6.6	1.3.6.1.2.1.6.6.0
tcpAttemptFails	1.3.6.1.2.1.6.7	1.3.6.1.2.1.6.7.0
tcpEstabResets	1.3.6.1.2.1.6.8	1.3.6.1.2.1.6.8.0
tcpCurrEstab	1.3.6.1.2.1.6.9	1.3.6.1.2.1.6.9.0
tcpInSegs	1.3.6.1.2.1.6.10	1.3.6.1.2.1.6.10.0
tcpOutSegs	1.3.6.1.2.1.6.11	1.3.6.1.2.1.6.11.0
tcpRetransSegs	1.3.6.1.2.1.6.12	1.3.6.1.2.1.6.12.0
tcpInErrs	1.3.6.1.2.1.6.14	1.3.6.1.2.1.6.14.0
tcpOutRsts	1.3.6.1.2.1.6.15	1.3.6.1.2.1.6.15.0

accessing objects without specifying them by name. With the use of lexicographical ordering, a management station can in effect traverse the structure of a MIB. At any point in the tree, the management station can supply an object or object instance identifier and ask for the object instance that occurs next in the ordering.

Figure 7.2 illustrates how object instance identifiers can be seen to be part of the hierarchical ordering of objects. The example shows the ipRouteTable in the MIB-II ip group, as seen through a MIB view that restricts the table to just three entries. The values in the table are as follows:

ipRouteDest	ipRouteMetric1	ipRouteNextHop
9.1.2.3	3	99.0.0.3
10.0.0.51	5	89.1.1.42
10.0.0.99	5	89.1.1.42

Note that the tree in Figure 7.2 is drawn to emphasize its logical interpretation as a two-dimensional table. The lexicographical ordering of the objects and object instances in the table can be seen by simply traversing the tree. The ordering is shown in Table 7.5.

FIGURE 7.2   An example subtree of objects and object instances

TABLE 7.5 Lexicographical Ordering of Objects and Object Instances in Figure 7.2

Object	Object Identifier	Next Object Instance in Lexicographical Order
ipRouteTable	1.3.6.1.2.1.4.21	1.3.6.1.2.1.4.21.1.1.9.1.2.3
ipRouteEntry	1.3.6.1.2.1.4.21.1	1.3.6.1.2.1.4.21.1.1.9.1.2.3
ipRouteDest	1.3.6.1.2.1.4.21.1.1	1.3.6.1.2.1.4.21.1.1.9.1.2.3
ipRouteDest.9.1.2.3	1.3.6.1.2.1.4.21.1.1.9.1.2.3	1.3.6.1.2.1.4.21.1.1.10.0.0.51
ipRouteDest.10.0.0.51	1.3.6.1.2.1.4.21.1.1.10.0.0.51	1.3.6.1.2.1.4.21.1.1.10.0.0.99
ipRouteDest.10.0.0.99	1.3.6.1.2.1.4.21.1.1.10.0.0.99	1.3.6.1.2.1.4.21.1.3.9.1.2.3
ipRouteMetric1	1.3.6.1.2.1.4.21.1.3	1.3.6.1.2.1.4.21.1.3.9.1.2.3
ipRouteMetric1.9.1.2.3	1.3.6.1.2.1.4.21.1.3.9.1.2.3	1.3.6.1.2.1.4.21.1.3.10.0.0.51
ipRouteMetric1.10.0.0.51	1.3.6.1.2.1.4.21.1.3.10.0.0.51	1.3.6.1.2.1.4.21.1.3.10.0.0.99
ipRouteMetric1.10.0.0.99	1.3.6.1.2.1.4.21.1.3.10.0.0.99	1.3.6.1.2.1.4.21.1.7.9.1.2.3
ipRouteNextHop	1.3.6.1.2.1.4.21.1.7	1.3.6.1.2.1.4.21.1.7.9.1.2.3
ipRouteNextHop.9.1.2.3	1.3.6.1.2.1.4.21.1.7.9.1.2.3	1.3.6.1.2.1.4.21.1.7.10.0.0.51
ipRouteNextHop.10.0.0.51	1.3.6.1.2.1.4.21.1.7.10.0.0.51	1.3.6.1.2.1.4.21.1.7.10.0.0.99
ipRouteNextHop.10.0.0.99	1.3.6.1.2.1.4.21.1.7.10.0.0.99	1.3.6.1.2.1.4.22.1.1.x

7.2   *Protocol Specification*

In this section, we examine the overall message format for SNMP and then describe each of the protocol data units (PDUs) that can be carried in a message.

7.2.1   SNMP Formats

With SNMP, information is exchanged between a management station and an agent in the form of an SNMP message. Each message includes a version number indicating the version of SNMP, a community name to be used for this exchange, and one of five types of protocol data units.[1] Figure 7.3 informally depicts this structure, and Table 7.6 defines

---

[1]The terminology chosen by the SNMP developers is unfortunate. It is common practice to designate the overall block of information being transferred as a *protocol data unit*. In the case of SNMP, this term is used to refer to only a portion of the information transferred.

Version	Community	SNMP PDU

(a) SNMP message

PDU type	request-id	0	0	variablebindings

(b) GetRequest PDU, GetNextRequest PDU, and SetRequest PDU

PDU type	request-id	error-status	error-index	variablebindings

(c) GetResponse PDU

PDU type	enterprise	agent-addr	generic-trap	specific-trap	time-stamp	variablebindings

(d) Trap PDU

name1	value1	name2	value2	. . .	namen	valuen

(e) variablebindings

FIGURE 7.3   SNMP formats

constituent fields. The ASN.1 definition is reproduced in Figure 7.4. Note that the GetRequest, GetNextRequest, and SetRequest PDUs have the same format as the GetResponse PDU, with the error-status and error-index fields always set to 0. This convention reduces by one the number of different PDU formats with which the SNMP entity must deal.

Note that although a PDU type field is depicted in Figure 7.3, no PDU type field is defined in the ASN.1 specification. However, each of the five different PDUs is defined as a separate ASN.1 type. Accordingly, since the basic encoding rules (BER) for ASN.1 use a (type, length, value) structure, the type of a PDU appears as an artifact of the BER encoding of the PDU.

7.2.1.1 Transmission of an SNMP Message

In principle, an SNMP entity performs the following actions to transmit one of the five PDU types to another SNMP entity:

1. The PDU is constructed, using the ASN.1 structure defined in RFC 1157.

2. This PDU is then passed to an authentication service, together with the source and destination transport addresses and a community name. The authentication service

then performs any required transformations for this exchange, such as encryption or the inclusion of an authentication code, and returns the result.

3. The protocol entity then constructs a message, consisting of a version field, the community name, and the result from step 2.

4. This new ASN.1 object is then encoded using the basic encoding rules and passed to the transport service.

In practice, authentication is not typically invoked.

TABLE 7.6   SNMP Message

Field	Description
version	SNMP version (RFC 1157 is version 1.)
community	A pairing of an SNMP agent with some arbitrary set of SNMP application entities (The name of the community acts as a password to authenticate the SNMP message.)
request-id	Used to distinguish among outstanding requests by providing each request with a unique ID
error-status	Used to indicate that an exception occurred while processing a request; values are noError (0), tooBig (1), noSuchName (2), badValue (3), readOnly (4), genErr (5)
error-index	When error-status is nonzero, may provide additional information by indicating which variable in a list caused the exception (A variable is an instance of a managed object.)
variablebindings	A list of variable names and corresponding values (In some cases, such as GetRequest PDU, the values are null.)
enterprise	Type of object generating trap; based on sysObjectID
agent-addr	Address of object generating trap
generic-trap	Generic trap type; values are coldStart (0), warmStart (1), linkDown (2), linkUp (3), authentication-Failure (4), egpNeighborLoss (5), enterprise-Specific (6)
specific-trap	Specific trap code
time-stamp	Time elapsed between the last (re)initialization of the network entity and the generation of the trap; contains the value of sysUpTime

```
RFC1157-SNMP DEFINITIONS ::=BEGIN

IMPORTS
     ObjectName, ObjectSyntax, NetworkAddress, IpAddress, TimeTicks
          FROM RFC1155-SMI;

--top-level message
```

FIGURE 7.4   SNMP formats (RFC 1157)

continued

```
Message ::= SEQUENCE {version INTEGER {version-1 (0)},          --version-1 for this RFC
                      community OCTET STRING,                   --community name
                      data ANY}    --e.g., PDUs if trivial authentication is being used
--protocol data units

PDUs ::= CHOICE {get-request        GetRequest-PDU,
                 get-next-request   GetNextRequest-PDU,
                 get-response       GetResponse-PDU,
                 set-request        SetRequest-PDU,
                 trap               Trap-PDU}

--PDUs

GetRequest-PDU     ::=  [0] IMPLICIT PDU
GetNextRequest-PDU ::=  [1] IMPLICIT PDU
GetResponsePDU     ::=  [2] IMPLICIT PDU
SetRequestPDU      ::=  [3] IMPLICIT PDU

PDU ::= SEQUENCE {request-id INTEGER,
                  error-status INTEGER {            --sometimes ignored
                                noError (0),
                                tooBig (1),
                                noSuchName (2),
                                badValue (3),
                                readOnly (4),
                                genError (5),
                  error-index INTEGER,              --sometimes ignored
                  variable-binding VarBindList}     --values are sometimes ignored

Trap-PDU ::= [4] IMPLICIT SEQUENCE {
                  enterprise OBJECT IDENTIFIER      --type of object generating trap,
                                                    --see sysObjectID in RFC1155
                  agent-addr NetworkAddress,        --address of object generating trap
                  generic-trap INTEGER {
                                coldStart (0)
                                warmStart (1),
                                linkDown (2),
                                linkUp (3),
                                authenticationFailure (4),
                                egpNeighborLoss (5),
                                enterpriseSpecific (6)},
                  specific-trap INTEGER,            --specific code, present even if
                                                    --generic-trap is not enterpriseSpecific
                  time-stamp TimeTicks,             --time elapsed between the last
                                                    --(re)initialization of the network
                                                    --entity and the generation of the trap
                  variable-bindings (VarBindList)   --"interesting" information
--variable binding

varBind ::= SEQUENCE {name ObjectName,
                      value ObjectSyntax}

VarBindList ::= SEQUENCE OF VarBind
END
```

FIGURE 7.4 *Continued*

7.2.1.2   Receipt of an SNMP Message

In principle, an SNMP entity performs the following actions upon reception of an SNMP message.

1. It does a basic syntax-check of the message and discards the message if it fails to parse.
2. It verifies the version number and discards the message if there is a mismatch.
3. The protocol entity then passes the user name, the PDU portion of the message, and the source and destination transport addresses (supplied by the transport service that delivered the message) to an authentication service.
   (a) If authentication fails, the authentication service signals the SNMP protocol entity, which generates a trap and discards the message.
   (b) If authentication succeeds, the authentication service returns a PDU in the form of an ASN.1 object that conforms to the structure defined in RFC 1157.
4. The protocol entity does a basic syntax-check of the PDU and discards the PDU if it fails to parse. Otherwise, using the named community, the appropriate SNMP access policy is selected and the PDU is processed accordingly.

In practice, the authentication service serves merely to verify that the community name authorizes the receipt of messages from the source SNMP entity.

7.2.1.3   Variable Bindings

All SNMP operations involve access to an object instance. Recall that only `leaf` objects in the object identifier tree may be accessed; that is, only scalar objects. However, it is possible in SNMP to group a number of operations of the same type (`get`, `set`, `trap`) into a single message. Thus, if a management station wants to get the values of all the scalar objects in a particular group at a particular agent, it can send a single message, requesting all values, and get a single response, listing all values. This technique can greatly reduce the communications burden of network management.

To implement multiple-object exchanges, all of the SNMP PDUs include a `variablebindings` field. This field consists of a sequence of references to object instances, together with the value of those objects. Some PDUs are concerned only with the name of the object instance (for example, `get` operations). In this case, the receiving protocol entity ignores the value entries in the `variablebindings` field. RFC 1157 recommends that in such cases the sending protocol entity use the ASN.1 value NULL for the value portion of the `variablebindings` field.

7.2.2   GetRequest PDU

The `GetRequest` PDU is issued by an SNMP entity on behalf of a network management station application. The sending entity includes the following fields in the PDU:

- *PDU type:* This indicates that this is a `GetRequest` PDU
- `request-id`: The sending entity assigns numbers such that each outstanding request to the same agent is uniquely identified. The `request-id` enables the SNMP application to correlate incoming responses with outstanding requests. It also enables an SNMP entity to cope with duplicated PDUs generated by an unreliable transport service.
- `variablebindings`: This lists the object instances whose values are requested.

The receiving SNMP entity responds to a `GetRequest` PDU with a `GetResponse` PDU containing the same `request-id` (Figure 7.5(a)). The `GetRequest` operation is atomic: Either all of the values are retrieved or none is. If the responding entity is able to provide values for all of the variables listed in the incoming `variablebindings` list, then the `GetResponse` PDU includes the `variablebindings` field, with a value supplied for each variable. If at least one of the variable values cannot be supplied, then no values are returned. The following error conditions can occur.

1. An object named in the `variablebindings` field may not match any object identifier in the relevant MIB view, or a named object may be of an aggregate type and

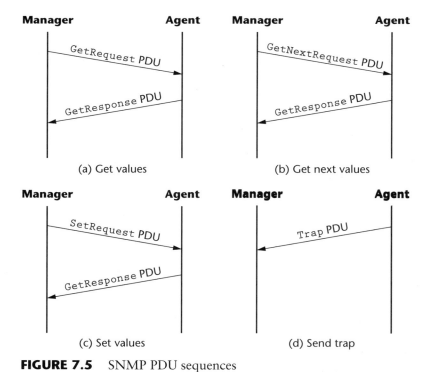

FIGURE 7.5   SNMP PDU sequences

therefore not have an associated instance value. In either case, the responding entity returns a GetResponse PDU with an error-status of noSuchName and a value in the error-index field that is the index of the problem object in the variable-bindings field. Thus, if the third variable listed in the incoming variable-bindings field is not available for a get operation, then the error-index field contains a 3.

2. The responding entity may be able to supply values for all variables in the list, but the size of the resulting GetResponse PDU may exceed a local limitation. In that case, the responding entity returns a GetResponse PDU with an error-status of tooBig.

3. The responding entity may not be able to supply a value for at least one of the objects for some other reason. In that case, the responding entity returns a GetResponse PDU with an error-status of genErr and a value in the error-index field that is the index of the problem object in the variablebindings field.

This logic is summarized in Figure 7.6.

Keep in mind that SNMP allows for only the retrieval of leaf objects in the MIB tree. It is not possible, for example, to retrieve an entire row of a table (for example, the IP routing table) simply by referencing the entry object (for example, ipRouteEntry) or to retrieve an entire table simply by referencing the table object (for example, ip-RouteTable). However, a management station can retrieve an entire row of a table at a time simply by including each object instance of the table in the variablebindings list. For example, for the table of Figure 7.2, the management station can retrieve the first row with

```
GetRequest (ipRouteDest.9.1.2.3, ipRouteMetric1.9.1.2.3,
            ipRouteNextHop.9.1.2.3)
```

The rules for responding to a GetRequest PDU place a burden on the network management station to be clever in the use of this PDU. If the network management station requires numerous values, then it is desirable to ask for a large number of values in a single PDU. On the other hand, if a response is not possible for even one of the objects—or if the response to all objects is too big for a single GetResponse PDU—then no information is returned.

One final note about the request-id field. RFC 1157 simply states that request-ids are used to distinguish among outstanding requests and that a Get-Response must include the same request-id value as the corresponding request PDU. No other use is made of this field in SNMP. For example, it is not required that the manager use monotonically increasing values of request-id, which would enable the agent to detect duplicates and replay responses. Thus, the value of this field depends on how it is implemented in SNMP and how it is used by network management applications using SNMP.

```
procedure receive-getrequest;
begin
   if object not available for get  then
      issue getresponse (noSuchName, index)
   else if  generated PDU too big  then
      issue getresponse (tooBig)
   else if  value not retrievable for some other reason  then
      issue getresponse (genErr, index)
   else      issue getresponse (variablebindings)
end;


procedure receive-getnextrequest;
begin
   if no next object not available for get  then
      issue getresponse (noSuchName, index)
   else if  generated PDU too big  then
      issue getresponse (tooBig)
   else if  value not retrievable for some other reason  then
      issue getresponse (genErr, index)
   else      issue getresponse (variablebindings)
end;


procedure receive-setrequest;
begin
   if object not available for set  then
      issue getresponse (noSuchName, index)
   else if  inconsistent object value  then
      issue getresponse (badValue, index)
   else if  generated PDU too big  then
      issue getresponse (tooBig)
   else if  value not settable for some other reason  then
      issue getresponse (genErr, index)
   else      issue getresponse (variable bindings)
end;
```

FIGURE 7.6   Receipt of SNMP PDUs

7.2.3   GetNextRequest PDU

The GetNextRequest PDU is almost identical to the GetRequest PDU. It has the same PDU exchange pattern (Figure 7.5(b)) and the same format (Figure 7.3(b)) as the Get-Request PDU. The only difference is the following: In the GetRequest PDU, each variable in the variablebindings list refers to an object instance whose value is to be returned. In the GetNextRequest PDU, for each variable, the respondent is to return the value of the object instance that is *next* in lexicographical order. [Since an agent can return only the value of a simple object instance (and not an aggregate object such as a subtree or a table), the "Next" in GetNextRequest refers to the next object *instance* in lexicographical order, not just the next object. Table 7.5 shows examples of this.] Like Get-Request, GetNextRequest is atomic: Either all requested values are returned or none is. The logic of GetNextRequest is summarized in Figure 7.6.

The apparently minor difference between GetRequest and GetNextRequest has tremendous implications. It allows a network management station to discover the structure of a MIB view dynamically. It also provides an efficient mechanism for searching a table whose entries are unknown. Table 7.7 summarizes the effects that can be achieved using GetNextRequest. We examine its principal uses in the following subsections.

7.2.3.1   Retrieving a Simple Object Value

Suppose that a network management station wished to retrieve the values of all of the simple objects in the udp group from an agent (see Figure 6.12). The management station could send a GetRequest PDU of the following form:

> GetRequest (udpInDatagrams.0, udpNoPorts.0, udpInErrors.0,
> udpOutDatagrams.0)

If the MIB view for this community at the agent supported all of these objects, then a GetResponse PDU would be returned with the values for all four objects:

> GetResponse ((udpInDatagrams.0 = 100), (udpNoPorts.0 = 1),
> (udpInErrors.0 = 2), (udpOutDatagrams.0 = 200))

where 100, 1, 2, and 200 are the correct values of the four respective object instances. However, if one of the objects was not supported, then a GetResponse PDU with an error code of noSuchName would be returned, but no values would be returned. To ensure getting all available values with the GetRequest PDU, the management station would have to issue four separate PDUs.

Now consider the use of the GetNextRequest PDU:

> GetNextRequest (udpInDatagrams, udpNoPorts, udpInErrors,
> udpOutDatagrams)

In this case, the agent will return the value of the lexicographically next object instance to each identifier in the list. Suppose now that all four objects are supported. The object identifier for udpInDatagrams is 1.3.6.1.2.1.7.1. The next instance identifier in lexicographical order is udpInDatagrams.0, or 1.3.6.1.2.1.7.1.0. Similarly, the next instance identifier after udpNoPorts is udpNoPorts.0, and so on. Thus, if all values are available, then the agent returns a GetResponse PDU of the form

> GetResponse ((udpInDatagrams.0 = 100), (udpNoPorts.0 = 1),
> (udpInErrors.0 = 2), (udpOutDatagrams.0 = 200))

TABLE 7.7 Possible Outcomes of a GetNextRequest PDU

Request	Example Form	Possible Responses	Comment
Object ID of a simple object in MIB	`Thing`	Value of `Thing.0` Value of next simple object in MIB view (e.g., `NextThing.0`) `noSuchName`	Object exists in MIB view; value is returned. Object does not exist in MIB view; value of lexicographically next object instance is returned. Object does not exist in MIB view; there is no object instance lexicographically beyond this ID.
Object instance ID of a simple object in MIB	`Thing.0`	Value of next simple object in MIB view (e.g., `NextThing.0`) `noSuchName`	Value of lexicographically next object instance is returned. There is no object instance lexicographically beyond this ID.
Object ID of a table	`someTable`	Value of first object instance in table `noSuchName`	Table exists in MIB view; value of entry in first column, first row is returned. Object does not exist in MIB view; there is no object instance lexicographically beyond this ID.
Object ID of a table entry	`someEntry`	Value of first object instance in table `noSuchName`	Table exists in MIB view; value of entry in first column, first row is returned. Object does not exist in MIB view; there is no object instance lexicographically beyond this ID.
Columnar object ID	`ColumnarThing`	Value of first instance of the columnar object (e.g., `ColumnarThing.x`) `noSuchName`	Table exists in MIB view; value of this columnar object in first row is returned. Object does not exist in MIB view; there is no object instance lexicographically beyond this ID.
Columnar object instance ID	`ColumnarThing.x`	Value of next object instance in table Value of first object instance beyond the end of the table `noSuchName`	Table exists in MIB view; value of next instance in same column or first instance of next column is returned. Table exists in MIB view; this object instance is the last in the table, and there is an object instance beyond the end of the table. There is no object instance lexicographically beyond this ID.
Object ID that does not match any object in MIB or that corresponds to a subtree		Value of next simple object in MIB view `noSuchName`	Object does not exist in MIB view; value of lexicographically next object instance is returned. Object does not exist in MIB view; there is no object instance lexicographically beyond this ID.

which is the same as before. Now, suppose that udpNoPorts is not visible in this view, and the same GetNextRequest PDU is issued. The response is

GetResponse ((udpInDatagrams.0 = 100), (udpInErrors.0 = 2),
        (udpInErrors.0 = 2), (udpOutDatagrams.0 = 200))

The identifier for udpNoPorts.0, which is 1.3.6.1.2.1.7.2.0, is not a valid identifier in this MIB view. Therefore, the agent returns the value of the next object instance in order, which in this case is 1.3.6.1.2.1.7.3.0 = udpInErrors.0.

In summary, when an agent receives a GetNextRequest PDU with the object identifiers of a set of objects, the result includes the value of the requested object instances for all those object instances that are available. For those that are not, the next object instance value in order is returned. Clearly, this is a more efficient way to retrieve a set of object values when some might be missing than the use of the GetRequest PDU.

7.2.3.2   Retrieving Unknown Objects

The rules for the use of the GetNextRequest PDU require that the agent retrieve the next object instance that occurs lexicographically after the identifier supplied. There is no requirement that the supplied identifier actually represent an actual object or object instance. For example, returning to the UDP group, since udpInDatagrams is a simple object, there is no object whose identifier is udpInDatagrams.2, or 1.3.6.1.2.1.7.1.2. However, if this identifier is supplied to an agent in a GetNextRequest, the agent simply looks for the next valid identifier; it doesn't check the validity of the supplied identifier! Thus, a value is returned for udpNoPorts.0, or 1.3.6.1.2.1.7.2.0.

Hence, a management station can use the GetNextRequest PDU to probe a MIB view and discover its structure. In our example, if the management station issues a Get-NextRequest (udp), the response will be the GetResponse (udpInDatagrams.0 = 100). The management station learns that the first supported object in this MIB view is udpInDatagrams, and it obtains the current value of that object at the same time.

7.2.3.3   Accessing Table Values

The GetNextRequest PDU can be used to search a table efficiently. Consider again the example in Figure 7.2. Recall that the table contains three rows with the following values:

ipRouteDest	ipRouteMetric1	ipRouteNextHop
9.1.2.3	3	99.0.0.3
10.0.0.51	5	89.1.1.42
10.0.0.99	5	89.1.1.42

Suppose that the management station wishes to retrieve the entire table and does not currently know any of its contents, or even the number of rows in the table. The management station can issue a `GetNextRequest` with the names of all of the columnar objects:

> `GetNextRequest (ipRouteDest, ipRouteMetric1, ipRouteNextHop)`

A review of Figure 7.2 reveals that the agent will respond with the values from the first row of the table:

`GetResponse ((ipRouteDest.9.1.2.3 = 9.1.2.3), (ipRouteMetric1.9.1.2.3`
`= 3), (ipRouteNextHop.9.1.2.3 = 99.0.0.3))`

The management station can then store those values and retrieve the second row with

> `GetNextRequest (ipRouteDest.9.1.2.3, ipRouteMetric1.9.1.2.3,`
> `ipRouteNextHop.9.1.2.3)`

The SNMP agent responds with

> `GetResponse ((ipRouteDest.10.0.0.51 = 10.0.0.51),`
> `(ipRouteMetric1.10.0.0.51 = 5), (ipRouteNextHop.10.0.0.51`
> `= 89.1.1.42))`

Then, the following exchange occurs:

> `GetNextRequest (ipRouteDest.10.0.0.51, ipRouteMetric1.10.0.0.51,`
> `ipRouteNextHop.10.0.0.51)`
> `GetResponse ((ipRouteDest.10.0.0.99 = 10.0.0.99),`
> `(ipRouteMetric1.10.0.0.99 = 5), (ipRouteNextHop.10.0.0.99`
> `= 89.1.1.42))`

The management station does not know that this is the end of the table, and so it proceeds with

> `GetNextRequest (ipRouteDest.10.0.0.99, ipRouteMetric1.10.0.0.99,`
> `ipRouteNextHop.10.0.0.99)`

However, no further rows are in the table, so the agent responds with those objects that are next in the lexicographical ordering of objects in this MIB view:

> `GetResponse ((ipRouteMetric1.9.1.2.3 = 3), (ipRouteNextHop.9.1.2.3`
> `= 99.0.0.3), (ipNetToMediaIfIndex.1.3 = 1))`

The example assumes that the next object instance is the one shown in the third entry of the response (see Figure 7.2). Since the object names in the list in the response do not match those in the request, this signals the management station that it has reached the end of the routing table.

7.2.4   SetRequest PDU

The SetRequest PDU is issued by an SNMP entity on behalf of a network management station application. It has the same PDU exchange pattern (Figure 7.5(c)) and the same format as the GetRequest PDU (Figure 7.3(b)). However, the SetRequest is used to write an object value rather than read one. Thus the variablebindings list in the Set-Request PDU includes both object instance identifiers and a value to be assigned to each object instance listed.

The receiving SNMP entity responds to a SetRequest PDU with a GetResponse PDU containing the same request-id. The SetRequest operation is atomic: Either all of the variables are updated or none is. If the responding entity is able to set values for all of the variables listed in the incoming variablebindings list, then the Get-Response PDU includes the variablebindings field, with a value supplied for each variable. If at least one of the variable values cannot be supplied, then no values are returned, and no values are updated. The same error conditions used in the case of Get-Request may be returned (noSuchName, tooBig, genErr). One other error condition may be reported: badValue. This is returned if the SetRequest contains at least one pairing of variable name and value that is inconsistent. The inconsistency could be in the type, length, or actual value of the supplied value. The logic for SetRequest is summarized in Figure 7.6.

7.2.4.1   Updating a Table

RFC 1157 does not provide any specific guidance on the use of the SetRequest command on columnar objects. In the case of an object that is not an INDEX object, the semantics of the command are obvious. Consider again the example table of Figure 7.2. Once again, assume that the following values exist:

ipRouteDest	ipRouteMetric1	ipRouteNextHop
9.1.2.3	3	99.0.0.3
10.0.0.51	5	89.1.1.42
10.0.0.99	5	89.1.1.42

If the management station issues the following:

SetRequest (ipRouteMetric1.9.1.2.3 = 9)

then the appropriate response would be

GetResponse (ipRouteMetric1.9.1.2.3 = 9)

The effect of this exchange is to update the value of ipRouteMetric1 in the first row.

Now, suppose that the management station wishes to add a new row to the table with values for ipRouteDest, ipRouteMetric1, and ipRouteNextHop of 11.3.3.12, 9, and 91.0.0.5, respectively. Then the management station would issue the following:

```
          SetRequest ((ipRouteDest.11.3.3.12 = 11.3.3.12),
(ipRouteMetric1.11.3.3.12 = 9), (ipRouteNextHop.11.3.3.12 = 91.0.0.5))
```

The columnar object ipRouteDest is the INDEX for the table. The value of ipRoute-Dest.x is always x, since the value of ipRouteDest is the index value appended to all columnar object identifiers. Thus if the *value* of 11.3.3.12 is assigned to the columnar object ipRouteDest, then the *name* of that object is ipRouteDest.11.3.3.12. This is an instance identifier currently unknown to the agent. RFC 1212 indicates three ways in which the agent could handle this request:

1. The agent could reject the operation and return a GetResponse with an error-status field of noSuchName.
2. The agent could attempt to accept the operation as requesting the creation of new object instances but find that one of the assigned values is inappropriate due to its syntax or value, and return a GetResponse with an error-status field of bad-Value.
3. The agent could accept the operation and create a new row, resulting in a table with four rows.

In the last case, the agent would return

```
          GetResponse ((ipRouteDest.11.3.3.12 = 11.3.3.12),
(ipRouteMetric1.11.3.3.12 = 9), (ipRouteNextHop.11.3.3.12 = 91.0.0.5))
```

SNMP does not dictate whether such a request should be rejected or an attempt should be made to add a new row.

Now, assume the original three-row table exists, and consider the following command:

```
          SetRequest (ipRouteDest.11.3.3.12 = 11.3.3.12)
```

There are two ways in which the agent could handle this request.

1. The agent could add a new row to the table, resulting in a table with four rows, and supply default values for the columnar objects not listed in the SetRequest.
2. The agent could reject the operation. This would be done if the agent requires that values be supplied for all objects within a row in one SetRequest.

Again, SNMP does not dictate which action will be taken; it is a policy and implementation matter for the agent.

7.2.4.2 Row Deletion

The `set` command can also be used to delete a row of a table. In the case of the `ipRoute-Table`, an object value is provided for this purpose. If the management station issues

SetRequest (ipRouteType.7.3.5.3 = invalid)

then the appropriate response would be

GetResponse (ipRouteDest.7.3.5.3 = invalid)

The effect of this exchange is to eliminate logically the row of the table indexed by an `ipRouteDest` value of 7.3.5.3. Whether the row is physically deleted from the agent's MIB or simply marked as null is implementation-specific.

Two tables provide a specific columnar object for row deletion. As we have just seen, the `ipRouteTable` includes an object `ipRouteType`, one of whose values is "invalid." Similarly, the `ipNetToMediaTable` includes the object `ipNetToMediaType`, which may take on the value "invalid." The other tables in MIB-II do not have such a handy device. Table 7.8 indicates what can be done with each table.

7.2.4.3 Performing an Action

SNMP provides no specific mechanism for issuing a command to an agent to perform an action. The only capabilities of SNMP are to read object values and to set object values within a MIB view. However, it is possible to use the set capability to issue a command. An object can be used to represent a command, so that a specific action is taken if the object is set to a specific value. For example, an agent could include a proprietary object `reBoot` with an initial value of 0; if a management station sets the object's value to 1, the agent system reboots and resets the object value to 0.

7.2.4.4 The Curious Case of `readOnly`

A close examination of Figure 7.4 reveals that one of the `error-status` values that may be returned in a `GetResponse` PDU is `readOnly(4)`. The obvious inference one would make is that this error status should be returned if a `Set` operation is attempted against a read-only object.

Unfortunately, in this case the obvious inference is wrong, and this has led to some confusion. The definition of the `SetRequest` PDU in RFC 1157 includes the following rule:

> *If, for any object named in the variable-bindings field, the object is not available for set operations in the relevant MIB view, then the receiving entity sends to the originator of the received message the GetResponse-PDU of identical form, except that the value of the error-status field is noSuchName, and the value of the error-index field is the index of said object name component in the received message.*

TABLE 7.8 Deleting/Nullifying Rows in MIB-II Tables

Group	Table	Relevant Object	Comment
interfaces	ifTable	ifAdminStatus	This is the only settable object in the table; a value of down(2) makes the interface unusable but does not erase the row.
address translation	atTable	—	No provision is made for row deletion; however, the entire group is deprecated in MIB-II.
ip	ipAddrTable	—	The entire table is read-only and may not be altered by a management station.
ip	ipRouteTable	ipRouteType	A row is invalidated by setting the value of this object to invalid(2).
ip	ipNetToMediaTable	ipNetToMediaType	A row is invalidated by setting the value of this object to invalid(2).
tcp	tcpConnTable	tcpConnState	The only value that may be set by the management station is deleteTCB(12). This has the effect of deleting the transmission control block that defines the connection and therefore invalidating the row.
udp	udpTable	—	The entire table is read-only and may not be altered by a management station.
egp	egpNeighTable	egpNeighEventTrigger	This is the only settable object in the table; a value of stop(2) causes a non-Idle peer to return to the Idle state but does not erase the row.

This rule is interpreted to mean the following.

1. If a Set operation is attempted for an object that is not in the MIB view of the manager, return noSuchName.

2. If a Set operation is attempted for an object that is in the MIB view of the manager but is read-only, return noSuchName.

One can reason that an object that is read-only is not in the MIB view of a manager for purposes of Set operations. There are two things "wrong" with this rule. First, information is lost; when a manager receives noSuchName in response to a set, the manager must also do a Get operation to determine if the error code refers to a missing object or a read-only object. Second, since the readOnly error code exists, it is clearly confusing not to use it in the obvious circumstances.

The solution to this mystery is that the use of readOnly was omitted in RFC 1157 due to a clerical error. The only occurrence of readOnly in RFC 1157 is in the ASN.1 PDU definitions. Therefore, to be compliant with the standard, one must not use this error code.

In Simple Network Management Protocol version 2 (SNMPv2), there is a new error code: notWritable, which means what readOnly should have meant in RFC 1157.

7.2.5 Trap PDU

The Trap PDU is issued by an SNMP entity on behalf of a network management agent application. It is used to provide the management station with an asynchronous notification of some significant event. Its format is quite different from that of the other SNMP PDUs. The fields are

- PDU type: indicating that this is a Trap PDU
- enterprise: identifies the network management subsystem that generated the trap (Its value is taken from sysObjectID in the System group.)
- agent-addr: the IP address of the object generating the trap
- generic-trap: one of the predefined trap types
- specific-trap: a code that indicates more specifically the nature of the trap
- time-stamp: the time between the last (re)initialization of the network entity that issued the trap and the generation of the trap
- variablebindings: additional information relating to the trap (The significance of this field is implementation-specific.)

The generic-trap field may take on one of seven values:

- coldStart(0): The sending SNMP entity is reinitializing itself such that the agent's configuration or the protocol entity implementation may be altered. Typically, this is an unexpected restart due to a crash or major fault.

- `warmStart(1)`: The sending SNMP entity is reinitializing itself such that neither the agent's configuration nor the protocol entity implementation is altered. Typically, this is a routine restart.
- `linkDown(2)`: signals a failure in one of the communications links of the agent. The first element in the `variablebindings` field is the name and value of the `ifIndex` instance for the referenced interface.
- `linkUp(3)`: signals that one of the communications links of the agent has come up. The first element in the `variablebindings` field is the name and value of the `ifIndex` instance for the referenced interface.
- `authenticationFailure(4)`: This signals that the sending protocol entity has received a protocol message that has failed authentication.
- `egpNeighborLoss(5)`: This signals that an EGP neighbor for whom the sending protocol entity was an EGP peer has been marked down and the peer relationship no longer exists.
- `enterpriseSpecific(6)`: signifies that the sending protocol entity recognizes that some enterprise-specific event has occurred. The `specific-trap` field indicates the type of trap.

Unlike the `GetRequest`, `GetNextRequest`, and `SetRequest` PDUs, the `Trap` PDU does not elicit a response from the other side (Figure 7.5(d)).

7.3   *Transport-Level Support*

SNMP requires the use of a transport service for the delivery of SNMP messages. The protocol makes no assumptions about whether the underlying service is reliable or unreliable, connectionless or connection-oriented.

7.3.1   Connectionless Transport Service

Most implementations of SNMP are within the TCP/IP architecture and use the User Datagram Protocol (UDP), which is a connectionless protocol (see Appendix B). It is also possible to support SNMP within the OSI architecture using the connectionless transport service (CLTS).

7.3.1.1   UDP Details

UDP segments are transmitted in IP datagrams. The UDP header includes source and destination port fields, enabling application-level protocols such as SNMP to address each other. It also includes an optional checksum that covers the UDP header and user data. If there is a checksum violation, the UDP segment is discarded. No other services are added to IP.

Two port numbers have been assigned for use by SNMP. Agents listen for incoming GetRequest, GetNextRequest, and SetRequest commands on port 161. Management stations listen for incoming Traps on port 162.

7.3.1.2   CLTS Details

As with UDP, the ISO connectionless transport service transmits each data unit independently. The connectionless transport protocol data unit includes source and destination transport service access points (TSAPs) and an optional checksum.

The TSAP address can be thought of as having two components: a network-layer address and a TSAP identifier, or *selector*. RFC 1283 dictates that agents listen for incoming GetRequest, GetNextRequest, and SetRequest commands at TSAP selector "snmp," and management stations listen for incoming Traps on TSAP selector "snmp-trap."

7.3.1.3   Loss of a PDU

Since both UDP and CLTS are unreliable, it is possible for an SNMP message to be lost. SNMP itself has no provision to guarantee delivery. Thus, the burden to cope with a lost PDU is with the application that is using SNMP.

The actions to be taken upon loss of an SNMP message are not covered in the standard. Some commonsense observations can be made. In the case of GetRequest and GetNextRequest, the management station can assume that either the message was lost or the responding GetResponse was lost if there is no response within a certain time period. The management station can repeat the request one or more times, eventually succeeding or giving up and assuming either that the agent is down or that it cannot be reached. Since a unique request-id accompanies each distinct request operation, there is no difficulty if duplicate messages are generated.

In the case of a SetRequest, the recovery should probably involve testing the object with a GetRequest to determine whether or not the set operation was performed. A duplicate SetRequest should be issued only if it is determined that the set operation was not performed.

Since no acknowledgment is provided in SNMP for traps, there is no easy way to detect the failure to deliver a trap. In SNMP, a trap should be used to provide early warning of a significant event. As a backup, the management station should also periodically poll the agent for the relevant status.

7.3.2   Connection-Oriented Transport Service

SNMP was intended for use over a connectionless transport service. The key reason for this is robustness. Network management operations become increasingly important as failures and outages of various sorts are experienced. If SNMP relies on the use of a transport connection, then the loss of that connection could impair the effectiveness of SNMP exchanges.

No provision has been made for the use of SNMP over TCP. However, RFC 1283 prescribes conventions for the use of SNMP over the ISO connection-oriented transport service (COTS). In order to issue a `GetRequest`, `GetNextRequest`, or a `SetRequest`, the management station must first set up a transport connection to the agent. Once the connection is set up, the management station can send requests and receive responses on that connection. If the management station anticipates additional requests to the same agent, it can hold the connection open, thus reducing the overhead associated with connection setup and tear-down. The agent may also break the connection if it needs the resources dedicated to managing the connection. Similarly, an agent would need to set up a connection to a management station prior to issuing a `trap`.

Although there is a single ISO connection-oriented transport service, this service is supported by five different transport protocols, labeled Class 0 through Class 4. Class 0 and Class 1 transport protocols assume the use of X.25 as the underlying network protocol and further restrict transport connections to be one-to-one with network connections. For these classes, the listening agent's address is the X.25 protocol-ID 03018200 and the listening management station's address is 0301900. For the other three transport classes, the same transport selectors used for CLTS are used for COTS.

7.4   *SNMP Group*

The `snmp` group defined as part of MIB-II contains information relevant to the implementation and operation of SNMP (Figure 7.7, Table 7.9). Some of the objects defined in the group are zero-valued in those SNMP implementations that support only SNMP station management functions or only SNMP agent functions.

With the exception of the last object in the group, all of the objects are read-only counters. The `snmpEnableAuthenTraps` may be set by a management station. It indicates whether the agent is permitted to generate authentication-failure traps. This setting overrides the agent's own configuration information. Thus, it provides a means whereby all authentication-failure traps may be disabled.

7.5   *Practical Issues*

7.5.1   Differences in SNMP Support

In Chapter 5, we looked at the results of tests conducted on various commercially available SNMP management station and agent products. The results showed some inconsistencies in the values generated for various MIB objects. Those same tests also looked at the support for SNMP provided by the various products. Unfortunately, some inconsistencies and areas of nonsupport were evident.

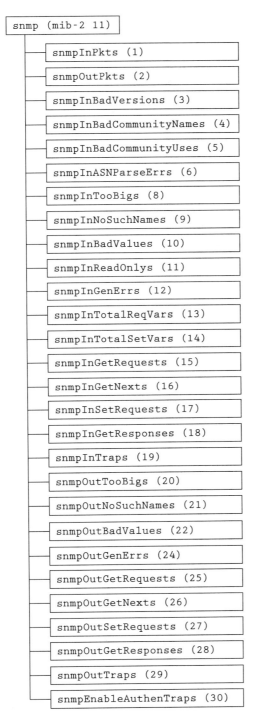

FIGURE 7.7 MIB-II snmp group

TABLE 7.9 snmp Group Objects

Object	Syntax	Access	Description
snmpInPkts	Counter	RO	Total number of messages delivered to the SNMP entity from the transport service
snmpOutPkts	Counter	RO	Total number of SNMP messages passed from the SNMP entity to the transport service
snmpInBadVersions	Counter	RO	Total number of SNMP messages delivered to the SNMP entity for an unsupported SNMP version
snmpInBadCommunityNames	Counter	RO	Total number of SNMP messages delivered to the SNMP entity that used an SNMP community name not known to the entity
snmpInBadCommunityUses	Counter	RO	Total number of SNMP messages delivered to the SNMP entity that represented an SNMP operation not allowed by the SNMP community named in the message
snmpInASNParseErrs	Counter	RO	Total number of ASN.1 or BER errors encountered when decoding received SNMP messages
snmpInTooBigs	Counter	RO	Total number of SNMP PDUs delivered to the SNMP entity for which the value of the error-status field is tooBig
snmpInNoSuchNames	Counter	RO	Total number of SNMP PDUs delivered to the SNMP entity for which the value of the error-status field is noSuchName
snmpInBadValues	Counter	RO	Total number of SNMP PDUs delivered to the SNMP entity for which the value of the error-status field is badValue
snmpInReadOnlys	Counter	RO	Total number of SNMP PDUs delivered to the SNMP entity for which the value of the error-status field is readOnly
snmpInGenErrs	Counter	RO	Total number of SNMP PDUs delivered to the SNMP entity for which the value of the error-status field is genErr
snmpInTotalReqVars	Counter	RO	Total number of MIB objects retrieved successfully by the SNMP entity as the result of receiving valid SNMP Get-Request and Get-Next PDUs
snmpInTotalSetVars	Counter	RO	Total number of MIB objects retrieved successfully by the SNMP entity as the result of receiving valid SNMP Set-Request PDUs
snmpInGetRequests	Counter	RO	Total number of SNMP Get-Request PDUs accepted and processed by the SNMP entity
snmpInGetNexts	Counter	RO	Total number of SNMP Get-Next PDUs accepted and processed by the SNMP entity

Name	Type	Access	Description
snmpInSetRequests	Counter	RO	Total number of SNMP Set-Request PDUs accepted and processed by the SNMP entity
snmpInGetResponses	Counter	RO	Total number of SNMP Get-Response PDUs accepted and processed by the SNMP entity
snmpInTraps	Counter	RO	Total number of SNMP Trap PDUs accepted and processed by the SNMP entity
snmpOutTooBigs	Counter	RO	Total number of SNMP PDUs generated by the SNMP entity for which the value of the error-status field is tooBig
snmpOutNoSuchNames	Counter	RO	Total number of SNMP PDUs generated by the SNMP entity for which the value of the error-status field is noSuchName
snmpOutBadValues	Counter	RO	Total number of SNMP PDUs generated by the SNMP entity for which the value of the error-status field is badValue
snmpOutGenErrs	Counter	RO	Total number of SNMP PDUs generated by the SNMP entity for which the value of the error-status field is genErr
snmpOutGetRequests	Counter	RO	Total number of SNMP Get-Request PDUs generated by the SNMP entity
snmpOutGetNexts	Counter	RO	Total number of SNMP Get-Next PDUs generated by the SNMP entity
snmpOutSetRequests	Counter	RO	Total number of SNMP Set-Request PDUs generated by the SNMP entity
snmpOutGetResponses	Counter	RO	Total number of SNMP Get-Response PDUs generated by the SNMP entity
snmpOutTraps	Counter	RO	Total number of SNMP Trap PDUs generated by the SNMP entity
snmpEnableAuthenTraps	INTEGER	RW	Authentication-failure traps enabled (1) or disabled (2)

Tables 7.10 and 7.11 summarize the key results. One common problem related to the reporting of the medium access control (MAC) addresses for LAN ports. In the configurations tested, all of the physical interfaces were Ethernet ports with 12-byte physical addresses. These addresses are not user-alterable and are fixed in the LAN interface. Clearly, it is important that the agent be able to provide the management station with the correct physical address for each of its interfaces. However, as the tables show, even this simple and basic piece of information is not always reliably reported. A number of the devices reported the same MAC address for all of their ports, and one device was unable to report at all.

Another very common problem is limited or nonexistent support for the `set` command. A number of the vendor products did not support the use of `set` at all, and others

TABLE 7.10   Variance in Bridges' SNMP Support (Mier 1991a)

Vendor	Could manager obtain the MAC-layer Ethernet addresses for all the bridge's LAN ports?	Was manager able to remotely change the values of SNMP standards-specified read-write variables?	Did bridge issue the appropriate SNMP alarm message in response to power interruption?
A	Yes	Agent supported set command for vendor's private-extension MIB objects, but not MIB-I or MIB-II read-write objects.	Agent issued a message, but format was not recognized as the expected `coldStart` SNMP message.
B	No; agent did not respond to manager's request.	No; unable to set values of MIB-I and MIB-II objects tested.	None within 5 minutes; bridge apparently loses address of manager when power is interrupted.
C	Agent responded with the same MAC address for two different LAN interfaces.	Agent supported set command for vendor's private-extension MIB objects, but not MIB-I or MIB-II read-write objects.	Yes; agent issued correct `Trap` message within about 20 seconds of power restoral.
D	Agent responded with the same MAC address for two different LAN interfaces.	Some; at least one read-write object was implemented as read-only.	Agent issued a message, but format was not recognized as the expected `coldStart` SNMP message.
E	Agent responded with the same MAC address for two different LAN interfaces.	No; unable to set values of MIB-I and MIB-II objects tested.	None within 5 minutes.
F	Yes	Some; at least one read-write object was implemented as read-only.	Yes; agent issued correct `Trap` message within about 2 minutes of power restoral.
G	Agent responded with the same MAC address for two different LAN interfaces.	No; unable to set values of MIB-I and MIB-II objects tested.	None within 5 minutes.

limited it to objects in private MIB extensions. The lack of a `set` support limits the network management capability. On the other hand, the basic SNMP specification provides only a password-type feature for security. Until such time as more robust security features are widely implemented, a number of users will be reluctant to allow object values to be remotely set.

TABLE 7.11   Variance in Routers' SNMP Support (Mier 1991b)

Vendor	Could manager obtain clear SNMP status, configuration, and address information on router and all interfaces?	Was manager able to remotely change the values of SNMP standards-specified read-write variables?	Did router issue the appropriate SNMP alarm message in response to power interruption?
1	Yes. However, textual interface descriptions are not explanatory.	Yes, for MIB-I objects and most of the vendor's private MIB objects that were tested.	No. Agent issued a `linkUp` message after 1.7 minutes rather than the expected `coldStart` message.
2	Yes. However, interface descriptions (Ethernet 0, 1) don't align with SNMP index numbers (interface 1, 2).	Yes, for MIB-I objects and most of the vendor's private MIB objects that were tested.	Yes; agent issued correct `Trap` message within about 0.3 minutes of power restoral.
3	Yes. However, vendor implements the same physical (MAC-layer) address for different LAN interfaces.	Yes, for MIB-I objects.	No. Agent issued a `Trap` message, but it contained a format error and was not recognized by managers as the expected trap.
4	Yes.	No; unable to set values of objects tested.	Yes; agent issued correct `Trap` message within about 1 minute of power restoral.
5	Partially. Operational status of serial link was reported incorrectly.	Yes, for MIB-I objects.	No. Agent issued `warmStart` and `linkUp` messages after about 1.5 minutes, but not the expected `coldStart` message.
6	Yes.	No; unable to set values of objects tested.	No. Traps not implemented in this agent.
7	Yes.	Some; at least one read-write object was implemented as read-only.	Yes; agent issued correct `Trap` message within about 2.1 minutes of power restoral.
8	Yes.	Some; at least one read-write object was implemented as read-only.	Yes; agent issued correct `Trap` message within about 0.3 minutes of power restoral.
9	Yes.	No; unable to set values of objects tested.	Yes; agent issued correct `Trap` message within about 2.2 minutes of power restoral.

Those devices that did support the `set` command could all be set up with a community name of "`public`," which gives any management system unrestricted access to the entire MIB. That is, the MIB view for community name `public` consists of the entire agent MIB. This is a useful feature; for a first-time SNMP implementation, the user can set all agents and managers to the `public` name to get some quick experience in the use of the system. The alternative is for the network management system to be configured with a set of community names, one for each device to be managed.

To test the ability of the agents to generate standard SNMP-defined traps, the testers literally pulled the plug on the device's power and then replugged it. The agent should issue a `coldStart` trap under these conditions. Only two of the bridges and four of the routers were able to generate the correct `trap` message. Again, this is bad news for the user. If agents cannot be trusted to issue traps reliably, then the trap-directed polling strategy is based on a false premise. The network management station either must rely more heavily on scheduled polling, which increases network overhead, or suffer a lack of up-to-date knowledge about the network.

7.5.2   Objects Not Supported

The MIB-I and MIB-II specifications dictate that for an implementation to claim support for a group, it must support all of the objects in a group. It is certainly permissible for an agent to support only some of the objects in a group, but in that case the vendor cannot claim that the group is supported.

Unfortunately, a number of vendors have tried to get around this restriction in the following way. If an agent does not count a quantity that is part of a group, it simply always returns the static value zero in response to a `get` command. This enables the vendor to say all the objects are "supported," since a value is returned for all objects. At first glance, this approach might seem entirely reasonable. If the agent has failed to count a particular event, its count is zero. If the agent never counts that event, its count will always be zero.

The problem with this approach is that, in some circumstances, it may be important for the management station to know whether the count is actually zero or whether the agent simply isn't counting. Consider the following example, due to Steven Waldbusser, one of the key developers of SNMP-related standards:

> As a network manager, I would be very angry if the following happened to me: While debugging a packet loss problem, I inspect ifInErrors on an interface and find that the interface has not received any error packets. Feeling confident of the link layer, I turn my attention up the stack to the network layer and above. Several hours or days later, I learn from my system vendor that ifInErrors is not implemented but is stating anyway that no errors have been received. If you can't trust your tools not to lie to you, you can't use them effectively. One still needs a healthy dose of skepticism, but if you need to second-guess everything you learn, you can't work efficiently.

Regardless of whether there is a deliberate attempt to mislead the user and the management station, or whether the agent vendor genuinely feels that a return of zero for an unimplemented counter is appropriate, the fact is that this practice can lead to confusion and inefficiency. The correct way to handle this situation is for the agent to return the error code noSuchName and for the vendor to admit that this particular group is not supported.

Since not all vendors are "doing the right thing," the user must beware.

7.5.3   Selection of a Network Management Station

The discussion earlier in this chapter and in Chapter 5, concerning interoperability, highlights the need to be concerned about the degree to which management and agent products conform to the standard and can operate with each other. In the case of agent products, one should also be concerned with ease of configuration and the range of MIB support.

For network management stations, conformance to standards is only a starting point in evaluating products. The network management station provides the user interface to the entire network management system and should therefore provide a powerful, flexible, and easy-to-use access point for network management. For example, the following list of features that should be included in a network management station is proposed in Wilkinson and Capen (1992):

- *Extended MIB support:* The full power of SNMP is realized only if the MIB support is open-ended. In particular, a network management station should be able to load MIB definitions for extended MIBs defined for agent products from other vendors.

- *Intuitive interface:* The interface should make network management as easy and powerful as possible for the user. When using a graphical window interface, the user should be able to open a separate window for each part of the network that he or she wishes to monitor. The interface should be capable of displaying topological and geographic maps of the network. Descriptive, intelligent icons can be used to represent key components such as bridges and users; when the user clicks on such an icon, the system should display the current status of the device and options for observing and controlling the device.

- *Automatic discovery:* The ideal network management station, when installed, should be able to discover agents in order to build maps and configure icons.

- *Programmable events:* The user should be able to define the actions to be taken when certain events occur. For example, in the event of a router failure, the management station could change the color of the router's icon or flash the icon, send an e-mail message to the responsible manager, and set off the network troubleshooter's beeper.

- *Advanced network control:* Ideally, the network management station should perform some predefined functions under certain conditions. For example, an administrator should be able to configure the management station automatically to shut off a bad or suspect hub or isolate an overactive network segment so that the whole network does not suffer. Of course, such features require the use of SNMP `set` commands. Because of SNMP's weak security, most products limit the scope of the `set` capability or forbid it altogether.

- *Object-oriented management:* Although the MIB and SMI specifications of SNMP refer to "objects," SNMP does not use object-oriented technology. However, an object-oriented system can be configured to support SNMP and can easily be upgraded to run multiple management protocols simultaneously.

- *Custom icons:* Descriptive icons are preferable to simple rectangles and circles for displaying network topology and geography. Ideally, the network management station should enable the user to create custom icons.

7.5.4   Polling Frequency

As we have seen, SNMP-defined traps are few in number. Although it is possible for proprietary traps to be implemented, these may not be understood by a network management station from another vendor. Thus, virtually all information that is gathered by the management station is gathered by polling (`GetRequest` and `GetNextRequest`). Furthermore, if polling is done only at start-up time and in response to a trap, the management station may have a very out-of-date view of the network. For example, the management station will not be alerted to congestion problems in the network.

It follows that a policy is needed for the frequency with which the management station polls. This, in turn, is related to the size of the network and therefore the number of agents that the management station can effectively manage. It is difficult to give guidance in this area, because performance will depend on the processing speed of the management station, the data rate of the various subnetwork segments, the congestion level in the network, and other factors. However, we can provide some simple formulas that give some idea of the scale of what is possible.

To simplify the problem, let us say that the management station can handle only one agent at a time. That is, when the management station polls a particular agent, it does no other work until it is done with that agent. The poll may involve a single get/response transaction or a series of such transactions. We can determine the maximum number of stations that the management station can handle by considering the situation in which the management station is engaged full-time in polling. We have the following equation:

$$N \leq \frac{T}{\Delta},$$

where

N = number of agents,

T = desired polling interval; that is, the desired elapsed time between successive polls of the same agent,

Δ = average time required to perform a single poll.

The quantity Δ depends on a number of factors:

- Processing time to generate a request at the management station
- Network delay from manager to agent
- Processing time at the agent to interpret message
- Processing time at the agent to generate response
- Network delay from agent to manager
- Processing time at manager to receive and interpret response
- Number of request/response exchanges to obtain all the desired information from an agent

The following example is provided in Ben-Artzi, Chandna, and Warrier (1990). The example consists of a single LAN, where each managed device is to be polled every 15 minutes (typical at many TCP/IP sites today). Assuming processing times on the order of 50 ms, and a network delay of about 1 ms (packet size of 1,000 bytes, no significant network congestion), then Δ is approximately 0.202 sec. Then

$$N \le \frac{15 \times 60}{0.202} \approx 4,500.$$

Thus, in this example, a single network manager could support a maximum of 4,500 devices with SNMP-based polling.

In a configuration that includes multiple subnetworks, especially wide area networks, the network delay component will be much greater. Typically, data rates are significantly lower on a WAN than on a LAN, the distances are greater, and there are delays introduced by bridges and routers. A total network delay of half a second would not be unusual. Using this as an example,

$$N \le \frac{15 \times 60}{(4 \times 0.05) + (2 \times 0.5)} \approx 750,$$

and the number of manageable devices is only 750.

In summary, four critical parameters are involved in these back-of-the-envelope calculations: the number of agents, the processing time for a request or a response, the network delay, and the polling interval. If the user can make rough estimates of any three of these, the fourth can be approximated. So, for a given network configuration and a known number of agents, the user can determine the minimum polling interval that can be supported. Alternatively, for a given network configuration and a desired polling interval, the user can determine the maximum number of agents that can be managed.

There is, however, yet another factor that must be considered, namely the load the polling traffic imposes on the network. For example, one firm with a large Ethernet installation set the polling interval at five minutes and found that this delay was considered too high for responding to network problems (Eckerson 1992).

7.5.5   Limitations of SNMP

The user who relies on SNMP for network management needs to be aware of its limitations. Ben-Artzi, Chandna, and Warrier (1990) list the following information.

1. SNMP may not be suitable for the management of truly large networks because of the performance limitations of polling, as just examined. With SNMP, you must send one packet out to get back one packet of information. This type of polling results in large volumes of routine messages and yields problem response times that may be unacceptable.

2. SNMP is not well suited for retrieving large volumes of data, such as an entire routing table.

3. SNMP traps are unacknowledged. In the typical case where UDP/IP is used to deliver trap messages, the agent cannot be sure that a critical message has reached the management station.

4. The basic SNMP standard provides only trivial authentication. Thus, basic SNMP is better suited for monitoring than control.

5. SNMP does not directly support imperative commands. The only way to trigger an event at an agent is indirectly, by setting an object value. This is a less flexible and powerful scheme than one that would allow some sort of remote procedure call, with parameters, conditions, status, and results to be reported.

6. The SNMP MIB model is limited and does not readily support applications that make sophisticated management queries based on object values or types.

7. SNMP does not support manager-to-manager communications. For example, there is no mechanism that allows a management system to learn about the devices and networks managed by another management system.

Many of these deficiencies are addressed in SNMPv2.

7.6   *Summary*

The heart of the SNMP framework is the simple network management protocol itself. The protocol provides a straightforward, basic mechanism for the exchange of management information between manager and agent.

The basic unit of exchange is the message, which consists of an outer message wrapper and an inner protocol data unit (PDU). The message header includes a community name, which allows the agent to regulate access. For any given community name, the agent may limit access to a subset of objects in its MIB, known as a MIB view.

Five types of PDUs may be carried in an SNMP message. The `GetRequest` PDU, issued by a manager, includes a list of one or more object names for which values are requested. The `GetNextRequest` PDU also is issued by a manager and includes a list of one or more objects. In this case, for each object named, a value is to be returned for the object that is lexicographically next in the MIB. The `SetRequest` PDU is issued by a manager to request that the values of one or more objects be altered. For all three of these PDUs, the agent responds with a `GetResponse` PDU, which contains the values of the objects in question, or an `error-status` explaining the failure of the operation.

The final PDU is the `Trap`, which is issued by an agent to provide information to a manager concerning an event.

SNMP is designed to operate over the connectionless User Datagram Protocol (UDP). However, SNMP can be implemented to operate over a variety of transport-level protocols.

APPENDIX 7A   *LEXICOGRAPHICAL ORDERING*

Given two sequences of nonnegative integers $(x_1, x_2, \ldots, x_n)$ and $(y_1, y_2, \ldots, y_m)$, we can say the $(x_1, x_2, \ldots, x_n)$ precedes $(y_1, y_2, \ldots, y_m)$ in lexicographic order if the following conditions are met:

$$[(x_j = y_j \text{ for } 1 \leq j \leq k) \text{ AND } (x_k < y_k \text{ for } k \leq n,m)]$$
$$\text{OR } [(x_j = y_j \text{ for } 1 \leq j \leq n) \text{ AND } (n < m)].$$

Lexicographical ordering in an object identifier tree is easily generated. The only restriction is that the tree must be drawn so that the branches under each node are

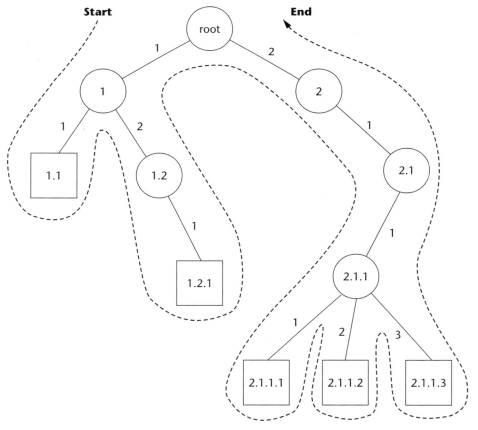

FIGURE 7.8   Traversing a tree

arranged in increasing order left to right. With this convention, the lexicographical order is generated by traversing the tree in what is referred to as a *preorder traversal,* which is defined recursively as follows.

- Visit the root.
- Traverse the subtrees from left to right.

This method of traversal is also known as a *depth-first search* of the tree. Figure 7.8 illustrates preorder traversal. As can be seen, the nodes of the tree are visited in lexicographic order.

PART THREE *RMON*

Remote Network Monitoring
Statistics Collection

The most important addition to the basic set of SNMP standards (SMI, MIB, SNMP) is the remote network monitoring (RMON) specification, which is currently defined in four documents (Table 8.1). RMON is a major step forward in internetwork management. It defines a remote monitoring MIB that supplements MIB-II and provides the network manager with vital information about the internetwork. The remarkable feature of RMON is that while it is simply a specification of a MIB, with no changes in the underlying SNMP protocol, it provides for a significant expansion in SNMP functionality.

This chapter introduces the original RMON and then goes on to examine the statistics-gathering portions of RMON. The next two chapters examine other aspects of RMON. For a review of the basic principles of network monitoring, please see Chapter 2.

8.1 Basic Concepts

With MIB-II, the network manager can obtain information that is purely local to individual devices. Consider a LAN with a number of devices on it, each with an SNMP agent. An SNMP manager can learn of the amount of traffic into and out of each device but, with MIB-II, cannot easily learn about the traffic on the LAN as a whole. Devices that traditionally have been employed to study the traffic on a network as a whole are called *network monitors*; they are also referred to as network analyzers, or probes. Typically, a monitor operates on a LAN in "promiscuous" mode, viewing every packet on the LAN. The monitor can produce summary information, including error statistics, such as a count of undersized packets and the number of collisions, and performance statistics, such as the number of packets delivered per second and the packet size distribution. The monitor may also store packets or partial packets for later analysis. Filters can be used to limit the number of packets counted or captured, based on packet type or other packet characteristics.

For the purposes of network management in an internetworked environment, there would typically need to be one monitor per subnetwork. The monitor may be a stand-alone device whose sole purpose is to capture and analyze traffic. In other cases, the

TABLE 8.1   RMON-Related RFCs

RFC	Date	Title
1513	September 1993	Token Ring Extensions to the Remote Network Monitoring MIB
1757	February 1995	Remote Network Monitoring Management Information Base
2021	January 1997	Remote Network Monitoring Management Information Base II
2074	January 1997	Remote Network Monitoring MIB Protocol Identifiers

monitoring function is performed by a device with other duties, such as a workstation, a server, or a router. For effective network management, these monitors need to communicate with a central network management station. In this latter context, they are referred to as *remote monitors*.

8.1.1   RMON Goals

The RMON specification is primarily a definition of a MIB. The effect, however, is to define standard network-monitoring functions and interfaces for communicating between SNMP-based management consoles and remote monitors. In general terms, the RMON capability provides an effective and efficient way to monitor subnetwork-wide behavior while reducing the burden both on other agents and on management stations. In addition, RFC 1757 lists the following design goals for RMON:

- *Off-line operation:* It might be desirable or necessary to limit or halt the routine polling of a monitor by a network manager. Limited polling saves on communications costs, especially where dial-up lines may have to be used to reach the monitor. Polling may cease if there is a communications failure or if the manager fails. In general, the monitor should collect fault, performance, and configuration information continuously, even if it is not being polled by a network manager. The monitor simply continues to accumulate statistics that may be retrieved by the manager at a later time. The monitor may also attempt to notify the management station if an exceptional event occurs.

- *Proactive monitoring:* If the monitor has sufficient resources, and if the practice is not considered to be disruptive, the monitor can continuously run diagnostics and log network performance. In the event of a failure somewhere in the Internet, the monitor may be able to notify the management station of the failure and provide the management station with information useful in diagnosing the failure.

- *Problem detection and reporting:* Preemptive monitoring involves an active probing of the network and the consumption of network resources to check for error and exception conditions. Alternatively, the monitor can passively (without polling) recognize certain error conditions and other conditions such as congestion on the basis of the traffic that it observes. The monitor can be configured to check continuously for such conditions. When one of these conditions occurs, the monitor can log the condition and attempt to notify the management station.

- *Value-added-data:* The network monitor can perform analyses specific to the data collected on its subnetwork, thus relieving the management station of this responsibility. For example, the monitor can analyze subnetwork traffic to determine which hosts generate the most traffic or errors on the subnetwork. This type of subnetwork-wide information is not otherwise accessible to a network management station that is not directly attached to the subnetwork.

- *Multiple managers:* An internetworking configuration may have more than one management station. Reasons for the additional managers include to improve reliability, to perform different functions (for example, engineering and operations), and to provide management capability to different units within an organization. The monitor can be configured to deal with more than one management station concurrently. (The requirements for support of multiple managers are discussed later in this section.)

Not all remote monitors may be capable of meeting all of these goals, but the RMON specification provides the base for supporting all of them.

Figure 8.1 is an example configuration for remote monitoring, showing an internet with five subnetworks. The three subnetworks in the lower left portion of the figure are located in the same building. The other two subnetworks are at two different remote sites. The subnetwork at the top of the figure is considered to be the central site. A dedicated management station with RMON management capability is attached to the central LAN. On two of the subnetworks, the RMON MIB is implemented in a personal computer, which may be dedicated to remote monitoring or, if the traffic on the subnetwork is light, may perform other duties, such as local network management or a server function. Attached to the FDDI backbone is a second management station with RMON management capability, concerned with management of the networks at that site. Finally, the RMON MIB functions for the token ring LAN are performed by the router that connects that LAN to the rest of the internet.

A note on terminology: A system that implements the RMON MIB is referred to as an RMON *probe*. The probe has an agent that is no different from any other SNMP agent. It also has an RMON probe process entity that provides the RMON-related functionality. The probe entity is capable of reading/writing the local RMON MIB in response to management action and in performing the various RMON-related functions described in this and the next two chapters. In the literature, you will sometimes see the term *RMON agent*. The term *RMON probe* is preferred.

8.1.2   Control of Remote Monitors

A remote monitor can be implemented either as a dedicated device or as a function available on a system for which processing and memory resources are specifically dedicated to

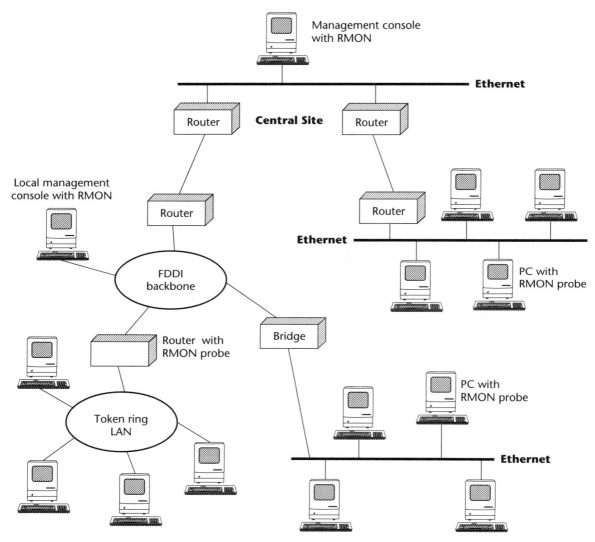

FIGURE 8.1   Example configuration using RMON

the monitoring function. With these dedicated resources, a remote monitor is capable of performing more complex tasks and a wider range of functions than would be expected of an agent that just supports MIB-II. In order to manage a remote monitor effectively, the RMON MIB contains features that support extensive control from the management station. These features fall into two general categories: configuration and action invocation.

8.1.2.1 Configuration

Typically, a remote monitor will need to be configured for data collection. *Configuration* dictates the type and form of data to be collected. The RMON MIB accommodates this as follows. The MIB is organized into a number of functional groups. Within each group, there may be one or more control tables and one or more data tables. A *control table*, which is typically read-write, contains parameters that describe the data in a *data table*, which is typically read-only. So, at configuration time, the management station sets the appropriate control parameters to configure the remote monitor to collect the desired data. The parameters are set by adding a new row to the control table or by modifying an existing row. As information is collected according to the parameter settings of a control row, the data are stored in rows of the corresponding data table.

Thus, functions to be performed by a monitor are defined and implemented in terms of table rows. For example, a control table may contain objects that specify the source of data to be collected, the type of data, the collection timing, and so on. By assigning specific values to the parameters (columnar objects) of the table, a single row of the control table defines a specific data collection function. Associated with that single control row are one or more rows in one or more data tables. The individual control row and its associated data rows are tied together by, in effect, interlocking pointers. The control row includes an index object that can be used to access one or more data rows in one or more data tables; each such data row includes an index that refers to the corresponding control table row. A number of examples of this structure are illustrated throughout the chapter.

To modify any parameters in a control table, it is necessary first to invalidate the control entry (row). This causes the deletion of that row and the deletion of all associated rows in data tables. The management station can then create a new control row with the modified parameters. The same mechanism is used simply to disable a particular data collection function. When a row of a control table is deleted, the associated data tables rows are deleted and the resources used by those rows are reclaimed.

In several cases, there is essentially a one-to-one relationship between the control parameters that define a data collection function, and a single row of objects used to hold collected data. In those cases, the control and data tables are combined into a single table.

8.1.2.2 Action Invocation

As was mentioned in Chapter 7, SNMP provides no specific mechanism for issuing a command to an agent to perform an action. The only capabilities of SNMP are to read object values and to set object values within a MIB view. However, it is possible to use the SNMP `Set` operation to issue a command, a process called *action invocation*. An object can be used to represent a command, so that a specific action is taken if the object is set to a specific value. A number of such objects are included in the RMON MIB. In general, these objects represent states, and an action is performed if the management station changes a state (by changing the value of the object). A request to set an object to its current value does not cause an action to be performed.

8.1.3   Multiple Managers

As Figure 8.1 illustrates, an RMON probe may be subject to management from multiple management stations. Any time concurrent access is allowed to a resource, there is a potential for conflict and unwanted results. In the case of a shared RMON probe, the following difficulties may arise.

1. Concurrent requests for resources could exceed the capability of the monitor to supply those resources.
2. A management station could capture and hold monitor resources for a long period of time, preventing their use for other desired management functions by other management stations.
3. Resources could be assigned to a management station that crashes without releasing the resources.

To deal with these problems, a combination of avoidance and resolution features are needed. It turns out that a relatively simple feature embedded in the RMON MIB supports these requirements. Associated with each control table is a columnar object that identifies the owner of a particular row of the table and of the associated function. The ownership label can be used in the following ways.

1. A management station may recognize resources it owns and no longer needs.
2. A network operator can identify the management station that owns a particular resource or function and negotiate for the resource or function to be freed.
3. A network operator may have the authority unilaterally to free resources another network operator has reserved.
4. If a management station experiences a reinitialization, it can recognize resources it had reserved in the past and free those it no longer needs.

The RMON specification suggests that the ownership label contain one or more of the following: IP address, management station name, network manager's name, location, or phone number.

Although the ownership concept is useful, it is important to note that the ownership label does not act as a password or access-control mechanism. Access control is enforced in SNMP only through the use of the MIB view mechanism associated with the community name. Thus, if a control table has read-write access, it is available for reading and writing by all management stations for which the table is visible in their MIB view. In general, a row of a control table should be altered or deleted only by its owner and read only by other management stations. The enforcement of this convention is beyond the scope of SNMP or the RMON specification.

If multiple network managers have access to a control table, some efficiencies can be achieved by sharing. When a management station wishes to utilize a certain function in a monitor, it should first scan the relevant control table to see if that function, or something close to that function, has already been defined by another management station. In that case, the management station may "share" the function by simply observing the corresponding read-only data rows associated with the control row. However, the management station that owns a control table row may modify or delete that row at any time. Thus, any management station that shares that row may find the function it desires modified or terminated.

Often, a monitor will be configured with a default set of functions that are set up when the monitor is initialized. The control rows that define these functions are owned by the monitor. By convention, each relevant ownership label is set to a string starting with `monitor`. The resources associated with the defined function are therefore owned by the monitor itself. A management station can make use of such functions in a read-only fashion if there is a functional match with the management station's requirements. A management station should not alter or delete a monitor-owned function, except under the direction of the administrator of the monitor, often the network administrator.

8.1.4   Table Management

In the SNMPv1 framework, the procedures for adding and deleting table rows are, to say the least, unclear. This lack of clarity has been the source of frequently asked questions and complaints.[1] The RMON specification includes a set of textual conventions and procedural rules that, while not violating or modifying the SNMP framework, provide a clear and disciplined technique for row addition and deletion. These conventions and procedures are summarized in this subsection.

8.1.4.1   Textual Conventions

Two new data types are defined in the RMON specification. In ASN.1, the definitions appear as follows:

```
OwnerString ::= DisplayString
EntryStatus ::= INTEGER { valid(1),
                          createRequest(2),
                          underCreation(3),
                          invalid(4) }
```

---

[1]SNMPv2 provides a clearer but much more complex set of procedures for adding and deleting rows, compared to that for SNMPv1. In order to enable RMON to remain compatible with both SNMPv1 and SNMPv2, these procedures are not adopted in the current RMON specification.

Associated with each read-write table (control or combination control/data) in the RMON MIB is an object whose value indicates the owner of that row.[2] This object has the type `OwnerString`. Recall from the definition of the macro for managed objects (Figure 5.3) that a `DisplayString` is an octet string of 0 to 255 octets. Thus, `Owner-String` is just a useful mnemonic name for `DisplayString`. In all cases, the object name ends in *Owner* and is thus easily identified.

Also associated with each read-write table in the RMON MIB is an object whose value gives the status of the row that contains that object instance. This object has the type `EntryStatus` and may take one of the four values listed in the ASN.1 definition of that type (`valid`, `createRequest`, `underCreation`, `invalid`). Objects of type `EntryStatus` are used in the creation, modification, and deletion of rows, as described ahead. In all cases, the object name ends in *Status* and is thus easily identified.

In the figures that follow, objects of type `EntryStatus` are indicated by an arrow with an open arrowhead. As in Chapters 6 and 7, `INDEX` objects are indicated by an arrow with a closed arrowhead.

RFC 1757 refers to these definitions as textual conventions. The purpose of these definitions is to enhance the readability of the specification. Objects defined in terms of these definitions are encoded by means of the rules that define the underlying primitive types (`INTEGER`, `OctetString`). Thus, no changes to the SMI or SNMP are needed to accommodate the RMON MIB. However, the textual convention `EntryStatus` does in fact add new semantics to the MIB, by defining a means for adding and deleting rows.

Figure 8.2 shows the general structure used for all control and data tables in the RMON MIB. These example definitions include the key elements typically found in RMON table definitions. The control table includes the following columnar objects:

- `rm1ControlIndex`: uniquely defines a unique row of `rm1ControlTable` and serves to identify a set of rows of `rm1DataTable`, all of which are controlled by this row
- `rm1ControlParameter`: applies to all of the data rows controlled by this control row (It somehow characterizes the set of data rows controlled by this control row. In this example, a single such parameter is indicated.)
- `rm1ControlOwner`: the owner of this row
- `rm1ControlStatus`: the status of this row

The data table is indexed by `rm1DataControlIndex` and then `rm1DataIndex`. The value of `rm1DataControlIndex` is the same as the value of `rm1ControlIndex` in `rm1ControlTable` that defines the control row for this data entry. For example, suppose that we are interested in the set of data rows controlled by the second control row and that we are further interested in the 89th member, or row, of that set. The instance of the value of that row would be named `rm1DataValue.2.89`.

---

[2]The need to specify the management station that owns a row is discussed in Section 8.1.3.

```
rm1ControlTable OBJECT-TYPE
   SYNTAX    SEQUENCE OF RM1ControlEntry
   ACCESS       not-accessible
   STATUS       mandatory
   DESCRIPTION
      "A control table."
   ::= { ex1 1}

rm1ControlEntry OBJECT-TYPE
   SYNTAX       RM1ControlEntry
   ACCESS       not-accessible
   STATUS       mandatory
   DESCRIPTION
      "Defines a parameter that controls a set
      of data table entries."
   INDEX   { rm1ControlIndex }
   ::= { rm1ControlTable 1}

rm1ControlEntry ::= SEQUENCE {
   rm1ControlIndex       INTEGER,
   rm1ControlParameter   Counter,
   rm1ControlOwner       OwnerString
   rm1ControlStatus      RowStatus    }

rm1ControlIndex OBJECT-TYPE
   SYNTAX       INTEGER
   ACCESS       read-only
   STATUS       mandatory
   DESCRIPTION
      "The value of this object uniquely iden-
      tifies this rm1Control entry."
   ::= { rm1ControlEntry 1}

rm1ControlParameter OBJECT-TYPE
   SYNTAX       Integer
   ACCESS       read-write
   STATUS       mandatory
   DESCRIPTION
      "The value of this object characterizes
      data table rows associated with this
      entry."
   ::= { rm1ControlEntry 2}

rm1ControlOwner OBJECT-TYPE
   SYNTAX       OwnerString
   ACCESS       read-write
   STATUS       mandatory
   DESCRIPTION
      "The entity that configured this entry."
   ::= { rm1ControlEntry 3}

rm1ControlStatus OBJECT-TYPE
   SYNTAX       EntryStatus
   ACCESS       read-write
   STATUS       mandatory
   DESCRIPTION
      "The status of this rm1Control entry."
   ::= { rm1ControlEntry 4}
```

```
rm1DataTable OBJECT-TYPE
   SYNTAX    SEQUENCE OF RM1CtrlEntry
   ACCESS       not-accessible
   STATUS       mandatory
   DESCRIPTION
      "A data table."
   ::= { ex1 2 }

rm1DataEntry OBJECT-TYPE
   SYNTAX       RM1DataEntry
   ACCESS       not-accessible
   STATUS       mandatory
   DESCRIPTION
      "A single data table entry."
   INDEX   { rm1DataControlIndex, rm1DataIndex }
   ::= { rm1DataTable 1 }

Rm1DataEntry ::= SEQUENCE {
   rm1DataControlIndex   INTEGER,
   rm1DataIndex          INTEGER,
   rm1DataValue          Counter }

rm1DataControlIndex OBJECT-TYPE
   SYNTAX       INTEGER
   ACCESS       read-only
   STATUS       mandatory
   DESCRIPTION
      "The control set of which this entry is a
      part. The control set identified by a
      value of this index is the same control
      set identified by the same value of
      rm1ControlIndex."
   ::= { rm1DataEntry 1 }

rm1DataIndex OBJECT-TYPE
   SYNTAX       INTEGER
   ACCESS       read-only
   STATUS       mandatory
   DESCRIPTION
      "An index that uniquely identifies a
      particular entry among all data entries
      associated with the same rm1Control-
      Entry."
   ::= { rm1DataEntry 2 }

rm1DataValue OBJECT-TYPE
   SYNTAX       Counter
   ACCESS       read-only
   STATUS       mandatory
   DESCRIPTION
      "The value reported by this entry."
   ::= { rm1DataEntry 3 }
```

FIGURE 8.2   Control and data tables in RMON1 style

Figure 8.3 is an example of a specific instance of these two tables. In this case, the control table has three rows. The first row has an owner of "monitor"; by convention, this means that the agent itself is the owner of this row. The second row is owned by manager `alpha`, and the third by manager `beta`. Each of these control rows controls one or more rows in the data table. For example, the row for manager `alpha` has a value of `rm1ControlIndex` of 2, which in some way characterizes all of the data rows controlled by this control row. All rows in the data table with an `rm1DataControlIndex` of 2 refer to this control row. Each such row has a unique value of `rm1DataIndex`.

8.1.4.2   Row Addition

The addition of a row to an RMON table by a management station using SNMP is achieved in the same fashion as described in Chapter 6. That is, a `SetRequest` PDU is issued that includes a list of columnar object identifiers for the table. Each object identifier is actually an object instance identifier consisting of the object identifier followed by the

FIGURE 8.3   Instance of tables defined in Figure 8.2

instance value for the index or indices for that table. Ideally, the `SetRequest variable-bindings` list should include all of the columnar objects in the table.

When an agent receives such a request, it must check the requested parameter settings to determine if they are permissible given restrictions defined in the RMON MIB as well as any implementation-specific restrictions, such as lack of resources. If row addition is not possible, a `GetResponse` with a `badValue` error status is returned; the `error-index` field indicates the first field in the `variablebindings` list for which the requested setting was invalid.

The RMON MIB supports a mechanism for coping with the problem posed by concurrent table addition attempts from multiple management stations. The problem occurs if two or more management stations attempt to create a row with the same parameters, including index parameters. To arbitrate this conflict, there is, in effect, a state machine built into the MIB structure defined by the `status` object. The management station and the agent engage in a multipacket exchange dubbed the "RMON Polka" to safely control the construction of the row and to prevent other managers from butting in.

The RMON Polka consists of the following steps.

1. If a management station attempts to create a new row, and the index object value or values do not already exist, the row is created with a status object value of `create-Request(2)`.

2. Immediately after completing the create operation, the agent sets the status object value to `underCreation(3)`.

3. Rows shall exist in the `underCreation(3)` state until the management station is finished creating all of the rows that it desires for its configuration. At that point, the management station sets the status object value in each of the created rows to `valid(1)`.

4. If an attempt is made to create a new row, with a `createRequest` status, and the row already exists, an error will be returned.

The effect of these conventions is that if multiple requests are made to create the same conceptual row, only the request received first will succeed, and the others will receive an error.

Another way in which a row could be added to a table is for a management station to activate an existing invalid row by changing the value of the status object from invalid to valid. The danger with this approach is that it may be impossible for the agent to activate that row if at least one of the parameter settings is not currently appropriate. In that case, there is no way for the agent to indicate to the management station which parameter is invalid, since the columnar object was not included in the `SetRequest`.

8.1.4.3 Row Modification and Deletion

A row is deleted by setting the status object value for that row to invalid. The owner of the row can therefore delete that row by issuing the appropriate `SetRequest` PDU. As

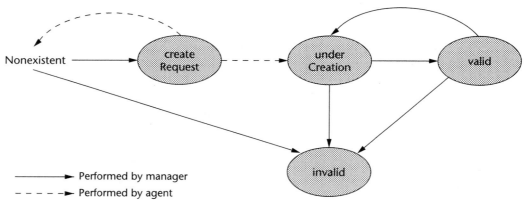

FIGURE 8.4 Transitions of EntryStatus state

was previously mentioned, a row may be modified by first invalidating the row and then providing the row with new parameter values.

Figure 8.4 summarizes the ways in which a manager may change the state of a row. Note that it is not applicable for a manager to move the state of a row from the create-Request state to any other state, because the manager will never find the EntryStatus variable for a row in that state. (Appendix 8A, taken from RFC 1757, provides a concise definition of the EntryStatus convention.)

8.1.5 Good and Bad Packets

In a number of the groups in RMON, there is reference to the counting of good and bad packets. RFC 1757 offers the following definitions:

Good packets are error-free packets that have a valid frame length. For example, on Ethernet, good packets are error-free packets that are between 64 octets long and 1518 octets long. They follow the form defined in IEEE 802.3 section 3.2.a11. Bad packets are packets that have proper framing and are therefore recognized as packets, but contain errors within the packet or have an invalid length. For example, on Ethernet, bad packets have a valid preamble and SFD, but have a bad CRC, or are either shorter than 64 octets or longer than 1518 octets.

8.1.6 The RMON MIB

The bulk of the RMON specification is devoted to a definition of the RMON management information base. This MIB is now incorporated into MIB-II with a subtree identifier of 16.

The RMON MIB is divided into ten groups (Figure 8.5):

- `statistics`: maintains low-level utilization and error statistics for each subnetwork monitored by the agent
- `history`: records periodic statistical samples from information available in the statistics group
- `alarm`: allows the management console user to set a sampling interval and alarm threshold for any counter or integer recorded by the RMON probe
- `host`: contains counters for various types of traffic to and from hosts attached to the subnetwork
- `hostTopN`: contains sorted host statistics that report on the hosts that top a list based on some parameter in the host table

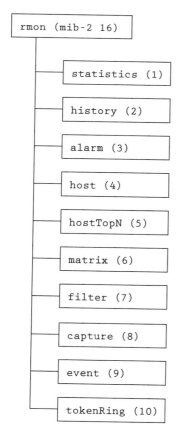

FIGURE 8.5   Remote network monitoring MIB

- matrix: shows error and utilization information in matrix form, so the operator can retrieve information for any pair of network addresses
- filter: allows the monitor to observe packets that match a filter (The monitor may capture all packets that pass the filter or simply record statistics based on such packets.)
- packet capture: governs how data is sent to a management console
- event: gives a table of all events generated by the RMON probe
- tokenRing: maintains statistics and configuration information for token ring subnetworks

Each group is used to store data and statistics derived from data collected by the monitor. A monitor may have more than one physical interface and hence may be connected to more than one subnetwork. The data stored in each group represent data gathered from one or more attached subnetworks, depending on how the monitor is configured for that particular group.

All of the groups in the RMON MIB are optional. However, there are some dependencies.

- The alarm group requires the implementation of the event group.
- The hostTopN group requires the implementation of the host group.
- The packet capture group requires the implementation of the filter group.

Many of the RMON groups are concerned primarily with the collection of traffic statistics for one or more subnetworks: statistics, history, host, hostTopN, matrix, and tokenRing. These groups are discussed in this chapter. The remainder of the groups (alarm, filter, packet capture, event) are concerned with various alarm conditions and with filtering of packets based on user-defined criteria; these groups are covered in Chapter 9.

8.2   statistics *Group*

The statistics group contains the basic statistics for each monitored subnetwork. RFC 1757 defines a single table (Figure 8.6) for this group, with one entry (row) for each monitored interface (subnetwork). The statistics are in the form of counters that start from zero when a valid entry is created. The table, etherStatsTable, collects a variety of counts for each attached subnetwork, including byte, packet, error, and frame size counts (Table 8.2). The table is for use with Ethernet interfaces. In addition, a table for token ring statistics is defined in RFC 1513 (discussed in Section 8.7). Future extensions of the MIB will accommodate other types of LANs, including FDDI.

FIGURE 8.6 RMON statistics group

TABLE 8.2 Counters in `etherStatsTable`

etherStatsDropEvents
Number of events in which packets were dropped by the monitor due to lack of resources. This is not necessarily the actual count of packets dropped, but the number of times this condition has been detected.

etherStatsOctets
Number of received octets of data (including those in bad packets).

etherStatsPkts
Number of received packets, including bad packets, broadcast packets, and multicast packets.

etherStatsBroadcastPkts
Number of good broadcast packets received.

etherStatsMulticastPkts
Number of good multicast packets received.

etherStatsCRCAlignErrors
Number of packets received of the proper size (between 64 and 1,518 octets) but with either a CRC error or an alignment error (not an integral number of octets).

etherStatsUndersizePkts
Number of packets received that were well formed but less than 64 octets long.

etherStatsOversizePkts
Number of packets received that were well formed but greater than 1,518 octets long.

etherStatsFragments
Number of packets received that were less than 64 octets long and with either a CRC error or an alignment error (not an integral number of octets).

etherStatsJabbers
Number of packets received that were greater than 1,518 octets long and with either a CRC error or an alignment error (not an integral number of octets).

etherStatsCollisions
The best estimate of the total number of collisions.

etherStatsPkts64Octets
Number of packets (including bad packets) received that were 64 octets in length.

etherStatsPkts65to127Octets
Number of packets (including bad packets) received that were between 65 and 127 octets in length.

etherStatsPkts128to255Octets
Number of packets (including bad packets) received that were between 128 and 255 octets in length.

etherStatsPkts256to511Octets
Number of packets (including bad packets) received that were between 256 and 511 octets in length.

etherStatsPkts512to1023Octets
Number of packets (including bad packets) received that were between 512 and 1,023 octets in length.

etherStatsPkts1024to1518Octets
Number of packets (including bad packets) received that were between 1,024 and 1,518 octets in length.

Two of the noncounter objects in the group warrant further explanation:

- etherStatsIndex: an integer index for this row. One row is defined for each monitored Ethernet interface on the device.

- etherStatsDataSource: identifies the interface and hence the Ethernet subnetwork that is the source of the data in this row. The value of this object instance is an object identifier that identifies the instance of ifIndex in the interfaces group of MIB-II that corresponds to this interface. For example, if this row refers to interface

#1, this object would be set to `ifIndex.1`. The statistics in this row reflect all packets transmitted on the Ethernet subnetwork attached to this interface.

The `statistics` group provides useful information about the load on a subnetwork and the overall health of the subnetwork, since various error conditions are counted, such as CRC alignment errors, collisions, and undersized and oversized packets.

Note that this group is used to collect statistics on traffic into the monitor across an interface. It is interesting to compare the objects in this group to the MIB-II `interfaces` group (Table 5.2), which is concerned with total traffic into and out of an agent's interface. There is some overlap, but the `statistics` group provides much more detail about Ethernet behavior.

It is also worthwhile to compare this table to the EtherLike MIB group (Table 6.10). The `dot3Stats` table in that group collects statistics for a single system on an ethernet, whereas the `etherStatsTable` collects statistics for all systems attached to an ethernet.

For the `statistics` group, the functions of control table and data table are combined. The only read-write objects in the table are `etherStatsDataSource`, `etherStatsOwner`, and `etherStatsStatus`. Thus, a management station can request that the monitor gather statistics on one or more of its Ethernet interfaces. The profile of statistics gathered is the same for all interfaces, all of which must be interfaces to Ethernet networks.

8.3   history *Group*

The `history` group is used to define sampling functions for one or more of the interfaces of the monitor. RFC 1757 defines two tables (Figure 8.7): `historyControlTable`, which specifies the interface and the details of the sampling function, and `etherHistoryTable`, which records the data. The latter is a media-specific table for Ethernet. There are similar tables for token ring defined in RFC 1513 (discussed in Section 8.7); other media-specific data tables may be added in the future.

Each row in the `historyControlTable` defines a set of samples at a particular sampling interval for a particular interface. As it is collected, each sample is stored in a new row of `etherHistoryTable`. The `historyControlTable` includes the following columnar objects:

- `historyControlIndex`: an integer that uniquely identifies a row in the `historyControlTable`. The same integer is also used to identify corresponding rows in the `etherHistoryTable` or another media-specific table.

- `historyControlDataSource`: This identifies the interface and hence the subnetwork that is the source of the data for samples defined by this row.

- `historyControlBucketsRequested`: the requested number of discrete sampling intervals over which data are to be saved in the part of the media-specific data table

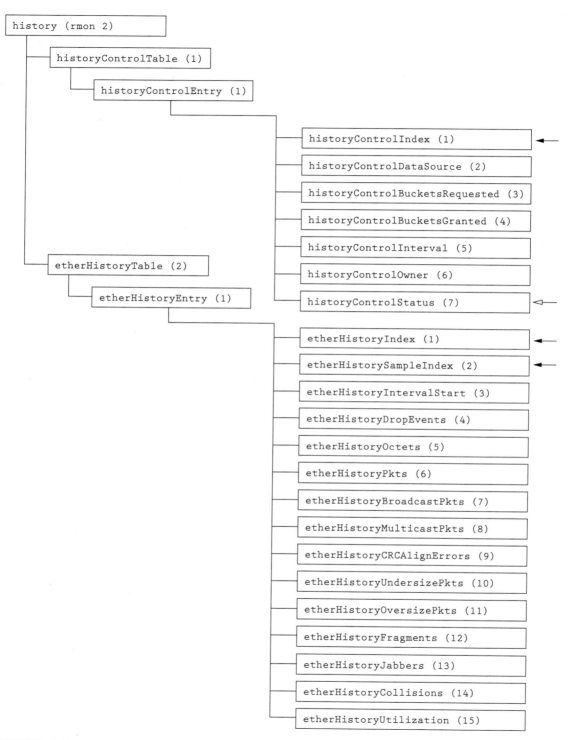

FIGURE 8.7 RMON history group

associated with this entry. A default value of 50 is assigned to this object if it is not provided by the creator of this row.

- `historyControlBucketsGranted`: the actual number of discrete sampling intervals over which data will be saved. When the associated `historyControlBuckets-Requested` is created or modified, the monitor should set this object as closely to the requested value as possible.

- `historyControlInterval`: The interval in seconds over which data are sampled for each bucket. The interval can be set to any number between 1 and 3,600 (1 hour). A default value of 1,800 is assigned to this object if it is not provided by the creator of this row.

The sampling scheme is dictated by `historyControlBucketsGranted` and `historyControlInterval`. For example, using the default values, the monitor would take a sample once every 1,800 seconds (30 minutes); each sample is stored in a row of `etherHistoryTable`, and the most recent 50 rows are retained.

The `etherHistoryTable` includes the following objects:

- `etherHistoryIndex`: the history of which this entry is a part. The history identified by a particular value of this index is the same as that identified by the same value of `historyControlIndex`.

- `etherHistorySampleIndex`: an index that uniquely identifies the particular sample this entry represents among all samples associated with the same row of the `historyControlTable`. This index starts at 1 and increases by one as each new sample is taken.

- `etherHistoryIntervalStart`: This is the value of `sysUpTime` (in the MIB-II `systems` group) at the start of the interval over which this sample was measured.

In addition, the table contains counters corresponding to the counters in `etherStats-Table`. Finally, the table includes an `INTEGER` object, `etherHistoryUtilization`. Two of the counters, `etherStatsOctets` and `etherStatsPkts`, can be used to measure the utilization of the subnetwork. To calculate utilization, sample the two objects before and after a common interval, and define the differences in the sampled values as `Octets` and `Pkts`, respectively. Then, the following calculation can be used:

$$\text{Utilization} = \frac{(\text{Packets} \times (96 + 64)) + (\text{Octets} \times 8)}{\text{Interval} \times 10^7} \times 100\%.$$

This equation can be explained as follows. The data rate on the medium is 10^7 bps; hence the total number of bits that could be transmitted during the interval is (Interval $\times$ 10^7). The actual number of bits transmitted includes the count of octets times 8, plus, for each packet, a 64-bit preamble and a 96-bit interframe gap.

Figure 8.8 shows the relationship between the control table and the data table. Each row of `historyControlTable` has a unique value of `historyControlIndex`. No two rows have the same combination of values of `historyControlDataSource` and `history-ControlInterval`. This means that for any given subnetwork, more than one sampling process can be in effect, but each must have a different sampling period (control interval). For example, the specification recommends that there be at least two history control entries per monitored interface, one with a 30-second sampling period and one with a 30-minute sampling period. The shorter period enables the monitor to detect sudden changes in traffic patterns; the longer period enables the steady-state behavior of the interface to be monitored.

For each of the K rows of `historyControlTable`, there is a set of rows of `ether-History`. In the figure, the number of rows of `etherHistoryTable` associated with control table row i is B_i. These are the B_i most recent samples for control entry i. The maximum value of B_i is the corresponding value of `historyControlBucketsGranted`.

The sampling scheme works as follows. The monitor or a management station can define a new "history" that is unique in terms of the interface and the sampling interval. This control table row is assigned a unique index, starting at 1, by the monitor. Associated with each history (that is, each row of `historyControlTable`) is a set of rows of `etherHistoryTable`. Each row of `etherHistoryTable`, also called a *bucket,* holds the statistics gathered during one sampling interval. Thus, `etherHistoryPkts` is a counter equal to the number of packets (including error packets) received during the corresponding sampling interval. Equivalently, the value of `etherHistoryPkts` for a given row equals the value of `etherStatsPkts` at the end of that sampling interval minus the value of `etherStatsPkts` at the start of that sampling interval.

As each sampling interval occurs, the monitor adds a new row to `etherHistory-Table` with the same `etherHistoryIndex` as the other rows for this history and with an `etherHistorySampleIndex` of one more than the value for the row corresponding to the previous sampling interval. Once the number of rows for a history becomes equal to `historyControlBucketsGranted`, the set of rows for that history functions as a circular buffer. As each new row is added to the set, the oldest row associated with this history is deleted. Similarly, if the number of rows granted to a history is reduced, by a change in `historyControlBucketsRequested` and `historyControlBuckets-Granted`, rows are deleted for that history to match the new granted size. For example, in Figure 8.8, the x oldest entries of `etherHistoryTable` that have an `etherHistory-Index` of 1 have already been discarded, and the y oldest entries of `etherHistory-Table` that have an `etherHistoryIndex` of 2 have already been discarded.

8.4   host *Group*

The host group is used to gather statistics about specific hosts on the LAN. The monitor learns of new hosts on the LAN by observing the source and destination MAC addresses

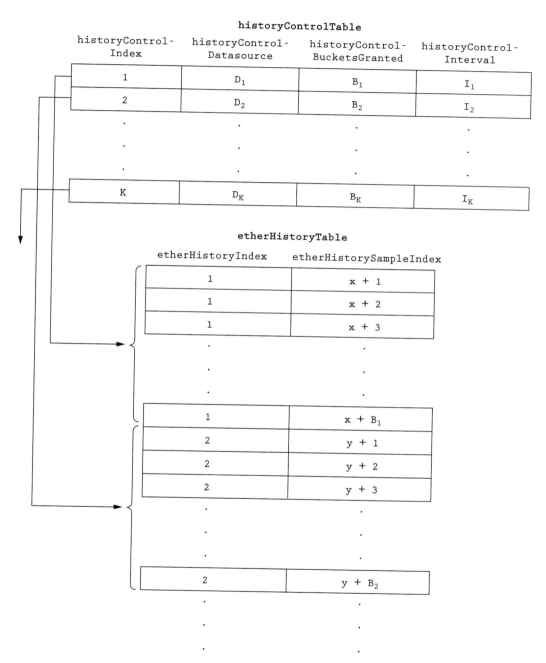

Note: Only selected fields in each table are shown.

FIGURE 8.8   An example of history tables

in good packets. For each host known to the monitor, a set of statistics is maintained. As usual, a control table determines for which interfaces (which subnetworks) this function is performed.

The host group consists of three tables: one control table and two data tables (Figure 8.9). The control table, hostControlTable, includes the following objects:

- hostControlIndex: an integer that uniquely identifies a row in the host-ControlTable. Each row in the control table refers to a unique interface of the monitor (unique subnetwork). The same integer is also used to identify corresponding rows in the hostTable and the hostTimeTable.
- hostControlDataSource: This identifies the interface and hence the subnetwork that is the source of the data for data-table entries defined by this row.
- hostControlTableSize: the number of rows in hostTable that are associated with this row. It is also the number of rows in hostTimeTable that are associated with this row. This is a read-only object set by the monitor.
- hostControlLastDeleteTime: the value of sysUpTime (in the MIB-II systems group) corresponding to the last time that an entry was deleted from the portion of the hostTable associated with this row. The value is zero if no deletions have occurred.

The relationship between hostControlTable and the data table, hostTable, is straightforward. For each interface specified by a row in hostcontrolTable, the hostTable contains one row for each MAC (medium access control) address discovered on that interface. Thus, the number of rows in the hostTable can be expressed as

$$N = \sum_{i=1}^{K} N_i,$$

where

N = number of rows in hostTable,
i = value of hostControlIndex,
K = number of rows in hostControlTable,
N_i = value of hostControlTableSize for row i of hostControlTable.

For example, Figure 8.10 shows an RMON probe with interfaces to two subnetworks ($K = 2$). Subnetwork X (interface #1; hostControlIndex = 1) has three hosts; therefore, once the monitor has learned of the existence of all three hosts, the corresponding value of hostControlTableSize will reach its maximum value of 3 ($N_1 = 3$). Subnetwork Y has two hosts ($N_2 = 2$).

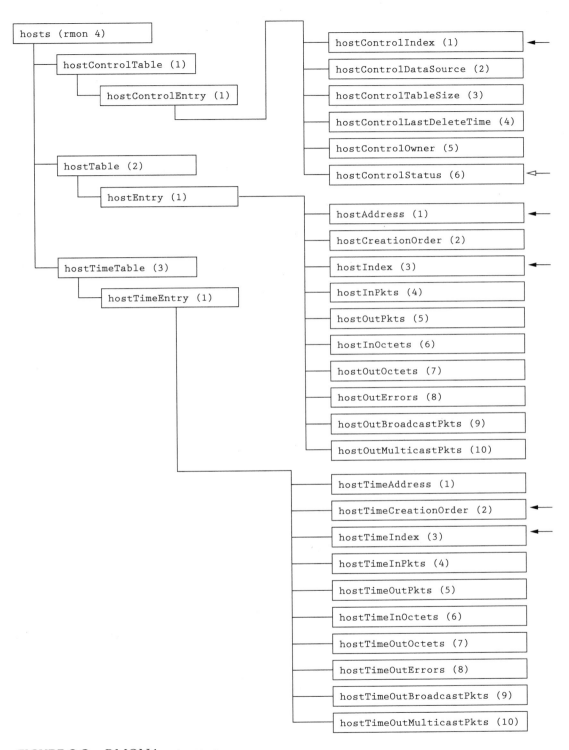

FIGURE 8.9 RMON host group

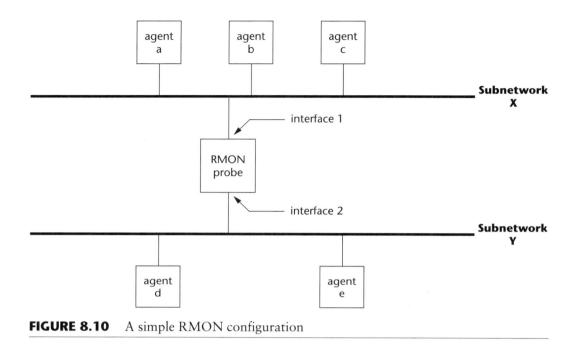

FIGURE 8.10   A simple RMON configuration

Each row of `hostTable` contains statistical data about the corresponding host. The table as a whole is indexed by the MAC address of the host as well as by the interface index. The table includes the following objects:

- `hostAddress`: This gives the MAC address of this host.

- `hostCreationOrder`: an index that defines the relative ordering of the creation time of hosts captured for a particular `hostControlEntry`. This index takes on a value between 1 and N_i, where N_i is the value of the associated `hostControlTableSize` (for row i of `hostControlTable`).

- `hostIndex`: the set of collected host statistics of which this entry is a part. The value of this object matches the value of `hostControlIndex` for one of the rows of `hostControlTable`. Thus, all entries in `hostTable` with the same value of `hostIndex` contain statistics for hosts on a single subnetwork.

As can be seen in Figure 8.9, the remaining objects in `hostTable` are used to collect basic statistics on traffic into and out of each discovered host (Table 8.3).

After a new row is defined in `hostControlTable`, the monitor begins to learn MAC addresses on the corresponding interface. Each time a new host is discovered on that interface, a row is added to `hostTable` and the value of `hostControlTableSize`

TABLE 8.3   Counters in `hostTable`

`hostInPkts`
  Number of good packets transmitted to this address
`hostOutPkts`
  Number of packets, including bad packets, transmitted by this address
`hostInOctets`
  Number of octets transmitted to this address, not including octets in bad packets
`hostOutOctets`
  Number of octets transmitted by this address, including octets in bad packets
`hostOutErrors`
  Number of bad packets transmitted by this address
`hostOutBroadcastPkts`
  Number of good broadcast packets transmitted by this address
`hostOutMulticastPkts`
  Number of good multicast packets transmitted by this address

is incremented by one. Ideally, the monitor should be able to maintain statistics on all hosts discovered on a subnetwork. However, if the monitor finds itself short of resources, it may delete entries as needed. In that case, the set of rows for that interface functions as a circular buffer. As each new row is added to the set, the oldest row associated with this interface is deleted. The value of `hostCreationOrder` for each of the existing rows for this interface is decremented by one, and the new row has a `hostCreationOrder` value of N_i. This change can potentially cause a problem to a management station if it is "remembering" a host on the basis of its `hostCreationOrder` number. Therefore, the specification recommends that management stations make use of `hostControlLast-DeleteTime` in the relevant row of `hostControlTable` to detect circumstances where a previous association between a value of `hostCreationOrder` and a specific row of `hostTable` is no longer valid.

The `hostTimeTable` contains the exact same information, row by row, as `hostTable` but is indexed by the creation order rather than by the host MAC address. This data table has two important uses.

1. The portion of `hostTimeTable` associated with a given interface is potentially quite large. The management station can exploit the fact that it knows the size of the table and the size of each row, to pack variables efficiently into SNMP `GetRequest` or `GetNextRequest` PDUs. Since each row has a unique index that runs from 1 to the table size, there is no confusion in having multiple packets outstanding.

2. The organization of `hostTimeTable` also supports efficient discovery by the management station of new entries for a particular interface, without having to download the entire table.

Figure 8.11 illustrates the relationship between the control table and the two data tables. Each row of `hostControlTable` has a unique value of `hostControlIndex` and a unique value of `hostControlDataSource`. For each of the *K* rows of `hostControl-Table`, there is a set of data rows. These data rows appear in both `hostTable` and `hostTimeTable`, but with a different ordering for each table: ordered by MAC address for `hostTable` and ordered by creation time for `hostTimeTable`.

The host group specification dictates that there are two logical views of the data: `hostTable` and `hostTimeTable`. This does not mean that the monitor must actually implement two separate tables with duplicate information. Depending on the database management system available at the monitor, it may be possible to store the information only once but provide two logical access methods to the data.

Finally, note that all of the information in this group is obtainable directly from each host via MIB-II information in the interfaces group. The reason for using this group instead is that it may not be cost effective to equip each host on the network with SNMP. Also, the monitor provides a single location of useful information in compact form.

8.5   `hostTopN` *Group*

The `hostTopN` group is used to maintain statistics about the set of hosts on one subnetwork that top a list based on some parameter. For example, a list could be maintained of the ten hosts that transmitted the most data during a particular day.

The statistics that are generated for this group are derived from data in the `host` group. The set of statistics for one `host` group object on one interface, or subnetwork, collected during one sampling interval is referred to as a *report*. Each report contains the results for only one variable, and that variable represents the amount of change in a host group object over the sampling interval. Thus, the report lists the hosts on a particular subnetwork with the greatest rate of change in a particular variable.

The `hostTopN` group consists of one control table and one data table (Figure 8.12). The `hostTopNControlTable` includes the following fields:

- `hostTopNControlIndex`: an integer that uniquely identifies a row in the `host-TopNControlTable`. Each row in the control table defines one top-N report prepared for one interface.

- `hostTopNHostIndex`: This value matches a value of `hostControlIndex` and `hostIndex` (Figure 8.9). Therefore, this value specifies a particular subnetwork. The top-N report defined by this row of the control table is prepared using the corresponding entries in `hostTable`.

- `hostTopNRateBase`: specifies one of seven variables from `hostTable` (Figure 8.9); the specified variable is the basis for the `hostTopNRate` variable in the row of

hostControlTable

hostControlIndex	hostControlDataSource	hostControlTableSize
1	D_1	N_1
2	D_2	N_2
.	.	.
.	.	.
.	.	.
K	D_K	N_K

hostTable

host-Address	host-CreationOrder	host-Index
$M(1,1)$	$C(1,1)$	1
$M(1,2)$	$C(1,2)$	1
$M(1,3)$	$C(1,3)$	1
.	.	.
.	.	.
$M(1,N_1)$	$C(1,N_1)$	1
$M(2,1)$	$C(2,1)$	2
$M(2,2)$	$C(2,2)$	2
$M(2,3)$	$C(2,3)$	2
.	.	.
.	.	.
$M(2,N_2)$	$C(2,N_2)$	2
.	.	.
.	.	.

hostTimeTable

hostTime-Address	hostTime-CreationOrder	hostTime-Index
$MT(1,1)$	1	1
$MT(1,2)$	2	1
$MT(1,3)$	3	1
.	.	.
.	.	.
$MT(1,N_1)$	N_1	1
$MT(2,1)$	1	2
$MT(2,2)$	2	2
$MT(2,3)$	3	2
.	.	.
.	.	.
$MT(2,N_2)$	N_2	2
.	.	.
.	.	.

$M(i,j) < M(i,j + 1)$
$C(i,j)$ for $j = 1$, Ni = permutation
on integers from 1 to Ni

$MT(i,j)$ for $j = 1$, Ni = permutation
on $M(i,j)$ for $j = 1, Ni$

Note: Only selected fields in each table are shown.

FIGURE 8.11 An example of host tables

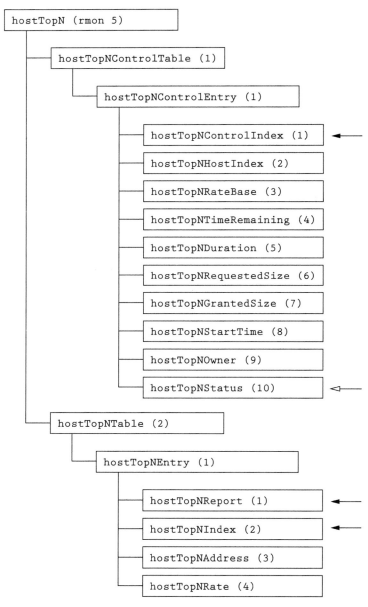

FIGURE 8.12 RMON hostTopN group

hostTopNTable defined by this control row. The type of this object is the following:

```
INTEGER { hostTopNInPkts (1),
          hostTopNOutPkts (2),
          hostTopNInOctets (3),
          hostTopNOutOctets (4),
          hostTopNOutErrors (5),
          hostTopNOutBroadcastPkts (6),
          hostTopNOutMulticastPkts (7) }
```

For example, if the value of this object is hostTopNInPkts, then the corresponding variable for which statistics are collected is hostInPkts from hostTable.

- hostTopNTimeRemaining: This tells the number of seconds left in the sampling interval for the report currently being collected.

- hostTopNDuration: This is the sampling interval, in seconds, for this report.

- hostTopNRequestedSize: This gives the maximum number of hosts requested for the top-N table for this report.

- hostTopNGrantedSize: This indicates the maximum number of hosts in the top-N table for this report.

- hostTopNStartTime: The value of sysUpTime (in the MIB-II systems group) when this top-N report was last started. In other words, this is the time when the associated hostTopNTimeRemaining object was modified to start the requested report, as explained later in this subsection.

The hostTopNTable includes the following objects:

- hostTopNReport: the report of which this entry is a part. The report identified by a particular value of this index is the same report as that identified by the same value of hostTopNControlIndex.

- hostTopNIndex: an index that uniquely identifies one row among all data rows associated with this report. Each row represents a unique host.

- hostTopNAddress: This gives the MAC address of this host.

- hostTopNRate: the amount of change in the selected variable during this sampling interval. The selected variable is specified by the value of hostTopNRateBase for this report.

The report preparation process works as follows. To begin, a management station creates a row of the control table to specify a new report. This control entry instructs the monitor to measure the difference between the beginning and ending values of a particular host group variable over a specified sampling period. The sampling period value is stored in both `hostTopNDuration` and `hostTopNTimeRemaining`. The first value is static; the second value counts the seconds down while the monitor is preparing the report. When `hostTopNTimeRemaining` reaches 0, the monitor calculates the final results and creates a set of N data rows, indexed by `hostTopNIndex`, with the top N hosts listed in decreasing order of the calculated rates.

Once the report is created, it remains as a set of read-only data rows available to the management station. If the management station wishes to generate an additional report for a new time period, it first gets the results of this report and then resets `hostTopN-TimeRemaining` to the value in `hostTopNDuration`. This causes the associated data rows to be deleted and a new report to be prepared.

Figure 8.13 illustrates the relationship between the control table and the data table. Each row of `hostTopNControlTable` has a unique value of `hostTopNControlIndex`. The value of `hostTopNHostIndex` references the relevant row of `hostControlTable` in the control group. The value of `hostTopNRateBase` identifies the host group variable to be sampled, and `hostTopNGrantedSize` indicates how many hosts are to be included in the ranking. For each of the K rows of `hostTopNControlTable`, there is a set of rows of `hostTopNTable`. Each row in the set of rows gives the MAC address and rate for that host on the subnetwork specified by `hostTopNHostIndex`.

8.6   `matrix` *Group*

The `matrix` group is used to record information about the traffic between pairs of hosts on a subnetwork. The information is stored in the form of a matrix. This method of organization is useful for retrieving specific pairwise traffic information, such as finding out which devices are making the most use of a server.

The `matrix` group consists of three tables: one control table and two data tables (Figure 8.14). The control table, `matrixControlTable`, includes the following objects:

- `matrixControlIndex`: an integer that uniquely identifies a row in the `matrixControlTable`. Each row in the control table defines a function that discovers conversations on a particular interface and places statistics about them in the two data tables.

- `matrixControlDataSource`: This identifies the interface and hence the subnetwork that is the source of the data in this row.

- `matrixControlTableSize`: the number of rows in the `matrixSDTable` that are associated with this row. It is also the number of rows in the `matrixDSTable` that are associated with this row. This is a read-only object set by the monitor.

- `matrixControlLastDeleteTime`: the value of `sysUpTime` (in the MIB-II `systems` group) corresponding to the last time that an entry was deleted from the portion of the `matrixSDTable` and the portion of the `matrixDSTable` associated with this row. The value is zero if no deletions have occurred.

hostTopNControl-Index	hostTopNHost-Index	hostTopNRate-Base	hostTopNGranted-Size
1	H_1	V_1	N_1
2	H_2	V_2	N_2
.	.	.	.
.	.	.	.
.	.	.	.
K	H_K	V_K	N_K

hostTopNTable

hostTopNReport	hostTopNIndex	hostTopNAddress	hostTopNRate
1	1	$M(1,1)$	$V_1(1)$
1	2	$M(1,2)$	$V_1(2)$
1	3	$M(1,3)$	$V_1(3)$
.	.	.	.
.	.	.	.
.	.	.	.
1	N_1	$M(1,N_1)$	$V_1(N_1)$
2	1	$M(2,1)$	$V_2(1)$
2	2	$M(2,2)$	$V_2(2)$
2	3	$M(2,3)$	$V_2(3)$
.	.	.	.
.	.	.	.
.	.	.	.
2	N_2	$M(2,N_2)$	$V_2(N_2)$
.	.	.	.
.	.	.	.
.	.	.	.

$$V_i(j) > V_i(j + 1)$$

Note: Only selected fields in the control table are shown.

FIGURE 8.13 An example of hostTopN tables

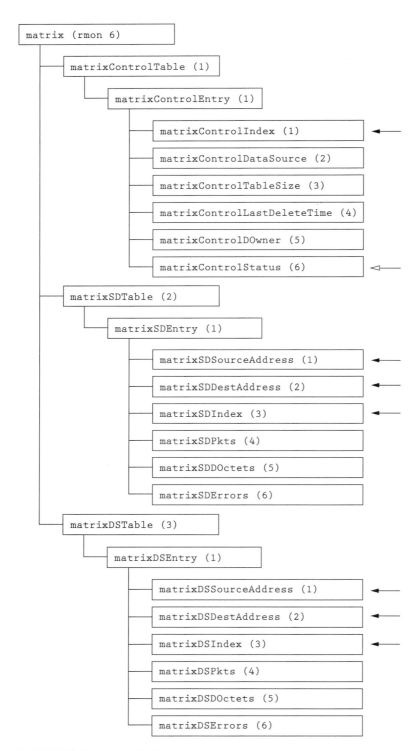

FIGURE 8.14 RMON matrix group

The `matrixSDTable` is used to store statistics on traffic from a particular source host to a number of destinations. The table includes the following objects:

- `matrixSDSourceAddress`: the source MAC address
- `matrixSDDestAddress`: the destination MAC address
- `matrixSDIndex`: the set of collected matrix statistics of which this row is a part (The set identified by a particular value of this index is the same as that identified by the same value of `matrixControlIndex`.)
- `matrixSDPkts`: number of packets transmitted from this source address to this destination address, including bad packets
- `matrixSDOctets`: number of octets contained in all packets transmitted from this source address to this destination address
- `matrixSDErrors`: number of bad packets transmitted from this source address to this destination address

The `matrixSDTable` is indexed first by `matrixSDIndex`, then by source address, and then by destination address. The `matrixDSTable` contains the same information as `matrixSDTable` but is indexed first by `matrixDSIndex`, then by destination address, and then by source address. The interpretation is as follows: Each row of the `matrix-ControlTable` identifies a single subnetwork. The `matrixSDTable` contains two rows for every pair of hosts on that subnetwork that have recently exchanged information: One of the rows reports the traffic in one direction between the two members of the pair; the other row reports the traffic in the opposite direction. The same set of rows also appears in `matrixDSTable`. Thus, the management station can easily index the information to find out about the traffic from one host to all others (use `matrixSDTable`) or about traffic from all hosts to one particular host (use `matrixDSTable`). Figure 8.15 depicts the logical matrix structure that results.

Whenever the monitor detects a new conversation that involves a new host pairing, it creates two new rows in both of the data tables. If the limit specified in `matrixControl-TableSize` is reached, then the monitor deletes rows as required. The specification suggests that the monitor delete the least recently used entries first.

Finally, note that, as with the `host` group, the two data tables in the `matrix` group contain the same information organized in two different ways. It is permissible to implement this as a single table or as two tables, so long as the logical view presented to the management station is of two data tables.

8.7 `tokenRing` *Extensions to RMON*

RFC 1513 defines extensions to the RMON MIB for managing 802.5 token ring networks.[3] Most of the object groups in RMON are relevant to all types of subnetworks.

---

[3]See Stallings (1996a) for a description of token ring LANs and the token ring MAC protocol.

Destination address

R = row in both `matrixSDTable` and `matrixDSTable` M(*i,j*) < M(*i,j* + 1)

FIGURE 8.15   Logical view of the `matrixSDTable` rows and the `matrixDSTable` rows associated with row *i* of the `matrixControlTable`

However, the detailed counter objects in the `statistics` group and the `history` group are media-specific. RMON itself defines media-specific objects for Ethernet subnetworks, whereas RFC 1513 defines new tables of objects within these groups for token ring subnetworks.

In addition, RFC 1513 defines some additional monitoring functions specifically for token ring subnetworks; these are defined in four new groups that are under the `token-Ring` group of the RMON MIB.

8.7.1   Extensions to Existing RMON Groups

RFC 1513 adds new tables to the `statistics` group and to the `history` group.

8.7.1.1   `statistics` Group

Statistics specific to token ring subnetworks are broken down into two tables: the Token Ring Mac-Layer Statistics Table (`tokenRingMLStatsTable`) and the Token Ring Promiscuous Statistics Table (`tokenRingPStatsTable`).

Unlike the Ethernet/802.3 CSMA/CD protocol, which involves transmission solely of MAC-level data packets, the token ring MAC protocol includes a variety of control packets to manage the token ring. The `tokenRingMLStatsTable` includes counts of these various MAC-level control packets, including error reports. Table 8.4 lists the counters in this table.

The `tokenRingPStatsTable` includes statistics on data packets collected promiscuously (Table 8.5). That is, the monitor reads all packets regardless of destination

TABLE 8.4   Counters in `tokenRingMLStatsTable`

`tokenRingMLStatsDropEvents`
　Number of events in which packets were dropped by the monitor due to lack of resources. This is not necessarily the actual count of packets dropped, but the number of times this condition has been detected.

`tokenRingMLStatsMacOctets`
　Number of octets of data in good MAC packets.

`tokenRingMLStatsMacPkts`
　Number of MAC packets received.

`tokenRingMLStatsRingPurgeEvents`
　Number of times ring enters ring purge state from normal ring state.

`tokenRingMLStatsRingPurgePkts`
　Number of ring purge packets detected.

`tokenRingMLStatsBeaconEvents`
　Number of times ring enters beaconing state from a nonbeaconing state.

`tokenRingMLStatsBeaconPkts`
　Number of beacon packets detected.

`tokenRingMLStatsClaimTokenEvents`
　Number of times ring enters claim token state from normal or purge state.

`tokenRingMLStatsClaimTokenPkts`
　Number of claim token packets detected.

`tokenRingMLStatsNAUNChanges`
　Number of NAUN changes detected.

`tokenRingMLStatsLineErrors`
　Number of line errors reported in error-reporting packets.

`tokenRingMLStatsInternalErrors`
　Number of adapter internal errors reported in error-reporting packets.

`tokenRingMLStatsBurstErrors`
　Number of burst internal errors reported in error-reporting packets.

`tokenRingMLStatsACErrors`
　Number of address-copied (AC) errors reported in error-reporting packets.

`tokenRingMLStatsAbortErrors`
　Number of abort delimiters reported in error-reporting packets.

`tokenRingMLStatsLostFrameErrors`
　Number of lost frame errors reported in error-reporting packets.

`tokenRingMLStatsPktsCongestionErrors`
　Number of receive congestion errors reported in error-reporting packets.

`tokenRingMLStatsFrameCopiedErrors`
　Number of frame-copied errors reported in error-reporting packets.

`tokenRingMLStatsFrequencyErrors`
　Number of frequency errors reported in error-reporting packets.

`tokenRingMLStatsTokenErrors`
　Number of token errors reported in error-reporting packets.

`tokenRingMLStatsSoftErrorReports`
　Number of soft error report frames.

`tokenRingMLStatsRingPollEvents`
　Number of ring poll events (i.e., the number of ring polls initiated by the active monitor that were detected).

address and accumulates statistics accordingly. This is the same technique as that used in the `etherStatsTable`.

8.7.1.2   `history` **Group**
RFC 1513 defines two new history tables, both of which are controlled by the RMON `historyControlTable` (Figure 8.7). The discussion in Section 8.3 concerning the way in which data tables are controlled by the `historyControlTable` applies. As before,

TABLE 8.5   Counters in `tokenRingPStatsTable`

`tokenRingPStatsDataOctets`
   Number of octets of data in good MAC data packets
`tokenRingPStatsDataPkts`
   Number of good data packets
`tokenRingPStatsDataBroadcastPkts`
   Number of good broadcast data packets
`tokenRingPStatsDataMulticastPkts`
   Number of good multicast data packets
`tokenRingPStatsDataPkts18to63Octets`
   Number of good data packets between 18 and 63 octets in length
`tokenRingPStatsDataPkts64to127Octets`
   Number of good data packets between 64 and 127 octets in length
`tokenRingPStatsDataPkts128to255Octets`
   Number of good data packets between 128 and 255 octets in length
`tokenRingPStatsDataPkts256to511Octets`
   Number of good data packets between 256 and 511 octets in length
`tokenRingPStatsDataPkts512to1023Octets`
   Number of good data packets between 512 and 1,023 octets in length
`tokenRingPStatsDataPkts1024to2047Octets`
   Number of good data packets between 1,024 and 2,047 octets in length
`tokenRingPStatsDataPkts2048to4095Octets`
   Number of good data packets between 2,048 and 4,095 octets in length
`tokenRingPStatsDataPkts4096to8191Octets`
   Number of good data packets between 4,096 and 8,191 octets in length
`tokenRingPStatsDataPkts8192to18000Octets`
   Number of good data packets between 8,192 and 18,000 octets in length
`tokenRingPStatsDataPktsGreaterThan18000Octets`
   Number of good data packets greater than 18,000 octets in length

each unique value of `historyControlIndex` identifies a set of rows in a history data table.

The Token Ring Mac-Layer History Table (`tokenRingMLHistoryTable`) collects information on the counter objects defined in `tokenRingMLStatsTable`. The Token Ring Promiscuous History Table (`tokenRingPHistoryTable`) collects information on the counter objects defined in `tokenRingPStatsTable`.

8.7.2   The Token Ring Group

RFC 1513 adds a new group to the RMON MIB, the `tokenRing` group. Beneath this group are four subordinate groups:

- Token Ring Ring Station Group

- Token Ring Ring Station Order Group
- Token Ring Ring Station Configuration Group
- Token Ring Ring Source Routing Group

8.7.2.1   Token Ring Ring Station Group

The Token Ring Ring Station group contains statistics and status information associated with each token ring station on the local ring. In addition, this group provides status information for each ring being monitored. The group consists of two tables: the ring-StationControlTable and the ringStationTable.

The ringStationControlTable contains a list of parameters related to the discovery of stations on a particular interface and the construction of a logical ring of those stations. The table contains one entry per subnetwork and includes the following objects:

- ringStationControlTableSize: the number of entries in the ringStation-Table associated with this interface (This is the number of stations currently monitored on this interface.)

- ringStationControlActiveStations: the number of active stations monitored on this interface

- ringStationControlRingState: has the value normalOperation(1), ring-PurgeState(2), claimTokenState(3), beaconFrameStreamingState(4), beaconBitStreamingState(5), beaconRingSignalLossState(6), beacon-SetRecoveryModeState(7)

- ringStationControlBeaconSender: the MAC address of the sender of the last beacon frame

- ringStationControlBeaconNAUN: the MAC address of the NAUN in the last beacon frame

- ringStationControlActiveMonitor: the MAC address of the active monitor on this subnetwork

- ringStationControlOrderChanges: the number of add and delete events in the ringStationOrderTable associated with this interface

The ringStationTable contains one row for each station that is now or has previously been detected as being physically present on a given subnetwork. The table collects statistics for each station, using counters that are essentially the same as those for the tokenRingMLStatsTable. The table also includes the following objects for each station:

- ringStationMacAddress: the MAC address of this station

- ringStationLastNAUN: the MAC address of the last known NAUN of this station

- ringStationStationStatus: indicates whether station is actively participating in logical ring

- `ringStationLastEnterTime`: the value of `sysUpTime` at the time this station last entered the logical ring
- `ringStationLastExitTime`: the value of `sysUpTime` at the time the monitor detected that this station last exited the logical ring

8.7.2.2   Token Ring Ring Station Order Group
The Token Ring Ring Station Order group provides the order of the stations on monitored rings. The group contains a single table, the `ringStationOrderTable`, with one entry for each station on each token ring subnetwork. The table consists of the following objects:

- `ringStationOrderIfIndex`: identifies the subnetwork for this entry
- `ringStationOrderOrderIndex`: denotes the location of this station on this ring with respect to other stations on the ring (This index is one more than the number of hops downstream to this station from the RMON monitor station.)
- `ringStationOrderMacAddress`: the MAC address of this station

8.7.2.3   Token Ring Ring Station Configuration Group
The Token Ring Ring Station Configuration group manages token ring stations through active means. Any station on a monitored ring may be removed or have configuration information downloaded from it. The group contains two tables: a control table (`ringStationConfigControlTable`) and a data table (`ringStationConfigTable`).

The `ringStationConfigControlTable` contains one entry for each active station in the `ringStationConfigTable`. This table consists of the following columnar objects:

- `ringStationConfigControlIfIndex`: identifies the subnetwork
- `ringStationConfigControlMacAddress`: the MAC address of the station controlled by this entry
- `ringStationConfigControlRemove`: has two possible values: `stable(1)` and `removing(2)` (Setting this object to 2 causes a Remove Station MAC frame to be sent.)
- `ringStationConfigControlUpdateStatus`: Set to `updating(2)` causes the configuration information associated with this entry to be updated

The corresponding data table, `ringStationConfigTable`, contains one entry per managed station, with the following objects:

- `ringStationConfigMacAddress`: the MAC address of this station
- `ringStationConfigUpdateTime`: the value of `sysUpTime` at the time this configuration information was last updated
- `ringStationConfigLocation`: assigned physical location of this location

TABLE 8.6   Counters in `sourceRoutingStatsTable`

`sourceRoutingStatsInFrames`
  Number of frames sent into this ring from another ring

`sourceRoutingStatsOutFrames`
  Number of frames sent from this ring to another ring

`sourceRoutingStatsThroughFrames`
  Number of frames sent from another ring, through this ring, to another ring

`sourceRoutingStatsAllRoutesBroadcast-Frames`
  Number of good frames received that were `AllRoutesBroadcast`

`sourceRoutingStatsSingleRoutesBroadcastFrames`
  Number of good frames received that were `SingleRoutesBroadcast`

`sourceRoutingStatsInOctets`
  Number of octets in good frames sent into this ring from another ring

`sourceRoutingStatsOutOctets`
  Number of octets in good frames sent from this ring to another ring

`sourceRoutingStatsThroughOctets`
  Number of octets in good frames sent from another ring, through this ring, to another ring

`sourceRoutingStatsAllRoutesBroadcast-Octets`
  Number of octets in good frames received that were `AllRoutesBroadcast`

`sourceRoutingStatsSingleRoutesBroadcastOctets`
  Number of octets in good frames received that were `SingleRoutesBroadcast`

`sourceRoutingStatsLocalLLCFrames`
  Number of frames received with no RIF (`RoutingInformationField`) and were not `AllRouteBroadcast` frames

`sourceRoutingStats1HopFrames`
  Number of frames received whose route had one hop, were not `AllRouteBroadcast` frames, and whose source or destination were on this ring (this ring number in the first or last entry of the RIF field)

`sourceRoutingStats2HopsFrames`
  Number of frames received whose route had two hops, were not `AllRouteBroadcast` frames, and whose source or destination were on this ring

`sourceRoutingStats3HopsFrames`
  Number of frames received whose route had three hops, were not `AllRouteBroadcast` frames, and whose source or destination were on this ring

`sourceRoutingStats4HopsFrames`
  Number of frames received whose route had four hops, were not `AllRouteBroadcast` frames, and whose source or destination were on this ring

`sourceRoutingStats5HopsFrames`
  Number of frames received whose route had five hops, were not `AllRouteBroadcast` frames, and whose source or destination were on this ring

`sourceRoutingStats6HopsFrames`
  Number of frames received whose route had six hops, were not `AllRouteBroadcast` frames, and whose source or destination were on this ring

`sourceRoutingStats7HopsFrames`
  Number of frames received whose route had seven hops, were not `AllRouteBroadcast` frames, and whose source or destination were on this ring

`sourceRoutingStats8HopsFrames`
  Number of frames received whose route had eight hops, were not `AllRouteBroadcast` frames, and whose source or destination were on this ring

`sourceRoutingStatsMoreThan8HopsFrames`
  Number of frames received whose route had more than eight hops, were not `AllRouteBroadcast` frames, and whose source or destination were on this ring

- `ringStationConfigMicrocode`: microcode version in this station
- `ringStationConfigGroupAddress`: low-order four octets of the group address recognized by this station
- `ringStationConfigFunctionalAddress`: functional addresses recognized by this station

8.7.2.4   Token Ring Ring Source Routing Group

The Token Ring Ring Source Routing group contains utilization statistics derived from source routing information optionally present in token ring packets. The group consists of a single table, `sourceRoutingStatsTable`, with one entry per interface. Table 8.6 on the previous page lists the counters in the table.

8.8   *Summary*

An important addition to the SNMP framework is the RMON (remote monitoring) MIB. RMON defines a set of managed objects that are useful for supporting the remote monitoring function. In addition, the specification of the RMON MIB has the effect of defining a set of functions for remote monitoring. The strength of the RMON approach is that it is compliant with the current SNMP framework; it requires no enhancements to the protocol.

In the context of the RMON MIB, the term "remote monitoring" refers to the use of an agent device connected to a broadcast network to collect statistics concerning traffic on that network. Typically, an agent is responsible only for management information that relates to the agent's device. Without a remote monitoring function, it is difficult—if not impossible—for a manager to construct a profile of the activity on an individual subnetwork as a whole.

APPENDIX 8A   EntryStatus *TEXTUAL CONVENTION (FROM RFC 1757)*

```
EntryStatus ::= INTEGER
        { valid(1),
        createRequest(2),
        underCreation(3),
        invalid(4)
        }
```

"The status of a table entry.

Setting this object to the value `invalid(4)` invalidates the corresponding entry. That is, it effectively disassociates the mapping identified with said entry. It is an implementation-specific matter as to whether the agent removes an invalidated entry from the table.

Accordingly, management stations must be prepared to receive tabular information from agents that corresponds to entries currently not in use. Proper interpretation of such entries requires examination of the relevant `EntryStatus` object.

An existing instance of this object cannot be set to `createRequest(2)`. This object may only be set to `createRequest(2)` when this instance is created. When this object is created, the agent may wish to create supplemental object instances with default values to complete a conceptual row in this table. Because the creation of these default objects is entirely at the option of the agent, the manager must not assume that any will be created but may make use of any that are created. Immediately after completing the create operation, the agent must set this object to `underCreation(3)`.

When in the `underCreation(3)` state, an entry is allowed to exist in a possibly incomplete, possibly inconsistent state, usually to allow it to be modified in multiple PDUs. When in this state, an entry is not fully active. Entries shall exist in the `underCreation(3)` state until the management station is finished configuring the entry and sets this object to `valid(1)` or aborts, setting this object to `invalid(4)`. If the agent determines that an entry has been in the `underCreation(3)` state for an abnormally long time, it may decide that the management station has crashed. If the agent makes this decision, it may set this object to `invalid(4)` to reclaim the entry. A prudent agent will understand that the management station may need to wait for human input and will allow for that possibility in its determination of this abnormally long period.

An entry in the `valid(1)` state is fully configured and consistent and fully represents the configuration or operation such a row is intended to represent. For example, it could be a statistical function that is configured and active, or a filter that is available in the list of filters processed by the packet capture process.

A manager is restricted to changing the state of an entry in the following ways:

From To	valid	createRequest	underCreation	invalid
valid	OK	NO	OK	OK
createRequest	N/A	N/A	N/A	N/A
underCreation	OK	NO	OK	OK
invalid	NO	NO	NO	OK
nonExistent	NO	OK	NO	OK

In the preceding table, it is not applicable to move the state from the create-Request state to any other state, because the manager will never find the variable in that state. The nonExistent state is not a value of the enumeration; rather, it means that the EntryStatus variable does not exist at all.

An agent may allow an EntryStatus variable to change state in additional ways, so long as the semantics of the states are followed. This allowance is made to ease the implementation of the agent and is made despite the fact that managers should never exercise these additional state transitions."

Remote Network Monitoring

Alarms and Filters

Chapter 8 describes the groups within RMON that are primarily concerned with the collection of traffic statistics. This chapter looks at the remainder of the RMON groups, which deal with alarms and the filtering and capturing of packets. Four groups are discussed:

- `alarm` group
- `filter` group
- Packet `capture` group
- `event` group

9.1 `alarm` *Group*

The `alarm` group is used to define a set of thresholds for network performance. If a threshold is crossed in the appropriate direction, an alarm is generated and sent to the central console. For example, an alarm could be generated if there are more than 500 CRC errors (the threshold) in any 5-minute period (the sampling interval).

The `alarm` group consists of a single table, `alarmTable` (Figure 9.1). Each entry in the table specifies a particular variable to be monitored, a sampling interval, and threshold parameters. The single entry in the table for that variable using that interval contains the most recent sampled value, that is, the value observed at the end of the last sampling interval. When the current sampling interval is completed, the new value for the sampled variable will be stored and the old value is lost.

The `alarmTable` includes the following objects:

- `alarmIndex`: an integer that uniquely identifies a row in the `alarmTable`. Each such row specifies a sample at a particular interval for a particular object in the monitor's MIB.

- `alarmInterval`: This is the interval in seconds over which the data are sampled and compared with the rising and falling thresholds.

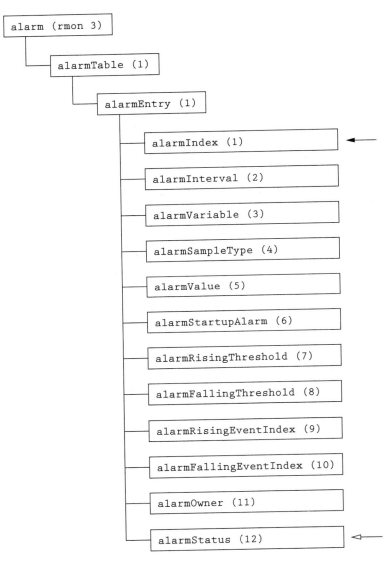

FIGURE 9.1 RMON alarm group

- `alarmVariable`: the object identifier of the particular variable in the RMON MIB to be sampled. The only object types allowed are `INTEGER`, `counter`, `gauge`, and `TimeTicks`. These are the only object types that resolve to ASN.1 type `INTEGER`.
- `alarmSampleType`: the method of calculating the value to be compared to the thresholds. If the value of this object is `absoluteValue(1)`, then the value of the selected variable will be compared directly with the thresholds. If the value of this object is `deltaValue(2)`, then the value of the selected variable at the last sample is subtracted from the current value, and the difference is compared to the thresholds.
- `alarmValue`: This gives the value of the statistic during the last sampling period.
- `alarmStartupAlarm`: has the value `risingAlarm(1)`, `fallingAlarm(2)`, or `risingOrFallingAlarm(3)`. This dictates whether an alarm will be generated if the first sample after the row becomes valid is greater than or equal to the `rising-Threshold`, less than or equal to the `fallingThreshold`, or both, respectively.
- `alarmRisingThreshold`: This is the rising threshold for the sampled statistic.
- `alarmFallingThreshold`: This is the falling threshold for the sampled statistic.
- `alarmRisingEventIndex`: the index of the `eventEntry` that is used when the rising threshold is crossed. The `eventTable` is part of the `event` group and is discussed later in this chapter.
- `alarmFallingEventIndex`: This is the index of the `eventEntry` that is used when the falling threshold is crossed.

The alarm scheme works as follows. The monitor or a management station can define a new alarm by creating a new row in the `alarmTable`. The combination of variable, sampling interval, and threshold parameters is unique to a given row. Two thresholds are provided: a rising threshold and a falling threshold. The rising threshold is crossed if the current sampled value is greater than or equal to the rising threshold and the value at the last sampling interval was less than the threshold. Similarly, a falling threshold is crossed if the current sampled value is less than or equal to the falling threshold and the value at the last sampling interval was greater than the threshold.

Two types of values are calculated for alarms. An `absoluteValue` is simply the value of an object at the time of sampling, whereas a `deltaValue` represents the difference in values for the object over two successive sampling periods. Thus, this latter value is concerned with a rate of change. Note that a counter, sampled as an `absoluteValue`, can never cross the falling threshold and will cross the rising threshold at most once. Both a counter sampled as a `deltaValue` and a gauge can cross both rising and falling thresholds any number of times.

The `alarm` group defines a mechanism designed to prevent relatively minor alarms from being generated repeatedly. The rules for the generation of rising-alarm events are as follows.

1. (a) If the first sampled value obtained after the row becomes valid is less than the rising threshold, then a rising-alarm event is generated the first time that the sample value becomes greater than or equal to the rising threshold.
   (b) If the first sampled value obtained after the row becomes valid is greater than or equal to the rising threshold, and if the value of alarmStartupAlarm is risingAlarm(1) or risingOrFallingAlarm(3), then a rising-alarm event is generated.
   (c) If the first sampled value obtained after the row becomes valid is greater than or equal to the rising threshold, and if the value of alarmStartupAlarm is FallingAlarm(2), then a rising-alarm event is generated the first time that the sample value again becomes greater than or equal to the rising threshold after having fallen below the rising threshold.
2. After a rising-alarm event is generated, another such event will not be generated until the sampled value has fallen below the rising threshold, reached the falling threshold, and then subsequently reached the rising threshold again.

The rules for the generation of falling-alarm events are the reverse of those just listed.

Figure 9.2 illustrates the alarm mechanism. The example is for an alarm with an alarmStartupAlarm value of risingAlarm or risingOrFallingAlarm. In this example, the first sampling produces a value that exceeds the rising threshold, and a rising-

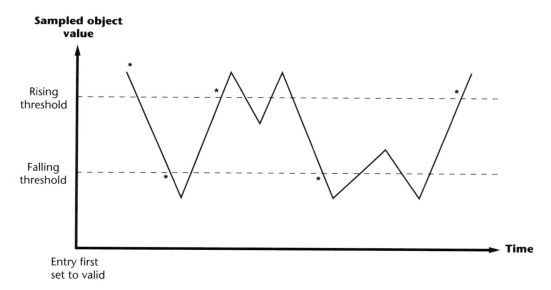

* = alarm event generated

FIGURE 9.2   Generation of alarm events

alarm event is generated. Subsequently, the falling threshold and then the rising threshold are crossed, generating two alarm events. Then the fluctuations in the value produce another crossing of the rising threshold; this crossing is not counted as an alarm event since it does not satisfy the rules spelled out in the preceding list. If these rules were not in force, a value that fluctuated around a threshold could generate many alarms, burdening the monitor.

The mechanism by which small fluctuations are prevented from causing alarms is referred to in the RMON specification as a *hysteresis mechanism*. The term refers to a phenomenon known as relay hysteresis and can be appreciated with the aid of Figure 9.3. We can think of the alarm-generation mechanism as having two states. While in the rising-alarm state, the mechanism will generate a rising alarm when the value of the observed variable reaches or exceeds the rising threshold; while in that state, the mechanism is disabled from generating a falling alarm. Once the rising alarm is generated, the mechanism is in a falling-alarm state and will remain so until the observed variable reaches or falls below the falling threshold. Similarly, while in the falling-alarm state, the mechanism will generate a falling alarm when the value of the observed variable reaches or falls below the falling-alarm threshold; while in that state, the mechanism is disabled from generating a rising alarm.

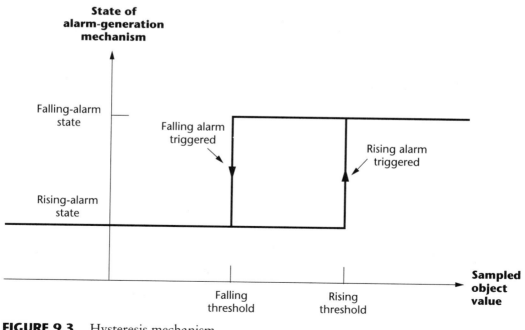

FIGURE 9.3   Hysteresis mechanism

One final point of interest. The specification recommends that a variable of type `deltaValue` be sampled with greater precision than indicated by `alarmInterval`: The delta sample should be taken twice per period, each time comparing the sum of the latest two samples to the threshold. This allows the detection of threshold crossings that span the sampling boundary. It would appear that a similar mechanism would be desirable for gauge variables sampled by `absoluteValue`; however, this is not mentioned in the specification.

To appreciate the significance of the double-sampling rule, consider the following sequence of counter values, observed at 10-second intervals:

Time (t)	0	10	20
Observed value	0	19	32
Delta value	0	19	13

If the rising threshold is 20, then no alarm is triggered. Now let us observe the same variable at 5-second intervals:

Time (t)	0	5	10	15	20
Observed value	0	10	19	30	32
Delta value	0	10	9	11	2

At $t = 15$, the sum of the last two delta samples is 20, which meets the rising-alarm threshold and triggers a rising-alarm event.

9.2 `filter` *Group*

The `filter` group provides a means by which a management station can instruct a monitor to observe selected packets on a particular interface (therefore a particular subnetwork). The basic building blocks defined in this group are two kinds of filters: a data filter and a status filter. The *data filter* allows the monitor to screen observed packets on the basis of a bit pattern that a portion of the packet matches (or fails to match); the *status filter* allows the monitor to screen observed packets on the basis of their status (for example, valid, CRC error, etc.). These filters can be combined using logical AND and OR operations to form a complex test to be applied to incoming packets. The stream of packets that pass the test is referred to as a *channel*, and a count of such packets is maintained. In addition, the channel can be configured to generate an event, defined in the `event` group (see Section 9.4), when a packet passes through the channel and the channel is in an enabled state. Finally, the packets passing through a channel can be captured if the mechanism is defined in the `capture` group (see Section 9.3). The logic defined for a single channel is quite complex. This gives the user enormous flexibility in defining the stream of packets to be counted.

Before examining the structure of the filter group, it is best to present the details of the filter logic and the channel logic.[1]

9.2.1   Filter Logic

At the lowest level of the filter logic, a single data filter or status filter defines characteristics of a packet. To begin, let us consider the logic for defining characteristics of a packet, using the following variables:

input	= the incoming portion of a packet to be filtered,
filterPktData	= the bit pattern to be tested for,
filterPktDataMask	= the relevant bits to be tested for,
filterPktDataNotMask	= indication of whether to test for a match or a mismatch.

The actual logical operations are rather complex, and we will approach them step by step. As an initial step, let us suppose that we simply want to test the input against a bit pattern for a match. For example, this could be used to screen for packets with a specific source address. The following expression would hold:

$$\texttt{if ((input = \^{} filterPktData) == 0)}$$
$$\texttt{filterResult = match;}$$

In this expression, we take the bitwise exclusive-or of input and filterPktData. The result has a 1-bit only in those positions where input and filterPktData differ. Thus, if the result is all 0s, then there is an exact match. Alternatively, we may wish to test for a mismatch. For example, suppose a LAN consists of a number of workstations and a server; a mismatch test could be used to screen for all packets that did not have the server as a source. The test for a mismatch would be just the opposite of the test for a match:

$$\texttt{if ((input = \^{} filterPktData) != 0)}$$
$$\texttt{filterResult = mismatch;}$$

So, if there is at least one 1-bit in the result, there is a mismatch.

The preceding tests assume that all bits in the input are relevant. There may, however, be some "don't-care" bits, which are not relevant to the filter. For example, we may wish to test for packets with any multicast destination address. Typically, a multicast address is indicated by one bit in the address field; the remaining bits of the address field

---

[1]In this discussion, the bitwise logical operators (AND, OR, NOT, XOR, EQUAL, NOT-EQUAL) are represented by the symbols used in the C language: $(\&, \ |, \ \sim, \ \^{}, \ ==, \ !=)$.

are irrelevant to a test for multicast address. To account for "don't-care" bits, the variable `filterPktDataMask` is introduced; this variable has a 1-bit in each position that is relevant and 0-bits in those positions considered irrelevant. The tests can be modified as follows:

```
if ( (((input = ^ filterPktData) & filterPktDataMask) == 0 )
     filterResult = match_on_relevant_bits;
else
     filterResult = mismatch_on_relevant_bits;
```

The XOR operation produces a result that has a 1-bit in every position where there is a mismatch. The AND operation produces a result that has a 1-bit in every *relevant* position where there is a mismatch. If all of the resulting bits are 0, then there is an exact match on the relevant bits; if any of the resulting bits is 1, there is a mismatch on the relevant bits.

Finally, we may wish to test for an input that matches in certain relevant bit positions and mismatches in others. For example, one could screen for all packets that had a particular host as a destination (exact match of the DA field) and did not come from the server (mismatch on the SA field). To enable these more complex tests to be performed, `filterPktDataNotMask` is used. This mask has the following interpretation:

1. The 0-bits in `filterPktDataNotMask` indicate the positions where an exact match is required between the relevant bits of input and `filterPktData` (all bits match).

2. The 1-bits in `filterPktDataNotMask` indicate the positions where a mismatch is required between the relevant bits of input and `filterPktData` (at least one bit does not match).

For convenience, let us make the following definition:

```
relevant_bits_different = (input ^ filterPktData) & filterPktDataMask
```

Now, incorporating `filterPktDataNotMask` into our test for a match, we have

```
if ( (relevant_bits_different & ~filterPktDataNotMask) = 0 )
     filterResult = successful_match;
```

The test for a mismatch is slightly more complex. If all of the bits of `filterPkt-DataNotMask` are 0-bits, then no mismatch test is needed.[2] Therefore, the test for mismatch is as follows:

---

[2]By the same line of reasoning, if all of the bits of `filterPktDataNotMask` are 1-bits, then no match test is needed. However, in that case, `~filterPktDataNotMask` is all 0s and the match test automatically passes: `relevant_bits_different & 0 == 0`.

```
if ( ((relevant_bits_different & filterPktDataNotMask) != 0)
    (filterPktDataNotMask = 0) )
    filterResult = successful_mismatch;
```

The logic for the filter test is summarized in Figure 9.4. The rules can be stated as follows. An incoming packet is to be tested for a bit pattern in a portion of the packet, located at a distance `filterPktDataOffset` from the start of the packet. The following operations are performed:

1. **TEST 1:** As a first test (not shown in the figure), the packet must be long enough so that there are at least as many bits in the packet following the offset as there are bits in `filterPktData`. If not, the packet fails this filter.

2. **TEST 2:** Each bit set to 0 in `filterPktDataNotMask` indicates a bit position in which the relevant bits of the packet portion should match `filterPktData`. If there is a match in every desired bit position, then the test is passed; otherwise the test is failed.

3. **TEST 3:** Each bit set to 1 in `filterPktDataNotMask` indicates a bit position in which the relevant bits of the packet portion should not match `filterPktData`. In this case, the test is passed if there is a mismatch in at least one desired bit position.

A packet passes this filter if and only if it passes all three tests.

As an example of the use of the filter test, consider that we wish to accept all Ethernet packets that have a destination address of 0xA5 (the prefix 0x indicates hexadecimal notation) and that do not have a source address of 0xBB. The first 48 bits of the Ethernet packet constitute the destination address, and the next 48 bits of the Ethernet packet constitute the source address. The test can be implemented as follows:

```
filterPktDataOffset  = 0
filterPktData        = 0x0000000000A50000000000BB
filterPktDataMask    = 0xFFFFFFFFFFFFFFFFFFFFFFFF
filterPktDataNotMask = 0x000000000000FFFFFFFFFFFF
```

The variable `filterPktDataOffset` indicates that the pattern matching should start with the first bit of the packet; `filterPktData` indicates that the pattern of interest consists of 0xA5 in the first 48 bits and 0xBB in the second 48 bits; `filterPktDataMask` indicates that all of the first 96 bits are relevant; and `filterPktDataNotMask` indicates that the test is for a match on the first 48 bits and a mismatch on the second 48 bits.

The logic for the status filter has the same structure as that for the data filter (Figure 9.4). For the status filter, the reported status of the packet is converted into a bit pattern. This is done as follows: Each error status condition has a unique integer value, corresponding to a bit position in the status bit pattern. To generate the bit pattern, each error value is raised to a power of 2 and the results are totaled. If there are no error con-

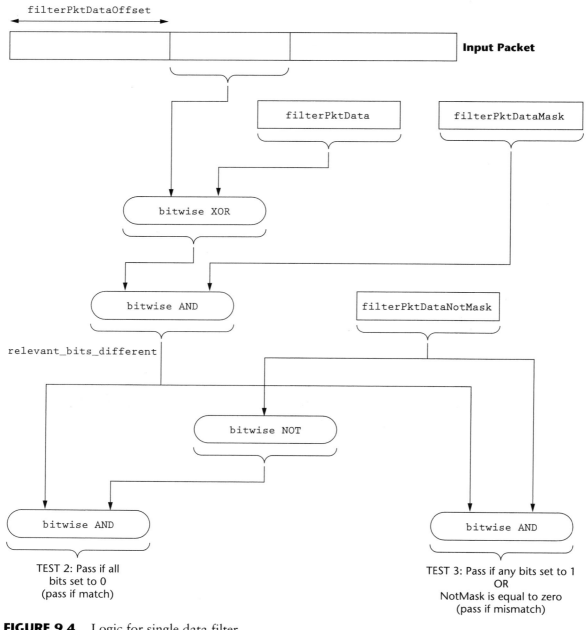

FIGURE 9.4   Logic for single data filter

ditions, then the status bit pattern is all 0s. For example, for an Ethernet interface, the following error values are defined:

Bit #	Error
0	Packet is longer than 1,518 octets
1	Packet is shorter than 64 octets
2	Packet experienced a CRC or alignment error

Therefore, an Ethernet fragment would have the status value of 6 ($2^1 + 2^2$).

9.2.2   Channel Definition

A channel is defined by a set of filters. For each observed packet, and for each channel, the packet is passed through each of the filters defined for that channel. The way in which these filters are combined to determine whether a packet is accepted for a channel depends on the value of an object associated with the channel, the channelAccept-Type. This object has the following syntax:

$$\text{INTEGER \{ acceptMatched(1), acceptFailed(2) \}}$$

If the value of this object is acceptMatched(1), packets will be accepted for this channel if they pass both the packet data and packet status matches of at least one of the associated filters. If the value of this object is acceptFailed(2), packets will be accepted to this channel only if they fail either the packet data match or the packet status match of every associated filter.

Figure 9.5 illustrates the logic by which filters are combined for a channel whose accept type is acceptMatched. A filter is passed if both the data filter and the status filter are passed; otherwise that filter is failed. If we define a pass as a logical 1 and a fail as a logical 0, then the result for a single filter is the AND of the data filter and status filter for that filter. The overall result for a channel is then the OR of all the filters. Thus, a packet is accepted for a channel if it passes at least one of the associated filter pairs for that channel.

If the accept type for a channel is acceptFailed, then the complement of the function just described is used. That is, a packet is accepted for a channel only if it fails every filter pair for that channel. This would be represented in Figure 9.5 by placing a NOT gate after the OR gate.

9.2.3   Channel Operation

The value of channelAcceptType and the set of filters for a channel determine whether or not a given packet is accepted for a channel. If the packet is accepted, then the counter

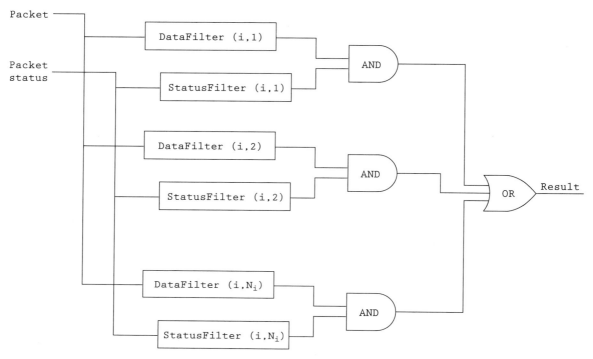

FIGURE 9.5   Filter logic for channel *i* if `channelAcceptType = acceptMatched(1)`

`channelMatches` is incremented. In addition, several additional controls are associated with the channel: `channelDataControl`, which determines whether the channel is on or off; `channelEventStatus`, which indicates whether the channel is enabled to generate an event when a packet is matched; and `channelEventIndex`, which specifies an associated event.

If `channelDataControl` has the value `off`, then, for this channel, no events may be generated as the result of packet acceptance, and no packets may be captured by the `capture` group (discussed in the next section). If `channelDataControl` has the value `on`, then these related actions are possible.

Figure 9.6 summarizes the channel logic. If `channelDataControl` is on, then an event will be generated if two conditions are met: (1) An event is defined for this channel in `channelEventIndex`, and (2) `channelEventStatus` has the value `eventReady` or `eventAlwaysReady`. If the event status is `eventReady`, then each time an event is generated, the event status is changed to `eventFired`. It then takes a positive action on the part of the management station to reenable the channel. This mechanism can therefore be used to control the flow of events from a channel to a management station. If the

```
#define      acceptMatched      1
#define      acceptFailed       2
#define      eventReady         1
#define      eventFired         2
#define      ON                 1

int   channelAcceptType, channelMatches, channelDataControl;
int   channelEventStatus, channelEventIndex;


/****************************** channel logic ***/

void PacketDataMatch( int result )
{
    if ( ((result = = 1) && (channelAcceptType = = acceptMatched))
         ((result = = 0) && (channelAcceptType = = acceptFailed)) )
    {
        channelMatches = channelMatches + 1;
        if ( channelDataControl == ON )
        {
            if ( (channelEventStatus != eventFired) &&
                 (channelEventIndex != 0) ) GenerateEvent();
            if ( channelEventStatus == eventReady)
                channelEventStatus = eventFired;
        }
    }
}
```

FIGURE 9.6   Channel operation logic

management station is not concerned about flow control, it may set the event status to
eventAlwaysReady, where it will remain until explicitly changed.

9.2.4   filter Group Structure

The filter group consists of two control tables (Figure 9.7). Each row of the channelTable defines a unique channel. Associated with that channel are one or more rows in the filterTable, which define the associated filters.

The channelTable includes the following objects:

- channelIndex: an integer that uniquely identifies one row in the channelTable. Each row defines one channel.

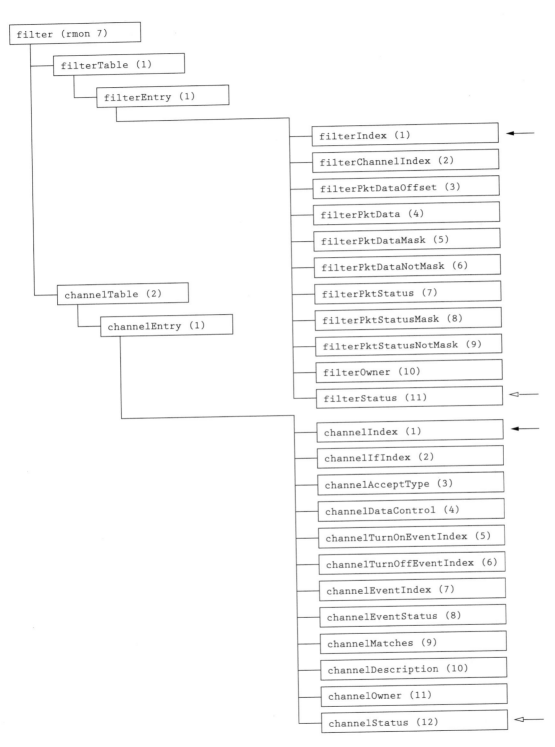

FIGURE 9.7 RMON filter group

- `channelIfIndex`: identifies the monitor interface, and hence the subnetwork, to which the associated filters are applied to allow data into this channel. The value of this object instance is an object identifier that identifies the instance of `ifIndex` in the `interfaces` group of MIB-II that corresponds to this interface.

- `channelAcceptType`: controls the action of the filters associated with this channel. If the value of this object is `acceptMatched(1)`, packets will be accepted to this channel if they pass both the packet data and packet status matches of at least one of the associated filters. If the value of this object is `acceptFailed(2)`, packets will be accepted to this channel only if they fail either the packet data match or the packet status match of every associated filter.

- `channelDataControl`: If this object has the value `on(1)`, the data, status, and events will flow through this channel. If this object has the value `off(2)`, the data, status, and events will not flow through this channel.

- `channelTurnOnEventIndex`: identifies the event that is configured to turn the associated `channelDataControl` from `off` to `on` when the event is generated. The value of this object identifies an object indexed by `eventIndex` in the `event` group. If no such event exists, then no association exists. If no event is intended, this object has the value 0.

- `channelTurnOffEventIndex`: identifies the event that is configured to turn the associated `channelDataControl` from `on` to `off` when the event is generated. The value of this object identifies an object indexed by `eventIndex` in the `event` group. If no such event exists, then no association exists. If no event is intended, this object has the value 0.

- `channelEventIndex`: identifies the event that is configured to be generated when the associated `channelDataControl` is on and a packet is matched. The value of this object identifies an object indexed by `eventIndex` in the `event` group. If no such event exists, then no association exists. If no event is intended, this object has the value 0.

- `channelEventStatus`: the event status of this channel. If the channel is configured to generate events when packets are matched, then the value of this object has the following interpretation. When the value is `eventReady(1)`, a single event will be generated for a packet match, after which this object is set to `eventFired(2)`. In the `eventFired(2)` state, no events are generated. This allows the management station to respond to the notification of an event and then reenable the object. While the value is `eventAlwaysReady(3)`, every packet match generates an event.

- `channelMatches`: a counter that records the number of packet matches. This counter is updated even when `channelDataControl` is set to off.

- `channelDescription`: This gives a text description of the channel.

The `filterTable` includes the following objects:

- `filterIndex`: an integer that uniquely identifies a row in the `filterTable` (Each such row defines one data filter and one status that is to be applied to every packet received on an interface.)
- `filterChannelIndex`: the channel of which this filter is a part
- `filterPktDataOffset`: offset from the beginning of each packet where a match of packet data will be attempted
- `filterPktData`: the data that is to be matched with the input packet
- `filterPktDataMask`: the mask that is applied to the match process
- `filterPktDataNotMask`: the inversion mask that is applied to the match process
- `filterPktStatus`: the status that is to be matched with the input packet
- `filterPktStatusMask`: the mask that is applied to the status match process
- `filterPktStatusNotMask`: the inversion mask that is applied to the status match process

9.3   *Packet* `capture` *Group*

The packet `capture` group can be used to set up a buffering scheme for capturing packets from one of the channels in the `filter` group. It consists of two tables (Figure 9.8): `bufferControlTable`, which specifies the details of the buffering function, and `captureBufferTable`, which buffers the data.

Each row in the `bufferControlTable` defines one buffer that is used to capture and store packets from one channel. The table includes the following objects:

- `bufferControlIndex`: an integer that uniquely identifies a row in the `buffer-ControlTable`. The same integer is also used to identify corresponding rows in the `captureBufferTable`.
- `bufferControlChannelIndex`: identifies the channel that is the source of packets for this row. The value matches that of `channelIndex` for one row of `channel-Table`.
- `bufferControlFullStatus`: If the value is `spaceAvailable(1)`, the buffer has room to accept new packets. If the value is `full(2)`, its meaning depends on the value of `bufferControlFullAction`.
- `bufferControlFullAction`: If the value is `lockWhenFull(1)`, the buffer will accept no more packets after it becomes full. If the value is `wrapWhenFull(2)`, the buffer acts as a circular buffer after it becomes full, deleting enough of the oldest packets to make room for new ones as they arrive.

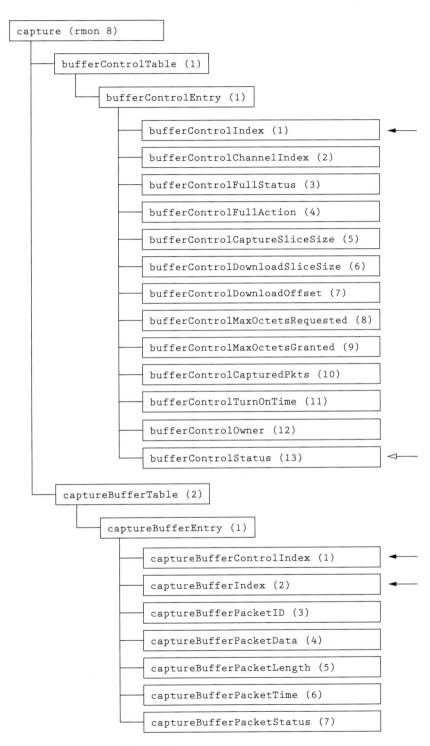

FIGURE 9.8 RMON packet capture group

- `bufferControlCaptureSliceSize`: maximum number of octets of each packet, starting with the beginning of the packet, that will be saved in this capture buffer. If the value is 0, the buffer will save as many octets as possible. The default value is 100.

- `bufferControlDownloadSliceSize`: This is the maximum number of octets of each packet in this buffer that will be returned in a single SNMP retrieval of that packet.

- `bufferControlDownloadOffset`: This gives the offset of the first octet of each packet in this buffer that will be returned in a single SNMP retrieval of that packet.

- `bufferControlMaxOctetsRequested`: the requested buffer size in octets. A value of −1 requests that the buffer be as large as possible.

- `bufferControlMaxOctetsGranted`: the granted buffer size in octets. This is the maximum number of octets that can be saved, including implementation-specific overhead.

- `bufferControlCapturedPackets`: This indicates the number of packets currently in this buffer.

- `bufferControlTurnOnTime`: This gives the value of `sysUpTime` (in the MIB-II `systems` group) when this buffer was first turned on.

The data table, `captureBufferTable`, contains one row for each packet captured. The table includes the following objects:

- `captureBufferControlIndex`: the buffer with which this packet is associated. The buffer identified by a particular value of this index is the same buffer as that identified by the same value of `bufferControlIndex`.

- `captureBufferIndex`: an index that uniquely identifies this particular packet among all packets associated with the same buffer. This index starts at 1 and increases by one as each new packet is captured. Thus, this variable serves as a sequence number for packets in one buffer.

- `captureBufferPacketID`: an index that describes the order of packets that are received on a particular interface. Thus, this variable serves as a sequence number for packets that are captured from one subnetwork, regardless of which buffer(s) they are stored in.

- `captureBufferPacketData`: This gives the actual packet data stored for this row.

- `captureBufferPacketLength`: the actual length of the packet as received (off the wire). As explained in the following paragraphs, it may be that only a part of the packet is actually stored in this entry.

- `captureBufferPacketTime`: This indicates the number of milliseconds that had passed from the time that the buffer was turned on to the time that this packet was captured.

- `captureBufferPacketStatus`: This indicates the error status of this packet.

A related set of parameters dictates how much of a packet is stored in the buffer and how much is available for delivery to a management station in one SNMP `Get` or `Get-Next` request. For convenience, use the following abbreviations:

CS = `bufferControlCaptureSliceSize`: the maximum number of octets of each packet that will be saved in this capture buffer

DS = `bufferControlDownloadSliceSize`: the maximum number of octets of each packet in this buffer that will be returned in an SNMP retrieval of that packet

DO = `bufferControlDownloadOffset`: the offset of the first octet of each packet in this buffer that will be returned in an SNMP retrieval of that packet

PL = `captureBufferPacketLength`: the actual length of the packet (off the wire)

PDL = length of `captureBufferPacketData`: the actual packet data stored for this row of `captureBufferTable`

The following expression holds:[3]

$$PDL = MIN[PL, CS].$$

This packet (if PL ≤ CS) or packet slice (if PL > CS) is stored as a single `OCTET STRING` in one row of `captureBufferTable`. However, this `OCTET STRING` may well be longer than will fit in a single SNMP message. The parameters DO and DS provide a tool to retrieve the captured packet in pieces. If you set DO to 0 and DS to 100, then get `captureBufferPacketData`, you will get octets 0. .MIN(actualStoredData − 1, 99); then if you set DO to 100, then get `captureBufferPacketData`, you will get octets 100. .MIN(actualStoredData − 1, 199); and so on. If the station reads "off the end of the packet," it gets a zero-length string.

Typically, a management station would set DO to 0, DS to 100 or so, then make a complete pass through the table, getting PL, the first 100 bytes of the packet, and maybe `PacketStatus`, and so forth. Then, the station would set DO to 100 and make another pass through to get more of each packet, and so on, until all of the captured data for those packets of interest had been retrieved.

Figure 9.9 illustrates the relationship between the control table and the data table. Each row of `bufferControlTable` has a unique value of `bufferControlIndex`.

---

[3]Unfortunately, the specification is not clear on these relationships. In fact, the definition of `captureBuffer-PacketData` seems to say that PDL = MIN[(PL − DO), (CS − DO), DS]. This is not correct and is not what is intended.

bufferControlTable

bufferControl- Index	bufferControl- ChannelIndex	bufferControl- CapturedPkts
1	C_1	N_1
2	C_2	N_2
.	.	.
.	.	.
.	.	.
K	C_K	N_K

captureBufferTable

captureBuffer- ControlIndex	captureBuffer- Index	captureBuffer- PacketData
1	1	$P(1,1)$
1	2	$P(1,2)$
1	3	$P(1,3)$
.	.	.
.	.	.
.	.	.
1	N_1	$P(1,N_1)$
2	$x + 1$	$P(2,x + 1)$
2	$x + 2$	$P(2,x + 2)$
2	$x + 3$	$P(2,x + 3)$
.	.	.
.	.	.
.	.	.
2	$x + N_2$	$P(2,x + N_2)$
.	.	.
.	.	.
.	.	.

Note: Only selected fields in each table are shown.

FIGURE 9.9   An example of packet capture tables

The value of `bufferControlChannelIndex` references the relevant row of the `channelTable`. For each of the *K* rows of `bufferControlTable`, there is a set of rows of `captureBufferTable`, which constitutes the buffer for that control row. In the example, the first buffer either is not full or has just become full, and the second buffer is acting as a circular buffer, storing only the last N_2 packets.

9.4   event *Group*

The `event` group supports the definition of events. An event is triggered by a condition located elsewhere in the MIB, and an event can trigger an action defined elsewhere in the MIB. An event may also cause information to be logged in this group and may cause an SNMP trap message to be issued.

Also, an event that is defined in this group can be used to trigger activity related to another group. For example, an event can trigger turning a channel on or off.

The `event` group consists of one control table and one data table (Figure 9.10). The control table, `eventTable`, contains event definitions. Each row of the table contains the parameters that describe an event to be generated when certain conditions are met. The table includes the following objects:

- `eventIndex`: an integer that uniquely identifies a row in the `eventTable` (The same integer is also used to identify corresponding rows in the `logTable`.)
- `eventDescription`: a textual description of this event
- `eventType`: takes on the value `none(1)`, `log(2)`, `snmp-trap(3)`, or `log-and-trap(4)` (In the case of `log`, an entry is made in the log table for each event. In the case of `snmp-trap`, an SNMP trap is sent to one or more management stations for each event.)
- `eventCommunity`: specifies the community of management stations to receive the trap if an SNMP trap is to be sent (See Section 7.1.2 for a definition of a community.)
- `eventLastTimeSent`: the value of `sysUpTime` (in the MIB-II `systems` group) at the time this event entry last generated an event

If an event is to be logged, entries will be created in the associated `logTable`, which includes the following objects:

- `logEventIndex`: identifies the event that generated this log entry. The value of this index refers to the same event as identified by the same value of `eventIndex`.
- `logIndex`: an index that uniquely identifies this particular log entry among all entries associated with the same event type. This index starts at 1 and increases by one as each new packet is captured.

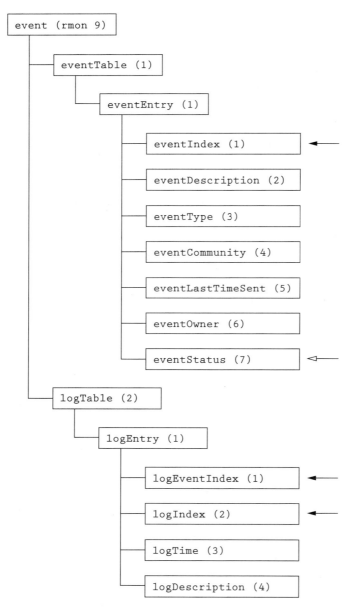

FIGURE 9.10 RMON event group

- `logTime`: This gives the value of `sysUpTime` when this log entry was created.
- `logDescription`: This is an implementation-dependent description of the event that activated this log entry.

The conditions for an event to occur are defined in other RMON groups. One key use of the event group is in conjunction with the `alarm` group. The `alarm` group can define rising-threshold and falling-threshold events that are referenced by indexing into the `eventTable`. Also, the `filter` group can reference an event that will occur when a packet is captured.

9.5   *Practical Issues*

9.5.1   Packet `capture` Overload

RMON is so rich that there is the very real danger of overloading the monitor, the internet between the monitor and the management station, and/or the management station. The network manager must avoid the temptation of "picking every possible cookie out of the jar."

As an extreme example, a system could be configured so that the management station would retrieve every single packet or even every single packet header in a defined channel. If the internet is moderately busy, this could put quite a stress on one or more of the affected subnetworks. Also, the monitor may not have the speed to capture all these packets while at the same time producing summary information and monitoring alarms. If not, the monitor may drop packets or fail to perform one of its other duties adequately.

A preferred alternative is to do much of the analysis locally, at the monitor, and send much more aggregated results to the management station. Thus, in addition to directly retrieving data from the RMON MIB via SNMP, the user could implement applications on the monitor to do some of the analytical work and then send the results to the management station via file transfer.

The packet capture feature of RMON can be useful if used intelligently. If, for example, a manager detects a specific problem area in the internet, it may be possible to zero in on a few nodes or a particular protocol as the suspected site(s) of the trouble and then, with appropriate filtering, use RMON to gather some raw data for diagnosis. For example, a common problem on a network is for all of the workstations to begin broadcasting one after another, a phenomenon known as a *broadcast storm*. Typically, the device that initiated the storm is the malfunctioning device or was triggered by a malfunctioning device. By noting the pattern of the storm, the network manager can usually pin this down. RMON can then be used to capture packets to and from the suspect device, for analysis by the network manager at the management station.

Even if the manager can develop RMON requests with some precision, it is still necessary to be aware of the tradeoffs involved. A complex filter will allow the monitor to capture and report a limited amount of data, thus avoiding an undue burden on the network. However, complex filters consume quite a bit of processing power at the monitor; if too many filters are defined, the monitor may not be able to keep up. This is especially true if its subnetworks are busy, which is probably the time when one is most interested in monitoring.

A vivid example of the effect of overload is a performance test of various RMON products conducted by Syracuse University (Boardman and Morrissey 1995). The experimenters used a 25-node network and configured a minimal number of RMON functions (one 30-second and one 30-minute History study, one Statistics, Matrix, and HostTopN study). Then, they set up a filter for the Ethernet source address and from that address transmitted a total of 602 packets, with a gap of 500 microseconds between packets. An additional 7,000 packets per second were generated to give a utilization level of about 70 percent. The experiment was run twice, once with 7,000 broadcast packets and once with 7,000 unicast packets providing the background load.

Figure 9.11 shows the results. Only two of the products captured all 602 packets in both tests. Two more captured all packets in the nonbroadcast case. The rest of the products had performance that ranged from not so good to horrible.

9.5.2   Network Inventory

As was just mentioned, it may not be practical or efficient to equip every device on an internet with SNMP. In addition, it may not even be practical or efficient to proxy every device. In that case, RMON provides a handy way to maintain an inventory of all devices on the network that are capable of sending or receiving packets of data (that is, objects like modems would not be included). By watching traffic on the various subnetworks, RMON monitors can quickly provide an inventory of network devices.

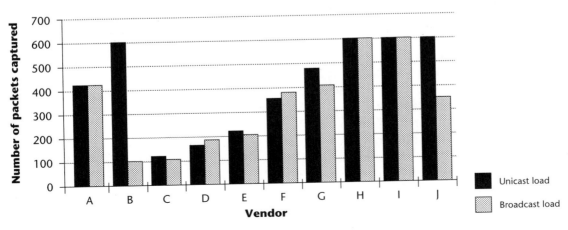

FIGURE 9.11   RMON probe performance

In fact, RMON is useful for this purpose even for SNMP-equipped devices. The SNMP design philosophy discourages agents from initiating communication strictly for the purpose of letting management stations know they exist. Thus, it may be difficult for a management station to determine the identity of all of the agents. RMON solves this problem.

9.5.3   Hardware Platform

Any platform that is to be used as an RMON monitor must, of course, support SNMP. Also, the logic to implement all of the RMON functionality, which is considerable, is added. The choice of platform is wide. It can be a personal computer or workstation dedicated solely to the RMON function. Alternatively, it can be a nondedicated host computer, an interconnect device such as a bridge or router, or even a network management station.

The choice of dedicated or nondedicated platform will depend on the size and complexity of the given subnetwork. For those subnetworks that have relatively light traffic and do not absolutely require 100 percent uptime, a nondedicated platform may be adequate and would save some money. An example of such a subnetwork is a departmental LAN. For such networks, a good choice for platform may be an interconnect device, such as a hub, router, or bridge. For a high-traffic subnetwork, such as an FDDI backbone, a dedicated platform is almost a necessity.

9.5.4   Interoperability

When all of the RMON equipment—managers and RMON probes—is from one vendor, interoperability is usually not a problem. Typically, the RMON products work together as advertised. Increasingly, however, there is a need for interoperability among RMON products. A principle reason is that more makers of network products such as hubs, LAN switches, and routers are including embedded RMON probes in their products. Thus, an RMON manager program must be able to work with a variety of RMON probes.

Unfortunately, interoperability is not always achieved. A recent series of tests by Winterfold Datacomm (Thomas 1995) found a number of interoperability problems. The tests, which involved RMON managers and agents from eight major vendors, uncovered the following problems.

1. Differences in the way RMON managers manipulate the tables that define the tasks running in probes and agents can prevent some RMON managers from retrieving needed information.

2. Those same differences also can prevent managers from getting a complete view of all the tasks assigned to a given RMON probe by other RMON managers. This leaves the manager unable to control the agent's resources, which means it may not be able to create new tasks to run the agent.

3. Packet capture, widely considered to be one of the most important features of RMON, is unreliable in a multivendor environment. Nearly one-fourth of the 54 manager-agent combinations tested failed to deliver captured packets. In some cases, managers were unable to set RMON probes to capture packets; in other cases, agents were set up properly, but managers failed to collect captured data.

These problems can generally be overcome by working with the various vendors, but it is a frustrating and time-consuming process for the user.

Similar interoperability problems were found in a series of tests run by Syracuse University (Boardman and Morrissey 1995).

9.6   *Summary*

In addition to providing a capability to collect traffic statistics from subnetworks, RMON provides features that enable the definition of events and alarms and that define packet stream filters and capturing logic. Four groups in RMON provide these functions:

- `alarm`: allows the person at the management console to set a sampling interval and alarm threshold for any counter or integer recorded by the RMON probe
- `filter`: allows the monitor to observe packets that match a filter (The monitor may either capture all packets that pass the filter or simply record statistics based on such packets.)
- packet `capture`: governs how data are sent to a management console
- `event`: a table of all events generated by the RMON probe

RMON2

Work began in 1994 on an extension to the RMON MIB specification to include monitoring of protocol traffic above the MAC level. This work, which is referred to as RMON2, resulted in two RFCs in 1997. This chapter provides a survey of the elements of RMON2.

10.1 *Overview*

RMON2 decodes packets at layers 3 through 7 of the OSI model. This has two important implications.

1. An RMON probe can monitor traffic on the basis of network-layer protocols and addresses, including the Internet Protocol (IP). This enables the probe to look beyond the LAN segments to which it is attached and to see traffic coming onto the LAN via routers.
2. Because an RMON probe can decode and monitor application-level traffic, such as e-mail, file transfer, and World Wide Web protocols, the probe can record traffic to and from hosts for particular applications.

Both of these new capabilities are important for network managers. Let us consider these two capabilities in turn.

10.1.1 Network-Layer Visibility

With the original RMON, now referred to as RMON1, an RMON probe can monitor all of the traffic on the LANs to which it is attached. It can capture all of the MAC-level frames and read the MAC-level source and destination addresses in those frames. The probe can provide detailed information about the MAC-level traffic to and from each host on each attached LAN. However, if a router is attached to one of these LANs, the RMON1 probe can only monitor the total traffic into and out of that router; it has no way of determining the ultimate source of incoming traffic arriving via the router or the ultimate destination of outgoing traffic leaving via the router.

With RMON2, the RMON probe now has the capability of seeing above the MAC layer by reading the header of the enclosed network-layer protocol, which is typically IP. This enables the probe to analyze traffic passing through the router to determine the ultimate source and destination. With this capability, the network manager can answer a number of new questions, such as:

1. If there is excessive load on the LAN due to incoming router traffic, what networks or hosts account for the bulk of that incoming traffic?

2. If a router is overloaded because of high amounts of outgoing traffic, what local hosts account for the bulk of that outgoing traffic, and to what destination networks or hosts is that traffic directed?

3. If there is a high load of pass-through traffic (arriving via one router and departing via another router), what networks or hosts are responsible for the bulk of this traffic?

With answers to questions such as these, the network manager may be able to take steps to contain traffic loads and improve performance. For example, the network manager can see which clients are communicating with which servers and place systems on the appropriate network segments to optimize traffic flow.

10.1.2 Application-Level Visibility

An RMON2 probe is not limited to monitoring and decoding network-layer traffic. It can also view higher-layer protocols running on top of the network-layer protocol. In particular, an RMON2 probe is capable of seeing above the IP layer by reading the enclosed higher-level headers such as TCP and viewing the headers at the application protocol level. This allows the network manager to monitor traffic in great detail.

With RMON2, a network management application can be implemented that will generate charts and graphs depicting traffic percentage by protocols or by applications. Again, such a level of detail is useful in controlling load and maintaining performance.

It is important to note that in RMON2 terms, any protocol above the network layer is considered "application level." From the RMON2 specification:

> *There are many cases in this MIB where the term Application Level is used to describe a class of protocols or a capability. This does not typically mean a protocol that is an OSI Layer 7 protocol. Rather, it is used to identify a class of protocols that is not limited to MAC-layer and network-layer protocols, but can also include transport, session, presentation, and application-layer protocols.*

10.1.3 The RMON2 MIB

The RMON2 MIB is simply an extension of the original RMON MIB that adds a number of new groups. Figure 10.1 illustrates the overall structure of the combined RMON1 and RMON2 MIB. The left-hand portion of the figure is identical to Figure 8.5. The

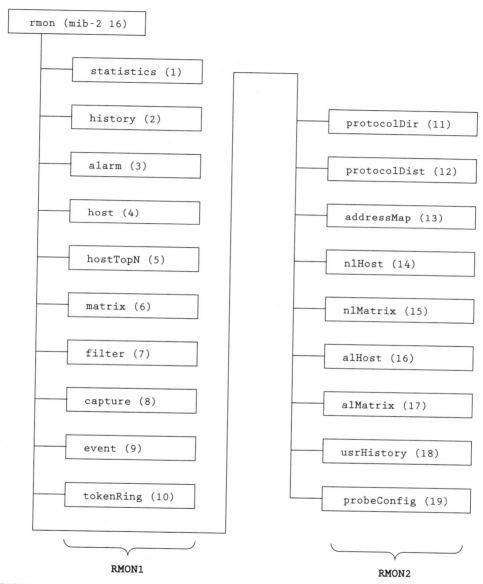

FIGURE 10.1   Remote network monitoring MIB

right-hand portion of the figure depicts the new `mib` groups defined in RMON2. Briefly, these groups are:

- *protocol directory* (`protocolDir`): a master directory of all of the protocols that the probe can interpret
- *protocol distribution* (`protocolDist`): aggregate statistics on the amount of traffic generated by each protocol, per LAN segment
- *address map* (`addressMap`): matches each network address to a specific MAC address and port on an attached device and the physical address on this subnetwork
- *network-layer host* (`nlHost`): statistics on the amount of traffic into and out of hosts on the basis of the network-layer address
- *network-layer matrix* (`nlMatrix`): statistics on the amount of traffic between pairs of hosts on the basis of network-layer address
- *application-layer host* (`alHost`): statistics on the amount of traffic into and out of hosts on the basis of application-level address
- *application-layer matrix* (`alMatrix`): statistics on the amount of traffic between pairs of hosts on the basis of application-level address
- *user history collection* (`usrHistory`): periodically samples user-specified variables and logs that data based on user-defined parameters
- *probe configuration* (`probeConfig`): defines standard configuration parameters for RMON probes

10.1.4 New Functional Features in RMON2

RMON2 introduces two new features not found in RMON1 that enhance the power and flexibility of RMON. Both are in the area of table indexing: the use of index objects that are not part of the table they index, and the use of time filter indexing.

10.1.4.1 Indexing with External Objects

In the structure of management information (SMI) for SNMPv1, and in particular in RFC 1212, which defines the use of the `INDEX` clause in `OBJECT-TYPE` macros, it is not clear whether an index object is required to be a columnar object in the table that it indexes. The SMI for SNMPv2 explicitly states that it is possible to use an object that is not part of a conceptual table as an index for that table. In such a case, the `DESCRIP-TION` clause for the conceptual row must include a textual explanation of how such objects are to be used in uniquely identifying a conceptual row instance.

RMON2 adopts this means of indexing and uses it frequently to tie together control tables and data tables. The way that this is done is best shown by example. Consider again the control and data tables defined in the style of RMON1 that are shown in

Figure 8.2. The data table is indexed by `rm1DataControlIndex` and then by `rm1Data-Index`. The value of `rm1DataControlIndex` is the same as the value of `rm1Control-Index` in `rm1ControlTable` that defines the control row for this data entry.

We saw an example of this type of structure in Figure 8.8, which shows the layout of the RMON1 `history` table. Each row of the data table includes both of the index objects. The first index object just replicates an index value from the index object for the control table.

Figure 10.2 shows the same type of control table and data table definition in the RMON2 style. The control table is the same. An important difference is that there is one less columnar object in the data table. In particular, there is no columnar object that indicates to which control row this data row belongs. Instead, the `rm2DataEntry` definition indicates that this data table is indexed by `rm2ControlIndex` and then by `rm2Data-Index`. Again, suppose that we are interested in the set of data rows controlled by the second control row and that we are further interested in the 89th member, or row, of that set. Again, the instance of the value of that row would be named `rm2DataValue.2.89`. In this case, the index value "2" refers to `rm2ControlIndex`. The manner in which the probe implements the table to use this index object is a local implementation manner.

The net result of this change is that there is one fewer object in the table definition for any table indexed by an external object. Another difference found in RMON2 is that status objects are specified as having syntax `RowStatus` rather than `EntryStatus`. `RowStatus` is a textual convention defined in SNMPv2 that provides a more elaborate method for adding and removing rows than that supported by `EntryStatus`. A discussion of `RowStatus` is deferred until Chapter 11.

10.1.4.2 Time Filter Indexing

A common function of a network management application is periodically to poll all probes subordinate to it for the values of objects maintained at the probe. For the sake of efficiency, it is desirable to have the probe return values only for those objects whose values have changed since the last poll. There is no direct way in SNMP or SNMPv2 to achieve this function. However, the RMON2 designers have come up with an innovative means of achieving the same functionality in the MIB definition.

The mechanism used in RMON2 relies on a new textual convention, defined as follows:[1]

```
TimeFilter ::= TEXTUAL-CONVENTION
    STATUS   CURRENT
    DESCRIPTION
         "  .  .  .  "

    SYNTAX TimeTicks
```

---

[1]The lengthy description clause is omitted here.

```
rm2ControlTable OBJECT-TYPE
   SYNTAX   SEQUENCE OF Rm2ControlEntry
   ACCESS      not-accessible
   STATUS      mandatory
   DESCRIPTION
      "A control table."
   ::= { ex1 1 }

rm2ControlEntry OBJECT-TYPE
   SYNTAX      Rm2ControlEntry
   ACCESS      not-accessible
   STATUS      mandatory
   DESCRIPTION
      "Defines a parameter that controls a
      set of data table entries."
   INDEX  { rm2ControlIndex }
   ::= { rm2ControlTable 1 }

rm2ControlEntry ::= SEQUENCE {
   rm2ControlIndex      INTEGER,
   rm2ControlParameter  Counter,
   rm2ControlOwner      OwnerString
   rm2ControlStatus     RowStatus   }

rm2ControlIndex OBJECT-TYPE
   SYNTAX     INTEGER
   ACCESS     read-only
   STATUS     mandatory
   DESCRIPTION
      "The unique index for this rm2Control
      entry."
   ::= { rm2ControlEntry 1 }

rm2ControlParameter OBJECT-TYPE
   SYNTAX     Integer
   ACCESS     read-write
   STATUS     mandatory
   DESCRIPTION
      "The value of this object character-
      izes data table rows associated with
      this entry."
   ::= { rm2ControlEntry 2 }

rm2ControlEntry OBJECT-TYPE
   SYNTAX     OwnerString
   ACCESS     read-write
   STATUS     mandatory
   DESCRIPTION
      "The entity that configured this
      entry."
   ::= { rm2ControlEntry 3 }
```

```
rm2ControlStatus OBJECT-TYPE
   SYNTAX     RowStatus
   ACCESS     read-write
   STATUS     mandatory
   DESCRIPTION
      "The status of this rm2Control
      entry."
   ::= { rm2ControlEntry 4 }

rm2DataTable OBJECT-TYPE
   SYNTAX   SEQUENCE OF Rm2CtrlEntry
   ACCESS      not-accessible
   STATUS      mandatory
   DESCRIPTION
      "A data table."
   ::= { ex1 2 }

rm2DataEntry OBJECT-TYPE
   SYNTAX     Rm2DataEntry
   ACCESS     not-accessible
   STATUS     mandatory
   DESCRIPTION
      "A single data table entry."
   INDEX { rm2ControlIndex, rm2DataIndex }
   ::= { rm2DataTable 1 }

rm2DataEntry ::= SEQUENCE
   rm2DataIndex       INTEGER,
   rm2DataValue       Counter   }

rm2DataIndex OBJECT-TYPE
   SYNTAX     Integer
   ACCESS     read-only
   STATUS     mandatory
   DESCRIPTION
      "An index that uniquely identifies
      a particular entry among all data
      entries associated with the same
      rm2ControlEntry."
   ::= { rm2DataEntry 1 }

rm2DataValue OBJECT-TYPE
   SYNTAX     Counter
   ACCESS     read-only
   STATUS     mandatory
   DESCRIPTION
      "The value reported by this entry."
   ::= { rm2DataEntry 2 }
```

FIGURE 10.2   Control and data tables in RMON2 style

An object of type `TimeFilter` has the syntax of `TimeTicks` (a time counter) but is used exclusively as an index to a table. The purpose of this index is to enable a manager to download from a probe's table only those rows that have changed since a specified time. That time is specified in the value of the `TimeFilter` index object.

The way in which this works is best shown by an example. Consider the following table definition, based on one in the RMON2 document:

```
fooTable OBJECT-TYPE
    SYNTAX     SEQUENCE OF FooEntry
    ACCESS     not-accessible
    STATUS     current
DESCRIPTION
    "A control table."
::= { ex 1 }


fooEntry OBJECT-TYPE
    SYNTAX     FooEntry
    ACCESS     not-accessible
    STATUS     current
DESCRIPTION
    "One row in fooTable."
INDEX { fooTimeMark, fooIndex }
::= { fooTable 1 }


FooEntry ::= SEQUENCE {
fooTimeMark    TimeFilter,
fooIndex       INTEGER,
fooCounts      Counter32 }
```

```
fooTimeMark OBJECT-TYPE
    SYNTAX     TimeFilter
    ACCESS     not-accessible
    STATUS     current
DESCRIPTION
    "A TimeFilter for this entry."
::= { fooEntry 1 }


fooIndex OBJECT-TYPE
    SYNTAX     FooEntry
    ACCESS     not-accessible
    STATUS     current
DESCRIPTION
    "Basic row index for this entry."
INDEX { fooTimeMark, fooIndex }
::= { fooEntry 2 }


fooCounts OBJECT-TYPE
    SYNTAX     Counter32
    ACCESS     read-only
    STATUS     current
DESCRIPTION
    "Current count for this entry."
::= { fooEntry 3 }
```

Suppose that `fooIndex` takes on only the values 1 and 2. If it were not for the presence of `fooTimeMark`, this would mean that only two counters and two rows would be in this table. With `fooTimeMark`, it is possible to request the values of these counters only if they have been updated since a given time.

For example, suppose that the current value of the counter associated with `foo-Index` = 1 is 5 and that the counter was most recently updated at time 6. Also suppose that the current value of the counter associated with `fooIndex` = 2 is 9 and that the counter was most recently updated at time 8. Then, suppose that at time 10, a manager issues the following request:[2]

```
GetRequest (fooCounts.7.1, fooCounts.7.2)
```

This requests the agent to return those counter values that have been updated since time 7. The response is

```
Response (fooCounts.7.2 = 9)
```

Conceptually, we can think of `fooTable` being constructed as follows. When `sysUpTime` at the probe is zero, the table is empty. A new `fooTimeMark` value is created for each new `sysUpTime` value as the clock ticks. Entries exist in the table for every columnar object for every `fooTimeMark` value, however, entries exist only for rows that have been updated since the corresponding `fooTimeMark` value. Thus, at $sysUpTime \geq 8$, `fooTable` can be viewed conceptually as shown in Figure 10.3(a). Several points need to be made.

1. There are two "basic" rows to this table, one for `fooIndex` = 1 and one for `foo-Index` = 2.
2. Basic row 1 does not exist for `fooTimeMark` values 7 and 8 since row 1 was last updated at time 6. Thus a `GetRequest` of `fooCounts.x.1` for $x \geq 7$ does not return a value. Similarly a `GetRequest` of `fooCounts.x.2` for $x \geq 9$ does not return a value.
3. All conceptual rows with the same value of `fooIndex` share the same value of `foo-Counts`, which is the last value assigned to `fooCounts`. Thus `fooCounts.0.1 = fooCounts.1.1 = fooCounts.2.1`, and so on.

In practice, no agent will implement a table with a `TimeFilter` index in this fashion. The time-filtered rows are only conceptual. The agent simply attaches to each basic row a time stamp that gives the time of the last update. This might look something like Figure 10.3(b). When an agent receives a request for a time-filtered access to a particular conceptual row, the agent filters the actual table as follows:

```
if (timestamp-for-this-fooIndex ≥ TimeFilter-value-in-Request)
        /* return this instance in a response PDU */
else /* skip this instance */
```

---

[2]This example uses the SNMPv2 version of `GetRequest`, which is a nonatomic. That is, if it is not possible to return values for all of the variables in the `GetRequest`, the agent returns those values that are available.

fooTimeMark (fooTable.1.1)	fooIndex (fooTable.1.2)	fooCounts (fooTable.1.3)
0	1	5
0	2	9
1	1	5
1	2	9
2	1	5
2	2	9
3	1	5
3	2	9
4	1	5
4	2	9
5	1	5
5	2	9
6	1	5
6	2	9
7	2	9
8	2	9

(a) Conceptual view of fooTable at sysUpTime ≥ 8

timeStamp	fooIndex (fooTable.1.2)	fooCounts (fooTable.1.3)
6	1	5
8	2	9

(b) Possible implementation view of fooTable at probe

FIGURE 10.3   Conceptual and implementation views of TimeFilter indexing

timestamp	fooIndex	fooCounts
0	1	0
0	2	0

(a) Time = 0

timestamp	fooIndex	fooCounts
500	1	1
0	2	0

(b) Time = 500

timestamp	fooIndex	fooCounts
900	1	2
0	2	0

(c) Time = 900

timestamp	fooIndex	fooCounts
900	1	2
1100	2	1

(d) Time = 1100

timestamp	fooIndex	fooCounts
900	1	2
1400	2	2

(e) Time = 1400

timestamp	fooIndex	fooCounts
2300	1	3
1400	2	2

(f) Time = 2300

FIGURE 10.4   Changes in agent's implementation view of a `TimeFilter` indexed table

Let us look at another example using the same table. Figure 10.4 shows the agent's view of the table. Assume that basic row 1 (`fooIndex` = 1) was updated as follows:

sysUpTime	fooCounts.*.1 value
500	1
900	2
2300	3

And assume that basic row 2 (`fooIndex` = 2) was updated as follows:

sysUpTime	fooCounts.*.2 value
1100	1
1400	2

Figure 10.4 shows the evolution of the table. Now let us look at a network management station that polls a probe every 15 seconds. The manager keeps a clock, nms, that records time in hundredths of a second. The following sequence occurs:

1. At nms = 1000, the manager does a baseline poll to get everything since the last agent restart (`TimeFilter` = 0).

    GetRequest (sysUpTime.0, fooCounts.0.1, fooCounts.0.2)

The agent responds with

```
Response (sysUpTime.0 = 600, fooCounts.0.1 = 1, fooCounts.0.2 = 0)
```

The agent received the request at a local time of 600; counter 1 was incremented at time 500.

2. At nms = 2500 (15 seconds later), the manager gets an update on all changes since the last report (agent time = 600).

```
GetRequest (sysUpTime.0, fooCounts.600.1, fooCounts.600.2)
```

The agent responds with

```
Response (sysUpTime.0 = 2100, fooCounts.600.1 = 2,
                    fooCounts.600.2 = 2)
```

The agent received the request at a local time of 2100; counter 1 was incremented at time 900; counter 2 was incremented at 1100 and 1400.

3. At nms = 4000, the manager gets an update on all changes since the last report:

```
GetRequest (sysUpTime.0, fooCounts.2100.1, fooCounts.2100.2)
```

The agent responds with

```
Response (sysUpTime.0 = 3600, fooCounts.2100.1 = 3)
```

Counter 1 was incremented at time 2300; counter 2 has not changed since time 2100 and so no value is returned.

4. At nms = 5500, the manager gets an update on all changes since the last report:

```
GetRequest (sysUpTime.0, fooCounts.3600.1, fooCounts.3600.2)
```

The agent responds with

```
Response (sysUpTime.0 = 5500)
```

Neither counter has been updated since time 3600.

The `TimeFilter` type enables a manager to "filter" a table efficiently, based on last update times.

10.2 *Protocol Directory Group*

The protocol directory (`protocolDir`) group addresses a key difficulty in the remote monitoring of protocol traffic above the MAC layer. On any particular network, many different protocols may be running. Some are standardized or at least well known, while others may be custom protocols developed for a particular application of a product. Since most of the objects in the RMON2 MIB deal with monitoring the activity of these protocols, some common framework is needed to support them all. This is the purpose of the protocol directory group, which provides a single central point for storing information about types of protocols.

In essence, the protocol directory group provides a way for an RMON2 manager to learn which protocols a particular RMON2 probe interprets. This information is especially important when the manager and probe are from different vendors. Figure 10.5 shows the structure of this group. The group includes a protocol directory table, with one entry for each protocol for which the probe can decode and count protocol data units (PDUs). The table covers MAC-, network-, and higher-layer protocols. The group also includes protocol `DirLastChange`, which contains the time of the last table update.

10.2.1 Protocol Identification

The first two columnar objects in `protocolDirTable`, which are `protocolDirID` and `protocolDirParameters`, are used as indexes that uniquely identify a single row and therefore uniquely identify one supported protocol. It is worthwhile examining these two components in some detail.

10.2.1.1 Protocol Identifier

The indexing works as follows. The `protocolDirID` object contains a unique octet string for a specific protocol. Octet string identifiers for protocols are arranged in a tree-structured hierarchy, similar to the hierarchy of MIB objects. In this case, the root of the tree is the identifier of a MAC-level protocol.

Each protocol layer is identified by one or more 32-bit values, and each such value is encoded as four subidentifiers, [a.b.c.d], where each subidentifier is one octet long. For example, the layer identifier for Ethernet is hexadecimal 1, which is encoded as [0.0.0.1] and referred to symbolically as `ether2`.

The first level of octet string identifiers under `protocolAssignments` is for MAC-level protocols. The following identifiers have been assigned values so far:

```
ether2        = 1 [ 0.0.0.1 ]
llc           = 2 [ 0.0.0.2 ]
snap          = 3 [ 0.0.0.3 ]
vsnap         = 4 [ 0.0.0.4 ]
ianaAssigned  = 5 [ 0.0.0.5 ]
```

Under each of these nodes in the identifier tree are protocols that are directly encapsulated by that MAC-level protocol. This structure continues through as many levels as necessary. For example, the Internet Protocol (IP) may be run directly on top of the

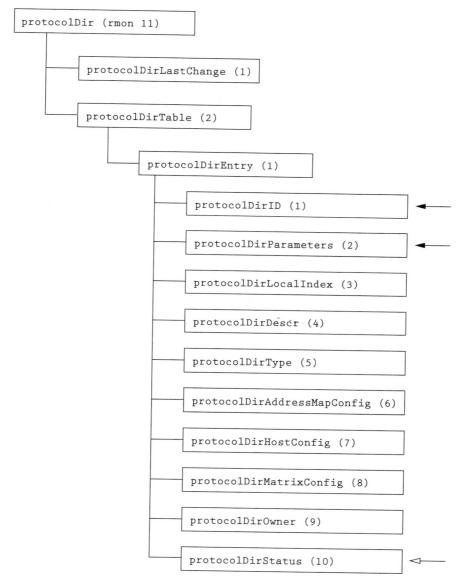

FIGURE 10.5   RMON2 protocol directory group

Ethernet MAC protocol. Symbolically, the identifier for IP running over Ethernet is `ether2.ip`. Similarly, the User Datagram Protocol (UDP) runs over IP and is encapsulated by IP. Thus, UDP running over IP on an Ethernet LAN has the octet string identifier `ether2.ip.udp`. Finally, a number of application-level protocols run on top of UDP. One example is SNMP. If this is operating over Ethernet, then the octet string identifier is `ether2.ip.udp.snmp`.

Let us look at this example in more detail. The actual structure of the `protocol-DirID` is shown in Figure 10.6 (for now, we ignore the `protocolDirParameters` portion). The value consists of a one-octet count of the number of octets in the remainder of the field, followed by a sequence of four-octet subfields. Each protocol layer is identified by a subfield of four octets. We have already seen that the identifier for Ethernet is [0.0.0.1]. Each protocol that is encapsulated by the Ethernet MAC protocol is identified by a unique 32-bit number of the form [0.0.a.b], where a and b contain the 16-bit value in the Type field of an Ethernet frame. This Type field is used to identify the protocol that is using the Ethernet MAC protocol. In the case of IP, this turns out to be [0.0.8.0]. In a similar fashion, the IP PDU includes an eight-bit Protocol field that identifies the user of IP. This value is encoded in the form [0.0.0.a] to identify uniquely the user of IP. In the IP standard, the value assigned to UDP is 17. Thus, the protocol identifier for UDP running over IP is [0.0.0.17]. Finally, the UDP PDU format includes a 16-bit Port field to identify a UDP user. The value assigned to SNMP is port 161. Again, each 16-bit value is encoded as [0.0.a.b]; thus, SNMP over UDP is

c n t	protocolDirID (object identifier)	c n t	protocolDirParameters (octet string)

(a) General format

	protocolDirID					protocolDirParameters			
c n t	protocol L2	protocol L3	protocol L4	protocol L5	c n t	para L2	para L3	para L4	para L5

octets	1	4 or 8	4	4	4	1	1/2	1	1	1

(b) Format for four encapsulated protocols

FIGURE 10.6   Format for index values for `protocolDirTable` encoded as [0.0.0.161]. Putting this all together, the `protocolDirID` that uniquely identifies SNMP running over UDP/IP on Ethernet is

$$16.0.0.0.1.0.0.8.0.0.0.0.17.0.0.0.161$$

The first number, 16, indicates that there are 16 octets to follow. The next group of four octets identify Ethernet; the next four identify IP running over Ethernet; the next four identify UDP running over IP; and the final four identify SNMP running over UDP.

Keep in mind that a separate entry is needed for each protocol that the probe can interpret and count. Suppose that the probe in this example is capable of

- interpreting all incoming Ethernet frames
- looking past the Ethernet header and trailer and interpreting the encapsulated IP datagram
- looking past the IP header and interpreting the encapsulated UDP segment
- looking past the UPD header and interpreting the encapsulated SNMP PDU

Then four entries are needed in `protocolDirEntry`. The corresponding `protocol-DirID` values would be

- `ether2` (4.0.0.0.1)
- `ether2.ip` (8.0.0.0.1.0.0.8.0)
- `ether2.ip.udp.` (12.0.0.0.1.0.0.8.0.0.0.0.17)
- `ether2.ip.udp.snmp` (16.0.0.0.1.0.0.8.0.0.0.0.17.0.0.0.161)

10.2.1.2 Protocol Parameters

The second index object for `protocolDirTable` is `protocolDirParameters`. This object instance contains information about the probe's capability with respect to a particular protocol. The value is structured as a one-octet count field followed by a set of N-octet parameters, one for each protocol layer in the corresponding `protocolDirID`, where N corresponds to the number of 32-bit blocks used for the identifier of that layer. Figure 10.6(a) shows the general structure, and Figure 10.6(b) shows the structure for a protocol at the fourth level of encapsulation. Note that the correspondence between protocols and parameters is one-to-one.

Each of the bits in the parameter octet is encoded separately to define a particular capability. The two least significant bits have reserved values that apply to all protocols:

- `countsFragments` (bit 0): Higher-layer protocols encapsulated within this protocol will be counted correctly even if this protocol fragments the upper-layer PDUs into multiple fragments.

- `tracksSessions` (bit 1): correctly attributes all packets of a port-mapped protocol; that is, a protocol that starts sessions on a well-known port or socket and then transfers them to dynamically assigned ports or sockets for the duration of the session. One example of such a protocol is the Trivial File Transfer Protocol (TFTP).

Continuing our example, consider the following encoding for the two objects (protocol DirID, protocol DirParameters:

$$16.0.0.0.1.0.0.8.0.0.0.0.17.0.0.0.161.4.0.1.0.0$$

This indexes an entry in `protocolDirTable` that refers to the protocol SNMP running over UDP/IP/Ethernet, with fragments counted correctly for IP and above.

As an aid in defining entries in this table, a new protocol descriptor macro has been specified. The macro is defined using a simple Backus–Naur Form (BNF) syntax rather than ASN.1. A simplified form is shown here:

```
protocol-identifier  :==
    <protocol-name>           "PROTOCOL-IDENTIFIER"
      "PARAMETERS"            "{" <param-bit-list> "}"
      "ATTRIBUTES"            "{" <attrib-bit-list> "}"
      "DESCRIPTION"           """ <protocol-description> """
    [ "CHILDREN"              """ <children-description> """        ]
    [ "ADDRESS-FORMAT"        """ <address-format-description> """  ]
    [ "DECODING"              """ <decoding-description> """        ]
    [ "REFERENCE"             """ <reference-description> """       ]
    "::=" "{" <protocol-encoding-identifiers> "}"
```

The macro includes the following clauses:

- `protocol-name`: a lowercase character string that matches a well-known name or acronym for this protocol
- PARAMETERS: a list of bit definitions that can be directly encoded into the parameter's octet (We have already discussed two reserved values for this definition: `countsFragments(0)`, `tracksSessions`.)
- ATTRIBUTES: a list of bit definitions, which are directly encoded into the `protocolDirType` value for this protocol, as explained ahead
- DESCRIPTION: a textual description of the protocol
- CHILDREN: a description of children protocols that are supported by this protocol (This clause has three subsections:
  (1) how the child protocol is indicated in the parent protocol: Typically, this is done by means of a field in the parent protocol header;
  (2) how the identifier of the child protocol is encoded in the protocol identifier octet string;
  (3) how the child protocol is named with respect to the parent protocol.)

- ADDRESS-FORMAT: a description of the OCTET STRING format used for addresses in this protocol
- DECODING: a description of the decoding procedure for the specified protocol; this deals with the format of the protocol packet or frame
- REFERENCE: references to publicly available specifications of the protocol
- protocol-encoding-identifiers: the identifier or alternative identifiers for this protocol

Figure 10.7 shows the use of this macro for the protocol example discussed here.

10.2.2 Protocol Directory Table

In addition to the two index objects for protocolDirTable, the table includes proto-colDirLocalIndex, which is an arbitrary unique index number associated with this entry. This index is a convenient way to refer to a specific entry and is used in the other RMON groups. The table also contains a textual description object, protocolDir-Descr, and owner and status objects. The remainder of the objects provide enumerated values that further define the protocol entry:

- protocolDirType: may be defined as extensible(0) if the agent or manager may extend this table by creating entries that are children of this protocol; and as addressRecognitionCapable(1), which indicates that the probe can not only count packets for this protocol but can also recognize source and destination address fields for finer-grained counting
- protocolDirAddressMapConfig: set to notSupported(1) if not capable of performing address mapping (see Section 10.4); if capable, then the value may be set to supportedOff(2) or supportedOn(3)
- protocolDirHostConfig: may be set to notSupported(1), supported-Off(2), or supportedOn(3) with respect to the network-layer and application-layer host table for this protocol (see Section 10.5)
- protocolDirMatrixConfig: may be set to notSupported(1), supported-Off(2), or supportedOn(3) with respect to the network-layer and application-layer matrix tables for this protocol

Table 10.1 summarizes these enumerated values.

10.3 Protocol Distribution Group

The protocol distribution (protocolDist) group summarizes how many octets and packets have been sent from each of the protocols supported. It consists of two tables

```
ether2 PROTOCOL-IDENTIFIER
   PARAMETERS { }
   ATTRIBUTES { hasChildren(0),
               addressRecognitionCapable(1) }
   DESCRIPTION
      "DIX Ethernet, also called Ethernet-II."
   CHILDREN
      "The Ethernet-II type field is used to select child protocols. This is a 16-bit
      field. Child protocols are deemed to start at the first octet after this type field.
         Children of this protocol are encoded as [ 0.0.0.1 ], the protocol identifier
      for 'ether2' followed by [ 0.0.a.b ] where 'a' and 'b' are the network byte order
      encoding of the MSB and LSB of the Ethernet-II type value. For example, a protocol-
      DirID-fragment value of:

      0.0.0.1.0.0.8.0

      defines IP encapsulated in ether2.
         Children of ether2 are named as 'ether2' followed by the type field value in
      hexadecimal. The above example would be declared as

      ether2 0x0800 "
   ADDRESS-FORMAT
      "Ethernet addresses are 6 octets in network order."
   DECODING
      "Only type values greater than or equal to 1500 decimal indicate Ethernet-II frames;
      lower values indicate 802.3 encapsulation."
   REFERENCE
      "RFC 894; the authoritative list of Ether Type values is identified by the URL:
      ftp://ftp.isi.edu/in-notes/iana/assignments/ethernet-numbers"
   ::= { 1 }


ip PROTOCOL-IDENTIFIER
   PARAMETERS { countsFragments (0) } --This parameter applies to all child protocols
   ATTRIBUTES { hasChildren(0),
               addressRecognitionCapable(1) }
   DESCRIPTION
      "The protocol identifier for IP. Note that IP may be encapsulated within itself, so
      more than one of the following identifiers may be present in a particular protocol-
      DirID string"
   CHILDREN
      "Children of 'ip' are selected by the value in the Protocol field, as defined in the
      PROTOCOL NUMBERS table within the Assigned Numbers Document.
         The value of the Protocol field is encoded into an octet string of the form
      [ 0.0.0.a ], where 'a' is the protocol field.
         Children of 'ip' are encoded as [ 0.0.0.a ], and named as 'ip a' where 'a' is
      the protocol field value. For example, a protocolDirID-fragment value of

      0.0.0.1.0.0.8.0.0.0.0.1

      defines an encapsulation of ICMP (ether2.ip.icmp)"
   ADDRESS-FORMAT
      "4 octets of the IP address, in network byte order. Each IP packet contains two
      addresses, the source address and the destination address."
```

FIGURE 10.7   Examples of protocol descriptor macros

DECODING
"Note: ether2/ip/ipip4/udp is a different protocolDirID than ether2/ip/udp, as
identified in the protocolDirTable. As such, two different local protocol index
values will be assigned by the agent. E.g.:
ether2/ip/ipip4/udp   16.0.0.0.1.0.0.8.0.0.0.0.4.0.0.0.17.4.0.0.0.0
ether2/ip/udp   12.0.0.0.1.0.0.8.0.0.0.0.17.3.0.0.0"
REFERENCE
"RFC 791; the following URL defines the authoritative repository for the PROTO-
COL NUMBERS Table:
        ftp://ftp.isi.edu/in-notes/iana/assignments/protocol-numbers"
::= { ether2 0x0800
      llc   0x06
      snap   0x0800
      ip   4
      ip   94   }

udp PROTOCOL-IDENTIFIER
    PARAMETERS { }
    ATTRIBUTES { hasChildren(0) }
    DESCRIPTION
        "User Datagram Protocol."
    CHILDREN
        "Children of UDP are identified by 16-bit Destination Port value specified in
        RFC 768. They are encoded as [0.0.a.b.], where 'a' is the MSB and 'b' is the
        LSB of the Destination Port value. Both bytes are encoded in network byte order.
        For example, a protocolDirID-fragment value of

        0.0.0.1.0.0.8.0.0.0.0.17.0.0.0.161

        identifies an encapsulation of SNMP (ether2.ip.udp.snmp)"
    REFERENCE
        "RFC 768; the following URL defines the authoritative repository for reserved
        and registered TCP port values:
            ftp://ftp.isi.edu/in-notes/iana/assignments/port-numbers"
::= { ip 17 }

snmp PROTOCOL-IDENTIFIER
    PARAMETERS { }
    ATTRIBUTES { }
    DESCRIPTION
        "Simple Network Management Protocol. Includes SNMPv1 and SNMPv2 protocol
        versions. Does not include SNMP trap packets."
    REFERENCE
        "Transport Mappings for SNMPv2: RFC 1906;
        SNMPv2 SMI: RFC 1902;
        SNMPv2 Protocol: RFC 1905;
        SNMP over IPX: RFC 1420;
        SNMP over AppleTalk: RFC 1419;"
::= { udp   161,
      ipx   0x900f, -- [0.0.144.15]
      atalk 8 }

FIGURE 10.7   *Continued*

TABLE 10.1   Enumerated Values in `protocolDirTable`

Object	Values
protocolDirType	extensible(0)
	addressRecognitionCapable(1)
protocolDirAddressMapConfig	notSupported(1)
	supportedOff(2)
	supportedOn(3)
protocolDirHostConfig	notSupported(1)
	supportedOff(2)
	supportedOn(3)
protocolDirMatrixConfig	notSupported(1)
	supportedOff(2)
	supportedOn(3)

(Figure 10.8): `protocolDistControlTable`, which controls collection of basic statistics for all supported protocols, and `protocolDistStatsTable`, which records the data.

Each row in `protocolDistControlTable` refers to a unique network interface for this probe and controls a number of rows of `protocolDistStatsTable`, one for each protocol recognized on that interface. The `protocolDistControlTable` includes the following columnar objects:

- `protocolDistControlIndex`: an integer that uniquely identifies a row in the `protocolDistControlTable` (The same integer is also used to index corresponding rows in `protocolDistStatsTable`.)

- `protocolDistControlDatasource`: identifies the interface—and hence the subnetwork—that is the source of the data for this row

- `protocolDistControlDroppedFrames`: total number of received frames for this interface that the probe chose not to count (Typically, a frame is not counted when the probe is out of some resources and decides to shed load from this collection.)

- `protocolDistControlCreateTime`: the value of `sysUpTime` when this control entry was activated

The `protocolDistStatsTable` includes one row for each protocol in `protocolDirTable` for which at least one packet has been seen. It is indexed by `protocolDistControlIndex` and by `protocolDirLocalIndex`, which uniquely identifies a particular protocol. The table includes the following objects:

- `protocolDistStatsPkts`: the number of packets received for this protocol

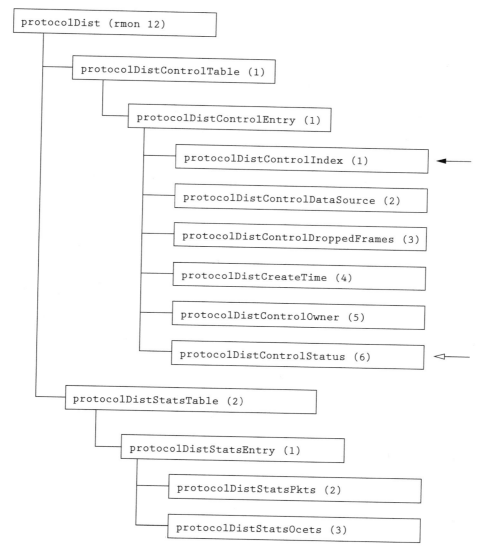

FIGURE 10.8   RMON2 protocol distribution group

- `protocolDistStatsOctets`: the number of octets transmitted to this address since it was added to the `nlHostTable` (see Section 10.5.1)

10.4 *Address Map Group*

The address map (`addressMap`) group matches each network address to a specific MAC-level address and therefore to a specific port on the network device. This is helpful in node discovery and network topology applications for pinpointing the specific paths of network traffic.

The address map group consists of three scalar objects, a control table (`addressMapControlTable`), and a data table (`addressMapTable`), as shown in Figure 10.9. The three scalar objects are

- `addressMapInserts`: the number of times an address-mapping entry has been inserted into the data table
- `addressMapDeletes`: the number of times an address-mapping entry has been deleted from the data table
- `addressMapMaxDesiredEntries`: the desired maximum number of entries in `addressMapTable` (If this value is set to −1, the probe may create any number of entries in `addressMapTable`.)

The current size of the data table is easily calculated:

$$\text{data table size} = \texttt{addressMapInserts} - \texttt{addressMapDeletes}.$$

Most of the control tables in RMON2 have an object with a name of the form `xControlMaxDesiredEntries`. The user may control how resources are allocated across all RMON2 functions by setting the values of these various objects appropriately.

The structure of the control and data tables in this group is not like that of the typical RMON group, in which each control table entry creates and controls a number of data table rows. Instead, there is a single "central" data table that contains entries that provide the mapping between network-layer (typically IP) addresses and MAC addresses. There is one entry in the control table for each subnetwork attached to the probe; each entry in this table enables the discovery of addresses on a new subnetwork and the placement of address mappings into the central data table. Thus, the data table is not indexed by a row of the control table. This arrangement is much cleaner from the viewpoint of a network management application. The application can see duplicates together instead of scanning through separate data tables.

The `addressMapControlTable` includes the following columnar objects:

- `addressMapControlIndex`: an integer that uniquely identifies a row in the `addressMapControlTable`

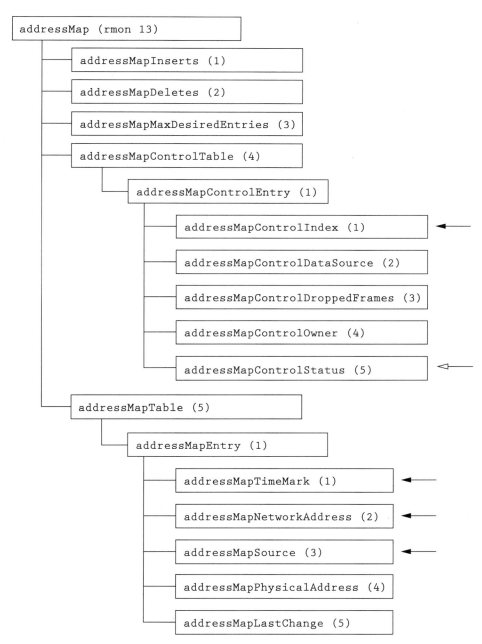

FIGURE 10.9   RMON2 address map group

- `addressMapControlDatasource`: identifies the interface, and hence the subnetwork, that is the source of the data for this row and that this row is configured to analyze
- `addressMapControlDroppedFrames`: total number of received frames for this interface that the probe chose not to count (Typically, this event occurs when the probe is out of some resources and decides to shed load by not collecting statistics.)

The `addressMapTable` will collect address mappings based on source MAC and network addresses seen in error-free MAC frames. The table will create entries for all protocols in the protocol directory table whose value of `protocolDirAddressMapConfig` is equal to `supportedOn(3)`. The table includes the following objects:

- `addressMapTimeMark`: a time filter for this entry (see Section 10.1 for a discussion of time filters)
- `addressMapNetworkAddress`: the network address for this entry
- `addressMapSource`: the last interface or repeater port on which the associated network address was seen
- `addressMapPhysicalAddress`: the last source MAC address on which the associated network address was seen
- `addressMapLastChange`: the value of `sysUpTime` at the time this entry was most recently updated

This table is indexed by four objects: a time filter, the identity of the protocol, the network address, and the interface on which the address was observed (`addressMap-TimeMark`, `protocolDirLocalIndex`, `addressMapNetworkAddress`, `addressMap-Source`). Thus, given a network address for a particular protocol observed on a particular interface within a particular amount of time, the MAC address for that network address can be read. There should be a unique MAC address (only one entry in the table) for any specific network address. On the other hand, a given MAC address may correspond to multiple network addresses and have multiple rows in the table.

This group can be used to detect duplicate IP addresses, which deals with a difficult problem that can affect routers and virtual LANs. The network management system can perform this function by interpreting the address map information in the table.

10.5 *RMON2 Host Groups*

Two RMON2 groups deal with the collection of statistics on a host basis: the network layer host group and the application analysis group. Both of these groups contain a data table that is controlled by a control table in the network-layer host group.

10.5.1 Network-Layer Host Group

The network-layer host (nlHost) group enables users to decode packets based on their network-layer address. This lets the network manager look beyond a router to the connected hosts. This table collects similar statistics to those collected in the RMON1 host group (Figure 8.9). However, the host group gathers statistics based on MAC address whereas the nlHost group gathers statistics based on network-layer address.

This group consists of a control table, nlHostControlTable, and a data table, nlHostTable (Figure 10.10). The control table, nlHostControlTable, includes the following objects:

- nlHostControlIndex: an integer that uniquely identifies a row in the nlHostControlTable (Each row in the control table refers to a unique interface of the monitor (unique subnetwork). The same integer is also used to identify corresponding rows in the nlHostTable and the alHostTable.)

- nlHostControlDatasource: identifies the interface, and hence the subnetwork, that is the source of the data for the data table entries defined by this row

- nlHostControlNlDroppedFrames: total number of received frames for this interface that the probe chose not to count for the associated nlHost entries

- nlHostControlNlInserts: the number of times an nlHost entry has been inserted into the nlHostTable data table

- nlHostControlNlDeletes: the number of times an nlHost entry has been deleted from the nlHostTable

- nlHostControlNlMaxDesiredEntries: the desired maximum number of entries in nlHostTable

- nlHostControlAlDroppedFrames: total number of received frames for this interface that the probe chose not to count for the associated alHost entries

- nlHostControlAlInserts: the number of times an alHost entry has been inserted into the alHostTable data table

- nlHostControlAlDeletes: the number of times an alHost entry has been deleted from the alHostTable

- nlHostControlAlMaxDesiredEntries: the desired maximum number of entries in alHostTable

Note that a separate count of inserts and deletes is kept for nlHostTable and alHostTable and that a separate MaxDesiredEntries value is specified for nlHostTable and alHostTable. This is because there is not a one-to-one relationship between entries in nlHostTable and alHostTable. Rather, each entry in nlHostTable refers to a unique network-layer address at some host, whereas each entry in alHostTable

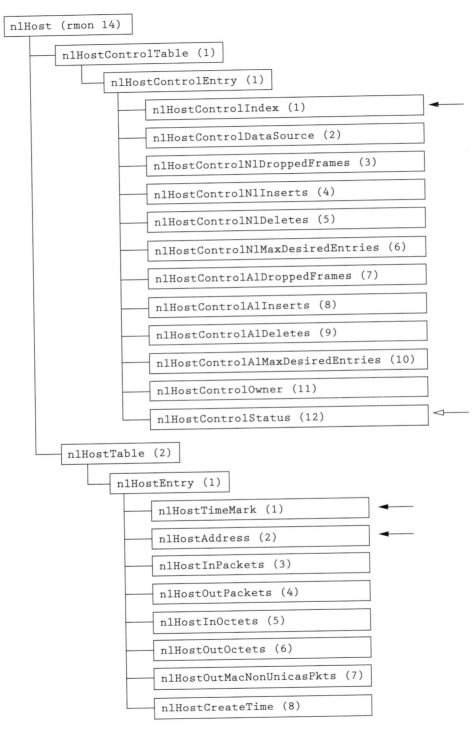

FIGURE 10.10   RMON2 network-layer host group

refers to a unique application-level protocol running at some host. There may be multiple application-level protocols active at the same network-layer host (for example, multiple applications running over IP on the same host).

The nlHostTable will create entries for all network-layer protocols in the protocol directory table whose value of protocolDirNlHostConfig is equal to supported-On(3). The probe adds entries to this table for all addresses seen as the source or destination address in all packets with no MAC errors. The table includes the following objects:

- nlHostTimeMark: a time filter for this entry (see Section 10.1 for a discussion of time filters)

- nlHostAddress: the network address for this entry

- nlHostInPackets: the number of error-free packets transmitted to this address since it was added to the table

- nlHostOutPackets: the number of error-free packets that were transmitted from this address since it was added to the table

- nlHostInOctets: the number of octets transmitted to this address since it was added to the table, not counting octets in packets containing errors

- nlHostOutOctets: the number of octets transmitted by this address since it was added to the table, not counting octets in packets containing errors

- nlHostCreateTime: the value of sysUpTime when this control entry was activated

- nlHostOutMacNonUnicastPkts: the number of packets transmitted by this address that were directed to the MAC broadcast address or to any MAC multicast address since this entry was added to the table

The purpose of nlHostTable is to collect basic statistics on traffic into and out of each discovered host, broken down by network-layer address. After a new row is defined in nlHostControlTable, the monitor begins to learn network-layer addresses on the corresponding interface. Each time a new network-layer address is discovered on that interface, a row is added to hostTable, and the value of nlHostControlNlInserts is incremented by one.

The nlHostTable is indexed by four objects: nlHostControlIndex, which defines the interface; nlHostTimeMark, a time filter; protocolDirLocalIndex, the identity of the protocol; and nlHostAddress, the network address. Thus, given a network address for a particular protocol observed on a particular interface within a particular amount of time, the traffic statistics for that address can be read.

Keep in mind that nlHostTable contains one entry for each known unique network-layer address. Since it is possible for a single host system to have multiple network-layer addresses, there may be more entries in this table than there are known hosts.

10.5.2 Application-Layer Host Group

The `nlHostControlTable` also controls `alHostTable` (Figure 10.11) in the application-layer host group. There is one entry in `alHostTable` for each application-level protocol discovered at each known network-layer address. Keep in mind that for RMON2, the term "application level" refers to all protocols above the network layer.

The `alHostTable` will create entries for all application-level protocols in the protocol directory table whose value of `protocolDirAlHostConfig` is equal to `supportedOn(3)`. The probe adds entries to this table for all addresses seen as the source or destination address in all packets with no MAC errors. The `alHostTable` includes the following objects:

- `alHostTimeMark`: a time filter for this entry (see Section 10.1 for a discussion of time filters)
- `alHostInPackets`: the number of error-free packets of this protocol type transmitted to this address since it was added to the table

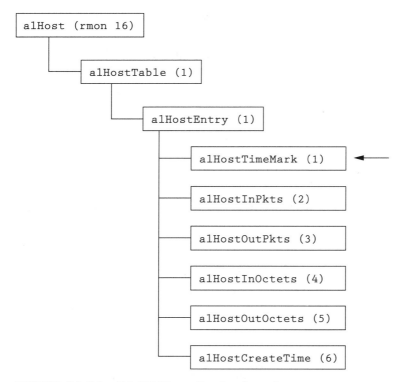

FIGURE 10.11   RMON2 application-layer host group

- `alHostOutPackets`: the number of error-free packets of this protocol type that were transmitted from this address since it was added to the table
- `alHostInOctets`: the number of octets of this protocol type transmitted to this address since it was added to the table, not counting octets in packets containing errors
- `alHostOutOctets`: the number of octets of this protocol type transmitted by this address since it was added to the table, not counting octets in packets containing errors
- `alHostCreateTime`: the value of `sysUpTime` when this control entry was activated

The `alHostTable` is indexed by five objects: `nlHostControlIndex`, which defines the interface; `alHostTimeMark`, a time filter; `protocolDirLocalIndex`, the identity of the network-layer protocol; `nlHostAddress`, the network address; and `protocolDirLocalIndex`, the application-level protocol. Thus, given a network address and particular network-layer and application-level protocols observed on a particular interface within a particular amount of time, the traffic statistics for that application-level protocol can be read. Note that the object `protocolDirLocalIndex` is used twice to index the table. However, two distinct object instances are used for the two indexes: one for a network-layer protocol and one for an application-level protocol.

The `alHostTable` enables a user to trace the traffic into and out of a host on the basis of application protocol. For example, the user could learn of the amount of traffic generated or received by Lotus Notes or Microsoft Mail, by a given host.

10.6 RMON2 Matrix Groups

A pair of RMON2 groups deal with the collection of statistics on pairs of hosts: the network-layer matrix (`nlMatrix`) group and the application-layer matrix (`alMatrix`) group. The data tables in these groups collect similar statistics to those collected in the RMON1 `matrix` group (Figure 8.14) and `hostTopN` group (Figure 8.12). However, the RMON1 groups gather statistics based on MAC address whereas the RMON2 groups gather statistics based on network-layer address and on application-level protocol.

10.6.1 Network-Layer Matrix Group

The network-layer matrix group consists of five tables: two control tables (Figure 10.12) and three data tables. One of the control tables and its two associated data tables deal with the collection of matrix statistics, while the other control table and its associated data table deal with the collection of `topN` statistics.

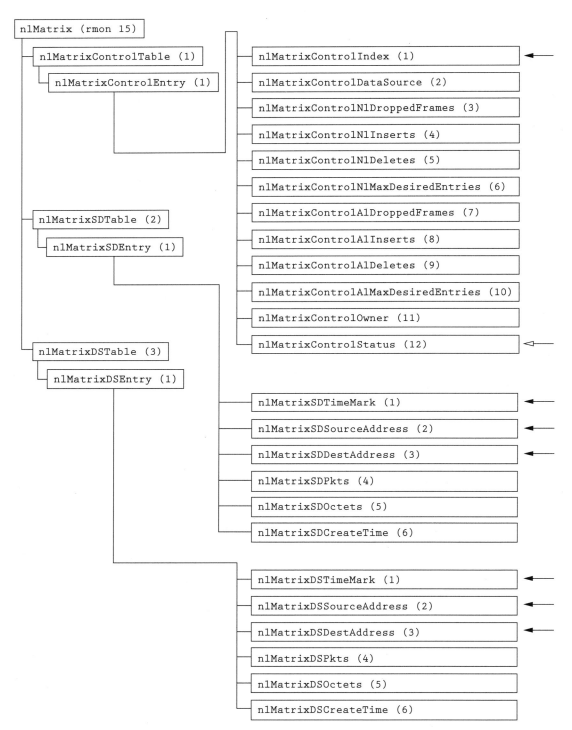

FIGURE 10.12 RMON2 network-layer matrix group: source/destination tables

10.6.1.1 Network-Layer Source/Destination Statistics

The `nlMatrixControlTable` includes the following objects:

- `nlMatrixControlIndex`: an integer that uniquely identifies a row in the `nlMatrixControlTable` (Each row in the control table refers to a unique interface of the monitor (unique subnetwork) and defines a function that discovers conversations on a particular interface and places statistics about them in `nlMatrixSDTable` and `nlMatrixDSTable`, and optionally in `alMatrixSDTable` and `alMatrixDSTable`.)

- `nlMatrixControlDatasource`: identifies the interface—and hence the subnetwork—that is the source of the data for the data table entries defined by this row

- `nlMatrixControlNlDroppedFrames`: total number of received frames for this interface that the probe chose not to count for this entry

- `nlMatrixControlNlInserts`: the number of times an `nlMatrix` entry has been inserted into the `nlMatrix` data tables

- `nlMatrixControlNlDeletes`: the number of times an `nlMatrix` entry has been deleted from the `nlMatrix` data tables

- `nlMatrixControlNlMaxDesiredEntries`: the desired maximum number of entries in the `nlMatrix` data tables

- `nlMatrixControlAlDroppedFrames`: total number of received frames for this interface that the probe chose not to count for the associated `alMatrix` entries

- `nlMatrixControlAlInserts`: the number of times an `alMatrix` entry has been inserted into the `alMatrix` data tables

- `nlMatrixControlAlDeletes`: the number of times an `alMatrix` entry has been deleted from the `alMatrix` data tables

- `nlMatrixControlAlMaxDesiredEntries`: the desired maximum number of entries in the `alMatrix` data tables

The `nlMatrixSDTable` is used to store statistics on traffic from a particular source network-layer address to a number of destinations. The `nlMatrixSDTable` will create entries for all network-layer protocols in the protocol directory table whose value of `protocolDirNlMatrixConfig` is equal to `supportedOn(3)`. The table includes the following objects:

- `nlMatrixSDTimeMark`: a time filter for this entry (see Section 10.1 for a discussion of time filters)

- `nlMatrixSDSourceAddress`: the source network address for this entry

- `nlMatrixSDDestAddress`: the destination network address for this entry

- `nlMatrixSDPackets`: the number of error-free packets transmitted from this source address to this destination address

- nlMatrixSDOctets: the number of octets, excluding packets with errors, transmitted from this source address to this destination address

- nlMatrixSDCreateTime: the value of sysUpTime when this control entry was activated

The nlMatrixSDTable is indexed first by the row of nlMatrixControlTable that controls it; then by a time filter; then by the network-layer protocol; then by the network-layer source address; and then by the network-layer destination address (hlMatrix-ControlIndex, nlMatrixSDTimeMark, protocolDirLocalIndex, nlMatrixSD-SourceAddress, nlMatrixSDDestAddress). The matrixDSTable contains the same information as matrixSDTable but is indexed by the destination address before the source address. The interpretation is as follows: Each row of the nlMatrixControl-Table identifies a single subnetwork. The matrixSDTable contains two rows for every pair of hosts on that subnetwork that have recently exchanged information: One of the rows reports the traffic in one direction between the two members of the pair; the other row reports the traffic in the opposite direction. The same set of rows also appears in matrixDSTable. Thus, the management station can easily index the information to find out about the traffic from one host to all others (use nlMatrixSDTable) or about traffic from all hosts to one particular host (use nlMatrixDSTable). This is the same type of arrangement used at the MAC level in the RMON1 matrix group, and Figure 8.14 depicts the logical matrix structure that results.

Whenever the monitor detects an exchange that involves a new host pairing, it creates a new row in both of the data tables. If the limit specified in nlMatrixControlNl-MaxDesiredEntries is reached, then the monitor deletes rows as required.

These two data tables contain the same information organized in two different ways. It is permissible to implement this as a single table or as two tables, as long as the logical view presented to the management station is of two data tables.

10.6.1.2 Network-Layer TopN Statistics

The network-layer matrix group also contains a control table and a data table that deal with TopN statistics (Figure 10.13). However, the philosophy here differs from that of RMON1. In RMON1, the HostTopN group maintains statistics that rank individual hosts on one subnetwork based on some parameter. In the case of the RMON2 TopN statistics table, the ranking is of the traffic between pairs of hosts based on some parameter. Thus, the network-layer TopN statistics can be used to determine which pairs of hosts rank in the top *N* according to some metric.

The nlMatrixTopNControlTable includes the following fields:

- nlMatrixTopNControlIndex: an integer that uniquely identifies a row in the nl-MatrixTopNControlTable (Each row in the control table defines one topN report prepared for one interface.)

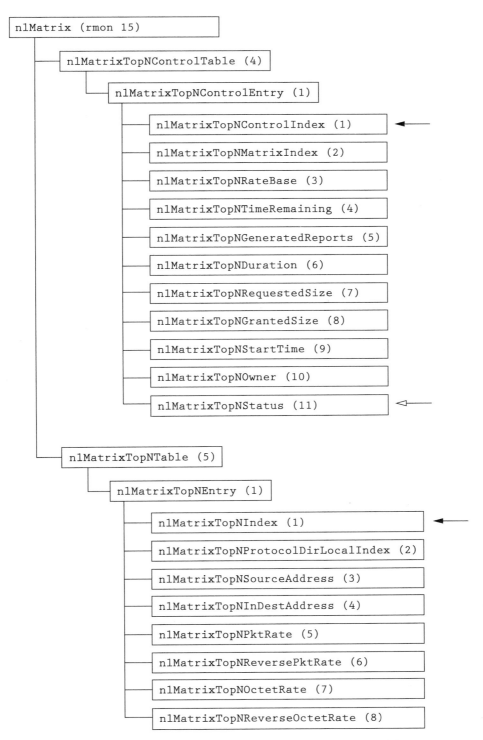

FIGURE 10.13 RMON2 network-layer matrix group: TopN tables

- `nlMatrixTopNMatrixIndex`: specifies a particular subnetwork, since this value matches a value of `nlMatrixControlIndex`, `nlMatrixSDIndex`, and `nlMatrix-DSIndex` (The `topN` report defined by this row of the control table is prepared using the corresponding entries in `nlMatrixSDTable` or `nlMatrixDSTable`.)

- `nlMatrixTopNRateBase`: specifies one of two variables in `nlMatrixTopNTable` that is to be used to sort the table; the type of this object is the following:

$$\text{INTEGER} \{ \text{ nlMatrixTopNPkts(1)}, \\ \text{nlMatrixTopNOctets(2)} \}$$

- `nlMatrixTopNTimeRemaining`: the number of seconds left in the sampling interval for the report currently being collected

- `nlMatrixTopNGeneratedReports`: the number of reports that have been generated by this entry

- `nlMatrixTopNDuration`: the sampling interval, in seconds, for this report

- `nlMatrixTopNRequestedSize`: the maximum number of matrix entries requested for the `topN` table

- `nlMatrixTopNGrantedSize`: the maximum number of entries in the `topN` table

- `nlMatrixTopNStartTime`: the value of `sysUpTime` when this `topN` report was last started (In other words, this is the time when the associated `hostTopNTime-Remaining` object was modified to start the requested report, as explained later in this subsection.)

The `nlMatrixTopNTable` includes the following objects:

- `nlMatrixTopNIndex`: an index that uniquely identifies one row among all data rows associated with a particular report (Each row represents a unique source–destination pair of hosts.)

- `nlMatrixTopNProtocolDirLocalIndex`: the `protocolDirLocalIndex` value that uniquely identifies a particular network-layer protocol

- `nlMatrixTopNSourceAddress`: the network-layer address of the source host in this pairing

- `nlMatrixTopNInDestAddress`: the network-layer address of the destination host in this pairing

- `nlMatrixTopNPktRate`: the number of packets seen from the source host to the destination host during this sampling interval

- `nlMatrixTopNReversePktRate`: the number of packets seen from the destination host to the source host during this sampling interval

- `nlMatrixTopNOctetRate`: the number of octets seen from the source host to the destination host during this sampling interval

- `nlMatrixTopNReverseOctetRate`: the number of octets seen from the destination host to the source host during this sampling interval

The `nlMatrixTopNTable` is indexed by `nlMatrixTopNControlIndex` and then by `nlMatrixTopNIndex`. The first index defines a set of rows that constitute a single report. The report will create a ranking for one of the two `nlMatrixTopNRateBase` variables on one subnetwork attached to the probe. The second index is used to rank the top *N* source–destination pairs in terms of the amount of traffic observed between the two in either packets or octets, depending on the `nlMatrixTopNRate` variable. That is, if `nlMatrixTopNRateBase = nlMatrixTopNPkts(1)`, then the report is sorted on `nl-MatrixTopNPktRate`; and if `nlMatrixTopNRateBase = nlMatrixTopNOctets(2)`, then the report is sorted on `nlMatrixTopNOctetRate`.

The report preparation process works as follows. To begin, a management station creates a row of the control table to specify a new report. This control entry instructs the monitor to measure the difference between the beginning and ending values of a particular host group variable over a specified sampling period. The sampling period value is stored in both `nlMatrixTopNDuration` and `nlMatrixTopNTimeRemaining`. The first value is static; the second value counts down the seconds while the monitor is preparing the report. When `nlMatrixTopNTimeRemaining` reaches 0, the monitor calculates the final results and creates a set of *N* data rows, indexed by `nlMatrixTopNIndex`, with the top *N* hosts listed in decreasing order of the calculated rates. The ordering is not made on the observed rate only; the observed reverse rate is reported but does not affect the rankings.

Unlike RMON1, RMON2 `TopN` tables automatically retrigger when the sort completes. In this way, the sorted report is updated every `TopNDuration` seconds automatically. Once the report is created, it remains as a set of read-only data rows available to the management station until it is overwritten by a new report. A network management system can determine whether a new report is available yet by polling the `TopNGenerated-Reports` object. The network management system must retrieve a new report within `TopNDuration` or else lose it.

10.6.2 Application-Layer Matrix Group

The application-layer matrix group consists of three data tables and one control table (Figure 10.14). Two of the data tables deal with the collection of matrix statistics, while the other data table deals with the collection of `topN` statistics.

10.6.2.1 Application-Layer Source/Destination Statistics

The two data tables that deal with application-level source/destination statistics are controlled by `nlMatrixControlTable`. The `alMatrixSDTable` is used to store statistics on traffic from a particular source application-layer address to a number of destinations. The `alMatrixSDTable` will create entries for all application-layer protocols in the protocol

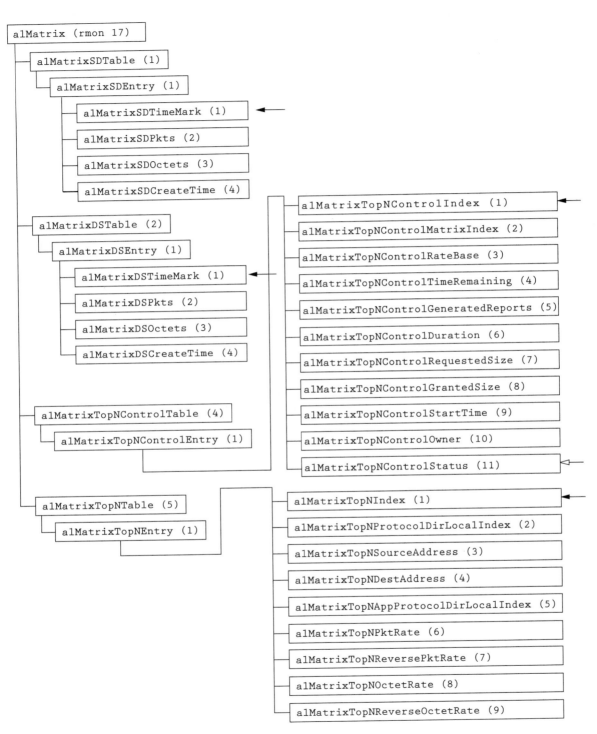

FIGURE 10.14 RMON2 application-layer matrix group

directory table whose value of `protocolDirAlMatrixConfig` is equal to `supported-On(3)`. The table includes the following objects:

- `alMatrixSDTimeMark`: a time filter for this entry (see Section 10.1 for a discussion of time filters)
- `alMatrixSDPackets`: the number of error-free packets transmitted from this source address to this destination address
- `alMatrixSDOctets`: the number of octets, excluding packets with errors, transmitted from this source address to this destination address
- `alMatrixSDCreateTime`: the value of `sysUpTime` when this control entry was activated

This table (and `alMatrixDSTable`) provides an extreme example of using objects that are not columnar objects in the table for indexing. The indexes for this table, in the order used, are

1. `nlMatrixControlIndex`: identifies a unique subnetwork and a unique row of `nlMatrixControlTable`. This selects all of the rows of `alMatrixSDTable` controlled by this row.
2. `alMatrixSDTimeMark`: a time filter index. This narrows the selection to those rows determined by a time filter.
3. `protocolDirLocalIndex`: identifies a unique network-layer protocol. This narrows the selection to statistics for a particular network-level protocol within a given time filter on a given subnetwork.
4. `nlMatrixSDSourceAddress`: identifies the unique source address on this subnetwork with this network-layer protocol. This narrows the selection to a particular source host using a particular network-level protocol within a given time filter on a given subnetwork.
5. `nlMatrixSDDestAddress`: identifies the unique destination address on this subnetwork with this network-layer protocol. This narrows the selection to statistics for traffic from the specified source host to this destination host.
6. `protocolDirLocalIndex`: identifies a unique application-level protocol that runs on the selected network-layer protocol. Thus, for the source–destination pair selected by the first five indexes, this index selects a single row that gathers statistics for a single application-level protocol operating between the source and destination hosts.

Thus, the indexing of this table involves six index objects from three different tables. As always, when index objects are not columnar objects in the table itself, it is up to the implementor to implement `alMatrixDSTable` in such a way that these indexes work.

The RMON2 MIB document includes the following example of the selection of a single object instance of `alMatrixSDPkts` in a single row of `alMatrixSDTable`:

> `alMatrixSDPkts.1.783495.18.4.128.2.6.6.4.128.2.6.7.34`

The subidentifier [1] specifies the first row of `nlMatrixControlTable`. The subidentifier [783495] specifies the time in time ticks for this row. The subidentifier [18] specifies the network-layer protocol defined by row 18 of `protocolDirTable`. The subidentifier sequence [4.128.2.6.6] specifies the network-layer source address; in this case, the address is an IP address consisting of four octets with an address value of 128.2.6.6. The subidentifier sequence [4.128.2.6.7] specifies the IP address of the destination host. Finally, the subidentifier [34] specifies the application-level protocol defined by row 34 of `protocolDirTable`.

The `alMatrixDSTable` contains the same information as `alMatrixSDTable` but is indexed by destination address before source address.

10.6.2.2 Application-Layer `TopN` Statistics

The application-layer `TopN` statistics control table and data table have almost exactly the same structure and functionality as the network-layer `TopN` statistics control and data tables.

First, consider the control table. The `alMatrixTopNControlTable` has the same structure as the `nlMatrixTopNControlTable`, with the same number of columnar objects, with essentially the same meanings. The one difference is the definition of the rate base object:

- `alMatrixTopNRateBase`: specifies one of two objects in `alMatrixTopNTable` that is to be used to sort the table, as well as the selector of the view of the matrix table that will be used. The type of this object is the following:

```
INTEGER { alMatrixTopNTerminalsPkts (1),
          alMatrixTopNTerminalsOctets (2),
          alMatrixTopNAllPkts (1),
          alMatrixTopNAllOctets (2) }
```

- The values `alMatrixTopNTerminalsPkts` and `alMatrixTopNTerminals-Octets` collect data only from protocols that have no child protocols that are counted, whereas the other two values collect data from all `alMatrix` entries.

The data table, `alMatrixTopNTable`, performs the same function as `nlMatrix-TopNTable`, but at the application level. The same types of columnar objects are included. In addition, `alMatrixTopNTable` includes `alMatrixTopNProtocolDirLocalIndex`, which specifies the application-level protocol being counted.

10.7 *User History Collection Group*

The user history collection (usrHistory) group periodically polls particular statistics and variables and then logs that data based on user-defined parameters. With this new feature, the network manager can configure history studies of any counter in the system, such as a specific history on a particular file server or router-to-router connection. In the RMON1 specification, historical data are collected only on a predefined set of statistics.

The structure of this group is the most complex of all of the RMON groups. In effect, this group consists of a three-level hierarchy of tables (Figure 10.15). At the top level is the usrHistoryControlTable; this control table specifies the details of the sampling function. Subordinate to this are one or more instances of usrHistory-ObjectTable; each of these control tables[3] specifies the variables to be sampled. Subordinate to each instance of usrHistoryObjectTable are one or more instances of usrHistoryTable; each of these data tables records the specified data.

As suggested in the RMON2 document, a useful way to characterize this structure is the following: The usrHistoryControlTable is a one-dimensional table consisting of a sequence of rows. Each row configures a set of user-history buckets, similar to each row in historyControlTable. The difference is that the creation of a row in usr-HistoryControlTable causes the creation of one or more instances of usrHistory-ObjectTable. Thus, we can think of usrHistoryObjectTable as being two-dimensional, consisting of a set of one-dimensional tables. Finally, each row of usrHistoryObjectTable refers to a single mib object instance and configures an instance of usrHistoryTable to collect a history for that object instance. Each row of a single instance of usrHistoryTable represents the value of a single mib object instance during a specific sampling interval.

The usrHistoryControlTable includes the following columnar objects:

- usrHistoryControlIndex: an integer that uniquely identifies a row in the usr-HistoryControlTable. Each entry configures a set of samples at a particular interval for a specified set of mib object instances.

- usrHistoryControlObjects: This is the number of mib objects for which data are to be collected in the portion of usrHistoryTable associated with this entry.

- usrHistoryControlBucketsRequested: the requested number of discrete sampling intervals over which data are to be saved in the part of usrHistoryTable

---

[3]In RMON terminology, the term "control table" refers to a table in which the manager can dynamically create rows using a random index; control tables like these have index, owner, and status objects; in this sense usr-HistoryObjectTable is not a control table. In a wider context, if all tables are either control or data, then this must be a control table. Perhaps the best way to describe it is as an extension of the usrHistoryControlTable. If SNMP had tables within tables, then this one would have been embedded in the usrHistoryControlTable.

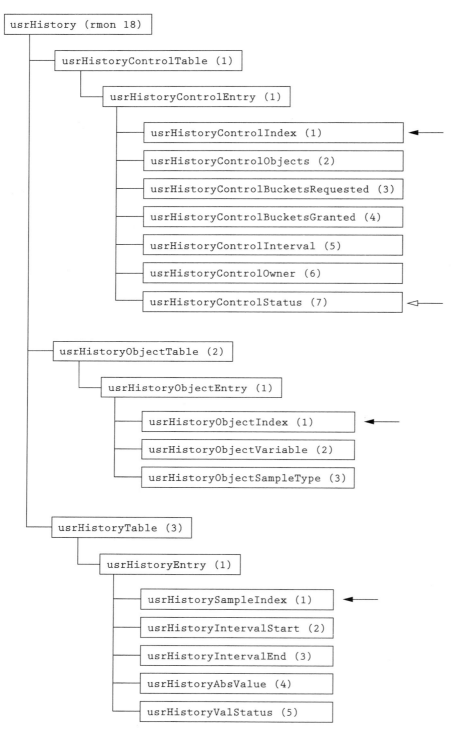

FIGURE 10.15 RMON2 user history collection group

associated with this entry. A default value of 50 is assigned to this object if it is not provided by the creator of this row.

- `usrHistoryControlBucketsGranted`: the actual number of discrete sampling intervals over which data will be saved in the part of `usrHistoryTable` associated with this entry. When the associated `usrHistoryControlBucketsRequested` is created or modified, the monitor should set this object as closely to the requested value as possible.

- `usrHistoryControlInterval`: the interval (in seconds) over which data are sampled for each bucket in the part of `usrHistoryTable` associated with this entry. The interval can be set to any number between 1 and $2^{31} - 1$ (over 68 years!). A default value of 1800 seconds (30 minutes) is assigned to this object if it is not provided by the creator of this row.

The sampling scheme is dictated by `usrHistoryControlBucketsGranted` and `usrHistoryControlInterval`. For example, using the default values, the monitor would take a sample of each of the objects (number of objects = `usrHistoryControl-Objects`) once every 30 minutes; each sample of each object is stored in a row of `etherHistoryTable`, and the most recent 50 rows are retained.

The `usrHistoryObjectTable` is a control table that includes the following columnar objects:

- `usrHistoryObjectIndex`: an integer that uniquely identifies a row in the `usrHistoryObjectTable`. Each entry defines a `mib` object instance to be sampled periodically.

- `usrHistoryObjectVariable`: The value of this object is an object identifier that specifies the particular `mib` object instance to be sampled. Only variables that resolve to the ASN.1 primitive type of `Integer32` (`Integer32`, `Counter`, `Gauge`, and `TimeTicks`) may be sampled.

- `usrHistoryObjectSampleType`: takes on the value `absoluteValue(1)` or `deltaValue(2)`. If the value of this object is `absoluteValue(1)`, then the value of the selected variable will be copied directly into the `history` bucket. If the value of this object is `deltaValue(2)`, then the value of the selected variable at the last sample is subtracted from the current value, and the difference is copied into the `history` bucket.

The `usrHistoryTable` is a data table that includes the following columnar objects:

- `usrHistorySampleIndex`: an index that uniquely identifies the particular sample this entry represents among all samples associated with the same row of the `usrHistoryControlTable`. This index starts at 1 and increases by one as each new sample is taken.

- `usrHistoryIntervalStart`: This gives the value of `sysUpTime` (in the MIB-II `systems` group) at the start of the interval over which this sample was measured.

- usrHistoryIntervalEnd: This indicates the value of sysUpTime at the end of the interval over which this sample was measured.

- usrHistoryAbsValue: the absolute value of the user-specified statistic during the last sampling period. This object has a syntax of Gauge32 and therefore ranges from 0 to $2^{32} - 1$.

- usrHistoryValStatus: takes on the values valueNotAvailable(1), valuePositive(2), valueNegative(3). Thus, in effect, the sample value is a 33-bit signed integer.

Figure 10.16 illustrates the relationship between the two control tables and the data table. Each row of usrHistoryControlTable has a unique value of usrHistoryControlIndex. This index also serves as the primary index into usrHistoryObjectTable so that, in effect, each row of usrHistoryControlTable has its own usrHistoryObjectTable. This latter table defines the list of objects to be sampled for this row of usrHistoryControlTable. It is possible for two different instances of usrHistoryObjectTable to list the same set of variables, as long as the controlling values of usrHistoryControlInterval are different. This means that for any given set of variables, more than one sampling process can be in effect.

For each of the M rows of usrHistoryControlTable, there is a set of rows of usrHistoryObjectTable. In the figure, the number of rows of usrHistoryObjectTable associated with usrHistoryControlTable row j is N_j. These are the N_j objects to be sampled, a value that is equal to usrHistoryControlObjects.j. Similarly, for each of the M rows of usrHistoryControlTable, there is a set of instances of usrHistoryTable subordinate to the corresponding part of usrHistoryObjectTable. The number of sets is equal to the value of usrHistoryControlObjects for that row of usrHistoryControlTable. The number of rows of each of these instances of usrHistoryTable associated with usrHistoryControl table row j is B_j. These are the B_j most recent samples for control entry j. The maximum value of B_j is the corresponding value of usrHistoryControlBucketsGranted.

The sampling scheme works as follows. The monitor or a management station can define a new "history," which is unique in terms of the set of objects and the sampling interval. This usrHistoryControlTable row is assigned a unique index by the monitor. Associated with each history (that is, each row of usrHistoryControlTable) are an instance of usrHistoryObjectTable, which specifies the objects to be sampled, and a set of instances of usrHistoryTable. Each row of each instance of usrHistoryTable, also called a *bucket*, holds the statistics gathered during one sampling interval for one of the objects.

As each sampling interval occurs, the monitor adds a new row to each instance of usrHistoryTable with a usrHistorySampleIndex of one more than the value for the row corresponding to the previous sampling interval. Once the number of rows for a history becomes equal to usrHistoryControlBucketsGranted, the set of rows for

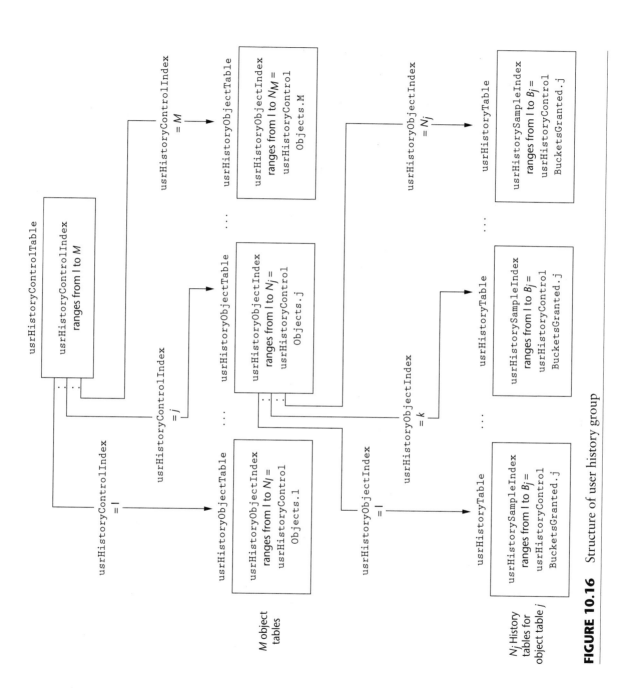

FIGURE 10.16 Structure of user history group

319

that history functions as a circular buffer. As each new row is added to the set, the oldest row associated with this history is deleted. Similarly, if the number of rows granted to a history is reduced, by a change in usrHistoryControlBucketsRequested and usrHistoryControlBucketsGranted, rows are deleted for that history to match the new granted size.

10.8 *Probe Configuration Group*

The probe configuration (probeConfig) group is designed to enhance interoperability among RMON probes and managers by defining a standard set of configuration parameters for probes. This makes it easier for one vendor's RMON application to be able to configure remotely another vendor's RMON probe.

The probe configuration group consists of a set of scalar objects plus four tables (Figure 10.17). The scalar objects are

- probeCapabilities: indicates which RMON groups are supported
- probeSoftwareRev: software revision of this device
- probeHardwareRev: hardware revision of this device
- probeDateTime: probe's current date and time
- probeResetControl: takes on the values running(1), warmBoot(2), and coldBoot(3)
- probeDownloadFile: the name of the file that contains the boot image to be downloaded from the TFTP (Trivial File Transfer Protocol) server
- probeDownloadTFTPServer: the IP address of the TFTP server that contains the boot image to load
- probeDownloadAction: takes on the values imageValid(1), downloadTo-PROM(2), and downloadToRAM(3) (When this object is set to (2) or (3), the device discontinues normal operation, downloads the boot image, and then does a warm boot to restart the newly loaded application.)
- probeOutDownloadStatus: defined as follows:

```
INTEGER { downloadSuccess(1),
          downloadStatusUnknown(2),
          downloadGeneralError(3),
          downloadNoResponseFromServer(4),
          downloadChecksumError(5),
          downloadIncompatibleImage(6),
          tftpFileNotFound(7),
          tftpAccessViolation(8) }
```

FIGURE 10.17   RMON2 probe configuration group

10.8.1 Control Strings

For use by several of the tables in the probe configuration group, a textual convention is defined with the assignment

$$\texttt{ControlString ::= DisplayString}$$

A *control string* is used to communicate with a modem or serial data switch and contains embedded commands to control how the device will interact with the remote device through the serial interface. Commands are represented by two-character sequences beginning with the ^ character. The following commands are defined.

^s   Send the string that follows, up to the next command or the end of the string.
^c   Delay for the number of seconds that follows.
^t   Set timeout to the value represented by the decimal digits that follow.
^w   Wait for the reply string that follows, up to the next command or the end of the string.
^!   Send the ^ character.
^d   Delay for the number of seconds represented by the decimal digits that follow.
^b   Send break for the number of milliseconds specified by the decimal digits that follow.

10.8.2 Serial Configuration Table

This table contains one row for each serial interface on the probe. It consists of the following elements:

- serialMode: incoming connection may be direct(1) or modem(2)
- serialProtocol: data link protocol to use may be slip(2) or other(1)
- serialTimeout: the number of seconds of inactivity allowed before terminating the connection on this interface
- serialModemInitString: a control string that specifies the initialization string for this modem
- serialModemHangUpString: a control string that specifies how to disconnect a modem connection on this interface
- serialModemConnectResp: an ASCII string that describes the modem response code and associated bps rate
- serialModemNoConnectResp: an ASCII string containing response codes that may be generated by a modem to report connection attempt failure
- serialDialoutTimeout: timeout value for dialing out

10.8.3 Network Configuration Table

This table contains one row for each network interface on the probe. It consists of the following elements:

- netConfigIpAddress: IP address of this interface
- netConfigSubnetMask: IP subnet mask of this interface

  In addition, a scalar object is associated with this table:

- netDefaultGateway: the IP address of the default gateway, or router

10.8.4 Trap Destination Table

This table defines the destination addresses for traps generated from this device. The table maps a community to one or more trap destination entries. The same trap will be sent to all destinations specified in the rows that have the same trapDestCommunity as the eventCommunity object in the RMON event group. The table includes the following objects:

- TrapDestIndex: a unique index for this row
- TrapDestCommunity: the community (see Section 7.1.2 for a definition of "community") to which these destination IP addresses belong
- TrapDestProtocol: the protocol with which to send this trap
- TrapDestAddress: the IP address to which to send traps

  This table is to be used in conjunction with the eventTable in the RMON1 event group. In essence, eventTable defines traps that are to be sent to specified communities, and trapDestTable specifies the IP addresses for sending traps to the members of that community.

10.8.5 Serial Connection Table

This table stores the parameters needed for initiating a SLIP (Serial Line Interface Protocol) connection to a management station. The table includes the following objects:

- serialConnectIndex: a unique index for this row
- serialConnectDestIpAddress: the IP address that can be reached at the other end of this SLIP connection
- serialConnectType: takes on the values direct(1), modem(2), switch(3), modemSwitch(4)

- `serialConnectDialString`: a control string that specifies how to dial the phone number to establish a modem connection
- `serialConnectSwitchConnectSeq`: a control string that specifies how to establish a data switch connection
- `serialConnectDisconnectSeq`: a control string that specifies how to terminate a data switch connection
- `serialConnectSwitchResetSeq`: a control string that specifies how to reset a data switch connection in the event of a timeout

10.9   *Extensions to RMON1 for RMON2 Devices*

The RMON2 specification includes the definition of a number of objects to be added to RMON1 tables. Table 10.2 lists these additions, which can be summarized as follows.

1. A `createTime` object is added to all control tables.
2. A `droppedFrames` object is added to a number of tables, included as a filter object in all filter definitions.
3. The object `filterProtocolDirLocalIndex` is added to `filterTable`.

The object `filterProtocolDirLocalIndex` is defined as follows.

> *DESCRIPTION*
> *"When this object is set to a non-zero value, the filter that it is associated with performs the following operations on every packet:*
>   *1. If the packet doesn't match the protocol directory entry, discard and exit.*
>   *2. If the associated* `filterProtocolDirLocalIndex` *is non-zero and the packet doesn't match the protocol directory entry, discard the packet and exit.*
>   *3. If the packet matches, perform the regular filter algorithm as if the beginning of the named protocol is the beginning of the packet, potentially applying the filterOffset value to move further into the packet."*

In other words, if this object has a nonzero value, its value indicates a protocol defined in `protocolDirTable`. All packets that do not match this protocol and any associated filters are discarded. For packets that do match this protocol, the headers of all lower-level protocols are stripped off and the regular filter algorithm is performed on the remainder. For example, if the protocol specified is IP, then the filter removes the MAC-level header and trailer from all incoming IP packets and then performs the filtering operation on the IP packet.

TABLE 10.2   Extensions to the RMON1 MIB

Augmented Table	Object	Description
etherStatsTable	etherStatsDroppedFrames probe but not counted	Number of frames received by
	etherStatsCreateTime	Value of sysUpTime when this row was activated
historyControlTable	historyControlDroppedFrames	Number of frames received by probe but not counted
hostControlTable	hostControlDroppedFrames	Number of frames received by probe but not counted
	hostControlCreateTime	Value of sysUpTime when this row was activated
matrixControlTable	matrixControlDroppedFrames	Number of frames received by probe but not counted
	matrixControlCreateTime	Value of sysUpTime when this row was activated
channelTable	channelDroppedFrames	Number of frames received by probe but not counted
	channelCreateTime	Value of sysUpTime when this row was activated
tokenRingMLStatsTable	tokenRingMLStatsDroppedFrames	Number of frames received by probe but not counted
	tokenRingMLStatsCreateTime	Value of sysUpTime when this row was activated
tokenRingPStatsTable	tokenRingPStatsDroppedFrames	Number of frames received by probe but not counted
	tokenRingPStatsCreateTime	Value of sysUpTime when this row was activated
ringStationControlTable	ringStationControlDroppedFrames	Number of frames received by probe but not counted
	ringStationControlCreateTime	Value of sysUpTime when this row was activated
sourceRoutingStatsTable	sourceRoutingStatsDroppedFrames	Number of frames received by probe but not counted
	sourceRoutingStatsCreateTime	Value of sysUpTime when this row was activated
filterTable	filterProtocolDirDataLocalIndex	Filters on the basis of the source or destination address
	filterProtocolDirLocalIndex	Filters on the basis of protocol directory entry

10.10 *Practical Issues*

We discussed, in Section 9.5, the performance limitations of RMON1. These limitations are of even greater concern with RMON2. Compared with RMON1, RMON2 must keep track of many more protocol types. Thus, it is a finer-grained data collection and aggregation tool, requiring more processing. To cope with these demands, RMON2 vendors are offering stand-alone probes which run on high-power platforms, equivalent to high-end workstations or servers. Despite this, keeping up with network traffic turns out to be a difficult task.

In this section, we look at the results from a recent performance study of six vendors of stand-alone RMON2 probes (Newman, Giorgis, and Melson, 1998). The probes were tested on a fast Ethernet (100 Mbps) LAN segment, to which was attached the probe plus two traffic generators, one for TCP segments and one for UDP segments. To report the results, each probe was connected by a separate port to a 10-Mbps Ethernet segment, to which an RMON2 management application station was also attached. Thus, results from the testing were reported "out-of-band" and did not generate traffic on the 100-Mbps segment.

Three separate tests were run for each probe. In each test, the RMON2 network-layer matrix group was enabled, and test traffic at a known rate was offered on the network segment. The results at the management application were then observed to see whether all of the traffic was reported. The tests ranged from a very light load to a maximum load.

The first test was at a very light load of 650 UDP packets per second (pps), using 64-octet packets, which is well below 1 percent of the capacity of the Ethernet. The traffic consisted of four streams of segments, each with a different UDP port number. All of the probes successfully identified the traffic as UDP, and there were only minor differences in the traffic counts reported.

The second test loaded up the network to about 50 percent capacity. The UDP load remained constant at 650 pps, while the rest of the load consisted of unidirectional TCP segments, with no acknowledgements coming back to the traffic generator. The results, shown in Figure 10.18(a), were disappointing. Only two of the probes came close to measuring the actual TCP load. One probe virtually collapsed, reporting only about 11 percent of the load. Further, the probes could not keep up with the modest UDP traffic either. Only one probe reported this traffic accurately. Both these results should raise alarm signals to (human) managers. With respect to the TCP traffic, the test showed that under a heavy load, but one that is still well within the capacity of the network, most probes are unable to report the extent of the load accurately. With respect to the UDP traffic, the test showed that probes may not be able to keep an accurate count of small traffic streams when there is a lot of background traffic. In the corporate world, many applications (for example, SNA applications) fit a profile of consuming a small percentage of the capacity but carrying the most mission-critical data. To be unable to capture this important traffic in the face of a relatively heavy load is bad news.

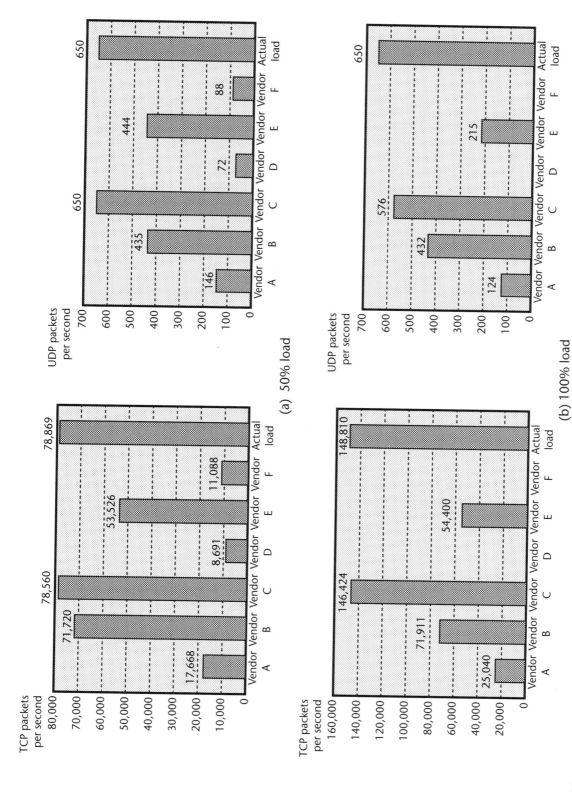

FIGURE 10.18 RMON2 probe performance

The results are even worse when the network is loaded to its maximum, as shown in Figure 10.18(b). For the TCP traffic, only one of the vendor products could make a reasonably accurate estimate of the load. None of the other probes captured even one-half of the traffic. Further, for two of the probes, this heavy load preempted the probe-to-manager link so that nothing at all was reported. Again, for the light UDP traffic, the reports that did come in varied widely from each other and all underestimated that actual UDP load. Of course, networks don't (or at least shouldn't) operate at full capacity load most of the time, but for many networks, occasional peak demand will push the network to near its limit. The probes should be able to handle this demand. Indeed, network management information is often most valuable when the network is stressed.

10.11 *Summary*

RMON2 extends the capability of the original RMON MIB to include protocols above the MAC level. The inclusion of network-layer protocols, such as IP, enables a probe to monitor traffic through routers attached to the local subnetwork. The probe can therefore monitor the sources of off-network traffic arriving by a router and the destinations of off-network traffic that leaves by a router. The inclusion of higher-layer protocols, such as those at the application level, enables the probe to provide a detailed breakdown of traffic on the basis of application.

SNMPv2

SNMPv2

Management Information

To address the deficiencies in SNMP, a major upgrade to the standard has been published, known as version 2 of SNMP (SNMPv2). SNMPv2 expands the functionality of SNMP and broadens its applicability to include OSI-based as well as TCP/IP-based networks. This chapter introduces SNMPv2 and then examines the management information aspects of the standard. Chapter 12 covers the protocol itself, and Chapter 13 discusses the additional MIB-related aspects of SNMPv2.

11.1 Background

We begin with a short history of the development of SNMPv2, plus a summary of the enhancements to SNMP provided in SNMPv2.

11.1.1 The Development of SNMPv2

The Simple Network Management Protocol (SNMP) was originally developed as a stop-gap measure to provide a minimal network management capability. SNMP had two advantages.

1. SNMP, its associated structure of management information (SMI), and its management information base (MIB) are quite simple and therefore can be easily and quickly implemented.
2. SNMP is based on the Simple Gateway Monitoring Protocol (SGMP), for which a great deal of operational experience had been gained.

By 1988 it became clear that network management was a critical need, both in the short term—to deal with the current level of network complexity—and in the long term—to deal with even more complex environments. Accordingly, a two-track policy was adopted: SNMP would be used to meet immediate network management needs, and an OSI-based solution would be pursued for long-term needs. The OSI-based solution was

CMOT (CMIP over TCP/IP), which essentially enabled OSI system management protocols to operate on top of TCP. This two-track strategy has not worked out, for several reasons.

1. It was initially intended that the SMI and MIB of SNMP be subsets of those for OSI systems management. This was planned to enable a relatively easy transition. However, the complex object-oriented approach of OSI was incompatible with quick deployment of SNMP, and so this linkage was dropped, allowing the SNMP framework to pursue the use of a simple scalar MIB. A result of this decision is to make the transition to OSI more difficult.

2. The development of stable OSI standards for network management, and the subsequent availability of product implementations, has taken much longer than anticipated. This delay opened up a window of opportunity that SNMP filled: SNMP has been implemented by a broad range of vendors and is widely deployed.

There is general agreement that for many of the large, complex network configurations now becoming common, SNMP is reaching the end of its useful life. There are, and will be for some time, many configurations for which SNMP provides adequate service. However, many users are faced with the choice between an inadequate facility (SNMP) and one that is not yet available (OSI systems management). Accordingly, there has been much interest in "fixing" SNMP to extend its useful lifetime.

One major flaw that has inhibited the use of SNMP is that it provides no security facilities. Specifically, there is no capability to authenticate the source of a management message nor any capability to prevent eavesdropping. The existence of the community name in the message header is useless from the viewpoint of security. An attacker can observe a message and learn a community name for the target device for subsequent use. Because of the lack of authentication capability, SNMP is vulnerable to attacks that can modify or disable a network configuration. As a result, many vendors have chosen not to implement the Set command, effectively crippling the management suite by reducing it to a monitoring facility. To address this problem, a set of RFCs referred to as "secure SNMP" was issued as proposed standards in July 1992.

However, secure SNMP does not address other deficiencies related to performance and functionality. To overcome these deficiencies, another proposal, known as Simple Management Protocol (SMP), was developed. SMP was the product of four individuals who have each played a major role in the history of SNMP:

- Jeffrey Case, SNMP Research, Inc.
- Keith McCloghrie, Cisco Systems
- Marshall Rose, Dover Beach Consulting, Inc.
- Steven Waldbusser, International Network Services

The SMP proposal was issued in July of 1992 as a set of eight documents. These documents were *not* RFCs. They constituted a privately issued proposal to the Internet community for an upgrade to SNMP. The extensions defined in the SMP proposal fall into four categories:

- *Scope:* SMP is designed to facilitate management of arbitrary resources, not just "network" resources. Thus, SMP can be used for applications management, systems management, and manager-to-manager communication. The SMP framework provides a more concise but more flexible framework for describing information, promoting extensibility. SMP also provides a means for describing both conformance requirements and implementation capabilities.

- *Size, speed, and efficiency:* SMP remains "simple," to enable the development of small, fast implementations. The major change in this category is the development of a bulk transfer capability for the efficient exchange of large amounts of management information.

- *Security and privacy:* SMP incorporates the enhancements found in secure SNMP.

- *Deployment and compatibility:* SMP is designed to run on top of TCP/IP, OSI, and other communications architectures. SMP is also designed to interoperate with SNMP platforms, using a subset of SMP capabilities.

After the publication of secure SNMP and SMP, both in July of 1992, a consensus emerged within the Internet community that it was highly desirable to enable users and vendors to make a single transition from the original SNMP to a second-generation SNMP that would include both security and functional enhancements. Accordingly, attempts to develop products based solely on secure SNMP were discouraged, and SMP was accepted as a baseline for beginning the process of defining a new SNMP standard, known as SNMP version 2 (SNMPv2). The original standard is now referred to as SNMPv1.

Two working groups were formed: one to deal with the security aspects of SNMPv2, and one to deal with all other aspects, including protocol and management information. Work officially began on SNMPv2 in October 1992. The charter called for the work to be completed in March of 1993. In fact, a more aggressive schedule was followed, and work on SNMPv2 was substantially complete by the end of 1992. The SNMPv2 functional working group completed its work in December of 1992, and the SNMPv2 security working group completed its work in January of 1993. The combined effort was then published as a set of proposed Internet standards in March of 1993.

After several years of experience with SNMPv2, IETF directed that a working group revisit the specification and make any needed revisions. The result was a new set of RFCs issued in 1996. In this new set of documents, the security aspects of SNMPv2 were dropped, while the rest of the specification experienced only modest changes. In addition, SNMPv2 makes use of the SNMPv1 message wrapper, with its use of the community concept. This "administrative framework" for SNMPv2 is termed "community-based SNMPv2," or SNMPv2C.

The elimination of the security features in SNMPv2 is, unfortunately, a major failure in the process of specifying the new SNMP. In a nutshell, what happened is this. There was little enthusiasm among vendors and users for the way in which security was specified in the 1993 documents. When the work began on the 1996 documents, it was hoped that some minor tune-ups to the security portion would suffice. Overall, the working group was operating on a rather tight time schedule to produce a revised version of SNMPv2 so that vendors could move forward with products. As the effort was nearing completion, one of the participants demonstrated to the satisfaction of the working group as a whole that the security portion of SNMPv2 was fatally flawed. To make a long and not very pretty story short, this is what happened next. There was an extension of the deadline for completing the new SNMPv2 documents to allow time for a new consensus to develop on a new security specification. Deadlock occurred and no such consensus was reached. Rather than extend this process indefinitely, the plug was pulled on the process and the new SNMPv2 was issued without security enhancements. This decision had the advantage of solidifying the specification of the many functional enhancements found in SNMPv2.

Table 11.1 lists the documents that constitute the specification for SNMPv2. Given that the specification now comprises eight documents, some might question the "Simple" in SNMPv2. Nevertheless, SNMPv2 does represent a natural progression from SNMPv1 and does retain, to some extent, the characteristics of ease of implementation and clarity of that earlier specification.

11.1.2 SNMPv2 Enhancements

Before listing specific enhancements that are part of SNMPv2, we need to note an overall change in the capability provided by SNMPv2. SNMPv2 can support either a highly centralized network management strategy or a distributed one. In the latter case (for example, see Figure 1.4), some systems operate in the role of both manager and agent. In

TABLE 11.1   SNMPv2 RFCs

Number	Title
1901	Introduction to Community-Based SNMPv2
1902	Structure of Management Information for SNMPv2
1903	Textual Conventions for SNMPv2
1904	Conformance Statements for SNMPv2
1905	Protocol Operations for SNMPv2
1906	Transport Mappings for SNMPv2
1907	Management Information Base for SNMPv2
1908	Coexistence Between Version 1 and Version 2 of the Internet-Standard Network Management Framework

its agent role, such a system will accept commands from a superior management system; these commands may deal with access to information stored locally at the intermediate manager or may require the intermediate manager to provide summary information about agents subordinate to itself. In addition, an intermediate manager can issue trap information to a superior manager.

The key enhancements to SNMP that are provided in SNMPv2 fall into the following categories:

- Structure of management information (SMI)
- Manager-to-manager capability
- Protocol operations

The SNMPv2 SMI expands the SNMP SMI in several ways. The macro used to define object types has been expanded to include several new data types and to enhance the documentation associated with an object. A very noticeable change is that a new convention has been provided for creating and deleting conceptual rows in a table. This convention is inspired by the one used in the RMON (remote network monitoring) MIB, but it is much more elaborate.

One important MIB is defined as part of the SNMPv2 effort. The SNMPv2 MIB contains basic traffic information about the operation of the SNMPv2 protocol; this is analogous to the `snmp` group in MIB-II. The SNMPv2 MIB also contains other information related to the configuration of an SNMPv2 manager or agent.

The most noticeable change in protocol operations is the inclusion of two new PDUs. The `GetBulkRequest` PDU enables the manager to retrieve large blocks of data efficiently. In particular, it is well suited to retrieving multiple rows in a table. The `InformRequest` PDU enables one manager to send trap type of information to another.

11.2 *Structure of Management Information*

The structure of management information (SMI) for SNMPv2 is based on the SMI for SNMP. The SNMPv2 SMI provides for more elaborate specification and documentation of managed objects and MIBs. Much of what has been added to the SNMPv2 SMI compared to the SNMP SMI codifies existing practices. The SNMPv2 SMI is nearly a proper superset of the SNMP SMI.

The SNMPv2 SMI introduces four key concepts:

- Object definitions
- Conceptual tables
- Notification definitions
- Information modules

11.2.1 Object Definitions

As with the SNMP SMI, object definitions in the SNMPv2 SMI are used to describe managed objects. The ASN.1 macro OBJECT-TYPE is used to convey the syntax and semantics of all managed objects in a systematic way.

Figure 11.1 reproduces from the SNMPv2 specification the OBJECT-TYPE macro; Figure 11.2 reproduces some associated definitions. This macro has the same general structure as the OBJECT-TYPE macro defined in RFC 1155 (SNMP SMI), with refinements in RFC 1212 (Concise MIB Definitions).

```
OBJECT-TYPE MACRO ::= BEGIN

TYPE NOTATION ::= "SYNTAX" Syntax
                  UnitsPart
                  "MAX-ACCESS" Access
                  "STATUS" Status
                  "DESCRIPTION" Text
                  ReferPart
                  IndexPart
                  DefValPart

VALUE NOTATION ::= value (VALUE ObjectName)

Syntax ::= type(ObjectSyntax) | "BITS" "{" Kibbles "}"

Kibbles ::= Kibble | Kibbles "," Kibble

Kibble ::= identifier "(" nonNegativeNumber ")"

UnitsPart ::= "UNITS" Text | empty

Access ::="not-accessible" | "accessible-for-notify" | "read-only" | "read-write" | "read-create"

Status ::= "current" | "deprecated" | "obsolete"

ReferPart ::= "REFERENCE" Text | empty

IndexPart ::= "INDEX" "{" IndexTypes "}" | "AUGMENTS" "{" Entry "}" | empty

IndexTypes ::= IndexType | IndexTypes "," IndexType

IndexType ::= "IMPLIED" Index | Index

Index ::= value (indexobject ObjectName)    --use the SYNTAX value of the
                                            --correspondent OBJECT-TYPE invocation

Entry ::= value (entryobject ObjectName)    --use the INDEX value of the
                                            --correspondent OBJECT-TYPE invocation

DefValPart ::= "DEFVAL" "{" value (Defval ObjectSyntax) "}" | empty

--uses the NVT ASCII character set
Text ::= """" string """"

END
```

FIGURE 11.1   SNMPv2 macro for object definition

Table 11.2 provides a comparison between the macro defined in the SNMPv2 documents and the macro defined for SNMP in RFCs 1155 and 1212. Those differences will be noted in the discussion that follows.

11.2.1.1 Data Types

Table 11.3 lists the data types of SNMPv1 and SNMPv2. For both SNMPv1 and SNMPv2, the type of an object may either be simple or application-based. The simple types for SNMPv2 are

- INTEGER (-2147483648..2147483647): represents integer-valued information between -2^{31} and $2^{31} - 1$ inclusive. This type can be used to define an enumerated list of integers. In this case, only the enumerated values may be used.
- OCTET STRING (SIZE (0..65535))

```
objectName ::= OBJECT IDENTIFIER

ObjectSyntax ::= CHOICE { simple            SimpleSyntax,
                   application-wide  ApplicationSyntax }

SimpleSyntax ::= CHOICE {
              integer-value    INTEGER {-2147483648..2147483647),   includes Integer32
              string-value     OCTET STRING (SIZE (0..65535) ),
              objectID-value   OBJECT IDENTIFIER }
--indistinguishable from INTEGER, but never needs more
--than 32 bits for a two's complement representation
Integer32 ::= [UNIVERSAL 2] IMPLICIT INTEGER (-2147483648..2147483647)

ApplicationSyntax ::= CHOICE { ipAddress-value          IpAddress,
                       counter-value            Counter32,
                       timeticks-value          TimeTicks,
                       arbitrary-value          Opaque,
                       big-counter-value        Counter64,
                       unsigned-integer-value   Unsigned32} --includes Gauge32
IpAddress ::= [APPLICATION 0] IMPLICIT OCTET STRING (SIZE (4) )

Counter32 ::= [APPLICATION 1] IMPLICIT INTEGER (0..4294967295)       --this wraps

Gauge32 ::= [APPLICATION 2] IMPLICIT INTEGER (0..4294967295)         --this doesn't wrap
--unsigned 32-bit quantity indistinguishable from Gauge32
Unsigned32 ::= [APPLICATION 2] IMPLICIT INTEGER (0..4294967295)
--hundredths of seconds since an epoch
TimeTicks ::= [APPLICATION 3] IMPLICIT INTEGER (0..4294967295)

Opaque ::= [APPLICATION 4] IMPLICIT OCTET STRING --for backward-compatibility only
--for counters that wrap in less than one hour with only 32 bits
Counter64 ::= [APPLICATION 6] IMPLICIT INTEGER (0..18446744073709551615)
```

FIGURE 11.2   Definitions associated with SNMPv2 macro for object definition

TABLE 11.2 A Comparison of the SMI for SNMPv2 and SNMP

SNMPv2

```
TYPE NOTATION ::= "SYNTAX" Syntax
Syntax ::= type(ObjectSyntax) |    "BITS" "{" Kibbles "}"
ObjectSyntax ::= CHOICE { simple SimpleSyntax,
            application-wide Application Syntax,
SimpleSyntax ::= CHOICE {
integer-value       INTEGER  (-2147483648..
                             2147483647),
string-value        OCTET STRING (SIZE (0..65535)).
objectID-value      OBJECT IDENTIFIER }
ApplicationSyntax ::= CHOICE {
ipAddress-value        IpAddress,
counter-value          Counter32,
timeticks-value        TimeTicks,
arbitrary-value        Opaque,
big-counter-value      Counter64,
unsigned-integer-value Unsigned32 }
UnitsPart ::= "UNITS" Text | empty


"MAX-ACCESS" Access
Access ::= "read-only" | "read-write" | "read-create" |
          "not-accessible" | "accessible-for-notify"


"STATUS" Status
Status ::= "current" | "obsolete" | "deprecated"


"DESCRIPTION" Text
ReferPart ::= "REFERENCE" Text | empty


IndexPart ::= "INDEX" "{" IndexTypes "}" |
              "AUGMENTS" "{" Entry "}" | empty
IndexTypes ::= IndexType | IndexTypes ", " IndexType
IndexType ::= "IMPLIED" Index | Index
Index ::= value (indexobject ObjectName)
Entry ::= value (entryobject ObjectName)


DefValPart ::= "DEFVAL" "{" value (defval Syntax) "}" |
    empty

VALUE NOTATION ::= value (VALUE ObjectName)
```

SNMP (RFC 1212)

```
TYPE NOTATION ::= "SYNTAX" type (ObjectSyntax)
ObjectSyntax ::= CHOICE { simple SimpleSyntax,
            application-wide Application Syntax }
SimpleSyntax ::= CHOICE {
number      INTEGER,
string      OCTET STRING,
object      OBJECT IDENTIFIER,
empty       NULL }
ApplicationSyntax ::= CHOICE {
internet    IpAddress,
counter     Counter,
gauge       Gauge,
ticks       TimeTicks,
arbitrary   Opaque }


"ACCESS" Access
Access ::= "read-only" | "read-write" | "write-only" |
          "not-accessible"


"STATUS" Status
Status ::= "mandatory" | "optional" | "obsolete" |
          "deprecated"


"DESCRIPTION" value (description DisplayString)

ReferPart ::= "REFERENCE" value (reference
              DisplayString) | empty


IndexPart ::= "INDEX" "{" IndexTypes "}"
IndexTypes ::= IndexType | IndexTypes ", " IndexType
IndexType ::= value (indexobject ObjectName)


DefValPart ::= "DEFVAL" "{" value (defvalue
               ObjectSyntax) "}" | empty

VALUE NOTATION ::= value (VALUE ObjectName)
```

TABLE 11.3   SNMPv1/SNMPv2 Data Types

Data Type	SNMPv1	SNMPv2
INTEGER	X	X
Unsigned32		X
Counter32	X	X
Counter64		X
Gauge32	X	X
TimeTicks	X	X
OCTET STRING	X	X
IpAddress	X	X
OBJECT IDENTIFIER	X	X
Opaque	X	X

- OBJECT IDENTIFIER: a unique identifier of an object, consisting of a sequence of integers, known as subidentifiers. The sequence, read from left to right, denotes the location of the object in the MIB tree structure.

Here is an example of the use of enumerated integers, taken from `ifTestTable` in RFC 1573 (Evolution of the Interfaces Group of MIB-II).

```
ifTestResult OBJECT-TYPE
    SYNTAX      INTEGER {
        none(1),    —no test yet requested
        success(2),
        inProgress(3),
        notSupported(4),
        unAbleToRun(5) —due to state of system
        aborted(6),
        failed(7)
        }
    MAX-ACCESS read-only
    STATUS current
    DESCRIPTION
        "This object contains the result of the most recently
        requested test, or the value none(1) if no tests have
        been requested since the last reset. Note that this
        facility provides no provision for saving the results
        of one test when starting another, as could be
        required if used by multiple managers concurrently."
    ::= { ifTestEntry 4 }
```

The following application types are defined in SNMPv2:

- `IpAddress`: This is a 32-bit address using the format specified in IP.
- `Counter32`: a nonnegative integer that may be incremented but not decremented. A maximum value of $2^{32} - 1$ (4,294,967,295) is specified; when the counter reaches its maximum, it wraps around and starts increasing again from zero. The SNMPv2 specification states that counters have no defined "initial" value, and thus a single value of a counter has no information content; it is only the difference between two readings of a counter that is significant.
- `Counter64`: a nonnegative integer that may be incremented but not decremented. A maximum value of $2^{64} - 1$ (18,446,744,073,709,551,615) is specified; when the counter reaches its maximum, it wraps around and starts increasing again from zero.
- `Unsigned32`: represents integers in the range 0 to $2^{32} - 1$ (4,294,967,296). This type is also used for `Gauge32`; the two are indistinguishable in ASN.1.
- `Gauge32`: a nonnegative integer that may increase or decrease, with a maximum value of $2^{32} - 1$. If the maximum value is reached, the gauge remains latched at that value until reset.
- `TimeTicks`: a nonnegative integer that counts the time, modulo 2^{32}, in hundredths of a second between two epochs. When an object type is defined in the MIB that uses this type, the definition of the object type identifies the two reference epochs.
- `Opaque`: This is provided for backward compatibility with SNMPv1.
- `BITS`: This is an enumeration of named bits.

Both SNMPv2 and SNMP include a 32-bit gauge type. The SNMPv2 document includes the following statement.

> *The Gauge32 type represents a non-negative integer, which may increase or decrease, but shall never exceed a maximum value. The maximum value cannot be greater than $2^{32} - 1$. The value of a Gauge has its maximum value whenever the information being modeled is greater than or equal to that maximum value; if the information being modeled subsequently decreases below the maximum value, the Gauge also decreases.*

There are two noteworthy points to this definition. First, the maximum value of a gauge can be set at any positive less than 2^{32}; in contrast, in SNMPv1, a gauge always has a maximum value of exactly $2^{32} - 1$. Figure 11.3 illustrates this feature (compare to Figure 5.2(b)). This is an example of what is referred to in the SMI document as "refinement," which is in essence a form of subtyping in ASN.1 (see Appendix B.2.4). Table 11.4 shows the allowable refinements for SNMPv2 data types.

The second noteworthy point about the definition of `Gauge32` is that it removes an ambiguity in the SNMP SMI. RFC 1155 states merely that a gauge latches at its maximum

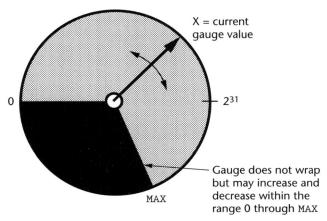

X = current
gauge value

0

2^{31}

Gauge does not wrap
but may increase and
decrease within the
range 0 through MAX

MAX

FIGURE 11.3   Limited-range gauge

TABLE 11.4   Refined Syntax Restrictions

Object Syntax	Range	Enumeration	Size	Repertoire
INTEGER	(1)	(2)		
Integer32	(1)			
Unsigned32	(1)			
OCTET STRING			(3)	(4)
OBJECT IDENTIFIER				
BITS		(2)		
IpAddress				
Counter32				
Counter64				
Gauge32	(1)			
TimeTicks				

[1]The range of permitted values may be refined by raising the lower bounds, by reducing the upper bounds, and/or by reducing the alternative value/range choices.

[2]The enumeration of named values may be refined by removing one or more named values (note that for BITS, a refinement may cause the enumerations no longer to be contiguous).

[3]The size in characters of the value may be refined by raising the lower bounds, by reducing the upper bounds, and/or by reducing the alternative size choices.

[4]The repertoire of characters in the value may be reduced by further subtyping.

value. The word "latch" is not defined, and it is not specified whether a gauge can decrease after it has attained its maximum value. There had been no agreement within the SNMP community on this point.

11.2.1.2 UnitsPart

An SNMPv2 OBJECT-TYPE macro includes an optional UNITS clause, which contains a textual definition of the units associated with an object. This clause is useful for any object that represents a measurement in some kind of units, such as time.

11.2.1.3 MAX-ACCESS Clause

The SNMPv2 MAX-ACCESS clause is similar to the SNMP ACCESS clause. The prefix MAX emphasizes that this is the maximal level of access, independent of any administrative authorization policy. The SNMPv2 definition does not include the "write-only" category. A new category, "read-create," has been added; it is used in connection with conceptual rows, as explained later in this chapter. Another new category is "accessible-for-notify." The five possibilities, ordered from least to greatest capability, are defined as follows:

- not-accessible: not accessible by a manager for any operation
- accessible-for-notify: an object that is accessible only via a notification (for example, snmpTrapOID)
- read-only: read access
- read-write: read access and write access
- read-create: read access, write access, and create access

Here is an example of the use of accessible-for-notify, taken from the Traps group of the SNMPv2 MIB (RFC 1907):

```
snmpTrapOID  OBJECT-TYPE
        SYNTAX      OBJECT IDENTIFIER
        MAX-ACCESS  accessible-for-notify
        STATUS      current
        DESCRIPTION
            "The authoritative identification of the trap currently
            being sent. This variable occurs as the second varbind in
            every SNMPv2-Trap-PDU and InformRequest-PDU."
        := { snmpTrap 1 }
```

11.2.1.4 STATUS Clause

The STATUS clause, which must be present, indicates whether this definition is current or historic. The STATUS clause for SNMPv2 does not contain the "optional" or "mandatory" categories defined for SNMPv1. An object with "current" status is valid for the current standard. A status of "obsolete" means that this object should not be implemented. A status of "deprecated" indicates that the definition is obsolete but that an implementor may wish to support that object to foster interoperability with older implementations.

11.2.1.5 Other Clauses

`ReferPart` is a textual cross-reference to an object defined in some other MIB module. This clause is optional. The `IndexPart` definition for SNMPv2 is more complex than that for SNMPv1. A discussion of this part is included in the discussion of tables, later in this section. `DefValPart` defines an acceptable default value that may be used when an object instance is created, at the discretion of the agent. This clause is optional. `VALUE NOTATION`: indicates the name used to access this object via SNMPv2.

11.2.2 SNMPv2 Tables

As with SNMPv1, management operations in SNMPv2 apply only to scalar objects. More complex information can be represented conceptually as a table.

11.2.2.1 Table Definition

A table has zero or more rows, each of which contains one or more scalar objects. In both SNMPv1 and SNMPv2, the following conventions apply.

1. A conceptual table has a `SYNTAX` clause of the form:

    SEQUENCE OF `<entry>`

    where `<entry>` refers to its subordinate conceptual row.

2. A conceptual row has a `SYNTAX` clause of the form:

    SEQUENCE { `<type1>`, . . . , `<typeN>` }

    where there is one `<type>` for each columnar object, and each `<type>` is of the form

    `<descriptor>` `<syntax>`

    where `<descriptor>` is the name of a columnar object, and `<syntax>` has the value of that object's `SYNTAX` clause. All columnar objects are always present; that is, the `DEFAULT` and `OPTIONAL` clauses are not allowed in the `SEQUENCE` definition.

3. Each columnar object is defined in the usual manner with an `OBJECT-TYPE` macro.

    SNMPv2 enhances conventions used in RFC 1212 and in the RMON specification (RFC 1757) to facilitate row creation, deletion, and access. Essentially, two categories of conceptual tables are allowed in SNMPv2:

    * *Tables that prohibit row creation and deletion by a manager:* These tables are controlled completely by the agent. The highest level of access allowed on any object is

read-write. In many cases, the entire table will consist of read-only objects. This type of table is useful when the number of rows corresponds to a fixed attribute (for example, the number of physical interfaces) or to a quantity that is controllable only by the agent.

- *Tables that allow row creation and deletion by a manager:* Such a table may be initialized with no rows, with only the manager causing row creation and deletion. It is also possible for the number of rows in the table to vary both by manager action and by independent agent action.

Both types of tables provide conventions and facilities for accessing rows in the table by indexing, and we look at this feature first. In addition, tables that allow row creation and deletion have additional features to facilitate these functions; we look at those features next.

11.2.2.2 Table Indexing

In the following discussion, it will be useful to refer to Figure 11.4, which shows a table definition using the SNMPv2 SMI. The table in this case is one that does not permit row creation or deletion.

Each conceptual row definition must include either an INDEX or an AUGMENTS clause, but not both. The INDEX clause defines a *base conceptual row*. The INDEX component of the row definition determines which object value(s) will unambiguously distinguish one row in the table.[1] That is, the INDEX objects (or objects) determine a conceptual row instance.

The one difference between the SNMPv2 convention for the INDEX clause and the RFC 1212 convention is the optional use of the IMPLIED modifier to an object name in SNMPv2. This modifier comes into play in defining instance identifiers. The rules for constructing the instance identifier of a columnar object instance are as follows. Given an object whose object identifier is y, in a table with INDEX objects i1, i2, . . . , iN, then the instance identifier for an instance of object y in a particular row is

$$y.(i1).(i2). . . . .(iN)$$

where each term in parentheses is interpreted as follows:

- *Integer-valued*: A single subidentifier takes the integer value (valid only for nonnegative integers).
- *String-valued, fixed-length*: Each octet of the string is encoded as a separate subidentifier, for a total of *n* subidentifiers for a string of length *n* octets.

---

[1]Note that the SNMPv2 document explicitly states that the INDEX objects must be sufficient to distinguish a conceptual row unambiguously. This rule was not always followed in SNMP; see the discussion in Section 7.1.3.2.

```
petTable OBJECT-TYPE
   SYNTAX     SEQUENCE OF PetEntry
   MAX-ACCESS  not-accessible
   STATUS      current
   DESCRIPTION
      "The (conceptual) table listing the characteristics of all pets living at this agent."
   ::= { A }

petEntry OBJECT-TYPE
   SYNTAX      PetEntry
   MAX-ACCESS  not-accessible
   STATUS      current
   DESCRIPTION
      "An entry (conceptual row) in the petTable. The Table is indexed by type of animal. Within
      each animal type, individual pets are indexed by a unique numerical sequence number"
   INDEX      { petType, petIndex }
   ::= { petTable 1 }

petEntry ::= SEQUENCE {
            petType            OCTET STRING,
            petIndex           INTEGER,
            petCharacteristic1  INTEGER,
            petCharacteristic2  INTEGER }

petType OBJECT-TYPE
   SYNTAX      OCTET STRING
   MAX-ACCESS  not-accessible
   STATUS      current
   DESCRIPTION
      "An auxiliary variable used to identify instances of the columnar objects in the petTable."
   ::= { petEntry 1 }

petIndex OBJECT-TYPE
   SYNTAX      INTEGER
   MAX-ACCESS  not-accessible
   STATUS      current
   DESCRIPTION
      "An auxiliary variable used to identify instances of the columnar objects in the petTable."
   ::= { petEntry 2 }

petCharacteristic1 OBJECT-TYPE
   SYNTAX      INTEGER
   MAX-ACCESS  read-only
   STATUS      current
   ::= { petEntry 3 }

petCharacteristic2 OBJECT-TYPE
   SYNTAX      INTEGER
   MAX-ACCESS  read-only
   STATUS      current
   ::= { petEntry 4 }
```

FIGURE 11.4   An example of a table for which row creation and deletion are not permitted

- *String-valued, variable length preceded by the* IMPLIED *keyword:* Each octet of the string is encoded as a separate subidentifier, for a total of *n* subidentifiers for a string of length *n* octets.
- *String-valued, variable length not preceded by the* IMPLIED *keyword:* For a string of length *n* octets, the first subidentifier is *n*; this is followed by each octet of the string encoded as a separate subidentifier, for a total of *n*+1 subidentifiers.
- *Object-identifier-valued preceded by the* IMPLIED *keyword:* For an object identifier with *n* subidentifiers, the encoding is one value for each subidentifier in order, for a total of *n* subidentifiers.
- *Object-identifier-valued not preceded by the* IMPLIED *keyword:* For an object identifier with *n* subidentifiers, the first subidentifier is *n*; this is followed by the value of each subidentifier in order, for a total of *n*+1 subidentifiers.
- IpAddress-*valued:* This means four subidentifiers, in the familiar a.b.c.d notation.

The IMPLIED keyword enables a small savings in the instance identifier when one of the index objects is a variable string. To avoid ambiguity, the IMPLIED keyword can be associated only with the last object in the INDEX clause. For example, if a table has two index objects, both of which are variable-length strings, the use of the IMPLIED keyword on both objects may be ambiguous.

As an example, consider Figure 11.4. The objects petType and petIndex serve as a pair of indices into the table; each row of the table will have a unique pair of values for these two objects. Figure 11.5 depicts an instance of this table, showing the values in the

petType (A.1.1)	petIndex (A.1.2)	petCharacteristic1 (A.1.3)	petCharacteristic2 (A.1.4)
DOG	1	23	10
DOG	5	16	10
DOG	14	24	16
CAT	2	6	44
CAT	1	33	5
WOMBAT	10	4	30
.	.	.	.
.	.	.	.
.	.	.	.

FIGURE 11.5   Example of table indexing

first six rows. Now, suppose that it is desired to reference the object instance in the second row, fourth column. The instance identifier is constructed as follows:

1. Take object identifier for desired column (A.1.4).

2. Append representation of value of first index object in desired row. In this case, `petType` is a variable-length `OCTET STRING`, and the value for this row is the `DOG`. The value has a string length of 3; the ASCII codes for each letter are 68, 79, 71, respectively. Thus the instance is represented by 3.68.79.71.

3. Append representation of value of second index object in desired row. The object `petIndex` is `INTEGER` with a value of 5 and so is represented by 5.

4. The complete instance identifier is A.1.4.3.68.79.71.5.

As an alternative to the `INDEX` clause, a conceptual row definition may include the `AUGMENTS` clause. The object name associated with the `AUGMENTS` clause must refer to a base conceptual row, and the object that includes the `AUGMENTS` clause is referred to as a *conceptual row extension*. In essence, the `AUGMENTS` feature is used to increase the number of columns in a table without rewriting the table definition. The subordinate scalar objects to the conceptual row extension object become additional columnar objects in the base conceptual row. The resulting table is treated in the same fashion as if it had been defined in a single table definition. Further, it is possible to augment a base conceptual row with multiple conceptual row extensions. Figure 11.6 is an example of the use of the `AUGMENTS` feature.

The `AUGMENTS` clause is useful in a situation where a core of information is to be stored in a table and one of several possible extensions to the table depending on configuration. For example, a vendor can easily specify vendor-specific objects as extensions to a standard MIB table. It should be easier for applications to access these objects than if they were defined as a new, separate table.

Any object that is specified in the `INDEX` clause of a conceptual row and is also a columnar object of that row is termed an *auxiliary object*. The `MAX-ACCESS` clause for auxiliary objects is `not-accessible`. This restriction makes sense:

- *Read:* In order to read any columnar object instance, it is necessary to know the value of the `INDEX` object(s) of the row instance; therefore, the only way to read the contents of an auxiliary variable is to know those contents already.

- *Write:* If a manager updates the value of an auxiliary object instance, the identity of the row is changed. This is not a permissible operation.

- *Create:* The create operation, as explained later in this section, involves assigning a value to a columnar object instance at the time of row instance creation; this is a task performed by the agent and not the manager.

It is also possible to use an object that is not part of the conceptual row (that is, not part of the conceptual table) as an index for that conceptual row. In that case, there is no

```
moreTable OBJECT-TYPE
   SYNTAX    SEQUENCE OF MoreEntry
   MAX-ACCESS  not-accessible
   STATUS      current
   DESCRIPTION
      "A table of additional pet objects."
   ::= { B }


moreEntry OBJECT-TYPE
   SYNTAX        MoreEntry
   MAX-ACCESS  not-accessible
   STATUS      current
   DESCRIPTION
      "Additional objects for a petTable entry."
   AUGMENTS    { petEntry }
   ::= { moreTable 1 }


moreEntry ::= SEQUENCE {
            nameOfVet         OCTET STRING,
            dateOfLastVisit  DateAndTime }


nameOfVet OBJECT-TYPE
   SYNTAX        OCTET STRING
   MAX-ACCESS  read-only
   STATUS        current
   ::= { moreEntry 1 }


dateOfLastVisit OBJECT-TYPE
   SYNTAX        DateAndTime
   MAX-ACCESS  read-only
   STATUS        current
   ::= { moreEntry 2 }
```

FIGURE 11.6   An example of a table that augments the table of Figure 11.4

restriction to the not-accessible access category. The DESCRIPTIONS clause for the conceptual row must include a textual explanation of how such objects are used in uniquely identifying a conceptual-row instance.

11.2.2.3 Row Creation and Deletion

Of all the issues addressed in evolving from SNMPv1 to SNMPv2, none was more controversial, consumed more time, or generated more heat than the issue of row creation and deletion. Two general strategies were considered.

1. Define two new protocol data units, `Create` and `Delete`, to be used for explicit row creation and deletion.

2. Embed the semantics for row creation and deletion into the MIB with a new textual convention called `RowStatus`. Row creation and deletion is performed using `set` and `get` operations, in the manner of the "RMON Polka" described in Section 8.1.4.2.

There are problems with both approaches, in terms of both the complexity of the algorithm and the communications overhead. Ultimately, the second strategy was adopted, and it is described in this subsection. In the following discussion, it will be useful to refer to Figure 11.7, which shows a table definition used as an example in the SNMPv2 specification.

A conceptual table may be defined in such a way as to allow the creation of new rows and the deletion of existing rows. Such tables have all of the indexing features described in the preceding subsection. To support row creation and deletion, there must be one columnar object in the table with a `SYNTAX` clause value of `RowStatus` and a `MAX-ACCESS` clause value of `read-create`. By convention, this is termed the *status column* for the conceptual row.

The definition of this textual convention is quite long.[2] However, it does provide a reasonably clear description of the intended use of this convention. It is therefore reproduced in full in Appendix 11A. *This appendix should be read before proceeding with the remainder of this subsection.* A flowchart that depicts the process of conceptual row creation is shown in Figure 11.8.

Reading the `RowStatus` definition shows that two methods are allowed for row creation, known as `createAndWait` and `createAndGo`. Let us briefly summarize the two methods.

First consider the `CreateAndWait` method. The manager begins by instructing the agent to create a new row with a given instance identifier (index value). If this succeeds, the agent creates the row and assigns values to those objects in the row with default values. If all `read-create` objects have default values, the row is placed in the `notInService` state, indicating that the row has been completed but is not active. If some `read-create` objects do not have default values, the row is placed in the `notReady` state, indicating that the row cannot be activated because some values are missing. The manager then issues a `Get` to determine the status of each `read-create` object in the row. The agent responds with a value for each object that has default values: `noSuchInstance` for each supported object that has no default value; `noSuchObject` for each object that is defined in the MIB but not supported by this agent. The manager must then

---

[2]The `EntryStatus` definition in the RMON specification was less than one page long. The `RowStatus` definition originally proposed in the SMP specification ran to two pages. The SNMPv2 `RowStatus` definition, in all its glory, consumes 11 pages in the RFC!

```
evalSlot OBJECT-TYPE
    SYNTAX        INTEGER
    MAX-ACCESS    read-only
    STATUS        current
    DESCRIPTION
        "The index number of the first
        unassigned entry in the evaluation
        table.

        A management station should create
        new entries in the evaluation table
        using this algorithm: first, issue a
        management protocol retrieval
        operation to determine the value of
        evalSlot; and, second, issue a
        management protocol set operation to
        create an instance of the evalStatus
        object setting its value to
        createAndGo (4) or
        createAndWait(5). If this latter
        operation succeeds, then the
        management station may continue
        modifying the instances
        corresponding to the newly created
        conceptual row, without fear of
        collision with other management
        stations."
    ::= { eval 1 }


evalTable OBJECT-TYPE
    SYNTAX    SEQUENCE OF EvalEntry
    MAX-ACCESS  not-accessible
    STATUS        current
    DESCRIPTIION
        "The (conceptual) evaluation table."
    ::= { eval 2 }


evalEntry OBJECT-TYPE
    SYNTAX        EvalEntry
    MAX-ACCESS  not-accessible
    STATUS        current
    DESCRIPTION
        "An entry (conceptual row) in the
        evaluation table."
    INDEX         { evalIndex }
    ::= { evalTable 1 }
```

```
EvalEntry ::= SEQUENCE {
                evalIndex    Integer32,
                evalString   DisplayString,
                evalValue    Integer32,
                evalStatus   RowStatus }

evalIndex OBJECT-TYPE
    SYNTAX        Integer32
    MAX-ACCESS  not-accessible
    STATUS        current
    DESCRIPTION
        "The auxiliary variable used to
        identify instances of the columnar
        objects in the evaluation table."
    ::= { evalEntry 1 }

evalString OBJECT-TYPE
    SYNTAX        DisplayString
    MAX-ACCESS  read-create
    STATUS        current
    DESCRIPTION
        "The string to evaluate."
    ::= { evalEntry 2 }

evalValue OBJECT-TYPE
    SYNTAX        Integer32
    MAX-ACCESS  read-only
    STATUS        current
    DESCRIPTION
        "The value when evalString was last
        executed."
    DEFVAL { 0 }
    ::= { evalEntry 3 }

evalStatus OBJECT-TYPE
    SYNTAX        RowStatus
    MAX-ACCESS  read-create
    STATUS        current
    DESCRIPTION
        "The status column used for creating,
        modifying, and deleting instances of
        the columnar objects in the evaluation
        table."
    DEFVAL { active }
    ::= { evalEntry 4 }
```

FIGURE 11.7   An example of a table for which row creation and deletion are permitted

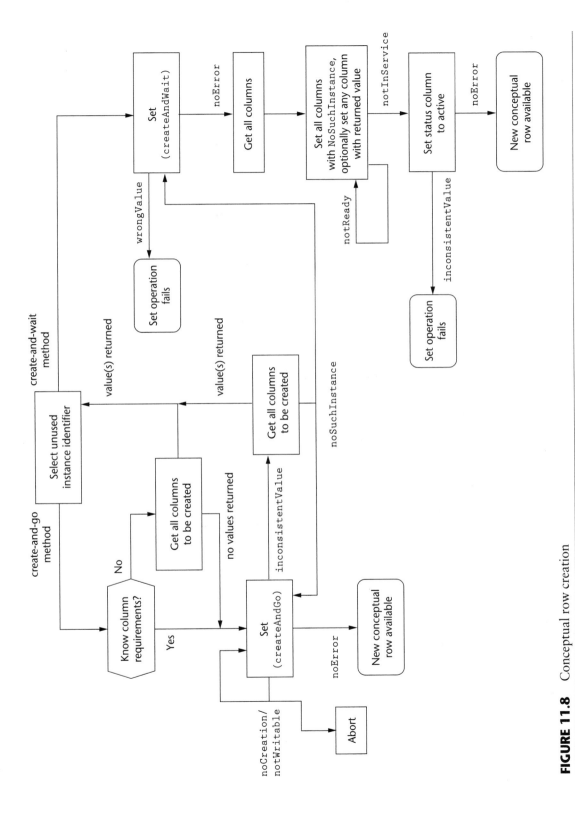

FIGURE 11.8 Conceptual row creation

351

use a Set to assign a value to all noSuchInstance objects and may also assign new values to default-value objects. Once all supported columnar objects with a read-create access category have been created, the manager can issue a Set to set the value of the status column to active.

The createAndGo method is simpler, but it is restricted in two ways. First, it must be limited to tables whose objects can fit into a single Set or Response PDU; second, the manager does not automatically learn of default values. The manager begins by selecting an instance identifier. It may then issue a Get PDU to determine which read-create objects are noSuchInstance, or it may already have this information from prior knowledge of the agent. The manager then issues a Set PDU that creates a new row and assigns values to objects in that row. The manager must assign values to all read-create objects that do not have default values and may assign values to read-create objects that do have default values. If the Set operation succeeds, the row is created and put in the active state.

To understand the tradeoffs between the two methods, consider the following checklist of features for row creation, which was constructed by the designers of the Row-Status algorithm:

MANDATORY FEATURES

1. *It must handle rows larger than one PDU.* For some tables, the number of creatable variables in a row is so large that a variable-list assignment of all rows will not fit into a single Set PDU.

2. *It must allow management station to learn of columns not implemented in agent.* An agent may support a particular table but not some of the objects in that table. It must be possible to create a row for such a table.

3. *It must allow management station to learn of columns not accessible in agent.* A columnar object with a MAX-ACCESS value of not-accessible exists, but no value can be set for that object. An example is the INDEX object for the table.

4. *It must arbitrate between multiple managers accessing same row.* If two managers attempt to create a row with the same instance identifier (the same value for the INDEX object), the agent must be able to enforce the creation of a single row for one of the managers and inform the other manager to try again with a different INDEX value.

5. *It must protect create operations from reordering.*

6. *It must allow protocol entity to detect* tooBig *before create is executed.* An agent must not create a row only to discover that it cannot respond properly in a single Response PDU.

7. *It must allow* read-only *and* read-create *objects to coexist in same row.*

VERY IMPORTANT FEATURES

8. It should allow simplified agent.

9. It should keep protocol entity ignorant of row relationships. The agent should not have to take into account any semantic relationship between rows while performing row creation and deletion.

10. It should not add a new PDU type.

USEFUL FEATURES

11. It should perform operations in one transaction.

12. It should allow the management station blindly to accept default values for columns it does not care about.

13. It should allow the management station to learn of the agent's default values and optionally override them.

14. It should allow the agent to choose index when it is arbitrary. For some tables, the index has significance (for example, a table indexed by an IP address). For other tables, the index is simply an arbitrary unique integer.

15. It should have the agent choose index as part of create operation. This would relieve the manager of the necessity of learning an unused index value before commencing row creation.

Based on this checklist, the two methods evaluate as shown below.[3]

Feature	Category	createAndWait	createAndGo
1	Must	Yes	No
2	Must	Yes	Yes
3	Must	Yes	Yes
4	Must	Yes	Yes
5	Must	Yes	Yes
6	Must	Yes	Yes
7	Must	Yes	Yes
8	Important	No	Yes
9	Important	Yes	Yes
10	Important	Yes	Yes
11	Useful	No	No
12	Useful	Yes	No
13	Useful	Yes	No
14	Useful	Yes	Yes
15	Useful	No	No

[3]Table contributed by Steve Waldbusser.

The `createAndWait` method places greater burden on the agent, which must be able to maintain conceptual rows in the `notInService` state. However, it is more powerful than `createAndGo` and can handle arbitrary row creations. On the other hand, the `createAndGo` method involves only one or two PDU exchanges and is therefore more efficient of communications resources, management station time, and agent complexity. However, it cannot handle arbitrary row creations. Both options are available and an agent implementor may decide which option to support for each table.

Once we have defined the PDUs for SNMPv2, we will return to the topic of row creation in Chapter 12 and work through an example.

To delete a conceptual row, a management station issues a `set` operation that sets the value of the status column instance to `destroy(6)`. If the operation succeeds, the agent immediately removes the entire conceptual row from the table.

A management station may also suspend a row that is currently active. To do this, the management station issues a `set` operation that sets the value of the status column instance to `notInService(2)`. If the agent is not willing to suspend the row, it returns with an error of `wrongValue`. Otherwise, the agent takes the specified row out of service and returns a response with `noError`.

11.2.2.4 Access Category Restrictions

Table 11.5 summarizes the restrictions on the access category of various objects associated with conceptual tables. Note that the restrictions differ, depending on whether or not the table supports row creation and deletion by management stations.

TABLE 11.5   Allowable Values of the `MAX-ACCESS` Clause for Table-related Objects

(a) Columnar Objects

Object	Table That Permits Row Creation and Deletion	Table That Does Not Permit Row Creation and Deletion
INDEX object (auxiliary)	`not-accessible`	`not-accessible`
Status object	`read-create`	—
Other columnar objects	`read-create` or `read-only` or `accessible-for-notify`	`read-write` or `read-only` or `accessible-for-notify`

(b) Noncolumnar Objects Related to the Table

Object	Table That Permits Row Creation and Deletion	Table That Does Not Permit Row Creation and Deletion
Table object	`not-accessible`	`not-accessible`
Entry (row) object	`not-accessible`	`not-accessible`
INDEX object (not included in table)	no restriction	no restriction

11.2.3 Notification Definitions

The NOTIFICATION-TYPE macro is used to define the information that is sent by an SNMPv2 entity when an exceptional event occurs at the entity. Figure 11.9 shows the NOTIFICATION-TYPE macro. A simple example, taken from RFC 1573 (Evolution of the Interfaces Group of MIB-II), is the linkUp trap:

```
linkUp NOTIFICATION-TYPE
    OBJECTS { ifIndex, ifAdminStatus, ifOperStatus }
    STATUS current
    DESCRIPTION
        "A linkUp trap signifies that the SNMPv2 entity, acting in an
        agent role, has detected that the ifOperStatus object for one of
        its communication links has transitioned out of the down state."
    ::= { snmpTraps 4 }
```

The optional OBJECTS clause defines the ordered sequence of MIB objects that are contained within every instance of the notification. The values of these objects are communicated to a manager when a notification occurs. The DESCRIPTION clause contains a textual definition of the semantics of the notification. The optional REFERENCE clause contains a textual cross-reference to an event or trap defined in some other MIB module. The value of an invocation of the NOTIFICATION-TYPE macro is an object identifier

```
NOTIFICATION-TYPE MACRO ::= BEGIN

TYPE NOTATION ::= ObjectsPart
                  "STATUS" Status
                  "DESCRIPTION" Text
                  ReferPart

VALUE NOTATION ::= value (VALUE NotificationName)

ObjectsPart ::= "OBJECTS" "{" Objects "}" | empty

Objects ::= Object | Objects "," Object

Object ::= value (Name ObjectName)

Status ::= "current" | "deprecated" | "obsolete"

ReferPart ::= "REFERENCE" Text | empty

Text ::= """" string """"

END
```

FIGURE 11.9   NOTIFICATION-TYPE macro

assigned to the notification. The procedure for issuing a notification using SNMPv2 is described in Chapter 12.

11.2.4 Information Modules

SNMPv2 introduces the concept of an *information module,* which specifies a group of related definitions. Three kinds of information modules are used:

1. MIB (management information base) modules, which contain definitions of interrelated managed objects and make use of the OBJECT-TYPE and NOTIFICATION-TYPE macros

2. Compliance statements for MIB modules, which make use of the OBJECT-GROUP and MODULE-COMPLIANCE macros

3. Capability statements for agent implementations that make use of the AGENT-CAPABILITIES macros.

These latter two modules are discussed in Section 13.2.

Figure 11.10 shows the MODULE-IDENTITY macro. All information modules start with exactly one invocation of the MODULE-IDENTITY macro, which provides contact and revision history. For example, the module identity statement for the main SNMPv2 MIB is as follows:

```
snmpMIB MODULE-IDENTITY
   LAST-UPDATED "9511090000Z"
   ORGANIZATION "IETF SNMPv2 Working Group"
   CONTACT-INFO
      "     Marshall T. Rose
        Postal: Dover Beach Consulting, Inc.
                420 Whisman Court
                Mountain View, CA 94043-2186
                US
        Tel: +1 415 968 1052
        E-mail: mrose@dbc.mtview.ca.us"
   DESCRIPTION
      "The MIB module for SNMPv2 entities."
   REVISION "9304010000Z"
   DESCRIPTION
      "The initial revision of this MIB module was published as
       RFC 1450."
   ::= { snmpModules 1 }
```

In addition, SNMPv2 includes the definition of an OBJECT-IDENTITY macro, which is used to document the objects used in a MIB.

```
MODULE-IDENTITY MACRO ::= BEGIN

TYPE NOTATION ::= "LAST-UPDATED" value(Update UTCTime)
                  "ORGANIZATION" Text
                  "CONTACT-INFO" Text
                  "DESCRIPTION" Text
                  RevisionPart

VALUE NOTATION ::= value(VALUE OBJECT IDENTIFIER)

RevisionPart ::= Revisions | empty

Revisions ::= Revision | Revisions Revision

Revision ::= "REVISION" value(Update UTCTime)
             "DESCRIPTION" Text
   --uses the NVT ASCII character set

Text ::= """" string """"

END

OBJECT-IDENTITY MACRO ::= BEGIN

TYPE NOTATION ::= "STATUS" Status
                  "DESCRIPTION" Text
                  ReferPart

VALUE NOTATION ::= value(VALUE OBJECT IDENTIFIER)

Status ::= "current" | "deprecated" | "obsolete"

ReferPart ::= "REFERENCE" Text | empty

Text ::= """" string """"

END
```

FIGURE 11.10   SNMPv2 MODULE-IDENTITY and OBJECT-IDENTITY macros

11.3 *Summary*

The SNMPv2 framework is a set of specifications for a second-generation SNMP framework. SNMPv2 incorporates the enhancements provided by secure SNMP plus additional functional enhancements to the SNMP framework.

The SNMPv2 SMI provides for more elaborate specification and documentation of managed objects and MIBs. Much of the new material codifies existing SNMP practices. The OBJECT-TYPE macro includes several features not found in the SNMP object definition macro. These include additional ASN.1 types, a UNITS clause, and a more elaborate indexing feature for tables. This latter enhancement provides a systematic and more powerful technique for row creation and deletion. The SNMPv2 SMI also includes new macros for defining object groups, traps, compliance characteristics, and capability characteristics.

| APPENDIX 11A | *RO W-STATUS TEXTUAL CONVENTION* |

RowStatus ::= TEXTUAL-CONVENTION
    STATUS current
    DESCRIPTION
        "The RowStatus textual convention is used to manage the creation and dele-
    tion of conceptual rows, and is used as the value of the SYNTAX clause for the sta-
    tus column of a conceptual row.
        The status column has six defined values:

- 'active', which indicates that the conceptual row is available for use by the managed device;
- 'notInService', which indicates that the conceptual row exists in the agent, but is unavailable for use by the managed device (see NOTE below);
- 'notReady', which indicates that the conceptual row exists in the agent, but is missing information necessary in order to be available for use by the managed device;
- 'createAndGo', which is supplied by a management station wishing to create a new instance of a conceptual row and to have its status automatically set to active, making it available for use by the managed device;
- 'createAndWait', which is supplied by a management station wishing to create a new instance of a conceptual row (but not make it available for use by the managed device); and
- 'destroy', which is supplied by a management station wishing to delete all of the instances associated with an existing conceptual row.

Whereas five of the six values (all except 'notReady') may be specified in a management protocol set operation, only three values will be returned in response to a management protocol retrieval operation: 'notReady', 'notInService', or 'active'. That is, when
queried, an existing conceptual row has only three states: it is either available for use by
the managed device (the status column has value 'active'); it is not available for use by the
managed device, though the agent has sufficient information to make it so (the status
column has value 'notInService'); or, it is not available for use by the managed device,
and an attempt to make it so would fail because the agent has insufficient information
(the state column has value 'notReady').

Note Well

*This textual convention may be used for a MIB table, irrespective of whether the
values of that table's conceptual rows are able to be modified while it is active, or
whether its conceptual rows must be taken out of service in order to be modified.
That is, it is the responsibility of the DESCRIPTION clause of the status column to*

specify whether the status column must not be 'active' in order for the value of some other column of the same conceptual row to be modified. If such a specification is made, affected columns may be changed by an SNMP set PDU if the RowStatus would not be equal to 'active' either immediately before or after processing the PDU. In other words, if the PDU also contained a varbind that would change the RowStatus value, the column in question may be changed if the RowStatus was not equal to 'active' as the PDU was received, or if the varbind sets the status to a value other than 'active'.

Also note that whenever any elements of a row exist, the RowStatus column must also exist.

To summarize the effect of having a conceptual row with a status column having a SYNTAX clause value of RowStatus, consider the following state diagram:

ACTION	A status column does not exist	B status column is notReady	C status column is notInService	D status column is active
set status column to createAndGo	noError → D or inconsistentValue	inconsistentValue	inconsistentValue	inconsistentValue
set status column to createAndWait	no Error see (1) or wrongValue	inconsistentValue	inconsistentValue	inconsistentValue
set status column to active	inconsistentValue	inconsistentValue or see (2) → D	noError → D	noError → D
set status column to notInService	inconsistentValue	inconsistentValue or see (3) → C	noError → C	noError → C or wrongValue
set status column to destroy	noError → A	noError → A	noError → A	noError → A
set any other column to some value	see (4)	noError see (1)	noError → C	see (5) → D

(1) goto B or C, depending on information available to the agent.

(2) if other variable bindings included in the same PDU, provide values for all columns which are missing but required, then return noError and goto D.

(3) if other variable bindings included in the same PDU, provide values for all columns which are missing but required, then return noError and goto C.

(4) at the discretion of the agent, the return value may be either:
inconsistentName: because the agent does not choose to create such an instance when the corresponding RowStatus instance does not exist, or
inconsistentValue: if the supplied value is inconsistent with the state of some other MIB object's value, or
noError: because the agent chooses to create the instance.

If noError is returned, then the instance of the status column must also be created, and the new state is B or C, depending on the information available to the agent. If inconsistentName or inconsistentValue is returned, the row remains in state A.

(5) depending on the MIB definition for the column/table, either noError or inconsistentValue may be returned.

NOTE: Other processing of the set request may result in a response other than noError being returned (e.g., wrongValue, noCreation, etc.).

Conceptual Row Creation

There are four potential interactions when creating a conceptual row: selecting an instance-identifier which is not in use; creating the conceptual row; initializing any objects for which the agent does not supply a default; and making the conceptual row available for use by the managed device.

Interaction 1: Selecting an Instance-Identifier

The algorithm used to select an instance-identifier varies for each conceptual row. In some cases, the instance-identifier is semantically significant (e.g., the destination address of a route), and a management station selects the instance-identifier according to the semantics.

In other cases, the instance-identifier is used solely to distinguish conceptual rows, and a management station without specific knowledge of the conceptual row might examine the instances present in order to determine an unused instance-identifier. (This approach may be used, but it is often highly sub-optimal; however, it is also a questionable practice for a naive management station to attempt conceptual row creation.)

Alternately, the MIB module that defines the conceptual row might provide one or more objects which provide assistance in determining an unused instance-identifier. For example, if the conceptual row is indexed by an integer-value, then an object having an integer-valued SYNTAX clause might be defined for such a purpose, allowing a management station to issue a management protocol retrieval operation. In order to avoid unnecessary collisions between competing management stations, 'adjacent' retrievals of this object should be different.

Finally, the management station could select a pseudo-random number to use as the index. In the event that this index was already in use and an inconsistentValue was returned in response to the management protocol set operation, the management station should simply select a new pseudo-random number and retry the operation.

A MIB designer should choose between the two latter algorithms based on the size of the table (and therefore the efficiency of each algorithm). For tables in which a large number of entries are expected, it is recommended that a MIB object be defined that returns an acceptable index for creation. For tables with small numbers of entries, it is recommended that the latter pseudo-random index mechanism be used.

Interaction 2: Creating the Conceptual Row

Once an unused instance-identifier has been selected, the management station determines if it wishes to create and activate the conceptual row in one transaction or in a negotiated set of interactions.

Interaction 2a: Creating and Activating the Conceptual Row

The management station must first determine the column requirements (i.e., it must determine those columns for which it must or must not provide values). Depending on the complexity of the table and the management station's knowledge of the agent's capabilities, this determination can be made locally by the management station. Alternately, the management station issues a management protocol get operation to examine all columns in the conceptual row that it wishes to create. In response, for each column, there are three possible outcomes:

- A value is returned, indicating that some other management station has already created this conceptual row. We return to interaction 1.

- The exception 'noSuchInstance' is returned, indicating that the agent implements the object-type associated with this column, and that this column in at least one conceptual row would be accessible in the MIB view used by the retrieval were it to exist. For those columns to which the agent provides read-create access, the 'noSuchInstance' exception tells the management station that it should supply a value for this column when the conceptual row is to be created.

- The exception 'noSuchObject' is returned, indicating that the agent does not implement the object-type associated with this column or that there is no conceptual row for which this column would be accessible in the MIB view used by the retrieval. As such, the management station cannot issue any management protocol set operations to create an instance of this column.

Once the column requirements have been determined, a management protocol set operation is accordingly issued. This operation also sets the new instance of the status column to 'createAndGo'.

When the agent processes the set operation, it verifies that it has sufficient information to make the conceptual row available for use by the managed device. The information available to the agent is provided by two sources: the management protocol set operation which creates the conceptual row, and implementation-specific defaults supplied by the agent (note that an agent must provide implementation-specific defaults for at least those objects which it implements as read-only). If there is sufficient information available, then the conceptual row is created, a 'noError' response is returned, the status column is set to 'active', and no further interactions are necessary (i.e., interactions 3 and 4 are skipped). If there is insufficient information, then the conceptual row is not created, and the set operation fails with an error of 'inconsistentValue'. On this error, the management station can issue a management protocol retrieval operation to determine if this was because it failed to specify a value for a required column, or because the selected instance of the status column already existed. In the latter case, we return to interaction 1. In the former case, the management station can re-issue the set operation with the additional information, or begin interaction 2 again using 'createAndWait' in order to negotiate creation of the conceptual row.

Note Well

> *Regardless of the method used to determine the column requirements, it is possible that the management station might deem a column necessary when, in fact, the agent will not allow that particular columnar instance to be created or written. In this case, the management protocol set operation will fail with an error such as 'noCreation' or 'notWritable'. In this case, the management station decides whether it needs to be able to set a value for that particular columnar instance. If not, the management station reissues the management protocol set operation, but without setting a value for that particular columnar instance; otherwise, the management station aborts the row creation algorithm.*

Interaction 2b: Negotiating the Creation of the Conceptual Row

The management station issues a management protocol set operation which sets the desired instance of the status column to 'createAndWait'. If the agent is unwilling to process a request of this sort, the set operation fails with an error of 'wrongValue'. (As a consequence, such an agent must be prepared to accept a single management protocol set operation, i.e., interaction 2a above, containing all of the columns indicated by its column requirements.) Otherwise, the conceptual row is created, a 'noError' response is returned, and the status column is immediately set to either 'notInService' or 'notReady', depending on whether it has sufficient information to make the conceptual row available for use by the managed device. If there is sufficient information available, then the status column is set to 'notInService'; otherwise, if there is insufficient information, then the status column is set to 'notReady'. Regardless, we proceed to interaction 3.

Interaction 3: Initializing Non-Defaulted Objects

The management station must now determine the column requirements. It issues a management protocol get operation to examine all columns in the created conceptual row. In the response, for each column, there are three possible outcomes:

- A value is returned, indicating that the agent implements the object-type associated with this column and had sufficient information to provide a value. For those columns to which the agent provides read-create access (and for which the agent allows their values to be changed after their creation), a value return tells the management station that it may issue additional management protocol set operations, if it desires, in order to change the value associated with this column.

- The exception 'noSuchInstance' is returned, indicating that the agent implements the object-type associated with this column, and that this column in at least one conceptual row would be accessible in the MIB view used by the retrieval were it to exist. However, the agent does not have sufficient information to provide a value, and until a value is provided, the conceptual row may not be made available for use by the managed device. For those columns to which the agent provides read-create access, the 'noSuchInstance' exception tells the management station that it must issue additional management protocol set operations, in order to provide a value associated with this column.

- The exception 'noSuchObject' is returned, indicating that the agent does not implement the object-type associated with this column or that there is no conceptual row for which this column would be accessible in the MIB view used by the retrieval. As such, the management station cannot issue any management protocol set operations to create an instance of this column.

If the value associated with the status column is 'notReady', then the management station must first deal with all 'noSuchInstance' columns, if any. Having done so, the value of the status column becomes 'notInService', and we proceed to interaction 4.

Interaction 4: Making the Conceptual Row Available

Once the management station is satisfied with the values associated with the columns of the conceptual row, it issues a management protocol set operation to set the status column to 'active'. If the agent has sufficient information to make the conceptual row available for use by the managed device, the management protocol set operation succeeds (a 'noError' response is returned). Otherwise, the management protocol set operation fails with an error of 'inconsistentValue'.

Note Well

A conceptual row having a status column with value 'notInService' or 'notReady' is unavailable to the managed device. As such, it is possible for the managed device to create its own instances during the time between the management protocol set operation which sets the status column to 'createAndWait' and the management protocol set operation which sets the status column to 'active'. In this case, when the management protocol set operation is issued to set the status column to 'active', the values held in the agent supersede those used by the managed device.

If the management station is prevented from setting the status column to 'active' (e.g., due to management station or network failure) the conceptual row will be left in the 'notInService' or 'notReady' state, consuming resources indefinitely. The agent must detect conceptual rows that have been in either state for an abnormally long period of time and remove them. It is the responsibility of the DESCRIPTION clause of the status column to indicate what an abnormally long period of time would be. This period of time should be long enough to allow for human response time (including 'think time') between the creation of the conceptual row and the setting of the status to 'active'. In the absence of such information in the DESCRIPTION clause, it is suggested that this period be approximately 5 minutes in length. This removal action applies not only to newly created rows, but also to previously active rows which are set to, and left in, the notInService state for a prolonged period exceeding that which is considered normal for such a conceptual row.

Conceptual Row Suspension

When a conceptual row is 'active', the management station may issue a management protocol set operation which sets the instance of the status column to 'notInService'. If the agent is unwilling to do so, the set operation fails with an error of 'wrongValue'. Otherwise, the conceptual row is taken out of service, and a 'noError' response is returned. It is the responsibility of the DESCRIPTION clause of the status column to indicate under what circumstances the status column should be taken out of service (e.g., in order for the value of some other column of the same conceptual row to be modified).

Conceptual Row Deletion

For deletion of conceptual rows, a management protocol set operation is issued which sets the instance of the status column to 'destroy'. This request may be made regardless of the current value of the status column (e.g., it is possible to delete conceptual rows which are either 'notReady', 'notInService', or 'active'). If the operation succeeds, then all instances associated with the conceptual row are immediately removed."

```
SYNTAX INTEGER {
—the following two values are states; these values may be read or
written:
active(1),
notInService(2),

—the following value is a state; this value may be read, but not
written:
notReady(3),

—the following three values are actions; these values may be
written, but are never read
createAndGo(4),
createAndWait(5),
destroy(6)        }
```

SNMPv2
Protocol

We begin this chapter with a description of the SNMPv2 protocol. This is followed by a discussion of transport mappings defined for SNMPv2. Finally, we examine strategies for the coexistence of SNMPv2 and SNMPv1 entities on the same network.

12.1 *Protocol Operations*

As mentioned earlier, SNMPv2 is an extension of SNMPv1. As with SNMPv1, SNMPv2 PDUs are encapsulated in a message. The SNMPv2 message format provides the functionality required for the security features of SNMPv2. That is, the form and meaning of the message header are determined by an administrative framework that defines both authentication and privacy policies.

SNMPv2 provides three types of access to management information:

- *Manager–agent request-response:* An SNMPv2 entity acting in a manager role sends a request to an SNMPv2 entity acting in an agent role, and the latter SNMPv2 entity then responds to the request. This type is used to retrieve or modify management information associated with the managed device.

- *Manager–manager request-response:* An SNMPv2 entity acting in a manager role sends a request to an SNMPv2 entity acting in a manager role, and the latter SNMPv2 entity then responds to the request. This type is used to notify an SNMPv2 entity acting in a manager role of management information associated with another SNMPv2 entity also acting in a manager role.

- *Agent–manager unconfirmed:* An SNMPv2 entity acting in an agent role sends an unsolicited message, termed a "trap," to an SNMPv2 entity acting in a manager role, and no response is returned. This type is used to notify an SNMPv2 entity acting in a manager role of an exceptional event that has resulted in changes to management information associated with the managed device.

Only the second item is new to SNMPv2; the other two types of interaction are found in SNMPv1.

12.1.1 SNMPv2 Messages

As with SNMPv1, information is exchanged using SNMPv2 in the form of a message containing a protocol data unit (PDU). The outer message structure includes a community name that may be used for authentication, as described in Section 7.1.

The structure of a message is specified in SNMPv2 as follows:

```
Message ::= SEQUENCE   {
            version   INTEGER { version(1) }, —version = 2 for SNMPv2
            community OCTET STRING,           —community name
            data      ANY                     —an SNMPv2 PDU
            }
```

The discussion in Section 7.1 concerning community names, community profiles, and access policies (Figure 7.1) is valid for SNMPv2. In this case, the message header has a version field value of 1, referring to SNMPv2 (SNMPv1 is version 0).

The use of the SNMPv1 message format as the outer wrapper for SNMPv2 PDUs is referred to as community-based SNMPv2, or SNMPv2C. This refers to the fact that, at present, any security provided for SNMPv2 must rely on the SNMPv1 community concept. If there is future agree ment on a new security framework, this could be implemented in the form of a new message format.

12.1.1.1 Transmission of an SNMPv2 Message

In general terms, an SNMPv2 entity performs the following actions to transmit a PDU to another SNMPv2 entity.

1. The PDU is constructed, using the ASN.1 structure defined in the protocol specification.
2. This PDU is then passed to an authentication service, together with the source and destination transport addresses and a community name. The authentication service then performs any required transformations for this exchange, such as encryption or the inclusion of an authentication code, and returns the result.
3. The protocol entity then constructs a message, consisting of a version field, the community name, and the result from step (2).
4. This new ASN.1 object is then encoded, using the basic encoding rules (BER), and passed to the transport service.

In practice, authentication is typically not invoked.

12.1.1.2 Receipt of an SNMPv2 Message

In general terms, an SNMPv2 entity performs the following actions upon reception of an SNMPv2 message.

1. It does a basic syntax-check of the message and discards the message if it fails to parse.

TABLE 12.1   Relationship Between SNMPv2 MIB MAX-ACCESS Value
and Protocol Access Mode

MAX-ACCESS Value	SNMPv2 Access Mode	
	READ-ONLY	READ-WRITE
read-only	Available for get and trap operations	
read-write	Available for get and trap operations	Available for get, set, and trap operations
read-create	Available for get and trap operations	Available for get, set, create, and trap operations
accessible-for-notify	Available for trap operations	
not-accessible	Unavailable	

2. It verifies the version number and discards the message if there is a mismatch.

3. The protocol entity then passes the user name, the PDU portion of the message, and the source and destination transport addresses (supplied by the transport service that delivered the message) to an authentication service.

   (a) If authentication fails, the authentication service signals the SNMPv2 protocol entity, which generates a trap and discards the message.

   (b) If authentication succeeds, the authentication service returns a PDU in the form of an ASN.1 object that conforms to the structure defined in the protocol specification.

4. The protocol entity does a basic syntax-check of the PDU and discards the PDU if it fails to parse. Otherwise, using the named community, the appropriate SNMPv2 access policy is selected and the PDU is processed accordingly. Table 12.1 shows how the access policy is enforced (compare with Table 7.1).

In practice, the authentication service merely serves to verify that the community name authorizes receipt of messages from the source SNMPv2 entity.

12.1.2 PDU Formats

The PDU formats for SNMPv2 are depicted informally in Figure 12.1; their relationship to the overall SNMPv2 message is shown in Figure 12.2. The ASN.1 definition is reproduced in Figure 12.3. Note that the GetRequest, GetNextRequest, SetRequest, and SNMPv2-Trap PDUs have the same format as the Response and InformRequest PDUs, with the error-status and error-index fields always set to 0. This convention reduces by one the number of different PDU formats with which the SNMPv2 entity

PDU type	request-id	0	0	variable-bindings

(a) GetRequest-PDU, GetNextRequest-PDU, SetRequest-PDU, SNMPv2-Trap-PDU, InformRequest-PDU

PDU type	request-id	error-status	error-index	variable-bindings

(b) Response-PDU

PDU type	request-id	non-repeaters	max-repetitions	variable-bindings

(c) GetBulkRequest-PDU

name1	value1	name2	value2	· · ·	namen	valuen

(e) variable-bindings

FIGURE 12.1   SNMPv2 PDU formats

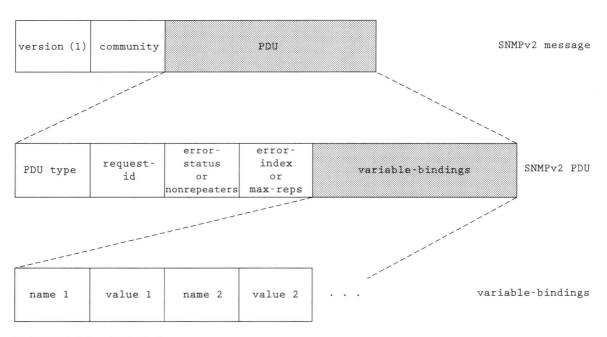

FIGURE 12.2   SNMPv2 message structure

```
SNMPv2-PDU DEFINITIONS ::= BEGIN

PDUs ::= CHOICE { get-request       GetRequest-PDU,
                  get-next-request  GetNextRequest-PDU,
                  get-bulk-request  GetBulkRequest-PDU,
                  response          Response-PDU,
                  set-request       SetRequest-PDU,
                  inform-request    InformRequest-PDU,
                  snmpV2-trap       SNMPv2-Trap-PDU,
                  report            Report-PDU        }

--PDUs

GetRequest-PDU      ::=  [0] IMPLICIT PDU
GetNextRequest-PDU  ::=  [1] IMPLICIT PDU
Response-PDU        ::=  [2] IMPLICIT PDU
SetRequest-PDU      ::=  [3] IMPLICIT PDU
GetBulkRequest-PDU  ::=  [5] IMPLICIT BulkPDU
InformRequest-PDU   ::=  [6] IMPLICIT PDU
SNMPv2-Trap-PDU     ::=  [7] IMPLICIT PDU
Report-PDU          ::=  [8] IMPLICIT PDU

max-bindings  INTEGER ::= 2147483647

PDU ::= SEQUENCE {request-id Integer32,
              error-status INTEGER {            --sometimes ignored
                          noError (0),
                          tooBig (1),
                          noSuchName (2), --for proxy compatibility
                          badValue (3),   --for proxy compatibility
                          readOnly (4),   --for proxy compatibility
                          genError (5),
                          noAccess (6),
                          wrongType (7),
                          wrongLength (8),
                          wrongEncoding (9),
                          wrongValue (10),
                          noCreation (11),
                          inconsistentValue (12),
                          resourceUnavailable (13),
                          commitFailed (14),
                          undoFailed (15),
                          authorizationError (16),
                          notWritable (17),
                          inconsistentName (18) },
              error-index INTEGER (0..max-bindings),    --sometimes ignored
              variable-binding VarBindList } --values are sometimes ignored
```

FIGURE 12.3   SNMPv2 PDU format definitions

```
BulkPDU ::= SEQUENCE {                       --MUST be identical in structure to PDU
                    request-id      Integer32,
                    non-repeaters   INTEGER (0..max-bindings),
                    max-repetitions INTEGER (0..max-bindings),
                    variable-binding VarBindList }        --values are ignored
--variable binding

VarBind ::= SEQUENCE {name ObjectName,
                    CHOICE {value           ObjectSyntax,
                            unspecified     NULL,    --in retrieval requests
                                                    --exceptions in responses:
                            noSuchObject [0]    IMPLICIT NULL,
                            noSuchInstance [2] IMPLICIT NULL,
                            endOfMibView [2]    IMPLICIT NULL } }
--variable-binding list

VarBindList ::= SEQUENCE (SIZE (0..max-bindings)) OF VarBind

END
```

FIGURE 12.3 *Continued*

---

must deal. Also, as with SNMPv2, there is no PDU type field defined in the ASN.1 specification, but it appears as an artifact of the BER encoding of the PDUs.

Figure 12.4 shows the PDU sequences defined in SNMPv2 (compare to Figure 7.5), and Table 12.2 compares SNMPv1 and SNMPv2 PDUs.

Before examining each of the PDUs in turn, let us comment briefly on the common fields in the SNMPv2 PDUs:

- request-id: The value of this field in a response PDU must equal the value in the corresponding field of a request PDU. The manager can assign a unique number to each outstanding request to the same agent in order to distinguish responses to multiple outstanding requests.

- error-status: A nonzero value indicates that an exception occurred while processing a request. Table 12.3 indicates which error status codes are appropriate in response to which request PDUs. Note that noSuchName(2), badValue(3), and readOnly(4) are only used for coexistence with SNMPv1; this is explained in Section 12.3.2.

- error-index: When the error-status field is nonzero, the error-index value identifies the variable (object) in the variable-bindings list that caused the error. The first variable in the list has index 1, the second has index 2, and so on.

- variable-bindings: This field enables a single operation to be applied to a group of object instances. The field consists of a sequence of pairs. The first element in

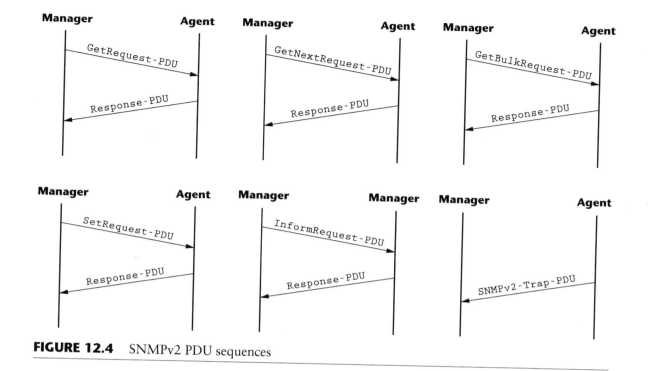

FIGURE 12.4   SNMPv2 PDU sequences

each pair is an object identifier. The second element in each pair is one of the following:

value: the value associated with each object instance; specified in a request PDU
unSpecified: a NULL value is used in retrieval requests
noSuchObject: indicates agent does not implement the object referred to by this object identifier
noSuchInstance: indicates that this object instance does not exist for this operation
endOfMibView: indicates an attempt to reference an object identifier that is beyond the end of the MIB at the agent

Table 12.4 indicates which of the above values can be used in which PDUs.

12.1.3 GetRequest PDU

The SNMPv2 GetRequest PDU is identical, in format and semantics, to the SNMPv1 GetRequest PDU. The only difference is in the way that responses are handled. Recall that the SNMPv1 GetRequest operation is atomic: Either all of the values are retrieved or none is retrieved. If the responding entity is able to provide values for all of the variables

TABLE 12.2 Comparison of SNMPv1 and SNMPv2 PDUs

SNMPv1 PDU	SNMPv2 PDU	Direction	Description
GetRequest	GetRequest	Manager to agent	Request value for each listed object
GetNextRequest	GetNextRequest	Manager to agent	Request next value for each listed object
—	GetBulkRequest	Manager to agent	Request multiple values
SetRequest	SetRequest	Manager to agent	Set value for each listed object
—	InformRequest	Manager to manager	Transmit unsolicited information
GetResponse	Response	Agent to manager or manager to manager (SNMPv2)	Respond to manager request
Trap	SNMPv2-Trap	Agent to manager	Transmit unsolicited information

TABLE 12.3 Use of Error Status Codes in Response-PDU

	GetRequest, GetNextRequest, GetBulkRequest	SetRequest	InformRequest
noError(0)	X	X	X
tooBig(1)	X	X	X
noSuchName(2)			
badValue(3)			
readOnly(4)			
genError(5)	X	X	X
noAccess(6)		X	
wrongType(7)		X	
wrongLength(8)		X	
wrongEncoding(9)		X	
wrongValue(10)		X	
noCreation(11)		X	
inconsistentValue(12)		X	
resourceUnavailable(13)		X	
commitFailed(14)		X	
undoFailed(15)		X	
authorizationError(16)	X	X	X
notWritable(17)		X	
inconsistentName(18)		X	

listed in the incoming variable-bindings list, then the GetResponse PDU includes the variable-bindings list, with a value supplied for each variable. If at least one of the variable values cannot be supplied, then no values are returned but an error response is returned. Thus, in SNMPv1, a variable-bindings list in a response consists of a sequence of pairs, with each pair consisting of the name of a variable and its associated value.

In contrast, in SNMPv2, a variable-bindings list is prepared even if values cannot be supplied for all variables. If an exception condition related to a variable is found (noSuchObject, noSuchInstance, endOfMibView), then that variable name is paired with an indication of the exception rather than a value. In SNMPv2, a response PDU is

TABLE 12.4 Allowable Values in `variable-bindings` List

	Object Instance Value	Unspecified or ignored	noSuch-Object	noSuch-Instance	endOfMibView
GetRequest		X			
Response to GetRequest		X	X	X	
GetNextRequest		X			
Response to GetNextRequest		X			X
GetBulkRequest		X			
Response to GetBulkRequest		X			X
SetRequest	X				
Response to SetRequest		X			
SNMPv2-Trap	X				
InformRequest	X				
Response to InformRequest	X				

constructed by processing each variable in the incoming variable list, according to the following rules.

1. If the variable does not have an OBJECT IDENTIFIER prefix that exactly matches the prefix of any variable accessible by this request, then its value field is set to noSuchObject.

2. Otherwise, if the variable's name does not exactly match the name of a variable accessible by this request, then its value field is set to noSuchInstance.

3. Otherwise, the value field is set to the value of the named variable.

If the processing of a variable name fails for any other reason, then no values are returned. Instead, the responding entity returns a response PDU with an error-status of genErr and a value in the error-index field that is the index of the problem object in the variable-bindings field.

If the size of the message that encapsulates the generated response PDU exceeds a local limitation or the maximum message size of the request's source party, then the response PDU is discarded and a new response PDU is constructed. The new response PDU has an error-status of tooBig, an error-index of zero, and an empty variable-bindings field.

A further word needs to be said about alternative (2) in the preceding list. Unless the management station has made an error, the conditions of this alternative will occur only for columnar objects, not for scalar values. Consider these two cases.

1. A scalar object type with the object identifier x has an instance identifier x.0. If the variable x.0 appears in a get PDU, the agent first determines if the object type x is in its MIB. If so, the only instance of that object is x.0, and the appropriate value may be returned.

2. A columnar object with the object identifier y has an instance identifier y.i, where i is a series of one or more subidentifiers containing the values of the index variable(s) for this table. If the variable y.i appears in a get PDU, the agent first determines if the object type y appears in its MIB. If so, it must then determine if the row indexed by i exists. If both of these conditions are met, then the value of object instance y.i may be returned.

The noSuchInstance code should therefore be returned only in the case of a columnar object for a nonexistent row or for a row under creation. This feature is used in row creation, as explained in Section 11.2.2.3.

The modification of GetRequest to permit partial responses is a significant improvement. In SNMPv1, if one or more of the variables in a GetRequest is not supported, the agent returns an error message with a status of noSuchName. In order to cope with such an error, the SNMPv1 manager must either return no values to the requesting application or include an algorithm that responds to an error by removing the missing variables, resending the request, and then sending a partial result to the application. Waldbusser (1992) reports that due to the complexity of the code needed to generate a partial response, many management stations do not implement such an algorithm and therefore cannot effectively interoperate with agents that have unimplemented variables. This has given rise to the practice among agent vendors of returning an arbitrary value for unimplemented objects rather than a noSuchName error, a problem discussed in Section 7.5.2. The provision of partial responses by SNMPv2 agents should eliminate this problem.

12.1.4 GetNextRequest PDU

The SNMPv2 GetNextRequest PDU is identical to the SNMPv1 GetNextRequest PDU, in format and semantics. As with the GetRequest PDU, the only difference is that the SNMPv1 GetNextRequest is atomic, while the SNMPv2 GetNextRequest processes as many variables as possible.

In SNMPv2, a response PDU for a GetNextRequest is constructed by processing each variable in the incoming variable list, according to the following rules.

1. The variable (object instance) is determined that is next in lexicographic order to the named variable. The resulting variable-bindings pair is set to the name and value of the located variable.

2. If no lexicographic successor exists, then the resulting `variable-bindings` pair consists of the name of the variable in the request and a value field set to `endOf-MibView`.

If the processing of any variable fails for any other reason, or if the resulting response is too big, the same procedures as for `GetRequest` are followed.

As an example (taken from the SNMPv2 specification), consider an SNMPv2 application that wishes to retrieve the media-dependent physical address and the address-mapping type for each entry in the IP net-to-media address translation table (Figure 6.5) of a particular network element. It also wishes to retrieve the value of `sysUpTime` at which the mappings existed. Suppose that the table contains three rows with the following values:

Interface Number	Network Address	Physical Address	Type
1	10.0.0.51	00:00:10:01:23:45	dynamic
1	9.2.3.4	00:00:10:54:32:10	static
2	10.0.0.15	00:00:10:98:76:54	dynamic

Figure 12.5 indicates the logical order of the object instances in this tree.

Suppose that the management station wishes to retrieve the entire table and does not currently know any of its contents, or even the number of rows in the table. The management station can issue a `GetNextRequest` with the names of all of the desired columnar objects:

```
GetNextRequest (sysUpTime, ipNetToMediaPhysAddress, ipNetToMediaType)
```

The agent responds with the value of `sysUpTime` and the values from the first row of the table:

```
Response ( (sysUpTime.0 = "123456"),
           (ipNetToMediaPhysAddress.1.9.2.3.4 = "000010543210"),
           (ipNetToMediaType.1.9.2.3.4 = "dynamic") )
```

The management station can then store these values and retrieve the second row with

```
GetNextRequest (sysUpTime, ipNetToMediaPhysAddress.1.9.2.3.4,
                ipNetToMediaType.1.9.2.3.4)
```

The SNMPv2 agent responds with

```
Response ( (sysUpTime.0 = "123461"),
           (ipNetToMediaPhysAddress.1.10.0.0.51 = "000010012345"),
           (ipNetToMediaType.1.10.0.0.51 = "static") )
```

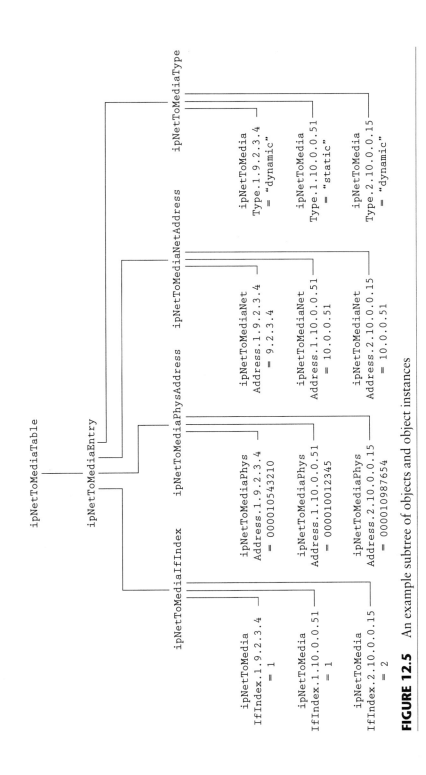

FIGURE 12.5 An example subtree of objects and object instances

Then, the following exchange occurs:

```
GetNextRequest (sysUpTime, ipNetToMediaPhysAddress.1.10.0.0.51,
                ipNetToMediaType.1.10.0.0.51)
Response ( ((sysUpTime.0 = "123466"),
           (ipNetToMediaPhysAddress.2.10.0.0.15 = "000010987654"),
           (ipNetToMediaType.2.10.0.0.15 = "dynamic") )
```

The management station does not know that this is the end of the table, and so it proceeds with

```
GetNextRequest (sysUpTime, ipNetToMediaPhysAddress.2.10.0.0.15,
                ipNetToMediaType.2.10.0.0.15)
```

However, there are no further rows in the table, so the agent responds with those objects that are next in the lexicographical ordering of objects in this MIB view:

```
Response ( (sysUpTime.0 = "123471"),
           (ipNetToMediaNetAddress.1.9.2.3.4 = "9.2.3.4"),
           (ipRoutingDiscards.0 = "2") )
```

Since the object names in the list in the response do not match those in the request, this signals the management station that it has reached the end of the routing table.

12.1.5 GetBulkRequest PDU

One of the major enhancements SNMPv2 provides is the GetBulkRequest PDU. Its purpose is to minimize the number of protocol exchanges required to retrieve a large amount of management information. The GetBulkRequest PDU allows an SNMPv2 manager to request that the response be as large as possible given the constraints on message size.

The GetBulkRequest operation uses the same selection principle as the GetNextRequest operation; that is, selection is always of the next object instance in lexicographic order. The difference is that, with GetBulkRequest, it is possible to specify that multiple lexicographic successors be selected.

In essence, the GetBulkRequest operation works in the following way. The GetBulkRequest includes a list of $(N + R)$ variable names in the variable-bindings list. For each of the first N names, retrieval takes place as for GetNextRequest. That is, for each variable in the list, the next variable in lexicographic order plus its value are returned; if there is no lexicographic successor, then the named variable and a value of endOfMibView are returned. For each of the last R names, multiple lexicographic successors are returned.

The GetBulkRequest PDU has two fields not found in the other PDUs: non-repeaters and max-repetitions. The non-repeaters field specifies the number of variables in the `variable-bindings` list for which a single lexicographic successor is to be returned. The `max-repetitions` field specifies the number of lexicographic successors to be returned for the remaining variables in the `variable-bindings` list. To explain the algorithm, let us define the following:

L = number of variable names in the `variable-bindings` field of the `GetBulk-Request` PDU

N = the number of variables, starting with the first variable in the `variable-bindings` field, for which a single lexicographic successor is requested

R = the number of variables, following the first N variables, for which multiple lexicographic successors are requested

M = the number of lexicographic successors requested for each of the last R variables

The following relationships hold:

N = MAX [MIN (`non-repeaters`, L), 0]
M = MAX [`max-repetitions`, 0]
$R = L - N$

The effect of the MAX operator is that if the value of either `non-repeaters` or `max-repetitions` is less than zero, a value of 0 is substituted. Figure 12.6 illustrates these relationships.

If N is greater than 0, then the first N variables are processed as for `GetNext-Request`. If R and M are both greater than 0, then for each of the last R variables, its M lexicographic successors are retrieved. For each variable, the following steps are performed.

• Obtain the value of the lexicographic successor of the named variable.

• Obtain the value of the lexicographic successor to the object instance retrieved in the previous step.

name1 name2   · · ·   nameN   nameN+1   · · ·   nameN+R

First N variable names:
provide one value each
(first lexicographic successor)

Last R variable names:
provide M values each
(first M lexicographic successors)

L = number of names in `variable-bindings` field
N = MAX [MIN (`non-repeaters` , L), 0]
M = MAX [`max-repetitions` , 0]
$R = L - N$

FIGURE 12.6   Interpretation of `GetBulkRequest` fields

- Obtain the value of the lexicographic successor to the object instance retrieved in the previous step.
- Continue this until *M* object instances have been retrieved.

If, at any point in this process, there is no lexicographic successor, then the `endOf-MibView` value is returned, paired with the name of the last lexicographic successor or, if there were no successors, with the name of the variable in the request.

Using these rules, the total number of `variable-bindings` pairs that can be produced is $N + (M \times R)$. The order in which the last $(M \times R)$ of these `variable-bindings` pairs are placed in the response PDU can be expressed as follows:

```
for ( m = 1 ; m <= M ; m++ )
    for ( r = 1 ; r <= R ; r++ )
        retrieve mth successor of (N + r)th variable;
```

The effect of this definition is that the successors to the last *R* variables are retrieved row by row, rather than retrieving all of the successors to the first variable, followed by all of the successors to the second variable, and so on. This matches the way in which conceptual tables are lexicographically ordered, so that if the last *R* values in the `Get-BulkRequest` are columnar objects of the same table, then the response will return conceptual rows of the table. Figure 12.7 illustrates the ordering, and Figure 12.8 depicts an example of the use of `GetBulkRequest`.

The maximum number of variable bindings returned is $N + (M \times R)$. A fewer number of pairs (possibly zero) may be generated for one of the following three reasons.

1. If the size of the message that encapsulates the generated response PDU exceeds a local limitation or the maximum message size of the request's source party, then the response is generated with a fewer number of variable-binding pairs. In essence, the response PDU is constructed by placing variable-binding pairs in the PDU in the proper order until the maximum size is reached.

2. If, during the iteration depicted earlier in this section, all of the subsequent variable-binding pairs have a value of `endOfMibView`, the variable bindings may be truncated at that point.

3. If the processing of the `GetBulkRequest` requires a significantly greater amount of processing time at the agent than a normal request, the agent may terminate the request after one or more iterations and return a partial result.

If the processing of a variable name fails (either one of the first *N* or one of the last *R*) for any reason other than `endOfMibView`, then no values are returned. Instead, the responding entity returns a response PDU with an `error-status` of `genErr` and a value in the `error-index` field that is the index of the problem object in the `variable-bindings` field.

FIGURE 12.7   Ordering of variable bindings in response to GetBulkRequest

The example that was used in the discussion of GetNextRequest can be used here to demonstrate the superior efficiency of the GetBulkRequest operation. Let us assume the minimal max-repetitions value that provides an improvement over GetNext-Request, namely a value of 2. Then, the manager issues

```
GetBulkRequest [ non-repeaters = 1, max-repetitions = 2 ]
              (sysUpTime, ipNetToMediaPhysAddress, ipNetToMediaType)
```

The agent responds with

```
Response ( (sysUpTime.0 = "123456"),
           (ipNetToMediaPhysAddress.1.9.2.3.4 = "000010543210"),
           (ipNetToMediaType.1.9.2.3.4 = "dynamic"),
           (ipNetToMediaPhysAddress.1.10.0.0.51 = "000010012345"),
           (ipNetToMediaType.1.10.0.0.51 = "static") )
```

FIGURE 12.8   GetBulkRequest command

Then, the following exchange occurs:

```
GetBulkRequest [ non-repeaters = 1, max-repetitions = 2 ]
               (sysUpTime, ipNetToMediaPhysAddress.1.10.0.0.51,
                ipNetToMediaType.1.10.0.0.51)
  Response ( (sysUpTime.0 = "123466"),
            (ipNetToMediaPhysAddress.2.10.0.0.15 = "000010987654"),
            (ipNetToMediaType.2.10.0.0.15 = "dynamic"),
            (ipNetToMediaNetAddress.1.9.2.3.4 = "9.2.3.4"),
            (ipRoutingDiscards.0 = "2") )
```

This signals the end of the table.

The GetBulkRequest operation removes one of the major limitations of SNMP, which is its inability to retrieve large blocks of data efficiently. Moreover, this use of this operator can actually enable reducing the size of management applications that are supported by the management protocol, realizing further efficiencies. There is no need for the management application to concern itself with some of the details of packaging requests. It need not perform a trial-and-error procedure to determine the optimal number of variable bindings to put in a request PDU. Also, if a request is too big, even for Get-BulkRequest, the agent will send back as much data as it can, rather than simply send a tooBig error message. Thus, the manager simply has to retransmit the request for the missing data; it does not have to figure out how to repackage the original request into a series of smaller requests.

12.1.6 SetRequest PDU

The SNMPv2 SetRequest PDU is identical to the SNMPv1 SetRequest PDU in format and semantics. The only difference is in the way that responses are handled.

First, the responding agent determines the size of a message encapsulating a response PDU with the same variable-bindings list of names and values. If this size exceeds a local limitation or the maximum message size of the request's source party, a response PDU is constructed with an error-status of tooBig, an error-index of zero, and an empty variable-bindings field. Otherwise, a response PDU is constructed in which all of the fields have the same values as the corresponding fields in the received request except as indicated later in this section.

The variable bindings are conceptually processed in two phases. In the first phase, each variable-binding pair, which constitutes an individual set operation, is validated. If all variable-binding pairs are validated, then each variable is altered in the second phase; that is, each individual set operation is performed in the second phase. Thus, as with SNMPv1, the SNMPv2 set operation is atomic: Either all variables are updated or none is.

12.1.6.1 Validation

The following validations are performed in order in the first phase on each variable binding (variable name, variable value pair) until they are all successful or until one fails.

1. If the variable is not accessible, then the error-status is noAccess.

2. If there are no variables that share the same object identifier as that in the variable binding and that are able to be created or modified no matter what new value is specified, then the error-status is notWritable.

3. If the value specifies a type that is inconsistent with that required for the variable, then the error-status is wrongType.

4. If the value specifies a length that is inconsistent with that required for the variable, then the error-status is wrongLength.

5. If the value contains an ASN.1 encoding that is inconsistent with that field's ASN.1 tag, then the error-status is wrongEncoding.

6. If the value cannot under any circumstances be assigned to the variable, then the error-status is wrongValue.

7. If the variable does not exist and could never be created, then the `error-status` is `noCreation`.

8. If the variable does not exist and cannot be created under the present circumstances, then the error status is `inconsistentName`.

9. If the variable exists but cannot be modified, then the `error-status` is `notWritable`.

10. If the value could, under other circumstances, be assigned to the variable but is presently inconsistent, then the `error-status` is `inconsistentValue`.

11. If the assignment of the value to the variable requires the allocation of a resource that is presently unavailable, then the `error-status` is `resourceUnavailable`.

12. If the processing of the variable binding fails for a reason other than those just listed, then the `error-status` is `genErr`.

If any of the preceding conditions is encountered on any of the variables, then a response PDU is issued with the `error-status` field set appropriately and the value of the `error-index` field set to the index of the failed variable binding. The use of a number of different error codes is an improvement over SNMP; it enables a management station to more readily determine the cause of a failed request and take the needed action to solve the problem.

12.1.6.2 Variable Update

If no validation errors are encountered, then an attempt is made to update all of the variables in the `SetRequest` PDU. For each variable in the list, the named variable is created if necessary and the specified value is assigned to it. If any assignment fails (despite the validation phase), then all assignments are undone, and a response PDU is issued with an `error-status` of `commitFailed` and the value of the `error-index` field set to the index of the failed variable binding. If, however, it is not possible to undo all of the assignments, then a response PDU is issued with an `error-status` of `undoFailed` and the value of the `error-index` field set to zero.

12.1.7 `SNMPv2-Trap` PDU

The `SNMPv2-Trap` PDU is generated and transmitted by an SNMPv2 entity acting in an agent role when an unusual event occurs. This PDU fulfills the same role as the SNMP `Trap` PDU, but with a different format. The `SNMPv2-Trap` PDU uses the same format as all other SNMPv2 PDUs except `GetBulkRequest`, thus easing the processing task at the receiver.

The `variable-bindings` field in the `SNMPv2-Trap` PDU contains the following pairs of object names and values:

- `sysUpTime.0`
- `snmpTrapOID.0`: part of the `trap` group in the SNMPv2 MIB, described in Section 13.1

- If the OBJECTS clause is present in the corresponding invocation of the macro NOTIFICATION-TYPE (Figure 11.8), then each corresponding variable and its value are copied to the variable-bindings field.
- Additional variables may be included at the option of the agent.

As with the SNMP Trap PDU, no response is issued to an SNMPv2-Trap PDU.

12.1.8 InformRequest PDU

The InformRequest PDU is sent by an SNMPv2 entity acting in a manager role, on behalf of an application, to another SNMPv2 entity acting in a manager role, to provide management information to an application using the latter entity.

The format of the InformRequest PDU is shown in Figure 12.1. The PDU includes a variable-bindings field with the same elements as for the SNMPv2-Trap PDU.

When an InformRequest PDU is received, the receiving SNMPv2 entity first determines the size of a message encapsulating a response PDU with the same values in its request-id, error-status, error-index, and variable-bindings fields as the received InformRequest PDU. If this size exceeds a local limitation or the maximum message size of the request's source party, a response PDU is constructed with an error-status of tooBig, an error-index of zero, and an empty variable-bindings field.

If the incoming PDU is not too big, the receiving SNMPv2 entity passes its contents to the destination application and generates a response PDU with the same values in its request-id and variable-bindings fields as the received InformRequest PDU, with an error-status field of noError and with a value of zero in its error-index field. This PDU is sent to the manager that originated the InformRequest PDU.

12.1.9 Report PDU

The SNMPv2 specification includes a Report PDU, accompanied by this comment:

Usage and precise semantics of Report-PDU are not presently defined. Any SNMP administrative framework making use of this PDU must define its usage and semantics.

There is no definition of how or when to use Report-PDU, because all of the text on usage of Report-PDUs occurred in security-related documents that were subsequently dropped. A reference to this PDU was retained in the protocol specification document.

12.1.10 Table Operations

Having introduced the SNMPv2 protocol operations, we can now return to the topic of SNMPv2 tables. This section provides an example of the use of the various features in

SNMPv2 for operating on tables.[1] We first look at the row creation operation and then examine the implications of augmenting a table.

12.1.10.1 Row Creation

Figure 12.9 defines a table, known as a `pingTable`, that can be used to provide a remote echo capability at an agent. This capability is part of the Internet Control Message Protocol (ICMP), which enables end systems and routers to exchange basic information needed to route Internet Protocol (IP) datagrams. ICMP is a user of IP (see Appendix A).

Two of the messages that can be sent using ICMP are `echo` and `echo reply`. These messages provide a mechanism for testing that communication is possible between entities (end systems and routers). The recipient of an `echo` message is obligated to return an `echo reply` message. An identifier and sequence number are associated with the `echo` message, to be matched in the `echo reply` message. The identifier might be used like a port to identify a particular session, and the sequence number might be incremented on each echo request sent. The echo is sometimes referred to as a *ping*.

Each row of the `pingTable` corresponds to a particular system that is remote from the agent. A manager can set up a row to instruct an agent to "ping" another system at regular intervals. Suppose that this table exists at an agent and currently has only one entry, with the following columnar object values:

Index	IpAddress	Delay	Remaining	Total	Received	Rtt	Status
1	128.2.13.21	1000	0	10	9	3	active

Note that the table does not contain the `pingSize` object. Let us assume that `pingSize` was defined in version 2 of this MIB and that this agent has an older version of software.

Now suppose that a manager wishes to add a new row using the `createAndWait` method. It determines that the next available index is 2, and it wishes the new row to have the following values:

Index	IpAddress	Delay	Remaining	Total	Received	Status
2	128.2.13.99	1000	20	20	0	active

To add this entry, the manager begins by issuing a set command:

SetRequest (pingStatus.2 = createAndWait)

If this is successful, the agent responds with

Response (pingStatus.2 = notReady)

---

[1] The author is indebted to Steve Waldbusser for providing this example.

```
pingTable OBJECT-TYPE
  SYNTAX   SEQUENCE OF PingEntry
  MAX-ACCESS  not-accessible
  STATUS      current
  DESCRIPTION
    "A table of ping request entries."
  ::= { ping 1 }

pingEntry OBJECT-TYPE
  SYNTAX      PingEntry
  MAX-ACCESS  not-accessible
  STATUS      current
  DESCRIPTION
    "A ping request entry."
  INDEX  { pingIndex }
  ::= { pingTable 1 }

PingEntry ::= SEQUENCE {
          pingIndex       Integer32,
          pingIPAddress   IpAddress,
          pingDelay       Integer32,
          pingsRemaining  Integer32,
          pingsTotal      Integer32,
          pingsReceived   Integer32,
          pingRtt         Integer32,
          pingStatus      RowStatus,
          pingSize        Integer32 }

pingIndex OBJECT-TYPE
  SYNTAX       Integer32
  MAX-ACCESS   not-accessible
  STATUS       current
  DESCRIPTION
    "A unique index for each entry."
  ::= { pingEntry 1 }

pingIPAddress OBJECT-TYPE
  SYNTAX       IpAddress
  MAX-ACCESS   read-create
  STATUS       current
  DESCRIPTION
    "The IP address to send ICMP echo
    packets to.

    An attempt to modify this object will
    fail with an 'inconsistentValue'
    error if the associated pingStatus
    object would be equal to active(1)
    both before and after the modifica-
    tion attempt."
  ::= { pingEntry 2 }
```

```
pingDelay OBJECT-TYPE
  SYNTAX       Integer32
  MAX-ACCESS   read-create
  STATUS       current
  DESCRIPTION
    "The number of milliseconds to delay
    between sending ICMP echo packets.

    An attempt to modify this object will
    fail with an 'inconsistentValue'
    error if the associated pingStatus
    object would be equal to active(1)
    both before and after the modifica-
    tion attempt."
  DEFVAL       { 1000 }
  ::= { pingEntry 3 }

pingsRemaining OBJECT-TYPE
  SYNTAX       Integer32
  MAX-ACCESS   read-create
  STATUS       current
  DESCRIPTION
    "The number of ICMP echos left to
    send in this sequence. When this
    object is modified by a management
    station, a new sequence of pings is
    started, possibly aborting a cur-
    rently running sequence. Whenever a
    sequence is started, the value of
    pingsTotal is loaded into pings-
    Remaining and the pingsReceived
    object is initialized to zero."
  DEFVAL       { 5 }
  ::= { pingEntry 4 }

pingsTotal OBJECT-TYPE
  SYNTAX       Integer32
  MAX-ACCESS   read-create
  STATUS       current
  DESCRIPTION
    "The total number of ICMP echos to be
    sent in this sequence."
  DEFVAL       { 5 }
  ::= { pingEntry 5}
```

FIGURE 12.9 PingTable example

pingsReceived OBJECT-TYPE
  SYNTAX   Integer32
  MAX-ACCESS read-only
  STATUS   current
  DESCRIPTION
    "The total number of ICMP echo reply
    packets received in this sequence.
    The success rate may be calculated
    as:
pingsReceived/(pingsTotal-pingsRemaining)"
  DEFVAL { 0 }
  ::= { pingEntry 6 }

pingRtt OBJECT-TYPE
  SYNTAX   Integer32
  MAX-ACCESS read-only
  STATUS   current
  DESCRIPTION
    "The round trip time of the last ICMP
    echo, in milliseconds.

    This object will be created by the
    agent after the first ICMP echo reply
    in a sequence is received. It will
    only exist when this entry is
    active(1). The agent shall delete it
    if this entry changes from the
    active(1) state."
  ::= { pingEntry 7 }

pingStatus OBJECT-TYPE
  SYNTAX   RowStatus
  MAX-ACCESS read-create
  STATUS   current
  DESCRIPTION
    "The status of this pingEntry. This
    object may not be set to active(1)
    unless the pingIPAddress, pings-
    Remaining and pingDelay columnar
    objects exist in this row.

    The first ping sequence is started
    when this object is set to
    active(1)."
  ::= { pingEntry 8 }

pingSize OBJECT-TYPE
  SYNTAX   Integer32
  MAX-ACCESS read-create
  STATUS   current
  DESCRIPTION
    "The size of ICMP echo packets to be
    sent.

    An attempt to modify this object will
    fail with an 'inconsistentValue'
    error if the associated pingStatus
    object would be equal to active(1)
    both before and after the modifica-
    tion attempt."
  DEFVAL { 64 }
  ::= { pingEntry 9 }

FIGURE 12.9 *Continued*

The status value of notReady indicates that there is insufficient information to make the conceptual row available for use by the managed device. For the row to be available, the manager must supply a value for all implemented read-create objects that do not have a default value. The management station next issues a get request to examine all of the columns in the new conceptual row, except for pingIndex, which is not accessible, and pingsReceived and pingRtt, which are read-only and therefore not of interest for row creation.

```
GetRequest ( pingIPAddress.2, pingDelay.2, pingsRemaining.2,
             pingsTotal.2, pingStatus.2, pingSize.2 )
```

The agent returns with

```
Response ( (pingIPAddress.2 = noSuchInstance), (pingDelay.2 = 1000),
           (pingsRemaining.2 = 5), pingsTotal.2 = 5),
           (pingsReceived.2 = 0), (pingStatus.2 = notReady),
           (pingSize.2 = noSuchObject ) )
```

This response indicates that default values have been assigned to pingDelay, pings Remaining, pingsTotal, and pingsReceived. No value has been assigned to ping IPAddress, so this must be assigned by the manager to complete the definition of the table. This makes sense, because this object specifies the target address for the ping operation requested by the manager. Until this value is assigned, the status of the row remains notReady. Finally, the agent does not support the object pingSize.

The manager is happy with the suggested delay but wants a total count of 20 rather than 5. Therefore, it issues the following:

```
SetRequest ( (pingIPAddress.2 = 128.2.13.99), (pingsRemaining.2 = 20),
             (pingsTotal.2 = 20), (pingStatus.2 = active) )
```

In summary, the first PDU exchange claimed the row, the second learned of the agent's suggestions and limitations, and the third finalized the parameters and activated the row. In effect, a negotiation has occurred between the management station and the agent.

This example highlights these important features of SNMPv2.

1. Occasionally, an agent will be unable to implement one or more columnar objects in a table. If those objects are mandatory, the agent is noncompliant but still should be able to interoperate with willing managers. The row creation exchange enables the manager to learn about such objects efficiently.

2. The agent can often choose a better value for a columnar object than the management station can. In effect, the agent suggests the default value as part of the row creation dialogue. If the suggested value is acceptable to the management station, it can leave it alone; otherwise it can set a new value.

12.1.10.2 Augmenting a Table

Figure 12.10 defines an augmentation to the `pingTable`. This augmentation adds several useful parameters to the table. Let us suppose that the current contents of `pingTable` are the following:

Index	IpAddress	Delay	Remaining	Total	Received	Rtt	Status
1	128.2.13.21	1000	0	10	9	3	active
2	128.2.13.99	1000	5	20	13	3	active

and let's suppose that the two entries in `pingTable` are augmented as follows:

Index	cmuPingTotalRtt	cmuPingsDropped
1	27	1
2	468	2

Now, it is interesting to note that the table is split with respect to the object identifiers. The original `pingTable` may be part of a standard MIB, while the augmented portion may be part of the `enterprises` subtree. Thus, a lexicographic walk using the `get-next` operation will not find the two portions of the table contiguous. A lexicographic walk through the relevant portion of the MIB (as in Figure 7.8) would encounter the following:

```
pingIPAddress.1 = 128.2.13.21
pingIPAddress.2 = 128.2.13.99
pingDelay.1 = 1000
pingDelay.2 = 1000
pingsRemaining.1 = 0
pingsRemaining.2 = 5
[ rest of table . . . ]
[ other tables and other MIBs . . . ]
enterprises.cmu . . . cmuPingTotalRtt.1 = 27
enterprises.cmu . . . cmuPingTotalRtt.2 = 468
enterprises.cmu . . . cmuPingsDropped.1 = 1
enterprises.cmu . . . cmuPingsDropped.2 = 2
```

However, this sort of split table presents no problems to the `get-bulk` operator. Consider the following request:

```
GetBulkRequest [non-repeaters = 0, max-repetitions = 2]
            (pingIPAddress, pingDelay, pingsRemaining,
            pingsReceived, pingRtt, pingStatus, cmuPingTotalRtt,
            cmuPingsDropped)
```

```
cmuPingTable OBJECT-TYPE
  SYNTAX    SEQUENCE OF CmuPingEntry
  MAX-ACCESS not-accessible
  STATUS      current
  DESCRIPTION
    "A table of additional ping objects."
  ::= { cmuPing 1 }

cmuPingEntry OBJECT-TYPE
  SYNTAX      CmuPingEntry
  MAX-ACCESS not-accessible
  STATUS      current
  DESCRIPTION
    "Additional ping objects for a ping entry."
  AUGMENTS { pingEntry }
  ::= { cmuPingTable 1}

CmuPingEntry ::= SEQUENCE {
      cmuPingTotalRtt  Integer32,
      cmuPingsDropped  Integer32 }

cmuPingTotalRtt OBJECT-TYPE
  SYNTAX      Integer32
  MAX-ACCESS read-only
  STATUS      mandatory
  DESCRIPTION
    "The sum of the round trip times of successful pings received in this sequence. A
    management station may calculate the average round trip time as:
                      cmupingTotalRtt/(pingsTotal-pingsRemaining)"
  DEFVAL { 0 }
  ::= { cmuPingEntry 1 }

cmuPingDropped OBJECT-TYPE
  SYNTAX      Integer32
  MAX-ACCESS read-only
  STATUS      mandatory
  DESCRIPTION
    "The number of ICMP echo reply packets dropped since this ping sequence was
    started. The success rate may be calculated as:
    pingsReceived/(pingsReceived + pingsDropped)"
  DEFVAL { 0 }
  ::= { cmuPingEntry 2 }
```

FIGURE 12.10   Augmented `pingTable` example

The response is

```
Response ( (pingIPAddress.1 = 128.2.13.21), (pingDelay.1 = 1000),
           (pingsRemaining.1 = 0), (pingsTotal.1 = 10),
           (pingsReceived.1 = 9), (pingRtt.1 = 3),
           (pingStatus.1 = active), (cmuPingTotalRtt.1 = 27),
           (cmuPingsDropped.1 = 1), (pingIPAddress.2 = 128.2.23.99),
           (pingDelay.2 = 1000), (pingsRemaining.2 = 5),
           (pingsTotal.2 = 20), (pingsReceived.2 = 13),
           (pingRtt.2 = 3), (pingStatus.2 = active),
           (cmuPingTotalRtt.2 = 468), (cmuPingsDropped.2 = 2) )
```

Thus, the objects in the combined table plus augmented table come back in row order, even though they are retrieved from different parts of the object identifier hierarchy.

12.2 Transport Mappings

The SNMPv2 specification includes a discussion of the mapping of SNMPv2 onto various transport-level protocols. The following are included:

- User Datagram Protocol (UDP)
- OSI Connectionless-Mode Network Service (CLNS)
- OSI Connection-Oriented Network Service (CONS)
- Novell Internetwork Packet Exchange (IPX)
- Appletalk

The SNMPv2 document states that UDP is the preferred mapping.

The SNMPv2 specification for transport mappings also spells out the following restrictions for the use of basic encoding rules (BER).

1. When the length field is being encoded, only the definite form is used; the indefinite form is prohibited.
2. The primitive form is used to encode the value field whenever possible.
3. When a BITS construct is serialized, all named bits are transferred regardless of their truth value.

12.3 Coexistence with SNMPv1

The SNMPv2 framework is derived from the SNMPv1 framework, as its designers intended that the evolution from SNMP to SNMPv2 be as smooth as possible. The easiest way to accomplish such an evolution on an existing network is to upgrade the manager systems to support SNMPv2 in a way that allows the coexistence of SNMPv2 managers, SNMPv2 agents, and SNMPv1 agents. The SNMPv2 specification provides some guidance in achieving this coexistence, and this section briefly summarizes that guidance. The issues raised fall into two categories:

- Management information
- Protocol operations

12.3.1 Management Information

The SNMPv2 specification notes that

- The structure of management information (SMI) for SNMPv2 is nearly a proper superset of the SMI for SNMPv1.
- The SNMPv2 approach largely codifies the existing practice for defining MIB modules.

The key design feature of the SNMPv2 SMI, from the viewpoint of coexistence, is that modules defined using the current SNMPv1 SMI may continue to be used with the SNMPv2 protocol. For the MIB modules to conform to the SNMPv2 SMI, certain changes are necessary. However, it is important to note that these changes are necessary to conform to the SNMPv2 SMI, but not necessary for interoperability. That is, it is possible for an agent to maintain an SNMPv1 MIB unchanged and still coexist in an SNMPv2–SNMPv1 environment.

The changes required for conformance to SNMPv2 provide a concise summary of the differences between the SNMPv2 and SNMPv1 SMIs. The changes fall into four categories:

- Object definitions
- Trap definitions
- Compliance definitions
- Capabilities definitions

12.3.1.1 Object Definitions
The following changes to object definitions are required.

1. The `IMPORTS` statement should reference SNMPv2-SMI instead of RFC1155-SMI and RFC-1212.
2. The `MODULE-IDENTITY` must be invoked immediately after any `IMPORTS` statement.
3. Remove the hyphen character from any descriptor containing that character.
4. Remove the hyphen character from any label for a named-number enumeration containing that character.

5. An INTEGER type with no range restriction should be defined as Integer32.

6. Remove the hyphen character from any SYNTAX clause value for a named-number enumeration containing that character.

7. Any Counter type should be defined as Counter32.

8. Any Gauge type should be defined as Gauge32.

9. Replace the ACCESS clause with a MAX-ACCESS clause. Use the same access category unless some other category makes "protocol sense." In particular, the read-create category should be used for object types for which object instances can be created by a set operation. If the value of the ACCESS clause is write-only, then the value of the MAX-ACCESS clause is read-write.

10. Replace each STATUS clause value of mandatory with current.

11. Replace each STATUS clause value of optional with obsolete.

12. A DESCRIPTION clause should be added if it is not present.

13. For any conceptual row without an INDEX clause, either an INDEX or AUGMENTS clause should be added.

14. For any object with an INDEX clause that references an object with a syntax of Network-Address, change the value of the STATUS clause of both objects to obsolete.

15. In any DEFVAL clause, replace an OJBECT IDENTIFIER value expressed as a collection of subidentifiers with a single ASN.1 identifier.

Other changes are desirable but not necessary:

1. The scheme used for row creation and deletion in SNMPv1 is inconsistent with that of SNMPv2. It would be desirable to deprecate the columnar objects in SNMPv1 tables that allow row creation and deletion and replace them with objects defined using the SNMPv2 approach.

2. For any string-valued object for which there are no bounds on the corresponding OCTET STRING type, bounds could be added.

3. Textual conventions can be formally defined using the TEXTUAL-CONVENTIONS macro.

4. For any object that represents a measurement in some kind of units, a UNITS clause could be added.

5. For any conceptual row that is an extension of another conceptual row, the AUGMENTS clause could be used.

12.3.1.2 Trap Definitions

To update trap definitions, each occurrence of the TRAP-TYPE macro should be mapped into the corresponding NOTIFICATION-TYPE macro as follows.

1. The IMPORTS clause must not reference RFC-1215.

2. The ENTERPRISE clause must be removed.

3. The VARIABLES clause must be renamed as the OBJECTS clause.

4. The STATUS clause must be added.

5. In SNMPv2, traps are assigned object identifiers. These must be incorporated into the object identifier tree.

12.3.1.3 Compliance Statements

A MODULE-COMPLIANCE macro should be added to those modules that are "standard." To update these definitions, the macro name AGENT-CAPABILITIES should be used.

12.3.1.4 Capabilities Statements

RFC-1303 defines a convention for describing SNMP agents using the MODULE-CONFORMANCE macro. The following steps will update these descriptions to the SNMPv2 framework.

1. Use the macro name AGENT-CAPABILITIES instead of MODULE-CONFORMANCE.

2. Add the STATUS clause.

3. For all occurrences of the CREATION-REQUIRES clause, note the slight change in semantics, and omit this clause if appropriate.

12.3.2 Protocol Operations

The protocol defined in the SNMPv2 framework is very similar to that of the SNMPv1 framework, using the same PDU formats. The major changes are an extension of the set of PDUs to include the GetBulkRequest PDU and the InformRequest PDU, and a change in semantics to allow get operations to provide partial results rather than operate in an atomic manner.

The coexistence strategy deals with two issues: the use of proxy agents and bilingual manager behavior.

12.3.2.1 Proxy Agent Behavior

The simplest way to achieve coexistence at the protocol level is to allow existing SNMPv1 agents to remain in place, but to reach them from an SNMPv2 manager by means of a proxy agent. An SNMPv2 entity acting in an SNMPv2 agent role can be implemented and configured to act in the role of a proxy agent on behalf of SNMPv1 agents. This would allow conversion between the SNMPv2 and SNMPv1 protocols.

The proxy agent needs to perform two mappings, as illustrated in Figure 12.11. SNMPv2 PDUs coming from an SNMPv2 manager are converted to SNMPv1 PDUs to be sent to an SNMPv1 agent according to the following rules.

1. GetRequest, GetNextRequest, and SetRequest PDUs are passed unchanged.

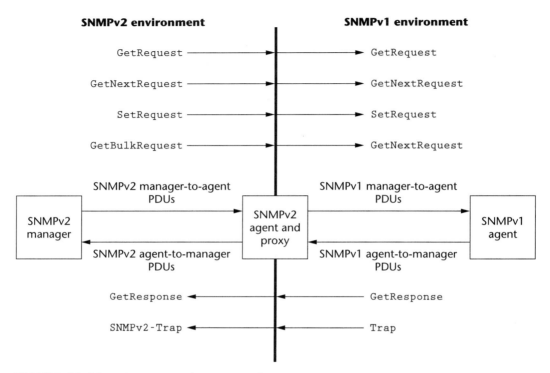

FIGURE 12.11   Coexistence by means of proxy agent

2. A `GetBulkRequest` PDU is converted to a `GetNextRequest` PDU with the same `variable-bindings` list. The effect of this mapping is that only the first "row" of the `max-repetitions` portion of the `variable-bindings` list will be retrieved.

SNMPv1 PDUs coming from an SNMP agent are converted to SNMPv2 PDUs to be sent to an SNMPv2 manager according to the following rules:

1. A `GetResponse` PDU is passed unchanged. Note that the `error-status` values of `noSuchName`, `badValue`, and `readOnly` are not used in SNMPv2; however, these values are recognized by an SNMPv2 manager (Figure 12.3) in order to be able to properly interpret responses from an SNMPv1 agent. In SNMPv1, if a response is too big, a `GetResponse` that includes the `variable-bindings` field is returned. In SNMPv2, this field is empty. Accordingly, if a `GetResponse` PDU is received by the proxy agent with an `error-status` field value of `tooBig`, the proxy agent will remove the contents of the `variable-bindings` field before propagating the response. Also note that an SNMPv2 agent will never generate a response to a `Get-`

`BulkRequest` with an `error-status` of `tooBig`; instead, the agent will return as many variable-binding pairs as possible. However, the proxy agent will pass a response to a `GetBulkRequest` with an `error-status` of `tooBig`.

2. A `Trap` PDU is converted into an SNMPv2-Trap PDU. This is done by prepending two new pairs onto the `variable-bindings` field: `sysUpTime.0` and `SNMPv2-TrapOID.0`.

12.3.2.2 Bilingual Manager Behavior

An alternative way to achieve coexistence is to employ management stations that "speak" both SNMPv2 and SNMPv1 (Figure 12.12). When a management application needs to contact a protocol entity acting in an agent role, the entity acting in a manager role uses either SNMPv2 or SNMPv1 PDUs based on information in a local database that assigns each correspondent agent to one of the two protocols.

This dual capability in the management station should be visible only at the SNMPv2/SNMPv1 level. Management applications can be written as if they were using only SNMPv2. For communication with SNMPv1 agents, the manager can map operations as if it were acting as a proxy agent.

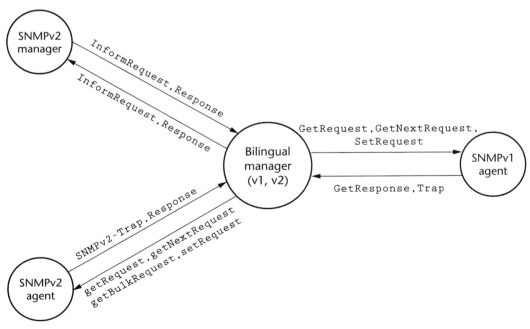

FIGURE 12.12   Coexistence by means of bilingual manager

12.4 *Summary*

There are two major enhancements in the protocol operations for SNMPv2. The Get-Bulk Request PDU allows for the retrieval of multiple rows of a table with a single PDU exchange. The InformRequest PDU enables a manager to transmit management information to another manager. Another change included in SNMPv2 is that the get operations are not atomic; partial results are allowed.

The SNMPv2 specification includes a strategy statement for evolution from SNMPv1 to SNMPv2 by means of a period of coexistence. The two elements of that strategy are as follows.

1. Minor changes to an SNMPv1 MIB are needed to bring it into conformance with SNMPv2 SMI.

2. A mixed SNMPv1/SNMPv2 environment can be managed by using a proxy agent that communicates with SNMPv2 managers and SNMPv1 agents, or by using bilingual managers.

SNMPv2

MIBs and Conformance

We begin this chapter with a description of the SNMPv2 MIB, which instruments both SNMPv1 and SNMPv1. Next conformance statements are examined; these are used to specify conformance requirements for standardized MIBs and to enable vendors to document the scope of their implementation. Finally, we look at the MIB extensions to the `interfaces` group, which are defined using SNMPv2 SMI and depend on some of the protocol features of SNMPv2.

13.1 *SNMPv2 Management Information Base*

The SNMPv2 MIB defines objects that describe the behavior of an SNMPv2 entity. This MIB consists of three groups:

- *System group:* an expansion of the original MIB-II `system` group to include a collection of objects allowing an SNMPv2 entity acting in an agent role to describe its dynamically configurable object resources
- *SNMP group:* a refinement to the original MIB-II `snmp` group, consisting of objects providing basic instrumentation of protocol activity
- *MIB objects group:* a collection of objects that deal with `SNMPv2-Trap` PDUs and that allow several cooperating SNMPv2 entities, all acting in a manager role, to coordinate their use of the SNMPv2 set operation

We consider each group in the MIB in turn.

13.1.1 System Group

The `system` group defined in the SNMPv2 MIB is actually the same group defined in MIB-II, with the addition of some new objects. Figure 13.1 shows the revised `system` group, which is still part of the MIB-II hierarchy.

A comparison of Figure 13.1 with the original `system` group (Figure 6.1) shows that all of the new objects have names beginning with the prefix `sysOR`. These objects

399

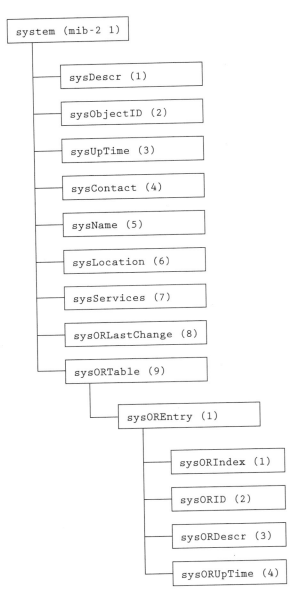

FIGURE 13.1 Revised system group

TABLE 13.1   SNMPv2 Additions to `system` Group

Object	Syntax	Description
sysORLastChange	TimeStamp	The value of `sysUpTime` at the time of the most recent change in state or value of any instance of `sysORID`.
sysORTable	SEQUENCE OF SysOREntry	Table of dynamically configurable object resources in an SNMPv2 entity acting in an agent role.
sysOREntry	SEQUENCE	Information on a particular dynamically configurable object resource.
sysORIndex	INTEGER	Integer used as index into `sysORTable`.
sysORID	OBJECT IDENTIFIER	The object ID of this entry. This is analogous to the `sysObjectID` object in MIB-II.
sysORDescr	DisplayString	A textual description of the object resource. This is analogous to the `sysDescr` object in MIB-II.
sysORUpTime	TimeStamp	The value of `sysUpTime` at the time this row was last instantiated.

relate to system resources and are used by an SNMPv2 entity acting in an agent role to describe those object resources that it controls that are subject to dynamic configuration by a manager. Table 13.1 lists the objects contained in the group.[1] There is a single scalar object and an object-resource table. The scalar object is `snmpORLastChange`, which records the value of `sysUpTime` at the time of the most recent change in state or value of any object instance included in the object-resource table; in other words, this is the last time that there was a change in the collection of manageable resources controlled by this agent. The object-resource table is a read-only table consisting of one entry for each object resource that can be dynamically configured.

13.1.2 SNMP Group

This is the same group defined in MIB-II but with the addition of some new objects and the deletion of some of the original objects. The `snmp` group contains some basic traffic information relating to the operation of SNMPv2. All but one of the objects are 32-bit read-only counters; these are listed in Table 13.2. The remaining object, `snmpEnable-AuthenTraps`, is a read-write enumerated integer, with the values `enabled(1)` and `disabled(2)`, that indicates whether the SNMPv2 entity is permitted to generate `authenticationFailure` traps.

A comparison with the original MIB-II `snmp` group (Figure 7.7) shows that the revised group (Figure 13.2) has far fewer parameters. The reason for this is that these

---

[1]The following acronyms are used: `read-only` (RO), `read-write` (RW), `read-create` (RC), `not-accessible` (NA).

TABLE 13.2   Counters in Revised SNMP Group

snmpInPackets
> Total number of packets received by SNMPv2 entity from transport service.

snmpInBadVersions
> Total number of SNMP messages delivered to the SNMP entity for an unsupported SNMP version.

snmpInBadCommunityNames
> Total number of SNMP messages delivered to the SNMP entity that used an SNMP community name not known to the entity.

snmpInBadCommunityUses
> Total number of SNMP messages delivered to the SNMP entity that represented an SNMP operation not allowed by the SNMP community named in the message.

snmpInASNParseErrs
> Total number of ASN.1 or BER errors encountered when decoding received SNMP messages.

snmpSilentDrops
> Total number of GetRequest, GetNextRequest, GetBulkRequest, SetRequest, and Inform-Request PDUs that were silently dropped because the size of a reply containing an alternate Response-PDU with an empty variable-bindings field was greater than either a local constraint or the maximum message size of the request's source party.

snmpProxyDrops
> Total number of GetRequest, GetNextRequest, GetBulkRequest, SetRequest, and Inform-Request PDUs that were silently dropped because the context indicated a proxy SNMPv2 context and the transmission of the (possibly translated) message to a proxy target failed in a manner (other than a time-out) such that no Response-PDU could be returned to the original request's source party.

detailed statistics are not essential to debugging real problems and they add quite a bit to the size of an agent. Accordingly, a more streamlined group of objects was adopted.

13.1.3 MIB Objects Group

The MIB objects group contains additional objects pertinent to the control of MIB objects (Figure 13.3). The first portion of this group is a subgroup, snmpTrap, consisting of two objects related to traps:

- snmpTrapOID, which is the object identifier of the trap or notification currently being sent. The value of this object occurs as the second varbind in every SNMPv2-Trap PDU and InformRequest PDU.

- snmpTrapEnterprise, which is the object identifier of the enterprise associated with the trap currently being sent. When an SNMPv2 proxy agent is mapping an RFC-1157 Trap PDU into an SNMPv2-Trap PDU, this variable occurs as the last varbind.

FIGURE 13.2   Revised SNMP group

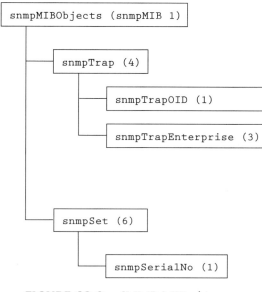

FIGURE 13.3   SNMP MIB objects group

The second portion of the MIB objects group is a subgroup, `snmpSet`, consisting of the single object `snmpSerialNo`. This object is used to solve two problems that can occur with the use of the set operation.

1. Multiple set operations on the same MIB object may be issued by a manager, and it may be essential that these operations be performed in the order that they were issued, even if they are reordered in transmission.

2. Concurrent use of set operations by multiple managers may result in an inconsistent or inaccurate database.

To see the second problem, consider a simple example. Suppose that the value of a MIB object corresponds to the address of a slot in a buffer and that the buffer is to be used for collecting data downloaded from a manager using some sort of file transfer protocol. The object's value indicates the next available slot. To use this value, a manager first reads the value, then increments it to the following slot, and then downloads its data. But the following sequence could occur.

1. Manager A gets the object's value, which is x.

2. Manager B gets the same value.

3. Manager A requires y octets of buffer space, and so issues a set to the agent to update the object to a value of $x + y$.

4. Manager B requires z octets of buffer space, and so issues a set to the agent to update the object to a value of $x + z$.

5. Both manager A and B are now prepared to send data into the buffer starting at location x.

The result will be that either A will overwrite B's data or vice versa. Furthermore, if $z < y$ and A sends its data after B, not only are B's data overwritten, but part of A's data will be overwritten by the next manager to use the buffer.

This problem, in which the outcome depends on the order in which independent events occur, is referred to as a race.[2]

The single object in the set group is defined as follows:

```
snmpSetSerialNo  OBJECT TYPE
   SYNTAX       TestAndIncr
   MAX-ACCESS   read-write
   STATUS       current
   DESCRIPTION
      "An advisory lock used to allow several cooperating SNMPv2
      entities, all acting in a manager role, to coordinate their
      use of the SNMPv2 set operation. This object is used for
      coarse-grain coordination. To achieve fine-grain coor-
      dination, one or more similar objects might be defined
      within each MIB group, as appropriate."
   ::= { snmpSet 1 }
```

TestAndIncr is a textual convention that has a type of INTEGER (0..2147483647), which is the range 0 to $2^{31} - 1$. The rule for modifying this object is as follows. Suppose that the current value of the object at an agent is K. Then,

1. If the agent receives a set operation for this object with a value of K, then the value of the object is incremented to $(K + 1)$ mod 2^{31}, and the operation succeeds with the value K being returned.

2. If the agent receives a set operation for this object with a value not equal to K, then the operation fails with an error of inconsistentValue.

The definition of the TestAndIncr textual convention is reproduced in Appendix 13A.

---

[2]See Stallings (1995b) for a discussion of issues related to distributed concurrent access.

Recall that the set operation is performed in an atomic fashion; that is, if a `Set-Request` PDU is received, the set operations specified by the variable bindings are all performed if all operations are valid, or none is performed if at least one operation is invalid. Thus, the `snmpSet` object can be used in the following way: When a manager wishes to set one or more object values in an agent, it first retrieves the value of the `snmpSet` object. It then issues a `SetRequest` PDU whose variable-binding list includes the `snmpSet` object with its retrieved value, together with a variable-bindings pair for each object value to be set. If two or more managers issue `SetRequests` using the same value of `snmpSet`, the first to arrive at the agent will succeed (assuming no other problems exist), resulting in an increment of `snmpSet`; the remaining set operations will fail due to an inconsistent `snmpSet` value. In addition, if a manager wishes to issue a series of set operations and guarantee that these are executed in the proper order, then the `snmpSet` object can be included in each operation.

As the definition states, this is a coarse-grained coordination technique: If all managers use the `snmpSet` object, then only one manager at a time can successfully issue a set to an agent, for all objects in the MIB. If a `TestAndIncr` object is associated with a single group, then concurrency restrictions can be confined to just the objects in that group.

13.2 *Conformance Statements*

The SNMPv2 specification includes a document dealing with conformance. The purpose of the conformance statements document is to define a notation to be used to specify acceptable lower bounds of implementation, along with the actual level of implementation achieved.

Four macros are defined in the conformance statements document:

- `OBJECT-GROUP`: indicates those objects in a MIB module that are part of a conformance group
- `NOTIFICATION-GROUP`: identifies a collection of notifications
- `MODULE-COMPLIANCE`: defines compliance requirements for an agent with respect to MIB modules and objects
- `AGENT-CAPABILITIES`: defines the capabilities provided by a particular agent implementation

13.2.1 OBJECT-GROUP **Macro**

The `OBJECT-GROUP` macro is used to specify a grouping of related managed objects. As in the SNMP SMI, a group of managed objects in SNMPv2 is the basic unit of conformance. The `OBJECT-GROUP` macro provides a systematic means for a vendor to describe its degree of conformance by indicating which groups are implemented.

The SNMPv2 specification clears up an ambiguity in SNMP that was discussed in Section 7.5. The SNMPv2 specification specifies that an object is "implemented" only if a reasonably accurate value can be returned for a read operation. In addition, for writable objects, the implementation must be able reasonably to influence the underlying managed entity in response to a set operation. If an agent cannot implement an object, it must return an error, such as noSuchObject, in response to a protocol operation. The agent is not permitted to return a value for an object that it does not implement.

Figure 13.4 shows the OBJECT-GROUP macro, which consists of the following major clauses:

- OBJECTS *clause:* lists all of the objects in the group that have a MAX-ACCESS clause value of accessible-for-notify, read-only, read-write, or read-create (Thus, objects that have a MAX-ACCESS clause value of not-accessible are not included in the OBJECT-GROUP macro; this includes conceptual table, conceptual row, and row index objects. Each of the named objects must be defined with an OBJECT-TYPE macro in the same module in which the OBJECT-GROUP module exists.)
- STATUS *clause:* indicates whether this definition is current or historic
- DESCRIPTION *clause:* contains a textual definition of the group, along with a description of any relations to other groups (The value of an invocation of the OBJECT-GROUP macro is an object identifier assigned to the group.)
- REFERENCE *clause:* may be used to include a textual cross-reference to a group defined in some other information module

```
OBJECT-GROUP MACRO ::= BEGIN

TYPE NOTATION ::= ObjectsPart
                  "STATUS" Status
                  "DESCRIPTION" Text
                  ReferPart

VALUE NOTATION ::= value (VALUE OBJECT IDENTIFIER)

ObjectsPart ::= "OBJECTS" "{" Objects "}"

Objects ::= Object | Objects "," Object

Object ::= value (Name ObjectName)

Status ::= "current" | "deprecated" | "obsolete"

ReferPart ::= "REFERENCE" Text | Empty

Text ::= """" string """"

END
```

FIGURE 13.4   OBJECT-GROUP macro

A simple example of an OBJECT-GROUP definition is that for the snmp group:

```
snmpGroup OBJECT-GROUP
    OBJECTS { snmpInPkts,
              snmpInBadVersions,
              snmpInASNParseErrs,
              snmpBadOperations,
              snmpSilentDrops,
              snmpProxyDrops,
              snmpEnableAuthenTraps }
    STATUS current
    DESCRIPTION
    "A collection of objects providing basic instrumentation and
    control of an SNMPv2 entity."
    ::= { snmpMIBGroups 8 }
```

13.2.2 NOTIFICATION-GROUP Macro

The NOTIFICATION-GROUP macro is used to define a collection of notifications for conformance purposes. Figure 13.5 shows this macro, which consists of the following major clauses:

- NOTIFICATIONS *clause:* lists each notification contained in the conformance group (Each of the named objects must be defined with a NOTIFICATION-TYPE macro in the same module in which the NOTIFICATION-GROUP module exists.)
- STATUS *clause:* indicates whether this definition is current or historic
- DESCRIPTION *clause:* contains a textual definition of the group, along with a description of any relations to other groups (The value of an invocation of the NOTIFICATION-GROUP macro is an object identifier assigned to the group.)
- REFERENCE *clause:* may be used to include a textual cross-reference to a group defined in some other information module

A simple example of a NOTIFICATION-GROUP definition is that for the SNMPv2 MIB:

```
snmpBasicNotificationsGroup NOTIFICATION-GROUP
    NOTIFICATIONS { coldStart, authenticationFailure }
    STATUS    current
    DESCRIPTION
      "The two notifications which an SNMPv2 entity is required to
      implement."
    ::= { snmpMIBGroups 7 }
```

```
NOTIFICATION-GROUP MACRO ::= BEGIN

TYPE NOTATION ::= NotificationsPart
                  "STATUS" Status
                  "DESCRIPTION" Text
                  ReferPart

VALUE NOTATION ::= value(VALUE OBJECT IDENTIFIER)

NotificationsPart ::= "NOTIFICATIONS" "{" Notifications "}"

Notifications ::= Notification | Notifications "," Notification

Notification ::= value(Name NotificationName)

Status ::= "current" | "deprecated" | "obsolete"

ReferPart ::= "REFERENCE" Text | empty

Text ::= """" string """"

END
```

FIGURE 13.5   NOTIFICATION-GROUP macro

13.2.3 MODULE-COMPLIANCE Macro

The MODULE-COMPLIANCE macro specifies a minimum set of requirements with respect to the implementation of one or more MIB modules. Figure 13.6 shows the MODULE-COMPLIANCE macro. The STATUS, DESCRIPTION, and REFERENCE clauses are similar in meaning to those for the OBJECTS-GROUP and NOTIFICATION-GROUP macros.

The MODULE clause is used one or more times to name each module included in the compliance requirements. The clause that refers to this module need not include a module name. Other MODULE clauses are identified by their module name and, optionally, their object identifier.

Each MODULE section specifies those groups that are mandatory and those that are optional for the implementation. If there is at least one mandatory group, then the MANDATORY-GROUPS clause is included, which lists all of the mandatory groups for the specified module. In order to be compliant with the module, an implementation must implement all objects in all mandatory groups.

For each group that is conditionally mandatory or unconditionally optional, there is a separate GROUP clause. The DESCRIPTION clause is used to specify those conditions under which a group is conditionally mandatory (for example, if a particular protocol is implemented, or if another group is implemented).

It is also possible, with the OBJECT clause, to specify refinements in the requirements for objects that are in one of the specified groups. For each such object, a separate OBJECT clause is included. Three types of refinements are possible. The first two refinements apply

```
MODULE-COMPLIANCE MACRO ::= BEGIN

TYPE NOTATION ::= "STATUS" Status
                    "DESCRIPTION" Text
                    ReferPart
                    ModulePart

VALUE NOTATION ::= value (VALUE OBJECT IDENTIFIER)

Status ::= "current" | "deprecated" | "obsolete"

ReferPart ::= "REFERENCE" Text | Empty

ModulePart ::= Modules | empty

Modules ::= Module | Modules Module

Module ::= "MODULE" ModuleName        --name of module
            MandatoryPart
            CompliancePart

ModuleName ::= modulereference ModuleIdentifier | empty

ModuleIdentifier ::= value (moduleID OBJECT IDENTIFIER) | empty

MandatoryPart ::= "MANDATORY-GROUPS" "{" Groups "}" | empty

Groups ::= Group | Groups "," Group

Group ::= value (group OBJECT IDENTIFIER)

CompliancePart ::= Compliances | empty

Compliances ::= Compliance | Compliances Compliance

Compliance ::= ComplianceGroup | Object

ComplianceGroup ::= "GROUP" value (Name OBJECT IDENTIFIER)
                    "DESCRIPTION" Text

Object ::= "OBJECT" value (Name ObjectName)
            SyntaxPart
            WriteSyntaxPart
            AccessPart
            "DESCRIPTION" Text

--must be a refinement for object's SYNTAX clause
syntaxPart::= "SYNTAX" type (SYNTAX) | empty

--must be a refinement for object's SYNTAX clause
WriteSyntaxPart ::= "WRITE-SYNTAX" type (WriteSYNTAX) | empty

AccessPart ::= "MIN-ACCESS" Access | empty

Access ::= "not-accessible" | "accessible-for-notify" | "read-only" | "read-write" | read-create"

Text ::= """" string """"

END
```

FIGURE 13.6   MODULE-COMPLIANCE macro

to the syntax of an object when it is read or written. The following refinements are allowed:

- *Range*: For INTEGER and Gauge32 types, the range of permitted values may be re-fined by raising the lower bounds, by reducing the upper bounds, and/or by reducing the alternative value/range choices.

- *Enumeration*: For INTEGER and BIT STRING types, the enumeration of named values may be refined by removing one or more named values.

- *Size*: For OCTET STRING types, the size in characters of the value may be refined by raising the lower bounds, by reducing the upper bounds, and/or by reducing the alternative size choices.

- *Repertoire*: For OCTET STRING types, the repertoire of characters in the value may be reduced by further subtyping (see Appendix B.1 for a discussion of subtyping).

These refinements are defined in the SYNTAX clause for read-only objects and in the WRITE-SYNTAX clause for writable objects.

The third type of refinement possible is in the access category of an object. The MIN-ACCESS clause is used to define a minimal level of access. An implementation is compliant if the level of access it provides is greater than or equal to this minimal level and less than or equal to the level specified in the MAX-ACCESS clause of the object definition.

The value of an invocation of the MODULE-COMPLIANCE macro is an object identifier assigned to the compliance definition. For example, the compliance statement for the SNMPv2 MIB is

```
snmpBasicCompliance MODULE-COMPLIANCE
   STATUS   current
   DESCRIPTION
     "The compliance statement for SNMPv2 entities which implement the
   SNMPv2 MIB."
   MODULE
     MANDATORY-GROUPS { snmpGroup, snmpSetGroup, systemGroup,
                         snmpBasicNotificationsGroup }
   GROUP   snmpCommunityGroup
   DESCRIPTION
      "This group is mandatory for SNMPv2 entities which support
      community-based authentication."
::= { snmpMIBCompliances 2 }
```

This module states that to be compliant an agent must implement all of the groups listed in the MANDATORY-GROUPS clause and that it must also support SNMPv1 community-based authentication.

13.2.4 Capability Definitions

The AGENT-CAPABILITIES macro is used to document the capabilities present in an SNMPv2 protocol entity acting in an agent role. The macro is used to describe the precise level of support that an agent claims with respect to a MIB group. The definition may indicate that some objects have restricted or augmented syntax or access levels. In essence, the capabilities statement specifies refinements or variations with respect to OBJECT-TYPE macros in MIB modules. Note that these refinements and variations are not specified with respect to MODULE-CAPABILITIES macros.

A formal definition of agent capabilities can be useful in promoting and optimizing interoperability. If a management station has the capabilities statement for each of the agents with which it interacts, it can adjust its behavior accordingly to optimize the use of resources: its own, the agent's, and the network's.

Figure 13.7 shows the AGENT-CAPABILITIES macro. The PRODUCT-RELEASE clause contains a textual description of the product release that includes this agent, and the DESCRIPTION clause contains a textual description of this agent. The remainder of the definition includes one section for each MIB module for which the agent claims a complete or partial implementation.

```
AGENT-CAPABILITIES MACRO ::= BEGIN

TYPE NOTATION ::= "PRODUCT-RELEASE" Text
                  "STATUS" Status
                  "DESCRIPTION" Text
                  ReferPart
                  ModulePart

VALUE NOTATION ::= value (VALUE OBJECT IDENTIFIER)

Status ::= "current" | "obsolete"

ReferPart ::= "REFERENCE" Text | Empty

ModulePart ::= Modules | empty

Modules ::= Module | Modules Module

Module ::= "SUPPORTS" ModuleName
           "INCLUDES" "{" Groups "}"
           VariationPart

ModuleName ::= identifier ModuleIdentifier

ModuleIdentifier ::= value (moduleID OBJECT IDENTIFIER) | empty

Groups ::= Group | Groups "," Group
```

FIGURE 13.7   AGENT-CAPABILITIES macro

```
Group ::= value (Name OBJECT IDENTIFIER)

VariationPart ::= Variations | empty

Variations ::= Variation | Variations Variation

Variation ::= ObjectVariation | NotificationVariation

NotificationVariation ::= "VARIATION" value (Name NotificationName)
                          AccessPart
                          "DESCRIPTION" Text

ObjectVariation ::= "VARIATIONS" value (Name Objectname)
                    SyntaxPart
                    WriteSyntaxPart
                    AccessPart
                    CreationPart
                    DefValPart
                    "DESCRIPTION" value (description Text)

SyntaxPart ::= "SYNTAX" type (SYNTAX) | empty

WriteSyntaxPart ::= "WRITE-SYNTAX" type (WriteSYNTAX) | empty

AccessPart ::= "ACCESS" Access | empty

Access ::= "not-implemented" | "accessible-for-notify" | "read-only |
           "read-write" | "read-create" | "write-only"

CreationPart ::= "CREATION-REQUIRES" "{" Cells "}" empty

Cells ::= Cell | Cells "," Cell

Cell ::= value (Cell ObjectName)

DefValPart ::= "DEFVAL" "{" value (Defval ObjectSyntax) "}" | empty

Text ::= """" string """"

END
```

FIGURE 13.7   *Continued*

The description of each MIB module begins with a SUPPORTS clause, which names the module. Then, the INCLUDES clause specifies the list of MIB groups from this MIB module that the agent claims to implement. Finally, for each supported MIB group, the definition may specify zero or more objects that the agent implements in some variant or refined fashion compared with the OBJECT-TYPE macro definition of the object. For each such object, the following are provided. First, the VARIATIONS clause names the object. Then, there may be one or more parts that specify refinements. The SyntaxPart and WriteSyntaxPart have the same semantics as the corresponding parts in the MODULE-COMPLIANCE macro. The AccessPart is used to indicate that the agent provides less than the access level specified in the MAX-ACCESS clause of the object definition. The

CreationPart names the columnar objects for a conceptual row to which values must be explicitly assigned, by a management protocol set operation, before the agent will allow the instance of the status column for that row to be set to active (4). The Def-Val part provides a refined DEFVAL value for the object. The DESCRIPTION clause contains a textual description of the variant or refined implementation.

The value of an invocation of the AGENT-CAPABILITIES macro is an object identifier assigned to the capabilities definition.

The SNMPv2 specification includes the usage example shown in Figure 13.8. In this example, the agent implements the SNMPv2, Interfaces, IP, TCP, UDP, and EVAL MIB modules. For each of these modules, the scope of the implementation is documented.

13.3 *Evolution of the* interfaces *Group of MIB-II*

As was explained in Chapter 6, RFC 1573 (Evolution of the Interfaces Group of MIB-II) clarifies and improves on the interfaces group in RFC 1213 (MIB-II) and uses SMIv2 for definition.

The interfaces group of MIB-II defines a generic set of managed objects such that any network interface can be managed independently of the specific type of interface. This generic approach is suited to typical protocol architectures, which have an internetworking-level protocol such as IP that is designed to run over any network interface. In addition, through the use of media-specific modules, such as the Ethernet and token ring MIBs, additional managed objects can be provided for particular types of network interfaces.

Experience with the interfaces group and the media-specific modules has shown that there are deficiencies in the interfaces group as defined in MIB-II. RFC 1573 is intended to address these deficiencies by clarifying, revising, and extending the MIB structure provided for interfaces. In particular, RFC 1573 notes the following problem areas:

1. *Interface numbering:* The interfaces group in MIB-II (Figure 6.2) defines the object ifNumber as the number of network interfaces present on the system and specifies that each value of ifIndex must be in the range from 1 to the value ifNumber and must remain constant. This requirement is problematic for devices that allow dynamic addition/removal of network interfaces, such as SLIP/PPP connections.

2. *Interface sublayers:* There is a need to distinguish between the multiple sublayers beneath the internetwork layer.

3. *Virtual circuits:* Some accommodation is needed of the fact that there may be multiple virtual circuits below the internetwork layer on the same network interface.

4. *Bit, character, and fixed-length interfaces:* The packet-transmission orientation of ifTable may not be appropriate for interfaces that are not inherently packet-based, including character-oriented (for example, PPP over EIA-232), bit-oriented (for example, DS1), and fixed-length transmission-oriented (for example, ATM).

```
example-agent AGENT-CAPABILITIES
  PRODUCT-RELEASE              "ACME agent release 1.1 for 4BSD"
  STATUS                       current
  DESCRIPTION                  "ACME agent for 4BSD"

  SUPPORTS                     SNMPv2-MIB
    INCLUDES                   { systemGroup, snmpGroup, snmpSetGroup,
                               snmpBasicNotificationsGroup }

      VARIATION                coldStart
        DESCRIPTION            "A coldStart trap is generated on all reboots."

  SUPPORTS                     IF-MIB
    INCLUDES                   { ifGeneralGroup, ifPacketGroup }

      VARIATION                ifAdminStatus
        SYNTAX                 INTEGER { up(1), down(2) }
        DESCRIPTION            "Unable to set test mode on 4BSD"

      VARIATION                ifOperStatus
        SYNTAX                 INTEGER { up(1), down(2) }
        DESCRIPTION            "Information limited on 4BSD"

  SUPPORTS                     IP-MIB
    INCLUDES                   { ipGroup, icmpGroup }

      VARIATION                ipDefaultTTL
        SYNTAX                 INTEGER (255..255)
        DESCRIPTION            "Hard-wired on 4BSD"

      VARIATION                ipInAddrErrors
        ACCESS                 not-implemented
        DESCRIPTION            "Information not available on 4BSD"

      VARIATION                ipNetToMediaEntry
        CREATION-REQUIRES      { ipNetToMediaPhysAddress }
        DESCRIPTION            "Address mappings on 4BSD require both protocol
                               and media addresses"

  SUPPORTS                     TCP-MIB
    INCLUDES                   { tcpGroup }
    VARIATION                  tcpConnState
      ACCESS                   read-only
      DESCRIPTION              "Unable to set this on 4BSD"

  SUPPORTS                     UDP-MIB
    INCLUDES                   { udpGroup }

  SUPPORTS                     EVAL-MIB
    INCLUDES                   { functionsGroup, expressionsGroup }
    VARIATION                  exprEntry
      CREATION-REQUIRES        { evalString }
      DESCRIPTION              "Conceptual row creation supported"

  ::= { acmeAgents 1 }
```

FIGURE 13.8   Example of AGENT-CAPABILITIES statement

5. *Counter size:* As the speed of network media has increased, the minimum time for a 32-bit counter has decreased, causing wraparound problems.

6. *Interface speed:* The range of ifSpeed is limited to a maximum of $2^{31} - 1$ bps, or less than 2.2 Gbps. This data rate is approached or surpassed by some network interface specifications (for example, SONET OC-48 at 2.448 Gbps).

7. *Multicast/broadcast counters:* Counters in ifTable are provided for combined multicast/broadcast transmission. Separate counters for multicast and broadcast packets are sometimes useful.

8. *Addition of new* ifType *values:* New ifType enumerated values are needed on an ongoing basis. The way in which ifType is defined in MIB-II dictates that these new numbers are only available with each new publication of the MIB, which occurs only every several years.

9. ifSpecific: The definition of ifSpecific in MIB-II is ambiguous. Some implementors have given this object a value that is the OBJECT IDENTIFIER of a media-specific MIB. Others have used the OBJECT IDENTIFIER of the media-specific table, or the entry object for that table, or even the index object within that table.

We will see how these concerns are addressed in the description that follows.

RFC 1573 restates, with minor modifications, the interfaces group from MIB-II. In addition, four new tables are introduced (Figure 13.9):

- Extensions table (ifXTable)
- Stack table (ifStackTable)
- Test table (ifTextTable)
- Receive address table (ifRcvAddressTable)

13.3.1 Interfaces Group

The interfaces group in RFC 1573 has the identical structure as the interfaces group in MIB-II; namely, it consists of the object ifNumber and the table ifTable. An important difference is the description clause attached to ifIndex, which reads as follows:

> *A unique value, greater than zero, for each interface or interface sub-layer in the managed system. It is recommended that values are assigned contiguously starting from 1. The value for each interface sub-layer must remain constant at least from one re-initialization of the entity's network management system to the next re-initialization.*

The object ifNumber still reflects the number of interfaces and therefore the number of rows in ifTable. However, it is not necessary to limit the numbering scheme of inter-

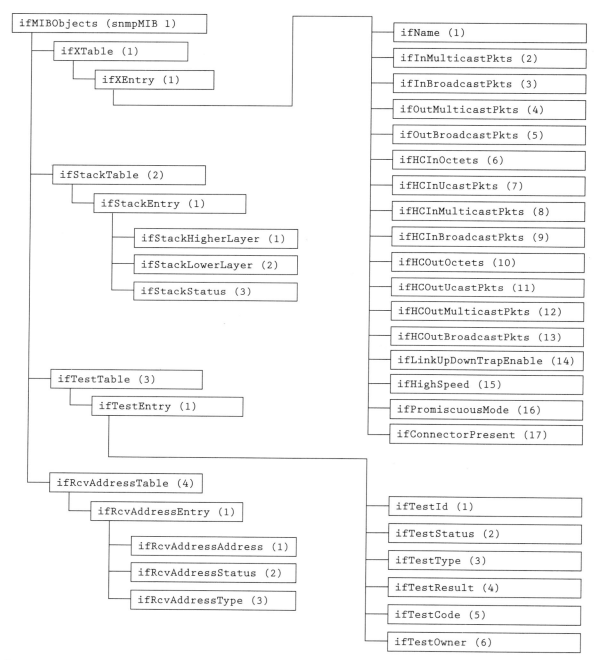

FIGURE 13.9   SNMPv2 additions to the `interfaces` group

faces to the range from 1 through the value of ifNumber. This allows for the dynamic addition/deletion of interfaces.

RFC 1573 allows for the existence of multiple rows in ifTable for a single physical interface, with one row per logical sublayer. However, the document recommends that this strategy be used sparingly. Also, RFC 1573 recommends that there not be a separate row in ifTable for each virtual circuit.

Several objects in ifTable have been deprecated. The objects ifInNUcastPkts and ifOutNUcastPkts, which count all nonunicast packets, are deprecated because new counters are defined in ifXTable to count multicast and broadcast packets separately. The object ifOutQLen was deprecated because frequently it was not implemented. The object ifSpecific is deprecated because it is ambiguous and yields no additional information beyond that provided in ifType.

Another change to ifTable is that the syntax of ifType is changed to be the textual convention IANAifType, which can be respecified (with additional values) without issuing a new version of the MIB. The Internet Assigned Number Authority (IANA) is responsible for updating IANAifType as needed.

13.3.2 Extension to the Interface Table

The ifXTable provides additional information to that provided in ifTable. The table and entry objects are defined as follows:

```
ifXTable   OBJECT-TYPE
   SYNTAX        SEQUENCE OF IfXEntry
   MAX-ACCESS    not-accessible
   STATUS        current
   DESCRIPTION
     "A list of interface entries. The number of entries is given by the
     value of ifNumber. This table contains additional objects for the
     interface table."
   ::= { ifMIBObjects 1 }
ifXEntry   OBJECT-TYPE
   SYNTAX        IfXEntry
   MAX-ACCESS    not-accessible
   STATUS        current
   DESCRIPTION
     "An entry containing additional management information applicable
     to a particular interface."
   AUGMENTS { ifEntry }
   ::= { ifXTable 1 }
```

```
IfXEntry ::= SEQUENCE { ifName                   DisplayString,
                        ifInMulticastPkts        Counter32,
                        ifInBroadcastPkts        Counter32,
                        ifOutMulticastPkts       Counter32,
                        ifOutBroadcastPkts       Counter32,
                        ifHCInOctets             Counter64,
                        ifHCInUcastPkts          Counter64,
                        ifHCInMulticastPkts      Counter64,
                        ifHCInBroadcastPkts      Counter64,
                        ifHCOutOctets            Counter64,
                        ifHCOutUcastPkts         Counter64,
                        ifHCOutMulticastPkts     Counter64,
                        ifHCOutBroadcastPkts     Counter64,
                        ifLinkUpDownTrapEnable   INTEGER,
                        ifHighSpeed              Gauge32,
                        ifPromiscuousMode        TruthValue,
                        ifConnectorPresent       TruthValue }
```

As you can see, `ifXTable` augments the revised `ifTable`. Thus, it is indexed by `ifIndex` from `ifTable`. The table includes the object `ifName`, which is the textual reference to the interface. If several entries in the table refer to different sublayers of the same interface, then they all have the same value of `ifName`.

The next four columnar objects (`ifInMulticastPkts`, `ifInBroadcastPkts`, `ifOutMulticastPkts`, `ifOutBroadcastPkts`) count the number of multicast and broadcast packets received and transmitted across the interface. These counters replace the deprecated `ifInNUcastpkts` and `ifOutNUcastPkts` of `ifTable`.

The next eight objects (`ifHCInOctets`, `ifHCInUcastPkts`, `ifHCInMulticast-Pkts`, `ifHCInBroadcastPkts`, `ifHCOutOctets`, `ifHCOutUcastPkts`, `ifHCOut-MulticastPkts`, `ifHCOutBroadcastPkts`) are referred to as "high-capacity" counter objects. They are all 64-bit versions of the corresponding `ifTable` counters, with the same semantics. On interfaces with data rates that are appropriately high, the agent will maintain the counts in these counters.

The `ifLinkUpDownTrapEnable` object has an enumerated INTEGER syntax with values `enabled(1)` and `disabled(2)`. This object indicates whether `linkUp` and `linkDown` traps should be generated for this entry. By default, this object should have the value `disabled(2)` [cj3,4,5]if this entry defines an interface that operates on top of another interface (as specified in `ifStackTable`). Otherwise, it is appropriate to generate `linkUp` and `linkDown` traps, and the value should be `enabled(1)`.

The next object, `ifHighSpeed`, is a gauge that estimates the current data rate of the interface in units of megabits per second (Mbps). If this object reports a value of n, then the data rate of the interface is in the half-closed interval $(n - 0.5, n + 0.5]$.

The `ifPromiscuousMode` object has an enumerated `INTEGER` syntax with values `true(1)` and `false(2)`. The value is true if the interface accepts all frames/packets transmitted on the media and `false(2)` if it accepts only packets or frames addressed to this station. Broadcast and multicast packets are not considered in this definition.

Finally, `ifConnectorPresent` has the value `true(1)` if the interface sublayer has a physical connector and the value `false(2)` otherwise.

13.3.3 Interface Stack Table

The `ifStackTable` shows the relationship among multiple rows in `ifTable` that are supported by the same physical interface to the medium. It indicates which sublayers run on top of which other sublayers. Each entry in the `ifStackTable` defines a relationship between two entries in `ifTable`. The object `ifStackHigherLayer` contains the `ifIndex` value corresponding to the higher sublayer of the relationship, while `ifStackLowerLayer` contains the `ifIndex` value corresponding to the lower sublayer of the relationship. This table is doubly indexed by these two objects. Finally, `ifStackStatus` has the syntax `RowStatus` (see Appendix 11A) and is used to create/destroy entries in this table.

13.3.4 Interface Test Table

The `ifTestTable` defines objects that enable a manager to instruct an agent to test an interface for various faults. The table contains one entry per interface. Table 13.3 defines the objects in this table.

Each entry in `ifTestTable` provides three capabilities.

1. It enables a manager to specify a particular test to be performed on the interface, by setting the value of `ifTestType`. When this value is successfully set, the agent runs the test.

2. It enables a manager to obtain the results of a test, by getting the values of `ifTestResult` and `ifTestCode`. When an agent has completed the running of a test, it records the results in these two object instances.

3. It provides a mechanism to ensure that only one manager at a time can successfully invoke a test—and that no test can be requested while a test is currently underway—using the objects `ifTestId` and `ifTestStatus`.

Figure 13.10, taken from the definition of `ifTestTable` in the document, describes the logic for the use of this table. When a manager wishes to invoke a test on a particular interface, it first issues a `GetRequest` for the appropriate row of the table for the values of `ifTestId` and `ifTestStatus`. If the test status is `notInUse`, then the manager may proceed; otherwise the manager must keep trying until the row is free.

TABLE 13.3   Objects in `ifTestTable`

Object	Syntax	Access	Description
ifTestTable	SEQUENCE OF IfTestEntry	NA	Table that enables managers to conduct tests
ifTestEntry	SEQUENCE	NA	Test specification for a single interface
ifTestId	TestAndIncr	RW	Identifies the current invocation of the interface's test
ifTestStatus	INTEGER	RW	Indicates whether some manager currently has the ownership of this entry required to invoke a test on this interface, values are not-InUse(1) and InUse(2)
ifTestType	AutonomousType	RW	Identifies the test to be initiated or currently underway
ifTestResult	INTEGER	RO	An indication of the result of the most recently requested test
ifTestCode	OBJECT IDENTIFIER	RO	A code that contains more specific information on the test result
ifTestOwner	OwnerString	RW	Identifies the entity that currently has the ownership of this entry

Once the row is found to be free, the manager will attempt to request a test, using the value of `ifTestId` that it just received. This value is used to identify each test uniquely. The manager issues a `SetRequest`, which attempts to set the value of `ifTestId` to the same value just received by this manager. The syntax of `ifTestId` is `TestAndIncr`. Recall from Section 12.3.5 that an object with this syntax is used in the following way: If the current value of the object instance at the agent is K and a manager request to set the value to K is received, then the set succeeds and the value is incremented by 1. If the received value is not equal to K, then the test fails. Thus, if a manager has retrieved `ifTestId` and then attempts to set `TestId` to that same value, it will succeed only if no other manager has intervened and invoked its own test.

If the setting of `ifTestId` succeeds, then the agent will also set `ifTestStatus` to `inUse`, to block other manager attempts, and will set `ifTestOwner` as requested by the manager. The agent then transmits a response PDU that indicates success to the requesting manager. That manager now has temporary ownership of that row.

Once the manager achieves ownership of the row, it may proceed to invoke the test. This is done by issuing a `SetRequest` that sets `ifTestType` with a value that indicates the test to be run. The agent responds by running the requested test and setting `if-TestResult` to the value `inProgress(3)`. When the test is complete, the agent places the result in `ifTestResult`, which takes one of the possible values listed at the top of page 422.

```
try_again:
      get (ifTestId, ifTestStatus)
      while (ifTestStatus !=notInUse) {
             /*
              *Loop while a test is running or some other
              *manager is configuring a test
              */
             short delay
             get (ifTestId, ifTestStatus)
             }
      /*
       *Is not being used right now --let's compete
       *to see who gets it.
       */
      lock_value = ifTestId

      if ( set(ifTestId = lock_value, ifTestStatus = inUse,
             ifTestOwner = 'my-IP-address') == FAILURE)
             /*
              *Another manager got the ifTestEntry -- go
              *try again
              */
             goto try_again;
      /*
       *I have the lock
       */
      set up any test parameters.

      /*
       *This starts the test
       */
      set(ifTestType = test_to_run);

      wait for test completion by polling ifTestResult

      when test completes, agent sets ifTestResult
             agent also sets ifTestStatus = 'notInUse'

      retrieve any additional test results, and ifTestId

      if (ifTestId == lock_value+1) results are valid
```

FIGURE 13.10   Logic for `ifTestTable`

- `none(1)`: no test as yet requested
- `success(2)`
- `inProgress(3)`
- `notSupported(4)`
- `unAbletoRun(5)`: due to state of system
- `aborted(6)`
- `failed(7)`

Additional information may be supplied in `ifTestCode`.

13.3.5   Generic Receive Address Table

This table contains one entry for each address (broadcast, multicast, and unicast) for which the system will receive packets on a particular interface, except when operating in promiscuous mode. That is, this table lists the addresses that this system recognizes and for which this system will capture the packets containing one of these addresses as a destination address.

The table consists of three columnar objects:

- `ifRcvAddressAddress`: a specific unicast, multicast, or broadcast address that the system will recognize as an appropriate destination address for capturing packets
- `ifRcvAddressStatus`: used to create and delete rows in this table; has the syntax RowStatus
- `ifRcvAddressType`: indicates whether the address is `other(1)`, `volatile(2)`, or `nonVolatile(3)` (A nonvolatile address will continue to exist after a system restart, whereas a volatile address will be lost. An address labeled as `other` indicates that this information is not being made available in this table.)

13.4   *Summary*

Two MIBs related to the SNMPv2 specification are described in this chapter. The SNMPv2 MIB includes information related to the utilization of the protocol itself. The extension to the `interfaces` group, defined in RFC 1573, is defined using SMIv2 and makes use of some of the features of SNMPv2 discussed in this chapter.

The SNMPv2 specification includes a technique for documenting the conformance requirements for a given MIB and a means by which vendors can specify the scope of their implementations. The following four macros are defined in the conformance statements document:

- OBJECT-GROUP: indicates those objects in a MIB module that are part of a conformance group
- NOTIFICATION-GROUP: identifies a collection of notifications
- MODULE-COMPLIANCE: defines compliance requirements for an agent with respect to MIB modules and objects
- AGENT-CAPABILITIES: defines the capabilities provided by a particular agent implementation

APPENDIX 13A `TestAndIncr` *TEXTUAL CONVENTION*

TestAndIncr ::= TEXTUAL-CONVENTION
    STATUS   current
    DESCRIPTION
"Represents integer-valued information used for atomic operations. When the management protocol is used to specify that an object instance having this syntax is to be modified, the new value supplied via the management protocol must precisely match the value presently held by the instance. If not, the management protocol set operation fails with an error of 'inconsistentValue'. Otherwise, if the current value is the maximum value of 2^{31} (2147483647 decimal), then the value held by the instance is wrapped to zero; otherwise, the value held by the instance is incremented by one. (Note that regardless of whether the management protocol set operation succeeds, the variable-binding in the request and response PDUs are identical.)

    The value of the ACCESS clause for objects having this syntax is either 'read-write' or 'read-create'. When an instance of a columnar object having this syntax is created, any value may be supplied via the management protocol.

    When the network management portion of the system is re-initialized, the value of every object instance having this syntax must either be incremented from its value prior to the re-initialization, or (if the value prior to the re-initialization is unknown) be set to a pseudo-randomly generated value."
SYNTAX INTEGER (0. .2147483647)

SNMPv3

Cryptographic Algorithms in SNMPv3

SNMPv3 specifies the use of four cryptographic algorithms. This chapter provides a brief overview of each. For a more detailed treatment of these algorithms, see Stallings (1999).

14.1 Conventional Encryption with DES

14.1.1 Conventional Encryption

Conventional encryption, also referred to as symmetric encryption or single-key encryption, was the only type of encryption in use prior to the introduction of public-key encryption in the late 1970s. Conventional encryption has been used for secret communication by countless individuals and groups, from Julius Caesar to the German U-boat force to present-day diplomatic, military, and commercial users. It remains by far the more widely used of the two types of encryption.

A conventional encryption scheme has five ingredients (Figure 14.1):

- *Plaintext:* This is the readable message or data that is fed into the algorithm as input.
- *Encryption algorithm:* The encryption algorithm performs various substitutions and transformations on the plaintext.
- *Secret key:* The secret key is also input to the algorithm. The exact substitutions and transformations performed by the algorithm depend on the key.
- *Ciphertext:* This is the scrambled message produced as output. It depends on the plaintext and the secret key. For a given message, two different keys will produce two different ciphertexts.
- *Decryption algorithm:* This is essentially the encryption algorithm run in reverse. It takes the ciphertext and the same secret key and produces the original plaintext.

There are two requirements for secure use of conventional encryption.

1. A strong encryption algorithm is required. At a minimum, the algorithm should be such that an opponent who knows the algorithm and has access to one or more

FIGURE 14.1   Conventional encryption

ciphertexts would be unable to decipher the ciphertext or figure out the key. This requirement is usually stated in a stronger form: The opponent should be unable to decrypt ciphertext or discover the key even if he or she is in possession of a number of ciphertexts together with the plaintext that produced each ciphertext.

2. Sender and receiver must have obtained copies of the secret key in a secure fashion and must keep the key secure. If someone can discover the key and knows the algorithm, all communication using this key is readable.

There are two general approaches to attacking a conventional encryption scheme. The first attack is known as *cryptanalysis*. Cryptanalytic attacks rely on the nature of the algorithm plus perhaps some knowledge of the general characteristics of the plaintext or even some sample plaintext-ciphertext pairs. This type of attack exploits the characteristics of the algorithm to attempt to deduce a specific plaintext or to deduce the key being used. Of course, if the attack succeeds in deducing the key, the effect is catastrophic; all future and past messages encrypted with that key are compromised.

The second method, known as the *brute-force* attack, is to try every possible key on a piece of ciphertext until an intelligible translation into plaintext is obtained. On average, half of all possible keys must be tried to achieve success. Table 14.1 shows how much time is involved for various key sizes. The table shows results for each key size, assuming that it takes 1 μs to perform a single decryption, a reasonable order of magnitude for today's computers. With the use of massively parallel organizations of microprocessors, it may be possible to achieve processing rates many orders of magnitude greater. The final column of the table considers the results for a system that can process 1 million keys per microsecond.

TABLE 14.1 Average Time Required for Exhaustive Key Search

Key size (bits)	Number of alternative keys	Time required at 1 encryption/µs	Time required at 10^6 encryptions/µs
32	$2^{32} = 4.3 \times 10^9$	2^{31} µs = 35.8 minutes	2.15 milliseconds
56	$2^{56} = 7.2 \times 10^{16}$	2^{55} µs = 1142 years	10.01 hours
128	$2^{128} = 3.4 \times 10^{38}$	2^{127} µs = 5.4×10^{24} years	5.4×10^{18} years

14.1.2 Data Encryption Standard

The most widely used encryption scheme is based on the Data Encryption Standard (DES) adopted in 1977 by the National Bureau of Standards, now the National Institute of Standards and Technology (NIST), as Federal Information Processing Standard 46 (FIPS PUB 46). For DES, data are encrypted in 64-bit blocks using a 56-bit key. The algorithm transforms 64-bit input in a series of steps into a 64-bit output. The same steps, with the same key, are used to reverse the encryption.

The overall scheme for DES encryption is illustrated in Figure 14.2. As with any encryption scheme, there are two inputs to the encryption function: the plaintext to be encrypted and the key. In this case, the plaintext must be 64 bits in length and the key is 56 bits in length.[1]

The left-hand side of the figure shows that the processing of the plaintext proceeds in three phases. First, the 64-bit plaintext passes through an initial permutation (IP) that rearranges the bits to produce the *permuted input*. This is followed by a phase consisting of 16 rounds of the same function, which involves both permutation and substitution functions. The output of the last (sixteenth) round consists of 64 bits that are a function of the input plaintext and the key. The left and right halves of the output are swapped to produce the *preoutput*. Finally, the preoutput is passed through a permutation (IP⁻¹) that is the inverse of the initial permutation function, to produce the 64-bit ciphertext.

The right-hand portion of Figure 14.2 shows the way in which the 56-bit key is used. Initially, the key is passed through a permutation function. Then, for each of the 16 rounds, a *subkey* (K$_i$) is produced by the combination of a left circular shift and a permutation. The permutation function is the same for each round, but a different subkey is produced because of the repeated iteration of the key bits.

Figure 14.3 shows the internal structure of a single round. The left and right halves of each 64-bit intermediate value are treated as separate 32-bit quantities, labeled L (*left*) and R (*right*). Each round involves a complex sequence of operations involving permutations, substitutions, and the exclusive-OR function.

---

[1]Actually, the function expects a 64-bit key as input. However, only 56 of these bits are used; the other 8 bits can be used as parity bits or simply set arbitrarily.

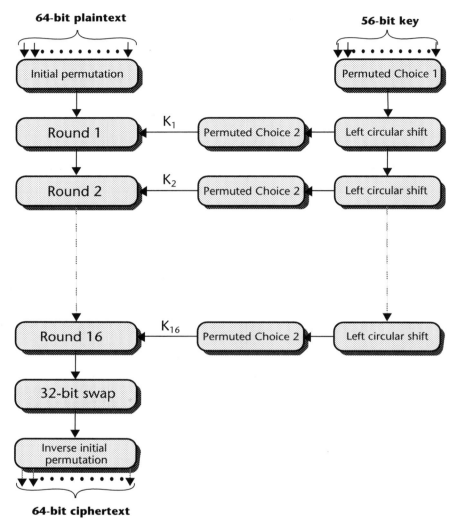

FIGURE 14.2 General depiction of DES encryption algorithm

14.1.3 Cipher Block Chaining Mode

DES processes only one 64-bit block of data at a time. For longer amounts of plaintext, it is necessary to break the plaintext up into 64-bit blocks (padding the last block if necessary). The simplest way to proceed is what is known as electronic codebook (ECB) mode, in which plaintext is handled 64 bits at a time and each block of plaintext is encrypted using the same key. The term *codebook* is used because, for a given key, there is

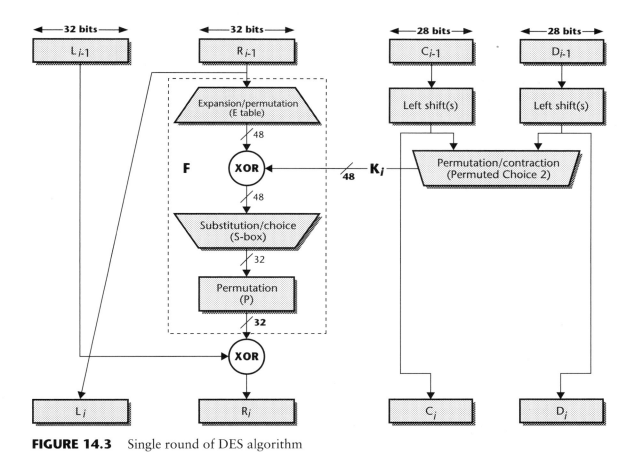

FIGURE 14.3   Single round of DES algorithm

a unique ciphertext for every 64-bit block of plaintext. Therefore, one can imagine a gigantic codebook in which there is an entry for every possible 64-bit plaintext pattern showing its corresponding ciphertext.

With ECB, if the same 64-bit block of plaintext appears more than once in the message, it always produces the same ciphertext. Because of this, for lengthy messages, the ECB mode may not be secure. If the message is highly structured, it may be possible for a cryptanalyst to exploit these regularities. For example, if it is known that the message always starts out with certain predefined fields, then the cryptanalyst may have a number of known plaintext-ciphertext pairs to work with. If the message has repetitive elements, with a period of repetition a multiple of 64 bits, then these elements can be identified by the analyst. This may help in the analysis or may provide an opportunity for substituting or rearranging blocks.

To overcome the security deficiencies of ECB, we would like a technique in which the same plaintext block, if repeated, produces different ciphertext blocks. A simple way to satisfy this requirement is the Cipher Block Chaining (CBC) mode (Figure 14.4). In this scheme, the input to the encryption algorithm is the XOR of the current plaintext block and the preceding ciphertext block; the same key is used for each block. In effect, we have chained together the processing of the sequence of plaintext blocks. The input to the encryption function for each plaintext block bears no fixed relationship to the plaintext block. Therefore, repeating patterns of 64 bits are not exposed.

For decryption, each cipher block is passed through the decryption algorithm. The result is XORed with the preceding ciphertext block to produce the plaintext block. To see that this works, we can write:

$$C_n = E_K[C_{n-1} \oplus P_n]$$

where $E_K[X]$ is the encryption of plaintext X using key K, and $\oplus$ is the exclusive-OR operation. Then,

$$D_K[C_n] = D_K[E_K(C_{n-1} \oplus P_n)]$$
$$D_K[C_n] = (C_{n-1} \oplus P_n)$$
$$C_{n-1} \oplus D_K[C_n] = C_{n-1} \oplus C_{n-1} \oplus P_n = P_n$$

where $D_K[X]$ is the decryption of plaintext X using key K.

To produce the first block of ciphertext, an initialization vector (IV) is XORed with the first block of plaintext. On decryption, the IV is XORed with the output of the decryption algorithm to recover the first block of plaintext.

The IV must be known to both the sender and receiver. For maximum security, the IV should be protected as well as the key. This could be done by sending the IV using ECB encryption. One reason for protecting the IV is that if an opponent is able to fool the receiver into using a different value for IV, then the opponent is able to invert selected bits in the first block of plaintext. To see this, consider the following:

$$C_1 = E_K(IV \oplus P_1)$$
$$P_1 = IV \oplus D_K(C_1)$$

Now use the notation that $X[i]$ denotes the ith bit of the 64-bit quantity X. Then,

$$P_1[i] = IV[i] \oplus D_K(C_1)[i]$$

Then, using the properties of XOR, we can state

$$P_1[i]' = IV[i]' \oplus D_K(C_1)[i]$$

where the prime notation denotes bit complementation. This means that if an opponent can predictably change bits in IV, the corresponding bits of the received value of P_1 can be changed.

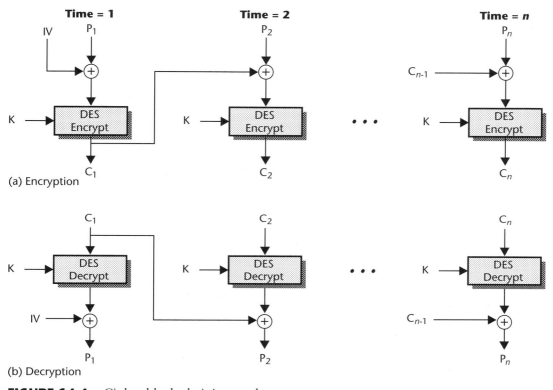

Time = 1   **Time = 2**   **Time = n**

(a) Encryption

(b) Decryption

FIGURE 14.4   Cipher block chaining mode

14.2 The MD5 Secure Hash Function

An essential element of most authentication and digital signature schemes is a secure hash function. A hash function accepts a variable-length message M as input and produces a fixed size hash code H(M), sometimes called a message digest, as output. In Section 14.4, we look at a standard way of using a hash function for message authentication. In this section and the next, we look at the two hash functions specified for use with SNMPv3.

The MD5 message-digest algorithm (RFC 1321) was developed by Ron Rivest at MIT (the "R" in the RSA [Rivest-Shamir-Adleman] public-key encryption algorithm). Until the last few years, when both brute-force and cryptanalytic concerns have arisen, MD5 was the most widely used secure hash algorithm.

The algorithm takes as input a message of arbitrary length and produces as output a 128-bit message digest. The input is processed in 512-bit blocks. Figure 14.5 depicts the

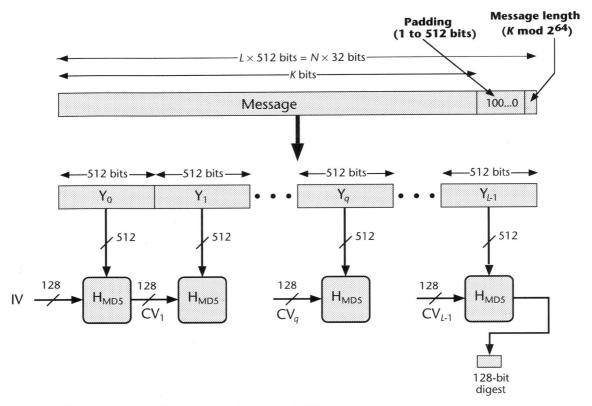

FIGURE 14.5   Message digest generation using MD5

overall processing of a message to produce a digest. The processing consists of the following steps.

1. *Append padding bits.* The message is padded so that its length in bits is congruent to 448 modulo 512. That is, the length of the padded message is 64 bits less than an integer multiple of 512 bits. Padding is always added, even if the message is already of the desired length. For example, if the message is 448 bits long, it is padded by 512 bits to a length of 960 bits. Thus, the number of padding bits is in the range of 1 to 512. The padding consists of a single 1-bit followed by the necessary number of 0-bits.

2. *Append length.* A 64-bit representation of the length in bits of the original message (before the padding) is appended to the result of step 1 (least significant byte first). If the original length is greater than 2^{64}, then only the low-order 64 bits of the length are used. Thus, the field contains the length of the original message, modulo 2^{64}. The

inclusion of a length value at the end of the message makes a type of attack known as a padding attack more difficult.

The outcome of the first two steps yields a message that is an integer multiple of 512 bits in length. In Figure 14.5, the expanded message is represented as the sequence of 512-bit blocks $Y_0, Y_1, \ldots, Y_{L-1}$, so that the total length of the expanded message is $L \times 512$ bits. Equivalently, the result is a multiple of 16 32-bit words. Let $M[0 \ldots N-1]$ denote the words of the resulting message, with N an integer multiple of 16. Thus, $N = L \times 16$.

3. *Initialize MD buffer.* A 128-bit buffer is used to hold intermediate and final results of the hash function. The buffer can be represented as four 32-bit registers (A, B, C, D). These registers are initialized to the following 32-bit integers (hexadecimal values):

$$
\begin{aligned}
A &= 67452301 \\
B &= EFCDAB89 \\
C &= 98BADCFE \\
D &= 10325476
\end{aligned}
$$

These values are stored in little-endian format, which is the least significant byte of a word in the low-address byte position. As 32-bit strings, the initialization values (in hexadecimal) appear as follows:

```
word A:   01 23 45 67
word B:   89 AB CD EF
word C:   FE DC BA 98
word D:   76 54 32 10
```

4. *Process message in 512-bit (16-word) blocks.* The heart of the algorithm is a function that consists of four "rounds" of processing; this module is labeled H_{MD5} in Figure 14.5, and its internal logic is illustrated in Figure 14.6. The four rounds have a similar structure, but each uses a different primitive logical function, referred to as F, G, H, and I in the specification. Each function takes three 32-bit words as input and produces a 32-bit word output. Each function performs a set of bitwise logical operations; that is, the nth bit of the output is a function of the nth bit of the three inputs. The functions are:

$$
\begin{aligned}
F(X,Y,Z) &= (X \bullet Y) + (X' \bullet Z) \\
G(X,Y,Z) &= (X \bullet Z) + (Y \bullet Z') \\
H(X,Y,Z) &= X \oplus Y \oplus Z \\
I(X,Y,Z) &= Y \oplus (X + Z')
\end{aligned}
$$

where the logical operators (AND, OR, NOT, XOR) are represented by the symbols ($\bullet$, $+$, $'$, $\oplus$). Function F is a conditional function: If X then Y else Z. Similarly, G can

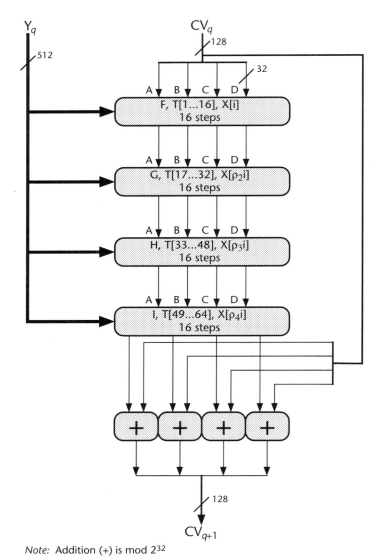

FIGURE 14.6   MD5 processing of a single 512-bit block

Note: Addition (+) is mod 2^{32}

be stated as: If Z then X else Y. Function H produces a parity bit. Table 14.2(a) is a truth table of the four functions.

The algorithm also makes use of a 64-element table T[1 . . . 64] constructed from the sine function. The *i*th element of T, denoted T[*i*], has the value equal to the integer part of $2^{32} \times \text{abs}(\sin(i))$, where i is in radians. Since abs(sin(i)) is a number

TABLE 14.2   Key Elements of MD5

(a) Truth table of logical functions

b	c	d	F	G	H	I
0	0	0	0	0	0	1
0	0	1	1	0	1	0
0	1	0	0	1	1	0
0	1	1	1	0	0	1
1	0	0	0	0	1	1
1	0	1	0	1	0	1
1	1	0	1	1	0	0
1	1	1	1	1	1	0

(b) Table T, constructed from the sine function

T[1]	=	D76AA478	T[17]	=	F61E2562	T[33]	=	FFFA3942	T[49] = F4292244
T[2]	=	E8C7B756	T[18]	=	C040B340	T[34]	=	8771F681	T[50] = 432AFF97
T[3]	=	242070DB	T[19]	=	265E5A51	T[35]	=	699D6122	T[51] = AB9423A7
T[4]	=	C1BDCEEE	T[20]	=	E9B6C7AA	T[36]	=	FDE5380C	T[52] = FC93A039
T[5]	=	F57C0FAF	T[21]	=	D62F105D	T[37]	=	A4BEEA44	T[53] = 655B59C3
T[6]	=	4787C62A	T[22]	=	02441453	T[38]	=	4BDECFA9	T[54] = 8F0CCC92
T[7]	=	A8304613	T[23]	=	D8A1E681	T[39]	=	F6BB4B60	T[55] = FFEFF47D
T[8]	=	FD469501	T[24]	=	E7D3FBC8	T[40]	=	BEBFBC70	T[56] = 85845DD1
T[9]	=	698098D8	T[25]	=	21E1CDE6	T[41]	=	289B7EC6	T[57] = 6FA87E4F
T[10]	=	8B44F7AF	T[26]	=	C33707D6	T[42]	=	EAA127FA	T[58] = FE2CE6E0
T[11]	=	FFFF5BB1	T[27]	=	F4D50D87	T[43]	=	D4EF3085	T[59] = A3014314
T[12]	=	895CD7BE	T[28]	=	455A14ED	T[44]	=	04881D05	T[60] = 4E0811A1
T[13]	=	6B901122	T[29]	=	A9E3E905	T[45]	=	D9D4D039	T[61] = F7537E82
T[14]	=	FD987193	T[30]	=	FCEFA3F8	T[46]	=	E6DB99E5	T[62] = BD3AF235
T[15]	=	A679438E	T[31]	=	676F02D9	T[47]	=	1FA27CF8	T[63] = 2AD7D2BB
T[16]	=	49B40821	T[32]	=	8D2A4C8A	T[48]	=	C4AC5665	T[64] = EB86D391

between 0 and 1, each element of T is an integer that can be represented in 32 bits. The table provides a "randomized" set of 32-bit patterns, which should eliminate any regularities in the input data. Table 14.2(b) lists the values of T.

Each round takes as input the current 512-bit block being processed (Y_q) and the 128-bit buffer value ABCD and updates the contents of the buffer. Each round also makes use of one-fourth of a 64-element table T[1 . . . 64], constructed from the sine function. The output of the fourth round is added to the input to the first round (CV_q) to produce CV_{q+1}. The addition is done independently for each of the four words in the buffer with each of the corresponding words in CV_q, using addition modulo 2^{32}.

5. *Output.* After all *L* 512-bit blocks have been processed, the output from the *L*th stage is the 128-bit message digest.

The MD5 algorithm has the property that every bit of the hash code is a function of every bit in the input. The complex repetition of the basic functions (F, G, H, I) produces results that are well mixed; that is, it is unlikely that two messages chosen at random, even if they exhibit similar regularities, will have the same hash code. The author of MD5 conjectures that the difficulty of generating two messages with the same MD5 digest is on the order of 2^{64} operations, and the difficulty of generating a message that produces a given digest is on the order of 2^{128} operations.

14.3 *The SHA-1 Secure Hash Function*

The Secure Hash Algorithm (SHA) was developed by the National Institute of Standards and Technology (NIST) and published as a federal information processing standard (FIPS PUB 180) in 1993; a revised version was issued as FIPS PUB 180-1 in 1995 and is generally referred to as SHA-1. SHA is based on the MD4 algorithm, a precursor to MD5, and its design closely models MD4.

The algorithm takes as input a message with a maximum length of less than 2^{64} bits and produces as output a 160-bit message digest. The input is processed in 512-bit blocks.

The overall processing of a message follows the structure shown for MD5 in Figure 14.5, with a block length of 512 bits and a hash length and chaining variable length of 160 bits. The processing consists of the following steps.

1. *Append padding bits.* The message is padded so that its length is congruent to 448 modulo 512. Padding is always added, even if the message is already of the desired length. Thus, the number of padding bits is in the range of 1 to 512. The padding consists of a single 1-bit followed by the necessary number of 0-bits.

2. *Append length.* A block of 64 bits is appended to the message. This block is treated as an unsigned 64-bit integer (most significant byte first) and contains the length of the original message (before the padding).

3. *Initialize MD buffer.* A 160-bit buffer is used to hold intermediate and final results of the hash function. The buffer can be represented as five 32-bit registers (A, B, C, D, E). These registers are initialized to the following 32-bit integers (hexadecimal values):

```
A = 67452301
B = EFCDAB89
C = 98BADCFE
D = 10325476
E = C3D2E1F0
```

Note that the first four values are the same as those used in MD5. However, in the case of SHA-1, these values are stored in big-endian format, which is the most significant byte of a word in the low-address byte position. As 32-bit strings, the initialization values (in hexadecimal) appear as follows:

word A: 67 45 23 01
word B: EF CD AB 89
word C: 98 BA DC FE
word D: 10 32 54 76
word E: C3 D2 E1 F0

4. *Process message in 512-bit (16-word) blocks.* The heart of the algorithm is a module that consists of four rounds of processing of 20 steps each. The logic is illustrated in Figure 14.7. The four rounds have a similar structure, but each uses a different primitive logical function, which we refer to as f_1, f_2, f_3, and f_4.

Each round takes as input the current 512-bit block being processed (Y_q) and the 160-bit buffer value ABCDE, and updates the contents of the buffer. Each round also makes use of an additive constant K_t, where $0 \leq t \leq 79$ indicates one of the 80 steps across five rounds. In fact, only four distinct constants are used. The values, in hexadecimal and decimal, are as follows:

Step number	Hexadecimal	Take integer part of:
$0 \leq t \leq 19$	$K_t = \text{5A827999}$	$\left[2^{30} \times \sqrt{2} \right]$
$20 \leq t \leq 39$	$K_t = \text{6ED9EBA1}$	$\left[2^{30} \times \sqrt{3} \right]$
$40 \leq t \leq 59$	$K_t = \text{8F1BBCDC}$	$\left[2^{30} \times \sqrt{5} \right]$
$60 \leq t \leq 79$	$K_t = \text{CA62C1D6}$	$\left[2^{30} \times \sqrt{10} \right]$

The output of the fourth round (eightieth step) is added to the input to the first round (CV_q) to produce CV_{q+1}. The addition is done independently for each of the five words in the buffer with each of the corresponding words in CV_q, using addition modulo 2^{32}.

5. *Output.* After all L 512-bit blocks have been processed, the output from the Lth stage is the 160-bit message digest.

14.4 *Message Authentication with HMAC*

Message authentication is a procedure that allows communicating parties to verify that received messages are authentic. The two important aspects are to verify that the contents of the message have not been altered and that the source is authentic. The message

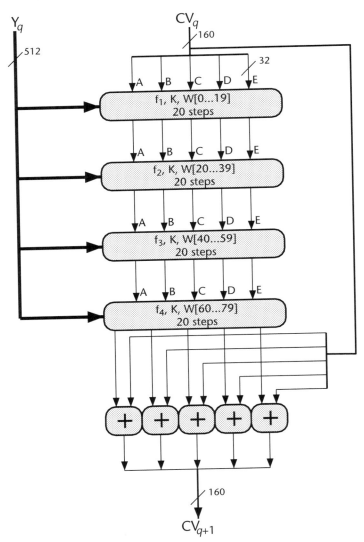

Note: Addition (+) is mod 2^{32}

FIGURE 14.7 SHA-1 processing of a single 512-bit block

authentication code (MAC) is a widely used technique for performing message authentication, and one MAC algorithm has emerged as the Internet standard for a wide variety of applications: HMAC.

14.4.1 Message Authentication Codes

A MAC algorithm involves the use of a secret key to generate a small block of data, known as a message authentication code, that is appended to the message. This technique assumes that two communicating parties, say A and B, share a common secret key K. When A has a message to send to B, it calculates the message authentication code as a function of the message and the key. The message plus code are transmitted to the intended recipient. The recipient performs the same calculation on the received message, using the same secret key, to generate a new message authentication code. The received code is compared to the calculated code (Figure 14.8). If we assume that only the receiver and the sender know the identity of the secret key, and if the received code matches the calculated code, then:

1. The receiver is assured that the message has not been altered. If an attacker alters the message but does not alter the code, then the receiver's calculation of the code will differ from the received code. Because the attacker is assumed not to know the secret key, the attacker cannot alter the code to correspond to the alterations in the message.

2. The receiver is assured that the message is from the alleged sender. Because no one else knows the secret key, no one else could prepare a message with a proper code.

3. If the message includes a sequence number (such as is used with X.25, HDLC, and TCP), then the receiver can be assured of the proper sequence, because an attacker cannot successfully alter the sequence number.

A number of algorithms could be used to generate the code. The National Bureau of Standards, in its publication *DES Modes of Operation*, recommends the use of the DES algorithm. The DES algorithm is used to generate an encrypted version of the message,

FIGURE 14.8   Use of a message authentication code

and the last number of bits of ciphertext are used as the code. A 16- or 32-bit code is typical. A more efficient and increasingly popular alternative is HMAC.

The process just described is similar to encryption. One difference is that the authentication algorithm need not be reversible, as it must be for decryption. It turns out that because of the mathematical properties of the authentication function, it is less vulnerable to being broken than encryption.

14.4.2 HMAC

In recent years, there has been increased interest in developing a MAC derived from a cryptographic hash code, such as MD5, SHA-1, or RIPEMD-160. There are several motivations for this interest.

1. Cryptographic hash functions generally execute faster in software than conventional encryption algorithms such as DES.
2. Library code for cryptographic hash functions is widely available.
3. There are no export restrictions from the United States or other countries for cryptographic hash functions, whereas conventional encryption algorithms, even when used for MACs, are restricted.

A hash function such as MD5 was not designed for use as a MAC and cannot be used directly for that purpose because it does not rely on a secret key. There have been a number of proposals for the incorporation of a secret key into an existing hash algorithm. The approach that has received the most support is HMAC (Bellare et al. 1996a; Bellare et al. 1996b). HMAC has been issued as RFC 2104, has been chosen as the mandatory-to-implement MAC for IP Security, and is used in other Internet protocols, such as Transport Layer Security (TLS, soon to replace Secure Sockets Layer) and Secure Electronic Transaction (SET).

14.4.2.1 HMAC Design Objectives

RFC 2104 lists the following design objectives for HMAC:

- To use, without modifications, available hash functions. In particular, hash functions that perform well in software, and for which code is freely and widely available.
- To allow for easy replaceability of the embedded hash function in case faster or more secure hash functions are found or required.
- To preserve the original performance of the hash function without incurring a significant degradation.
- To use and handle keys in a simple way.
- To have a well-understood cryptographic analysis of the strength of the authentication mechanism based on reasonable assumptions about the embedded hash function.

The first two objectives are important to the acceptability of HMAC. HMAC treats the hash function as a "black box." This has two benefits. First, an existing implementation of a hash function can be used as a module in implementing HMAC. In this way, the bulk of the HMAC code is prepackaged and ready to use without modification. Second, if it is ever desired to replace a given hash function in an HMAC implementation, all that is required is to remove the existing hash function module and drop in the new module. This could be done if a faster hash function were desired. More important, if the security of the embedded hash function were compromised, the security of HMAC could be retained simply by replacing the embedded hash function with a more secure one (for example, replacing MD5 with SHA-1).

The last design objective in the preceding list is, in fact, the main advantage of HMAC over other proposed hash-based schemes. HMAC can be proven secure provided that the embedded hash function has some reasonable cryptographic strengths. We return to this point later in this section, but first we examine the structure of HMAC.

14.4.2.2 HMAC Algorithm

Figure 14.9 illustrates the overall operation of HMAC. Define the following terms as:

H = embedded hash function (for example, MD5, SHA-1, RIPEMD-160)

M = message input to HMAC (including the padding specified in the embedded hash function)

Y_i = ith block of M, $0 \leq i \leq (L-1)$

L = number of blocks in M

b = number of bits in a block

n = length of hash code produced by embedded hash function

K = secret key; if key length is greater than b, the key is input to the hash function to produce an n-bit key; recommended length is $\geq n$

K^+ = K padded with zeros on the left so that the result is b bits in length

ipad = 00110110 (36 in hexadecimal) repeated $b/8$ times

opad = 01011100 (5C in hexadecimal) repeated $b/8$ times

Then HMAC can be expressed as follows:

$$\text{HMAC}_K = H[(K^+ \oplus \text{opad}) \| H[(K^+ \oplus \text{ipad}) \| M]]$$

In words:

1. Append zeros to the left end of K to create a b-bit string K^+ (for example, if K is of length 160 bits and $b = 512$, then K will be appended with 44 zero bytes 0x00).
2. XOR (bitwise exclusive-OR) K^+ with ipad to produce the b-bit block S_i.
3. Append M to S_i.
4. Apply H to the stream generated in step 3.

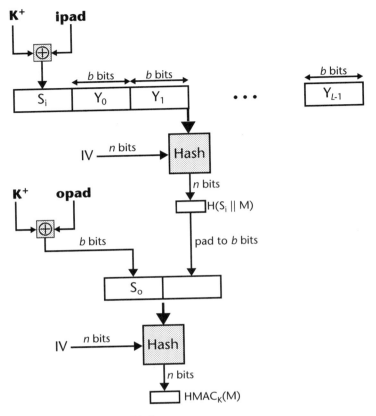

FIGURE 14.9   HMAC structure

5. XOR K^+ with opad to produce the b-bit block S_o.

6. Append the hash result from step 4 to S_o.

7. Apply H to the stream generated in step 6 and output the result.

Note that the XOR with ipad results in flipping one-half of the bits of K. Similarly, the XOR with opad results in flipping one-half of the bits of K, but a different set of bits. In effect, by passing S_i and S_o through the hash algorithm, we have pseudorandomly generated two keys from K.

HMAC should execute in approximately the same time as the embedded hash function for long messages. HMAC adds three executions of the hash compression function (for S_i, S_o, and the block produced from the inner hash).

14.4.2.3 Security of HMAC

The security of any MAC function based on an embedded hash function depends in some way on the cryptographic strength of the underlying hash function. The appeal of HMAC is that its designers have been able to prove an exact relationship between the strength of the embedded hash function and the strength of HMAC.

The security of a MAC function is generally expressed in terms of the probability of successful forgery with a given amount of time spent by the forger and a given number of message-MAC pairs created with the same key. In essence, it can be shown that, for a given level of effort (time, message-MAC pairs), on messages generated by a legitimate user and seen by the attacker, the probability of successful attack on HMAC is equivalent to one of the following attacks on the embedded hash function.

1. The attacker is able to compute an output of the compression function even with an IV that is random, secret, and unknown to the attacker.

2. The attacker finds collisions in the hash function even when the IV is random and secret.

In the first attack, we can view the compression function as equivalent to the hash function applied to a message consisting of a single b-bit block. For this attack, the IV of the hash function is replaced by a secret, random value of n bits. An attack on this hash function requires either a brute-force attack on the key, which is a level of effort on the order of 2^n, or a birthday attack, which is a special case of the second attack, discussed next.

In the *second attack*, the attacker is looking for two messages M and M' that produce the same hash: H(M) = H(M'). It can be shown that this requires a level of effort of $2^{n/2}$ for a hash length of n. On this basis, the security of MD5 is called into question, because a level of effort of 2^{64} looks feasible with today's technology. Does this mean that a 128-bit hash function such as MD5 is unsuitable for HMAC? The answer is no, because of the following argument. To attack MD5, the attacker can choose any set of messages and work on these off-line on a dedicated computing facility to find a collision. Because the attacker knows the hash algorithm and the default IV, the attacker can generate the hash code for each of the messages that the attacker generates. However, when attacking HMAC, the attacker cannot generate message/code pairs off-line because the attacker does not know K. Therefore, the attacker must observe a sequence of messages generated by HMAC under the same key and perform the attack on these known messages. For a hash code length of 128 bits, this requires 2^{64} observed blocks (2^{73} bits) generated using the same key. On a 1-Gbps link, one would need to observe a continuous stream of messages with no change in key for about 250,000 years in order to succeed. Thus, if speed is a concern, it is fully acceptable to use MD5 rather than SHA-1 as the embedded hash function for HMAC.

SNMPv3

Architecture and Applications

SNMPv2, in its final form, contains no provisions for security. This deficiency is reme-died in SNMPv3. The documents issued by the SNMPv3 working group are, in fact, not a complete specification for a network management protocol. Rather, these documents define a set of security capabilities and a framework that enables that set to be used with the SNMPv2 or SNMPv1 functional capabilities.[1] The framework also is suitable for use with new functional capabilities and accommodates security enhancements and modifi-cations. We begin this chapter with an introduction to SNMPv3, showing the context within which it evolved. Then we look at the overall SNMPv3 framework. Finally, the functional capabilities that may be employed within the SNMPv3 framework, known as applications, are examined.

15.1 Background

This section provides a summary of the history leading to SNMPv3 and an outline of the way in which SNMPv3 is presented in Chapters 15 through 17.

15.1.1 The Development of SNMPv3

Chapters 4 and 11 presented a history of the evolution of SNMP and SNMPv2. Figure 15.1 captures the key milestones in the development of SNMP-related standards. The starting point was the simple gateway monitoring protocol (SGMP) issued in November of 1987. The SGMP provided a straightforward means for monitoring gateways (OSI level 3 routers). When the need for a more general-purpose network management tool was identified, SGMP was taken as the baseline and adapted to produce the simple net-work management protocol (SNMP) first issued in August of 1988. SNMP provided a minimal but powerful set of facilities for monitoring and control of network elements

---

[1] By functional capabilities, we mean the capabilities supported by the SNMP PDU. Security features are reflected in the SNMP message that encloses the SNMP PDU.

FIGURE 15.1   The evolution of SNMP

using a straightforward structure of management information (SMI), management information base (MIB), and protocol. One notable deficiency in SNMP was the difficulty of monitoring networks, as opposed to nodes on networks. Remarkably, a quite substantial functional enhancement to SNMP was achieved simply by the definition of a set of standardized management objects referred to as the remote network monitoring (RMON) MIB, first issued in November of 1991. RMON represented the first, and last, major functional enhancement to the first version of SNMP.

Another deficiency in SNMP was the complete lack of security facilities. To remedy this problem, a set of documents referred to as secure SNMP (S-SNMP) was issued as proposed standards in July of 1992. In that same month, the simple management protocol (SMP) was issued outside the Internet standards structure. SMP provided functional enhancements to SNMP and incorporated, with minor modifications, the security enhancements of S-SNMP. SMP also incorporated some of the concepts from RMON, including the specifications of alarms and events, and the use of a status columnar object to facilitate row creation and deletion. SMP was accepted as the baseline for developing a second-generation SNMP, known as SNMP version 2 (SNMPv2). The first generation came to be called SNMPv1.

To produce SNMPv2, two working groups were set up. The SNMPv2 working group was charged with all nonsecurity aspects, including SMI, MIB, protocol, confor-

TABLE 15.1   SNMPv3 Documents

Number	Title	Date
RFC 2271	An Architecture for Describing SNMP Management Frameworks	January 1998
RFC 2272	Message Processing and Dispatching for SNMP	January 1998
RFC 2273	SNMPv3 Applications	January 1998
RFC 2274	User-Based Security Model for SNMPv3	January 1998
RFC 2275	View-Based Access Control Model (VACM) for SNMP	January 1998
Internet Draft	Introduction to Version 3 of the Internet Network Management Framework	October 1998

mance statements, and coexistence strategies with SNMPv1. This work was substantially based on SMP. After many iterations, this working group completed its work in December of 1992 and issued a set of nine Internet draft documents that were ready to enter the standardization process as proposed Internet standards.

The second working group, known as the SNMPv2 security working group, proceeded at a slightly slower pace to develop the security aspects of SNMPv2. This work was substantially based on S-SNMP, as revised for SMP. After many iterations, this group produced Internet draft documents in January of 1993 that represented broad agreement but with some unresolved issues.

As discussed in Chapter 11, SNMPv2 was revised and reissued in 1996 without the security features, because of a lack of consensus on what should constitute SNMP security. To remedy this lack of security, a number of independent groups began work on a security enhancement to SNMPv2. Two competing approaches emerged as front-runners: SNMPv2u and SNMPv2*. Ultimately, these two approaches served as input to a new IETF SNMPv3 working group, which was chartered in March of 1997. By January of 1998, this group had produced a set of Proposed Internet standards published as RFCs 2271–2275 (Table 15.1). This document set defines a framework for incorporating security features into an overall capability that includes either SNMPv1 or SNMPv2 functionality. In addition, the documents define a specific set of capabilities for network security and access control.[2]

A brief clarification of the term *SNMPv3* is perhaps in order. RFCs 2271 through 2275, produced by the SNMPv3 working group, describe an overall architecture plus specific message structures and security features, but do not define a new SNMP PDU format. Thus, the existing SNMPv1 or SNMPv2 PDU format must be used within the new architecture. An implementation referred to as SNMPv3 consists of the security and architectural features defined in RFCs 2271 through 2275 plus the PDU format and functionality

---

[2] Three of the developers of the SNMPv3 documents have authored a book on the subject, whose target audience is protocol implementors and network administrators (Blumenthal et al. 1998)

defined in the SNMPv2 documents. This is expressed in the SNMPv3 introduction document (Table 15.1) as follows: "SNMPv3 is SNMPv2 plus security and administration."

15.1.2 Plan of Attack

We present the material on SNMPv3 in three chapters.

- This chapter describes the overall management framework for SNMPv3 and the applications (functional elements) for SNMP management-agent interaction. These elements are defined in RFCs 2271 and 2273, respectively.
- Chapter 16 looks at the general message-processing functionality of the SNMPv3 framework and the specific message-processing security functions of SNMPv3. These elements are defined in RFCs 2272 and 2274, respectively.
- Chapter 17 examines access control, which is defined in RFC 2275.

15.2 *SNMPv3 Overview*

RFC 2271 defines an overall SNMP architecture. This architecture is, in effect, a modular description of the major functional and security elements that may go into the implementation of an SNMP manager or agent system.

15.2.1 Design Requirements

The following design goals guided the development of the SNMP architecture.

- Use existing work, for which there is implementation experience and some consensus as to its value. As a result, the SNMP architecture and SNMPv3 security features rely heavily on SNMPv2u and SNMPv2*.
- Address the need for secure `Set request` messages over real-world networks, which is the most important deficiency of SNMPv1 and SNMPv2.
- Design a modular architecture that will (1) allow implementation over a wide range of operational environments, some of which need minimal, inexpensive functionality and some of which may support additional features for managing large networks; (2) make it possible to move portions of the architecture forward in the standards track even if consensus has not been reached on all pieces; and (3) accommodate alternative security models.
- Keep SNMP as simple as possible.

Based on these goals, a number of design decisions were made in the process of developing the SNMPv3 documents. It is worth quoting these decisions in their entirety, as put forth in RFC 2271:

- *Architecture:* An architecture should be defined which identifies the conceptual boundaries between the documents. Subsystems should be defined which describe the abstract services provided by specific portions of an SNMP framework. Abstract service interfaces, as described by service primitives, define the abstract boundaries between documents, and the abstract services that are provided by the conceptual subsystems of an SNMP framework.

- *Self-contained documents:* Elements of procedure plus the MIB objects which are needed for processing for a specific portion of an SNMP framework should be defined in the same document and, as much as possible, should not be referenced in other documents. This allows pieces to be designed and documented as independent and self-contained parts, which is consistent with the general SNMP MIB module approach. As portions of SNMP change over time, the documents describing other portions of SNMP are not directly impacted. This modularity allows, for example, Security Models, authentication and privacy mechanisms, and message formats to be upgraded and supplemented as the need arises. The self-contained documents can move along the standards track on different time lines.

- *Remote configuration:* The Security and Access Control Subsystems add a whole new set of SNMP configuration parameters. The Security Subsystem also requires frequent changes of secrets at the various SNMP entities. To make this deployable in a large operational environment, these SNMP parameters must be able to be remotely configured.

- *Controlled complexity:* It is recognized that producers of simple managed devices want to keep the resources used by SNMP to a minimum. At the same time, there is a need for more complex configurations which can spend more resources for SNMP and thus provide more functionality. The design tries to keep the competing requirements of these two environments in balance and allows the more complex environments to logically extend the simple environment.

- *Threats:* The Security Models in the Security Subsystem SHOULD protect against the principal threats: modification of information, masquerade, message stream modification, and disclosure. They do not need to protect against denial of service and traffic analysis.

In terms of security threats (see Section 3.2 for a discussion of security threats), SNMPv3 has essentially the same design objectives as were first used to guide the development of Secure SNMP in 1992. SNMPv3, as with Secure SNMP and the initial version of SNMPv2, is designed to secure against the following principal threats:

- *Modification of information:* An entity could alter an in-transit message generated by an authorized entity in such a way as to effect unauthorized management operations, including the setting of object values. The essence of this threat is that an unauthorized entity could change any management parameter, including those related to configuration, operations, and accounting.

- *Masquerade:* Management operations that are not authorized for some entity may be attempted by that entity by assuming the identity of an authorized entity.
- *Message stream modification:* SNMP is designed to operate over a connectionless transport protocol. There is a threat that SNMP messages could be reordered, delayed, or replayed (duplicated) to effect unauthorized management operations. For example, a message to reboot a device could be copied and replayed later.
- *Disclosure:* An entity could observe exchanges between a manager and an agent and thereby learn the values of managed objects and learn of notifiable events. For example, the observation of a set command that changes passwords would enable an attacker to learn the new passwords.

SNMPv3 is not intended to secure against the following two threats.

- *Denial of service:* An attacker may prevent exchanges between manager and agent.
- *Traffic analysis:* An attacker may observe the general pattern of traffic between managers and agents.

The lack of a counter to the denial-of-service threat may be justified on two grounds: First, denial-of-service attacks are in many cases indistinguishable from the type of network failures with which any viable network management application must cope as a matter of course; and second, a denial-of-service attack is likely to disrupt all types of exchanges and is a matter for an overall security facility, not one embedded in a network management protocol. As to traffic analysis, many network management traffic patterns are predictable (for example, entities may be managed via SNMP commands issued on a regular basis by one or a few management stations) and therefore there is no significant advantage to protecting against observing these traffic patterns.

15.2.2   Document Overview

RFCs 2271 through 2275, referred to collectively as SNMPv3, do not stand alone. They are insufficient to define a complete SNMP implementation. RFC 2271 indicates which other documents may be used in conjunction with SNMPv3 to define a complete implementation and also provides guidance for creating additional documents.

Figure 15.2 indicates the documents that fit within the SNMP architecture defined in RFC 2271. The top three boxes refer to documents that are planned for future publication. The *Document Roadmap* will list all nonobsolete RFCs for SNMP and indicate how sets of documents taken together form specific Frameworks. *Applicability Statements* will describe the environments to which certain versions of SNMP or models within SNMP would be appropriately applied, and those which may be inappropriate for a given envi-

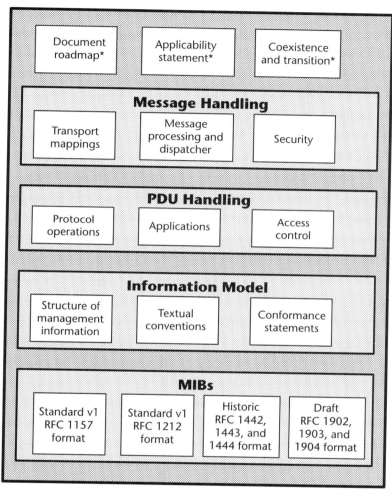

* = expected to be written in the future

FIGURE 15.2   SNMP document roadmap (RFC 2271)

ronment. *Coexistence and Transition* documents provide guidance for enabling the coexisting of implementations of different versions of SNMP and for a gradual transition from one version to another; RFC 1908, which describes the coexistence between SNMPv1 and SNMPv2, is the only document in this category so far published (see Section 12.3).

15.2.2.1 Message Handling Documents

The outermost data block handled within SNMP is the message. It is the message that is transmitted across the network by means of some lower-layer protocol such as UDP. On incoming messages, the message header must be processed prior to examining the enclosed SNMP PDU, and for outgoing data, a message header must be prepared for the outgoing PDU. The message header contains security-related information that determines the security operations for this message. Message handling documents that deal with all of these aspects of message processing fall into three categories:

- *Transport mappings:* A transport mapping describes the manner in which SNMP messages are mapped onto various transport-layer protocols. An example is RFC 1906, which indicates the mapping for community-based SNMPv2 messages (Section 12.2).

- *Message processing and dispatcher:* A message processing model document defines a message format. The document may also define one or more MIB modules for use in message processing and for instrumenting message traffic.

- *Security:* A security document describes security functions, such as authentication and privacy, and defines the semantics of security-related fields in the message header.

15.2.2.2 PDU Handling Documents

Enclosed within a message header is an SNMP PDU, which supports management functions. PDU handling documents fall into three categories.

- *Protocol operations:* A protocol operations document defines a set of PDU formats corresponding to various specific management functions and defines the operations of the protocol with respect to processing PDUs.

- *Applications:* An application document defines the functions supported by means of the SNMP PDU. In this context, an application is a low-level set of management functions, such as `get` and `set` commands, notifications, and proxy operations.

- *Access control:* Access control is a security function performed at the PDU level. An access control document defines mechanisms for determining whether access to a managed object should be allowed.

15.2.2.3 Information Model Documents

Information model documents define the structure and syntax of management information. These documents fall into three categories.

- *Structure of management information:* An SMI document defines the syntax used in constructing MIBs and for defining the managed objects and other elements of a management information base.

- *Textual conventions:* Textual conventions are used to enhance the readability of a MIB specification. A textual convention defines a new syntactic type similar to those defined in an SMI, but with more precise semantics.

- *Conformance statements:* A conformance statement specifies an acceptable lower bound on implementations and provides a notation for indicating the actual level of implementation achieved.

15.2.2.4 MIB Documents

MIB documents describe collections of managed objects that contain representations of managed information. Figure 15.2 indicates four sets of documents of interest. RFCs 1157 and 1212 define the format used for SNMPv1. Table 4.1 indicates some of the MIB documents defined using these formats. RFCs 1442 through 1444 defined the SMI, textual conventions, and conformance statement notation for the original version of SNMPv2. These have been supplanted by RFCs 1902 through 1904 for the revised version of SNMPv2.

15.3 *SNMP Architecture*

The SNMP architecture, as envisioned by RFC 2271, consists of a distributed, interacting collection of SNMP entities. Each entity implements a portion of the SNMP capability and may act as an agent node, a manager node, or a combination of the two. Each SNMP entity consists of a collection of modules that interact with each other to provide services. These interactions can be modeled as a set of abstract primitives and parameters. In this section, we look first at the internal structure of an SNMP entity, and then consider the service definitions for the modules of an SNMP entity.

15.3.1 SNMP Entities

Figure 15.3 shows a general block diagram of an SNMP entity. Each SNMP entity includes a single SNMP engine. An SNMP engine implements functions for sending and receiving messages, authenticating and encrypting/decrypting messages, and controlling access to managed objects. These functions are provided as services to one or more applications that are configured with the SNMP engine to form an SNMP entity.

As Figure 15.3 illustrates, both the SNMP engine and the applications it supports are defined as a collection of discrete modules. This architecture provides several advantages. First, as we shall see, the role of an SNMP entity is determined by which modules are implemented in that entity. For example, a certain set of modules is required for an SNMP agent, while a different (though overlapping) set of modules is required for an SNMP manager. Second, the modular structure of the specification lends itself to defining different versions of each module. This in turn makes it possible to (1) define alternative or enhanced capabilities for certain aspects of SNMP without needing to go to a new version of the entire standard (for example, SNMPv4), and (2) clearly specify coexistence and transition strategies.

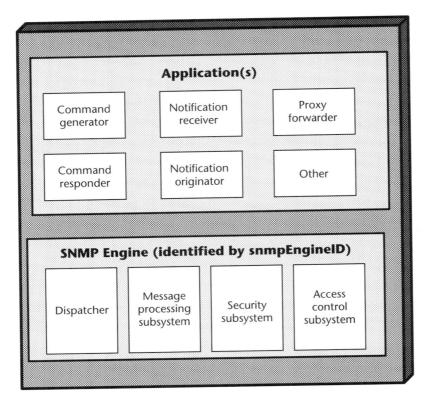

FIGURE 15.3 SNMP entity (RFC 2271)

Table 15.2 provides a brief definition of each of the modules defined in the SNMP architecture specified in RFC 2271. To get a better understanding of the role of each module and its relationship to other modules, it is best to look at their use in traditional SNMP managers and agents. The term *traditional*, equivalent to *pure*, is used to emphasize the fact that a given implementation need not be a pure manager or agent but may have modules that allow the entity to perform both management and agent tasks.

15.3.1.1 Traditional SNMP Manager

Figure 15.4, based on a figure in RFC 2271, is a block diagram of a traditional SNMP manager. In SNMPv3 terminology, a traditional SNMP manager includes three categories of applications. The *Command Generator Applications* monitor and manipulate management data at remote agents; they make use of SNMPv1 and/or SNMPv2 PDUs, including Get, GetNext, GetBulk, and Set. A *Notification Originator Application* initiates asynchronous messages; in the case of a traditional manager, the InformRequest PDU is used for this application. A *Notification Receiver Application* processes incoming asynchro-

TABLE 15.2   Components of an SNMP Entity (RFC 2271 and 2273)

Dispatcher

Allows for concurrent support of multiple versions of SNMP messages in the SNMP engine. It is responsible for (1) accepting PDUs from applications for transmission over the network and delivering incoming PDUs to applications; (2) passing outgoing PDUs to the Message Processing Subsystem to prepare as messages, and passing incoming messages to the Message Processing Subsystem to extract the incoming PDUs; (3) sending and receiving SNMP messages over the network.

Message Processing Subsystem

Responsible for preparing messages for sending, and for extracting data from received messages.

Security Subsystem

Provides security services such as the authentication and privacy of messages. This subsystem potentially contains multiple Security Models.

Access Control Subsystem

Provides a set of authorization services that an application can use for checking access rights. Access control can be invoked for retrieval or modification request operations and for notification generation operations.

Command Generator

Initiates SNMP `Get`, `GetNext`, `GetBulk`, and/or `Set request` PDUs and processes the response to a request that it has generated.

Command Responder

Receives SNMP `Get`, `GetNext`, `GetBulk`, and/or `Set request` PDUs destined for the local system as indicated by the fact that the `contextEngineID` in the received request is equal to that of the local engine through which the request was received. The command responder application will perform the appropriate protocol operation, using access control, and will generate a response message to be sent to the request's originator.

Notification Originator

Monitors a system for particular events or conditions, and generates `Trap` and/or `Inform` messages based on these events or conditions. A notification originator must have a mechanism for determining where to send messages, and which SNMP version and security parameters to use when sending messages.

Notification Receiver

Listens for notification messages, and generates response messages when a message containing an `Inform` PDU is received.

Proxy Forwarder

Forwards SNMP messages. Implementation of a proxy forwarder application is optional.

nous messages; these include `InformRequest`, `SNMPv2-Trap`, and `SNMPv1 Trap` PDUs. In the case of an incoming `InformRequest` PDU, the Notification Receiver Application will respond with a `Response` PDU.

All of the applications just described make use of the services provided by the SNMP engine for this entity. The SNMP engine performs two overall functions, as follows.

FIGURE 15.4 Traditional SNMP manager

1. It accepts outgoing PDUs from SNMP applications, performs the necessary processing, including inserting authentication codes and encrypting, and then encapsulates the PDUs into messages for transmission.

2. It accepts incoming SNMP messages from the transport layer, performs the necessary processing, including authentication and decryption, and then extracts the PDUs from the messages and passes these on to the appropriate SNMP application.

In a traditional manager, the SNMP engine contains a Dispatcher, a Message Processing Subsystem, and a Security Subsystem. The *Dispatcher* is a simple traffic manager. For outgoing PDUs, the Dispatcher accepts PDUs from applications and performs the following functions. For each PDU, the Dispatcher determines the type of message processing required (that is, for SNMPv1, SNMPv2c, or SNMPv3) and passes the PDU on to the appropriate message processing module in the Message Processing Subsystem. Subsequently, the Message Processing Subsystem returns a message containing that PDU and including the appropriate message headers. The Dispatcher then maps this message onto a transport layer for transmission.

For incoming messages, the Dispatcher accepts messages from the transport layer and performs the following functions. The Dispatcher routes each message to the appropriate message processing module. Subsequently, the Message Processing Subsystem returns the PDU contained in the message. The Dispatcher then passes this PDU to the appropriate application.

The *Message Processing Subsystem* accepts outgoing PDUs from the Dispatcher and prepares these for transmission by wrapping them in the appropriate message header and returning them to the Dispatcher. The Message Processing Subsystem also accepts incoming messages from the Dispatcher, processes each message header, and returns the enclosed PDU to the Dispatcher. An implementation of the Message Processing Subsystem may support a single message format corresponding to a single version of SNMP (SNMPv1, SNMPv2c, SNMPv3), or it may contain a number of modules, each supporting a different version of SNMP.

The *Security Subsystem* performs authentication and encryption functions. Each outgoing message is passed to the Security Subsystem from the Message Processing Subsystem. Depending on the services required, the Security Subsystem may encrypt the enclosed PDU, and it may generate an authentication code and insert it into the message header. The processed message is then returned to the Message Processing Subsystem. Similarly, each incoming message is passed to the Security Subsystem from the Message Processing Subsystem. If required, the Security Subsystem checks the authentication code and performs decryption. It then returns the processed message to the Message Processing Subsystem. An implementation of the Security Subsystem may support one or more distinct security models. So far, the only defined security model is the User-Based Security Model (USM) for SNMPv3, specified in RFC 2274.

15.3.1.2 Traditional SNMP Agent

Figure 15.5, based on a figure in RFC 2271, is a block diagram of a traditional SNMP agent. The traditional agent may contain three types of applications. *Command Responder Applications* provide access to management data. These applications respond to incoming requests by retrieving and/or setting managed objects and then issuing a Response PDU. A *Notification Originator Application* initiates asynchronous messages; in the case of a traditional agent, the SNMPv2-Trap or SNMPv1 Trap PDU is used for this application. A *Proxy Forwarder Application* forwards messages between entities.

The SNMP engine for a traditional agent has all of the components found in the SNMP engine for a traditional manager, plus an *Access Control Subsystem*. This subsystem provides authorization services to control access to MIBs for the reading and setting of management objects. These services are performed on the basis of the contents of PDUs. An implementation of the Security Subsystem may support one or more distinct access control models. So far, the only defined security model is the View-Based Access Control Model (VACM) for SNMPv3, specified in RFC 2275.

Note that security-related functions are organized into two separate subsystems: security and access control. This is an excellent example of good modular design, because the two subsystems perform quite distinct functions and therefore it makes sense to allow standardization of these two areas to proceed independently. The Security Subsys-

FIGURE 15.5 Traditional SNMP agent

tem is concerned with privacy and authentication, and operates on SNMP messages. The Access Control Subsystem is concerned with authorized access to management information, and operates on SNMP PDUs.

15.3.2 Terminology

Table 15.3 briefly defines some terms that are introduced in RFC 2271. Some of these are textual conventions and are defined in greater detail in Appendix 15A. Associated with each SNMP entity is a unique `snmpEngineID`. For purposes of access control, each SNMP entity is considered to manage a number of contexts of managed information, each of which has a `contextName` that is unique within that entity. To emphasize that there is a single manager of contexts within an entity, each entity has a unique `context-EngineID` associated with it; because there is a one-to-one correspondence between the context engine and the SNMP engine at this entity, the `contextEngineID` is identical in value to the `snmpEngineID`. Access control is governed by the specific context for which access is attempted and the identity of the user requesting access; this latter identity is expressed as a principal, which may be an individual or an application or a group of individuals or applications.

Other terms of importance relate to the processing of messages. The `snmpMessage-ProcessingModel` determines the message format and the SNMP version for message processing. The `snmpSecurityModel` determines which security model is to be used. The `snmpSecurityLevel` determines which security services are requested for this specific operation. The user may request just authentication, or authentication plus privacy (encryption), or neither.

15.3.3 Abstract Service Interfaces

The services between modules in an SNMP entity are defined in the RFCs in terms of primitives and parameters. A *primitive* specifies the function to be performed, and the *parameters* are used to pass data and control information. We can think of these primitives and parameters as a formalized way of defining SNMP services. The actual form of a primitive is implementation dependent; an example is a procedure call. An interface defined using primitives and parameters is referred to as an *abstract service interface*.

The SNMPv3 documents make a distinction between three kinds of values: input values, output values, and primitive values.[3] An *input value* is a parameter passed as an argument in a primitive from the calling entity to the called entity. An *output value* is a parameter passed as an argument in a primitive from the called entity to the calling entity; that is, an output value is passed with the return from the called entity to the call-

---

[3] These three terms are not used in the RFCs but are defined here for clarity.

TABLE 15.3   SNMPv3 Terminology

snmpEngineId
> Unique and unambiguous identifier of an SNMP engine, as well as the SNMP entity that corresponds to that engine. It is defined by a textual convention, with a syntax of Octet String.

contextEngineID
> Uniquely identifies an SNMP entity that may realize an instance of a context with a particular contextName.

contextName
> Identifies a particular context within an SNMP engine. It is passed as a parameter to the Dispatcher and Access Control Subsystem.

scopedPDU
> A block of data consisting of a contextEngineID, a contextName, and an SNMP PDU. It is passed as a parameter to/from the Security Subsystem.

snmpMessageProcessingModel
> Unique identifier of a message processing model of the Message Processing Subsystem. Possible values include SNMPv1, SNMPv2c, and SNMPv3. It is defined by a textual convention, with a syntax of Integer.

snmpSecurityModel
> Unique identifier of a security model of the Security Subsystem. Possible values include SNMPv1, SNMPv2c, and USM. It is defined by a textual convention, with a syntax of Integer.

snmpSecurityLevel
> A level of security at which SNMP messages can be sent or with which operations are being processed, expressed in terms of whether or not authentication and/or privacy are provided. The alternative values are noAuthnoPriv, authNoPriv, and authPriv. It is defined by a textual convention, with a syntax of Integer.

principal
> The entity on whose behalf services are provided or processing takes place. A principal can be an individual acting in a particular role; a set of individuals, with each acting in a particular role; an application or set of applications; and combinations thereof.

securityName
> A human-readable string representing a principal. It is passed as a parameter in all of the SNMP primitives (Dispatcher, Message Processing, Security, Access Control).

ing entity. A *primitive value* is a value assigned to the primitive as a whole upon return. For example, consider the following expression:

$$\text{functioncode} = \text{requestservice} (\text{IN } w \text{ IN } x \text{ OUT } y \text{ OUT } z)$$

In this case, requestservice is the name of a primitive used to request a particular service. The parameters w and x are input values and are provided by the calling entity. The parameters y and z are output values; these are just placeholders when the call is made, but when `requestservice` returns, the values of *y* and *z* are provided. This particular primitive also returns a primitive value, named `functioncode`.

In the tables that follow, input values, output values, and primitive values are labeled as IN, OUT, and PV, respectively. In the discussion that follows, it may be useful to refer to Figure 15.6, based on a figure in RFC 2271, to see how all of these primitives fit together. Figure 15.6(a) shows the sequence of events in which a Command Generator or Notification Originator application requests that a PDU be sent, and subsequently how the matching response is returned to that application; these events occur at a manager. Figure 15.6(b) shows the corresponding events at an agent. The figure shows how an incoming message results in the dispatch of the enclosed PDU to an application, and how that application's response results in an outgoing message. Note that some of the arrows in the diagram are labeled with a primitive name, representing a call. Unlabeled arrows represent the return from a call, and the shading indicates the matching between call and return.

15.3.3.1 Dispatcher Primitives

Dispatcher primitives define the interface between SNMP applications and the Dispatcher. Table 15.4 lists these primitives and the parameters associated with each primitive. In each case, the parameters are passed by the calling entity (application or Dispatcher) to the called entity (Dispatcher or application).

The Dispatcher primitives are as follows:

- `sendPdu`: Used by a command generator to send an SNMP `request` or `notification` PDU to another SNMP entity. This primitive returns a primitive value of `statusInformation`. If the Dispatcher is successful in preparing a message for transmission for this PDU, then `statusInformation` has a value of type `sendPdu-Handle`; this is a unique identifier assigned to this PDU so that the application can later match up an incoming response PDU with this outgoing `request` or `notification` PDU. Note that the application provides the transport domain and address of the destination for this PDU, specifies a message processing model and a security model, identifies a principal and the level of security requested (authentication, authentication and privacy, neither), the context for this PDU (the `contextEngineID` and the local `contextName` for the management information being requested), and the PDU itself. The application also indicates whether a response is expected.

- `processResponsePdu`: Used by the Dispatcher to pass an incoming SNMP `response` PDU to an application. The `statusInformation` parameter indicates the success or failure of the operation requested in the matching preceding `request` or `notification` PDU. That matching `request` or `notification` PDU is identified by the `sendPduHandle` parameter. The remaining input parameters are from the incoming response message.

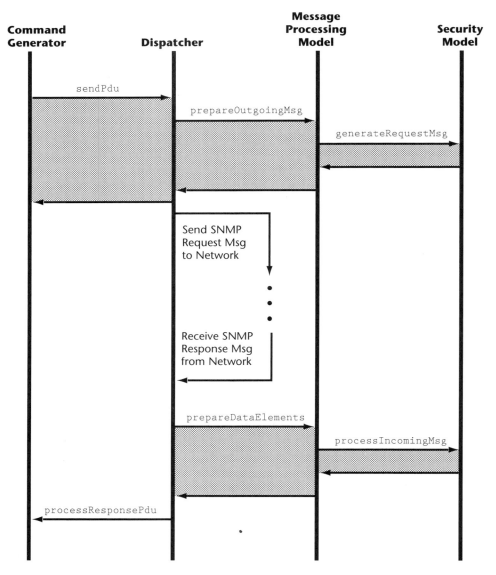

(a) Command Generator or Notification Originator

FIGURE 15.6   Scenario diagrams

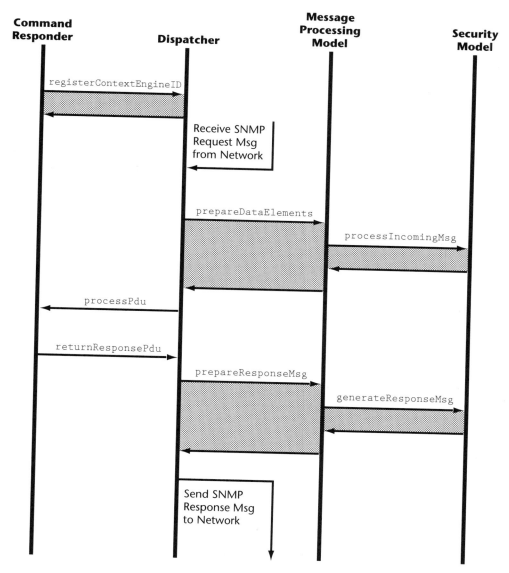

(b) Command Responder

FIGURE 15.6 *Continued*

TABLE 15.4 Dispatcher Primitives

Parameter	sendPdu	processPdu	returnResponsePdu	processResponsePdu	registerContextEngineID	unregisterContextEngineID	Description
transportDomain	IN						Transport domain to be used
transportAddress	IN						Transport address to be used
messageProcessingModel	IN	IN	IN	IN			Typically, SNMP version
securityModel	IN	IN	IN	IN			Security Model to use/in use
securityName	IN	IN	IN	IN			On behalf of this principal
securityLevel	IN	IN	IN	IN			Level of security requested/in use
contextEngineID	IN	IN	IN	IN			Data from/at this SNMP entity
contextName	IN	IN	IN	IN			Data from/in this context
pduVersion	IN	IN	IN	IN			Version of the PDU
PDU	IN	IN	IN	IN			SNMP protocol data unit
expectResponse	IN						TRUE or FALSE
maxSizeResponseScopedPDU		IN	IN				Maximum size of the Response PDU
stateReference		IN	IN				Reference to state information
statusInformation	PV		IN	IN	PV		sendPduHandle or error indication
sendPduHandle				IN			Handle from sendPDU
contextEngineID					IN	IN	Take/give up responsibility for this context
pduType					IN	IN	pduType(s) to be registered/unregistered

- processPdu: Used by the Dispatcher to pass an incoming SNMP request or notification PDU to an application. The stateReference parameter contains security-related state information generated by the Security Subsystem. The purpose of this parameter is as follows. In processing an incoming message, the Security Subsystem may create state information needed to generate a matching response message. This information needs to be passed back to the Security Subsystem with the outgoing response message. The pduVersion parameter indicates the version of this PDU. The remaining parameters are from the received message.

- returnResponsePdu: Used by a command responder to return an SNMP response PDU, in response to an incoming request or notification PDU. This primitive includes the following parameters: an indication of the maximum allowable size of the delivered PDU; a stateReference parameter that matches the value in the corresponding processPdu; and a statusInformation parameter to indicate the success or failure of the operation requested in the corresponding incoming request or notification PDU. The remaining parameters, as well as the stateReference parameter, are from the corresponding processPdu call.

- registerContextEngineID: Used to register responsibility for a specific contextEngineID, for specific pduTypes.

- unregisterContextEngineID: Used to unregister responsibility for a specific contextEngineID, for specific pduTypes.

15.3.3.2 Message Processing Subsystem Primitives

Message Processing Subsystem primitives define the interface between the Dispatcher and Message Processing Subsystem. Table 15.5 lists these primitives and the parameters associated with each primitive.

All three of the primitives represent calls from the Dispatcher to the Message Processing Subsystem:

- prepareOutgoingMessage: Used to request the preparation of a message containing an outgoing SNMP request or notification PDU. This primitive returns a primitive value of statusInformation, indicating the success or failure of message preparation. The Dispatcher provides a PDU as an input parameter and, if message preparation is successful, receives a message containing that PDU as an output parameter.

- prepareDataElements: Used to extract a PDU from an incoming message. The Dispatcher provides a message as input and, if message processing is successful, receives a PDU as output, together with an indication of PDU type. The stateReference output parameter contains state information to be used in a possible response.

- prepareResponseMessage: Used to request the preparation of a message containing an outgoing SNMP response PDU, in response to an incoming request or notification

TABLE 15.5   Message Processing Subsystem Primitives

Parameter	prepareOutgoingMessage	prepareResponseMessage	prepareDataElements	Description
transportDomain	IN		IN	Origin transport domain
transportAddress	IN		IN	Origin transport address
messageProcessing Model	IN	IN	OUT	Typically, SNMP version
securityModel	IN	IN	OUT	Security Model to use/in use
securityName	IN	IN	OUT	On behalf of this principal
securityLevel	IN	IN	OUT	Level of security requested/in use
contextEngineID	IN	IN	OUT	Data from/at this SNMP entity
contextName	IN	IN	OUT	Data from/in this context
pduVersion	IN	IN	OUT	Version of the PDU
PDU	IN	IN	OUT	SNMP protocol data unit
expectResponse	IN			TRUE or FALSE
sendPduHandle	IN		OUT	Handle for matching incoming responses
maxSizeResponseScopedPDU		IN	OUT	Maximum size of the Response PDU
stateReference		IN	OUT	Reference to state information as presented with the request
statusInformation	PV	IN	OUT	Success or error indication
wholeMsg			IN	As received from the network
wholeMsgLength			IN	As received from the network
destTransportDomain	OUT	OUT		Destination transport domain
destTransportAddress	OUT	OUT		Destination transport address
outgoingMessage	OUT	OUT		Message to send
outgoingMessageLength	OUT	OUT		Message length
pduType			OUT	SNMP PDI type
result		PV	PV	SUCCESS or FAILURE

PDU. This primitive returns a primitive value of result, indicating the success or failure of message preparation. The stateReference input parameter contains state information contained in the corresponding prepareDataElements primitive.

15.3.3.3 Security Subsystem Primitives

Security Subsystem primitives define the interface between the Message Processing Subsystem and Security Subsystem. Table 15.6 lists these primitives and the parameters associated with each primitive.

TABLE 15.6   Security Subsystem Primitives

Parameter	generateRequestMsg	processIncomingMsg	generateResponseMsg	Description
messageProcessing Model	IN	IN	IN	Typically, SNMP version
globalData	IN		IN	Message header, admin data
maxMessageSize	IN	IN	IN	Of the sending SNMP entity
securityModel	IN	IN	IN	For the outgoing message
securityEngineID	IN	OUT	IN	Authoritative SNMP entity
securityName	IN	OUT	IN	On behalf of this principal
securityLevel	IN	IN	IN	Level of security requested/in use
scopedPDU	IN	OUT	IN	Message (plaintext) payload
securityParameters	OUT	IN	OUT	Filled in by Security Model/for the received message
wholeMsg	OUT	IN	OUT	Complete generated message/message received on wire
wholeMsgLength	OUT	IN	OUT	Length of the generated/received message
maxSizeResponseScopedPDU		OUT		Maximum size of the Response PDU
securityStateReference		OUT	IN	Reference to security state information, needed for response
statusInformation	PV	PV	PV	Success or error indication

All three of the primitives represent calls from the Message Processing Subsystem to the Security Subsystem:

- generateRequestMessage: Used to generate a message containing an outgoing SNMP request or notification PDU. This primitive returns a primitive value of statusInformation, indicating the success or failure of message generation. The Message Processing Subsystem provides a message header and a scopedPDU (contextEngineID, contextName, PDU) as input parameters, and receives a prepared message (possibly with authentication and encryption applied) and associated security parameters as output parameters.

- processIncomingMessage: Used to provide security processing for an incoming message. This primitive returns a primitive value of statusInformation, indicating the success or failure of security processing. The Message Processing Subsystem provides the message received from the network as an input parameter and, if message processing is successful, receives a PDU as output, together with an indication of PDU type. The `securityStateReference` output parameter contains state information to be used in a possible response.

- `generateResponseMessage`: Used to generate a message containing an outgoing SNMP `response` PDU, in response to an incoming `request` or `notification` PDU. This primitive returns a primitive value of `statusInformation`, indicating the success or failure of message generation. The `stateReference` input parameter contains state information presented with the corresponding `processIncoming-Message` primitive. The Message Processing Subsystem provides a message header and a `scopedPDU` as input parameters, and receives a prepared message (possible with authentication and encryption applied) and associated security parameters as output parameters.

15.3.3.4 Access Control Subsystem Primitives

The Access Control Subsystem provides a single primitive to define the interface between SNMP applications and the Access Control Subsystem. Table 15.7 lists this primitive, `isAccessAllowed`, and the parameters associated with it. The parameters are all input parameters passed by the calling entity (application) to the called entity (Access Control Subsystem). The application specifies the principal who wants access, the security model in use, the level of security involved, the type of operation to be performed, the `context-Name`, and an object identifier for the managed object for which access is requested. The primitive returns a primitive value that indicates whether access is allowed.

15.4 SNMPv3 Applications

RFC 2273 defines, in general terms, the procedures followed by each type of application when generating PDUs for transmission or processing incoming PDUs. In all cases, the procedures are defined in terms of interaction with the Dispatcher by means of the Dispatcher primitives. The description in RFC 2273 is detailed and clear. Here we give a brief account.

TABLE 15.7   Access Control Subsystem Primitives

Parameter	`isAccessAllowed`	Description
`securityModel`	IN	Security Model in use
`securityName`	IN	Prinipal who wants access
`securityLevel`	IN	Level of security
`viewType`	IN	read, write, or notify view
`contextName`	IN	Context containing `variableName`
`variableName`	IN	OID for the managed object
`statusInformation`	PV	Success or error indication

15.4.1 Command Generator Applications

A command generator application makes use of the `sendPdu` and `processResponsePdu` Dispatcher primitives. As we have seen, the `sendPdu` provides the Dispatcher with information about the intended destination, security parameters, and the actual PDU to be sent. The Dispatcher then invokes the Message Processing Model, which in turn invokes the Security Model, to prepare the message. The Dispatcher hands the prepared message over to the transport layer (for example, UDP) for transmission. If message preparation fails, the return primitive value of the `sendPdu`, set by the Dispatcher, is an error indication. If message preparation succeeds, the Dispatcher assigns a `sendPduHandle` identifier to this PDU and returns that value to the command generator as the return primitive value of the `sendPdu`. The command generator stores the `sendPduHandle` so that it can match the subsequent response PDU to the original request.

The Dispatcher delivers each incoming response PDU to the correct command generator application, using the `processResponsePdu` primitive. The command generator then performs the following steps.

1. First, the command generator examines the parameters in the `processResponse-Pdu` primitive. It compares the received values of `messageProcessingModel`, `securityModel`, `securityName`, `contextEngineID`, `contextName`, and `pdu-Version` to those in the corresponding `request` PDU (using `sendPduHandle` to identify the request PDU). If not all of these parameters match, the response is discarded. If `statusInformation` indicates the request failed, an implementation-dependent action is taken, such as resending the request or notifying the principal.

2. Next, the command generator examines the contents of the response PDU. It extracts the `operation type`, `request-id`, `error-status`, `error-index`, and `variable-bindings`. If the `request-id` is not equal to the value used in the original request, the response is discarded.

3. If steps 1 and 2 succeed, the command generator takes an implementation-dependent action.

15.4.2 Command Responder Applications

A command responder application makes use of four Dispatcher primitives (`register-ContextEngineID`, `unregisterContextEngineID`, `processPdu`, `returnResponse-Pdu`) and one Access Control Subsystem primitive (`isAccessAllowed`).

The `registerContextEngineID` primitive enables a command responder application to associate itself with an SNMP engine for the purpose of processing certain PDU types for a context engine. Once a command responder has registered, all asynchronously received messages containing the registered combination of `contextEngineID` and `pduType` supported are sent to the command responder that registered to support that combination. A command responder can disassociate from an SNMP engine using the `unregisterContextEngineID` primitive.

The Dispatcher delivers each incoming request PDU to the correct command responder application, using the `processPdu` primitive. The command responder then performs the following steps.

1. The command responder examines the contents of the `request` PDU. The operation type must match one of the types previously registered by this application.

2. The command responder determines if access is allowed for performing the management operation requested in this PDU. For this purpose, the `isAccessAllowed` primitive is called. The `securityModel` parameter indicates which security model the Access Control Subsystem is to use in responding to this call. The Access Control Subsystem determines if the requesting principal (`securityName`) at this security level (`securityLevel`) has permission to request the management operation (`viewType`) on the management object (`variableName`) in this context (`context-Name`).

3. If access is permitted, the command responder performs the management operation and prepares a `response` PDU. If access fails, the command responder prepares the appropriate `response` PDU to signal that failure.

4. The command responder calls the Dispatcher with a `returnResponsePdu` primitive to send the `response` PDU.

15.4.3 Notification Generator Applications

A notification generator application follows the same general procedures used for a command generator application. If an `Inform` PDU is to be sent, both the `sendPdu` and `processResponsePdu` primitives are used, in the same fashion as for command generator applications. If a `trap` PDU is to be sent, only the `sendPdu` primitive is used.

15.4.4 Notification Receiver Applications

A notification receiver application follows a subset of the general procedures as for a command responder application. The notification receiver must first register to receive `Inform` and/or `trap` PDUs. Both types of PDUs are received by means of a `processPdu` primitive. For an `Inform` PDU, a `returnResponsePdu` primitive is used to respond.

15.4.5 Proxy Forwarder Applications

A proxy forwarder application makes use of Dispatcher primitives to forward SNMP messages. The proxy forwarder handles four basic types of messages:

- *Messages containing PDU types from a command generator application:* The proxy forwarder determines either the target SNMP engine or an SNMP engine that is closer, or downstream, to the target, and sends the appropriate `request` PDU.
- *Messages containing PDU types from a notification originator application:* The proxy forwarder determines which SNMP engines should receive the notification and sends the appropriate `notification` PDU or PDUs.
- *Messages containing a `response` PDU type:* The proxy forwarder determines which previously forwarded request or notification, if any, is matched by this response, and sends the appropriate `response` PDU.
- *Messages containing a `report` indication:* `report` PDUs are SNMPv3 engine-to-engine communications described in Chapter 16. The proxy forwarder determines which previously forwarded request or notification, if any, is matched by this `report` indication, and forwards the `report` indication back to the initiator of the request or notification.

15.5 *MIBs for SNMPv3 Applications*

RFC 2273 defines three MIBs to support SNMPv3 applications: the management target MIB, the notification MIB, and the proxy MIB. We examine each of these in turn.

15.5.1 Management Target MIB

The SNMP-TARGET-MIB contains objects for defining management targets and includes a single group, the `snmpTargetsObjects` group.

A management target refers to a management entity that can be the recipient of messages generated by notification generators and proxy forwarders. These applications require a mechanism for determining where and how to send generated messages. Two kinds of information are needed:

- *Destination information:* consisting of a transport domain and a transport address. This combination is also referred to as a *transport endpoint*.
- *SNMP message parameters:* consisting of message processing model, security model, security level, and security name information.

The `snmpTargetObjects` group contains one table for each of these two types of information. A many-to-many relationship exists between the two types of information. That is, there may be multiple sets of SNMP message parameters for a single transport endpoint and there may be multiple transport endpoints for a single set of SNMP message parameters.

Figure 15.7 shows the structure of the snmpTargetObjects group. In addition to the two tables there are two counter objects and an object of syntax TestandIncr. The snmpUnavailableContexts object contains a count of the total number of packets received by the SNMP engine that were dropped because the context contained in the message was unavailable. The snmpUnknownContexts object contains a count of the total number of packets received by the SNMP engine that were dropped because the context contained in the message was unknown. The snmpTargetSpinLock object regulates modification of table entries by multiple managers (see Appendix 13A). In particular, it assures that only one manager at a time can read and then set snmpTargetAddrTagList in the target address table.

15.5.1.1 Target Address Table

This is a table of transport addresses to be used in the generation of SNMP messages. It includes the following columnar objects:

- snmpTargetAddrName: A locally arbitrary, but unique, identifier used to index the table.
- snmpTargetAddrTDomain: The transport type of the target address (for example, UDP).
- snmpTargetAddrTAddress: A transport address. For example, if the transport type is UDP, then this is a 6-octet value; the first four octets contain the IP address of the target and the last two octets contain the UDP port number.
- snmpTargetAddrTimeout: Reflects the expected maximum round trip time for communicating with the target transport address. The time interval that an application may wait could be longer than this value (for example, if authentication is required, extra time may be allowed for that).
- snmpTargetAddrRetryCount: A default number of retries to be attempted when a response is not received for a generated message.
- snmpTargetAddrTagList: A list of tag values, explained below.
- snmpTargetAddrParams: An identifier (typically human-readable) that identifies an entry in snmpTargetParamsTable. The identified entry contains parameters to be used when generating messages to be sent to this transport address.
- snmpTargetAddrStorageType: Storage type for this row.
- snmpTargetAddrStatus: Status of this row (see Appendix 11A) used to govern row creation.

Associated with each entry in snmpTargetAddrTable are zero or more tag values, which are used to select groups of entries in the table. A tag value is typically human-readable and refers to a class of targets to which messages may be sent. Examples of tag values are "router," "host," and "acme." An instance of the columnar object snmp-

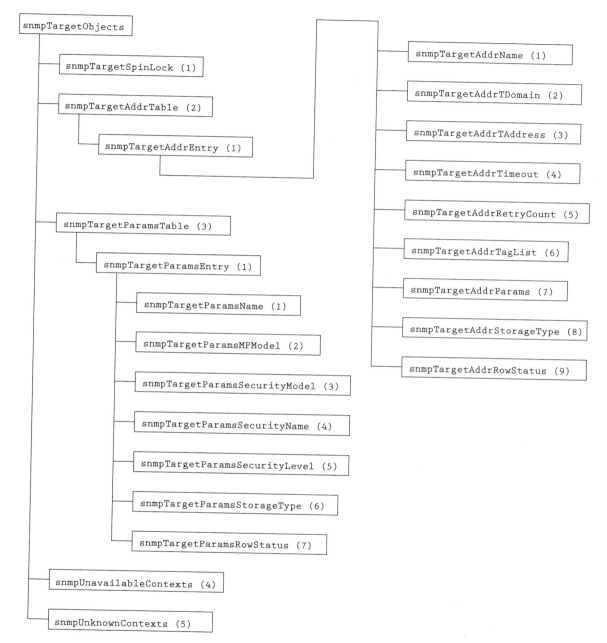

FIGURE 15.7 The snmpTargetObjects group

`TargetAddrTagList` contains a list of these tag values. The list may be empty, consist of a single tag value, or consist of a sequence of tag values separated by one of the reserved delimiters (space, tab, carriage return, line feed). A given tag value may appear in more than one of the tag lists. For example, a number of the entries may include the tag value "router," so that when a notification is to be sent to all routers, those entries in `snmp-TargetAddrTable` whose `snmpTargetAddrTagList` value includes "router" are used. In this way, a single notification message, for example, can be automatically generated for multiple transport endpoints. On the other hand, because a single entry in `snmp-TargetAddrTable` may have an `snmpTargetAddrTagList` value that contains multiple tag values, that single entry may be used in multiple message generation operations.

15.5.1.2 Target Parameters Table

This table contains parameters to be used in generating a message. The parameters include the message processing model (for example, SNMPv3, SNMPv2c, SNMPv1), the security model (for example, USM), security name (identifies a principal), and security level (noAuthnoPriv, authNoPriv, authPriv). The table is indexed by `snmpTarget-ParamsName`; this columnar object links `snmpTargetParamsTable` to `snmpTarget-AddrTable` through `snmpTargetAddrParams` in the latter table.

15.5.2 Notification MIB

The SNMP-NOTIFICATION-MIB contains objects for the remote configuration of the parameters used by an SNMP entity for the generation of notifications, and includes a single group, `snmpNotifyObjectsGroup` (Figure 15.8). The group consists of three tables:

- `snmpNotifyTable`: Each entry in this table selects one or more entries in `snmp-TargetAddrTable` to be used for notification generation.
- `snmpNotifyFilterProfileTable`: Augments `snmpTargetAddrTable` so as to potentially associate a set of filters with a particular management target.
- `snmpNotifyFilterTable`: Defines filters used to limit the number of notifications generated for a particular management target.

To explain the use of these tables we first discuss the mechanism by which a notification originator identifies management targets. Then we describe notification filtering.

15.5.2.1 Identification of Management Targets for Notifications

An SNMP entity uses `snmpNotifyTable` to select management targets to receive notifications. The key columnar objects in the table are:

- `snmpNotifyName`: An arbitrary, locally unique identifier for this entry. An SNMP entity can be configured so that an `snmpNotifyName` is associated with a particular notification to be sent out under certain conditions.

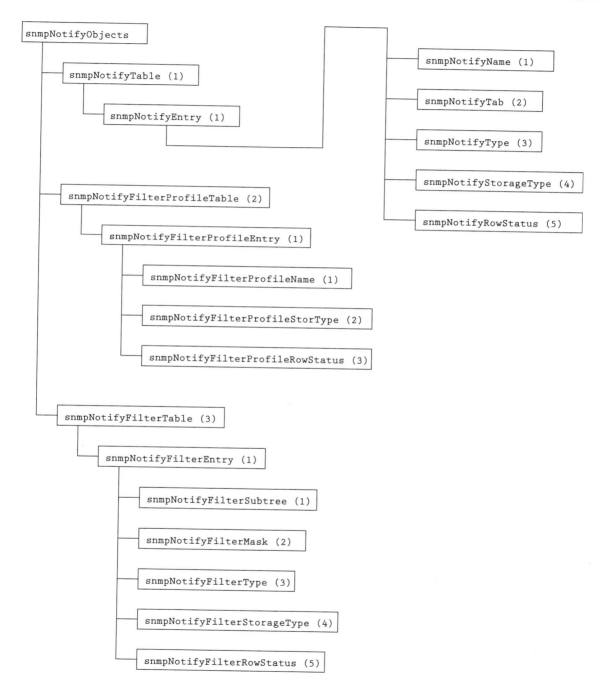

FIGURE 15.8 The snmpNotifyObjects group

- snmpNotifyTag: A tag value used to select zero or more entries in snmpTarget-AddrTable. For a given value, all rows in snmpTargetAddrTable in which snmp-TargetAddrTagList includes that value are selected.
- SnmpNotifyType: Trap or inform.

A typical scenario would be as follows. A notification originator application determines that a certain condition or set of conditions has been met that requires notification be sent out. Associated with this condition is a name, used to index into snmpNotify-Table. The selected instance of snmpNotifyTag determines which target addresses in snmpTargetAddrTable will receive the notification, and for each target, snmpNotify-Type determines whether a trap or inform PDU will be sent. For each target address (selected in snmpTargetAddrTable), snmpTargetParamsTable provides the parameters needed to generate the message.

Note that, because each entry in snmpTargetAddrTable may have multiple tag values, a given entry may be selected by more than one entry in snmpNotifyTable. Thus, multiple different notifications may be defined for a single target address.

An example from RFC 2273 should help clarify the relationship between snmp-NotifyTable and the snmpTargetObjects group. Table 15.8 shows instances of the two snmpTargetObjects tables and of snmpNotifyTable; for conciseness, the storage type and row status objects in each table are omitted.[4] These tables define two groups of management targets, shown in Table 15.9.

15.5.2.2 Notification Filtering

Notification filtering makes use of two tables, snmpNotifyFilterProfileTable and snmpNotifyFilterTable (Figure 15.8). Before describing the filtering mechanism, we need to describe the way in which these two tables are organized. The organization makes for a concise representation, but is a little confusing to follow.

The snmpNotifyFilterProfileTable is indexed by snmpTargetParamsName, which is the index object for snmpTargetParamsTable (Figure 15.7). This is an example of indexing with an external object, which was described in Section 10.1.4.1. The snmp-NotifyFilterProfileTable must be implemented in such a way that, by using snmp-TargetParamsName, a unique entry in snmpNotifyFilterProfileTable is selected. It is not necessary that there be an entry in snmpNotifyFilterProfileTable for every value of snmpTargetParamsName. The only columnar object defined in snmp-NotifyFilterProfileTable (other than storage type and row status) is snmpNotify-FilterProfileName, which is a name assigned to a filter profile. Now we turn to snmpNotifyFilterTable. This table is indexed by two objects. The first is snmp-Notify-FilterProfileName, which is an external object. The second index is

---

[4]A minor error in the RFC 2273 example is corrected in Table 15.8.

TABLE 15.8 Trap Configuration Example: Table Definitions

(a) snmpTargetAddrTable

snmpTargetAddrName	snmpTargetAddrTDomain	snmpTargetAddrTAddr	snmpTargetAddrTagList	snmpTargetAddrParams
"addr1"	snmpUDPDomain	128.1.2.3:162	"group1"	"AuthNoPriv-joe"
"addr2"	snmpUDPDomain	128.2.4.6:162	"group1"	"AuthNoPriv-joe"
"addr3"	snmpUDPDomain	128.1.5.9:162	"group2"	"AuthPriv-bob"

(b) snmpTargetParamsTable

snmpTargetParams-Name	snmpTargetParams-MPModel	snmpTargetParams-SecurityModel	snmpTargetParams-SecurityName	snmpTargetParams-SecurityLevel
"AuthNoPriv-joe"	3 (SNMPv3)	3 (USM)	"joe"	authNoPriv(2)
"AuthPriv-bob"	3 (SNMPv3)	3 (USM)	"bob"	authPriv(3)

(c) snmpNotifyTable

snmpNotifyName	snmpNotifyTag	snmpNotifyType
"group1"	"group1"	trap(1)
"group2"	"group2"	trap(1)

TABLE 15.9 Trap Configuration Example: Management Targets

	GROUP 1		GROUP 2
	First Target	**Second Target**	**Target**
messageProcessingModel	SNMPv3	SNMPv3	SNMPv3
securityModel	3 (USM)	3 (USM)	3 (USM)
securityName	"joe"	"joe"	"bob"
securityLevel	authNoPriv(2)	authNoPriv(2)	authPriv(3)
transportDomain	snmpUDPDomain	snmpUDPDomain	snmpUDPDomain
transportAddress	128.1.2.3:162	128.2.4.6:162	128.1.5.9:162

snmpNotifyFilterSubtree, which defines a single subtree entry in the table, as explained below. Thus, snmpNotifyFilterTable is tied indirectly to snmpTarget-ParamsTable by means of the external index object snmpNotifyFilterProfileName.

Each entry in snmpNotifyFilterTable defines a family of MIB subtrees, using the subtree, mask, and type columnar objects. This technique is also used in access control, described in Chapter 17. Appendix 17A provides a detailed explanation of how a subtree family is defined. In essence, a subtree consists of a MIB object plus all objects that are subordinate to it in the naming hierarchy. It is possible to exclude certain portions of this subtree so that one is left not with a complete subtree but only a partial subtree, consisting of a MIB object and some of its subordinate objects. This is a family of subtrees. If we then group multiple entries, we can define an arbitrary collection of MIB objects to be used for some purpose.

With this background, we can describe notification filtering. When a notification is to be generated, the notification originator uses snmpNotifyTable to identify one or more targets for the notification with the corresponding entries in snmpTarget-ParamsTable. The notification originator then generates notification messages using the parameters in snmpTargetParamsTable. For each entry that is used in snmpTarget-ParamsTable, the notification generator checks to see if there is an index in snmp-NotifyFilterProfileTable equal to the index of the entry in snmpTarget-ParamsTable. If not, filtering is not performed in generating this message for this management target. If an entry does exist, then the value of snmpNotifyFilter-ProfileName is used to index into snmpNotifyFilterTable. Recall that this table has a second index, snmpNotifyFilterSubtree. Thus, there may be multiple entries in snmpNotifyFilterTable, each with the same index value of snmpNotifyFilter-ProfileName but different values of snmpNotifyFilterSubtree. All of these entries are used in the filtering process for this message.

The filtering logic is somewhat complicated but may be briefly summarized. The notification (inform or trap) includes an snmpTrapOID.0 plus a list of MIB object identifiers (see Sections 12.1.7 and 12.1.8). If the filtering logic associated with this message

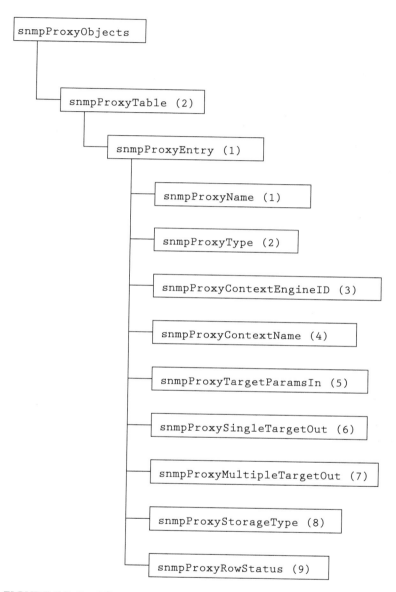

FIGURE 15.9 The snmpProxyObjects group

includes all of these object identifiers, then the notification may be sent to this target. If any of these object identifiers is excluded, then the notification is not sent to this target.

15.5.3 Proxy MIB

The SNMP-PROXY-MIB contains objects for the remote configuration of the parameters used by an SNMP entity for the proxy forwarding operations. The MIB includes a single group, snmpProxyObjectsGroup (Figure 15.9), which consists of a single table, snmp-ProxyTable. Each entry of the table contains a set of translation parameters used by the proxy forwarder. In addition to storage type and row status, the columnar objects are:

- snmpProxyName: A locally unique name used to index into the table.
- snmpProxyType: The type of message that may be forwarded using the translation parameters defined by this entry: read(1), write(2), trap(3), inform(4).
- snmpProxyContextEngineID: The contextEngineID contained in messages that may be forwarded using the translation parameters defined by this entry.
- snmpProxyContextName: The contextName contained in messages that may be forwarded using the translation parameters defined by this entry. This object is optional.
- snmpProxyTargetParamsIn: Selects an entry in snmpTargetParamsTable. The selected entry is used for a potential match with the parameters in the incoming message.
- snmpProxySingleTargetOut: Used to index into snmpTargetAddrTable. The selected entry is the one whose index object snmpTargetAddrName matches the value of snmpProxySingleTargetOut.
- snmpProxyMultipleTargetOut: A tag value used to select multiple entries in snmpTargetAddrTable. All entries containing this tag value are selected.

For an incoming request message, the proxy forwarder needs to select the appropriate entry in snmpProxyTable. The entry is selected as follows:

1. If the message contains a Get, GetNext, or GetBulk, the snmpProxyType must be read(1). If the message contains a Set, the type must be write(2).
2. The contextEngineID in the message must equal snmpProxyContextEngineID.
3. If the snmpProxyContextName object is supported, it must equal the context-Name in the message.
4. The snmpProxyTargetParamsIn instance identifies a row in snmpTarget-ParamsTable. The message security parameters in that row must match the corresponding fields in the incoming message (message processing model, security model, security name, security level).

If there is no entry that meets all of these conditions, then the message should not be forwarded, and the proxy forwarder may take some implementation-dependent action. There may be multiple entries that match these conditions. If so, the matching entry whose snmpProxyName has the lexicographically smallest value is used.

If a matching entry is selected, then a message is forwarded. The proxy forwarder uses the entry in snmpTargetAddrTable identified by snmpProxySingleTargetOut to obtain the target address and timeout and retry values for the message and the associated entry in snmpTargetParamsTable to construct the security-related parameters.

For an incoming notification message, the proxy forwarder selects the appropriate entries in snmpProxyTable as follows.

1. If the message contains a trap, the snmpProxyType must be trap(3). If the message contains an Inform, the type must be inform(4).
2. The contextEngineID in the message must equal snmpProxyContextEngineID.
3. If the snmpProxyContextName object is supported, it must equal the context-Name in the message.
4. The snmpProxyTargetParamsIn instance identifies a row in snmpTarget-ParamsTable. The message security parameters in that row must match the corresponding fields in the message (message processing model, security model, security name, security level).

If there is no entry that meets all of these conditions, then the notification should not be forwarded, and the proxy forwarder may take some implementation-dependent action. If there are one or more matches, then all matching entries are selected. Using the snmpProxyMultipleTargetOut tag value from each selected entry yields a set of tag values. Each entry in snmpTargetAddrTable with a matching tag value is selected. Each such entry provides the transport parameters needed to send an outgoing message; it also provides an index into snmpTargetParamsTable to obtain the security parameters needed for message generation.

Thus, a properly configured snmpProxyTable will enable a proxy forwarder to accept an incoming message, determine for each message the target or targets, and construct the security parameters for the outgoing message.

15.6 *Summary*

RFCS 2271 through 2275 define a new architecture for SNMP which can accommodate existing SNMPv1 and SNMPv2c implementations, provide a framework for SNMPv3, and provide a framework for future revisions and enhancements to elements of SNMP. These documents also define SNMPv3.

The SNMP architecture defines five generic applications for generating and receiving SNMP PDUs: command generator, command responder, notification originator, notification receiver, and proxy forwarder. The architecture also defines an SNMP engine, which is responsible for preparing messages from PDUs for transmission, extracting PDUs from incoming messages for delivery to applications, and for doing security-related processing of outgoing and incoming messages. The SNMP engine consists of four components: Dispatcher, Message Processing Subsystem, Security Subsystem, and Access Control Subsystem.

SNMPv3 defines two security-related capabilities. The user-based security model (USM) and the view-based access control (VACM) model. USM provides authentication and privacy (encryption) functions and operates at the message level. VACM determines whether a given principal is allowed access to particular MIB objects to perform particular functions, and operates at the PDU level.

| APPENDIX 15A | *TEXTUAL CONVENTIONS FOR THE SNMP MANAGEMENT ARCHITECTURE* |

This appendix contains abridged versions of the textual conventions that are defined in RFC 2271.

SnmpEngineID ::= TEXTUAL-CONVENTION
    STATUS current
    DESCRIPTION   "An SNMP engine's administratively unique identifier.

The value for this object may not be all zeros or all 'ff'H or the empty (zero length) string.

The initial value for this object may be configured via an operator console entry or via an algorithmic function. In the latter case, the following example algorithm is recommended.

In cases where there are multiple engines on the same system, the use of this algorithm is NOT appropriate, as it would result in all of those engines ending up with the same ID value.

1. The very first bit is used to indicate how the rest of the data is composed.

   0–as defined by enterprise using former methods that existed before SNMPv3. See item 2 below.

   1–as defined by this architecture, see item 3 below.

   Note that this allows existing uses of the engineID (also known as AgentID [RFC 1910]) to co-exist with any new uses.

2. The snmpEngineID has a length of 12 octets.

   The first four octets are set to the binary equivalent of the agent's SNMP management private enterprise number as assigned by the Internet Assigned Numbers Authority (IANA). The remaining eight octets are determined via one or more enterprise-specific methods.

3. The length of the octet strings varies.

   The first four octets are set to the binary equivalent of the agent's SNMP management private enterprise number as assigned by the Internet Assigned Numbers Authority (IANA). The fifth octet indicates how the rest (6th and following octets) are formatted. The values for the fifth octet are:

   0–reserved, unused
   1–IPv4 address (4 octets)   lowest non-special IP address
   2–IPv6 address (16 octets)   lowest non-special IP address
   3–MAC address (6 octets)   lowest IEEE MAC address, canonical order
   4–Text, administratively assigned   Maximum remaining length 27

5–Octets, administratively assigned   Maximum remaining length 27
6-127–reserved, unused
127-255–as defined by the enterprise   Maximum remaining length 27"
SYNTAX   OCTET STRING (SIZE(1..32))

SnmpSecurityModel ::= TEXTUAL-CONVENTION
STATUS   current
DESCRIPTION   "An identifier that uniquely identifies a securityModel of the Security Subsystem within the SNMP Management Architecture.

The values for securityModel are allocated as follows:

- The zero value is reserved.
- Values between 1 and 255, inclusive, are reserved for standards-track Security Models and are managed by the Internet Assigned Numbers Authority (IANA).
- Values greater than 255 are allocated to enterprise-specific Security Models. An enterprise-specific securityModel value is defined to be:

enterpriseID * 256 + security model within enterprise

For example, the fourth Security Model defined by the enterprise whose enterpriseID is 1 would be 260.

This scheme for allocation of securityModel values allows for a maximum of 255 standards-based Security Models, and for a maximum of 255 Security Models per enterprise.

As of this writing, there are several values of securityModel defined for use with SNMP or reserved for use with supporting MIB objects. They are as follows:

0–reserved for 'any'
1–reserved for SNMPv1
2–reserved for SNMPv2c
3–User-Based Security Model (USM)"
SYNTAX   INTEGER(0..2147483647)

SnmpMessageProcessingModel ::= TEXTUAL-CONVENTION
STATUS   current
DESCRIPTION   "An identifier that uniquely identifies a Message Processing Model of the Message Processing Subsystem within an SNMP Management Architecture.

The values for messageProcessingModel are allocated as follows:

- Values between 0 and 255, inclusive, are reserved for standards-track Message Processing Models and are managed by the Internet Assigned Numbers Authority (IANA).

– Values greater than 255 are allocated to enterprise-specific Message Processing Models. An enterprise messageProcessingModel value is defined to be:

enterpriseID * 256 + messageProcessingModel within enterprise

For example, the fourth Message Processing Model defined by the enterprise whose enterpriseID is 1 would be 260.

This scheme for allocation of securityModel values allows for a maximum of 255 standards-based Message Processing Models, and for a maximum of 255 Message Processing Models per enterprise.

As of this writing, there are several values of messageProcessingModel defined for use with SNMP. They are as follows:

0–reserved for SNMPv1
1–reserved for SNMPv2c
2–reserved for SNMPv2u and SNMPv2*
3–reserved for SNMPv3"

SYNTAX INTEGER(0..2147483647)

SnmpSecurityLevel ::= TEXTUAL-CONVENTION
STATUS current
DESCRIPTION "A Level of Security at which SNMP messages can be sent or with which operations are being processed; in particular, one of:

noAuthNoPriv – without authentication and without privacy
authNoPriv   – with authentication but without privacy
authPriv   – with authentication and with privacy

These three values are ordered such that noAuthNoPriv is less than authNoPriv and authNoPriv is less than authPriv."

SYNTAX INTEGER { noAuthNoPriv(1), authNoPriv(2), authPriv(3) }

SnmpAdminString ::= TEXTUAL-CONVENTION
DISPLAY-HINT "255a"
STATUS current
DESCRIPTION "An octet string containing administrative information, preferably in human-readable form."
SYNTAX OCTET STRING (SIZE (0..255))

SNMPv3

Message Processing and
User-Based Security Model

This chapter examines message handling and the security-related processes related to message transmission and reception. First, we look at the message handling functions of the Dispatcher and Message Processing Subsystem; this description is part of the overall SNMP architecture and is not specific to SNMPv3. Then, we examine the user-based security model (USM) introduced for secure message processing as part of SNMPv3.

16.1 Message Processing

We begin with a look at the message format defined for SNMPv3. The remainder of this section describes message processing by the Dispatcher and Message Processing Subsystem.

16.1.1 SNMPv3 Message Format

As with previous versions of SNMP, in SNMPv3, information is exchanged between SNMP entities in the form of a message. Each message includes a message header and a PDU. The message structure is illustrated informally in Figure 16.1; the shaded fields are those created and processed by the Message Processing Subsystem. Figure 16.2 contains the ASN.1 definition of the message format from RFC 2272. The message includes the following fields:

- `msgVersion`: Set to `snmpv3(3)`.
- `msgID`: A unique identifier used between two SNMP entities to coordinate request and response messages, and by the message processor to coordinate the processing of the message by different subsystem models within the architecture. The range of this ID is 0 through $2^{31} -1$.
- `msgMaxSize`: Conveys the maximum size of a message in octets supported by the sender of the message, with a range of 484 through $2^{31} -1$. This is the maximum segment size that the sender can accept from another SNMP engine (whether a response or some other message type).

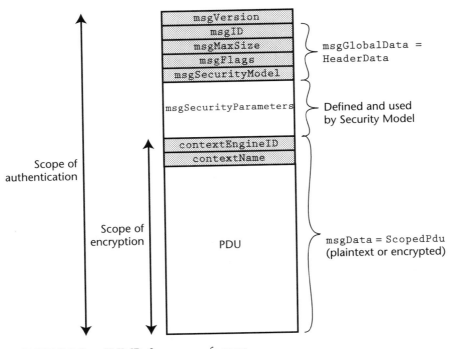

FIGURE 16.1   SNMPv3 message format

- msgFlags: An octet string containing three flags in the least significant three bits: reportableFlag, privFlag, authFlag. If reportableFlag = 1, then a Report PDU must be returned to the sender under those conditions that can cause the generation of a Report PDU; when the flag is zero, a Report PDU may not be sent. The reportableFlag is set to 1 by the sender in all messages containing a request (Get, Set) or an Inform, and set to 0 for messages containing a Response, a Trap, or a Report PDU. The reportableFlag is a secondary aid in determining when to send a Report. It is only used in cases in which the PDU portion of the message cannot be decoded (for example, when decryption fails due to incorrect key). The privFlag and authFlag are set by the sender to indicate the security level that was applied to the message. For privFlag = 1, encryption was applied and for authFlag = 1, authentication was applied. All combinations are allowed except (privFlag = 1 AND authFlag = 0); that is, encryption without authentication is not allowed.
- msgSecurityModel: An identifier in the range of 0 through $2^{31} - 1$ that indicates which security model was used by the sender to prepare this message and therefore which security model must be used by the receiver to process this message. Reserved values include 1 for SNMPv1, 2 for SNMPv2c, and 3 for USM.

```
SNMPv3MessageSyntax DEFINITIONS IMPLICIT TAGS ::= BEGIN

        SNMPv3Message ::= SEQUENCE {
            -- identify the layout of the SNMPv3Message
            -- this element is in same position as in SNMPv1
            -- and SNMPv2c, allowing recognition
            msgVersion INTEGER { snmpv3 (3) } ,
            -- administrative parameters
            msgGlobalData HeaderData,
            -- security model-specific parameters
            -- format defined by Security Model
            msgSecurityParameters OCTET STRING,
            msgData   ScopedPduData
        }

        HeaderData ::= SEQUENCE {
            msgID       INTEGER (0..2147483647),
            msgMaxSize  INTEGER (484..2147483647),

            msgFlags    OCTET STRING (SIZE(1)),
                    --  .... ...1   authFlag
                    --  .... ..1.   privFlag
                    --  .... .1..   reportableFlag
                    --             Please observe:
                    --  .... ..00   is OK, means noAuthNoPriv
                    --  .... ..01   is OK, means authNoPriv
                    --  .... ..10   reserved, must NOT be used.
                    --  .... ..11   is OK, means authPriv

            msgSecurityModel INTEGER (0..2147483647)
        }

ScopedPduData ::= CHOICE {
        plaintext   ScopedPDU,
        encryptedPDU OCTET STRING  -- encrypted scopedPDU value
    }

        ScopedPDU ::= SEQUENCE {
            contextEngineID  OCTET STRING,
            contextName      OCTET STRING,
            data             ANY -- e.g., PDUs as defined in RFC1905
        }
    END
```

FIGURE 16.2   SNMPv3 message format definition

- `msgSecurityParameters`: An octet string that contains parameters generated by the Security Subsystem in the sending SNMP entity and processed by the Security Subsystem in the receiving entity. The contents of this string are not interpreted by the Message Processing Subsystem or the Dispatcher.

- `contextEngineID`: An octet string that uniquely identifies an SNMP entity. For incoming messages, this field determines which application the `scopedPDU` will be sent to for processing. For outgoing messages, this value is provided by the application when it issues a request for a message to be sent.

- `contextName`: An octet string that uniquely identifies a particular context within the scope of the associated context engine.

- `data`: A PDU. The SNMPv3 message processing model specifies that this must be an SNMPv2 PDU.

Figure 16.1 indicates how these fields are organized. The second through fifth fields (`msgID`, `msgMaxSize`, `msgFlags`, and `msgSecurityModel`) are referred to in the ASN.1 definition by the name `msgGlobalData`. This block contains parameters needed by the message processing subsystem to coordinate message handling and processing. The final three fields (`contextEngineID`, `contextName`, and `data`) are referred to by the name `msgData` and have a type of `scopedPduData`. A *scoped* PDU is a PDU containing information named in the context that is unambiguously identified by the `contextEngineID` and the `contextName`. This block contains information needed by the application for PDU processing.

16.1.2 Command Generator Message Processing

Figure 16.3 repeats Figure 15.6(a) and adds some additional detail concerning the way in which some key information is passed and coordinated. In this subsection, we trace through the message handling steps involved in generating a command and receiving a response; similar operations are involved in notification generation/response. A more detailed description can be found in RFC 2272. Here we are concerned with highlighting the critical steps and also in following the progression of critical information, such as the transport domain and address and the PDU handle; it is sometimes difficult to follow how these elements are generated and managed in the discussion in RFC 2272.

16.1.2.1 Preparing an Outgoing Request Message

Once a Command Generator has prepared a PDU for transmission, the following steps occur.

1. The Command Generator issues a `sendPdu` primitive to the Dispatcher including the PDU to be sent, the requested `securityLevel`, and the `transportDomain` and `transportAddress` (see Table 15.4) as parameters. For convenience, we refer to the combination of these last two parameters as `TAddress`. The `sendPdu` also

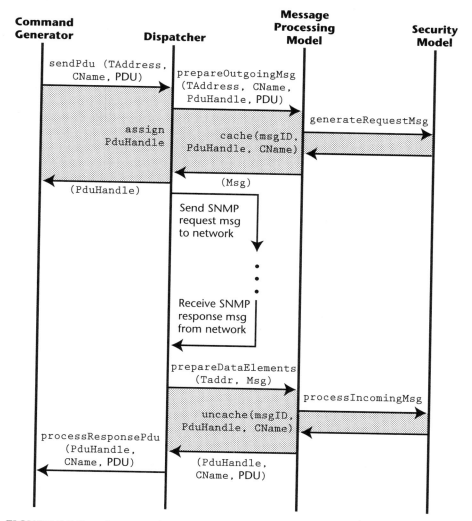

FIGURE 16.3   Command generator messsage processing

includes the `contextEngineID` and `contextName`, which we will refer to as CName. The Dispatcher assigns a unique `sendPduHandle` to this PDU.[1]

2. The Dispatcher issues a `prepareOutgoingMessage` primitive to the Message Processing Subsystem (Table 15.5) that includes the `TAddress` and `CName` provided by the

---

[1]This assignment is indicated in the shaded area between the `sendPdu` call and return; actions indicated in shaded areas refer to actions by the entity on the right (in this case, the Dispatcher).

Command Generator, as well as the PDU, `securityLevel`, and `sendPduHandle`. The Message Processor assigns a unique `msgID` to the message that has been requested.

3. The Message Processor prepares a `scopedPdu` from the CName and PDU information. It prepares the `msgGlobalData` portion of the message header including the `msgID` just generated and sets the `msgFlags` based on the `securityLevel` parameter passed down from the Dispatcher.

4. The Message Processor passes the prepared message to the Security Model using `generateRequestMessage`. The Security Model fills in the `msgSecurity-Parameters` and returns the generated message.

5. The Message Processor caches the following information about the outgoing message:
   - `sendPduHandle` (parameter from `prepareOutgoingMessage` primitive)
   - `msgID` (generated by Message Processor)
   - `securityModel` (parameter from `prepareOutgoingMessage` primitive)
   - `securityName` (parameter from `prepareOutgoingMessage` primitive)
   - `securityLevel` (parameter from `prepareOutgoingMessage` primitive)
   - `contextEngineID` (parameter from `prepareOutgoingMessage` primitive)
   - `contextName` (parameter from `prepareOutgoingMessage` primitive)

6. The Message Processor returns from `prepareOutgoingMessage` to the Dispatcher with the prepared message as a parameter.

7. The Dispatcher returns from the `sendPdu` to the Command Generator with `send-PduHandle` as a primitive value. The Dispatcher also passes the message down to the transport layer (for example, UDP) for transmission, using the `TAddress` associated with this message.

16.1.2.2 Receiving an Incoming Response Message

Some time after the transmission of a request message from an SNMP entity, a matching response message should be received back. When the message is received, the following steps occur.

1. The transport layer (for example, UDP) passes the received message to the Dispatcher, together with `Taddr` information.

2. The Dispatcher issues a `prepareDataElements` primitive to the Message Processor that includes `TAddr` and the message as parameters.

3. The Message Processor extracts the fields from the message. If the value of `msg-SecurityModel` does not match a supported security model (for example, USM), a `Report` PDU is generated and the message is discarded. If `authFlag` = 0 and `priv-Flag` = 1, then a `Report` PDU is generated and the message is discarded; all other combinations of `authFlag` and `privFlag` are used to assign a value to `security-Level`.

4. The Message Processor passes the received message to the Security Model using `processIncomingMessage`. The Security Model processes `msgSecurityParameters` and returns the `scopedPdu` (CName and PDU) as a parameter plus `status-Information` as a primitive value. If an error indication is returned, the Message Processor generates a `Report` PDU, and message processing is complete.

5. If Security Model processing succeeds, the Message Processor extracts the CName and PDU from `scopedPdu`. The value of the `msgID` is used to find the cached information for the corresponding outstanding `Request` message (see Section 16.1.2.1, step 5). The `securityModel`, `securityName`,[2] `securityLevel`, `contextEngineID`, and `contextName` values from the incoming message are matched against those from the cached block. If any of these values do not match, the incoming message is discarded and a failure returned to the Dispatcher. If all of these values match, the `sendPduHandle` value from the cached block is retrieved, and the Message Processor returns from `prepareDataElements` to the Dispatcher with the PDU, CName, and `sendPduHandle` among the parameters.

6. The Dispatcher determines which application is waiting for a `response` PDU associated with this `sendPduHandle`. The response is dispatched to the application using `processResponsePdu` with `sendPduHandle`, CName, and the PDU among the parameters.

If a `Report` PDU is generated by the Message Processor, then the message containing this report is passed to the Dispatcher for transmission. When a Message Processor receives a message containing a `Report` PDU, it performs some implementation-dependent processing.

16.1.3 Command Responder Message Processing

Figure 16.4 repeats Figure 15.6(b) and adds some additional detail concerning the way in which some key information is passed and coordinated. In this subsection, we will trace through the message handling steps involved in receiving a command and generating a response.

16.1.3.1 Receiving an Incoming `Request` Message

Command Responder message processing begins with the arrival of a `request` message at an SNMP entity. When the message is received, the following steps occur.

1. The transport layer (for example, UDP) passes the received message to the Dispatcher, together with `Taddr` information.

---

[2]The `securityName` parameter is derived by the Security Model from the `msgSecurityParameters` portion of the message and returned to the Message Processor.

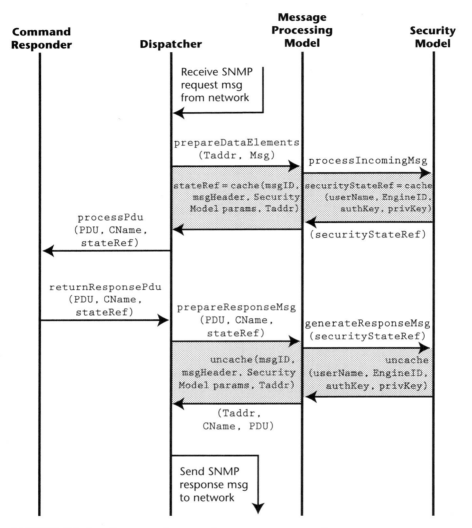

FIGURE 16.4   Command responder message processing

2. The Dispatcher issues a prepareDataElements primitive to the Message Processor that includes TAddr and the message as parameters.

3. The Message Processor extracts the fields from the message. If the value of msgSecurityModel does not match a supported security model (for example, USM), a Report PDU is generated and the message is discarded. If authFlag = 0 and privFlag = 1, then a Report PDU is generated and the message is discarded; all other combinations of authFlag and privFlag are used to assign a value to securityLevel.

4. The Message Processor passes the received message to the Security Model using `processIncomingMessage`. The Security Model processes `msgSecurityParameters` and returns the `scopedPdu` (CName and PDU) as a parameter plus `statusInformation` as a primitive value. If an error indication is returned, the Message Processor generates a `Report` PDU, and message processing is complete.

5. If Security Model processing succeeds, the Message processor caches the following information about the incoming message:

   - `msgVersion` (from message header)
   - `msgID` (from message header)
   - `msgMaxSize` (from message header)
   - `msgFlags` (from message header)
   - `securityLevel` (derived from `msgFlags` from message header)
   - `contextEngineID` (from message header)
   - `contextName` (from message header)
   - `securityModel` (from message header)
   - `securityName` (from Security Model)
   - `maxSizeResponseScopedPdu` (from Security Model)
   - `securityStateReference` (from Security Model)
   - `transportDomain` (from Dispatcher)
   - `transportAddr` (from Dispatcher)

   A `stateReference` value is created; this is an implementation-specific reference that identifies this block of cached data.

6. The Message Processor returns from `prepareDataElements` to the Dispatcher with `stateReference`, CName, and the PDU among the parameters. The `sendPduHandle` parameter is null.

7. The Dispatcher uses the combination of `contextEngineID` and `pduType` to determine which application has registered for this request and dispatches the PDU to the application with `processPdu`. Parameters include security-related parameters, CName, and `stateReference`.

16.1.3.2 Preparing an Outgoing Response Message

Having received a `request` PDU from the Dispatcher, the application invokes the Access Control Subsystem to determine if access is allowed and, if so, processes the `request` PDU and prepares a `Response` PDU. The following steps then occur.

1. The Command Generator issues a `returnResponsePdu` primitive to the Dispatcher with `stateReference`, CName, and the PDU to be sent among the parameters.

2. The Dispatcher issues a `prepareResponseMsg` primitive to the Message Processing Subsystem that includes the `stateReference`, CName, and PDU provided by the Command Responder.

3. The Message Processor retrieves the cached information for the original request via the `stateReference`. The Message Processor prepares a `scopedPdu` from the CName and PDU information from the Dispatcher. It prepares the `msgGlobalData` portion of the message header based on values retrieved from the cache.

4. The Message Processor passes the prepared message to the Security Model using `generateResponseMessage`. The Security Model fills in the `msgSecurity-Parameters` and returns the generated message.

5. The Message Processor returns from `prepareResponseMsg` to the Dispatcher with `TAddr` (from the cache) and the prepared message as parameters.

6. The Dispatcher passes the message down to the transport layer (for example, UDP) for transmission, using the `TAddress` associated with this message.

16.2 *The SNMPv3 User-Based Security Model*

RFC 2274 defines the user-based security model (USM) for SNMPv3. This specification encompasses:

- *Authentication:* Provides data integrity and data origin authentication. The message authentication code HMAC, with either the hash function MD5 or SHA-1, provides authentication.
- *Timeliness:* Protects against message delay or replay.
- *Privacy:* Protects against disclosure of message payload. The cipher block chaining (CBC) mode of DES is used for encryption.
- *Message format:* Defines format of `msgSecurityParameters` field, which supports the functions of authentication, timeliness, and privacy.
- *Discovery:* Defines procedures by which one SNMP engine obtains information about another SNMP engine.
- *Key management:* Defines procedures for key generation, update, and use.

We begin this section with a description of the `msgSecurityParameters` field in the SNMPv3 message format. This is followed by a discussion of the timeliness mechanisms for USM. Next, we describe the `usmUser` group; this MIB contains objects used by an SNMP engine to control the operation of USM to process messages to/from a particular user. Then we summarize the cryptographic functions that have been defined for USM. We are then in a position to describe the USM message processing functions. Finally, we examine the areas of discovery and key management.

16.2.1 USM Security Parameters

RFC 2274 defines a structure, `UsmSecurityParameters`, that specifies the internal format of the `msgSecurityParameters` field in an SNMPv3 message. Figure 16.5 shows the ASN.1 definition and Figure 16.6 illustrates the SNMPv3 message format when USM is in use; the shaded fields are those whose values are created/processed by the USM (compare Figure 16.1).

16.2.1.1 Authoritative SNMP Engine

Before examining the fields within `msgSecurityParameters`, we need to define the concept of an authoritative SNMP engine. In any message transmission, one of the two entities, transmitter or receiver, is designated as the authoritative SNMP engine, according to the following rules.

- When an SNMP message contains a payload which expects a response (for example, a `Get`, `GetNext`, `GetBulk`, `Set`, or `Inform` PDU), then the receiver of such messages is authoritative.

- When an SNMP message contains a payload which does not expect a response (for example, an `SNMPv2-Trap`, `Response`, or `Report` PDU), then the sender of such a message is authoritative.

Thus, for messages sent on behalf of a Command Generator and for `Inform` messages from a Notification Originator, the receiver is authoritative. For messages sent on

```
USMSecurityParametersSyntax DEFINITIONS IMPLICIT TAGS ::= BEGIN

    UsmSecurityParameters ::=
        SEQUENCE {
            -- global User-based security parameters
            msgAuthoritativeEngineID      OCTET STRING,
            msgAuthoritativeEngineBoots   INTEGER (0..2147483647),
            msgAuthoritativeEngineTime    INTEGER (0..2147483647),
            msgUserName                   OCTET STRING (SIZE(1..32)),
            -- authentication protocol specific parameters
            msgAuthenticationParameters   OCTET STRING,
            -- privacy protocol specific parameters
            msgPrivacyParameters          OCTET STRING
        }
    END
```

FIGURE 16.5   User security model security parameters definition

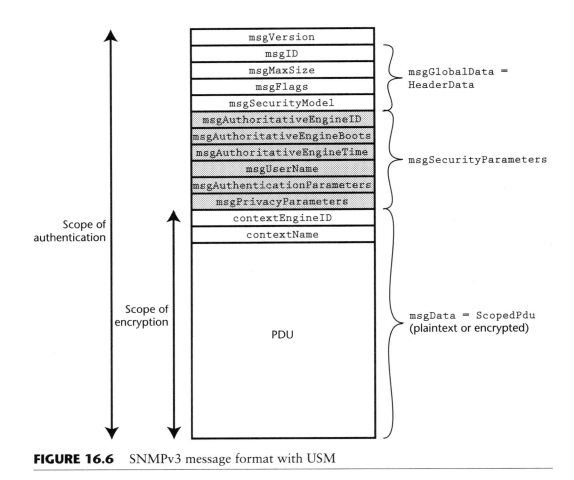

FIGURE 16.6 SNMPv3 message format with USM

behalf of a Command Responder or for `Trap` messages from a Notification Originator, the sender is authoritative. This designation serves two purposes.

1. The timeliness of a message is determined with respect to a clock maintained by the authoritative engine. When an authoritative engine sends a message (`Trap`, `Response`, `Report`), it contains the current value of its clock, so that the nonauthoritative recipient can synchronize on that clock. When a nonauthoritative engine sends a message (`Get`, `GetNext`, `GetBulk`, `Set`, `Inform`), it includes its current estimate of the time value at the destination, allowing the destination to assess the message's timeliness.

2. A key localization process, described later, enables a single principal to own keys stored in multiple engines; these keys are localized to the authoritative engine in

such a way that the principal is responsible for a single key but avoids the security risk of storing multiple copies of the same key in a distributed network.

It makes sense to designate the receiver of Command Generator and `Inform` PDUs as the authoritative engine, and therefore the possessor of the authoritative clock in an exchange. If a response or trap is delayed or replayed, little harm should occur. However, Command Generator and, to some extent, `Inform` PDUs result in management operations, such as reading or setting MIB objects. Thus, it is important to guarantee that such PDUs are not delayed or replayed, which could cause undesired effects.

16.2.1.2 Elements of `UsmSecurityParameters`

When an outgoing message is passed to the USM by the Message Processor, the USM fills in the `msgSecurityParameters` field. When an incoming message is passed to the USM by the Message Processor, the USM processes the values contained in `msgSecurity-Parameters`. The security parameters field consists of the following elements:

- `msgAuthoritativeEngineID`: The `snmpEngineID` of the authoritative SNMP engine involved in the exchange of this message. Thus, this value refers to the source for a `Trap`, `Response`, or `Report`, and to the destination for a `Get`, `GetNext`, `Get-Bulk`, `Set`, or `Inform`.

- `msgAuthoritativeEngineBoots`: The `snmpEngineBoots` value of the authoritative SNMP engine involved in the exchange of this message. The object `snmp-EngineBoots` is an integer in the range 0 through $2^{31} - 1$ that represents the number of times that this SNMP engine has initialized or reinitialized itself since its initial configuration.

- `msgAuthoritativeEngineTime`: The `snmpEngineTime` value of the authoritative SNMP engine involved in the exchange of this message. The object `snmpEngine-Time` is an integer in the range 0 through $2^{31} - 1$ that represents the number of seconds since this authoritative SNMP engine last incremented the `snmpEngineBoots` object. Each authoritative SNMP engine is responsible for incrementing its own `snmpEngineTime` value once per second. A nonauthoritative engine is responsible for incrementing its notion of `snmpEngineTime` for each remote authoritative engine with which it communicates.

- `msgUserName`: The user (principal) on whose behalf the message is being exchanged.

- `msgAuthenticationParameters`: Null if authentication is not being used for this exchange. Otherwise, this is an authentication parameter. For the current definition of USM, the authentication parameter is an HMAC message authentication code.

- `msgPrivacyParameters`: Null if privacy is not being used for this exchange. Otherwise, this is a privacy parameter. For the current definition of USM, the privacy parameter is a value used to form the initial value (IV) in the DES CBC algorithm.

16.2.2 USM Timeliness Mechanisms

The set of USM timeliness mechanisms includes the following:

- Management of authoritative clocks
- Synchronization
- Timeliness checking

16.2.2.1 Management of Authoritative Clocks

Each SNMP engine that can ever act in the capacity of an authoritative engine must maintain two objects, snmpEngineBoots and snmpEngineTime, that refer to its local time. Thus, all engines that act as agents or that act as managers that can receive Inform PDUs must maintain these two objects. When an SNMP engine is first installed, these two object values are set to 0. Thereafter, snmpEngineTime is incremented once per second. If snmpEngineTime ever reaches its maximum value ($2^{31} - 1$), snmpEngineBoots is incremented, as if the system had rebooted, and snmpEngineTime is set to 0 and begins incrementing again.

If an authoritative engine is ever unable to determine its latest snmpEngineBoots value, it sets that value to its maximum value of $2^{31} - 1$. Once the local value of snmpEngineBoots equals $2^{31} - 1$, it remains latched at that value and an authenticated message always causes a notInTimeWindow authentication failure. To recover from a latched snmpEngineBoots value, it is necessary to manually reconfigure the system with a new snmpEngineID value, or with new secret key values for the authentication and privacy protocols of all users known to that SNMP engine. However, barring some kind of failure or sabotage, it would take about 68 years for the snmpEngineID value to reach its maximum.

16.2.2.2 Synchronization

An SNMP engine that operates in a nonauthoritative role (it may also operate in an authoritative role) must remain loosely synchronized with each authoritative SNMP engine with which it communicates. For this purpose, the nonauthoritative engine keeps a local copy of three variables for each authoritative SNMP engine that is known to this engine:

- snmpEngineBoots: the most recent value of snmpEngineBoots for the remote authoritative engine.
- snmpEngineTime: this engine's notion of snmpEngineTime for the remote authoritative engine. This value is synchronized to the remote authoritative engine by the synchronization process described below. Between synchronization events, this value is logically incremented once per second to maintain a loose synchronization with the remote authoritative engine.

- `latestReceivedEngineTime`: the highest value of `msgAuthoritativeEngine-Time` that has been received by this engine from the remote authoritative engine; this value is updated whenever a larger value of `msgAuthoritativeEngineTime` is received. The purpose of this variable is to protect against a replay message attack that would prevent the nonauthoritative SNMP engine's notion of `snmpEngine-Time` from advancing, as we will see in the subsequent discussion.

One set of these three variables is maintained for each remote authoritative engine known to this engine. Logically, the values are maintained in some sort of cache, indexed by the unique `snmpEngineID` of each remote authoritative engine. Initially, a nonauthoritative SNMP engine can retrieve `snmpEngineBoots` and `snmpEngineTime` from an authoritative engine, using the discovery process described in Section 16.2.6. Subsequently, synchronization occurs automatically as incoming messages are received, as explained in the following paragraphs.

To enable nonauthoritative engines to maintain time synchronization, each authoritative engine inserts its current boot and time values, as well as its value of `snmpEngineID`, in each outgoing `Response`, `Report`, or `Trap` message in the fields `msgAuthoritative-EngineBoots`, `msgAuthoritativeEngineTime`, and `msgAuthoritativeEngineID` (Figure 16.6). If the message is authentic, then the receiving nonauthoritative engine updates its local variables (`snmpEngineBoots`, `snmpEngineTime`, and `latestReceivedEngineTime`) for that remote engine according to the following rules.

1. An update occurs if at least one of the two following conditions is true:
   - (`msgAuthoritativeEngineBoots` > `snmpEngineBoots`) OR
   - [(`msgAuthoritativeEngineBoots` = `snmpEngineBoots`) AND (`msgAuthoritativeEngineTime` > `latestReceivedEngineTime`)]

   The first condition says that an update should occur if the boot value from the authoritative engine has increased since the last update. The second condition says that if the boot value has not increased, then an update should occur if the incoming engine time is greater than the latest received engine time. The incoming engine time will be less than the latest received engine time if two incoming messages arrive out of order, which can happen, or if a replay attack is underway; in either case, the receiving engine will not perform an update.

2. If an update is called for, then the following changes are made:
   - set `snmpEngineBoots` to the value of `msgAuthoritativeEngineBoots`
   - set `snmpEngineTime` to the value of `msgAuthoritativeEngineTime`
   - set `latestReceivedEngineTime` to the value of `msgAuthoritativeEngine-Time`

   If we turn the logic around, we see that if `msgAuthoritativeEngineBoots` < `snmpEngineBoots`, then no update occurs. Such a message is considered not authentic and must be ignored. If `msgAuthoritativeEngineBoots` = `snmpEngineBoots` but `msgAuthoritativeEngineTime < latestReceivedEngineTime`, then again no update occurs. In this case, the message may be authentic, but it may be misordered, in which case an update of `snmpEngineTime` is not warranted.

Note that synchronization is only employed if the authentication service is in use for this message and the message has been determined to be authentic via HMAC. This restriction is essential because the scope of authentication includes `msgAuthoritative-EngineID`, `msgAuthoritativeEngineBoots`, and `msgAuthoritativeEngineTime`, thus assuring that these values are valid.

16.2.2.3 Timeliness Checking by Authoritative Receiver

SNMPv3 dictates that a message must be received within a reasonable time window, to avoid delay and replay attacks. The time window should be chosen to be as small as possible given the accuracy of the clocks involved, round-trip communication delays, and the frequency with which clocks are synchronized. If the time window is set too small, authentic messages will be rejected as unauthentic. On the other hand, a large time window increases the vulnerability to malicious delays of messages. The actual test for timeliness depends on whether the message recipient is authoritative or nonauthoritative. Table 16.1 summarizes the tests, as well as showing the clock synchronization algorithm.

First, consider the more important case of an authoritative receiver. With each incoming message that has been authenticated and whose `msgAuthoritativeEngineID`

TABLE 16.1   Timeliness Calculations on Received Messages

	Authoritative Receiver (receiver of Get, GetNext, GetBulk, Set, Inform PDUs) (MEAB, MAET from incoming message; SEB, SET refer to this local engine)	Nonauthoritative Receiver (receiver of Trap, Response, Report PDUs) (MEAB, MAET from incoming message; SEB, SET, LRET refer to remote engine that sent this message)

Clock synchronization	Not applicable	IF
		   (MAEB > SEB) **OR**
		     [(MAEB = SEB) **AND** (MAET > LRET)]
		 THEN
		   SEB ← MAEB
		   SET ← MAET
		   LRET ← MAET

Timeliness check	Inside Time Window **IF**
	   (SEB ≠ $2^{31} - 1$) **AND**
	   (MAEB = SEB) **AND**
	   (SET − 150 ≤ MAET ≤ SET + 150)
		Inside Time Window **IF**
		   (SEB ≠ $2^{31} - 1$) **AND**
		   [(MAEB > SEB) **OR**
		   (MAEB = SEB) **AND** (SET − 150 ≤ MAET)]]

MEAB = `msgAuthoritativeEngineBoots`; MAET = `msgAuthoritativeEngineTime`; SEB = `snmpEngineBoots`; SET = `snmpEngineTime`; LRET = `latestReceivedEngineTime` is the same as the value of snmpEngineID for this engine, the engine compares the values of msgAuthoritativeEngineBoots and msgAuthoritativeEngineTime from the incoming message with the values of snmpEngineBoots and snmpEngineTime that this engine maintains for itself. The incoming message is considered outside the time window if any one of the following conditions is true:

- snmpEngineBoots = $2^{31} - 1$ OR

- msgAuthoritativeEngineBoots ≠ snmpEngineBoots OR

- the value of msgAuthoritativeEngineTime differs from that of snmpEngine-Time by more than ±150 seconds

The first condition says that if snmpEngineBoots is latched at its maximum value, no incoming message can be considered authentic. The second condition says that a message must have a boot time equal to the local engine's boot time; for example, if the local engine has rebooted and the remote engine has not synchronized with the local engine since the reboot, the messages from that remote engine are considered not authentic. The final condition says that the time on the incoming message must not be less than the local time by greater than 150 seconds nor more than the local time by greater than 150 seconds.

If a message is considered to be outside the time window, then the message is considered not authentic, and an error indication (notInTimeWindow) is returned to the calling module.

Again, as with synchronization, timeliness checking is only done if the authentication service is in use and the message is authentic, assuring the validity of the message header fields. This is true both for authoritative receivers and for nonauthoritative receivers, discussed next.

16.2.2.4 Timeliness Checking by Nonauthoritative Receiver

The RFC 2274 specification for timeliness checking by a nonauthoritative receiver differs somewhat from that of an authoritative receiver. With each incoming message to be authenticated whose msgAuthoritativeEngineID is not equal to the value of snmp-EngineID for this engine, the engine compares the values of msgAuthoritative-EngineBoots and msgAuthoritativeEngineTime from the incoming message with the values of snmpEngineBoots and snmpEngineTime that this engine maintains for the corresponding remote SNMP engine. The incoming message is considered outside the time window if any one of the following three conditions is true:

- snmpEngineBoots = $2^{31} - 1$ OR

- msgAuthoritativeEngineBoots < snmpEngineBoots OR

- [(msgAuthoritativeEngineBoots = snmpEngineBoots) AND msgAuthoritativeEngineTime < snmpEngineTime − 150]

The first condition says that if this engine's notion of the remote `snmpEngineBoots` is latched at its maximum value, no incoming message can be considered authentic. The second condition says that a message may not have a boot time that is less than the local notion of boot time; if the message's boot time is less than the local notion of boot time, then this message appears to have been sent by the remote engine prior to its most recent boot. The final condition says that if the boot times match, then an incoming message must be no older than 150 seconds compared to the local notion of the remote authoritative engine's clock time.

Note that the condition (`msgAuthoritativeEngineBoots > snmpEngineBoots`) is permitted. This makes it possible for the receiving engine to accept a message as authentic when received from an authoritative engine that has rebooted since the receiving engine last synchronized.

Finally, Table 16.1 highlights a difference in the time window definition for authoritative and nonauthoritative receivers. For an authoritative receiver, the time window is defined as

$$(\texttt{snmpEngineTime} - 150) \leq \texttt{msgAuthoritativeEngineTime} \leq (\texttt{snmpEngineTime} + 150)$$

But for a nonauthoritative receiver, the time window is defined as

$$(\texttt{snmpEngineTime} - 150) \leq \texttt{msgAuthoritativeEngineTime}$$

To explain this difference, let us ignore the delays caused by network transit time, which will usually be one or two orders of magnitude less than 150 seconds. Now consider the two cases:

- *Nonauthoritative receiver.* Suppose the received timer value (`msgAuthoritativeEngineTime`), which represents the remote engine's actual timer value, is greater than the receiver's notion of the remote timer value (`snmpEngineTime`). The authoritative engine obviously knows its clock better than the receiver does, so the receiver must accept that the authoritative clock advanced faster than the receiver's notion of that clock, no matter how much faster that is—even greater than 150 seconds faster. The message is accepted as authentic and the receiver has the opportunity to resynchronize its notion of the remote clock. The same reasoning does not apply to the authoritative engine's clock being much slower than the receiver's notion, because that could indicate a replay attack.

- *Authoritative receiver.* Suppose the received timer value (`msgAuthoritativeEngineTime`), which represents the remote engine's notion of the receiver's actual timer value, is greater than the receiver's local timer value (`snmpEngineTime`). This could simply indicate that the remote engine's clock is running faster than the local clock. However, if the remote engine's notion of the local time is greater than 150 seconds more than the actual local time, this may indicate some problem at the remote engine, and the message is not accepted as authentic.

16.2.3 The `usmUser` Group

Each SNMP entity maintains a MIB, the `usmUser` Group, with information about local and remote principals. Figure 16.7 shows the structure of this group, which consists of a single scalar object, `usmUserSpinLock`, and the table `usmUserTable`. The object `usmUserSpinLock`, of type `TestandIncr` (see Appendix 13A), enables cooperating Command Generator applications to coordinate their use of facilities to change keys using the `usmUserTable`. In addition to the usual storage type and row status objects, `usmUserTable` includes the following columnar objects:

- `usmUserEngineID`: The identifier of an authoritative SNMP engine. In a simple agent, this is the agent's `snmpEngineID`. The value can also be that of a remote SNMP engine with which this user can communicate.

- `usmUserName`: A human-readable string representing the name of the user in USM-dependent format; this value functions as the identifier, or `securityName`, of this principal.

- `usmUserSecurityName`: A human-readable string representing the name of the user in a format that is independent of the security model; this value functions as the identifier, or `securityName`, of this principal. The default relationship between this object and `usmUserName` is identity; that is, the two values are identical for a given entry in the table.

- `usmUserCloneFrom`: A pointer to another conceptual row in this table. When a new user is created (that is, a new row is created in this table), this newly created object instance refers to an existing row from which the privacy and authentication parameters of the new user are copied into the new row. In addition, the secret authentication and encryption keys for the new user are copied from the `cloneFrom` user; these keys are not kept in `usmUserTable` because they are not accessible via SNMP. The first time an instance of this object is set by a management operation, the cloning process is invoked.

- `usmUserAuthProtocol`: An object identifier that indicates whether messages sent on behalf of this user to/from the SNMP engine identified by `usmUserEngineID` can be authenticated and, if so, the type of authentication protocol to be used. Possible values are the objects `usmNoAuthProtocol`, `usmHMACMD5AuthProtocol`, and `usmHMACSHAAuthProtocol`. The default is `usmHMACMD5AuthProtocol`.

- `usmUserAuthKeyChange`: An octet string with the syntax `KeyChange`. When this object is modified, it causes the secret authentication key used for messages sent on

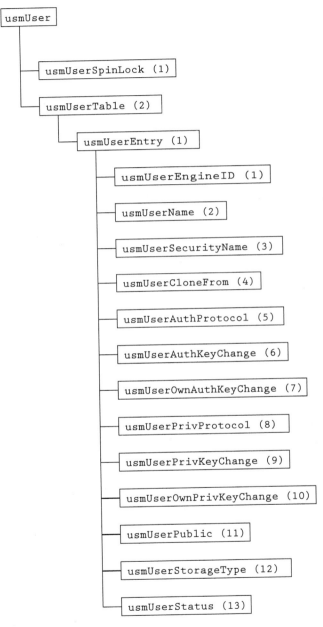

FIGURE 16.7 The usmUser group

behalf of this user to/from the SNMP engine identified by `usmUserEngineID` to be modified by a one-way function (described in Section 16.2.7.3). When creating a new user, this object may only be set (that is, the key may only be changed) if it is previously or concurrently initialized through a set operation on the corresponding value of `usmUserCloneFrom`.

- `usmUserOwnAuthKeyChange`: An octet string with the syntax `KeyChange`. Behaves exactly as `usmUserAuthKeyChange` with one exception: In order for the `Set` operation to succeed, the `usmUserName` of the operation requester must match the `usm-UserName` that indexes this row. This object only allows a user to change his/her own secret authentication key, and therefore access can be public.

- `usmUserPrivProtocol`: An object identifier that indicates whether messages sent on behalf of this user to/from the SNMP engine identified by `usmUserEngineID` can be protected by encryption and, if so, the type of privacy protocol to be used. Possible values are the objects `usmNoPrivProtocol` and `usmDESPrivProtocol`. The default is `usmNoPrivProtocol`.

- `usmUserPrivKeyChange`: An octet string with the syntax `KeyChange`. When this object is modified, it causes the secret encryption key used for messages sent on behalf of this user to/from the SNMP engine identified by `usmUserEngineID` to be modified by a one-way function. When creating a new user, this object may only be set (that is, the key may only be changed) if it is previously or concurrently initialized through a set operation on the corresponding value of `usmUserCloneFrom`.

- `usmUserOwnPrivKeyChange`: An octet string with the syntax `KeyChange`. Behaves exactly as `usmUserPrivKeyChange` with one exception: In order for the `Set` operation to succeed, the `usmUserName` of the operation requester must match the `usm-UserName` that indexes this row.

- `usmUserPublic`: This is an octet string, defined in RFC 2274 as follows: "A publicly-readable value that is written as part of the procedure for changing a user's secret authentication and/or privacy key, and later read to determine whether the change of the secret was effected." No further explanation of the use of this object is given anywhere in RFC 2274. A future extension of USM may define a procedure for using this object.

The table is indexed by `usmUserEngineID` and `usmUserName`. Thus, more than one `usmUserName` can be associated with each `usmUserEngineID`. Each such `usmUserName` represents a separate principal that has a security relationship with the SNMP engine represented by `usmUserEngineID`.

16.2.4 Cryptographic Functions

Two cryptographic functions are defined for USM: authentication and encryption. To support these functions, an SNMP engine requires two values: a privacy key (`privKey`) and an authentication key (`authKey`). Separate values of these two keys are maintained for the following users:

- *Local users:* Any principal at this SNMP engine for which management operations are authorized.

- *Remote users:* Any principal at a remote SNMP engine for which communication is desired.

These values are user attributes stored for each relevant user. The values of `privKey` and `authKey` are not accessible via SNMP.

16.2.4.1 Authentication

USM allows the use of one of two alternative authentication protocols: HMAC-MD5-96 and HMAC-SHA-96. For HMAC-MD5-96, the HMAC message authentication code described in Chapter 14 is used, with MD5 as the underlying hash function. A 16-octet (128-bit) `authKey` is used as input to the HMAC algorithm. The algorithm produces a 128-bit output, which is truncated to 12 octets (96 bits). This value is the message authentication code to be inserted in the `msgAuthenticationParameters` field of the SNMPv3 message (Figure 16.6).

For HMAC-SHA-96, the underlying hash function is SHA-1. The `authKey` is 20 octets in length. The algorithm produces a 20-octet output, which is again truncated to 12 octets.

16.2.4.2 Encryption

USM uses the cipher block chaining (CBC) mode of the Data Encryption Standard (DES) for encryption, which is described in Chapter 14. A 16-octet `privKey` is provided as input to the encryption protocol. The first 8 octets (64 bits) of this `privKey` are used as a DES key. Because DES only requires a 56-bit key, the least significant bit of each octet is ignored.

For CBC mode, a 64-bit initialization vector (IV) is required. This is produced in the following manner.

- The last 8 octets of the 16-octet privKey are used as a pre-IV.

- To ensure that the two different IVs are used for two different plaintext inputs encrypted with the same key, an 8-octet *salt value* is produced. The salt value is equal to the concatenation of the current value of this engine's `snmpEngineBoots` value, which is 4 octets in length, and a local 4-octet integer maintained by the local encryption protocol. This 4-octet integer is implementation-dependent and should be modified after each use.

- The salt value is bit-by-bit XORed with the pre-IV to produce the IV.

The salt value is placed in the `msgPrivacyParameters` field of the SNMPv3 message (Figure 16.6) to enable the receiving entity to compute the correct IV. This scheme accomplishes the following: First, because the salt value changes for each use, a different IV is used for different plaintexts. Second, only the salt value is transmitted via SNMP, and therefore an attacker cannot determine the IV.

16.2.5 USM Message Processing

Figure 16.8 depicts, in general terms, the procedures followed by USM for processing outgoing and incoming messages. We look at each of the two operations in more detail in this section. In Section 16.2.5.1, we first trace through the USM steps involved in generating a command and receiving a response; similar operations are involved in notification generation/response. We then look at the steps involved in receiving a command and generating a response in Section 16.2.5.2.

16.2.5.1 Command Generator Message Processing

Figure 16.3 shows the context in which the USM is involved in command generator message processing. We begin with the steps taken by USM when it is invoked with a `generateRequestMsg` primitive from the Message Processing Subsystem. Recall from Table 15.6 that the Message Processor provides the following input parameters with the primitive call:

- `messageProcessingModel`: Identifies the calling message processing model (not used by USM)
- `globalData`: The first portion of a message header, which includes `msgVersion`, `msgID`, `msgMaxSize`, `msgFlags`, and `msgSecurityModel` (not used by USM)
- `maxMessageSize`: Maximum message size for this message (not used by USM)
- `securityModel`: Security model in use; should identify USM
- `securityEngineID`: The `snmpEngineID` of the authoritative SNMP engine to which this request message is to be sent
- `securityName`: Identifies the principal on whose behalf the message is to be generated. Together with `securityEngineID`, it identifies a row in the `usmUserTable` that is to be used for securing the message (Figure 16.7). Note that the selected row in `usmUserTable` identifies a local principal and the remote engine to which the principal is sending a `command` or `Inform` PDU.
- `securityLevel`: The requested security services (none, authentication, authentication plus privacy).
- `scopedPDU`: The message payload, which is opaque to the USM.

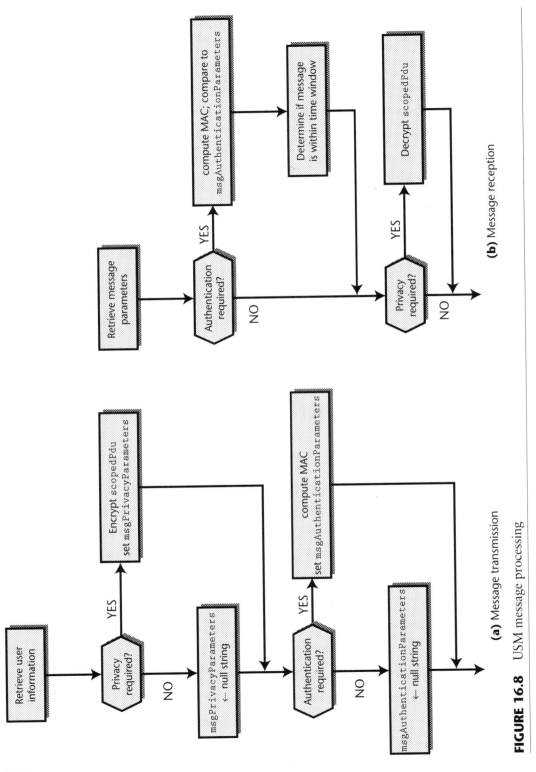

FIGURE 16.8 USM message processing

(a) Message transmission

(b) Message reception

Note that many of the input parameters are ignored by USM; other security models may use these parameters, which are part of the general abstract service interface to the Security Subsystem.

In what follows, we ignore some basic error-checking steps that may stop the process, such as an invalid `msgSecurityParameters` field. The USM performs the following steps upon receipt of `generateRequestMsg`.

1. USM determines if there is an entry in `usmUserTable` for the destination `security-EngineID` and the source `securityName`. If not, an error indication is returned.

2. USM determines if the requested `securityLevel` is supported for this user and, if not, returns an error indication.

3. If the `securityLevel` requests privacy, then the `scopedPdu` value is encrypted using CBC-DES and the localized private encryption key (`privKey`) for this user. The resulting ciphertext is stored in the `scopedPdu` field, and the salt value derived from the `privKey` value (described in Section 16.2.4.2) is stored in the `msgPrivacy-Parameters` field of the SNMPv3 message (Figure 16.6). If privacy is not requested, then the `msgPrivacyParameters` field is set to the NULL string.

4. The `snmpEngineID` parameter is stored in the `msgAuthoritativeEngineID` field of the message.

5. The `securityName` parameter is stored in the `msgUserName` field.

6. If the `securityLevel` requests authentication, the current values of `snmpEngine-Boots` and `snmpEngineTime` corresponding to the `snmpEngineID` parameter are stored in the `msgAuthoritativeEngineBoots` and `msgAuthoritativeEngine-Time` fields, respectively. Then, the message authentication code is calculated over the entire message, using HMAC and the localized authentication key (`authKey`) for this user, and stored in `msgAuthenticationParameters`. If the `security-Level` does not request authentication, a zero value is stored in the `msgAuthoritativeEngineBoots` and `msgAuthoritativeEngineTime` fields and the `msg-AuthenticationParameters` field is set to the NULL string.

7. The completed message with its length is returned to the calling Message Processing Module.

Some time after the transmission of a request message from an SNMP entity, a matching response message should be received back. This message is handled by the Dispatcher and the Message Processor. The latter invokes USM with a `processIncoming-Message` primitive. Recall from Table 15.6 that the Message Processor provides the following input parameters with the primitive call:

- `messageProcessingModel`: Identifies the calling message processing model (not used by USM).

- `maxMessageSize`: Maximum message size as included in this message. USM uses this value to calculate the `maxSizeResponseScopedPdu`.
- `securityParameters`: Security parameters as received in the message.
- `securityModel`: Security model in use; should identify USM.
- `securityLevel`: The requested security services (none, authentication, authentication plus privacy).
- `wholeMsg`: The whole message as it was received.
- `wholeMsgLength`: The length of the whole message as it was received.

Processing includes the following steps (again, some of the details are omitted).

1. The security parameter values are extracted from `securityParameters`.

2. If the value of `msgAuthoritativeEngineID` in `securityParameters` is unknown, and if this SNMP engine performs discovery (Section 16.2.6), it may optionally create a new entry in its `usmUserGroup` MIB. Otherwise, an error indication is returned.

3. USM determines if there is an entry in `usmUserTable` for the remote authoritative `securityEngineID` and the local `securityName`. If not, an error indication is returned.

4. USM determines if the requested `securityLevel` is supported for this user and, if not, returns an error indication.

5. If the `securityLevel` specifies that this message is to be authenticated, then the message is authenticated using HMAC and the localized authentication key (`auth-Key`) for this user, by calculating the message authentication code for this message and comparing the result to the `msgAuthenticationParameters` field in the message. If there is no match, USM halts processing and returns an error indication. If there is a match, the message is declared authentic and processing continues.

6. USM performs time synchronization, as described in Section 16.2.2.2.

7. USM performs timeliness checking, as described in Section 16.2.2.4. If the message is not within the time window, USM halts processing and returns an error indication. If the message is within the time window, processing continues.

8. If the `securityLevel` indicates that encryption was performed, then the `scopedPdu` portion of the message is decrypted using CBC-DES and the localized private encryption key (`privKey`) for this user.

9. The `scopedPdu` is returned to the calling Message Processing Module.

Note: In RFC 2274, clock synchronization (step 6 in our numbering) occurs before time window verification (step 7 in our numbering), as indicated above. This means that a nonauthoritative engine may update its notion of the authoritative engine's clock if the received message is authentic, even if the message is not within the time window. Since the publication of the RFC, there has been an ongoing dispute about this on the SNMPv3 mailing list, but as of this writing, it appears that the wording in the standard will not change. It is instructive to look at the implications of this. Define:

MAEB = `msgAuthoritativeEngineBoots`
MAET = `msgAuthoritativeEngineTime`
SEB   = local notion of `snmpEngineBoots` for the remote authoritative engine
SET   = local notion of `snmpEngineTime` for the remote authoritative engine
LRET = `latestReceivedEngineTime`

Then suppose a nonauthoritative engine receives a message so that

$$(MAEB = SEB) \text{ AND } [LRET < MAET < (SET - 150)]$$

Then, the conditions are right for a clock update, so it gets done:

$$SET := MAET; \quad LRET := MAET$$

Now, when we come to the time window check, we have

$$(MAEB = SEB) \text{ AND } (MAET = SET)$$

so we declare that the message is timely. However, if we had done the time window check first, we would have declared the message untimely because MAET < (SET − 150). That doesn't seem good, but that is what the RFC says.

Related to all of this, the RFC states: "Note that this procedure does not allow for automatic time synchronization if the nonauthoritative SNMP engine has a real out-of-sync situation whereby the authoritative SNMP engine is more than 150 seconds behind the nonauthoritative SNMP engine." This statement is not always true. In the example just given, the authoritative SNMP engine is more than 150 seconds behind the nonauthoritative engine (because `msgAuthoritativeEngineTime` < (`snmpEngineTime` − 150)) but time synchronization occurs (because `latestReceivedEngineTime` < `msgAuthoritativeEngineTime`).

16.2.5.2 Command Responder Message Processing

Figure 16.4 shows the context in which the USM is involved in command responder message processing. Many of the steps are the same as for the Command Generator context, but there are a few important differences. We begin with the steps taken by USM when it is invoked with a `processIncomingMessage` primitive from the Message Processing

Subsystem. This is done while the Message Processor is handling an incoming `Request` message. The steps are as follows.

1. The security parameter values are extracted from `securityParameters`. A `cachedSecurityData` block is prepared to cache the following information:
   - `msgUserName`
   - `securityEngineID`
   - `securityLevel`

2. If the value of `msgAuthoritativeEngineID` in `securityParameters` is unknown, an error indication is returned.

3. USM determines if there is an entry in `usmUserTable` for the local authoritative `securityEngineID` and the remote `securityName`. If not, an error indication is returned.

4. USM determines if the requested `securityLevel` is supported for this user and, if not, returns an error indication.

5. If the `securityLevel` specifies that this message is to be authenticated, then the message is authenticated using HMAC and the localized authentication key (`authKey`) for this user, by calculating the message authentication code for this message and comparing the result to the `msgAuthenticationParameters` field in the message. If there is no match, USM halts processing and returns an error indication. If there is a match, the message is declared authentic and processing continues.

6. USM performs timeliness checking, as described in Section 16.2.2.3. If the message is not within the time window, USM halts processing and returns an error indication. If the message is within the time window, processing continues.

7. If the `securityLevel` indicates that encryption was performed, then the `scopedPdu` portion of the message is decrypted using CBC-DES and the localized private encryption key (`privKey`) for this user.

8. The following information is added to the `cachedSecurityData` block prepared in step 1:
   - `usmUserAuthProtocol`
   - `usmUserAuthKey`
   - `usmUserPrivProtocol`
   - `usmUserPrivKey`

9. A reference or pointer to this cached block is placed in the output parameter `securityStateReference`.

10. The `scopedPdu` is returned to the calling Message Processing Module.

After the return from USM to the Message Processor, the Message Processor subsequently returns the recovered PDU to the Command Responder. Meanwhile, the Message

Processor caches the value of `securityStateReference` that it received in the return from USM, as part of the set of Security Model parameters that it caches (Figure 16.4). Subsequent to that, the Command Responder may prepare a `Response` PDU and then invoke the Message Processor with a `prepareResponseMsg` primitive. The Message Processor will then invoke USM with a `generateResponseMsg` primitive, which has the same input and output parameters as `generateRequestMsg` with one exception: `generateResponseMsg` includes `securityStateReference` as an input parameter. The Message Processor retrieves this value from its cache and passes the value of `security-StateReference` for the incoming `Request` that matches this outgoing `Response`.

The USM performs the following steps upon receipt of `generateResponseMsg`.

1. Using the incoming value of `securityStateReference`, USM retrieves the user information stored in the cache. This is the information from the matching `Request` message processed previously.

2. USM determines if the requested `securityLevel` is supported for this user and, if not, returns an error indication.

3. If the `securityLevel` requests privacy, then the `scopedPdu` value is encrypted using CBC-DES and the localized private encryption key (`privKey`) for this user. The resulting ciphertext is stored in the `scopedPdu` field, and the salt value derived from the `privKey` value is stored in the `msgPrivacyParameters` field of the SNMPv3 message. If privacy is not requested, then the `msgPrivacyParameters` field is set to the NULL string.

4. The `snmpEngineID` parameter is stored in the `msgAuthoritativeEngineID` field of the message.

5. The `securityName` parameter is stored in the `msgUserName` field.

6. The current values of `snmpEngineBoots` and `snmpEngineTime` for this local authoritative engine are stored in the `msgAuthoritativeEngineBoots` and `msg-AuthoritativeEngineTime` fields, respectively. If the `securityLevel` requests authentication, the message authentication code is calculated over the entire message, using HMAC and the localized authentication key (`authKey`) for this user, and stored in `msgAuthenticationParameters`. If the `securityLevel` does not request authentication, the `msgAuthenticationParameters` field is set to the NULL string.

7. The completed message with its length is returned to the calling Message Processing Module.

Step 6 highlights an interesting difference between authoritative and nonauthoritative engines. For a nonauthoritative engine, the values of `msgAuthoritativeEngine-Boots` and `msgAuthoritativeEngineTime` in the message header are set only if the message is to be authenticated by the authoritative receiver. This restriction makes sense, because the authoritative receiver will only check those fields if the message is to be authenticated. However, for a `Response` message from an authoritative engine, the values of `msgAuthoritativeEngineBoots` and `msgAuthoritativeEngineTime` in the message header are always set. Keep in mind that in the case of the authoritative sender, these values represent the "official" local values of `snmpEngineBoots` and `snmp-EngineTime`. When the `Response` message is received by the nonauthoritative engine, it may only use these values for synchronization if the message is authenticated. However, an implementation might perhaps use these values for a "reality check" even on nonauthenticated `Response` messages.

16.2.6 Discovery

USM requires the use of a discovery process to obtain sufficient information about other SNMP engines in order to communicate with them. In particular, a nonauthoritative SNMP engine must learn the `snmpEngineID` value of an authoritative engine before communication may proceed. This process takes one or two steps.

- The nonauthoritative engine sends a `Request` message to the authoritative engine it wishes to discover with a requested `securityLevel` of `noAuthnoPriv`. The message includes a `msgUserName` field with the value "initial" and a null `msg-AuthoritativeEngineID`. The enclosed `Request` PDU has an empty `varBindList`. The authoritative engine will respond with a `Report` message containing its `snmpEngineID` in the `msgAuthoritativeEngineID` field.
- If authenticated communication is required, the nonauthoritative engine needs to establish time synchronization with the authoritative engine. To do this, the nonauthoritative engine sends an authenticated `Request` message with the `msgAuthoritativeEngineID` field set to the value of the newly learned remote `snmpEngineID` and with the values of `msgAuthoritativeEngineBoots` and `msgAuthoritative-EngineTime` set to zero. The response to this authenticated message will be a `Report` message from the authoritative engine with current values of its `snmpEngineBoots` and `snmpEngineTime` carried in the `msgAuthoritativeEngineBoots` and `msg-AuthoritativeEngineTime` fields.

16.2.7 Key Management

A requirement for the use of the authentication and privacy services of SNMPv3 is that, for any communication between a principal on a nonauthoritative engine and a remote authoritative engine, a secret authentication key and a secret privacy key must be shared. These keys enable a user at a nonauthoritative engine (typically a management system) to employ authentication and privacy with remote authoritative systems that the user manages (typically, agent systems). RFC 2274 provides guidelines for the creation, update, and management of these keys.

To simplify the key management burden on principals, each principal is only required to maintain a single authentication key and a single encryption key. These keys are not stored in a MIB and are not accessible via SNMP. In this section we look first at the technique for generating these keys from a password. Then we look at the concept of key localization, which enables a principal to share a unique authentication and encryption key with each remote engine while only maintaining a single authentication and encryption key locally. Finally, we examine the mechanism for key update.

16.2.7.1 Password to Key Algorithm

Recall from Section 16.2.4 that a user requires a 16-octet privacy key and an authentication key either 16 or 20 octets in length. For keys owned by human users, it is desirable that the user be able to employ a human-readable password rather than a bit-string key. Accordingly, RFC 2274 defines an algorithm for mapping from the user password to a 16- or 20-octet key. USM places no restriction on the password itself, but local management policies should dictate that users employ passwords that are not easily guessed. See Stallings (1999) for a discussion of password selection.

Password to key generation is performed as follows.

1. Take the user's password as input and produce a string of length 2^{20} octets (1,048,576 octets) by repeating the password value as many times as necessary, truncating the last value if necessary, to form the string digest0. For example, an 8-character password (2^3 octets) would be concatenated with itself 2^{17} times to form digest0.

2. If a 16-octet key is desired, take the MD5 hash of digest0 to form digest1. If a 20-octet key is desired, take the SHA-1 hash of digest0 to form digest1. The output is the user's key.

One advantage of this technique is that it greatly slows down a brute-force dictionary attack, in which an adversary tries many different potential passwords, generating the key from each one, and then tests whether the resulting key works with the authentication or encryption data available to him or her. For example, if an attacker intercepts an authenticated message, the attacker could try generating the HMAC value with different possible user keys. If a match occurs, the attacker can assume that the password has been discovered. The two-step process outlined above significantly increases the amount of time such an attack will take.

Another advantage of this technique is that it decouples the user's keys from any particular network management system (NMS). No NMS need store values of user keys. Instead, when needed, a user key is generated from that user's password. Blumenthal et al. (1997a) lists the following considerations that motivate the use of a password approach that is independent of NMS.

1. If a key is to be stored rather than generated from a password, one alternative is to maintain a centralized repository of secret keys. But this adversely affects overall reliability and can make troubleshooting impossible if the repository itself is not accessible when needed.

2. On the other hand, if duplicate repositories are maintained, this endangers overall security by providing potential breakers with more targets to attack.

3. If either centralized or multiple duplicate repositories are used, they must be maintained in secure locations. This may reduce the opportunity for "forward camp" establishment during firefighting (that is, troubleshooting when unpredictable segments of the network are inoperative and/or inaccessible for an unpredictable length of time).

A single password could be used to generate a single key for both authentication and encryption. A more secure scheme is to use two passwords, one to generate an authentication key and one to generate a distinct encryption key.

16.2.7.2 Key Localization

A localized key is defined in RFC 2274 as a secret key shared between a user and one authoritative SNMP engine. The objective is that the user need only maintain a single key (or two keys of both authentication and privacy are required) and therefore need only remember one password (or two). The actual secrets shared between a particular user and each authoritative SNMP engine are different. The process by which a single user key is converted into multiple unique keys, one for each remote SNMP engine, is referred to as key localization. Blumenthal et al. (1997b) gives a motivation for this strategy, which we summarize here.

We can define the following goals for key management.

- Every SNMP agent system in a distributed network has its own unique key for every user authorized to manage it. If multiple users are authorized as managers, the agent has a unique authentication key and a unique encryption key for each user. Thus, if the key for one user is compromised, the keys for other users are not compromised.

- The keys for a user on different agents are different. Thus, if an agent is compromised, only the user keys for that agent are compromised and not the user keys in use for other agents.

- Network management can be performed from any point on the network, regardless of the availability of a preconfigured network management system (NMS). This allows a user to perform management functions from any management station. This capability is provided by the password-to-key algorithm described previously.

We can also define the following as things to avoid.

- A user has to remember (or otherwise manage) a large number of keys, a number that grows with the addition of new managed agents.
- An adversary who learns a key for one agent is now able to impersonate any other agent to any user, or any user to any other agent.

To address the preceding goals and considerations, a single user key is mapped by means of a nonreversible one-way function (a secure hash function) into different localized keys for different authenticated engines (different agents). The procedure is as follows.

1. Form the string `digest2` by concatenating `digest1` (described in Section 16.2.7.1), the authoritative engine's `snmpEngineID` value, and `digest1`.
2. If a 16-octet key is desired, take the MD5 hash of `digest2`. If a 20-octet key is desired, take the SHA-1 hash of `digest2`. The output is the user's localized key.

The resulting localized key can then be configured on the agent's system in some secure fashion. Because of the one-way nature of MD5 and SHA-1, it is infeasible for an adversary to learn a user key even if the adversary manages to discover a localized key.

Figure 16.9 summarizes the key localization process.

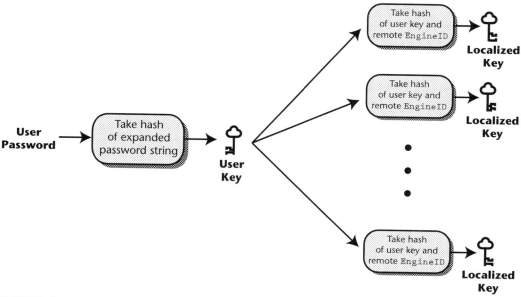

FIGURE 16.9   Key localization

16.2.7.3 Key Update

SNMPv3 assumes that there is some secure means of delivering localized keys to authenticated (agent) systems. This secure delivery is beyond the scope of SNMPv3; it may be manual or by some other secure protocol. Once an initial key (or pair of keys for authentication and privacy) is delivered to an agent, SNMPv3 provides a mechanism for securely updating keys. It is desirable that keys be changed from time to time to enhance security.

A user, on his or her own, could initiate the key change process by request and supply a new password. Alternatively, the NMS could initiate the process by requesting a new password. In either case, the user key at the NMS is updated. The NMS can then calculate a localized key for each communicating agent. The NMS must then securely communicate to each agent to cause that agent to update its localized key. Obviously, the NMS cannot simply send the key in plaintext over the network. Two options present themselves.

- Encrypt the new key using the old key as the encryption key.
- Use some sort of one-way function to produce a value from the old key. Exclusive-OR (XOR) this value with the new key and send the result to the agent. The agent can then XOR the incoming result with the same function applied to the old key to produce the new key.

The first method is straightforward but has the drawback that it requires the use of encryption even in systems that support only message authentication. A related drawback is that export restrictions from the United States and possibly other countries could complicate the use of an encryption-based approach. Accordingly, SNMPv3 uses a variation of the second approach listed above.

The SNMPv3 approach involves the use of the KeyChange objects in the usmUser-Group. A remote principal or NMS sets this object, which is then automatically used by the agent to update the corresponding key. The algorithm defined in RFC 2274 takes into account the possibility that a variable-length key may be used for a particular authentication or encryption algorithm, which complicates the key update algorithm. Here, we present a simplified version that works with the fixed-length DES, HMAC-MD5, and HMAC-SHA algorithms defined for SNMPv3. The algorithm is in two phases, one of which takes place at the requestor engine and one of which takes place at the remote agent engine.

The process begins when a requestor wishes to update an existing key keyOld to a new value keyNew. The requestor performs the following steps.

1. Generate a value *random* either from a pseudorandom number generator or a true random number generator.
2. Compute

$$digest = Hash(keyOld \mathbin{||} random)$$

where Hash is either MD5 or SHA-1, depending on whether a 16-octet or 20-octet key is desired, and the symbol $||$ represents concatenation.

3. Compute

$$delta = digest \oplus keyNew$$
$$protocolKeyChange = (random \mid\mid delta)$$

where $\oplus$ is the exclusive-OR operation.

The value `protocolKeyChange`, which is just the concatenation of `random` and `delta`, is then sent to the agent in a `Set` command to update a `KeyChange` object instance in `usmUserTable` (Figure 16.7). This update causes the receiver to perform the following steps.

1. Compute

$$digest = Hash(keyOld \mid\mid random)$$

2. Compute

$$keyNew = digest \oplus delta$$

The algorithm works as follows. The requestor computes a digest value from the old key and a random number, and sends the random number to the receiver. Because the old key is a shared secret key, the receiver has that key and uses the received random number to compute the same value of digest. The requestor also performs an XOR of the desired `keyNew` and `digest` and sends that value to the receiver as `delta`. The receiver is able to calculate

$$digest \oplus delta = digest \oplus (digest \oplus keyNew) = keyNew$$

By the rules of Boolean algebra, the first two terms in the middle expression cancel, leaving the receiver with the desired value of `keyNew`. Even though an attacker can observe the value of `random`, it is unable to calculate `digest` because the attacker does not know the value of `keyOld`. Similarly, even though the attacker can observe the value of `delta`, it is unable to calculate `keyNew` because the attacker does not know the value of `digest`.

Note that a far easier technique would be to XOR the `keyOld` with `keyNew` and transmit that value. The receiver then takes the XOR of the received value and `keyOld` to produce `keyNew`. Because the attacker does not know `keyOld`, the attacker cannot deduce the value of `keyNew`. However, there are advantages to using the random number and the secure one-way hash function, as pointed out in Blumenthal and Wijnen (1997a).

- The one-way function puts an impenetrable barrier between the old and new keys, so that if the new key is discovered, it is still infeasible to recover the older key.
- Deducing relationship between the bits of the old and new keys is intractable in both directions (forward and backward), so that the cryptanalyst only has the traffic protected by a given key to use in attempting to determine that key.

One other requirement needs to be addressed: Who has authority to update keys? SNMPv3 allows both a network administrator and a user to update a particular user's keys. A network administrator can configure the initial keys for a user and may require that the user change passwords from time to time, and take care of key update when that happens. In addition, a user can change his or her own password and key at any time. To accommodate these two requirements, the usmUser Group contains two key change objects for each of the user's two keys (Figure 16.7). For the authentication key, usmUserAuthKeyChange may be set by the network administrator to cause a key update. The agent system is configured so that only the network administrator has access to this object, permitted by the Access Control Subsystem. The object usmUserOwn-AuthKeyChange is not protected by access control but is defined in such a way that it only permits update if the requestor has the same userName as the usmUserName object for this row. Similarly, usmUserPrivKeyChange and usmUserOwnPrivKeyChange provide update capability for a user's encryption key to the network administrator and user, respectively.

16.3   Summary

RFC 2272 defines a general-purpose message processing capability that can be used with any Security Model. For outgoing messages, the Message Processor is responsible (1) for constructing the message header to attach to the outgoing PDU and (2) for passing the appropriate parameters to the Security Model so that it can perform authentication and privacy functions, if requested. For incoming messages, the Message Processor is responsible (1) for passing the appropriate parameters to the Security Model for authentication and privacy processing and (2) for processing and removing the message header to recover the incoming PDU.

SNMPv3 includes a user-based security model (USM) that uses DES for encryption and HMAC for authentication. USM includes a timeliness function to prevent delay and replay attacks. In addition, USM includes a key management capability that provides for key localization and key update.

SNMPv3

View-Based Access Control Model

This chapter examines the access control model defined in RFC 2275. We begin with a look at the key elements that make up the view-based access control model (VACM). Next, we examine the access control processing logic used to enforce access policy. Then the VACM MIB that supports access control is defined. An appendix to this chapter explains the concepts of view subtrees and view families.

17.1 The VACM Model

The view-based access control model has two important characteristics:

- The VACM determines whether access to a managed object in a local MIB by a remote principal should be allowed.
- The VACM makes use of a MIB that defines the access control policy for this agent, and makes it possible for remote configuration to be used.

In this section, we first look at the elements that make up the VACM model, and then summarize the motivations for this organization.

17.1.1 Elements of the VACM Model

RFC 2275 defines five elements that make up the VACM:

- Groups
- Security level
- Contexts
- MIB views
- Access policy

17.1.1.1 Groups

A group is defined as a set of zero or more <securityModel, securityName> tuples on whose behalf SNMP management objects can be accessed. A securityName refers to a principal, and access rights for all principals in a given group are identical. A unique group-Name is associated with each group. The group concept is a useful tool for categorizing managers with respect to access rights. For example, all top-level managers may have one set of access rights, while intermediate-level managers may have a different set of access rights.

Any given combination of securityModel and securityName can belong to at most one group. That is, for this agent, a given principal whose communications are protected by a given securityModel can only be included in one group.

17.1.1.2 Security Level

The access rights for a group may differ depending on the security level of the message that contains the request. For example, an agent may allow read-only access for a request communicated in an unauthenticated message but may require authentication for write access. Further, for certain sensitive objects, the agent may require that the request and its response be communicated using the privacy service.

17.1.1.3 Contexts

A MIB context is a named subset of the object instances in the local MIB. Contexts provide a useful way of aggregating objects into collections with different access policies.

The context is a concept that relates to access control. When a management station interacts with an agent to access management information at the agent, then the interaction is between a management principal and the agent's SNMP engine, and the access control privileges are expressed in a MIB view that applies to this principal and this context. Contexts have the following key characteristics.

- An SNMP entity, uniquely identified by a contextEngineID, may maintain more than one context.
- An object or an object instance may appear in more than one context.
- When multiple contexts exist, to identify an individual object instance, its context-Name and contextEngineID must be identified in addition to its object type and its instance.

RFC 2275 provides the following example. The managed object type ifDescr (Figure 6.2) provides textual information about an interface. To identify the description of device-X's first network interface, four pieces of information are needed: the contextEngineID of the SNMP entity that provides access to the management information at device-X, the contextName (device-X), the managed object type (ifDescr), and the instance ("1"). This is an example in which a single agent maintains management information for multiple devices.

Figure 17.1 shows an example of an SNMP engine that manages three contexts. The engine makes use of the bridge MIB defined in RFC 1493 (see Table 4.1), but the engine maintains management information for two different bridges, labeled `bridge1` and `bridge2`. This could be a case in which neither bridge implements SNMP and another device on the same LAN collects and maintains management information on behalf of the two bridges. Thus, some object instances within this engine's bridge MIB pertain to `bridge1` and some to `bridge2`. Accordingly, two separate contexts are set up. When a remote manager wishes to access bridge information, it specifies which bridge it is concerned about by using the appropriate context name. The remainder of the management information at this agent pertains to activity at this device and is maintained in a context with a default `contextName` of the empty string.

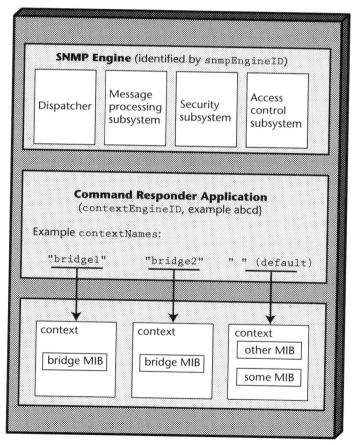

FIGURE 17.1   Example of SNMP contexts (RFC 2271)

17.1.1.4 MIB Views

It is often the case that we would like to restrict the access of a particular group to a subset of the managed objects at an agent. To achieve this objective, access to a context is by means of a MIB view, which defines a specific set of managed objects (and optionally specific object instances). VACM makes use of a powerful and flexible technique for defining MIB views, based on the concepts of view subtrees and view families. The MIB view is defined in terms of a collection, or family, of subtrees, with each subtree being included in or excluded from the view.

Recall that the managed objects in a local database can be organized into a hierarchy, or tree, based on the object identifiers of the objects. This local database comprises a subset of all object types defined according to the Internet standard Structure of Management Information (SMI) and includes object instances whose identifiers conform to the SMI conventions.

SNMPv3 includes the concept of a subtree.[1] A subtree is simply a node in the MIB's naming hierarchy plus all of its subordinate elements. More formally, a subtree may be defined as the set of all objects and object instances that have a common ASN.1 OBJECT IDENTIFIER prefix to their names. The longest common prefix of all of the instances in the subtree is the object identifier of the parent node of that subtree.

Associated with each entry in `vacmAccessTable` are three MIB views, one each for read, write, and notify access. Each MIB view consists of a set of view subtrees. Each view subtree in the MIB view is specified as being included or excluded. That is, the MIB view either includes or excludes all object instances contained in that subtree. In addition, a view mask is defined in order to reduce the amount of configuration information required when fine-grained access control is required (for example, access control at the object instance level). The conventions for defining view subtrees are examined in Appendix 17A.

17.1.1.5 Access Policy

VACM enables an SNMP engine to be configured to enforce a particular set of access rights. Access determination depends on the following factors:

- The *principal* making the access request. The VACM makes it possible for an agent to allow different access privileges for different users. For example, a manager system responsible for network-wide configuration may have broad authority to alter items in the local MIB, while an intermediate-level manager with monitoring responsibility may have read-only access and may further be limited to accessing

---

[1]The subtree concept, in essentially the same form as used in SNMPv3, was first introduced with Secure SNMP (RFC 1353) and was later used in the first version of SNMPv2 (RFC 1447).

only a subset of the local MIB. As was discussed, principals are assigned to groups and access policy is specified with respect to groups.

- The *security level* by which the request was communicated in an SNMP message. Typically, an agent will require the use of authentication for messages containing a set request (write operation).

- The *security model* used for processing the request message. If multiple security models are implemented at an agent, the agent may be configured to provide different levels of access to requests communicated by messages processed by different security models. For example, certain items may be accessible if the request message comes through USM, but not accessible if the Security Model is SNMPv1.

- The *MIB context* for the request.

- The specific *object instance* for which access is requested. Some objects hold more critical or sensitive information than others, and therefore the access policy must depend on the specific object instance requested.

- The *type of access* requested (read, write, notify). Read, write, and notify are distinct management operations, and different access control policies may apply for each of these operations.

17.1.2 Motivation

The concepts that make up VACM appear to result in a rather complex definition of access control. The motivations for introducing these concepts are to clarify the relationships involved in accessing management information and to minimize the storage and processing requirements at the agent. To understand these motivations, consider the following. In SNMPv1 and SNMPv2c, the community string is used to represent the following security-related information:

- The identity of the requesting entity (management station)
- The identity of the performing entity (agent acting for itself or for a proxied entity)
- The identity of the location of the management information to be accessed (agent or proxied entity)
- Authentication information
- Access control information (authorization to perform required operation)
- MIB view information

By lumping all of these concepts into a single variable, flexibility and functionality are lost. VACM provides a similar set of security-related information represented in the following fashion:

Item of Information	Source of Information
Requesting entity	`msgUserName` and `msgSecurityModel` in incoming request message; mapped into `groupName` by VACM
Performing entity	`contextEngineID` in incoming request message
Location of management information	`contextName` in incoming request message
Authentication information	`msgAuthenticationParameters` in incoming request message; not used directly by VACM; message requiring authentication is only accepted by SNMP engine if message is authenticated by USM
Access control information	entry in `vacmAccessTable`, which depends on `group-Name`, `contextName`, `securityModel`, and `security-Level`; the last element is derived from `msgFlags` in incoming request message
MIB view information	view objects in `vacmViewTreeFamilyTable`, which is determined by operation type (read, write, notify), indicated by PDU contained in incoming message and is indexed into from `vacmAccessTable`

This is a substantial improvement over SNMPv1. It uncouples various concepts so that values can be assigned to each one separately.

17.2 *Access Control Processing*

In this section, we look at the functionality of VACM.

17.2.1 Abstract Service Interface

The service provided by the Access Control Subsystem is defined by the Access Control Subsystem primitive, `isAccessAllowed`. This primitive takes the following form (see Table 15.7):

```
statusInformation = -- success or errorIndication isAccessAllowed (
IN   securityModel     -- Security Model in use
IN   securityName      -- principal who wants to access
IN   securityLevel     -- Level of Security
IN   viewType          -- read, write, or notify view
IN   contextName       -- context containing variableName
IN   variableName      -- OID for the managed object )
```

The primitive value `statusInformation` can return one of the following values:

- `accessAllowed`: A MIB view for the principal identified by this `securityName`, with the requested `securityModel`, `securityLevel`, `contextName`, and `viewType`, and which includes the requested `variableName`, was found, and access is granted.

- `notInView`: The MIB view was found, but access is denied because the `variableName` is not included in the MIB view for the specified `viewType`.

- `noSuchView`: No MIB view for the specified `viewType` was found.

- `noSuchContext`: This `contextName` is not supported.

- `noGroupName`: The group defined by the combination of `securityModel` and `securityName` is not supported.

- `noAccessEntry`: There are no MIB views for this combination of `securityModel`, `securityName`, `securityLevel`, and `contextName`.

17.2.2 Inputs to the Access Control Decision

The definition of the `isAccessAllowed` primitive specifies that the input parameters are `securityModel`, `securityName`, `securityLevel`, `viewType`, `contextName`, and `variableName`. All of these parameters are needed to make the access control decision. Put another way, the Access Control Subsystem is defined in such a way as to provide a very flexible tool for configuring access control at the agent, by breaking down the components of the access control decision into six separate variables.

Figure 17.2, adapted from a figure in RFC 2275, provides a useful way of looking at the input variables and shows how the various tables in the VACM MIB come into play in making the access control decision:

- *Who:* The combination of `securityModel` and `securityName` define the *who* of this operation; it identifies a given principal whose communications are protected by a given `securityModel`. This combination belongs to at most one group at this SNMP engine. The `vacmSecurityToGroupTable` provides the `groupName`, given the `securityModel` and `securityName`.

- *Where:* The `contextName` specifies *where* the desired management object is to be found. The `vacmContextTable` contains a list of the recognized `contextNames`.

- *How:* The combination of `securityModel` and `securityLevel` define *how* the incoming `request` or `Inform` PDU was protected. The combination of who, where, and how identify zero or one entries in `vacmAccessTable`.

- *Why:* The `viewType` specifies *why* access is requested: for a read, write, or notify operation. The selected entry in `vacmAccessTable` contains one MIB `viewName`

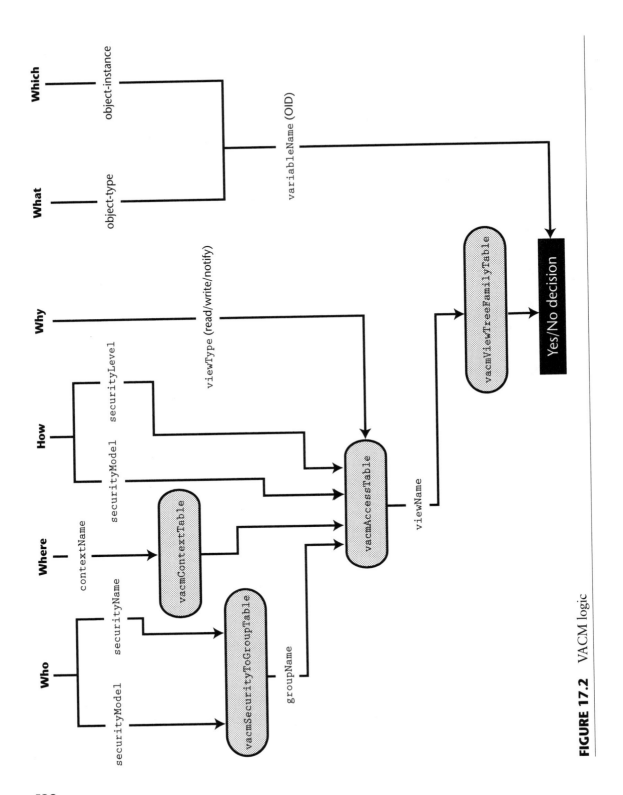

FIGURE 17.2 VACM logic

for each of these three types of operation, and `viewType` is used to select a specific `viewName`. This `viewName` selects the appropriate MIB view from `vacmViewTree-FamilyTable`.

- *What:* The `variableName` is an object identifier whose prefix identifies a specific object type and whose suffix identifies a specific object instance. The object type indicates *what* type of management information is requested.

- *Which:* The object instance indicates *which* specific item of information is requested.

Finally, the `variableName` is compared to the retrieved MIB view. If the `variable-Name` matches an element included in the MIB view, then access is granted.

17.2.3 Access Control Logic

We can now summarize the procedures used by VACM to determine if access is allowed. When `isAccessAllowed` is invoked by an application, VACM performs the following steps (Figure 17.3).

1. VACM checks to see if there is an entry in `vacmContextTable` for this `context-Name`. If so, then this context is known to this SNMP engine. If not, then an `errorIndication` of `noSuchContext` is returned.

2. VACM checks `vacmSecurityToGroupTable` to determine if there is a group assigned to this `<securityModel, securityName>` pair. If so, then this principal, operating under this `securityModel`, is a member of a group configured at this SNMP engine. If not, then an `errorIndication` of `noGroupName` is returned.

3. VACM next consults the `vacmAccessTable` with `groupName`, `contextName`, `securityModel`, and `securityLevel` as indices. If an entry is found, then an access control policy has been defined for this `groupName`, operating under this `securityModel`, at this `securityLevel`, for access to this `contextName`. If not, then an `errorIndication` of `noAccessEntry` is returned.

4. VACM then determines whether the selected `vacmAccessTable` entry includes reference to a MIB view of `viewType`. If so, then this entry contains a `viewName` for this combination of `groupName`, `contextName`, `securityModel`, `securityLevel`, and `viewType`. If not, then an `errorIndication` of `noSuchView` is returned.

5. The `viewName` from step 4 is used as an index into `vacmViewTreeFamilyTable`. If a MIB view is found, then a MIB view has been configured for this `viewName`. If not, then an `errorIndication` of `noSuchView` is returned.

6. VACM checks the `variableName` against the selected MIB view. If this variable is included in the view, then a `statusInformation` of `accessAllowed` is returned. If not, then an `errorIndication` of `notInView` is returned.

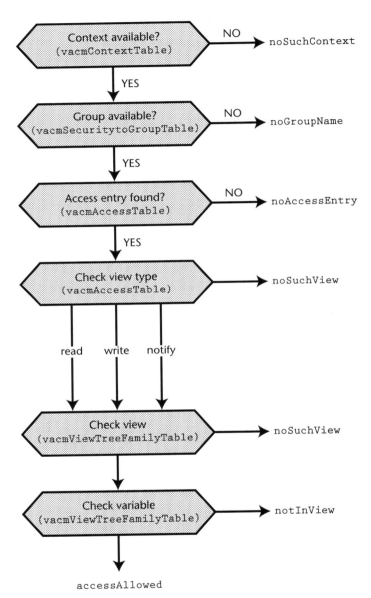

FIGURE 17.3   VACM flowchart

17.3 *The VACM MIB*

We now turn to a detailed look at the VACM MIB that supports access control processing. Figure 17.4 provides an overall view of the MIB structure. The VACM MIB contains information in the following categories:

- Local contexts
- Groups
- Access rights
- MIB Views

17.3.1 Information About Local Contexts

The `vacmContextTable` lists the locally available contexts by name; this information is used by Command Generator applications to configure the `vacmAccessTable` to control access to all contexts at the SNMP entity. The `vacmContextTable` itself is read-only and cannot be configured by SNMP operation. Each entry in the table is a human-readable name identifying a particular context at a particular SNMP entity. An empty (zero length) context name represents the default context.

The `vacmContextTable` is independent of the `vacmAccessTable`. That is, at any time there may be a context listed in `vacmContextTable` for which there are not entries in `vacmAccessTable` that reference that context, and there may be an entry in `vacm-AccessTable` that references a context that does not currently exist and that therefore has no current entry in `vacmContextTable`.

17.3.2 Information About Groups

This `vacmSecurityToGroupTable` provides a `groupName` given a `securityModel` and `securityName`. The `groupName` is used to define an access control policy for a group of principals (which may consist of a single principal) under a given security model. The table is indexed by `vacmSecurityModel` and `vacmSecurityName`, and the value of `vacmGroupName` is used to index into `vacmAccessTable`.

17.3.3 Information About Access Rights

The `vacmAccessTable` can be configured to define access rights for groups. For a given group, access rights may be defined for one or more contexts, one or more security models, and one or more security levels. Thus, there may be multiple entries in `vacmAccess-Table` for a particular `groupName`. To spell this out:

1. A context refers to a subset of the object instances at the local MIB. For a particular group, access rights may be defined for more than one context.

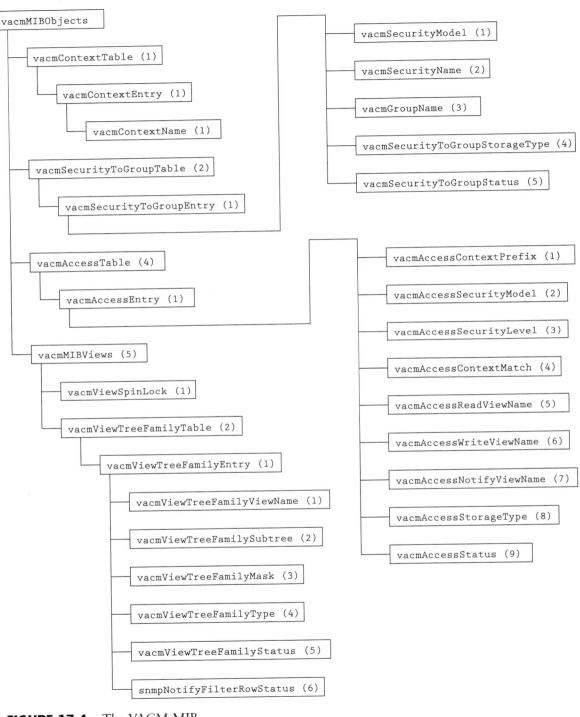

FIGURE 17.4 The VACM MIB

2. If an agent supports more than one Security Model, then access rights for a group may be defined separately with respect to each Security Model. Within a given Security Model, the group access rights may be enumerated for multiple contexts.

3. The access rights of a group to a particular context under a particular Security Model may depend on the security level of the exchange. Thus, a group may have greater access rights to a particular context under a particular Security Model if authentication is employed compared to when authentication is not employed.

Furthermore, for a given group, context, Security Model, and security level, the scope of information that may be accessed may differ for read, write, and notify actions.

We first list and briefly define the objects in `vacmAccessTable`. We then explain the rather complex logic by which an entry in this table is retrieved. In addition to the usual storage type and status objects, each row of the table contains the following objects:

- `vacmAccessContextPrefix`: This is an octet string that is either treated as a full context name or the prefix of a context name, depending on the value of `vacmAccessContextMatch` for this row.

- `vacmAccessSecurityModel`: Identifies a particular security model (for example, any, SNMPv1, SNMPv2c, USM). In order to gain the access rights allowed by this row, this `securityModel` must be in use.

- `vacmAccessSecurityLevel`: The minimum security level required in order to gain the access rights allowed by this row (for example, `noAuthnoPriv`, `authNoPriv`, `authPriv`).

- `vacmAccessContextMatch`: If the value of this object is `exact(1)`, then there must be an exact match between the `contextName` supplied and the value of `vacmAccessContextPrefix` in order to select this row. If the value is `prefix(2)`, then there need only be a match between `vacmAccessContextPrefix` and the starting octets of `contextName`. This allows for a simple form of wildcarding. For example, 'bridge' is a prefix of both 'bridge1' and 'bridge2'.

- `vacmAccessReadViewName`: The value of this object indexes into `vacmViewTreeFamilyTable`, and identifies the MIB view to which this conceptual row authorizes read access.

- `vacmAccessWriteViewName`: The value of this object indexes into `vacmViewTreeFamilyTable`, and identifies the MIB view to which this conceptual row authorizes write access.

- `vacmAccessNotifyViewName`: The value of this object indexes into `vacmViewTreeFamilyTable`, and identifies the MIB view to which this conceptual row authorizes access for notification.

The indices into this table are `vacmGroupName`, `vacmAccessContextPrefix`, `vacmAccessSecurityModel`, and `vacmSecurityLevel`. This makes it possible to select a row on the basis of four values: `groupName`, `contextName`, `securityModel`, and `securityLevel`. However, it is a bit more complicated than that, because RFC 2275 provides the user with great flexibility in setting up this table. Selection of a row is essentially a two-phase process. In the first phase, a set of rows is selected that is compatible with a given `groupName`, `contextName`, `securityModel`, and `security-Level`. If multiple rows are compatible, then a second phase is used to select the most "appropriate" row.

The first phase consists of the following steps.

1. Select all entries with `vacmGroupName` = `groupName`. That is, for a given supplied value of `groupName`, select all entries for which the index object `vacmGroupName` has a value of `groupName`. This is an example of indexing with an external object, which was described in Section 10.1.4.1.

2. Among those entries selected in step 1, discard all entries except for (1) those for which `vacmContextPrefix` = `contextName` plus (2) those for which `vacm-ContextMatch` = `'prefix'` and `vacmContextPrefix` is a prefix of `contextName`.

3. Among those entries remaining after step 2, discard all entries except for (1) those in which `vacmSecurityModel` = `securityModel` plus (2) those with `vacmSecurity-Model` = `'any'`.

4. Among those entries remaining after step 3, retain only those entries for which `vacmSecurityLevel` is less than or equal to `securityLevel`. The `security-Level` values are ordered such that `noAuthNoPriv` is less than `authNoPriv`, and `authNoPriv` is less than `authPriv`.

Figure 17.5 expresses this selection process in terms of the union and intersection of sets of table entries. If the result of this selection process is a single entry, then that is the entry to be used. If, on the other hand, multiple entries remain, then the second phase consists of the following steps, used to eliminate all but one entry.

1. If there is at least one entry with `vacmSecurityModel` = `securityModel`, discard all entries with `vacmSecurityModel` = `'any'`. A specific `securityModel` designation takes precedence over a wildcard designation.

2. If more than one entry remains after step 1, and there is at least one entry with `vacmContextPrefix` = `contextName`, discard all entries that do not have such an exact match. An exact match takes precedence over a prefix (wildcard) match.

3. If more than one entry remains after step 2, discard all entries with `vacmContext-Prefix` values shorter than the longest remaining entry.

4. If more than one entry remains after step 3, select the entry with the highest `securityLevel`.

Use groupName, contextName, securityModel, and securityLevel as index values to index into vacmAccessTable

Define the following sets:

G   = {entries with vacmGroupName = groupName}

C1   = {entries with vacmContextPrefix = contextName}

C2   = {entries with (vacmContextMatch = 'prefix') AND
          (vacmContextPrefix = prefix of contextName) }

SM1 = {entries with vacmSecurityModel = securityModel}

SM2 = {entries with vacmSecurityModel = 'any'}

SL   = {entries with vacmSecurityLevel ≤ securityLevel}

The set E of possible matches is:

$$E = G \cap (C2 \cup C2) \cap (SM1 \cup SM2) \cap SL$$

FIGURE 17.5   Set logic for vacmAccessTable

17.3.4 Information About MIB Views

The structure vacmMIBViews consists of a single scalar object, vacmViewSpinLock, and the table vacmViewTreeFamilyTable. The object vacmViewSpinLock, of type TestandIncr (see Appendix 13A), enables cooperating Command Generator applications to coordinate their use of the Set operation in creating and modifying views.

In addition to the usual storage type and row status objects, vacmViewTreeFamilyTable includes the following columnar objects:

- vacmViewTreeFamilyViewName: The name assigned to a set of rows constituting a single view.

- vacmViewTreeFamilySubtree: An object identifier which specifies a subtree that, in combination with the corresponding instance of vacmViewTreeFamilyMask, defines a family of subtrees.

- vacmViewTreeFamilyMask: The bit mask which, in combination with the corresponding instance of vacmViewTreeFamilySubtree, defines a family of subtrees.

- vacmViewTreeFamilyType: Takes on the value included(1) or excluded(2). Indicates whether the corresponding family of subtrees defined by Subtree and Mask is included or excluded from the definition.

The vacmViewTreeFamilyTable is indexed by two objects. The first is vacmViewTreeFamilyViewName, which is the object used to index from vacmAccessTable via vacmAccessReadViewName, vacmAccessWriteViewName, or vacmAccessNotifyViewName. The second index object is vacmViewTreeFamilySubtree, which defines a single subtree entry in the table, as explained below. There may be multiple subtrees (multiple entries) associated with a given `viewName`, in which case the MIB view for this `viewName` consists of the union of all such subtrees.

Each entry in `vacmViewTreeFamilyTable` defines a family of MIB subtrees, using the subtree, mask, and type columnar objects. This technique is also used in notification filtering, described in Chapter 15. Appendix 17A provides a detailed explanation of how a subtree family is defined. In essence, a subtree consists of a MIB object plus all objects that are subordinate to it in the naming hierarchy. It is possible to exclude certain portions of this subtree so that one is left not with a complete subtree but only a partial subtree, consisting of a MIB object and some of its subordinate objects. This is a family of subtrees. If we then group multiple entries, we can define an arbitrary collection of MIB objects to be used for some purpose.

17.3.5 Parameters for Initial Configuration

RFC 2275 suggests that an initial configuration of the VACM MIB be set up during installation of an SNMP engine that supports VACM. It will help clarify the relationship among the various tables in the VACM MIB to study one of these configurations.

Three possible security configurations are defined in the document:

- Initial-no-access-configuration
- Initial-semi-security-configuration
- Initial-minimum-security-configuration

For the initial-no-access-configuration, there is no initial configuration and no access is allowed to the local MIB at the time of system installation. The remaining two configurations have the same entries in `vacmContextTable`, `vacmSecurityToGroup-Table`, and `vacmAccessTable`, and differ only in the `vacmViewTreeFamilyTable`. Table 17.1 shows the parameters for the initial-semi-security-configuration. For all of the tables, the storage type and row status objects are omitted for conciseness.

The `vacmContextTable` is initially configured with a single entry that has the `contextName` of the empty string. By convention, this is the default context. Similarly, the `vacmSecurityToGroupTable` is initially configured with a single entry. This entry specifies the USM `securityModel`, a `securityName` of "initial," and a `groupName` of "initial." Access privileges will be configured for this `groupName`. Subsequently, if the configuration manager for this system wishes to expand the use of this semi-security configuration, he or she can add more `securityNames` to this `groupName`. No other changes would be required.

Having defined a context and a group, we need to define the MIB views within that context to which this group has access. Requests may arrive from the group with three levels of message protection: no protection, authentication only, and authentication plus

TABLE 17.1 VACM MIB Parameters for Initial Semi-Security Configuration

(a) vacmContextTable

vacmContextName
" "

(b) vacmSecurityToGroupTable

vacmSecurityModel	vacmSecurityName	vacmGroupName
3 (USM)	"initial"	"initial"

(c) vacmAccessTable

vacmGroupName (external index)	vacmAccess ContextPrefix	vacmAccess SecurityModel	vacmAccess SecurityLevel	vacmAccess ReadViewName	vacmAccess WriteViewName	vacmAccess NotifyViewName
"initial"	" "	3 (USM)	noAuthNoPriv	"restricted"	" "	"restricted"
"initial"	" "	3 (USM)	authNoPriv	"internet"	"internet"	"internet"
"initial"	" "	3 (USM)	authPriv	"internet"	"internet"	"internet"

(d) vacmViewTreeFamilyTable

vacmViewTreeFamilyViewName	vacmViewTreeFamilySubtree	vacmViewTreeFamilyMask	vacmViewTreeFamilyType
"internet"	1.3.6.1	" "	1 (included)
"restricted"	1.3.6.1.2.1.1	" "	1 (included)
"restricted"	1.3.6.1.2.1.11	" "	1 (included)
"restricted"	1.3.6.1.6.3.7.2.1	" "	1 (included)
"restricted"	1.3.6.1.6.3.8.2.1	" "	1 (included)
"restricted"	1.3.6.1.6.3.9.2.1	" "	1 (included)

541

privacy. The `vacmAccessTable` is configured for this `groupName`, `contextName`, and `securityModel` as follows.

1. For unprotected communication (`noAuthNoPriv`), access is allowed to a restricted MIB view for read and notify operations, and no access is allowed for write operations.
2. For communications protected either with authentication or authentication plus privacy, access is allowed to the "internet" MIB view, which, as we shall see, refers to the entire "internet" subtree of MIB-II (see Figure 5.1).

All that remains is to define the MIB views that correspond to the `viewNames` "internet" and "restricted." This is done in `vacmViewTreeFamilyTable`. There is one entry for "internet". This entry has a subtree value of 1.3.6.1, which is the object identifier for the MIB-II internet object. Thus, we can make the following statement: For all principals who are members of the "initial" group, who communicate a request using authentication or authentication plus privacy using the USM `securityModel`, access to the entire "internet" subtree under the `contextName` " " is granted for read, write, and notify operations. At installation time, the only principal that is a member of that group is the principal with `securityName` "initial".

The remaining five entries in `vacmViewTreeFamilyTable` have a `vacmViewTreeFamilyViewName` value of "restricted". Therefore, when this table is indexed using a `viewName` of "restricted", the MIB view is defined by the collection of these five entries. Each of these five entries has a type of `included`, and each includes a different subtree. Thus, the MIB view defined by these five entries consists of the union of the following subtrees of MIB-II:

- The MIB-II system group (1.3.6.1.2.1.1), which provides general information about the managed system.
- The MIB-II snmp group (1.3.6.1.2.1.11), which provides information related to the implementation and execution experience of SNMP on this system.
- `snmpEngine` (1.3.6.1.6.3.7.2.1), defined in RFC 2271. This subtree includes `snmpEngineID`, `snmpEngineBoots`, `snmpEngineTime`, and `snmpEngineMaxMessageSize` for this engine.
- `snmpMPDStats` (1.3.6.1.6.3.8.2.1), defined in RFC 2272. This subtree includes three counters related to SNMPv3 message traffic.
- `usmStats` (1.3.6.1.6.3.9.2.1), defined in RFC 2274. This subtree includes six counters related to USM processing of message traffic.

Thus, we can make the following statement: For all principals who are members of the "initial" group, who communicate a request without authentication using the USM `securityModel`, access to the "restricted" set of subtrees under the `contextName` " " is granted for read and notify operations. In addition, access to the "internet" set of sub-trees is granted for read, write, and notify operations for a request communicated with authentication. At installation time, the only principal that is a member of that group is the principal with `securityName` "initial".

17.4 Summary

The view-based access control model is defined in RFC 2275. The VACM implements the services required for the Access Control Subsystem. VACM makes an access control decision (access allowed/denied) on the basis of the principal asking for access, the security model and security level used for communicating the principal's request, the context to which access is requested, the type of access requested (read, write, notify), and the actual object for which access is requested.

APPENDIX 17A   *THE USE OF SUBTREES AND MASKS*

SNMPv3 defines the use of subtrees and masks to identify subsets of managed objects in a concise and flexible manner. This capability is used in the `snmpNotifyObjects` group, described in Chapter 15, and also for purposes of access control, described in this chapter.

In this appendix, we first introduce the concept of a table of subtrees. Next, an example is given to illustrate the use of subtrees and masks. Finally, the specific rules governing the definition of subtrees and masks are explained.

17A.1   Subtrees

In Section 17.1, we introduced the concept of a subtree, which is a node in the MIB's naming hierarchy plus all of its subordinate elements. More formally, a *subtree* may be defined as the set of all objects and object instances that have a common ASN.1 object identifier prefix to their names. The longest common prefix of all of the instances in the subtree is the object identifier of the parent node of that subtree.

Using an appropriately constructed SNMP table, it is possible to define a set of subtrees. Each subtree in the set is specified as being included or excluded. That is, the table either includes or excludes all object instances contained in that subtree. In addition, a mask is defined in order to reduce the amount of configuration information required when fine-grained definition is required (for example, definition at the individual object level).

A table that makes use of subtrees to define subsets of managed objects is organized as follows. Each conceptual row in the table includes an instance of the following columnar objects:

- *Subtree:* An object identifier which specifies a subtree that, in combination with the corresponding instance of Mask, defines a family of subtrees.
- *Mask:* The bit mask which, in combination with the corresponding instance of Subtree, defines a family of subtrees.
- *Type:* Takes on the value `included(1)` or `excluded(2)`. Indicates whether the corresponding family of subtrees defined by Subtree and Mask is included or excluded from the definition.

A set of entries in the table, chosen in some fashion, defines a collection of subtree families used for a purpose such as access control or filtering. Each entry in the table represents a family of subtrees that, according to the status of the entry, are either included or excluded.

17A.2 Subtree Examples

Perhaps the best way to explain the conventions for defining a family of subtrees is by first looking at an example.[2] Table 17.2(a) shows families defined for two principals, lucy and ricky.

The lucy group includes all of the objects in the subtree defined by the MIB-2 object identifier for the system group. That is, all of the objects in the system group are included in lucy's MIB family. The next entry for lucy specifies that the subtree identified by { if-Entry 0 2 } is included in the family. Referring back to Figure 6.2, we see that `ifEntry` defines a conceptual row in `ifTable` in the `Interfaces` group of MIB-2. This table is indexed by the columnar object `ifIndex`. Now, the object identifier for `ifEntry` is 1.3.6.1.2.1.2.2.1, which is derived as follows:

```
iso  org  dod  internet  mgmt  mib-2  interfaces  ifTable  ifEntry
 1    3    6      1        2      1        2          2        1
```

Recall that the rules for specifying object identifiers for object instances within a table dictate that the identifier consists of the identifier for the columnar object followed by the value of the index variable or variables. In this case, the index variable is `ifIndex`. So, for example, the object identifier for the columnar object `ifType` is { `ifEntry 3` }, which is 1.3.6.1.2.1.2.2.1.3. An object instance of `ifType` for interface number 2 (value of `if-Index` = 2) is therefore written as:

```
{ifEntry 3 2} = { ifType 2 } = 1.3.6.1.2.1.2.2.1.3.2
```

Now, there is no such columnar object that can be expressed as { `ifEntry 0` } and therefore no object instance that can be expressed as { `ifEntry 0 2` }. However, the latter expression can be interpreted to mean: "all object instances in `ifTable` for which `ifIndex` = 2"; that is, { `ifEntry 0 2` } refers to all object instances related to the second network interface. This interpretation is confirmed by the mask associated with this family name, as shown in Table 17.2(b). The mask has a hexadecimal value of FFA0. Reading from left to right, each bit of the mask is matched against the corresponding subidentifier of the family name. If the mask bit is 1, the subidentifier is used; if the mask bit is 0, then the corresponding subidentifier position is treated as a "wildcard" in which any value may appear. Thus it doesn't matter in this case what value of x appears in the expression { `ifEntry x 2` }; the mask dictates that all objects with identifiers of the form 1.3.6.1.2.1.2.2.1.x.2 are part of the family of subtrees defined by this entry.

The next entry in lucy's table has the name { `ifSpeed 2` }. The family mask is a zero-length string. By convention, such a bit mask is extended with 1's to be the same

---

[2]This example is based on one that appeared in RFC 1351, which dealt with the old Secure SNMP; it is valid for SNMPv3.

TABLE 17.2   An Example of the Use of Subtrees and Masks

(a) Subtrees and masks for lucy and ricky

Name	Type	Subtree	Mask
lucy	included	system	" "h
lucy	included	{ ifEntry 0 2 }	"FFA0"h
lucy	excluded	{ ifSpeed 2 }	" "h
ricky	included	icmp	" "h
ricky	included	{ ifEntry 0 5 }	"FFA0"h
ricky	included	{ ifInOctets 4 }	" "h

(b) Detail for lucy

Include:

Family Name = { ifEntry 0 2 }

1	3	6	1	2	1	2	2	1	0	2

Family Mask = "FFA0"h

1	1	1	1	1	1	1	1	1	0	1

Exclude:

Family Name = { ifSpeed 2 }

1	3	6	1	2	1	2	2	1	5	2

Family Mask = " "h

1	1	1	1	1	1	1	1	1	1	1

(c) Detail for ricky

Include:

Family Name = { ifEntry 0 5 }

1	3	6	1	2	1	2	2	1	0	5

Family Mask = "FFA0"h

1	1	1	1	1	1	1	1	1	0	1

Include:

Family Name = { ifInOctets 2 }

1	3	6	1	2	1	2	2	1	10	4

Family Mask = " "h

1	1	1	1	1	1	1	1	1	1	1

length in bits as the number of subidentifiers in the family name. Thus, there are no wild-cards and this entry identifies the subtree { ifSpeed 2 }. Now, according to the preceding entry, all object instances in the second row of ifTable are included, which would include ifSpeed for the second row. By this entry, ifSpeed for the second row is excluded. When an identifier is part of two or more families, the family name with the greatest number of subidentifiers dominates. If two or more family names have the same number of subidentifiers, then the family name that is lexicographically largest dominates. We have:

{ ifSpeed 2 } = 1.3.6.1.2.1.2.2.1.5.2 > 1.3.6.1.2.1.2.2.1.0.2 = { ifEntry 0 2 }

Therefore, the third entry in Table 17.2(a) takes precedence over the second entry. In summary, the subtree family for lucy consists of the system group plus the conceptual row of ifTable for which ifIndex = 2, with the exception of ifSpeed.

Three entries in the table serve to identify the subtree family for ricky. The first entry specifies that the icmp group of MIB-II is included. The second entry specifies that the conceptual row of ifTable for which ifIndex = 5 is included. Finally, the third entry specifies that the columnar object ifInOctets, from ifTable, for which ifIndex = 4 is included.

17A.3 Conventions

As was mentioned, a table for defining subtree families includes subtree, mask, and type columnar objects. Each instance of a mask object contains a bit mask that, in combination with the corresponding instance of a subtree object, defines a family of subtrees. Each bit of the mask corresponds to one subidentifier of the object identifier value of Subtree, according to the following conventions.

- The most significant bit of the mask corresponds to the first subidentifier; the second most significant bit of the mask corresponds to the second subidentifier; and so on.
- If there are more bits in the mask than subidentifiers in the subtree value, the excess least significant bits of the mask are ignored.
- If there are fewer bits in the mask than subidentifiers in Subtree, the mask is extended, from the least-significant side, with 1's to be the required length.
- If the mask bit is 1, the corresponding subidentifier is used; if the mask bit is 0, any value may appear in the corresponding subidentifier position (wildcard).

Consider an object instance x with the object identifier $x_1.x_2.x_3...x_n$ and consider an entry in the table with a subtree value of $v_1.v_2.v_3...v_k$ and a mask value of $m_1m_2m_3...m_k$. In the notation of the preceding sentence, x_i is the ith subidentifier of x, v_i is the ith subidentifier of the subtree, and m_i is the ith bit of the mask, where the mask has been adjusted to have the same length in bits as the subtree has in subidentifiers. Object instance x is said to be contained in the family of subtrees defined by an entry in a table if the following conditions are met:

- $n \geq k$, AND
- For each subidentifier v_i of the subtree, either:
$$m_i = 0 \quad \text{OR} \quad x_i = v_i$$

Finally, to determine if a specific object is included in the collection of subtree families defined by multiple rows of the defining table, the object identifier x of the object is compared to each relevant entry in the table, according to the following rules.

1. If none of the entries match (x is not contained in the family of subtrees defined by any entry), then x is not in the collection.

2. If exactly one of the entries match, then x is included in, or excluded from, the collection according to the value of the type object in that row.

3. If more than one of the entries match, then:

   a. If one of the matching entries has a subtree value with more subidentifiers than that of any other matching entry, then that entry determines inclusion or exclusion; otherwise

   b. Among those entries with the equal, largest number of subidentifiers, the lexicographically greatest instance of a subtree value determines the inclusion or exclusion.

Appendices

APPENDIX A   *The TCP/IP Protocol Suite*

When communication is desired among computers from different vendors, the software development effort can be a nightmare. Different vendors use different data formats and data exchange protocols. Even within one vendor's product line, different model computers may communicate in unique ways.

As the use of computer communications and computer networking proliferates, a one-at-a-time, special-purpose approach to communications software development is too costly to be acceptable. The only alternative is for computer vendors to adopt and implement a common set of conventions. For this to happen, standards are needed. Such standards have two benefits:

- Vendors feel encouraged to implement the standards because of an expectation that their products would be less marketable without them, because of wide usage of the standards.

- Customers are in a position to require that the standards be implemented by any vendor wishing to propose equipment to them.

Any distributed application, such as electronic mail or client/server interaction, requires a complex set of communications functions for proper operation. Many of these functions, such as reliability mechanisms, are common across many or even all applications. Thus, the communications task is best viewed as consisting of a modular architecture in which the various elements perform the various required functions. Hence, before one can develop standards, there should be a structure, or *protocol architecture*, that defines the communications tasks.

Two protocol architectures have served as the basis for the development of interoperable communications standards: the TCP/IP protocol suite and the OSI reference model (compared in Figure A.1). TCP/IP is the most widely used interoperable architecture. In this section, we provide a brief overview of TCP/IP.

The TCP/IP architecture is a result of protocol research and development conducted on the experimental packet-switched network, ARPANET, funded by the Defense Advanced Research Projects Agency (DARPA), and is generally referred to as the TCP/IP

FIGURE A.1   A comparison of the OSI and TCP/IP communications architectures

protocol suite. This protocol suite consists of a large collection of protocols that the Internet Activities Board (IAB) has issued as Internet standards.

A.1   Operation of TCP and IP

In general terms, communications can be said to involve three agents: applications, computers, and networks. Examples of applications include file transfer and electronic mail. The applications that we are concerned with here are distributed applications that involve the exchange of data between two computer systems. These applications, and others, execute on computers that can often support multiple simultaneous applications. Computers are connected to networks, and the data to be exchanged are transferred by the network from one computer to another. Thus, the transfer of data from one application to another involves first getting the data to the computer in which the application resides and then getting it to the intended application within the computer.

With these concepts in mind, it appears natural to organize the communication task into four relatively independent layers:

• Network access layer

- Internet layer
- Host-to-host layer
- Process layer

The *network access layer* is concerned with the exchange of data between an end system (server, workstation, etc.) and the network to which it is attached. The sending computer must provide the network with the address of the destination computer, so that the network may route the data to the appropriate destination. The sending computer may wish to invoke certain services, such as priority, that might be provided by the network. The specific software used at this layer depends on the type of network to be used; different standards have been developed for circuit switching, packet switching (for example, X.25), local area networks (for example, Ethernet), and others. Thus, it makes sense to separate those functions pertaining to network access into a separate layer. By doing this, the remainder of the communications software, above the network access layer, need not be concerned about the specifics of the network to be used. The same higher-layer software should function properly regardless of the particular network to which the computer is attached.

The network access layer is concerned with access to and routing data across a network for two end systems attached to the same network. In those cases where two devices are attached to different networks, procedures are needed to allow data to traverse multiple interconnected networks. This is the function of the *internet layer*. The Internet Protocol (IP) is used at this layer to provide the routing function across multiple networks. This protocol is implemented not only in the end systems but also in routers. A *router* is a processor that connects two networks and whose primary function is to relay data from one network to the other on its route from the source to the destination end system.

Regardless of the nature of the applications that are exchanging data, there is usually a requirement that data be exchanged reliably. That is, we would like to be assured that all of the data arrive at the destination application and in the same order in which they were sent. As we shall see, the mechanisms for providing reliability are essentially independent of the nature of the applications. Thus, it makes sense to collect those mechanisms in a common layer shared by all applications; this is referred to as the *host-to-host layer*. The Transmission Control Protocol (TCP) provides this functionality.

Finally, the *process layer* contains the logic needed to support the various user applications. For each different type of application, such as file transfer, a separate module is needed that is peculiar to that application.

A.2   *The TCP/IP Layers*

Figure A.2 indicates how these protocols are configured for communications. To make clear that the total communications facility may consist of multiple networks, the con-

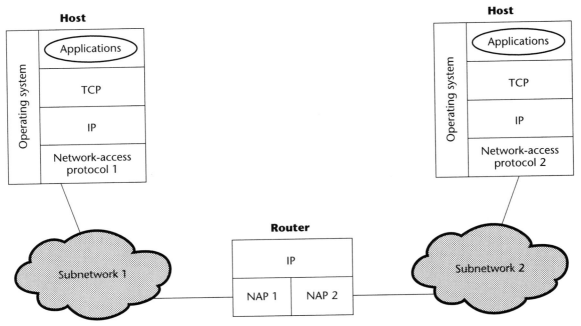

FIGURE A.2   Communications using the TCP/IP protocol architecture

stituent networks are usually referred to as *subnetworks*. Some sort of network access protocol, such as the Ethernet logic, is used to connect a computer to a subnetwork. This protocol enables the host to send data across the subnetwork to another host or, in the case of a host on another subnetwork, to a router. IP is implemented in all of the end systems and the routers. It acts as a relay to move a block of data from one host, through one or more routers, to another host. TCP is implemented only in the end systems; it keeps track of the blocks of data to assure that all are delivered reliably to the appropriate application.

For successful communication, every entity in the overall system must have a unique address. Actually, two levels of addressing are needed. Each host on a subnetwork must have a unique global internet address; this allows the data to be delivered to the proper host. Each process with a host must have an address that is unique within the host; this allows the host-to-host protocol (TCP) to deliver data to the proper process. These latter addresses are known as *ports*.

Let us trace a simple operation. Suppose that a process, associated with port 1 at host *A*, wishes to send a message to another process, associated with port 2 at host *B*. The process at *A* gives the message to TCP with instructions to send it to host *B*, port 2. TCP passes the message to IP with instructions to send it to host *B*. Note that IP need not be told the identity of the destination port. All that it needs to know is that the data are intended for host *B*. Next, IP relays the message to the network access layer (for example, Ethernet logic), with instructions to send it to router *X* (the first hop on the way to *B*).

To control this operation, control information as well as user data must be transmitted, as suggested in Figure A.3. Let us say that the sending process generates a block of data and passes this to TCP. TCP may break this block into smaller pieces to make the data more manageable. To each of these pieces, TCP appends control information known as the TCP header, forming a *TCP segment*. The control information is to be used by the peer TCP protocol entity at host *B*. Examples of items included in this header are as follows:

- *Destination port:* When the TCP entity at *B* receives the segment, it must know to whom the data are to be delivered.

- *Sequence number:* TCP numbers the segments that it sends to a particular destination port sequentially, so that if they arrive out of order, the TCP entity at *B* can reorder them.

- *Checksum:* The sending TCP includes a code that is a function of the contents of the remainder of the segment. The receiving TCP performs the same calculation and compares the result with the incoming code. A discrepancy results if there has been some error in transmission.

Next, TCP hands each segment over to IP, with instructions to transmit it to *B*. These segments must be transmitted across one or more subnetworks and relayed through one or more intermediate routers. This operation, too, requires the use of control information. Thus IP appends a header of control information to each segment, to

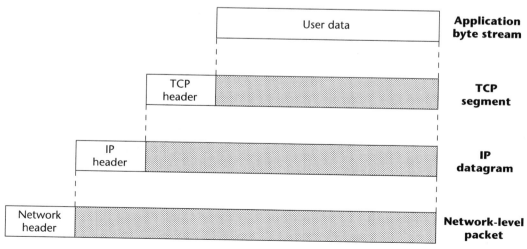

FIGURE A.3   Protocol data units in the TCP/IP architecture

form an *IP datagram.* An example of an item stored in the IP header is the destination host address (in this example, *B*).

Finally, each IP datagram is presented to the network access layer for transmission across the first subnetwork in its journey to the destination. The network access layer appends its own header, creating a *packet,* or *frame.* The packet is transmitted across the subnetwork to router *X*. The packet header contains the information that the subnetwork needs to transfer the data across the subnetwork. Examples of items that may be contained in this header include

- *Destination subnetwork address:* The subnetwork must know to which attached device the packet is to be delivered.
- *Facilities requests:* The network access protocol might request the use of certain subnetwork facilities, such as priority.

At router *X*, the packet header is stripped off and the IP header is examined. On the basis of the destination address information in the IP header, the IP module in the router directs the datagram out across subnetwork 2 to *B*. To do this, the datagram is again augmented with a network access header.

When the data are received at *B*, the reverse process occurs. At each layer, the corresponding header is removed, and the remainder is passed on to the next-higher layer, until the original user data are delivered to the destination process.

A.3   *TCP/IP Applications*

A number of applications have been standardized to operate on top of TCP, including SNMPv1 and SNMPv2. In this section, we mention three other common application protocols.

The *Simple Mail Transfer Protocol* (SMTP) provides a basic electronic-mail facility. It provides a mechanism for transferring messages among separate hosts. Features of SMTP include mailing lists, return receipts, and forwarding. SMTP does not specify the way in which messages are to be created; some local editing or native electronic-mail facility is required. Once a message is created, SMTP accepts the message and makes use of TCP to send it to an SMTP module on another host. The target SMTP module will make use of a local electronic-mail package to store the incoming message in a user's mailbox.

The *File Transfer Protocol* (FTP) is used to send files from one system to another under user command. Both text and binary files are accommodated, and the protocol provides features for controlling user access. When a user wishes to engage in file transfer, FTP sets up a TCP connection to the target system for the exchange of control messages. These messages allow user ID and password to be transmitted, and they permit the user to specify the file and file actions desired. Once a file transfer is approved, a second TCP connection is set up for the data transfer. The file is transferred over the data connection, without the overhead of any headers or control information at the application level. When the transfer is complete, the control connection is used to signal the completion and to accept new file transfer commands.

TELNET provides a remote log-on capability, which enables a user at a terminal or personal computer to log on to a remote computer and function as if directly connected to that computer. The protocol was designed to work with simple scroll-mode terminals. TELNET is actually implemented in two modules: User TELNET interacts with the terminal I/O module to communicate with a local terminal. It converts the characteristics of real terminals to the network standard, and vice versa. Server TELNET interacts with an application, acting as a surrogate terminal handler so that remote terminals appear as local to the application. Terminal traffic between User and Server TELNET is carried on a TCP connection.

A.4   User Datagram Protocol

In addition to TCP, one other transport-level protocol is commonly used as part of the TCP/IP protocol suite: the *User Datagram Protocol* (UDP) specified in RFC 768. The UDP provides a connectionless service for application-level procedures. UDP does not guarantee delivery, preservation of sequence, or protection against duplication. UDP enables a procedure to send messages to other procedures with a minimum of protocol mechanism. UDP is the preferred transport protocol for SNMPv1 and SNMPv2.

UDP sits on top of IP. Because it is connectionless, UDP has very little to do. Essentially, it adds a port-addressing capability to IP. This is best seen by examining the UDP header, shown in Figure A.4. The header includes a source port and a destination port, which identify the sending and receiving users of TCP. For example, port number 161

FIGURE A.4   UDP header

identifies an SNMP agent, and port number 162 identifies an SNMP manager. The length field contains the length in octets of the entire UDP segment, including header and data. The checksum is the same algorithm used for TCP and IP. It applies to the entire UDP segment plus a *pseudo-header* prefixed to the UDP header at the time of calculation. The pseudo-header includes the following fields from the IP header: source and destination internet address and protocol. By including the pseudo-header, UDP protects itself from misdelivery by IP. That is, if IP delivers a segment to the wrong host, even if the segment contains no bit errors, the receiving UDP entity will detect the delivery error. If an error is detected, the segment is discarded and no further action is taken.

The checksum field in UDP is optional. If it is not used, it is set to zero. However, it should be pointed out that the IP checksum applies only to the IP header and not to the IP data field, which in this case consists of the UDP header and the user data. Thus, if UDP does not perform a checksum calculation, no check is made on the user data.

A.5   *TCP/IP Standards*

Many of the protocols that make up the TCP/IP protocol suite have been standardized or are in the process of standardization. By universal agreement, an organization known as the Internet Architecture Board (IAB) is responsible for the development and publication of these standards, which are published in a series of documents called Requests for Comments (RFCs).

This section provides a brief description of the way in which standards for the TCP/IP protocol suite are developed.

A.5.1   The Internet and Internet Standards

The Internet is a large collection of interconnected networks, all of which use the TCP/IP protocol suite. The Internet began with the development of ARPANET and the subsequent support by the Defense Advanced Research Projects Agency (DARPA) for the development of additional networks to support military users and government contractors.

The IAB is the coordinating committee for Internet design, engineering, and management. Areas covered include the operation of the Internet itself and the standardization of protocols used by end systems on the Internet for interoperability. The IAB has two principal subsidiary task forces:

- Internet Engineering Task Force (IETF)
- Internet Research Task Force (IRTF)

The actual work of these task forces is carried out by working groups. Membership in a working group is voluntary; any interested party may participate.

The IETF is responsible for publishing the RFCs. The RFCs are the working notes of the Internet research and development community. A document in this series may be on essentially any topic related to computer communications and may be anything from a meeting report to the specification of a standard.

The final decision of which RFCs become Internet standards is made by the IAB, on the recommendation of the IETF. To become a standard, a specification must meet the following criteria.

- It must be stable and well understood.
- It must be technically competent.
- It must have multiple, independent, and interoperable implementations with operational experience.
- It must enjoy significant public support.
- It must be recognizably useful in some or all parts of the Internet.

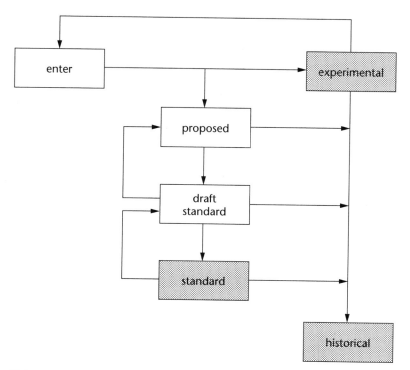

FIGURE A.5 Standards track diagram

The key difference between these criteria and those used for international standards is the emphasis here on operational experience.

A.5.2   The Standardization Process

Figure A.5 on the previous page illustrates the series of steps, called the *standards track,* that a specification goes through to become a standard. The steps involve increasing amounts of scrutiny and testing. At each step, the IETF must make a recommendation for advancement of the protocol, and the IAB must ratify it.

The white boxes in the diagram represent temporary states, which should be occupied for the minimum practical time. However, a document must remain a proposed standard for at least six months and a draft standard for at least four months to allow time for review and comment. The gray boxes represent long-term states that may be occupied for years.

A protocol or other specification that is not considered ready for standardization may be published as an experimental RFC. After further work, the specification may be resubmitted. If the specification is generally stable, has resolved known design choices, is believed to be well understood, has received significant community review, and appears to enjoy enough community interest to be considered valuable, then the RFC will be designated a proposed standard.

For a specification to be advanced to draft standard status, there must be at least two independent and interoperable implementations from which adequate operational experience has been obtained. After such experience has been obtained, a specification may be elevated to a standard. At this point, the specification is assigned an STD number as well as an RFC number. Finally, when a protocol becomes obsolete, it is assigned to the historic state.

Abstract Syntax Notation One

Abstract Syntax Notation One (ASN.1) is a formal language developed and standardized by CCITT (X.208) and ISO (ISO 8824). ASN.1 is important for several reasons. First, it can be used to define abstract syntaxes of application data. Although any formal language could be used for this purpose, in practice ASN.1 is likely to be used almost exclusively. In addition, ASN.1 is used to define the structure of application and presentation protocol data units (PDUs). Finally, ASN.1 is used to define the management information base for both SNMP and OSI systems management.

Before examining the details of ASN.1, we need to introduce the concept of an abstract syntax and discuss the three uses of ASN.1 mentioned in the preceding paragraph. Then, we will look at the fundamentals of ASN.1. Next, a special and important facility— the ASN.1 macro facility—is examined. Finally, the encoding of data whose values are defined in ASN.1 is introduced.

B.1   *Abstract Syntax*

Table B.1 defines some key terms relevant to a discussion of ASN.1, and Figure B.1 illustrates the underlying concepts. For purposes of this discussion, a communications architecture in an end system can be considered to have two major components. The *data transfer component* is concerned with the mechanisms for the transfer of data between end systems. In the case of the TCP/IP protocol suite, this component would consist of TCP or UDP on down. In the case of the OSI architecture, this component would consist of the session layer on down. The *application component* is the user of the data transfer component and is concerned with the end user's application. In the case of the TCP/IP protocol suite, this component would consist of an application, such as SNMP, FTP, SMTP, or TELNET. In the case of OSI, this component actually consists of the application layer, which is composed of a number of application service elements, and the presentation layer.

As we cross the boundary from the application to the data transfer component, there is a significant change in the way that data are viewed. For the data transfer component, the data received from an application are specified as the binary value of a sequence of

TABLE B.1   Terms Relevant to ASN.1

Abstract syntax	Describes the generic structure of data independent of any encoding technique used to represent the data. The syntax allows data types to be defined and values of those types to be specified.
Data type	A named set of values. A type may be simple, which is defined by specifying the set of its values, or structured, which is defined in terms of other types.
Encoding	The complete sequence of octets used to represent a data value.
Encoding rules	A specification of the mapping from one syntax to another. Specifically, encoding rules determine algorithmically, for any set of data values defined in an abstract syntax, the representation of those values in a transfer syntax.
Transfer syntax	The way in which data are actually represented in terms of bit patterns while in transit between presentation entities.

octets. This binary value can be directly assembled into service data units (SDUs) for passing between layers and into protocol data units (PDUs) for passing between protocol entities within a layer. The application component, however, is concerned with a user's view of data. In general, that view is one of a structured set of information, such as text in a document, a personnel file, an integrated database, or a visual display of image information. The user is primarily concerned with the semantics of data. The application component must provide a representation of this data that can be converted to binary values; that is, it must be concerned with the syntax of the data.

The approach illustrated in Figure B.1 to support application data is as follows. For the application component, information is represented in an abstract syntax that deals with data types and data values. The abstract syntax formally specifies data independently from any specific representation. Thus, an abstract syntax has many similarities to the data-type definition aspects of conventional programming languages such as Pascal, C, and Ada, and to grammars such as Backus-Naur Form (BNF). Application protocols describe their PDUs in terms of an abstract syntax.

This abstract syntax is used for the exchange of information between application components in different systems. The exchange consists of application-level PDUs, which contain protocol control information and user data. Within a system, the information represented using an abstract syntax must be mapped into some form for presentation to the human user. Similarly, this abstract syntax must be mapped into some local format for storage. Note that such a mapping is used in the case of a management information base (MIB). However, elements within the MIB are defined using the abstract syntax. Thus, the abstract syntax notation is employed by a user to define the MIB; the application must then convert this definition to a form suitable for local storage.

The component must also translate between the abstract syntax of the application and a transfer syntax that describes the data values in a binary form, suitable for interac-

FIGURE B.1   The use of abstract and transfer syntaxes

tion with the data transfer component. For example, an abstract syntax may include a data type of character; the transfer syntax could specify ASCII or EBCDIC encoding.

The transfer syntax thus defines the representation of the data to be exchanged between data transfer components. The translation from abstract syntax to the transfer syntax is accomplished by means of encoding rules that specify the representation of each data value of each data type.

This approach for the exchange of application data solves the two problems that relate to data representation in a distributed, heterogeneous environment.

- There is a common representation for the exchange of data between differing systems.
- Internal to a system, an application uses some particular representation of data. The abstract/transfer syntax scheme automatically resolves differences in representation between cooperating application entities.

The fundamental requirement for selection of a transfer syntax is that it support the corresponding abstract syntax. In addition, the transfer syntax may have other attributes that are not related to the abstract syntaxes that it can support. For example, an abstract syntax could be supported by any one of four transfer syntaxes, which are the same in all respects except that one provides data compression, one provides encryption, one provides both, and one provides neither. The choice of which transfer syntax to use would depend on cost and security considerations.

B.2 ASN.1 Concepts

The basic building block of an ASN.1 specification is the *module*. We begin this section by looking at the top-level structure of the module. Then, we introduce some lexical conventions used in ASN.1 definitions. Next, the data types defined in ASN.1 are described. Finally, examples of the use of ASN.1 are given.

B.2.1 Module Definition

ASN.1 is a language that can be used to define data structures. A structure definition is in the form of a named module. The name of the module can then be used to reference the structure. For example, the module name can be used as an abstract syntax name; an application can pass this name to the presentation service to specify the abstract syntax of the APDUs that the application wishes to exchange with a peer application entity.

Modules have the basic form

```
<modulereference> DEFINITIONS ::=
    BEGIN
        EXPORTS
        IMPORTS
        AssignmentList
    End
```

The `modulereference` is a module name followed optionally by an object identifier to identify the module. The `EXPORTS` construct indicates which definitions in this module may be imported by other modules. The `IMPORTS` construct indicates which type and value definitions from other modules are to be imported into this module. Neither the `IMPORTS` or `EXPORTS` constructs may be included unless the object identifier for the module is included. Finally, the assignment list consists of type assignments, value assignments, and macro definitions. Macro definitions are discussed later on in this appendix. Type and value assignments have the form

```
<name> ::= <description>
```

Figure B.2 defines the syntax for ASN.1 in Backus-Naur Form (BNF). The easiest way to describe the syntax is by example. First, we need to specify some lexical conventions.

```
ModuleDefinition ::= modulereference DEFINITIONS "::=" BEGIN ModuleBody END
ModuleBody ::= AssignmentList | empty
AssignmentList ::= Assignment | AssignmentList Assignment
Assignment ::= Typeassignment | Valueassignment
Typeassignment ::= typereference "::=" Type
Valueassignment ::= valuereference Type "::="Value
Type ::= BuiltinType | DefinedType
BuiltinType ::= BooleanType | IntegerType | BitStringType | OctetStringType | NullType |
                SequenceType | SequenceOfType | SetType | SetOfType | ChoiceType |
                SelectionType | TaggedType | AnyType | ObjectIdentifierType |
                CharacterStringType | UsefulType | EnumeratedType | RealType
Value ::= BuiltinValue | DefinedValue
BuiltinValue ::= BooleanValue | IntegerValue | BitStringValue | OctetStringValue | NullValue |
                SequenceValue | SequenceOfValue | SetValue | SetOfValue | ChoiceValue |
                SelectionValue | TaggedValue | AnyValue | ObjectIdentifierValue |
                CharacterStringValue | EnumeratedValue | RealValue
DefinedValue ::= Externalvaluereference | valuereference
BooleanType ::= BOOLEAN
BooleanValue ::= TRUE | FALSE
IntegerType ::= INTEGER | INTEGER {NamedNumberList}
NamedNumberList ::= NamedNumber | NamedNumberList, NamedNumber
NamedNumber ::= identifier(SignedNumber) | identifier(DefinedValue)
SignedNumber ::= number | -number
IntegerValue ::= SignedNumber | identifier
BitStringType ::= BIT STRING | BIT STRING {NamedBitList}
NamedBitList ::= NamedBit | NamedBitList, NamedBit
NamedBit ::= identifier(number) | identifier(DefinedValue)
BitStringValue ::= bstring | hstring | {IdentifierList} | {}
IdentifierList ::= Identifier | IdentifierList, identifier
OctetStringType ::= OCTETSTRING
OctetStringValue ::= bstring | hstring
NullType ::= NULL
NullValue ::= NULL
SequenceType ::= SEQUENCE {ElementTypeList} | SEQUENCE {}
ElementTypeList ::= ElementType | ElementTypeList, ElementType
ElementType ::= NamedType | NamedType OPTIONAL | NamedType DEFAULT Value |
                COMPONENTS OF Type
NamedType ::= identifier Type | Type | SelectionType
SequenceValue ::= {ElementValueList} | {}
ElementValueList ::= NamedValue | ElementValueList, NamedValue
SequenceOfType ::= SEQUENCE OF Type | SEQUENCE
SequenceOfValue ::= {ValueList} | {}
SetType ::= SET{ElementTypeList} | SET {}
SetValue ::= {ElementValueList} | {}
SetOfType ::= SET OF Type | SET
SetOfValue ::= {ValueList} | {}
ChoiceType ::= CHOICE {AlternativeTypeList}
```

Continued

FIGURE B.2   BNF grammar for ASN.1

```
AlternativeTypeList ::= NamedType | AlternativeTypeList, NamedType
ChoiceValue ::= NamedValue
SelectionType ::= identifier < Type
SelectionValue ::= NamedValue
TaggedType ::= Tag Type | Tag IMPLICIT Type
Tag ::= [Class ClassNumber]
ClassNumber ::= number | DefinedValue
Class ::= UNIVERSAL | APPLICATION | PRIVATE | empty
TaggedValue ::= Value
AnyType ::= ANY | ANY DEFINED BY identifier
AnyValue ::= Type Value
ObjectIdentifierType ::= OBJECT IDENTIFIER
ObjectIdentifierValue ::= {ObjIdComponentList} | {DefinedValue ObjIdComponent List}
ObjIdComponentList ::= ObjIdComponent | ObjIdComponent ObjIdComponentList
ObjIdComponent ::= NameForm | NumberForm | NameAndNumberForm
NameForm ::= identifier
NumberForm ::= number | DefinedValue
NameAndNumberForm ::= identifier(NumberForm)
CharacterStringType ::= typereference
CharacterStringValue ::= cstring
UsefulType ::= typereference
EnumeratedType ::= ENUMERATED {Enumeration}
Enumeration ::= NamedNumber | NamedNumber, Enumeration
EnumerationValue ::= identifier
RealType ::= REAL
RealValue ::= NumericRealValue | SpecialRealValue
NumericRealValue ::= {Mantissa, Base, Exponent} | 0
Mantissa ::= SignedNumber
Base ::= 2 | 10
Exponent ::= SignedNumber
SpecialRealValue ::= PLUS-INFINITY | MINUS-INFINITY
```

FIGURE B.2   *Continued*

B.2.2   Lexical Conventions

ASN.1 structures, types, and values are expressed in a notation similar to that of a programming language. The following lexical conventions are followed.

1. Layout is not significant; multiple spaces and blank lines can be considered as a single space.

2. Comments are delimited by pairs of hyphens (--) at the beginning and end of the comment, or by a pair of hyphens at the beginning of the comment and the end of the line at the end of the comment.

3. Identifiers (names of values and fields), type references (names of types), and module names consist of upper- and lowercase letters, digits, and hyphens.

4. An identifier begins with a lowercase letter.

5. A type reference or a module name begins with an uppercase letter.

6. A built-in type consists of all capital letters. A built-in type is a commonly used type for which a standard notation is provided.

B.2.3 Abstract Data Types

ASN.1 is a notation for abstract data types and their values. A *type* can be viewed as a collection of values. The number of values that a type may take may be infinite. For example, the type INTEGER has an infinite number of values.

We can classify types into four categories:

- *Simple:* These are atomic types, with no components.
- *Structured:* A structured type has components.
- *Tagged:* These are types derived from other types.
- *Other:* This category includes the CHOICE and ANY types, defined later in this section.

Every ASN.1 data type, with the exception of CHOICE and ANY, has an associated *tag*. The tag consists of a class name and a nonnegative integer tag number. There are four classes of data types, or four classes of tag:

- *Universal:* generally useful, application-independent types and construction mechanisms; these are defined in the standard and are listed in Table B.2.
- *Application-wide:* relevant to a particular application; these are defined in other standards
- *Context-specific*: also relevant to a particular application, but applicable in a limited context
- *Private:* types defined by users and not covered by any standard

A data type is uniquely identified by its tag. ASN.1 types are the same if and only if their tag numbers are the same. For example, UNIVERSAL 4 refers to OctetString, which is of class UNIVERSAL and has tag number 4 within the class.

B.2.3.1 Simple Types

A *simple type* is one defined by directly specifying the set of its values. We may think of these as the atomic types; all other types are built up from the simple types. The simple data types in the UNIVERSAL class can be grouped into several categories, as indicated in Table B.2; these are not "official" categories in the standard but are used here for convenience.

The first group of simple types can be referred to, for want of a better word, as "basic" types. The Boolean type is straightforward. The Integer type is the set of positive and negative integers and zero. In addition, individual integer values can be assigned

TABLE B.2 Universal Class Tag Assignments

Tag	Type Name	Set of Values
		BASIC TYPES
UNIVERSAL 1	BOOLEAN	TRUE or FALSE
UNIVERSAL 2	INTEGER	The positive and negative whole numbers, including zero
UNIVERSAL 3	BIT STRING	A sequence of zero or more bits
UNIVERSAL 4	OCTET STRING	A sequence of zero or more octets
UNIVERSAL 9	REAL	Real numbers
UNIVERSAL 10	ENUMERATED	An explicit list of integer values that an instance of a data type may take
		OBJECT TYPES
UNIVERSAL 6	OBJECT IDENTIFIER	The set of values associated with information objects allocated by this standard
UNIVERSAL 7	Object descriptor	Human-readable text providing a brief description of an information object
		CHARACTER STRING TYPES
UNIVERSAL 18	NumericString	Digits 0 through 9, and the space character
UNIVERSAL 19	PrintableString	Printable characters
UNIVERSAL 20	TeletexString	Character set defined by CCITT Recommendation T.61
UNIVERSAL 21	VideotexString	Set of alphabetic and graphical characters defined by CCITT Recommendations T.100 and T.101
UNIVERSAL 22	IA5String	International alphabet 5 (equivalent to ASCII)
UNIVERSAL 25	GraphicString	Character set defined by ISO 8824
UNIVERSAL 26	VisibleString	Character set defined by ISO 646 (equivalent to ASCII)
UNIVERSAL 27	GeneralString	General character string
		MISCELLANEOUS TYPES
UNIVERSAL 5	NULL	The single value NULL; commonly used where several alternatives are possible but none of them applies
UNIVERSAL 8	EXTERNAL	A type defined in some external document (It need not be one of the valid ASN.1 types.)
UNIVERSAL 23	UTCTime	Consists of the date—specified with a two-digit year, a two-digit month, and a two-digit day—followed by the time—specified in hours, minutes, and optionally seconds—followed by an optional specification of the local time differential from universal time
UNIVERSAL 24	GeneralizedTime	Consists of the date—specified with a four-digit year, a two-digit month, and a two-digit day—followed by the time—specified in hours, minutes, and optionally seconds—followed by an optional specification of the local time differential from universal time

TABLE B.2 *Continued*

UNIVERSAL 9-15	Reserved	Reserved for addenda to the ASN.1 standard
UNIVERSAL 28-	Reserved	Reserved for addenda to the ASN.1 standard
	STRUCTURED TYPES	
UNIVERSAL 16	SEQUENCE and SEQUENCE-OF	Sequence: defined by referencing a fixed, ordered list of types; each value is an ordered list of values, one from each component type
		Sequence-of: defined by referencing a single existing type; each value is an ordered list of zero or more values of the existing type
UNIVERSAL 17	SET and SET-OF	Set: defined by referencing a fixed, unordered list of types, some of which may be declared optional; each value is an unordered list of values, one from each component type
		Set-of: defined by referencing a single existing type; each value is an unordered list of zero or more values of the existing type

names to indicate a specific meaning. The BitString is an ordered set of zero or more bits; individual bits can be assigned names. The actual value of a BitString can be specified as a string of either binary or hexadecimal digits. Similarly, an OctetString can be specified as a string of either binary or hexadecimal digits. The Real data type consists of numbers expressed in scientific notation (mantissa, base, exponent); that is:

$$M \times B^E$$

The mantissa (M) and the exponent (E) may take any integer values, positive or negative; a base (B) of 2 or 10 may be used.

Finally, the Enumerated type consists of an explicitly enumerated list of integers, together with an associated name for each integer. The same functionality can be achieved with the Integer type by naming some of the integer values; but, because of the utility of this feature, a separate type has been defined. Note, however, that although the values of the Enumerated type are integers, they do not have integer semantics. That is, arithmetic operations should not be performed on enumerated values.

Object types are used to name and describe information objects. Examples of information objects are standards documents, abstract and transfer syntaxes, data structures, and managed objects. In general, an information object is a class of information (for example, a file format) rather than an instance of such a class (for example, an individual file). The Object Identifier is a unique identifier for a particular object. Its value consists of a sequence of integers. The set of defined objects has a tree structure, with the root of the tree being the object referring to the ASN.1 standard. Starting with the root of the object identifier tree, each object identifier component value identifies an arc in the tree. The `Object` descriptor is a human-readable description of an information object.

ASN.1 defines a number of character-string types. The values of each of these types consists of a sequence of zero or more characters from a standardized character set.

Some miscellaneous types have also been defined in the UNIVERSAL class. The `Null` type is used in places in a structure where a value may or may not be present. The `Null` type is simply the alternative of no value being present at that position in the structure. An `External` type is one whose values are unspecified in the ASN.1 standard; it is defined in some other document or standard and can be defined using any well-specified notation. `UTCTime` and `GeneralizedTime` are two different formats for expressing time. In both cases, either a universal or local time may be specified.

B.2.3.2   Structured Types

Structured types are those consisting of components. ASN.1 provides four structured types for building complex data types from simple data types:

- SEQUENCE
- SEQUENCE OF
- SET
- SET OF

The `Sequence` and `Sequence-of` types are used to define an ordered list of values of one or more other data types. This is analogous to the record structure found in many programming languages, such as COBOL. A sequence consists of an ordered list of elements, each specifying a type and, optionally, a name. The notation for defining the Sequence type is as follows:

```
SequenceType  ::= SEQUENCE {ElementTypeList} | SEQUENCE { }
ElementTypeList ::= ElementType | ElementTypeList, ElementType
ElementType ::=
  NamedType                |
  NamedType OPTIONAL       |
  NamedType DEFAULT Value  |
  COMPONENTS OF Type
```

A `NamedType` is a type reference with or without a name. Each element definition may be followed by the keyword OPTIONAL or DEFAULT. The OPTIONAL keyword indicates that the component element need not be present in a sequence value. The DEFAULT keyword indicates that if the component element is not present, then the value specified by the DEFAULT clause will be assigned. The COMPONENTS OF clause is used to define the inclusion, at this point in the `ElementTypeList`, of all the `ElementType` sequences appearing in the referenced type.

A `Sequence-of` consists of an ordered, variable number of elements, all of one type. A `Sequence-of` definition has the following form:

$$\text{SequenceOfType} ::= \text{SEQUENCE OF Type} \mid \text{SEQUENCE}$$

The notation `SEQUENCE` is to be interpreted as `SEQUENCE OF ANY`; the type `ANY` is explained in a later subsection.

A set is similar to a sequence, except that the order of the elements is not significant; the elements may be arranged in any order when they are encoded into a specific representation. A set definition has the following form:

$$\text{SetType} ::= \text{SET \{ElementTypeList\}} \mid \text{SET \{ \}}$$

Thus, a set may include optional, default, and `component-of` clauses.

A `Set-of` is an unordered, variable number of elements, all of one type. A `Set-of` definition has the following form:

$$\text{SetOfType} ::= \text{SET OF Type} \mid \text{SET}$$

The notation `SET` is to be interpreted as `SET OF ANY`; the type `ANY` is explained in a later subsection.

B.2.3.3   Tagged Types

The term *tagged type* is somewhat of a misnomer since all data types in ASN.1 have an associated tag. The ASN.1 standard defines a tagged type as follows.

> *A type defined by referencing a single existing type and a tag; the new type is isomorphic to the existing type, but is distinct from it. In all encoding schemes a value of the new type can be distinguished from a value of the old type.*

Tagging is useful to distinguish types within an application. It may be desired to have several different type names, such as `Employee_name` and `Customer_name`, which are essentially the same type. For some structures, tagging is needed to distinguish component types within the structured type. For example, optional components of a `SET` or `SEQUENCE` type are typically given distinct context-specific tags to avoid ambiguity.

There are two categories of tagged types: implicitly tagged types and explicitly tagged types. An implicitly tagged type is derived from another type by *replacing* the tag (old class name, old tag number) of the old type with a new tag (new class name, new tag number). For purposes of encoding, only the new tag is used.

An explicitly tagged type is derived from another type by *adding* a new tag to the underlying type. In effect, an explicitly tagged type is a structured type with one component, the underlying type. For purposes of encoding, both the new and old tags must be reflected in the encoding.

An implicit tag results in shorter encodings, but an explicit tag may be necessary to avoid ambiguity if the tag of the underlying type is indeterminate (for example, if the underlying type is CHOICE or ANY).

B.2.3.4   CHOICE and ANY Types

The CHOICE and ANY types are data types without tags. The reason for this setting is that when a particular value is assigned to the type, then a particular type must be assigned at the same time. Thus, the type is assigned at "runtime."

The CHOICE type is a list of alternative known types. Only one of these types will actually be used to create a value. It was stated earlier that a type can be viewed as a collection of values. The CHOICE type is the union of the sets of values of all of the component types listed in the type definition. This type is useful when the values to be described can be of different types depending on circumstance and all the possible types are known in advance.

The notation for defining the CHOICE type is as follows:

```
ChoiceType ::= CHOICE {AlternativeTypeList}
AlternativeTypeList ::= NamedType | AternativeTypeList, NamedType
```

The ANY type describes an arbitrary value of an arbitrary type. The notation is simply

```
AnyType ::= ANY
```

This type is useful when the values to be described can be of different types but the possible types are not known in advance.

B.2.4   Subtypes

A *subtype* is derived from a parent type by restricting the set of values defined for a parent type. That is, the set of values for the subtype is a subset of the set of values for the parent type. The process of subtyping can extend to more than one level: That is, a subtype may itself be a parent of an even more restricted subtype.

Six different forms of notation for designating the values of a subtype are provided in the standard. Table B.3 indicates which of these forms can be applied to particular parent types. The remainder of this subsection provides an overview of each form.

B.2.4.1   Single Value

A single-value subtype is an explicit listing of all of the values that the subtype may take on. For example,

```
SmallPrime ::= INTEGER ( 2 | 3 | 5 | 7 | 11 | 13 | 17 | 19 | 23 | 29 )
```

TABLE B.3   Applicability of Subtype Value Sets

Type (or derived from such a type by tagging)	Single Value	Contained Subtype	Value Range	Size Constraint	Permitted Alphabet	Inner Subtyping
BOOLEAN	✓	✓				
INTEGER	✓	✓	✓			
ENUMERATED	✓	✓				
REAL	✓	✓	✓			
OBJECT IDENTIFIER	✓	✓				
BIT STRING	✓	✓		✓		
OCTET STRING	✓	✓		✓		
CHARACTER STRING types	✓	✓		✓	✓	
SEQUENCE	✓	✓				✓
SEQUENCE OF	✓	✓		✓		✓
SET	✓	✓				✓
SET OF	✓	✓		✓		✓
ANY	✓	✓				
CHOICE	✓	✓				✓

In this case, SmallPrime is a subtype of the built-in type INTEGER. As another example, consider the following:

```
Months ::= ENUMERATED { january (1),
                        february (2),
                        march (3),
                        april (4),
                        may (5),
                        june (6),
                        july (7),
                        august (8),
                        september (9),
                        october (10),
                        november (11),
                        december (12) }
First-quarter ::= Months ( january | february | march )
Second-quarter ::= Months ( april | may | june )
```

First-quarter and Second-quarter are both subtypes of the enumerated type Months.

B.2.4.2 Contained Subtype

A *contained* subtype is used to form new subtypes from existing subtypes. The contained subtype includes all of the values of the subtypes that it contains. For example,

```
First-half ::= Months ( INCLUDES First-quarter |
                INCLUDES Second-quarter )
```

A contained subtype may also include listing explicit values:

```
First-third ::= Months ( INCLUDES First-quarter | april )
```

B.2.4.3 Value Range

A *value-range* subtype applies only to INTEGER and REAL types. It is specified by giving the numerical values of the endpoints of the range. The special values PLUS-INFINITY and MINUS-INFINITY may be used. The special values MIN and MAX may be used to indicate the minimum and maximum allowable values in the parent. Each endpoint of the range is either closed or open. When open, the specification of the endpoint includes the less-than symbol (<). The following are equivalent definitions:

```
PositiveInteger ::= INTEGER (0<..PLUS-INFINITY)
PositiveInteger ::= INTEGER (1..PLUS-INFINITY)
PositiveInteger ::= INTEGER (0<..MAX)
PositiveInteger ::= INTEGER (1..MAX)
```

The following definitions are also equivalent:

```
NegativeInteger ::= INTEGER (MINUS-INFINITY..<0)
NegativeInteger ::= INTEGER (MINUS-INFINITY..-1)
NegativeInteger ::= INTEGER (MIN..<0)
NegativeInteger ::= INTEGER (MIN..-1)
```

B.2.4.4 Permitted Alphabet

The *permitted alphabet* constraint may be applied only to character string types. A permitted alphabet type consists of all values (strings) that can be constructed using a sub-alphabet of the parent type. Examples follow:

```
TouchToneButtons ::= IA5String ( FROM
                     ( "0" | "1" | "2" | "3" | "4" | "5" | "6" | "7" | "8" |
                     "9" | "*" | "#" ) )
DigitString ::= IA5String ( FROM
                ( "0" | "1" | "2" | "3" | "4" | "5" | "6" | "7" | "8" | "9" ) )
```

B.2.4.5 Size Constraint

A *size* constraint limits the number of items in a type. It can be applied only to the string types (bit string, octet string, character string) and to `Sequence-of` and `Set-of` types. The item that is constrained depends on the parent type, as follows:

TYPE	UNIT OF MEASURE
bit string	bit
octet string	octet
character string	character
sequence-of	component value
set-of	component value

As an example of a string type, Recommendation X.121 specifies that international data numbers, which are used for addressing end systems on public data networks, including X.25 networks, should consist of at least 5 digits but not more than 14 digits. This could be specified as follows:

```
ItlDataNumber ::= DigitString ( SIZE ( 5..14 ) )
```

Now consider a parameter list for a message that may include up to 12 parameters:

```
ParameterList ::= SET SIZE ( 0..12 ) OF Parameter
```

B.2.4.6 Inner Subtyping

An *inner-type* constraint can be applied to the sequence, sequence-of, set, set-of, and choice types. An inner subtype includes in its value set only those values from the parent type that satisfy one or more constraints on the presence and/or values of the components of the parent type. This is a rather complex subtype, and only a few examples are given here.

Consider a protocol data unit (PDU) that may have four different fields, in no particular order:

```
PDU ::= SET { alpha   [0] INTEGER,
              beta    [1] IA5String OPTIONAL,
              gamma   [2] SEQUENCE OF Parameter,
              delta   [3] BOOLEAN }
```

The following code will specify a test that requires the Boolean value to be false and the integer value to be negative:

```
TestPDU ::= PDU ( WITH COMPONENTS
{ ..., delta (FALSE), alpha (MIN ... <0)})
```

To further specify that the beta parameter is to be present and either 5 or 12 characters in length, consider this code:

```
FurtherTestPDU ::= TestPDU (WITH COMPONENTS
              { ..., beta (SIZE (5 | 12) PRESENT})
```

As another example, consider the use of inner subtyping on a sequence-of construct:

```
Text-block ::= SEQUENCE OF VisibleString
Address ::= Text-block ( SIZE (1..6) WITH COMPONENT (SIZE (1..32)))
```

This indicates that the address contains from 1 to 6 text blocks and that each text block is from 1 to 32 characters in length.

B.2.5   Data Structure Example

Figure B.3, taken from the ASN.1 standard, is an example that defines the structure of a personnel record. Part (a) of the figure informally depicts the personnel record by giving an example of a specific record. Such a display might correspond to the user presentation in Figure B.1. In part (b), we see the formal description, or abstract syntax, of the data structure. In the notation, a structure definition has the form

```
<type name> ::= <type definition>
```

A simple example is

```
SerialNumber ::= INTEGER
```

There are no simple types defined in the example. A similar construction is

```
EmployeeNumber ::= [APPLICATION 2] IMPLICIT INTEGER
```

This definition makes use of the universal type Integer, but the user has chosen to give the type a new tag. The use of the term [APPLICATION 2] gives the tag (class and tag number) for this new type. Because the designation IMPLICIT is present, values of this type will be encoded only with the tag APPLICATION 2. If the designation were not present, then the values would be encoded with both the APPLICATION and UNIVERSAL tags. The use of the implicit option results in a more compact representation. In some applications, compactness may be less important than other considerations, such as the ability to carry out type checking. In the latter case, explicit tagging can be used by omitting the word IMPLICIT.

The definition of the Date type is similar to that of EmployeeNumber. In this case, the type is a character string consisting of characters defined in ISO 646, which is equivalent to ASCII. The double hyphen indicates that the rest of the line is a comment; the

```
Name:                   John P Smith
Title:                  Director
Employee Number:        51
Date of Hire:           17 September 1971
Name of Spouse:         Mary T Smith
Number of Children:     2

Child Information
    Name:               Ralph T Smith
    Date of Birth:      11 November 1957

Child Information
    Name:               Susan B Jones
    Date of Birth:      17 July 1959
```

(a) Informal description of personnel record

```
PersonnelRecord ::= [APPLICATION 0] IMPLICIT SET {
      Name,
      title [0] VisibleString,
      number EmployeeNumber,
      dateOfHire [1] Date,
      nameOfSpouse [2] Name,
      children [3] IMPLICIT SEQUENCE OF ChildInformation DEFAULT {} }

ChildInformation ::= SET {
      Name,
      dateOfBirth [0] Date}

Name ::= [APPLICATION 1] IMPLICIT SEQUENCE {
      givenName VisibleString,
      initial VisibleString,
      familyName VisibleString }

EmployeeNumber ::= [APPLICATION 2] IMPLICIT INTEGER

Date ::= [APPLICATION 3] IMPLICIT VisibleString -- YYYYMMDD
```

(b) ASN.1 description of the record structure

```
                {givenName "John", initial "P", familyName "Smith"},
title           "Director"
number          51
dateOfHire      "19710917"
nameOfSpouse    {givenName "Mary", initial "T", familyName "Smith"},
children
{  {            {givenName "Ralph", initial "T", familyName "Smith"},
   dateOfBirth  "19571111" },
                {givenName "Susan", initial "B", familyName "Jones"},
   dateOfBirth  "19590717" } } }
```

(c) ASN.1 description of a record value

FIGURE B.3   Example of use of ASN.1

format of the `Date` type will not be checked other than to determine that the value is an ISO 646 character string.

The type of `Name` is the `Sequence` type. In this case, each of the three elements in the sequence is named. `ChildInformation` is of the `SET` type. Note that no name is given to the first element of the set, but the second element is given the name `dateOfBirth`. The second element is the data type `Date`, defined elsewhere. This data type is used in two different locations, here and in the definition of `PersonnelRecord`. In each location, the data type is given a name and a context-specific tag, [0] and [1], respectively. This follows the general rule that when an implicit or explicit tag is defined, but only the tag number is provided, then the tag's class defaults to context-specific.

Finally, the overall structure, `PersonnelRecord`, is defined as a set with five elements. Associated with the last element is a default value of a null sequence, to be used if no value is supplied.

Part (c) of the figure is an example of a particular value for the personnel record, expressed in the abstract syntax.

B.2.6   PDU Example

As another example, consider the ASN.1 specification of the format of the protocol data units for the SNMPv2 protocol (described in Chapter 12). The specification from the standard is reproduced in Figure 12.3.

One new construct in this example is the `CHOICE` type. It is used to describe a variable selected from a collection. Thus, any instance of the type PDUs will be one of eight alternative types. Note that each of the choices is labeled with a name. All of the PDUs defined in this fashion have the same format but different labels. The format consists of a sequence of four elements. The second element, `error-status`, enumerates 18 possible integer values, each with a label. The last element, `variable-binding`, is defined as having syntax VarBindList, which is defined later in the same set of definitions. `VarBindList` is defined as a `Sequence-of` construct consisting of some number of elements of syntax VarBind, with a size constraint of up to 2,147,483,647, or $2^{31} - 1$, elements. Each element, in turn, is a sequence of two values; the first is a name, and the second is a choice among five elements.

The `BulkPDU` definition is also a sequence of four elements, but it differs from the other PDUs.

B.3   ASN.1 Macro Definitions

Included in the ASN.1 specification is the ASN.1 macro notation. This notation allows the user to extend the syntax of ASN.1 to define new types and their values. The subject of ASN.1 macros is complex, and this section serves only to introduce the subject.

Let us begin with several observations.

1. There are three levels, and they must be carefully distinguished:
   - The *macro notation*, used for defining macros
   - A *macro definition*, expressed in the macro notation and used to define a set of macro instances
   - A *macro instance*, generated from a macro definition by substituting values for variables

2. A macro definition functions as a `Super` type, generating a class of macro instances that function exactly like a basic ASN.1 type.[1]

3. A macro definition may be viewed as a template that is used to generate a set of related types and values.

4. The macro is used to extend the ASN.1 syntax but does not extend the encoding. Any type defined by means of a macro instance is simply an ASN.1 type and is encoded in the usual manner.

5. In addition to the convenience of defining a set of related types, the macro definition enables the user to include semantic information with the type.

We begin this section with a description of the general format of a macro definition. Then we look at an example. Finally, we define the overall macro definition process.

B.3.1   Macro Definition Format

A macro definition has the following general form:

```
<macroname> MACRO ::=
BEGIN
  TYPE NOTATION ::= <new-type-syntax>
  VALUE NOTATION ::= <new-value-syntax>
  <supporting-productions>
END
```

The macro name is written in all uppercase letters. A new ASN.1 type is defined by writing the name of the type, which begins with a capital letter, followed by the macro name, followed by a definition of the type dictated by the form of the macro body.

The type and value notations and the supporting productions are all specified using Backus-Naur Form (BNF). The `new-type-syntax` describes the new type. The `new-value-syntax` describes the values of the new type. The `supporting-productions`

---

[1]The ASN.1 standard uses the term "basic ASN.1 type" to refer to any ASN.1 type that is not a macro instance.

provide any additional grammar rules for either the type or value syntax; that is, any nonterminals within the `new-type-syntax` and/or `new-value-syntax` are expanded in the `supporting-productions`.

When specific values are substituted for the variables or arguments of a macro definition, a macro instance is formed. This macro instance has two results. First, it generates a representation of a basic ASN.1 type, called the *returned type*. Second, it generates a representation of a generic ASN.1 value; that is, a representation of the set of values that the type may take. This generic value is called the *returned value*.

B.3.2   Macro Example[2]

Suppose we wish to represent a pair of integers and to be able to refer to it as an ASN.1 type in various places within an ASN.1 module. We can define a new ASN.1 type as follows:

```
Pair-integers ::= SEQUENCE ( INTEGER, INTEGER )
```

We may also have a need for a type that represents pairs whose first member is an integer and whose second member is an octet string:

```
Pair-integer-octet-string ::= SEQUENCE ( INTEGER, OCTET STRING )
```

It may happen that there is a need for a number of paired structures in our module, and a large collection of defined types is assembled:

```
Pair-integers, Pair-octet-strings, Pair-printable-strings, Pair-
booleans, Pair-object-identifiers, Pair-integer-octet-string,
Pair-integer-character-string, Pair-reals, Pair-integer-real,
Pair-real-integer
```

And so on. We may also need pairs that contain pairs:

```
Pair-integer-Pair-octet-strings, Pair-integer-Pair-reals,
Pair-Pair-integers-Pair-integers
```

If such a proliferation occurs, much of our module definition is taken up with such definitions. It is therefore preferable to find a simple representation of the concept "pairs of types."

To begin, we need a macro name to represent this concept; we choose PAIRA. By convention, macro names are in all uppercase letters; they can be used freely anywhere a basic ASN.1 type may be used. Next, we need a general format for representing types.

---

[2]This example is found in the ASN.1 standard.

This can simply be PAIRA (type, type) as the way of expressing a macro instance, with "type" being an argument for which any ASN.1 type or any macro name may be substituted. When the substitution is made, the ASN.1 type returned by the macro instance is defined to be SEQUENCE { type, type }. We also need to be able to express values for the new type, and we choose the format (value, value).

For example, consider this fragment of an ASN.1 module:

```
SET { PAIRA ( INTEGER, INTEGER ), OCTET STRING }
```

By "executing" the macro and performing the substitution, we have the following result:

```
SET { SEQUENCE { INTEGER, INTEGER }, OCTET STRING }
```

One value of this type written using the macro instance value representation is

```
{ (4, 20), "April 20" }
```

The same value using the ASN.1 value representation is

```
{ {4, 20}, "April 20" }
```

Admittedly, in this example there is virtually no savings in using the macro definition versus directly using ASN.1 notation. We can, however, come up with a more "human-readable" form. We will call this new macro simply PAIR. The type definition format for a macro instance will be of the form

```
PAIR TYPE-X = type TYPE-Y = type
```

with a corresponding value notation:

```
(X = value, Y = value)
```

In this case, the definition

```
SET { ( PAIR TYPE-X = INTEGER TYPE-Y = INTEGER ), OCTET STRING }
```

yields the following type result:

```
{ (X = 4, Y = 20), "April 20" }
```

Let us look at two more macro instances from the PAIR macro:

```
T1 ::= PAIR TYPE-X = INTEGER
            TYPE-Y = BOOLEAN
T2 ::= PAIR TYPE-X = VisibleString
            TYPE-Y = T1
```

Then a value of type T1 might be

$$(X = 3, Y = TRUE)$$

and a value of type T2 might be

$$(X = "Name", Y = (X = 4, Y = FALSE))$$

Figure B.4 is the macro definition for PAIR. As with all macro definitions, it has two major parts. The first part defines the *type notation*. This part simply defines the syntax for the type definition to be used in a macro instance; it does not define the resulting type. The production includes the following key elements:

1. Character strings enclosed in quotation marks are to be reproduced exactly in the macro instance that declares a variable to be of the type of this macro.

2. An argument is any nonterminal in the macro definition other than nonterminals of type `local-type-reference` or `local-value-reference`. Such terms are variables, for which a substitution is made to form the macro instance.

3. The keyword `type` is used to specify that, at this point, each macro instance, using standard ASN.1, contains some ASN.1 type name.

```
PAIR MACRO ::=
BEGIN
  TYPE NOTATION ::=
    "TYPE-X" "=" type (Local-type-1)    --Expects any ASN.1 type and assigns it
                                        --to the variable Local-type-1
     "TYPE-Y" "=" type (Local-type-2)   --Expects a second ASN.1 type and assigns it
                                        --to the variable Local-type-2

  VALUE NOTATION ::=
    "("
    "X" "=" value (Local-value-1 Local-type-1)  --Expects a value for the type in
                                                --Local-type-1 and assigns it
                                                --to the variable Local-value-1
     "Y" "=" value (Local-value-2 Local-type-2)  --Expects a value for the type in
                                                --Local-type-2 and assigns it
                                                --to the variable Local-value-2

    <VALUE SEQUENCE {Local-type-1, Local-type-2}
      ::= {Local-value-1, Local-value-2} >   --This "embedded" definition returns
                                            --the final value as the value of a
                                            --sequence of the two types
    ")"
END
```

FIGURE B.4   ASN.1 MACRO example

The second major part of the macro definition is the *value notation*. This part determines the type of the macro instance and also defines the syntax for specifying values of the macro instance. The production includes the following key elements:

1. Character strings enclosed in quotation marks are to be reproduced exactly in specifying a value for a type defined by a macro instance.

2. An argument is any nonterminal in the macro definition other than nonterminals of type `local-type-reference` or `local-value-reference`. Such terms are variables, for which a substitution is made to form the macro instance.

3. The keyword `value` is used to specify that, at this point, each macro instance, using standard ASN.1, contains some value of a type specified in the macro definition.

4. The keyword `VALUE` is used to mark the place in the macro definition where the actual type of the macro is specified. The type appearing immediately after `VALUE` is the macro's returned type; that is, any value derived from the macro is encoded as a value of that type.

B.3.3 Macros Versus Defined Types

The ASN.1 macro facility provides tools for

1. Defining new types
2. Representing those types
3. Representing values of those types
4. Encoding specific values of those types

A similar capability already exists within ASN.1, which allows for the construction of defined types, either from built-in types or recursively from built-in types and defined types. The macro facility differs from the ASN.1 defined type capability in the following respects.

1. The macro facility allows the definition of a family of types. Each new type generated by a macro definition (a macro instance) is closely related to other types generated from the same macro. In contrast, there is no particular relationship between one basic ASN.1 defined type and other defined types.

2. A defined type is represented in a set way from the strings symbolizing the types from which it is constructed. A macro instance is represented in whatever way the writer of the macro chooses. Thus, the syntax of a type defined via macro instance can be chosen to correspond closely to the notation used within the particular application for which the macro was written. Furthermore, the macro instance may include commentary or semantic narrative. In this way types defined by a macro may be more readable and more writable.

3. In basic ASN.1, the representation of a value of a type is derived from the representation of the type in a relatively straightforward manner. The two representations are isomorphic; that is, they have similar or identical structure. This isomorphism is not required with a macro definition. The returned type and the returned generic value may have quite different syntaxes. Again, this allows for more readable and writable values.

B.3.4   Macro Paradigm

Figure B.5 illustrates the ASN.1 macro paradigm from conception through implementation to encoding. Let us follow the steps of this diagram.

1. Starting with a concept to be represented, a set of types that adequately represents the concept is chosen. We have referred informally to this set of types as a Super type.

2. A macro definition, which is a concrete realization of a Super type, is written according to the rules of the ASN.1 macro definition notation.

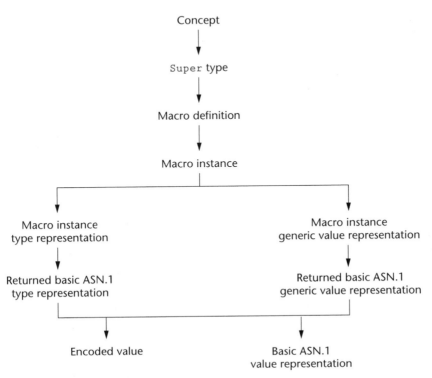

FIGURE B.5   ASN.1 macro paradigm

3. The macro definition is parameterized so that any of the types in the Super type may be generated via the substitution of arguments when writing a particular instance of the macro definition.

4. A macro instance defines an ASN.1 type, and since any ASN.1 has a defined type representation as well as a defined generic value representation, a macro instance provides a type representation and a generic value representation for the new ASN.1 type being defined.

5. The final result of the macro instance is returned as an argument and specifies the basic ASN.1 type representation. Since this is isomorphic to the corresponding generic value representation, the latter is also implicitly returned.

6. A specific value of the type defined by the macro instance can be encoded using the equivalent ASN.1 encoding and can be represented using the basic ASN.1 value representation.

Figure B.6 illustrates the process of defining the PAIR macro.

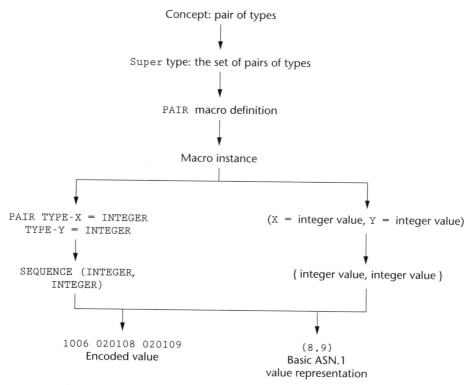

Concept: pair of types

Super type: the set of pairs of types

PAIR macro definition

Macro instance

```
PAIR TYPE-X = INTEGER
     TYPE-Y = INTEGER
```

(X = integer value, Y = integer value)

```
SEQUENCE (INTEGER,
          INTEGER)
```

{ integer value, integer value }

```
1006 020108 020109
```
Encoded value

{8,9}
Basic ASN.1
value representation

FIGURE B.6   ASN.1 macro paradigm applied to PAIR

B.4 Basic Encoding Rules

The *basic encoding rules* (BER) is an encoding specification developed and standardized by CCITT (X.209) and ISO (ISO 8825). It describes a method for encoding values of each ASN.1 type as a string of octets.

B.4.1 Encoding Structure

The basic encoding rules define one or more ways to encode any ASN.1 value as an octet string. The encoding is based on the use of a `type-length-value` (TLV) structure. That is, any ASN.1 value can be encoded as a triple with the following components:

- `type`: indicates the ASN.1 type, as well as the class of the type and whether the encoding is primitive or constructed, as explained later in this appendix
- `length`: indicates the length of the actual value representation
- `value`: represents the value of the ASN.1 type as a string of octets

This structure is recursive: For any ASN.1 value that consists of one or more components, the "value" portion of its TLV encoding itself consists of one or more TLV structures.

Figure B.7 illustrates the structure of the TLV encoding, and Figure B.8 illustrates its use for the example personnel record value. There are three methods for encoding an ASN.1 value:

1. Primitive, definite-length encoding
2. Constructed, definite-length encoding
3. Constructed, indefinite-length encoding

The method chosen depends on the ASN.1 type of the value to be encoded and whether or not the length of the value is known based on the type. Table B.4 summarizes the possibilities.

B.4.1.1 Primitive, Definite-Length Encoding

The primitive, definite-length encoding method can be used for simple types and types derived from simple types by implicit tagging. The BER format consists of three fields:

- *Identifier:* This field encodes the tag (class and tag number) of the ASN.1 type of the value. The first two bits indicate one of the four classes. The next bit is zero to indicate that this is a primitive encoding. The remaining five bits of the first octet can encode a tag number that distinguishes one data type from another within the designated class. For tags whose number is greater than or equal to 31, those five bits contain the binary value 11111, and the actual tag number is contained in the last

FIGURE B.7   BER encoding of values

Personnel Record 60	Length 8185	Contents						
		Name 61	Length 10	Contents				
				VisibleString 1A	Length 04	Contents "John"		
				VisibleString 1A	Length 01	Contents "P"		
				VisibleString 1A	Length 05	Contents "Smith"		
		Title A0	Length 0A	Contents				
				VisibleString 1A	Length 08	Contents "Director"		
		Employee Number 42	Length 01	Contents 33				
		Date of Hire A1	Length 0A	Contents				
				Date 43	Length 08	Contents "19710917"		
		Name of Spouse A2	Length 12	Contents				
				Name 61	Length 10	Contents		
						VisibleString 1A	Length 04	Contents "Mary"
						VisibleString 1A	Length 01	Contents "T"
						VisibleString 1A	Length 05	Contents "Smith"

Personnel Record 60	Length 8185	Contents				
		Name 61	Length 10	Contents		
				VisibleString 1A	Length 04	Contents "John"
				VisibleString 1A	Length 01	Contents "P"
				VisibleString 1A	Length 05	Contents "Smith"
		Title A0	Length 0A	Contents		
				VisibleString 1A	Length 08	Contents "Director"

FIGURE B.8   BER encoding of Figure B.3(c)

```
Employee    Length   Contents
Number      01       33
42
Date of     Length   Contents
Hire        0A
A1
                      Date      Length   Contents
                      43        08       "19710917"
Name of     Length   Contents
Spouse      12
A2
                      Name      Length   Contents
                      61        10
                                VisibleString   Length   Contents
                                1A              04       "Mary"
                                VisibleString   Length   Contents
                                1A              01       "T"
                                VisibleString   Length   Contents
                                1A              05       "Smith"
```

FIGURE B.8   *Continued*

TABLE B.4   BER Encoding Methods

	Primitive, Definite-length Encoding	Constructed, Definite-length Encoding	Constructed, Indefinite-length Encoding
Simple nonstring types	✓		
Simple string types	✓	✓	✓
Structured types		✓	✓
Explicit tagging		✓	✓

seven bits of one or more additional octets. The first bit of each additional octet is set to 1, except for the last octet, in which it is set to 0.

- *Length:* This field specifies the length in octets of the contents field. If the length is less than 128, the length field consists of a single octet beginning with a zero. If the length is greater than 127, the first octet of the length field contains a seven-bit integer that specifies the number of additional length octets; the additional octets contain the actual length of the contents field.

- *Contents:* This field directly represents the ASN.1 value as a string of octets. Details for particular types are given later in this section.

B.4.1.2   Constructed, Definite-Length Encoding

The constructed, definite-length encoding method can be used for simple string types, structured types (`Sequence`, `Sequence-of`, `Set`, `Set-of`), types derived from simple string types and structured types by implicit tagging, and any type defined by explicit tagging. This encoding method requires that the length of the value be known in advance. The BER format consists of three fields:

- *Identifier:* as described for primitive, definite-length encoding, except that the P/C bit is set to 1 to indicate that this is constructed encoding
- *Length:* as described for primitive, definite-length encoding
- *Contents:* contains the concatenation of the complete BER encodings (identifier, length, contents) of the components of the value; three cases are possible:
  1. Simple strings and types derived from simple strings by implicit tagging: the concatenation of the BER encodings of consecutive substrings of the value
  2. Structured types and types derived from structured types by implicit tagging: the concatenation of the BER encodings of components of the value
  3. Types defined by explicit tagging: the BER encoding of the underlying value

B.4.1.3   Constructed, Indefinite-Length Encoding

The constructed, indefinite-length encoding method can be used for simple string types, structured types, types derived from simple string types and structured types by implicit tagging, and any type defined by explicit tagging. This encoding method does not require that the length of the value be known in advance. The BER format consists of four fields:

- *Identifier:* as described for constructed, indefinite-length encoding
- *Length:* one octet, with the value 80_{16}
- *Contents:* as described for constructed, indefinite-length encoding
- *End-of-contents:* two octets, with the value 0000_{16}

B.4.2   Contents Encoding

Table B.5 summarizes the rules for encoding for the various ASN.1 types. The table gives only a concise definition of the rules; for more detail, the reader should consult the standard.

Most of the encoding rules for ASN.1 types are relatively straightforward. For some types, a few additional comments are warranted.

B.4.2.1   **Integer**

Integer values are represented using *two's complement notation*. This notation can be briefly summarized as follows.[3] Consider an integer in two's complement representation stored in an N-bit field. There are two cases: nonnegative and negative.

Nonnegative numbers are represented as follows. The leftmost (most significant) bit is zero and the remaining bits are the binary form of the magnitude of the number. A negative number whose magnitude is X and for which X has a value of less than or equal to 2^{N-1} is represented by calculating $2^N - X$. For all negative numbers, the leftmost bit has a value 1. Thus, this bit functions as a sign bit.

If an N-bit sequence of binary digits $b_{N-1}b_{N-2} \cdots b_1 b_0$ is interpreted as a two's complement representation, the value can be calculated as follows:

$$\text{value} = -b_{N-1} 2^{N-1} + \sum_{i=0}^{N-2} b_i 2^i.$$

The largest negative number that can be represented is -2^{N-1}, and the largest positive integer that can be represented is $2^{N-1} - 1$. Thus, in a single octet, the range of numbers that can be represented is $-128 \le \text{value} \le 127$.

An important characteristic of the two's complement representation is the way in which an N-bit number is padded out to form an M-bit number, where $M > N$. For nonnegative numbers, the representation is padded out by adding additional 0s to the left. For negative numbers, the representation is padded out by adding additional 1s to the left.

BER dictates that the minimum number of octets be used for representing integers. Thus, if the value is between -128 and $+127$, only a single octet is used. Note that care must be taken for unsigned variables, such as counters and gauges. If a 32-bit counter has a value of 2^{31} or greater, then five octets rather than four will be needed to encode it. For example, in the SNMP structure of management information, the counter type is defined as follows:

```
Counter ::= [APPLICATION 1] IMPLICIT INTEGER (0..4294967295)
```

This defines an unsigned 32-bit integer with a maximum value of $2^{32} - 1$.

Now consider a 32-bit counter that has its maximum value of $FFFFFFFF_{16}$. The correct encoding, in hexadecimal, is

```
41 05 00 FF FF FF FF
```

The identifier octet specifies that this is an application class type with tag number 1. The length octet specifies that the value length is five octets. Because of the use of two's complement representation, the value cannot be encoded in four octets.

---

[3]For a more complete discussion of two's complement representation and two's complement arithmetic, see Stallings (1996b).

TABLE B.5 BER Encoding Rules

ASN.1 type	BER encoding rules	Example value	Encoding of example value[1]
BOOLEAN	Primitive. A single octet with a content of zero for FALSE and a nonzero content for TRUE.	TRUE	01 01 FF
INTEGER	Primitive. Two's-complement representation with the minimum number of octets.	−129	02 02 FF 7F
ENUMERATED	Same as the integer value with which it is associated.		
REAL	Primitive. If the value is zero, there are no contents octets. Otherwise, the first contents octet indicates whether the base is 10, 2, 8, or 16, or a special real value ($+\infty$, $-\infty$). If base is 10, first contents octet also specifies one of three ISO 6093 character-encoding schemes for the remaining contents octets. If base is 2, 8, 16, first contents octet also specifies length of exponent, sign of mantissa, and scaling factor to align implied decimal point of mantissa with octet boundary; following the first contents are zero or one additional octets to specify exponent length, followed by octets for the exponent, followed by octets for the mantissa.	0	09 00

BIT STRING	Primitive or constructed. For primitive encoding, the contents consists of an initial octet followed by zero or more subsequent octets. The actual bit string begins with the first bit of the second octet and continues through as many octets as necessary. The first octet indicates how many bits in the last octet are unused. For constructed encoding, the bit string is broken up into substrings; each substring except the last must be a multiple of 8 bits in length. Each substring may be encoded as primitive or constructed, but usually the primitive encoding is used.	"0110111100101 110111"	primitive:
			03 04 06 6E 5D C0
			constructed:
			23 09
			  03 03 00 6E 5D
			  03 02 06 C0

OCTET STRING	Primitive or constructed. For primitive encoding, the contents octets are identical to the value of the octet string. For constructed encoding, the octet string is broken up into substrings; each substring may be encoded as primitive or constructed, but usually the primitive encoding is used.	01 23 45 67	primitive:
			04 04 01 23 45 67
			constructed:
			24 08
			  04 02 01 23
			  04 02 34 56

NULL	Primitive. There are no contents octets.	null	05 00
SEQUENCE	Constructed. The contents octets are the concatenation of the BER encodings of the values of the components of the sequence in order of definition. If the value of a component with the OPTIONAL or DEFAULT qualifier is absent from the sequence, no encoding is included for that component. If the value of a component with the DEFAULT qualifier is	definition: SEQUENCE (INTEGER, INTEGER) value: (3,8)	30 06 02 01 03 02 01 08

the default value, then encoding of that component may or may not be included.

Type	Description	Definition / Value	Encoding
SEQUENCE OF	Constructed. The contents octets are the concatenation of the BER encodings of the values of the occurrences in the collection, in the order of occurrence.	definition: SEQUENCE OF (INTEGER) value: (3,8)	30 06 02 01 03 02 01 08
SET	Constructed. The contents octets are the concatenation of the BER encodings of the values of the components of the sequence in any order. If the value of a component with the OPTIONAL or DEFAULT qualifier is absent from the sequence, no encoding is included for that component. If the value of a component with the DEFAULT qualifier is the default value, then encoding of that component may or may not be included.	definition: SET (INTEGER, INTEGER) value: (3,8)	31 06 02 01 03 02 01 08
SET OF	Constructed. The contents octets are the concatenation of the BER encodings of the values of the occurrences in the collection, in any order.	definition: SET OF (INTEGER) value: (3,8)	31 06 02 01 03 02 01 08
CHOICE	Primitive or constructed. The encoding of the CHOICE value is the encoding of the chosen alternative.		
IMPLICIT tag	Primitive or constructed. The encoding of the tag field replaces the underlying tag value. The encoding of the length and contents octets are the same as for the underlying value.	definition: [17] IMPLICIT BOOLEAN value: TRUE	91 01 FF
EXPLICIT tag	Constructed. The contents octets are the complete BER encoding of the underlying value.	definition: [17] BOOLEAN value: TRUE	B1 03 01 01 FF
ANY	Primitive or constructed. The encoding of the ANY value is the encoding of the actual value.		
OBJECT IDENTIFIER	Primitive. The first two components are combined using the formula $(X \times 40) + Y$ to form the first subidentifier. Each subsequent component forms the next subidentifier. Each subidentifier is encoded as a non-negative integer using as few 7-bit blocks as possible. The blocks are packed in octets with the first bit of each octet equal to 1 except for the last octet of each subidentifier.	{2 100 3}	06 03 81 34 03
Character String	Primitive or constructed. Encoded as if it had been declared [UNIVERSAL x] IMPLICIT OCTET STRING.	"Jones"	1A 05 4A 6F 6E 65 73

¹All encodings are depicted using hexadecimal notation.

B.4.2.2   Bit, Octet, and Character Strings

For the simple string types, the encoding can be either primitive or constructed. For the constructed encoding, the string is broken up into a number of substrings, each of which is encoded using BER rules. Since these rules are recursive, each substring can be further subdivided into sub-substrings using the constructed encoding.

The way in which a string is broken up into substrings is arbitrary and at the convenience of the encoding process. That is, the boundaries that define the substrings are arbitrary.

B.4.2.3   Object Identifier

An object identifier consists of a sequence of integers. The BER encoding packs the first two integers into a single subidentifier. Thus, an identifier consisting of N integers has $N-1$ subidentifiers. The first two integers can be combined because the first integer always takes on the value 0, 1, or 2, and the second integer must be less than 40 if the first integer is 0 or 1. The packing formula is

$$Z = (X \times 40) + Y,$$

where X is the first integer, Y is the second integer, and Z is the resulting subidentifier value. The result can be summarized as follows:

Subidentifier Value	First Integer	Second Integer
$0 \leq Z \leq 39$	0	Z
$40 \leq Z \leq 79$	1	$Z - 40$
$80 \leq Z$	2	$Z - 80$

B.5   *Alternative Encoding Rules*

BER provides options for encoding various values and does not result in a very compact representation. Currently, several new encoding rules for ASN.1 are being standardized that will become new parts to ISO 8825 and X.208. The new encoding rules are as follows:

- *Packed encoding rules (PER):* This results in a very compressed encoding. Unlike BER, PER is implicitly typed, and it relies on ASN.1 subtype information to minimize the size of encodings. For example, a type defined as `INTEGER (998..1001)` can be encoded in PER using two bits.

- *Distinguished encoding rules (DER):* This is a subset of BER, which gives exactly one way to represent any ASN.1 value.

- *Canonical encoding rules (CER):* Like DER, CER is a subset of BER. Whereas DER caters to applications that have a need for a single way to encode data using definite-length encoding, CER caters to applications that have a need for a single way to encode data using indefinite-length encoding.

- *Light-weight encoding rules (LWER):* This set of rules is intended to result in faster encoding of protocol data units (PDUs) at the expense of potentially generating longer encodings.

Glossary

Abstract Syntax Notation One (ASN.1)   A formal language used to define syntax. In the case of SNMP, ASN.1 notation is used to define the format of SNMP protocol data units and of objects.

Accounting Management   One of the five OSI systems management functional areas (SMFAs). Consists of facilities that enable the detection, isolation, and correction of abnormal operation of the OSI environment.

Agent   In the context of SNMP, a software module that performs the network management functions requested by network management stations. An agent module may be implemented in any network element that is to be managed, such as a host, bridge, or router. Agents and network management stations communicate by means of SNMP.

Application Layer   Layer 7 of the OSI model. This layer determines the interface of the system with the user and provides useful application-oriented services.

Authentication   A process used to verify the integrity of transmitted data, especially a message.

Availability   The percentage of time that a particular function or application is available for users.

Bridge*   A functional unit that interconnects two local area networks (LANs) that use the same logical link control protocol but may use different medium access control protocols.

Bus   A LAN topology in which stations are attached to a shared transmission medium. The medium is a linear cable; transmissions propagate the length of the medium and are received by all stations.

Byte   A group of bits, usually eight, used to represent a character of other data.

Ciphertext   The output of an encryption algorithm; the encrypted form of a message or data.

Columnar Object   An object that is part of an SNMP table. There is one instance of the columnar object for each row in the table.

Note: Some of the definitions in this glossary are from the *American National Standard Dictionary of Information Technology,* ANSI Standard X3.172, 1995. These are marked with an asterisk.

Communications Architecture   The hardware and software structure that implements the communications function.

Community   In the context of SNMP, a relationship between an agent and a set of SNMP managers that defines security characteristics. The community concept is a local one, defined at the agent. The agent establishes one community for each desired combination of authentication, access control, and proxy characteristics. Each community is given a unique (within this agent) community name, and the management stations within that community are provided with and must employ the community name in all get and set operations. The agent may establish a number of communities, with overlapping management station membership.

Configuration Management   One of the five OSI systems management functional areas (SMFAs). Consists of facilities that exercise control over, identify, collect data from, and provide data to managed objects for the purpose of assisting in providing for continuous operation of interconnection services.

Counter   A non-negative integer which may be incremented but not decremented. The maximum value is determined by the number of bits assigned to the counter. When the counter reaches its maximum, it wraps around and starts increasing again from zero. In SNMPv1, all counters are 32 bits; SNMPv2 also allows 64-bit counters.

Cyclic Redundancy Check (CRC)   An error-detecting code in which the code is the remainder resulting from dividing the bits to be checked by a predetermined binary number.

Datagram*   In packet switching, a packet, independent of other packets, that carries information sufficient for routing from the originating data terminal equipment (DTE) to the destination DTE without the necessity of establishing a connection between the DTEs and the network.

Data Link Layer*   In OSI, the layer that provides service to transfer data between network layer entities, usually in adjacent nodes. The data link layer detects and possibly corrects errors that may occur in the physical layer.

End System (ES)   A device other than an intermediate system attached to a subnetwork in an internet. End systems on different subnetworks exchange data by transmitting the data through one or more intermediate systems.

Encapsulation   The addition of control information by a protocol entity to data obtained from a protocol user.

Encrypt*   To convert plain text or data into unintelligible form by the use of a code in such a manner that reconversion to the original form is possible.

Error Detecting Code*   A code in which each coded representation conforms to specific rules of construction, so that their violation indicates the presence of errors.

Error Rate*   The number of errors per unit of time.

Fault Management   One of the five OSI systems management functional areas (SMFAs). Consists of facilities that enable the detection, isolation, and correction of abnormal operation of the OSI environment.

Flow Control   A function performed by a receiving entity to limit the amount or rate of data sent by a transmitting entity.

Frame   A group of bits that includes data plus one or more addresses and other protocol control information. Generally refers to a link layer (OSI layer 2) protocol data unit.

Frame Check Sequence (FCS)   An error-detecting code inserted as a field in a block of data to be transmitted. The code serves to check for errors upon reception of the data.

Gateway   An internetworking device that connects two computer networks that use different communications architectures.

Gauge   A non-negative integer which may increase or decrease with a range between 0 and some maximum value.

Hash Function   A function that maps a variable-length data block or message into a fixed-length value called a hash code. The function is designed in such a way that, when protected, it provides an authenticator to the data or message. Also referred to as a message digest.

Header   System-defined control information that precedes user data.

Intermediate System (IS)   A device attached to two or more subnetworks in an internet and that performs routing and relaying of data between end systems. Examples of intermediate systems are bridges and routers.

Internet   A collection of communication networks interconnected by bridges, routers, and/or gateways.

Internet Protocol*   A protocol designed for use in an interconnected system of packet networks. The internet protocol provides for transmitting blocks of data, called datagrams, from sources to destinations, where source and destination are hosts identified by fixed-length addresses. The internet protocol also provides for fragmentation and reassembly of long datagrams, if necessary, for transmission through small-packet networks.

Internetworking   Communication among devices across multiple networks.

Layer*   A group of services, functions, and protocols that is complete from a conceptual point of view, that is one out of a set of hierarchically arranged groups, and that extends across all systems that conform to the network architecture.

Logical Link Control (LLC)*   In a local area network, the protocol that governs the exchange of frames between data stations independently of how the transmission medium is shared.

Management Information Base (MIB)   In the context of SNMP, this term is used in two ways: (1) a structured set of data variables, called objects, in which each variable represents some resource to be managed. Each agent in a network maintains a MIB for the network element that it executes on; (2) the definition of a related collection of objects that represent some related collection of resources to be managed. A number of MIBs, in the sense of definition (2) have been issued as RFCs.

Medium Access Control (MAC)*   In a local area network, the protocol that governs access to the transmission medium, taking into account the topological aspects of the network, to enable the exchange of data between data stations.

Message Authentication Code (MAC)   An authenticator that is a cryptographic function of both the data to be authenticated and a secret key.

Network Layer   Layer 3 of the OSI model. Responsible for routing data through a communication network.

Network Management Station   In the context of SNMP, a software module that executes management applications that monitor and control network elements, such as hosts, bridges, and routers. A network management station communicates with an agent in a network element by means of SNMP.

Network Monitoring System   An integrated set of hardware and software that measures and analyzes communications-related parameters in a network.

Network Technical Control System   A system, consisting of hardware probes and supporting software, that deals with fault detection, fault isolation, and fault recovery.

Object   In the context of SNMP, a data variable that represents some resource or other aspect of a managed device; also referred to as a managed object. Note that this definition is quite different from the normal use of the term *object* in the context of object-oriented design.

Object Identifier   Uniquely identifies an object within a MIB. The form of an object identifier is a sequence of numbers separated by periods. This sequence defines the location of an object in the tree-structured MIB of which it is a part.

Object Instance   A specific instance of an object type that has been bound to a specific value.

Object Type   Defines a particular kind of managed object. The definition of an object type is therefore a syntactic description.

Octet   A group of eight bits, usually operated upon as an entity.

One-Way Function   A function that is easily computed, but the calculation of its inverse is infeasible.

Open Systems Interconnection (OSI) Reference Mode   A model of communications between cooperating devices. It defines a seven-layer architecture of communication functions.

Packet   A group of bits that includes data plus control information. Generally refers to a network layer (OSI layer 3) protocol data unit.

Packet Switching   A method of transmitting messages through a communications network, in which long messages are subdivided into short packets. Each packet is passed from source to destination through intermediate nodes. At each node, the entire message is received, stored briefly, and then passed on to the next node.

Performance Management   One of the five OSI systems management functional areas (SMFAs). Consists of facilities needed to evaluate the behavior of managed objects and the effectiveness of communication activities.

Physical Layer   Layer 1 of the OSI model. Concerned with the electrical, mechanical, and timing aspects of signal transmission over a medium.

Plaintext   The input to an encryption function or the output of a decryption function.

Presentation Layer*   Layer 6 of the OSI model. Provides for the selection of a common syntax for representing data and for transformation of application data into and from the common syntax.

Probe   In the context of RMON, a remote network monitor.

Propagation Delay   The delay between the time a signal enters a channel and the time it is received.

Protocol*   A set of semantic and syntactic rules that determines the behavior of entities in the same layer in performing communication functions.

Protocol Control Information*   Information exchanged between entities of a given layer, via the service provided by the next lower layer, to coordinate their joint operation.

Protocol Data Unit (PDU)*   A set of data specified in a protocol of a given layer and consisting of protocol control information of that layer, and possibly user data of that layer.

Proxy   In the context of SNMP, an agent (the proxy agent) that acts on behalf of another network element (the proxied device). A management station sends queries concerning a device to its proxy agent. The proxy agent is responsible for collecting the information or triggering the action requested of the proxied device by the management station.

Remote Network Monitor   An agent, implemented in a network element, that observes all of the traffic on the network or networks and maintains information and statistics concerning that traffic in its MIB. Also referred to as a probe.

Response Time   In a data system, the elapsed time between the end of transmission of an inquiry message and the beginning of the receipt of a response message, measured at the inquiry terminal.

Router   An internetworking device that connects two computer networks. It makes use of an internet protocol and assumes that all of the attached devices on the networks use the same communications architecture and protocols. A router operates at OSI layer 3.

Routing   The determination of a path that a data unit (frame, packet, message) will traverse from source to destination.

Security Management   One of the five OSI systems management functional areas (SMFAs). Addresses those aspects of OSI security essential to operate OSI network management correctly and to protect managed objects.

Service Access Point (SAP)   A means of identifying a user of the services of a protocol entity. A protocol entity provides one or more SAPs, for use by higher-level entities.

Session Layer   Layer 5 of the OSI model. Manages a logical connection (session) between two communicating processes or applications.

Software Monitor   A software module resident in main memory on a host or communications processor that can gather and report statistics on configuration and communications and software activity.

Subnetwork   Refers to a constituent network of an internet. This avoids ambiguity since the entire internet, from a user's point of view, is a single network.

Systems Management Function (SMF)   A part of OSI systems management activities which satisfy a set of logically related user requirements.

Systems Management Functional Area (SMFA)   A category of OSI systems management user requirements

Transport Layer   Layer 4 of the OSI model. Provides reliable, sequenced transfer of data between endpoints.

Trap   In the context of SNMP, an unsolicited message sent by an agent to a management station. The purpose is to notify the management station of some unusual event.

Virtual Circuit   A packet-switching mechanism in which a logical connection (virtual circuit) is established between two stations at the start of transmission. All packets follow the same route, need not carry a complete address, and arrive in sequence.

References

Bellare, M., Canetti, R., and Krawczyk, H. 1996a. "Keying Hash Functions for Message Authentication." *Proceedings, CRYPTO '96*, August; published by Springer-Verlag. An expanded version is available at http://www-cse.ucsd.edu/users/mihir.

Bellare, M., Canetti, R., and Krawczyk, H. 1996b. "The HMAC Construction." *CryptoBytes*, Spring.

Ben-Artzi, A., Chandna, A., and Warrier, U. 1990. "Network Management of TCP/IP Networks: Present and Future." *IEEE Network Magazine*, July.

Blumenthal, U., Hien, N., and Wijnen, B. 1997a. "Key Derivation for Network Management Applications." *IEEE Network*, May/June.

Blumenthal, U., and Wijnen, B. 1997b. "Security Features for SNMPv3." *The Simple Times*, December.

Blumenthal, U., Hien, N., and Wijnen, B. 1998. *SNMPv3 Handbook*. Reading, Mass.: Addison-Wesley.

Blumenthal, U. 1998. Private communication.

Boardman, B., and Morrissey, P. 1995. "Probing the Depths of RMON." *Network Computing*, February 1.

Case, J., and Partridge, C. 1989. "Case Diagrams: A First Step to Diagrammed Management Information Bases." *Computer Communication Review*, January. Reprinted in *Connexions*, March.

Cerf, V. 1988. *IAB Recommendations for the Development of Internet Management Standards*. RFC 1052, April.

Cerf, V. 1989. *Report of the Second Ad Hoc Network Management Review Group*. RFC 1109, August.

Chiu, D., and Sudama, R. 1992. *Network Monitoring Explained: Design and Application*. New York: Ellis Horwood.

Dupuy, A., et al. 1989. "Network Fault Management: A User's View." *Proceedings, First International Symposium on Integrated Network Management*, May; published by North-Holland.

Eckerson, W. 1992. "Net Management Traffic Can Sap Net Performance." *Network World*, May 14.

Fried, S., and Tjong, J. 1990. "Implementing Integrated Monitoring Systems for Heterogeneous Networks." In Kerchenbaum (1990).

Guynes, J. 1988. "Impact of System Response Time on State Anxiety." *Communications of the ACM,* March.

Jacobson, V. 1988. "Congestion Avoidance and Control." *Proceedings, SIGCOMM '88,* August.

Kerchenbaum, A., et al. 1990. *Network Management and Control.* New York: Plenum.

Martin, J. 1988. *Principles of Data Communication.* Englewood Cliffs, N.J.: Prentice-Hall.

Mazumdar, S., and Lazar, A. "Objective-Driven Monitoring. 1991." *Proceedings, Second International Symposium on Integrated Network Management,* April; published by North-Holland.

Mier, E. 1991a. "Network World, Bell Labs Evaluate SNMP on Bridges." *Network World,* April 22.

Mier, E. 1991b. "Network World, Bell Labs Test Routers' SNMP Agents." *Network World,* July 1.

Newman, D., Giorgis, T., and Melson, B. 1998. "Probing RMON2." *Data Communications,* May 21.

Shneiderman, B. 1984. "Response Time and Display Rate in Human Performance with Computers." *ACM Computing Surveys,* September.

Smith, D. 1983. "Faster Is Better: A Business Case for Subsecond Response Time." *Computerworld,* April 18.

Stallings, W. 1996a. *Local and Metropolitan Area Networks.* Fifth ed. Upper Saddle River, N.J.: Prentice-Hall.

Stallings, W. 1996b. *Computer Organization and Architecture.* Fourth ed. Upper Saddle River, N.J.: Prentice-Hall.

Stallings, W. 1997. *Data and Computer Communications.* Fifth ed. Upper Saddle River, N.J.: Prentice-Hall.

Stallings, W. 1998. *Operating Systems: Internals and Design Principles.* Third ed. Upper Saddle River, N.J.: Prentice-Hall.

Stallings, W. 1999. *Cryptography and Network Security: Principles and Practice.* Second ed. Upper Saddle River, N.J.: Prentice-Hall.

Terplan, K. 1992. *Communication Networks Management.* Englewood Cliffs, N.J.: Prentice-Hall.

Thadhani, A. 1981. "Interactive User Productivity." *IBM Systems Journal,* No. 1.

Thomas, R. 1995. "Interoperable RMON? Plug and Pray." *Data Communications,* May.

Waldbusser, S. 1992. "Applications Stand to Benefit from SNMP." *The Simple Times,* September/October.

Wilkinson, S., and Capen, T. 1992. "Remote Control." *Corporate Computing,* October.

Index

Addison-Wesley Computer and Engineering Publishing Group

How to Interact with Us

1. Visit our Web site

http://www.awl.com/cseng

When you think you've read enough, there's always more content for you at Addison-Wesley's web site. Our web site contains a directory of complete product information including:

- Chapters
- Exclusive author interviews
- Links to authors' pages
- Tables of contents
- Source code

You can also discover what tradeshows and conferences Addison-Wesley will be attending, read what others are saying about our titles, and find out where and when you can meet our authors and have them sign your book.

2. Subscribe to Our Email Mailing Lists

Subscribe to our electronic mailing lists and be the first to know when new books are publishing. Here's how it works: Sign up for our electronic mailing at **http://www.awl.com/cseng/mailinglists.html**. Just select the subject areas that interest you and you will receive notification via email when we publish a book in that area.

3. Contact Us via Email

cepubprof@awl.com
Ask general questions about our books.
Sign up for our electronic mailing lists.
Submit corrections for our web site.

bexpress@awl.com
Request an Addison-Wesley catalog.
Get answers to questions regarding your order or our products.

innovations@awl.com
Request a current Innovations Newsletter.

webmaster@awl.com
Send comments about our web site.

cepubeditors@awl.com
Submit a book proposal.
Send errata for an Addison-Wesley book.

cepubpublicity@awl.com
Request a review copy for a member of the media interested in reviewing new Addison-Wesley titles.

We encourage you to patronize the many fine retailers who stock Addison-Wesley titles. Visit our online directory to find stores near you or visit our online store: **http://store.awl.com/** or call **800-824-7799**.

Addison Wesley Longman
Computer and Engineering Publishing Group
One Jacob Way, Reading, Massachusetts 01867 USA
TEL 781-944-3700 • FAX 781-942-3076